The Handbook of
British Mammals

The Handbook of British Mammals

EDITED BY G.B.CORBET
AND H.N.SOUTHERN

SECOND EDITION

PUBLISHED FOR THE MAMMAL SOCIETY
BY BLACKWELL SCIENTIFIC PUBLICATIONS
OXFORD LONDON EDINBURGH MELBOURNE

© 1964, 1977 Blackwell Scientific Publications
Osney Mead, Oxford, OX2 0EL
8 John Street, London, WC1N 2ES
9 Forrest Road, Edinburgh, EH1 2QH
P.O. Box 9, North Balwyn, Victoria 3104, Australia

British Library Cataloguing in Publication Data

The handbook of British mammals.—2nd ed.
  1. Mammals—Great Britain
  I. Corbet, Gordon Barclay II. Southern,
  Henry Neville III. Mammal Society
  599′.0941   QL727

  ISBN 0–632–09080–4

First published 1964
Reprinted 1965
Second edition 1977

Distributed in the United States of America by
J. B. Lippincott Company, Philadelphia
and in Canada by
J. B. Lippincott Company of Canada Ltd, Toronto

Printed and bound in Great Britain by
Butler & Tanner Ltd
Frome and London

Contents

Preface

The first edition of *The Handbook of British Mammals* was published in 1964 and, in 1968, the decision was taken to prepare a second edition and allow the first to go out of print. At that point it was not easy to foresee the magnitude of the task in front of us which has occasioned this delay before the second edition could be completed and published.

One of the aims of the first *Handbook*, apart from being a guide to the identification and study of British mammals in the field, was to help stimulate interest and active research; in this aim it has succeeded beyond our wildest dreams. A flood of population and behaviour studies has made it possible for all the following accounts of species groups and many accounts of single species to have been written by authors who have made them their special study. This is a heartening contrast to the earlier state of affairs when the Editor had to be responsible for searching the literature to fill the many gaps. We wish to thank these authors not only for their careful labours but also for waiving royalties in favour of the Mammal Society. We also thank many people, especially Mr G.Kinns, who have allowed us to use their photographs free of charge.

The sheer bulk of knowledge that has accumulated since 1964 has meant that this new version is necessarily much longer than its predecessor. To keep the volume within a reasonable compass (and price) we, therefore, decided to telescope the original Part I on the Biology of British Mammals to the following relatively brief chapter entitled The Study of British Mammals, 1964–1976.

There are several reasons for doing this, apart from the need to save space. First, the description of techniques and technical aids, which occupied a long chapter in the first edition, is now being dealt with, in much greater detail, in the serial publication, Techniques in Mammalogy, appearing in *Mammal Review* under the care of G.I.Twigg and J.Clevedon Brown.

Secondly, these authors have in course of preparation a more general book on the biology of mammals which will cover much of the ground of Part I of the earlier *Handbook* and a great deal more besides, albeit with a different approach and at a different level.

Thirdly, literature and knowledge about mammals have proliferated so much in the last decade that it seems unnecessary to repeat the kind of information that was included in such chapters as 'What is a Mammal?' and 'Breeding'. One need cite only the excellent two-volume work, *The Life of Mammals*, by L.Harrison Matthews.

In view of these parallel and easily accessible publications, it has seemed to us best to provide a sketch (it can be no more) of the advances in our knowledge since 1964.

Oxford H.N.Southern
19 May 1976 *President*
Mammal Society

The Study of British Mammals 1964–1976

H.N.SOUTHERN & I.J.LINN

Home range and movements

With the exception of some large species, information about home range and movements prior to 1964 was mainly derived from the method of capture-mark-recapture, whether the subjects were mice, bats or seals. This still generates much argument about how to express such results on a common basis so that comparisons can be made between species and places (e.g. Watts 1970; Golley, Petrusewicz & Ryszkowski 1975; and many others). Nevertheless, the method is useful and can give valuable information, e.g. King (1975) was able to show that male weasels (*Mustela nivalis*) had territories of 7–15 ha in deciduous woodland near Oxford in contrast to the 1–5 ha observed by Lockie (1966) in young forestry plantations in Scotland but similar to those determined by Moors (1974) in Aberdeenshire farmland. She also showed that the territories of female weasels were much smaller (one quarter or less) than those of the males and had big gaps between them, which may account for the puzzling fact that males always outnumber females in trapped samples.

For shrews Croin-Michielson (1966) revealed the interesting fact that the home ranges of pygmy shrews were twice as large as those of common shrews living in the same area. Another surprising fact was discovered by Stoddart (1970) in his study of water voles, namely that females, having reared one family of young, may move considerable distances to another colony or occupied area and establish themselves in a new home range to have the next family.

He also showed that females not infrequently changed their ranges within one occupied area, whereas males stayed put—the opposite of what has generally been recorded for small rodents and shrews (Shillito 1963).

This new information about home ranges throws valuable light on the degree of isolation that exists between breeding groups and, therefore, on the pattern of intra-specific variation that may be expected. It also tells us how fast any variant may travel in a population and, of greater practical importance, how a disease may spread.

This last point has a particular urgency just now because of the possibility that rabies, having spread from eastern Europe into France during the last few decades, may re-enter the British Isles. Since, of our wild mammals, foxes are known to be the main carriers of this distressing and dangerous disease, they have become the focus for intensive researches into their numbers, home ranges and movements. The urgency to learn about such matters has justified considerable expenditure on equipment. Thus radio transmitters and modern gadgets for turning night into day (infra-red viewers and light intensifiers), far too expensive for the normal run of researchers, have brought a new dimension into the measurement of home range and movements. Results to date (Lloyd 1977, Macdonald 1977) have already shown that foxes in lowland England have far smaller ranges than those in mountainous areas. A further complication is the relatively recent expansion of the fox's habitat to include urban environments (dust-bin foxes!) where rabies could be more readily transmitted to the abounding population of pet dogs.

We already have with us the problem of the badger as a strongly suspected transmitter of bovine tuberculosis to cattle. In this instance, the infection is confined to the south-western counties of England, especially Gloucestershire and Cornwall. Although it is early days to draw conclusions about the possible spread of the disease, Kruuk (unpubl.), using the same machinery of radio transmitters, etc., has concluded that the badger is largely a sedentary animal. This shows how vital it is to obtain this kind of information.

An aspect of the organisation of home ranges which has received special attention during the last decade is the use of scent glands for proclaiming proprietorship of an area. This process of setting scent, familiar to anybody who has watched badgers, is well known in many ungulates and carnivores and Stoddart (1972) has shown that water voles transfer the secretions of their lateral glands by means of their feet to the substratum of latrine sites. Similarly, Flowerdew (1971) has described a sub-caudal gland in the male wood mouse. Analysis of these various 'chemical communications' by gas chromatography may give evidence on sex, age and breeding condition of animals and, possibly, distinguish individuals (see Gorman (1976) on the mongoose in Fiji).

So great has been the dissatisfaction with 'trap-revealed' home ranges of small mammals, that several ingenious methods have been tested to give information about movements without arresting them in traps. Footprints of toe-clipped mice and voles on smoked paper placed in the runways and the provision of bait including coloured wool or plastic fragments have yielded valuable information but a particularly ingenious method is that described by Randolph (1973). She removed individual wood mice from the field to the laboratory, fed each with a bait containing distinctive fibres (including polar bear fur!) and dyes and released them where caught. Movements were traced by placing massive numbers of containers with bait and collecting for analysis the faeces deposited in them. Thus not only were the mice's movements unimpeded, but a large number of individuals could be traced simultaneously.

The use of radioactive substances as markers has expanded greatly since the pioneer work mentioned in the first edition of the Handbook. Bailey, Linn & Walker (1973) have given us a comprehensive review of progress in this field. Leg-rings containing radioactive substances or bits of wire implanted under the skin are still favoured techniques for tracing home ranges; they can also be used in conjunction with automatic recorders to measure activity, e.g. visits to nests, passage along runways etc.

Another method is the injection of radioactive substances so that they diffuse through an animal's tissues. In this way such substances can be detected when passed on to offspring or even to ectoparasites. Furthermore, as they are excreted in the faeces and urine, very accurate measurements of movements and home ranges can be made. Stoddart (1970) showed in this way that tracer-revealed home ranges of water voles are usually larger than trap-revealed home ranges. The water vole's habit of using fairly obvious latrines is here very helpful.

Behaviour

Much information, both general and particular, has been collected since 1964, as a glance through the pages of Notes on British Mammals, published in the *Journal of Zoology*, will testify. This is a rewarding field for the amateur naturalist, even if he is unable to lay his hands on an infra-red viewer and has to be content with using stealth and a red torch.

Kruuk (unpubl.) working on badgers and Macdonald (unpubl.) on foxes have recently begun to reveal the way in which populations of these animals are structured socially and the effects this structure has on dispersal and reproductive success, promoting the former and reducing the latter. The full publication of their results is being eagerly awaited.

The elucidation of these relationships is, of course, easier with diurnal species such as the grey squirrel. The activities of this animal in stripping bark from trees has, for many years—at any rate since the reduction of rabbits by myxomatosis—made it the foremost pest for foresters. Yet this provoking habit is scarcely noticeable in the native American forests of this squirrel. Painstaking work by the staff of the Ministry of Agriculture's Infestation Control Division especially by J. C. Taylor (1970) has at last pieced together a reasonable explanation of this puzzle. It is based on the operation of the social structure revealed. All areas of good habitat have an entrenched resident population, especially of females, and at certain times of year a surplus of younger squirrels is expelled into unknown and poorer territories. Here, with no settled social structure, aggression is rife and one form that this takes is the stripping of bark. The most vulnerable areas are monocultures of young and middle-aged plantations, so beloved of foresters, and it is probable that bark also supplies a source of food in such areas, which are poor in other kinds of food. Sycamore, beech and oak, in that order, are the worst affected.

This may be contrasted with American forests which are richer in fruit-bearing species of trees, where there are still various species of natural predators and where the squirrel is a highly prized game animal.

It is now becoming clear that this distinction between residents and roamers, first pointed out by Evans (1942) and followed up by Polish ecologists, applies to many animal populations and is of the first importance in regulating numbers. Some fascinating recent work on the humble house mouse has revealed this in instructive detail.

First of all, Crowcroft and his co-workers (Crowcroft 1966) studied confined populations of wild mice and showed that, where cover was scant, one male mouse would be completely dominant in a small enclosure. However, if the enclosure was broken up by a series of criss-cross barriers, several social groups, each with a male and one or more females, could co-exist by occupying different areas. Even so, as numbers increased by breeding, more and more mice were thrust out of the groups and accumulated in a corner, fed slyly when the residents were not looking and refrained from breeding. These would have been roamers in the wild.

Secondly, Anderson (1970) confirmed this two-tiered structure in the field. On the Canadian prairies small permanent groups of house mice occupy grain stores, while the overflow lives in the surrounding fields and fluctuates widely in numbers. Anderson points out that these resident groups, which he calls demes, are isolated from each other and evolve genetic differences by in-breeding (see next section).

Finally, Berry (1970) discovered an even more complicated situation on the island of Skokholm off Pembrokeshire. Not only was the population of house mice divided into residents which lived along the cliff tops all year and the roamers which spilled over the centre of the island during the summer but each of these sections was characterised by different gene frequencies. These could be identified from details of skeletal structure but, more significantly, there were also physiological differences. Those mice with a higher metabolic rate were able to survive better through the rigours of the winter.

Some interesting aspects of behaviour have been revealed by studying food preferences, Macdonald (1977) exposed his tame foxes to a choice of small rodent species and shrews. Every time the favourite food was the short-tailed vole followed by the bank vole and, less favoured still, the wood mouse; shrews came lowest of all on the list. Here, then, is a trend in preference of prey from a total herbivore to a total carnivore and it may be that man's preference for the flesh of herbivores, except the pig, is not just a matter of which was easiest to domesticate.

The hiding of food in caches is a well-known habit of squirrels and foxes and naturalists have long debated whether the re-location of such caches was a chance affair. Macdonald (1976), in some elegant experiments with his tame foxes, proved beyond doubt that a fox can go unerringly to its own caches but is quite unable to find the caches of another fox or those provided by the experimenter. This illustrates how exceedingly intimate a resident animal can become with the minute topography of its own home range.

Over the general and fundamental question of what our wild mammals eat, much devoted labour in analysing faeces and gut contents has advanced our knowledge significantly, as may be seen from the sections on food under each species in the body of this volume.

In 1956 came the first report that ultrasounds are emitted, not only by bats, but by the nestling young of some species of rodents, presumably for communication with the mother. Since then a number of papers from J.D.Pye's group at King's College, London, e.g. Sales 1972, have added to the number of species known to use this kind of signal and have also shown that males emit ultrasounds when initiating copulation with females and that females emit them when searching for a lost litter. The interpretation of such signals is still rather speculative but no doubt further experiments will shed light in the matter.

The above are no more than the highlights of behavioural studies since 1964. The sections under this heading in the body of this volume will be found packed with new information.

Genetics and intra-specific variation

In the time of Linnaeus a species was regarded as the fundamental unit of classification, being, as we now say, genetically homogeneous. Since the work of the taxonomist is based on museum specimens, such a way of looking at species simplifies his herculean task considerably. Trouble arose first from having to cope with the geographical variation within species as it became revealed and a huge and cumbersome apparatus of subspecies, designated by trinomial scientific names, had to be injected below the species level. Worse was to come, for research done mainly during this century revealed that there were variations within species also in biological characters such as voice, behaviour, physiology and life histories. These, of course, are not amenable to storage in museums. Finally, the demonstration that every species which has been closely investigated has turned out to be tremendously heterogeneous genetically once and for all disposes of the 'homogeneous species'.

Some of these variations within species have already been glanced at in the section on Behaviour. Since the techniques of mammalian chromosome preparation have advanced enormously in the last two decades, many species, especially rodents and shrews, have been shown to be polymorphic in the structure and arrangement of their chromosomes (Meylan 1970, Ford & Hamerton 1970) and perhaps most startling is the situation disclosed for the common shrew. A paragraph in the first edition states 'Chromosome number variable . . . subject complex and still under investigation.' The picture that has emerged since that was written is as follows. European common shrews are sharply divided into two forms geographically separated except for some zones of overlap in Switzerland where they do not hybridise. Form A is found in lowland west Europe, Form B on higher ground and to the north and east of Europe. Form A's complement of chromosomes shows no variation, that of form B is polymorphic. Yet over the whole of the common shrew's range, no morphological characters have been found to signalise these variations. The detection and diagnosis of these and other examples of 'cryptospecies' is one of the most challenging problems now facing the taxonomist.

Another class of genetic variation, which has been the subject of recent study, concerns the so-called biochemical polymorphisms. In all species so far investigated, these have been shown to be widespread and abundant and may be used as markers to reveal genetic structure and its intra-specific patterning in mammal populations. Most enzymes and other proteins (and those of the blood haemoglobins and plasma have received most attention) exhibit a specific electric charge which causes them to move slower or faster in an electric field. This movement can be recorded in a starch gel and made visible by staining. The process is known as starch gel electrophoresis and is a sensitive indicator of the genetic heterogeneity of populations.

Pioneer work on wild mammals in this field was done by Semeonoff & Robertson (1968) on the short-tailed vole and by McDougall & Lowe (1968) on red deer, both in Scotland. The former showed that the frequency of certain allelomorphs changed with the phase of the 3–4 year cycle of numbers which is characteristic of this vole, while in the deer frequencies changed from east to west. Even more notable have been the results of Rasmussen (1970) who examined fourteen populations of deermice (*Peromyscus*) in Arizona in ponderosa pine forest separated by various distances and degrees of ecological discontinuity and found differences in gene frequencies between populations only two miles apart. Yet two populations separated by the huge cleft of the Grand Canyon of the Colorado River in the same state were alike.

This work confirms what has been noted under Behaviour about the detailed structure and organisation into demes of small mammal populations.

Gross changes in the pressure of natural selection have been engineered by man and the corresponding changes in genetic constitution of the animals subjected to such pressure have been observed. The pandemic of myxomatosis in the early 1950's was, perhaps, the most widespread and devastating 'experiment' ever performed and it was expected that adjustment, both by selection for resistant rabbits and for relatively benign strains of virus, would be achieved fairly rapidly. Nevertheless, even now after twenty years, the rabbit is still an uncommon animal in many parts of Great Britain.

Research on pest control during the last war revealed that brown rats and house mice had their own strategies for evading attempts to poison them. These involved an uncanny ability in detecting poisoned baits or a diffuseness of feeding activity which prevented a lethal dose being eaten. Soon after the war the blood anti-coagulant, warfarin, was introduced to the scene and revolutionized it. Warfarin is undetectable by taste or smell and its action is not violent and it was used widely and successfully against infestations of rats and mice. At the moment there is a strong movement to use it to poison grey squirrels but the difficulty here is to ensure that no other woodland animals eat the bait.

Events during the last two decades, however, (see Drummond 1970) have shown that the blanket use of warfarin produces stringent selection for genetic characters that provide resistance to its action. There are, by now, many areas in western Europe where old-fashioned methods of rodent control have had to be reintroduced. Our increasing awareness of the genetical heterogeneity of populations should have warned us that rats and mice might lose many battles and yet, eventually, win the war.

As a final example of the modern approach to the study of intra-specific variation, we may cite the work done on the British subspecies of wood mouse (*Apodemus sylvaticus*) by Berry and others. All the variants from the mainland form live on off-shore islands and an earlier interpretation was that they represented a previous stock which had been supplanted on the mainland by a later invader from the continent. In 1961 Corbet advanced the view that these island races had been introduced by man in relatively recent times and, since then, several workers, especially Delany and Berry (see Berry 1970), have been elucidating the pattern of these variations. Characters such as size and coat colour are tricky since they change with age but can be valuable if analysed with care (Delany 1970). Berry has used a number of minor variations in the skull, e.g. presence or absence of certain small foramina, whether others are single or double and so on. In this way twenty or so variants can be checked and the results give a very sensitive index of similarity and dissimilarity between populations.

Conclusions are that many of these island races of wood mice are notably different from each other as well as from mainland mice which is not surprising if an island has been colonised by a small number of animals, or, perhaps, by a single pregnant female. But even amid all this variability, Berry detects a general tendency for these island mice to resemble Scandinavian stock rather than British mainland or west European forms. Thus it is possible that these islands became populated through the agency of the Vikings during the first millenium A.D.

Population studies

It is a truism to say that the study of populations revolves around the counting or estimation of numbers of animals and the detection and analysis of change in their numbers. Only by understanding why these changes do or do not take place can we arrive at any predictions about the future course of events and the measures to take, if some form of management becomes necessary.

Techniques for measuring the distribution and abundance of animals have not changed greatly since 1964. Where we can make a total count, as with deer or seals, we do so. Where this is not possible, we resort to counting sample areas and multiplying up to obtain a figure for the whole area in which we are interested; or we employ a method of estimation such as capture-mark-recapture, which gives an estimated total from the proportion of marked to unmarked animals. Often we do not need such precision and are content to use an index to density such as counting tracks or faeces or by using a standard line or grid of traps for a standard period of time. Such indices will tell us clearly enough whether mice or voles are twice as numerous in one year as in another or whether their numbers are different in different habitats.

What advances have been made have been mainly in refining the statistical methods employed in such estimations and indices to make allowance for 'edge effect' (how many animals are drawn into a grid of traps from outside the grid), differences in trappability according to species, sex and age and so on. For small mammals a good review of recent research on the estimation of density is given in Smith *et al.* (1975) and on density indices in Linn & Downton (1975). For the less sophisticated there is a brief, partial examination of the problems by Southern (1973).

When we turn from methods to results, such extensive information has been published since 1964 that it is difficult to know where to begin or end. Perhaps the most significant advance in our knowledge has been the acquisition, for a number of species, of life-table data. Clearly information about densities of animals, even on change of densities from season to season and place to place does not get us very far in explaining the equilibrium of a population. We must know also what is the input from breeding and immigration and the output from death and emigration which trim the balance of numbers. In other words, we need to know what is the rate of turnover of a population, compounded of birth and death rates; for simplicity, in this discussion, we shall use these terms to include immigration and emigration respectively.

A life table is really a very simple way of displaying the survival and death rates of a population, though it is cloaked in the ciphers of actuaries and demographers. It starts with a number of animals born into a population at one time and gives the number that survive in subsequent periods of time until the last member has died. Naturally the acquisition of this sort of information for wild animals is far from simple and there are innumerable pitfalls in its interpretation; for some creatures, e.g. birds which have been extensively ringed and recovered, survival rates can be registered on a large scale but mammals present much greater difficulties.

One of the most straightforward examples of recently published life tables for wild mammals is that for the grey squirrel by Barkalow *et al.* (1970). It also illustrates well the information that can be condensed in life table form and explains the nomenclature of the different columns (Table A).

In this Table column 2 (l_x) gives the raw data; an initial cohort of 1000 will have declined to 247 by the beginning of the next age interval (1–2 years) and to 112 at the start of the 2–3 year age interval and so on. Column 3 (d_x) gives the complementary information of the number of deaths in each age interval and from this can be calculated the important information of what proportion of squirrels entering each age interval will have died by the beginning of the next one (q_x). Thus we are able to detect that mortality falls heavily on young squirrels in their first and second years of age (75% and 55% respectively). For the next three years their survival rate generally improves, though still something over a quarter of the squirrels in these age classes disappear each year. After this, in the age interval of 5–6 years, the death rate rises markedly again and the cohort rapidly fades out. The anomaly of the low death rate of the 6–7 year class is probably due to the paucity of figures at this stage. We shall revert to the final column (e_x) below.

TABLE A. Life table for the grey squirrel, based on 1023 individuals marked as nestlings, brought, for convenience, to a starting cohort of 1000 (after Barkalow *et al.* 1970)

Age (x)	Survivors (l_x)	Deaths* (d_x)	Death rate (q_x)	Expectation of further life (e_x)
0–1	1000	753	75%	0·99
1–2	247	135	55	1·82
2–3	112	30	27	2·41
3–4	82	26	32	2·10
4–5	56	15	26	1·84
5–6	41	25	59	1·32
6–7	16	1	2	1·48
7–8	15	15	100	—

*These will include some emigrants.

When the first edition of the Handbook was published, life tables were available for only about two British mammals and these were derived from laboratory stocks. These, of course, measured only how long an animal *can* live, not how long it *does* live under natural conditions. Again, in tracing the survival of wild animals, the following through of a cohort all born at one season can be excessively laborious with long-lived animals. A short cut to obtaining approximately the same information is to take a sample of animals from a population at one blow, determine the age of each individual and construct a frequency distribution of the age classes. Thus, if we find that 90% of the sample falls in the age class 0–1 years (or months, weeks, etc.), 9% in the age class 1–2 years and 1% in the age class 2–3 years, we can presume that of 100 animals born into this population at the same time, 90 will die in their first year, 9 in their second year and one in its third year, but we shall not have had to wait three years to find this out. A life table based on a cross section of a population is most descriptively designated as a 'vertical' life table, though other authors use the terms 'static' or 'time-specific'. A life table based on the following through of a cohort is called a 'horizontal' life table ('cohort' or 'dynamic' life table of other authors).

We must remember, however, that these somewhat simplified life tables can run into trouble with a wild population that is fluctuating in numbers considerably from year to year, as short-lived species may do, or undergoing a long-term trend. Fortunately, many mammal populations maintain a fairly even equilibrium of numbers and the proportions of their age classes remain roughly the same from year to year. The picture can be widely different in, e.g. fish such as the herring, in which the product of one prolific year may dominate the population for a number of subsequent years.

The construction of a vertical life table depends, of course, on the feasibility of determining the age of every individual in the sample and, since this is vital, much energy and research has been spent in the last twenty years on methods of ageing mammals. It would be inappropriate here to go into details (an expert review of the subject was published by Morris in 1972) but, broadly, whereas marking and tagging are needed for horizontal life tables, vertical ones depend on the measurement of morphological and physiological changes with age. Thus, increase in size, wear of teeth, deposition of annual rings in teeth, horns etc., the fusion of epiphyses and sutures and much other evidence have been pressed into service.

The last column (e_x) in Table A gives the 'mean expectation of further life', obviously a figure of great value to insurance companies where man is concerned and useful in wild animals for comparisons between species and age classes. Very roughly, at any point in time in a life table, a group of animals of the same age enters into an older age class; if we sum the total number of years to be lived in the future from this point in time (i.e. add up all the remaining entries of survivors) and divide by the initial number of the group, we arrive at a figure for e_x. The steps in the actual calculation of e_x are, however, somewhat more complicated than this description would suggest; for a very clear exposition Krebs (1972) should be consulted. The figures for expectation of further life in the case of the grey squirrel (Table A) show that, as with many mammals, it rises to a peak or a plateau in mature life and declines as the end of life approaches.

The expanding British population of grey seals has, during the last twenty years, aroused controversy and legislation over its management. Hewer (1974) has, with great labour, provided us with an approximation to a vertical life table by examining a sample of 239 cows and 254 bulls and determining their ages by counting the layers of cementum which are laid down, one each year, round the roots of the canine teeth. Unfortunately, the resulting frequency distribution cannot be rigorously analysed as a life table because, as the author admits, the samples are not an accurate representation of the age distribution of the population. Nevertheless, e_x figures, though very approximate, do reveal that, throughout life, cows may expect to live considerably longer than bulls. This fits in with the fact that no bulls in the sample exceeded the age of 23 years, whereas some cows were found that had lived for over 30 years. This may be connected with the wear and tear on bulls which the harem system involves, since they stay ashore without feeding and fight to defend their harem during the whole breeding season.

A particularly elegant example of the analysis of population processes is shown in the work of Lowe (1969) on the red deer of the Isle of Rhum. Up to 1957 these deer had been lightly culled (*c.* 6% per annum); in that year the then Nature Conservancy bought the island and the first census of the deer was done, a yearly procedure that was carried on until 1966. Throughout this period a higher rate of culling (16%) was imposed. Most of the natural deaths were monitored each year by combing the island for corpses and both these and the shot animals were aged from the progressive replacement, eruption and wear of the teeth.

From this it was possible to tell which of these deer had been present in 1957 at the start of the investigation and what were their ages at that time. Thus a vertical life table could be constructed for 1957 and checked to be in close agreement with the census of that year. This life table is assumed to show the equilibrium of the red deer population on Rhum under the regime of light culling. It shows that, during the first four or five years of life, stags had a higher expectation of further life than hinds (4 to 7 years compared with 3 to 5), after which the figures for each sex become roughly equal. It shows further that during the eighth and ninth year of life the mortality of both sexes suddenly increased, giving an e_x figure of under two years. After this setback, the figure increased again (to 3·3 years in stags and 3·5 in hinds) before finally tailing off up to the oldest age of 16 years.

At the same time a horizontal life table can be constructed for the calves born in 1956 and counted in 1957. It is a tragedy that these can be followed only until 1966, when the investigation was terminated. The main point of interest in comparing the two life tables is whether the change in cull from 1957 onwards affected the population dynamics. In fact, the figures for expectation of further life, though lower throughout than those in the vertical life table through the exclusion of older animals, show exactly the same trends. Young stags survive better than young hinds up to about their fourth year, after which the figures become equal, and there is the same sudden drop in life expectation at the ages of eight and nine years. It seems that the increased mortality due to shooting after 1957 very nearly replaced the natural mortality prior to that year—a finding very pertinent to principles of management.

At the other end of the size scale, we now have a very informative comparison of life tables for the common and pygmy shrews constructed from live-trapping data (i.e. horizontal life tables) by Croin-Michielson (1966). She followed the lives of three cohorts of common shrews launched between June and August and found that, apart from one cohort including very newly weaned animals some of which dispersed from her trapping area, their survival through the winter and through to the next spring was remarkably good, being usually around 90% per trapping interval (4–5 weeks). After this they died off rapidly and none survived after July of their second year. These shrews, therefore, once they had become established residents, almost lived out their physiological life span—in other words they died of old age, which is very unusual in wild animals. Parallel data, however, for the pygmy shrew showed that death struck at them throughout their lives and their life tables resembled the more usual kind exhibited by rodents and most other mammals. By the next spring all three cohorts that she followed had suffered a death rate between 70 and 90%.

In considering how common and pygmy shrews can occupy the same habitat and yet avoid direct competition, Croin-Michielson adduced evidence that, during the winter, common shrews spend most of their time in burrows, while pygmy shrews remain above ground. The notable difference between the two species in the incidence of mortality supports her hypothesis, since during the winter pygmy shrews will be more vulnerable to predation.

For most mammals we have to accept that a life table starts with a cohort of weaned animals, since it is rarely possible to measure the death rate between birth and weaning (the red deer being a notable exception). Sometimes we have to start from the age when the species studied will first come into live traps and that may be variable. Despite these imperfections, useful information may be obtained. Flowerdew (1974) found that, by accepting any unmarked, young wood mouse as a starter, he could construct horizontal life tables which showed important differences in expectation of further life between areas quite close together, e.g. 14 weeks in one area and 12 weeks in another, and between years, e.g. 14 weeks in 1968 and 10 weeks in 1969 on the same area. This warns us to be wary of lumping figures.

We have said enough now to show some of the advances that have been made recently in exploring the patterns of mortality in British wild mammals. For a full assessment of the turnover of a population, we need to know also the pattern of births, so that, by combining the 'income' and 'expenditure' of a population we can determine whether it is showing a net loss or a net gain or is remaining stationary.

Ideally the birth rate should be expressed as the number of female offspring born per mature female of each reproductive age group per unit of time. The drawing up of this information is known to demographers as an age-specific fertility table and does for the 'income' of a population what the life table does for the 'expenditure'. Such precision is desirable because the number of young produced by mammals usually varies with the age of the mother, rising as she grows to full productive maturity and falling as she approaches old age. Thus in constructing such a table it is vital to know the age composition of the females.

Clearly this information is very hard to obtain for wild mammals. It is feasible, of course, to derive it from a laboratory maintained stock, e.g. the pioneer work of Leslie & Ranson (1940) on *Microtus agrestis* and of Leslie *et al.* (1955) on *M. arvalis orcadensis*, but such figures give us only a physiological maximum; this, however, is useful for some purposes, e.g. comparing species.

Nevertheless, some progress has been made, of which it will have to suffice, within the confines of this Introduction, to cite two examples from researches already quoted. Barkalow *et al.* (1970) report the somewhat unusual condition in the grey squirrel that female offspring per female per year starts at a figure of 0·05 for those in their first year (the column labelled m_x in their Table 3), i.e. very few of them breed, rises to 1·3 in their second year and to 2·3 in the third year; from this point it stays steady at 2·3 for the remainder of the life time (to eight years). Lowe (1969), on the other hand, found a more normal state of affairs for the red deer on Rhum. Hinds do not breed there until their third year, when the m_x figure for the 1957 population was 0·3. This figure rose to 0·5 when the hinds were six years old and then declined again to 0·3 by the tenth year of life, after which it remained steady at 0·3 to the end of the table (16 years).

With all the accumulation of data on the equilibria of numbers in wild populations of British mammals we may well inquire next the reasons that these equilibria are what they are. This is, after all, the central problem of population ecology, towards the elucidation of which all these laborious countings and computations are directed. As Darwin stressed, all animals have a vast potential for increase in numbers; what factors, therefore, halt a growing population at a certain level and hold it there and why is this level different in different times and places?

Jewell *et al.* (1974) studied the feral Soay sheep on St Kilda and showed that their numbers were regulated quite simply by the amount and quality of the grazing available to them. They suffered periodic sudden declines and then, as the vegetation recovered, their numbers rose again. Similarly, Lowe's work on the red deer on the Isle of Rhum indicated that, during the time before his investigation started and while the deer were being lightly culled, most of the natural mortality had been due directly to starvation.

The regulation of numbers of wild animals is classically attributed to starvation, predators or disease or a combination of these factors. This is the stark condition revealed at St Kilda and Rhum. Matters, however, are rarely as straightforward as this. In ecological text-books a fourth factor is usually added—competition for space and this is becoming more and more recognised as a regulator, especially of vertebrate populations. It is a somewhat protean concept and may take almost as many forms as there are animals; it does not submit readily to quantification and, perhaps, this is one reason that its study appeals to the average, 'non-numerate' naturalist. It is not just a matter of dictation by the environment; now the animal itself is having a say in the matter and this is fascinating to observe.

Even in the apparently straightforward story of the deer on Rhum a hint of this influence is given at the close of the investigation. Partly through the difficulty of identifying the sexes at a distance during the census on which the cull was based, the proportion of stags was allowed to rise to 1·3 : 1 hind by 1964 and this was followed during the next two years by an unexplained disappearance of stags. Some corpses were washed up on the beaches and it is possible that pressure of numbers had forced some stags to attempt to emigrate.

Clearly one aspect of the demand for space is the holding and defending of a territory or home range whether by a single individual or pair, as in many passerine birds, or by a socially organised group, as in many mammals. We have already mentioned in previous sections the effects of aggressiveness by dominant animals in promoting dispersal and inhibiting reproduction of those lower in the social scale and these effects can doubtless be important in regulating the number of animals that can live in a particular area (see especially Wynne-Edwards (1964)). Such demands for space must have evolved against the background of basic environmental restraints already mentioned—starvation, predators and parasites, so that the whole pattern of the regulation of any animal population must be a complex one.

Much of the recent research on these problems has been done on mice and voles, partly because they supply abundant material for quantitative study, partly because their populations turn over rapidly, so that the influence of regulating factors can quickly be detected, and partly because their numbers sometimes rise to plague proportions with consequent economic losses to forestry and agriculture.

From the mass of information published on this topic during the last twenty years, there is space here to refer to only one major piece of research but one which delineates very clearly the complex interaction of the factors that regulate populations.

From 1950 to 1970, members of the now extinct Bureau of Animal Population at Oxford followed fairly closely the changes in numbers of wood mice and bank voles in the nearby deciduous woodlands of the Wytham Estate, belonging to the University (see Southern (1970)). Watts (1969) studied these changes intensively for three years and was able to check and confirm his results against the long series of records in the files of the Bureau. More recently his work has been verified and extended by Flowerdew (1974).

Watts concentrated his attention on the wood mouse and found his starting point for interpreting the yearly fluctuations in the fact that numbers returned with remarkable consistency to roughly the same level each winter. As winter gave way to spring and the breeding season approached, the numbers of mice declined. If the crop of acorns on which the mice fed largely during the winter was poor, the decline was steep; if the crop was rich, the decline was still evident but did not reach nearly so low a level. But, in that case, why was there any decline at all, and such a consistent one? Watts showed that the decline was due to a deterioration in the survival rate and argued that this was caused by the heightened aggression of mice coming into breeding condition; this has received support from the subsequent work of Flowerdew (1974).

The next point to be accounted for was that, having declined to a spring low, the mouse population remained at that level through to summer despite a full programme of reproduction. Again, Watts demonstrated a very poor survival rate for spring litters and attributed this to strife among the mice, since there is no evidence of food shortage at this time of year.

So here, already, we have two factors implicated, the supply of food during the winter and the dislike of mice for their fellow mice.

The last phase of the story concerns the resurgence of numbers during the autumn leading to the consistent winter peak. Again, since the mechanism of this is a notably improved survival rate of later litters, it seems probable that the aggressiveness of the adults has waned or the aggressive animals have died but the most significant feature to be observed here is the timing of the end of reproduction in relation to the summer density of the mice. If the spring decline was not severe and the population has jogged along through the summer at a moderate level, then breeding may cease as early as September. If, however, the spring decline was severe, breeding may continue to November or December. The end result is the same—a winter peak of numbers at about the same level year after year. The adjustment is so precise as to demonstrate a perfectly density-dependent (i.e. regulatory) process. It is instructive, indeed, to observe how many factors are geared to produce and maintain the complete annual picture.

It does not follow, of course, that other species or, indeed, wood mice in habitats different from Wytham Woods will exhibit just this pattern of regulation but it is heartening for the future to have some guide as to what to look for and how to look for it.

Distribution and status

If there is one thing that a Society with a widespread network of keen members can do better than individuals or small groups with professional expertise, it is to gather extensive information about such fundamental matters as distribution and status of our mammal species. Above all, and this is where the Mammal Society has contributed most signally since its founding, it can organize the acquisition of such information.

When this Handbook was first published, the only example of a detailed, country-wide distribution map was that for the grey squirrel by Shorten (1946), based on parishes, and an up-dated version, based on the 10 km squares of the National Grid, by Lloyd (1962). These documented the spread of this species at the expense of the red squirrel.

Now, not only are distributions of several species, some of which are mentioned below, known in reasonable detail but in 1965 the Mammal Society launched a National Distribution Scheme under the care of G.B.Corbet to gather and map data for all British mammals except deer which in 1967 came under the British Deer Society's own scheme. The initial aim was to rescue and record the mass of information hidden away in people's notebooks and heads and in miscellaneous publications. These, too, were based on presence in the 10 km National Grid squares and preliminary versions were published by Corbet (1971). In some instances the maps portrayed mainly the distribution of keen observers but, generally, they were sufficiently encouraging for the data to be transferred to the Biological Records Centre of the then Nature Conservancy at Monk's Wood, where 'instant' maps are available from which naturalists can see what empty squares they can helpfully examine. This is rewarding work, highly to be recommended and commended; only by the mapping of more and more data will the squares that are truly empty be revealed and a firm basis laid from which to measure future change. Some idea of the value of this scheme can be gained from the simplified distribution maps included in the body of this edition.

Surveys of particular species, organized through the Mammal Society, have, of course, yielded much more precise information. The Badger Survey, started by T.J.Pickvance in 1963, has evolved into a comprehensive network of observers with County Recorders checking and channelling the information to a central point. Data on density as well as distribution enable us to detect changes in status and, e.g., provide a background against which to assess the badger's involvement in the problem of bovine tuberculosis. The report by Neal (1972) shows the broad patterning of the distribution in the British Isles and for twenty-two counties, selected for their intensive cover, he presents figures for total sets found, the highest density noted in a 10 km square and details of the soils and habitats that the badgers favoured.

A striking example of the way in which one person's zeal can literally change the map concerns the harvest mouse. Corbet's map (1971) gives only three records north-west of a line drawn from the Severn to the Humber. In 1973 a special survey was begun and the energetic organiser, Stephen Harris, who has covered very large areas of the country himself, widely publicised the fact that summer nests can easily be found in the winter. This adroit move brought a flood of new records, so far extending the harvest mouse's known range northwards to Edinburgh and westwards to Pembrokeshire. It remains to be seen whether this is a phase of the expansion and contraction which seem to have alternated during this century.

A survey of the distribution and numbers of the otter has proved a rather more intractable project. It was initiated in 1968, partly because of a general impression that the otter's numbers were declining perhaps because of competition between it and the introduced American mink. An immediate stop-gap attempt to gain some objective evidence on the matter was made by H.R.Hewer in collaboration with the British Field Sports Society. Using the records of the otter hunts expressed as the number of otters 'found' per 100 days hunting, Hewer showed that the figures were relatively steady from the beginning of this century to about the middle of the 1960's when there was rather a sudden drop in most areas (Anon. [Hewer] 1969). A repeat survey on figures up to 1971 (Anon. [Hewer] 1974) suggested little change since 1967 except in the Midlands where the decline continued. The Mammal Society's survey, however, with the aim of collecting more satisfactory data based on extensive search for traces, is now getting into its stride and is revealing a more disturbing picture, especially in East Anglia. It is urgent to continue and expand this survey.

Other surveys are going on which can be mentioned only briefly here. Some are connected with the Mammal Society, e.g. the dormouse and one recently started on whales and dolphins; some are mainly the work of the Ministry of Agriculture, e.g. rabbits, foxes, grey squirrels, coypu, mink. Finally, the sterling labours of the Seals Research Division of the Natural Environment Research Council deserve notice. In the first edition of this Handbook only a 'guesstimate' could be given for the total population of grey seals in the British Isles. Now a fairly accurate account of numbers at each breeding colony is available (Bonner 1976). This, together with a deeper insight into life table data, has enabled a rational system of culling to be introduced at colonies that have become overpopulated in recent years.

Some of these surveys have revealed changes in range and/or status and this, of course, is one of their most valuable functions. They lay a base line for future work.

Other changes in status in the British Mammal fauna between 1964 and 1976 have been established. For a general account during historic times we refer readers to Corbet (1974).

To begin with, three species of bat have been added to the British list during this period. A small colony of the grey long-eared bat (*Plecotus austriacus*) is now known to exist in Dorset and, since its recognition in 1963, specimens have been recorded for Sussex and Hampshire as well. It is a close relative of our common long-eared bat (*P. auritus*) and was distinguished from it on the Continent only in 1960. Similarly in 1970, on the Continent, the whiskered bat (*Myotis mystacinus*) was found to have a very close relative, Brandt's bat (*M. brandti*), from which it had not previously been distinguished. By now Brandt's bat has been identified in England at a number of localities reaching as far north as Yorkshire. The third newcomer, Nathusius' pipistrelle (*Pipistrellus nathusii*), again with a close relative, the common pipistrelle, is now known from a single specimen found in Dorset in 1969.

The most arresting change in the distribution of the British mammal fauna was the discovery in 1964 of the bank vole in Ireland. It is more than probable that this is due to a recent introduction by man and, as such, will be considered by naturalists as a reprehensible action. Nevertheless, now the damage is done, it should form an interesting study on how a species spreads into a new environment. The latest information (Fairley 1971) indicates that the bank vole is almost confined to the area of south-west Ireland between the Rivers Shannon and Blackwater. Further information will be awaited eagerly.

There are some further examples of change of status in the period concerned. The American mink has made good its foothold in Britain and has now occupied most of our river systems, despite intensive trapping. There is so far no evidence to implicate it in the decline of the otter. The wild cat has now been recorded south of the Highland line and the polecat has spread to most of Wales and the English border counties (see provisional maps in Corbet (1971)). Deer continue to colonise new ground, especially the introduced sika and muntjac, and populations of Australian wallabies are now established in the Peak District and in Sussex.

On the other hand, bats generally seem to be on the decline, not only in Britain but also in Europe and North America (Racey & Stebbings 1972). It is thought that the disturbance of roosts and the pervasive effects of pesticides are the main causes and much energy and devotion have recently been spent on installing grilles over the entrances to caves which house roosting bats. The species now in the greatest danger are the greater horseshoe bat, whose numbers have fallen alarmingly over the last two decades, and the mouse-eared bat, whose prospects are very precarious in Britain anyway. Both these are now totally protected by the Conservation of Wild Creatures and Wild Plants Act, 1975.

Conservation and legislation

The concept of conservation, as opposed to protection, has made great strides into our everyday conversation of recent years. It is a term that is sometimes used rather glibly and can mean almost as many things as there are people who use it. Among many definitions we prefer the one put forward by Elton (1958)—'. . . some wise principle of coexistence between man and nature, even if it means a modified kind of man and a modified kind of nature'.

This embraces the view that nature conservation is not simply a matter of putting fences round certain areas and making them into nature reserves, though this is an essential element in the whole strategy and it is encouraging to know that the total area of Britain's nature reserves has now reached 300,000 acres. To this must be added many more areas that have been reserved by the burgeoning activity of local Naturalists' Trusts and other bodies.

Nevertheless, Elton's definition makes the important point that man cannot avoid being himself implicated in the ecological balance of the whole countryside and, where interests clash, management is necessary and, moreover, management based on sound ecological principles. This outlook is gradually becoming familiar to the public and is the linch pin on which the policies of the Nature Conservancy Council and the researches of the Institute of Terrestrial Ecology turn. This Introduction is no place to go into the battles that have been fought (and sometimes lost) to establish these principles but we would recommend a thoughtful little book by D.N.McVean and J.D.Lockie (1969), *Ecology and Land Use in Upland Scotland*. Though devoted to only one of our major habitats, the philosophy is applicable to the rest of Great Britain.

This principle of conservation was first established by legislation in the Deer (Scotland) Act, 1959, which is described in its title as 'an Act to further the conservation and control of red deer in Scotland'. It sets up a Red Deer Commission with the dual function of advising owners 'in the interests of conservation' on the stock carrying capacity of their land and of arranging for control where deer become too numerous and cause damage to agriculture or forestry. As hard evidence of the way in which our public conscience has matured in that direction, we may note the legislation concerning mammals that has been enacted since the first edition of this Handbook was published.

Earlier legislation had protected grey seals without making adequate provision for control. That had encouraged a great proliferation of their numbers which caused an outcry from various fishing interests and overcrowding at some colonies such that 'slum' conditions developed, causing a high mortality among the pups. The Conservation of Seals Act, 1970, prescribed close seasons for both grey and common seals during the breeding season when they are most accessible and most vulnerable but allows culling under licence and with approved weapons to prevent damage to fisheries, for management purposes and the exploitation of the surplus as a natural resource. Neither species is protected at other times of the year but the minimum size of the rifle that may be used is laid down.

The badger is a harmless animal which scarcely ever needs control. The Badgers Act, 1973, therefore gives it complete protection, save insofar as the owner or occupier of any land may kill the occasional rogue. Such unnecessary and undesirable practices as badger digging and the use of badger tongs are prohibited. Gassing badgers always has been and remains illegal but a loophole has recently been made whereby the Minister can authorise the gassing of specified sets where badgers have been convincingly implicated in the transmission of bovine tuberculosis.

More recently has come the Conservation of Wild Creatures and Wild Plants Act, 1975, which, as mentioned earlier, protects absolutely the greater horseshoe and mouse-eared bats and prohibits bat ringing except under licence from the Nature Conservancy Council. The schedule of protected wild creatures has to be reviewed by the Nature Conservancy Council every five years and is essentially fluid. Any other species may be added if its 'status as a British wild creature is being endangered by any action designated as an offence under the Act' (i.e. killing or taking) and an animal must be removed from it, if no longer endangered.

Though the Deer Act, 1963, lays down close seasons for deer in England, it is more an animal welfare Act than a conservation one. Indeed, most species of deer had become so numerous that it was profitable to poach them, often by cruel and undesirable methods. These are prohibited by the Act and the size and type of weapons and ammunition that may be used specified.

This may seem a brief tale but it shows more activity of a positive kind during the last fifteen years than during the previous century or so. We must remember that any law that cannot be enforced is a bad law and that it is best to move slowly in such matters and with due consideration of the facts. Good laws and the management they are designed to bring about must be based on knowledge, not on emotion, and, as we hope this Introduction has shown, the Mammal Society together with other bodies such as the British Deer Society has led the way in the necessary scientific study of our mammal fauna.

References

ANDERSON P.K. (1970) Ecological structure and gene flow in small mammals. *Symp. zool. Soc. Lond.* **26**, 299–325.

ANON. [HEWER H.R.] (1969) The otter in Britain. *Oryx*, **10**, 16–22.

ANON. [HEWER H.R.] (1974) The otter in Britain—a second report. *Oryx*, **12**, 429–35.

BAILEY G.N.A., LINN I.J. & WALKER P.J. (1973). Radioactive marking of small mammals. *Mammal Rev.* **3**, 11–23.

BARKALOW F.S., HAMILTON R.B. & SOOTS R.F. (1970). The vital statistics of an unexploited gray squirrel population. *J. Wildlife Manag.* **34**, 489–500.

BERRY R.J. (1970) Covert and overt variation, as exemplified by British mouse populations. *Symp. zool. Soc. Lond.* **26**, 3–26.

BONNER W.M. (1976). The stocks of Grey seals (*Halichoerus grypus*) and Common seals (*Phoca vitulina*) in Great Britain. *Nat. Env. Res. Council Publ.*, *Ser. C*, **no. 16**. Natural Environment Research Council, London.

CORBET G.B. (1961). Origin of the British insular races of small mammals and the 'Lusitanian' fauna. *Nature, Lond.* **191**, 1037–40.

CORBET G.B. (1971). Provisional distribution maps of British mammals. *Mammal Rev.* **1**, 95–142.

CORBET G.B. (1974). The distribution of mammals in historic times. *The changing flora and fauna of Britain* (ed. D.L.Hawksworth), pp. 179–202. Academic Press, London.

CROIN-MICHIELSON N. (1966). Intraspecific and interspecific competition in the shrews *Sorex araneus* L. and *S. minutus* L. *Arch. néerl. Zool.* **17**, 73–174.

CROWCROFT W.P. (1966). *Mice all over.* Foulis, London.

DELANY, M.J. (1970). Variation and ecology of island populations of the long-tailed field mouse (*Apodemus sylvaticus* (L)). *Symp. zool. Soc. Lond.* **26**, 283–95.

DRUMMOND D.C. (1970) Variations in rodent populations in response to control measures. *Symp. zool. Soc. Lond.* **26**, 351–67.

ELTON C.S. (1958). *The ecology of invasions by animals and plants.* Methuen, London.

EVANS F.C. (1942). Studies of a small mammal population in Bagley Wood, Berkshire. *J. Anim. Ecol.* **11**, 182–97.

FAIRLEY J.S. (1971). The present distribution of the bank vole *Clethrionomys glareolus* Schreber in Ireland. *Proc. R. Irish Acad.* **71**,(B), 183–9.

FLOWERDEW J.R. (1971). The subcaudal glandular area of *Apodemus sylvaticus. J. Zool. Lond.* **165**, 525–7.

FLOWERDEW J.R. (1974). Field and laboratory experiments on the social behaviour and population dynamics of the wood mouse (*Apodemus sylvaticus*). *J. Anim. Ecol.* **43**, 499–511.

FORD C.E. & HAMERTON J.L. (1970). Chromosome polymorphism in the common shrew *Sorex araneus. Symp. zool. Soc. Lond* **26**, 223–36.

GOLLEY F.B., PETRUSEWICZ K. & RYSZKOWSKI L. (1975). *Small mammals: their productivity and population dynamics.* University Press, Cambridge.

GORMAN M.L. (1976). A mechanism for individual recognition by scent in *Herpestes auropunctatus* (Carnivora: Viverridae). *Anim. Behav.* **24**, 141–5.

JEWELL P.A., MILNER C. & BOYD J. MORTON (1974). *Island survivors; the ecology of the Soay sheep of St. Kilda.* Athlone Press, London.

KING C.M. (1975). The home range of the weasel (*Mustela nivalis*) in an English woodland. *J. Anim. Ecol.* **44**, 639–69.

KREBS C.J. (1972). *Ecology.* Harper & Row, New York.

LESLIE P.H. & RANSON R.M. (1940). The mortality, fertility and rate of natural increase of the vole (*Microtus agrestis*) as observed in the laboratory. *J. Anim. Ecol.* **9**, 27–52.

LESLIE P.H., TENER J.S., VIZOSO M. & CHITTY H. (1955). The longevity and fertility of the Orkney vole, *Microtus orcadensis*, as observed in the laboratory. *Proc. zool. Soc. Lond.* **125**, 115–25.

LINN I.J. & DOWNTON F. (1975). The analysis of data obtained from small mammal index trappings. *Acta theriol.* **20**, 319–31.

LLOYD H.G. (1962). The distribution of squirrels in England and Wales, 1959. *J. Anim. Ecol.* **31**, 157–65.

LLOYD H.G. (1977). Tagging and radio-tracking of foxes in Wales. *Mammal Rev.* **7** (in press).

LOCKIE J.D. (1966). Territory in small carnivores. *Symp. zool. Soc. Lond.* **18**, 143–65.

LOWE V.P.W. (1969). Population dynamics of the red deer (*Cervus elaphus* L.) on Rhum. *J. Anim. Ecol.* **38**, 425–57.

MACDONALD D.W. (1976). Food caching by red foxes and some other carnivores. *Z. Tierpsychol.* **42**, 170–85.

MACDONALD D.M. (1977). Some behavioural consequences of food preference in the red fox, *Vulpes vulpes* L. *Mammal Rev.* 7, 7–23.

McDOUGAL E.I. & V.P.W. (1968). Transferrin polymorphism and serum proteins of some British deer. *J. Zool. Lond.* 155, 131–40.

McVEAN D.N. & LOCKIE J.D. (1969). *Ecology and land use in upland Scotland.* University Press, Edinburgh.

MEYLAN A. (1970). Chromosomal polymorphism in mammals. *Symp. zool. Soc. Lond.* 26, 211–22.

MOORS P.J. (1974). *The annual energy budget of a weasel* (Mustela nivalis *L.) population in-farmland.* Unpub. Ph.D. thesis, University of Aberdeen.

MORRIS P. (1972). A review of mammalian age determination methods. *Mammal Rev.* 2, 69–104.

NEAL E.G. (1972). The national badger survey. *Mammal Rev.* 2, 55–64.

RACEY P.A. & STEBBINGS R.E. (1972). Bats in Britain—a status report. *Oryx*, 11, 319–27.

RANDOLPH S.E. (1973). A tracking technique for comparing individual home ranges of small mammals. *J. Zool. Lond.* 170, 509–20.

RASMUSSEN D.I. (1970). Biochemical polymorphisms and genetic structure in populations of *Peromyscus. Symp. zool. Soc. Lond.* 26, 335–49.

SALES G.D. (1972). Ultrasound and mating behaviour in rodents with some observations on other behavioural situations. *J. Zool. Lond.* 168, 149–64.

SEMEONOFF R. & ROBERTSON F.W. (1968). A biochemical and ecological study of plasma esterase polymorphism in natural populations of the field vole, *Microtus agrestis* L. *Biochem. Genet.* 1, 205–27.

SHILLITO (BABINGTON) J.F. (1963). Observations in the range and movements of a woodland population of the common shrew *Sorex araneus* L. *Proc. zool. Soc. Lond.* 140, 533–46.

SHORTEN, M. (1946). A survey of the distribution of the American grey squirrel (*Sciurus carolinensis*) and the British red squirrel (*Sciurus vulgaris leucouros*) in England and Wales in 1944–5. *J. Anim. Ecol.* 15, 82–92.

SMITH M.H., GARDNER R.H., GENTRY J.B., KAUFMAN D.W. & O'FARRELL M.H. (1975). Density estimations of small mammal populations. *Small mammals: their productivity and population dynamics* (ed. F.B.Golley, K.Petrusewicz & L.Ryszkowski) pp. 25–53. University Press, Cambridge.

SOUTHERN H.N. (1970). The natural control of a population of Tawny owls (*Strescaluco*). *J. Zool. Lond.* 162, 197–285.

Southern H.N. (1970). The natural control of a population of Tawny owls (*Strixcaluco*). *Rev.* 3, 1–10.

STODDART D.M. (1970). Individual range, dispersion and dispersal in a population of water voles (*Arvicola terrestris* (L.)). *J. Anim. Ecol.* 39, 403–25.

STODDART D.M. (1972). The lateral scent organs of *Arvicola terrestris* (Rodentia: Microtinae). *J. Zool. Lond.* 166, 49–54.

TAYLOR J.C. (1970). The influence of arboreal rodents on their habitat and man. *European and Mediterranean Plant Protection Organization Publ. Ser. A*, no. 58, 217–23.

WATTS C.H.S. (1969). The regulation of wood mouse (*apodemus sylvaticus*) numbers in Wytham Woods, Berkshire. *J. Anim. Ecol.* 38, 285–304.

WATTS C.H.S. (1970). Correction for bias in movements of small mammals as revealed by trapping. *J. Mammal.* 51, 194–6.

WYNNE-EDWARDS V.C. (1964). *Animal dispersion in relation to social behaviour.* Oliver & Boyd, Edinburgh.

List of Species

In the following list the valid scientific name and most frequently used vernacular name are given for each species. The page at which each entry begins is given at the left. Synonyms and subspecific names are given in the main account of each species and can be traced through the index. Categories other than order, family, genus and species are used only in a few cases where they are stable and provide a useful subdivision of the groups found in the British Isles.

I	introduced	V	vagrant
E	extinct	D	domestic
F	feral	N	not yet recorded from British Isles but likely

Order Insectivora *continued*

45	FAMILY SORICIDAE	shrews		
46	*Sorex araneus*	common shrew		G. B. Corbet
54	*Sorex minutus*	pygmy shrew		G. B. Corbet
57	*Neomys fodiens*	water shrew		P. D. Jenkins
62	*Crocidura russula*	greater white-toothed shrew		P. D. Jenkins
65	*Crocidura suaveolens*	lesser white-toothed shrew		P. D. Jenkins

68	**Order Chiroptera**	bats		R. E. Stebbings
75	FAMILY RHINOLOPHIDAE	horseshoe bats		
76	*Rhinolophus ferrumequinum*	greater horseshoe bat		
80	*Rhinolophus hipposideros*	lesser horsehoe bat		
83	FAMILY VESPERTILIONIDAE			
84	*Myotis mystacinus*	whiskered bat		
87	*Myotis brandti*	Brandt's bat		
89	*Myotis nattereri*	Natterer's bat		
91	*Myotis bechsteini*	Bechstein's bat		
94	[*Myotis dasycneme*	pond bat]	N	
94	*Myotis myotis*	mouse-eared bat		
97	*Myotis daubentoni*	Daubenton's bat		
100	[*Myotis emarginatus*	notch-eared bat]	N	
100	*Vespertilio murinus*	parti-coloured bat	V	
102	*Eptesicus serotinus*	serotine		
105	*Nyctalus leisleri*	Leisler's bat		
108	*Nyctalus noctula*	noctule		
112	*Pipistrellus pipistrellus*	pipistrelle		
117	*Pipistrellus nathusii*	Nathusius' pipistrelle	?V	
118	*Barbastella barbastellus*	barbastelle		
121	*Plecotus auritus*	common long-eared bat		
125	*Plecotus austriacus*	grey long-eared bat		

129	**Order Lagomorpha**	lagomorphs		
129	FAMILY LEPORIDAE	rabbits and hares		
130	*Oryctolagus cuniculus*	rabbit	I	H. G. Lloyd
140	*Lepus capensis*	brown hare		R. Hewson
144	*Lepus timidus*	mountain hare		R. Hewson

151	**Order Rodentia**	rodents		
151	FAMILY CASTORIDAE			
151	*Castor fiber*	beaver	E	
152	FAMILY SCIURIDAE	squirrels		
153	*Sciurus vulgaris*	red squirrel		A. M. Tittensor
164	*Sciurus carolinensis*	grey squirrel	I	A. M. Tittensor
172	FAMILY CRICETIDAE	voles etc.		
172	SUBFAMILY MICROTINAE			
173	*Clethrionomys glareolus*	bank vole		J. R. Flowerdew
185	*Microtus agrestis*	field vole		D. Evans
193	*Microtus arvalis*	Orkney/Guernsey voles	?I	G. B. Corbet and S. J. Wallis
196	*Arvicola terrestris*	water vole		D. M. Stoddart
204	*Ondatra zibethicus*	musk rat	I, E	
204	FAMILY MURIDAE	rats and mice		
206	*Apodemus sylvaticus*	wood mouse		J. R. Flowerdew
217	*Apodemus flavicollis*	yellow-necked mouse		D. Corke
220	*Micromys minutus*	harvest mouse		R. Trout
227	*Mus musculus*	house mouse	I	F. P. Rowe
235	*Rattus rattus*	ship rat	I	K. D. Taylor
240	*Rattus norvegicus*	common rat	I	K. D. Taylor
247	FAMILY GLIRIDAE	dormice		
247	*Glis glis*	fat dormouse	I	G. B. Corbet
250	*Muscardinus avellanarius*	common dormouse		G. B. Corbet
256	FAMILY CAPROMYIDAE			
256	*Myocastor coypus*	coypu	I	L. M. Gosling
266	**Order Cetacea**	whales etc.		P. E. Purves
274	**Suborder Mysticeti**	baleen whales		
274	FAMILY BALAENIDAE	right whales		
275	*Balaena glacialis*	black right whale		

Order Cetacea *continued*

276   Family
      Balaenopteridae   rorquals etc.

276   *Megaptera novaeangliae*   humpback whale
279   *Balaenoptera physalus*   common rorqual
280   *Balaenoptera acutorostrata*   lesser rorqual
282   *Balaenoptera borealis*   sei whale
283   *Balaenoptera musculus*   blue whale

285   Suborder Odontoceti   toothed whales

285   Family Physeteridae   sperm whales

285   *Physeter catodon*   sperm whale
287   *Kogia breviceps*   pygmy sperm whale   V

288   Family Ziphiidae   beaked whales

288   *Hyperoodon ampullatus*   bottle-nosed whale
289   *Ziphius cavirostris*   Cuvier's whale
290   *Mesoplodon bidens*   Sowerby's whale
291   *Mesoplodon mirus*   True's beaked whale   V

292   Family Monodontidae

292   *Delphinapterus leucas*   white whale   V
293   *Monodon monoceros*   narwhal   V

295   Family Phocoenidae   porpoises

295   *Phocoena phocoena*   porpoise

296   Family Delphinidae   dolphins

296   *Orcinus orca*   killer whale
298   *Pseudorca crassidens*   false killer whale   V
299   *Globicephala melaena*   pilot whale
301   *Grampus griseus*   Risso's dolphin
302   *Lagenorhynchus
      albirostris*   white-beaked dolphin
303   *Lagenorhynchus acutus*   white-sided dolphin
305   *Tursiops truncatus*   bottle-nosed dolphin
306   *Stenella caeruleoalbus*   blue-white dolphin   V
308   *Delphinus delphis*   common dolphin

310   Order Carnivora   carnivores

311   Family Canidae   dogs

Order **Carnivora** *continued*

311	*Canis lupus*	wolf	E	
311	*Vulpes vulpes*	fox		H. G. Lloyd
321	FAMILY URSIDAE	bears		
321	*Ursus arctos*	brown bear	E	
321	FAMILY MUSTELIDAE			
323	*Martes martes*	pine marten		C. M. King
331	*Mustela erminea*	stoat		C. M. King
338	*Mustela nivalis*	weasel		C. M. King
345	*Mustela putorius*	polecat		K. C. Walton
352	*Mustela furo*	ferret	F	K. C. Walton
353	*Mustela vison*	mink	I	H. V. Thompson
357	*Meles meles*	badger		E. G. Neal
367	*Lutra lutra*	otter		C. M. King
375	FAMILY FELIDAE	cats		
375	*Felis silvestris*	wild cat		H. H. Kolb

383 Order **Pinnipedia**

383		pinnipedes		W. N. Bonner
383	FAMILY PHOCIDAE	seals		
384	*Phoca vitulina*	common seal		
394	*Halichoerus grypus*	grey seal		
403	*Phoca hispida*	ringed seal	V	
405	*Pagophilus groenlandicus*	harp seal	V	
405	*Erignathus barbatus*	bearded seal	V	
406	*Cystophora cristata*	hooded seal	V	
406	FAMILY ODOBENIDAE			
406	*Odobenus rosmarus*	**walrus**	V	

408 Order **Perissodactyla** odd-toed ungulates

408	FAMILY EQUIDAE	horses		
408	*Equus*	horse	D	

Introduction

This second edition of *The Handbook of British Mammals* deals fully with all species at present found in Britain, Ireland, the Channel Islands and the adjacent seas, including well-established introductions; and more briefly with occasional vagrants and species that have become extinct in historic times. All the authors of the systematic sections of the first edition have kindly agreed to allow their material to be re-used freely in compiling the present volume. All the accounts have been extensively rewritten. The author responsible for each species is named in the list of species and at the end of the account of that species, except in the case of the bats which are entirely the work of R. E. Stebbings, the cetaceans (P. E. Purves) and the seals (W. N. Bonner). All the introductory material, the accounts of orders, families and genera (other than bats, cetaceans and seals), the maps and the accounts of those extinct and introduced species that are dealt with very briefly are the responsibility of G. B. Corbet. The line drawings are by Robert Gillmor, Mrs Stephanie Durban and Mrs Elizabeth Sutton.

The same sequence of subheadings has been used for each species. The following explanatory notes are divided on a similar basis.

CLASSIFICATION

No innovations are made with respect to the higher classification. In general it follows that used in the first edition which in turn was based upon that of Simpson (1945). The only exception is that the pinnipedes are treated as an order, Pinnipedia, separate from the order Carnivora, as is done in most recent works. At the species level the only deviations from the treatment in the first edition are the following: the whiskered bat, *Myotis mystacinus*, of earlier works is now recognized as comprising two separate species, *M. mystacinus* and *M. brandti*; the long-eared bats are likewise known to comprise two species, *Plecotus auritus* and *P. austriacus*, previously confounded under the former name; the water vole, previously known as *Arvicola amphibius*, is considered to be conspecific with the continental *A. terrestris* and takes that name; the European brown hare is now considered conspecific with the African *Lepus capensis* and must take that name.

NOMENCLATURE

The original citation of the species name is given, with author, date and type locality. The synonyms that follow are only those that are based on British or Irish specimens or that have been widely used for the species as a whole. Subspecific names are included in the synonymy of the species name—any further discussion of subspecies is given under Variation. The more commonly used vernacular synonyms follow. All synonyms, vernacular and scientific, are included in the index. In quoting scientific names of British mammals it is quite unnecessary, except when specifically discussing nomenclature, to give the author and date of the name.

RECOGNITION

This section should be read in conjunction with the diagnostic characters given in the accounts of the higher categories or in the associated tables.

SIGN

Most of the signs mentioned are well illustrated by Bang & Dahlstrom (1974) and by Lawrence & Brown (1973).

DESCRIPTION

This section is normally limited to amplifying the characters most useful in recognition, pointing out the main specializations of the species, and describing variation correlated with sex, age and season. Coloured illustrations of most species can be found in van den Brink (1967) and many other popular books. More detailed descriptions of external structure, skulls and teeth can be found in Miller (1912).

MEASUREMENTS

Measurements of size can be more misleading than useful if variation with sex, age and season is not taken into account. Where figures are available with adequate qualifications they are usually tabulated. Otherwise only approximate indications of size are given in the text. Tables of cranial and dental measurements of most species were given by Miller (1912).

DISTRIBUTION

The distribution maps show the probable distribution at the present time, based mainly upon the results of the mapping programme being conducted jointly by the Mammal Society and the Biological Records Centre of the Institute of Terrestrial Ecology. Continuous black indicates widespread occurrence (in suitable habitat); stipple indicates areas where the species is likely to be less widespread. More detailed but provisional maps showing actual records by 10 km squares were published by Corbet (1971) for Britain and Ireland and by Crichton (1974, no date) for Ireland only.

VARIATION

Geographical variation is dealt with first, beginning with any differences between British and continental animals. Recent studies of geographical variation have generally shown that it is much less clear-cut and discrete than had previously been supposed and very few formally named subspecies can stand up to close scrutiny. Those that appear valid are diagnosed or their characters are tabulated. Many aspects of variation were dealt with in a symposium volume edited by Berry & Southern (1970).

HABITAT

The habitat occupied by most species of mammal can generally be defined in terms of adequate cover as protection against predators and disturbance, and an adequate food supply. For a guide to the description of habitat see Ferns (1967).

BEHAVIOUR

Information on behaviour is generally given in the following sequence: locomotion, diurnal rhythm of activity, home range, annual rhythm, social structure, communication and senses. Prominence is given to systematic studies of behaviour in natural conditions but these are scarce and for many species much of the information necessarily comes from observations of captive animals or from anecdotal accounts. These last commonly consist of single observations of behaviour that is reported because it seems unusual. They are by no means irrelevant to the study of normal behaviour but it is only when systematic observations of normal behaviour have been made that the significance of the anecdotal accounts can be appreciated. For a general text-book on mammalian behaviour see Ewer (1968).

FOOD

As with behaviour, there is a tendency for information on the normal diet to be swamped by records of the unusual. The 'anecdotal' literature on food is very extensive and has had to be quoted very sparingly. Normally, information on feeding behaviour is given here rather than under Behaviour.

BREEDING

The sequence normally followed is: synopsis, seasonality, courtship and mating, gestation, litter size, nesting behaviour, birth, development of young to weaning. Sources of general information on reproduction of mammals are Asdell (1964), a comprehensive survey dealing with all groups, and Austin & Short (1972), a series of five books dealing with the cytology, genetics and physiology of reproduction.

POPULATION STRUCTURE

Under this heading are presented data on the age structure of the population, longevity and density, including annual or non-annual fluctuations in density.

PREDATORS AND MORTALITY

Studies of predation that are relevant to most of the smaller species of mammals are those of Southern (1954, 1970) on the tawny owl, Glue (1967, 1974) on the barn owl, Day (1968) on mustelids and King (1971) on weasels.

PARASITES AND DISEASE

Rather than give exhaustive lists of parasites recorded, which would often include more stragglers than normal species, an attempt has been made to mention the species that occur frequently and regularly. The literature however is very scattered and there have been few attempts to collect together records relevant to one host species as distinct from records of hosts for each species of parasite. The main groups of parasites are shown in the following list which follows the sequence used in the text and includes the principal sources of information for each group.

Fleas—class Insecta, order Siphonaptera (Smit 1957a, b, George 1974).

Lice—class Insecta, order Phthiraptera (Hopkins 1949).

Mites—class Arachnida, order Acari (Evans *et al.* 1961).

Ticks—class Arachnida, order Acari, suborder Ixodoidea (Arthur 1963, Evans *et al.* 1961).

Tapeworms—phylum Platyhelminthes, class Cestoda.

Flukes—phylum Platyhelminthes, class Trematoda.

Roundworms—phylum Nematoda.

Protozoans—phylum Protozoa (Cox 1970).

RELATIONS WITH MAN

This section deals with the economic status of the species and, where relevant, its maintenance in captivity.

LITERATURE

References are given here to monographs or other useful and comprehensive compilations on a particular species. References to the source of specific facts are given throughout the text and relate to the bibliographies beginning on p. 465. The following publications are important sources of information that deal with all groups (or at least more than one order) of mammals.

Anderson & Jones (1967)—a concise account of each family of mammals.

Barrett-Hamilton & Hinton (1910–21)—a very detailed account of British mammals with a greal deal of historical information. Unfinished, including only the insectivores, bats, lagomorphs and rodents.

van den Brink (1967)—a field guide with coloured illustrations of most species and maps showing distribution in Europe.

Corbet (in press)—a review of the taxonomy and distribution of all mammals of the Palaearctic Region.

Ellerman & Morrison-Scott (1951)—a taxonomic checklist giving bibliographic references to all names of Palaearctic and Indian mammals up to 1946.

Fairley (1972)—a bibliography of literature on mammals in Ireland with 963 references.

Kurtén, B. (1968)—an account of the mammals of Europe during the Pleistocene Period, very relevant to a study of the origin of the present British fauna.

Miller (1912)—the most detailed taxonomic descriptions of European mammals, with illustrations of skulls and teeth.

Niethammer & Krapp (in press)—a detailed five-volume handbook on the mammals of Europe.

Ognev (1928–50)—very detailed accounts of the mammals of the USSR, including most species found in Britain. Includes much information on ecology and behaviour. Available in English translation.

Ovenden *et al.* (in press)—a field guide with coloured illustrations and maps of all European species.

Simpson (1945)—a comprehensive classification of fossil and recent mammals.

Walker (1964)—a genus-by-genus account of the mammals of the world with an extensive bibliography.

The principal journals dealing with British mammals are the following (official abbreviations in brackets):

Mammal Review (*Mammal Rev.*), published by Blackwell Scientific Publications for the Mammal Society. Mainly review articles covering all aspects of the study of mammals but with the emphasis on British mammals.

Journal of Zoology (*J. Zool., Lond.*), published by Academic Press for the Zoological Society of London. Contains batches of 'Notes from the Mammal Society', mainly on British mammals (these are distributed to members of the Mammal Society) as well as frequent longer papers on mammals.

Journal of Animal Ecology (*J. Anim. Ecol.*), published by Blackwell Scientific Publications for the British Ecological Society. Contains occasional papers on the ecology of British mammals.

Journal of Mammalogy (*J. Mammal.*), published by the American Society of Mammalogists. Mainly North American.

Mammalia, published by the Museum National d'Histoire Naturelle, Paris. Papers in French and English, many on European mammals.

Zeitschrift für Säugetierkunde (*Z. Säugetierk.*), published by Paul Parey for the Deutsche Gesellschaft für Säugetierkunde. Papers mainly in German, some in English, many on European mammals.

Acta Theriologica (*Acta theriol.*), published by the Polish Academy of Sciences. Almost entirely on European mammals with many papers in English.

Recognition of the Major Groups

There are probably somewhere in the region of 4000 species of living mammals, of which only about 100 occur, or have been recorded, in the British Isles. These represent 9 of the 19 major groups or orders of mammals that are recognised in most recent classifications, and of the really large orders only the Primates are unrepresented (except by man), although the Marsupialia are only represented by introduced and shakily established colonies of wallabies.

The number of species that can be said to be indigenous and resident in the British Isles and their coastal waters is 50, the remaining 50 or so being made up of vagrant bats, seals and cetaceans, introduced or feral species, and species that have become extinct within historical time.

Most mammals are nocturnal or otherwise difficult to see, so that their presence has very often to be detected by indirect means such as trapping, finding their remains or examining their tracks or other signs. This section on identification is divided into two parts dealing respectively with the whole animal and with the skull. In each case the object here is to place an animal in its correct order—further recognition or corroboration can be achieved by turning to the general account of the order or smaller group concerned.

THE WHOLE ANIMAL

Marsupials (p. 23)

Only species at present found in the wild is a wallaby: like a small kangaroo, about 60 cm tall in normal resting posture, distinguished from rabbit and hares by long tail, shorter ears and progression on hind feet only (when travelling fast).

Wallaby

Insectivores (p. 28)

Hedgehog: unmistakable—no other British species is spiny.

Mole: black, velvety fur; spade-like front feet; short tail; no visible ears. (Water vole, a rodent, may also be black and may burrow, but has shaggy fur, a longer tail and visible ears.)

Shrews: mouse-sized, but snout very pointed; fur velvety, black or brown.

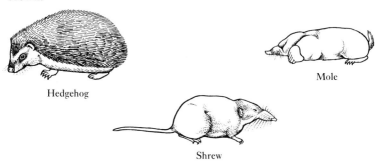

Hedgehog

Mole

Shrew

Bats (p. 68)

In flight, distinguished from birds by more fluttering and erratic flight, short, plump body and the continuity of wing and tail surfaces.

Horseshoe bat

Lagomorphs (p. 129)

Rabbit and hares: easily distinguished by long ears, very short tail and hopping or bounding run.

Hare

Rodents (p. 151)

Squirrels: in trees or, if on ground, invariably take to trees when disturbed. Distinguished from marten by shorter body, more bushy tail and erect posture when at rest. Only other strictly arboreal mammal is fat dormouse which is smaller and nocturnal.

Coypu and water vole: aquatic; shorter body than otter and mink; prominent orange incisors.

Rats, mice and voles: shorter in body than weasels and stoats; nose not prolonged as in shrews.

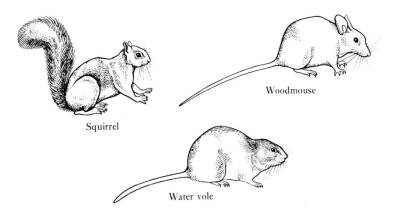

Squirrel

Woodmouse

Water vole

Cetaceans (p. 266)

Dolphins, porpoises and whales: in water only the dorsal fin is normally seen. Dorsal fin of basking shark may be mistaken for a whale but in the shark the vertical tail fin is usually seen following.

When stranded, cetaceans are easily distinguished from fish and seals by horizontal tail flukes, lack of hind limbs, blow-hole on top of head and smooth, naked skin.

Common dolphin

Pilot whale

Carnivores (p. 310)

Range in size from fox (head and body 60–70 cm) to weasel (head and body 20 cm). Most are rarely seen by day. Large ones individually distinctive.

Fox: red colour, bushy tail, pointed ears.

Badger: bold black and white head stripes, grey colour, short legs and tail.

Fox

Badger

Otter: sleek; long, thick, tapering tail; usually seen in water, including sheltered coastal water.

Wild cat: similar to large domestic tabby.

Remainder are weasel-like with long slender bodies and short legs, and range in size from the marten (head and body 50 cm) to weasel (20 cm). Marten may be in trees, others on ground. Mink is semi-aquatic.

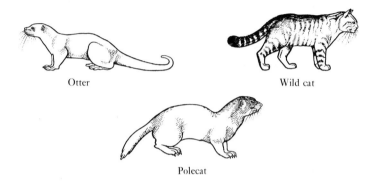

Otter   Wild cat

Polecat

Seals (p. 383)

In water usually only head is seen, looking very dog-like. Unmistakable when they come ashore.

Common seal

Ungulates (p. 409)

Deer and goats: in woodland often only fleeting glimpses may be obtained—large size, bounding gait, long, slender legs and often conspicuous pale patch around tail are distinctive. But remember that the smallest deer, muntjac, is only about the size of a fox and not very much larger than a hare.

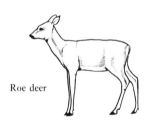

Roe deer

SKULLS

If the remains of a dead animal are found, whether it be the skeleton of a deer or whale or the remains of a shrew in an owl pellet, the skull is the most useful part to preserve for the purpose of identification of the species. Identification is often possible on the basis of a single lower jaw or in some cases even on the basis of a single tooth. The guide to identification given here and continued in the accounts of each order assumes an entire skull or at least the anterior half with all the teeth. The smaller the fragment available the more necessary it becomes to compare the specimen directly with a reference collection to achieve a satisfactory identification.

Skulls of young animals with milk teeth may cause confusion. They can usually be recognized as such if tooth replacement is in progress or by the overall fragility of the skull.

Marsupials (p. 23)

The skull of a wallaby is easily recognized by the combination of a long gap (diastema) between the incisors and the cheek-teeth, three upper incisors on each side and one very large, forward-projecting lower incisor on each side. Length up to 130 mm. Compare especially with those of rabbits, hares and small deer.

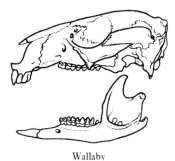

Wallaby

Insectivores (p. 28)

The tooth-rows are continuous (as in carnivores). Shrews and hedgehog differ from carnivores and bats in lacking enlarged canines. Moles have enlarged

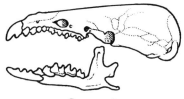

Common shrew

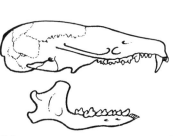

Mole

Hedgehog

canines but differ from carnivores in the sharply cusped cheek-teeth, slender zygomatic arches and lack of specialised carnassial teeth. Maximum length (hedgehog) *c.* 60 mm.

Bats (p. 68)

The skull is small (not over 24 mm), with a short rostrum, enlarged canines and sharply cusped cheek-teeth.

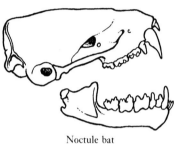

Noctule bat

Lagomorphs (p. 129)

Long diastema between incisors and cheek-teeth; large, chisel-shaped upper and lower incisors as in rodents but a second small pair of upper incisors behind the first. The transverse elongation of the cheek-teeth is not found in any rodent. Length up to 105 mm.

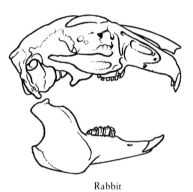

Rabbit

Rodents (p. 151)

Long diastema, single pair of curved, chisel-shaped incisors above and below, cheek-teeth not more than five per row, often only three. Maximum length *c.* 130 mm (coypu).

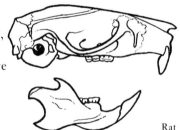

Rat

Cetaceans (p. 266)

Teeth are either absent, or numerous and similar in form (occasionally with one enlarged one in the lower jaw). The position of the nasal opening, far back on top of the skull, is characteristic.

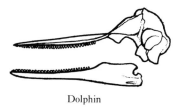

Dolphin

Lesser rorqual

Carnivores (p. 310)

The tooth-rows are continuous, the canines enlarged and one of the cheek-teeth in each row is enlarged, with a longitudinal shearing edge (the carnassial). This is the last premolar above and the first molar below. The

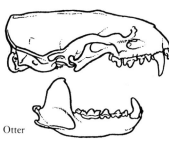

Otter

cheek-teeth (in any one species) are always very diverse in shape and size (cf. pinnipedes). Three pairs of lower incisors. Minimum size *c*. 30 mm.

Pinnipedes (p. 383)

As in carnivores but carnassials not differentiated and cheek-teeth show little variation in size or shape from front to back. Only two pairs of lower incisors. Length over 150 mm if adult.

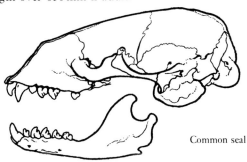

Common seal

Horse (p. 408)

Large size, long diastema, three pairs of upper incisors and high-crowned cheek-teeth are diagnostic.

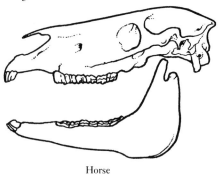

Horse

Artiodactyls (p. 409)

Pig unique in having continuous tooth-rows, three pairs of upper incisors, enlarged angular canines and very complex molars.

Remainder (ruminants) recognised by absence of upper incisors, apparently four pairs of lower incisors (i.e. three pairs plus incisiform canines), a long diastema and cheek-teeth with longitudinal crescentic ridges. Size from 150 mm (small deer—cf. wallaby) to 600 mm in a cow.

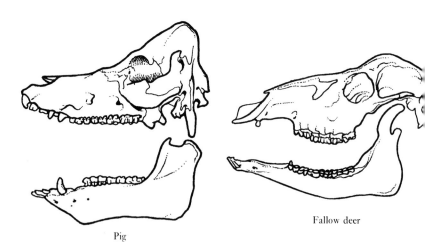

Fallow deer

Pig

Systematic Accounts

Order Marsupialia
Marsupials

As indigenous animals marsupials are typical of the Australasian and Neotropical regions, with one species of opossum extending into North America. One species of wallaby is feral in Britain.

FAMILY MACROPODIDAE
KANGAROOS AND WALLABIES

This family includes most of the larger herbivores of Australasia, with about 52 species in 17 genera.

GENUS *Macropus*

This genus contains most of the kangaroos and larger wallabies. The generic names *Wallabia* and *Protemnodon* have also been used for the wallabies, including *M. rufogriseus*.

Red-necked wallaby *Macropus rufogriseus*

Kangurus rufogriseus Desmarest, 1817; King Island, Bass Strait. *Kangurus ruficollis* Desmarest, 1817. *Macropus (Halmaturus) fruticus* Ogilby, 1838; Tasmania. *Macropus bennetti* Waterhouse, 1838; Tasmania. Scrub wallaby, red wallaby, Bennett's wallaby.

RECOGNITION Only this one species of wallaby is known to be at large in Britain. The skull is immediately recognisable from the combination of procumbent lower incisors with three pairs of upper incisors. The cheek teeth are also quite unlike those of any other British mammal.

SIGN The droppings are easier to observe than the animals, and fairly distinctive: the individual pellets are ovoid, *c.* 15 × 20 mm, with rounded ends, and composed of rather coarse fibrous material. They are at most only loosely clumped, perhaps 5–6 pellets in a loose string (whereas rumi-

FIGURE 1 Red-necked wallaby.

FIGURE 2 Red-necked wallaby. An animal in the Peak District showing attitude when hopping slowly. (Photo: D. W. Yalden)

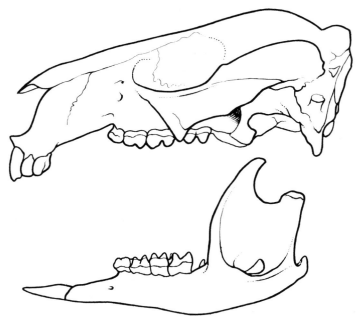

FIGURE 3 Red-necked wallaby.

nant pellets are usually in large piles). Tracks (e.g. in snow) are unmistakeable.

DESCRIPTION Generally grizzled greyish brown above, white below. The rusty patch over the shoulders is variable in intensity. The tail is silvery-grey, but tipped black; the paws, feet, muzzle and ears are also tipped black. There is a pale line along the upper lip and a spot over the eye. Fawn and silver individuals reported.

MEASUREMENTS See Table 1.

DISTRIBUTION See Fig. 4. Native to eastern Australia from central Queensland to South Australia and Tasmania. Introduced to Germany, to the South Island of New Zealand and to various zoos and parks in Britain, notably Whipsnade.

There are now two small feral colonies in Britain, in the Peak District (originating from Whipsnade stock) and the Sussex Weald. These date from escapes in about 1940. A small colony on Herm, Channel Islands, begun in the 1890s, was later exterminated.

TABLE 1 Measurements of red-necked wallabies from New Zealand, from Wodzicki & Flux (1967)

	Males ($n=10$)	Females ($n=12$)
Head and body	650 mm	610 mm
Tail	620 mm	620 mm
Hind foot	220 mm	200 mm
Ears	92 mm	94 mm
Weight	13·2 kg	10·5 kg
(range)	(6·8–22·7 kg)	(6·8–13·6 kg)

In all tables n signifies the number of specimens measured to give a mean

HABITAT This is a scrub wallaby, lying up in woodland but coming into the open to feed. One of the British colonies is living in scrub at the edge of heather moorland.

BEHAVIOUR In fast locomotion, a bipedal jumping gait as would be expected in a kangaroo. At slower speeds, e.g. during feeding, the hind limbs and the fore limbs plus tail act as alternate supports (Windsor &

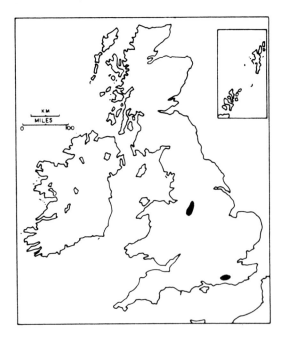

FIGURE 4 Red-necked wallaby: distribution.

Dagg 1971). Generally solitary, or in loose groups of two to five. Apparently silent. Sight poor, but hearing acute, and pinnae constantly in motion when suspicious. Seem to have no fixed home site.

FOOD Known to indulge in 'pseudorumination' (Mollison 1960) like other kangaroos. In Australia, regarded as a general grazer and browser, but no specific information. Peak District population feed predominantly on heather (*Calluna*) (50% in summer, 90% in winter), but also on bracken (*Pteridium*), bilberry (*Vaccinium*), pine (*Pinus*) and grasses (Yalden & Hosey 1971).

BREEDING In captivity, peak of births in England seems to be March–May, but can be any month (Yalden & Hosey 1971, Zuckerman 1952). One young per litter; replacement young usually produced if first lost from pouch early in development. Gestation lasts *c*. 30 days, pouch life about 280 days (Calaby & Poole 1971).

PREDATORS AND MORTALITY Severe winters, both in Tasmania and Britain, have caused heavy mortality. In Australia, man is the main enemy. In Britain road casualties are frequent.

RELATIONS WITH MAN In parts of Australia regarded as a pest of forestry, preventing natural regeneration of *Eucalyptus* woodland. Also regarded as a forestry pest in New Zealand, where 70 000 have been shot and more poisoned (the peak population was estimated as over 500 000). In Britain there seems no likelihood of such large populations occurring. The Peak District population may have reached 50 prior to the 1962–3 winter, but is now less. The species does well in captivity.

AUTHOR FOR THIS SPECIES D. W. Yalden.

Order Insectivora
Insectivores

The insectivores are mainly small, ground-dwelling mammals that feed upon invertebrates. They are found throughout the world except in Australasia and most of South America (where they are replaced ecologically by marsupials). In spite of diverse external form they have many primitive characters: plantigrade feet, five clawed digits on each foot, small brain, continuous tooth-rows with relatively few, pointed cusps, long muzzle and abdominal testes.

In Britain three families are represented including respectively the hedgehog, the mole and the shrews (p. 16). Although superficially very different, the moles and shrews are more closely related to each other than either is to the hedgehog.

Two families that have generally been included in the order Insectivora, the elephant-shrews (Macroscelididae) and the tree-shrews (Tupaiidae) are now excluded. As a result the name Lipotyphla has been used to replace Insectivora but this is not required by the rules of nomenclature and seems very undesirable.

FAMILY ERINACEIDAE

The spiny hedgehogs (subfamily Erinaceinae, with three closely related genera) occur in the deciduous woodland, steppe and desert zones of the Palaearctic, Ethiopian and Oriental Regions. The only other subfamily is the Echinosoricinae, or hairy hedgehogs, with five monospecific genera in the evergreen forest zones of the Oriental Region. All members of the family are ground-dwelling, predominantly nocturnal insectivores, and the family is well represented in the fossil record.

GENUS *Erinaceus*

Opinions vary as to the number of species in the genus, but there are probably four Palaearctic species and three more in subsaharan Africa. The British hedgehog is *E. europaeus*; the eastern European *E. concolor*

(= *E. roumanicus*) and the eastern Asiatic *E. amurensis* have been considered conspecific with it, but recent work in Eastern Europe casts doubt on this. *E. algirus* in N. Africa (and a few localities in S. Europe) is clearly distinct. The two other genera of spiny hedgehogs, *Hemiechinus* and *Paraechinus*, contain desert and dry-steppe species, basically similar to *Erinaceus* and included in that genus by some authors; neither occurs in Europe.

Hedgehog *Erinaceus europaeus*

Erinaceus europaeus Linnaeus, 1758; Wamlingbo, South Gothland Island, Sweden. *Erinaceus europaeus occidentalis* Barrett-Hamilton, 1900; Haddington, Scotland.
Urchin, hedgepig.

RECOGNITION Quite unmistakable by virtue of spiny pelage. Skull has continuous tooth-rows without enlarged canines, and widely flared, robust zygomatic arches (Fig. 5).

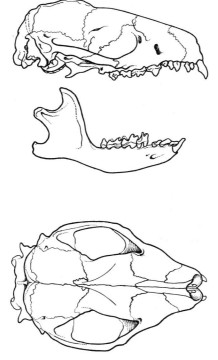

FIGURE 5 Hedgehog. Skull with permanent teeth.

FIGURE 6 Hedgehog showing how it lifts the body well clear of the ground when it is walking rapidly. When it is moving around tentatively investigating things, the attitude is more crouching, while real alarm causes the animal to curl up.

SIGN Presence in area often revealed by road casualties. Footprints are fairly distinctive, with five claw marks, but need careful comparison with those of rats and water vole although they are usually larger. Droppings are characteristic, being long (15–50 mm), cylindrical (10 mm diameter), usually hard and firmly compressed and dark grey or black studded with shiny fragments of insects. Animals can be found by searching after dark with a torch, especially in moist grassy areas. In winter, nests may be found by searching under low cover, e.g. bramble bushes.

DESCRIPTION Several thousand spines completely replace hair on upper surface except for face. Spines about 22 mm long, pale creamy brown with dark band near tip. No seasonal moult, spines long-lasting, replaced irregularly; individual marked spines still present after 18 months (Herter 1938).

Ventral pelage sparse and coarse, usually uniform brown but rather variable in intensity.

Rest of body relatively unspecialised. Feet plantigrade with five well-developed and well-clawed toes. Sexes similar, but in male penis far forward, in position of navel; in female vagina opens very close to anus. Testes permanently abdominal. Five pairs of nipples in both sexes, evenly spaced from axilla to groin.

Tooth formula

$$\frac{3.1.3.3}{2.1.2.3},$$

first incisors large, caniniform; remainder, canines and first premolars small, almost unicuspid, last premolars and molars larger with low-cusped crowns. Deciduous teeth

$$\frac{3.1.3}{2.1.2},$$

replaced from about 24th day. Skeleton unremarkable. Musculature of skin highly specialised to erect spines, and to enable animal to flex into ball and pull spiny part of skin down over rest of body, chief muscle being the *orbicularis* which encircles body at limit of spines (Herter 1965). Anatomy of soft parts described by Carlier (1892–3).

Chromosomes: $2n = 48$; F.N. $= 92$ (material from Czechoslovakia, described in detail by Kral 1967).

MEASUREMENTS Head and body c. 160 mm at weaning, increasing to 260 mm or more in large adults. Condylobasal length of skull similarly increases from c. 40 mm up to 58 mm. Males are usually bigger than females, but sex differences are obscured by differences due to age and growth. Body weight increases from 120 g at weaning to over 1100 g. Age changes marked, but overshadowed by enormous annual fluctuation due to accumulation of fat and subsequent loss of reserves over winter (causing 30% reduction in body weight, Kristoffersson & Suomalainen 1964).

DISTRIBUTION See Fig. 7. In deciduous woodland and Mediterranean zones of western Europe from the Mediterranean coast to central Sweden and Finland and east to a line from about the Oder to the Adriatic, beyond which it is replaced by *E. concolor* ($= E.$ *roumanicus*).

Found throughout mainland of Britain and Ireland up to tree line. Present on the following islands (known introductions marked *, but many others probably introduced also): Shetland (mainland)*, Unst*, Yell*, Foula*, Fetlar*, Muckle Roe*, Bressay*, Whalsay*, E.Burra*, W.Burra*, Ventray*; Orkney (mainland)*, Skye, Soay (Skye), Canna*, Coll, Mull, Luing, Bute, Man, Anglesey, Wight, Guernsey, Jersey. Sub-fossil remains show presence in Britain since the Mesolithic period (Star Carr, Yorks., Fraser & King 1954). British hedgehogs introduced to New Zealand late 19th century, very abundant there now.

VARIATION British population not discretely distinguishable from continental. Extent to which processes of premaxillae and frontals approach

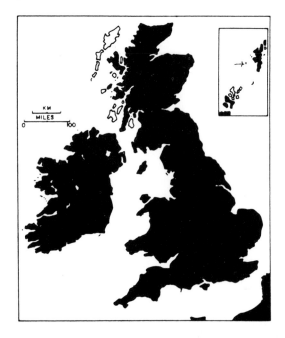

FIGURE 7 Hedgehog: distribution.

FIGURE 8 Hedgehog nest. (Photo: G. Kinns)

each other variable—these processes meet in 11 out of 16 skulls (69%) from mainland Britain and 12 out of 44 (27%) from continental W. Europe. This character was the basis of description of *E. e. occidentalis* but does not justify recognition of British subspecies. Ventral colour tends to be darker in Ireland.

Partial and complete albinos have been recorded.

HABITAT Most abundant where there is close proximity of grassland to woodland, scrub or hedgerow, e.g. edge of woods, hedgerows in meadowland, or sand-dunes with shrubs. Present in virtually all lowland habitats where there is sufficient cover for nesting. Notably common in suburban areas but scarce in coniferous woods, marshy and moorland areas.

BEHAVIOUR Gait rather hesitant with frequent stops to sniff the air. Crouches and erects spines at least sign of danger, reacting especially to noise. Rolls up tightly when disturbed with head and extremities completely protected by spines. Swims and climbs surprisingly well.

Almost entirely nocturnal but may be seen at dawn and dusk. Often do not build nests during summer but spend the day in the shelter of vegetation, without occupying one site for more than a few days. Snuffles and snorts regularly when searching for food; also sometimes emits loud, pig-like squeal when alarmed. Eyesight poor, smell and hearing acute.

Hibernation in carefully built nest usually of leaves and grass under cover, e.g. bramble or brushwood, sometimes in rabbit burrow or in garden shed, etc. More than one nest usually built; most animals move at least once during winter (Morris, P. 1973). Some evidence of territoriality in building winter nests, which are rarely in very close proximity. Hibernation usually begins about October, males before females; younger animals (especially late litter) may remain active until December; ends early in April in southern England. Preceded by accumulation of white fat under the skin and around the viscera, and brown fat (a thermogenic tissue='hibernating gland' of earlier authors) around the shoulders. Onset induced at least partly by low temperature. In hibernation temperature falls from normal 34°C to match that of the environment. Optimal hibernation temperature about 4°C. Heart beat slows from 190 to about 20/min., respiration reduced to about 10 intermittent breaths per minute. Histological changes much studied, e.g. by Smit-Vis (1962).

Social structure unknown. Captives established 'peck-order' (Lindemann 1951); males especially are agressive and presumed territorial. Little evidence in wild, and some suggestion to contrary. Home ranges

FIGURE 9 Hedgehog applying saliva to its spines—'self anointing'. (Photo: P. Morris)

may overlap completely, many hedgehogs may visit same area, but at different times. Possible temporal separation rather than spatial. Extent of home range doubtless varies seasonally and with nature of habitat, probably governed by food supply. Some 'homing' instinct, and ability to recognise landmarks; may follow well-used paths (Lindemann 1951).

Communication unlikely to be by acoustic or visual means, except perhaps at very short range. Possible use of droppings as scent markers, but no evidence.

'Self-anointing' is intriguing activity in which the hedgehog is stimulated to produce masses of frothy saliva which is liberally plastered all over the animal's body (Burton 1957). Purpose is a complete mystery; explanatory theories reviewed by Brockie (1976).

FOOD Almost entirely ground level invertebrates, but small number of birds' eggs and chicks (Kruuk 1964); carrion also taken. Only detailed study in Britain (Yalden 1969), from a variety of habitats, showed scarabeid beetles and caterpillars to be most frequent (each 21% by weight) followed by earthworms, carabid beetles, flies, centipedes, harvestmen and spiders. Slugs also important but difficult to evaluate. Average nightly intake believed to be about 70 g (Kruuk 1964). Food caught and dealt with entirely by the mouth.

Folk-tales of hedgehogs carrying fruit (usually apples) on spines frequently repeated. Validity disputed, though stories of wide currency. Similarly oft-repeated tales of hedgehogs taking milk from cows.

Frequently claimed to kill snakes for food (Ognev 1928) and to be resistant to adder venom. Little evidence of former assertion in Britain; regarding latter, hedgehogs are not immune to venom, but dense spines observed to protect skin from puncture by fangs.

BREEDING Males fecund early April to late August; pregnant females found May to October with early peak May to July and later peak September (Morris, B. 1961). 'Courtship' consists of the male walking round and round the female with much snorting and often inconclusive results. Ovulation is spontaneous and early cycles are often infertile. Gestation 31–35 days; embryo number 2–7, means recorded 5·0 (Deanesly 1934, $n = 10$) and 4·6 (Morris, B. 1961, $n = 42$). Loss of embryos small (maximum recorded 3·3% but postnatal mortality c 20% prior to weaning.) Birth in large, specially built nest. Mother eats young if disturbed soon after birth, later reacts to interference by carrying litter to safer place. Babies suckle for about 4 weeks; no post-partum oestrus. Some females may produce second litter. Male takes no part in rearing family.

Young blind at birth, weighing 11–25 g; sex ratio about equal. First coat of white spines appears soon after birth, second pelage of dark spines with white tips visible by 36 hours between first white spines. Capable of rolling up from 11th day. Eyes open at 14 days, begin to leave nest at about 22 days. Replacement of milk teeth begins about 24th day, weaned at between 4 and 6 weeks. Young disperse to lead solitary lives thereafter. Young from early summer litters are fully grown before hibernation in autumn; those from later litters hibernate at a subadult size and are unlikely to survive the winter (a weight of 400 g or more is required to survive hibernation). First breed in year following birth, at about 11 months old.

POPULATION Little known. Preliminary studies suggest 60–70% mortality in first year, good survival over next two years, and decline in survival rate after 4th or 5th year (author's data). Live at least 7 years in captivity; 7 years certainly in wild, 10 years probably near maximum. (Age determination: Morris, P. 1970, 1971.)

Adult sex ratios, revealed by trapping and road casualties, change seasonally—excess males in spring, excess females in autumn. Not accurate reflection of true sex ratio; juveniles have 1 : 1 ratio. Population fluctuations unknown—no accurate census method. Vermin bag records equivocal and anyway unreliable. Population density varies with habitat and season. Road mortality used as index suggests much higher density in New Zealand than in England (Davies 1957; Brockie 1960) and a higher density in suburban areas than in rural ones.

PREDATORS AND MORTALITY Spines adequate protection against most predators, though a few young or sickly animals may be killed by foxes, badgers and dogs. Very occasionally taken by polecat, tawny owl and golden eagle. Large numbers killed on roads, many die in hibernation, especially during first winter. Despite ability to swim many drown in garden ponds.

PARASITES AND DISEASE Flea *Archaeopsylla erinacei* is highly specific to the hedgehog and usually present in large numbers, up to 500 on one animal. Ticks and mites are nonspecific, but the ticks *Ixodes hexagonus* and *I. ricinus* are frequent, as are the parasitic mites *Demodex canis* and *Otodectes cynotis*, the last causing 'otodectic mange' of the ears. In New Zealand the mange mite *Caparinia tripilis* causes substantial mortality (Brockie 1974). Lice have not been recorded.

A ringworm fungus, *Trichophyton mentagrophytes* var. *erinacei*, is specific to the hedgehog, infecting the skin, especially of the head, of about 20% of British animals, more prevalent in older animals and those living at higher densities (Morris, P. & English 1969). Hedgehogs carry the virus of foot and mouth disease (McLaughlan & Henderson 1947) and leptospires (Twigg *et al.* 1968).

RELATIONS WITH MAN Traditionally persecuted for predation on eggs of game-birds although damage is relatively insignificant. Formerly eaten in some areas, especially by gypsies who baked them in mud. Frequently kept as pets and thereby introduced to city gardens and to islands. Probably a useful predator of horticultural pests such as slugs. Easy to keep and breed in captivity (Morris, B. 1967). Has been used for experimental work on viruses (foot-and-mouth disease, influenza and yellow fever).

LITERATURE Herter (1938)—a detailed monograph in German; Herter (1965)—an English translation of a more popular German work; Burton (1969)—a general popular account.

AUTHOR FOR THIS SPECIES P. A. Morris.

FAMILY TALPIDAE

The mole is the only member of this family found in Britain. The family is represented throughout much of Eurasia and North America. Besides the moles it includes also several species of shrew-mole in eastern Asia

FIGURE 10 Mole. Note the cylindrical body with heavy fossorial fore-limbs and small tail carried vertically.

and the aquatic desmans of Russia and Iberia. Related to the shrews (Soricidae), but the dentition is less specialised.

GENUS *Talpa*

All Eurasian moles can be regarded as belonging to the genus *Talpa*, although the Asiatic species have frequently been placed in separate genera. There are about 11 species. The two (or possibly three) European species have the maximum dentition normally found in placental mammals, the dental formula being

$$\frac{3 \cdot 1 \cdot 4 \cdot 3}{3 \cdot 1 \cdot 4 \cdot 3}.$$

The nearest relative of *T. europaea* is the smaller Mediterranean mole, *T. caeca*, found throughout the Mediterranean region of Europe where its range overlaps slightly with that of *T. europaea*.

Mole *Talpa europaea*

Talpa europaea Linnaeus, 1758; South Sweden.
Moldwarp, want.

RECOGNITION The short, black, velvety fur, wide, heavily clawed fore feet, short tail, absence of ear-pinnae and minute eyes (usually hidden in fur) are all highly distinctive. The long, tapering snout resembles that of shrews which are, however, much smaller and lack all these other specialisations. Rarely seen on surface of ground, but mole-hills are conspicuous (see below under SIGN).

The skull, about 35 mm long, has continuous tooth-rows each with 11 teeth, enlarged upper canines (4th teeth) and very slender zygomatic arches. The very short humerus (Fig. 11) is also distinctive, e.g. when found in owl pellets.

SIGN Fresh mole-hills, circular mounds of soil without any openings, are distinctive signs of their presence provided they are distinguished from ant-hills. By the time they become covered with vegetation mole-hills are generally flattened and inconspicuous, whereas hills of the yellow ant in pasture remain high and steep-sided. Larger, more permanent mounds or 'fortresses' incorporating a nesting chamber are sometimes made—they can be recognised by the associated smaller mole-hills. Tunnelling just below the surface, especially noticeable in woodland and arable land, pushes up characteristic ridges of soil.

DESCRIPTION Highly modified for subterranean life. The body is cylindrical, *c*. 110–160 mm in length, with very short legs. The front limbs are adapted for digging, with very short and massive humerus and the hand almost circular with five large, strong claws. Associated muscles arise from elongate scapulae and a strongly keeled sternum (described in detail by Yalden 1966). The eyes are extremely small but functional, and there are no ear pinnae. The tail is about one quarter the length of the head and body, has a constriction at the base and is carried erect.

The external genitalia of males and non-breeding females are very similar but they can be distinguished by the length of the prepuce ($>$6 mm in males, $<$6 mm in females) and the length of the perineum ($>$5 mm in males, $<$4 mm in females) (Matthews 1935). The vulva opens only during the breeding season.

Scent glands are associated with the anus, consisting of a pair of lateral and one median gland on the dorsal side of the rectum. There is, in addition, a skin gland in the centre of the back in the lumbar region (Lehmann 1969).

The pelage is uniformly short, erect and velvety black, although in some lights a slight greyish or brownish cast is visible. Short vibrissae on the muzzle are associated with specialised sensory receptors (Eimer's organs), and the hairs of the tail-tip are also sensory. There is no sexual dimorphism in pelage and no seasonal nor age changes other than in length. There are three moults, one in spring, with males almost a month later than females, another July to September which may not be completed, and a third from early October to December occurring concurrently in all age groups and both sexes (Godfrey & Crowcroft 1960).

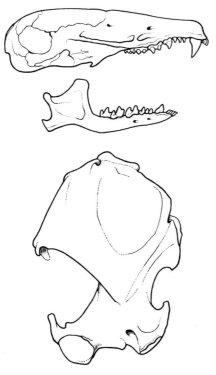

FIGURE 11 Mole. Skull and humerus. The latter is so different from the humerus of any other mammal that it is very easily recognised, e.g. in owl pellets.

The skull is narrow, with very slender zygomatic arches and well-formed, but flattened, tympanic bullae. The incisors are small, followed in the upper jaw by large canines but in the lower jaw by small canines and large, caniniform first premolars. The other anterior premolars are small, almost rudimentary. The milk (deciduous) dentition is rudimentary, does not erupt and is not detectable after birth except for DP_1, which persists as the functional tooth and is not replaced.

The vagina and uterus merge to form a long, S-shaped median uterovaginal canal into which the two uterine horns open at right angles. The testes remain abdominal.

Chromosomes: $2n=34$; F.N.$=68$ (Bovey 1949).

<small>MEASUREMENTS</small> Very variable. See Table 2.

<small>TABLE</small> 2 External measurements of moles from Suffolk (Godfrey & Crowcroft 1960)

	Males ($n=42$)	Females ($n=57$)
Head and body	143 mm (121–159)	135 mm (113–144)
Tail	33 mm (26–40)	32 mm (25–38)
Weight	110 g (87–128)	85 g (72–106)

<small>DISTRIBUTION</small> See Fig. 12. Europe, and into West Siberia as far as River Ob, beyond which it is replaced by *T. altaica*. North to South Sweden, South Finland and to Arctic Circle in Russia; south to Mediterranean, but absent southern Iberia and Balkans where it is replaced by *T. caeca*.

Throughout mainland of Britain, but absent from Ireland. Of small

<small>FIGURE</small> 12 Mole: distribution.

islands, present only on Skye, Mull, Anglesey, Wight, Alderney and Jersey. Reported to have been first introduced to Mull in ballast early in 19th century (Harvey-Brown & Buckley 1892).
Found up to 1000 m where the habitat is suitable.

VARIATION British moles have not been shown to differ from the continental form, which is best considered as *T. e. europaea*, although Stein (1960) distinguished a western continental race, *T. e. cinerea*. No regional variation within Britain has been described, but considerable variation in size between moles from neighbouring localities has been reported (Larkin 1948).

Abnormal colour is probably more frequent than in any other British mammal, but no figures of frequency are available from Britain. In Poland 51 out of 50 000 (0·1%) were found to have abnormal colour (Skoczeń 1961b). Main variants are (i) pale, varying from rare true albinos through cream to apricot or rust-coloured, (ii) piebald or patched and (iii) grey or silver-grey.

The premolars are variable and may show absence or duplication of one or more teeth. Absence of at least one upper premolar was found in 0·3% of 8184 specimens from throughout the range (in none of 880 from England); absence of some lower premolars in 0·6% of 8653 (0·2% of 978 from England); supplementary (or bicuspid) upper premolars in 0·1% of 8184 (3 out of 880 from England); and supplementary lower premolars in 2·1% of 8653 (1·7% of 978 from England) (all figures from Stein 1963).

HABITAT Found wherever there is suitable soil, avoiding only soils that are extremely shallow or stony, heavily waterlogged, or very acid (pH below 4·4) (Milner & Ball 1970). Because of this they are scarce in heather moors, coniferous woodland and at high altitude, but they have been recorded up to 1000 m. Most abundant in permanent pasture and deciduous woodland, although less conspicuous in the latter.

BEHAVIOUR Moles spend almost their entire lives in tunnels that they dig themselves, varying in depth from immediately below the surface to about 70 cm, occasionally deeper. Digging is done by alternate use of the front feet which are thrust sideways and backwards by rotation of the humerus. The loose soil is pushed up a vertical or sloping shaft by similar movements to form a mole-hill. The hind feet are pressed against the sides of the tunnel during digging (Skoczeń 1958, Yalden 1966). Above ground only the inner edges of the fore feet touch the ground. They swim well using all four limbs.

Moles are active day and night: periods of almost continuous activity last $c.$ $4\frac{1}{2}$ hours and alternate with periods of $c.$ $3\frac{1}{2}$ hours in the nest (Godfrey 1955). Some evidence that there is relatively more activity during hours of daylight than of darkness (Meese & Cheeseman 1969). Sleep in nest in upright position with head tucked between fore legs.

Each animal is normally sole occupant of a system of tunnels. Length of home range in pasture about 30–40 m for females; 50 m for males in winter but increasing with onset of sexual activity in spring to about 150 m (Larkin 1948, Godfrey & Crowcroft 1960, Haeck 1969.) Tunnels usually branch, but in spring males often make long straight tunnels entering those of neighbouring females. Possibly some sharing of tunnels, subordinate animals coming out when dominant one is at rest (Stein 1950a). Fighting has been recorded (Godfrey & Crowcroft 1960).

Tactile sense organs are very highly developed, especially on the tip of the snout which is erectile and contains specialised receptors (Eimer's organs). Senses of hearing and smell are moderately developed and the eyes are functional although vision is probably poor (Quilliam 1966c). The entire sensory apparatus was reviewed by Quilliam (1966b). Make scarcely audible twitter when excited and single raucous squeaks when fighting.

FOOD Food is sought in the semi-permanent tunnels, by further digging and on the surface, the last by far the least important (Haeck 1969). Almost confined to larger members of soil fauna, especially earthworms and insects (mainly larvae of beetles and flies). Two other constant items (but not nearly so abundant) are myriapods and molluscs, especially slugs. Vegetable matter found occasionally in stomachs is probably accidental. Larkin (1948) showed how earthworms predominated in winter (90–100% by volume) and declined in summer ($c.$ 50%) when proportion of insects increased; also how general proportion of insects increased during dry weather. (See also Schaerffenberg 1940, Haeck 1969, Funmilayo 1971.)

From weight of stomach contents (3–6 g) Godfrey & Crowcroft (1960) suggested intake of 40–50 g of food per day; laboratory experiments on energy requirements indicated that a mole of $c.$ 80 g needed $c.$ 50 g of earthworms per day ($=c.$ 0·5 Kcal/g/day) (Hawkins & Jewell 1962). This is probably comparable to energy requirements of rodents (cf. Hawkins, Jewell & Tomlinson 1960). Mellanby (1967), however, maintained the body weight of captive moles for several days on much smaller quantities of worms and insect larvae. Food is commonly stored in or near the nest chamber in autumn and winter. Stores consist mainly of earthworms with the anterior segments mutilated, and up to 470 worms (820 g) have been found (Evans 1948, Skoczeń 1961a).

BREEDING Breeding season very short, between March and May, with very rapid growth and subsequent decline of organs in both sexes. Usually single litter of 3 or 4 born in May or June.

Testes and prostate glands grow rapidly from January, reaching peak in February or March and declining to minimum in late May. Female has two parts to ovary, one part, the interstitial gland, being homologue of testis and active during anoestrus (Matthews 1935, Deanesly 1966). Sudden swing to ovarian activity during February and early March when secondary sexual organs also grow rapidly. After very short period of heat almost all females are pregnant. Second or late oestrus in very small proportion of animals recorded in Britain and on the Continent, perhaps related to abundance of food. Oestrus may last only 20–30 hours, and ovulation may depend upon copulation. Gestation *c*. 4 weeks. Average number of embryos (from various British sources) *c*. 3·8 (Godfrey & Crowcroft 1960), contrasting with higher numbers on Continent; up to 5·7 in Russia. Rate of reproduction perhaps controlled by absorption of embryos. Larkin (1948) found loss of 6% and Morris (1961) 25% including 20% of litters totally resorbed.

Young naked at birth, begin to grow fur at 14 days, open eyes at 22 days. Weight at birth *c*. 3·5 g, at 3 weeks *c*. 60 g. Growth may be slower if food is scarce. Lactation probably 4–5 weeks: Godfrey (1957) found that one litter marked with radio-active rings first left nest 33 days after birth and nest usually abandoned when young are *c*. 5 weeks old. Sexual maturity not attained until following spring.

POPULATION STRUCTURE Sex ratio probably 1 : 1, but males more trappable and especially in breeding season may outnumber females by 2 or 3 : 1 in trapping catch. Density in grassland has been estimated by Larkin (1948) as about 8 per hectare in winter and 16 per hectare in summer. Difficult to assess from density of hills. Mead-Briggs & Woods (1973) utilised an index of activity to assess short-term reductions in numbers.

Life span *c*. 3 years: in some populations three year-classes are distinguishable by wear of teeth (Larkin 1948, Funmilayo 1976), but in others this is too variable. If population remains static about two-thirds must die each year, giving mean expectancy of further life *c*. 1 year, if mortality is evenly spread amongst age groups. Figures from Larkin suggest this may be correct, though first-year mortality may be unevenly spread.

Populations, wherever studied, seem reasonably steady, compared with fluctuations of small rodents. Densities have increased, especially in cultivated and drained land, with decline of mole-catching as a lucrative activity.

PREDATORS AND MORTALITY Intra-uterine and nestling mortality may be heavy when food is scarce, e.g. in drought when earthworms are hard to obtain. Predation on post-nestling young heavy during dispersal, by birds of prey, e.g. tawny owl (Southern 1954), and small carnivores. Frequently caught and killed by cats and foxes but may not be eaten.

PARASITES AND DISEASE Permanence of nest conducive to heavy infestation by ectoparasites, and nests also contain rich fauna of commensals, e.g. mites (Oudemans 1913). Host-specific fleas are *Palaeopsylla minor*, *P. kohauti* and *Ctenophthalmus bisoctodentatus*. Species found commonly on moles but also on other small mammals are *Hystrichopsylla talpae*, *Ctenophthalmus nobilis* and *Rectofrontia pentacanthis*. No lice have been recorded. The fur mite *Labidophorus soricis* is found, attached to individual hairs, and the tick *Ixodes hexagonus* has been recorded.

A number of internal parasites are known including the thread-like intestinal trematodes *Ityogonimus* spp., studied by Frankland (1959).

Protozoa recorded from the blood are *Trypanosoma talpae* and *Babesia microti* (Cox 1970).

Spherules of the fungus *Haplosporangium parvum* have been found in the lungs of moles (McDiarmid & Austwick 1954) and may sometimes be pathogenic.

Moles in Czechoslovakia have been found to be a reservoir of tick-borne encephalitis virus (Kozuch *et al.* 1966).

RELATIONS WITH MAN Regarded as a pest by most farmers, with least complaint from smaller arable holdings where constant tillage restricts infestation. Moles, by tunnelling beneath seed drill lines in search of insect larvae attacking some of the seeds, may subsequently cause wilting and destruction of the young plants. Damage is more often caused to pasture and hayfields. Stones brought up to the mole-hill may damage cutting machinery, and soil fouling silage may lead to harmful fermentation. Mole-hills which are not quickly dispersed by extra harrowing serve as ideal seed beds for the more vigorous colonisers including several weed species, producing an insidious pasture degradation.

It is unlikely that moles take sufficient worms to have any substantial effect on their numbers. The deeper tunnels made by moles, especially in damp land, are probably beneficial by improving the drainage.

Formerly controlled by professional trappers; now mainly by poisoning with strychnine.

Can be kept in captivity with difficulty. Techniques of live-trapping and keeping were described by Rudge (1966).

LITERATURE Godfrey & Crowcroft (1960), Mellanby (1971)—two books giving a general account of the species as well as many original observations. Quilliam (1966a)—a collection of 15 research papers on many aspects of the species.

AUTHOR FOR THIS SPECIES A. R. Mead-Briggs.

FAMILY SORICIDAE
SHREWS

A widespread family containing a multitude of small forms, all insectivorous or carnivorous, which live mainly on the ground in leaf litter and grass. An important element in any community, breaking down animal tissue and returning materials to the soil.

Characterised externally by narrow pointed snout, small eyes, short

TABLE 3 Identification of the genera of shrews

	Sorex	*Neomys*	*Crocidura*
Colour of back	Brown	Black	Greyish brown
Scattered long hairs on tail	No	No	Yes
Keel of stiff hairs on underside of tail	No	Yes	No
Fringes of stiff hairs of hind feet	Slight	Prominent	Slight
Colour of teeth	Red-tipped	Red-tipped	White
Upper unicuspid teeth	5	4	3
First lower tooth (upper edge)	Wavy	Smooth	Smooth

rounded ears with complex lobes in the conch, short legs, plantigrade feet with five digits, slender tail of even width throughout the length and rather short, dense pelage. There are scent glands on the flanks, marked when well developed by a line of short white hairs. Sexes indistinguishable by external genitalia.

No functional milk dentition. First incisors very large, followed in upper jaw by up to five small, single-cusped (unicuspid) teeth representing I²–P². Remaining premolars and molars (P³–M³) large, with high pointed cusps. Braincase very rounded and delicate, tympanic bone annular and loosely attached to the skull, zygomatic arches lacking, mandibles with double articulating surfaces.

Prominent, very large lymph-gland in abdomen ('pancreas of Aselli'—see Twigg & Hughes 1970). Testes ventral but internal; female tract T-shaped; no pubic symphysis.

Shrews are very voracious, with little resistance to starvation, and are active day and night and throughout the winter.

There are over a hundred species, in about twenty genera. The two dominant genera, *Sorex* and *Crocidura*, are both represented in Britain. Aquatic forms, represented in Britain by the water shrew, are also found in eastern Asia (*Nectogale* and *Chimarrogale*) and in North America (*Sorex palustris*). Some species are mōle-like and fossorial, e.g. *Anourosorex squamipes* in South East Asia. Allied to *Crocidura* is the genus *Suncus* with a large, commensal species in tropical Asia as well as the smallest of all mammals, *S. etruscus*, in the Mediterranean region which weighs under 2 g. The characters of the three genera in Britain are compared in Table 3.

GENUS *Sorex*

The dominant genus of shrews in the northern parts of Eurasia and North America, with about thirty-five species almost equally divided between the two continents. The teeth are red-tipped, there are five pairs of unicuspid teeth behind the large first incisors and the tail lacks the protruding tactile hairs found in *Crocidura*.

The two species in Britain can be distinguished as in Table 4.

Common shrew *Sorex araneus*

Sorex araneus Linnaeus, 1758; Upsala, Sweden. *Sorex vulgaris* Nilsson, 1848. *Sorex tetragonurus* Hermann, 1780; France. *Sorex tetragonurus castaneus* Jenyns, 1838; Burwell Fen, Cambridgeshire, England. *Sorex araneus fretalis* Miller, 1909; Trinity, Jersey, Channel Islands. *Sorex grantii* Barrett-Hamilton & Hinton, 1913; Islay, Inner Hebrides, Scotland.
Shrew-mouse, ranny.

RECOGNITION Distinguished from water shrew by brown upper surface, smaller size, and, in the hand, by the evenly haired tail, lobed first

TABLE 4 Identification of shrews of the genus *Sorex*

	Common shrew, *S. araneus*	Pygmy shrew, *S. minutus*
Pelage	3-coloured, flanks contrasting with back and belly	2-coloured, flanks not distinctively coloured
Head and body length	Usually 60–80 mm	Usually 40–60 mm
Tail: head and body	50–60%	65–70%
Hind feet	12–13 mm	10–11 mm
3rd unicuspid tooth	Smaller than 2nd	Larger than 2nd
Upper toothrow	8·0–8·8 mm	6·2–6·6 mm

FIGURE 13 (a) Common shrew; (b) pygmy shrew; (c) water shrew; (d) lesser white-toothed shrew.

lower teeth and the presence of a very small, fifth upper unicuspid tooth on each side. More difficult to distinguish from pygmy shrew without experience, but sharp contrast between colour of back and flank is distinctive, as are the relatively shorter tail and larger overall size (especially clear-cut in length of hind feet and of skull—see measurements in Table 4).

DESCRIPTION In winter and second summer (adult) pelage, back is very dark brown contrasting rather sharply with paler brown flanks which in turn contrast sharply with grey, yellow-tinged under parts. Juvenile (first summer) pelage is much lighter above, contrasting less with flanks. Tail bicoloured, of even width, well-haired and with a prominent terminal pencil of hair in juveniles, but the hairs are not renewed and by the second summer the tail is almost naked.

Sexes externally similar except for development of prominent lateral glands in breeding males. Breeding females often with patch of grey hair on back of neck where they have been held during copulation.

Moult in autumn from juvenile to winter pelage starts at rump and moves forwards to head, dorsal surface being ahead of ventral. Two spring moults proceed in opposite direction, starting on the head, and are completed earlier in females than in males. Length of hair (measured in terms of the black zone only) increases from about 2 mm in summer to about 6 mm in winter. Size of brain and brain-case is greatest in newly weaned animals and thereafter decreases until the following spring when there is an increase (without recovering the juvenile size) followed by a further decrease in the second autumn (Crowcroft & Ingles 1959, Bielak & Pucek 1960).

Unicuspid teeth decreasing rather evenly in size from front to back.

Chromosome number variable, 22 to 27 in male, 22 to 25 in female, due to Robertsonian polymorphism affecting elements that may form metacentric and/or acrocentric chromosomes; F.N. (autosomes) = 36; sex chromosomes XX ($\female$) and XYY ($\male$) (Meylan 1964).

MEASUREMENTS See Table 5.

TABLE 5 Measurements of common shrews, from Crowcroft (1954b).

	June–July (juveniles only)			Oct.–Nov.			Feb.			May		
	n	Mean	Range	n	Mean	Range	n	Mean	Range	n	Mean	Range
Head and body	77	70 mm	62–75	68	72 mm	66–75	65	67 mm	57–71	38	79 mm	74–85
Tail	76	40 mm	32–45	67	40 mm	35–47	64	40 mm	35–45	37	38 mm	34–42
Weight	77	7.2 g	5·4–9·0	64	7·0 g	5·8–9·3	64	6·0 g	4·8–7·7	37	10·4 g	8·5–1·

DISTRIBUTION See Fig. 14. The whole of Europe except for the Mediterranean region, but population south-west of a line from north-east France through Switzerland, and on Jersey, may represent a sibling species which is almost identical morphologically, but has a distinctive chromosome complement. North to the Arctic coast and east into Siberia as far as the River Yenesei.

Throughout the mainland of Britain at all altitudes, but absent from Ireland. Present on the following islands: Raasay, Crowlin, Skye, Scalpay (Skye), Soay (Skye), Colonsay, Mull, Ulva, Lismore, Scarba, South Shuna, Luing, Jura, Islay, Gigha, Arran, Bute, Anglesey, Skomer, Isle of Wight and Jersey. Definitely absent from the Shetlands, Orkneys, Outer Hebrides and Scilly Islands, from the remaining larger islands of the Inner Hebrides, and from the other Channel Islands.

VARIATION British population has been distinguished subspecifically from continental as *S. a. castaneus* on basis of duller dorsal colour, but this does not stand up to scrutiny on the larger samples now available. No good evidence of discrete subspecies within continental range and therefore British population can be allocated to *S. a. araneus*.

No evidence for geographical variation within British mainland, but some island populations show slight differentiation. Most distinctive is that on Islay, *S. a. granti*, characterised by very grey flanks and frequent lack of 5th unicuspid teeth. Fifth unicuspids absent on at least one side in 52% on Islay ($n=23$); 5% on island of Skomer ($n=126$); 1·1% on British mainland ($n=465$).

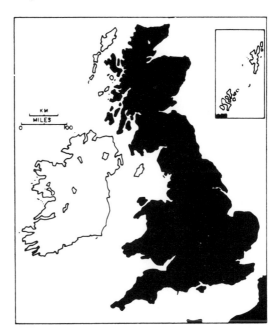

FIGURE 14 Common shrew: distribution.

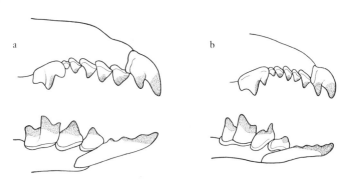

FIGURE 15 Anterior teeth of (a) common shrew and (b) pygmy shrew. These are
young individuals with relatively unworn teeth. The serrations on the lower incisors
are much less distinct in adults.

The form on Jersey (*fretalis*) differs marginally from mainland British
animals in having a blunter snout, reflected in the rostrum of the skull
being shorter, broader and deeper. It also differs considerably in karyotype, which agrees with that of a southwestern chromosome race on the
continent. It is likely that these animals should be considered specifically
distinct from *S. araneus*, but until clear-cut morphological differences
are found it is best to treat them as a 'chromosome race' of *S. araneus*.

Mainland populations exhibit chromosome polymorphism, the Jersey
population does not (described in detail by Ford & Hamerton 1970).

Gross colour variation extremely rare: only one case of melanism
recorded in Britain (Gurney 1879), albinos more frequent. Minor albinism of the ear tufts is frequent (20% reported by Crowcroft 1957) and
that of the tail tip seems to vary geographically: 4·5% in England and
Wales, 8·8% in Scotland (Corbet 1963).

HABITAT In almost every habitat, provided some low cover is present.
Most abundant in thick grass, hedgerows, bushy scrub, bracken etc. At
high altitudes found sparsely amongst heather and more abundantly in
stable scree (to at least 1000 m).

BEHAVIOUR Movements swift and bustling, exploring busily with
mobile snout and vibrissae and occasionally rearing up and appearing
to sniff the air. Make runways in litter and tunnels through soil (recognisable by small size and flat cross-section) using nose and front paws. Burrows of other animals are also used but the tight fit of its own burrows
keeps a shrew's fur clean. Swims readily.

Active day and night, with about ten periods of almost continuous
activity alternating with shorter periods of rest. Peaks of activity at about

10.00 hrs and 22.00 hrs; most active at night, least in early afternoon (Crowcroft 1954a).

Young disperse within a few weeks of weaning and both sexes establish mutually exclusive territories—in a Dutch dune area these were about 200–800 m² (Michielsen 1966). Michielsen estimated that in winter 80% of time is spent below ground, in contrast to 50% in pygmy shrew. Territoriality is abandoned when breeding begins in spring.

Touch, hearing and probably kinaesthetic sense more important than sight and smell. Make soft twittering during normal movements and shrill screams during contacts between individuals (which are invariably aggressive except between a male and a sexually receptive female).

FOOD Mainly invertebrates of soil and litter, especially earthworms and beetles but including most other groups available—insects (adults and larvae), spiders, centipedes, woodlice, snails and slugs. A detailed study (Rudge 1968) showed earthworms and beetles to be dominant in all three localities examined. Laboratory tests have shown a distaste for millipedes and molluscs (Rudge 1968) and that one species of woodlouse (*Philoscia muscorum*) was greatly preferred to three others (Crowcroft 1957). Diet composed of significantly larger items than that of pygmy shrew (Pernetta 1973b).

Invertebrate faunas have been compared in samples of litter exposed to and protected from shrews (Shillito 1960). Mainly removed were springtails, spiders, beetles and flies, discrepancy being greatest in late autumn and winter, and again in June and July. Animals eaten as second choice were woodlice, pseudoscorpions, myriapods and lumbricid worms. Those rejected were enchytraeid worms, mites and small beetles.

Food intake about three-quarters of body weight per day, rising to $1\frac{1}{2}$ times body weight when lactating (Crowcroft 1957). A shrew of 8 g ate its own weight of wet food ($=2$–4 g dry weight) per day, i.e. about 2 Kcal/g body wt/day (Hawkins & Jewell 1962). Seen to lick fluid from everted rectum—function not clear (Crowcroft 1957).

BREEDING Breed in spring and summer of second year when a succession of litters is produced, each of about 5–7 young.

Sexual organs rapidly reach maturity after winter, males late February to early March, females March to April. Almost no courtship behaviour, female receptive for less than 24 hours. Male holds female by scruff during mating—behaviour described in detail by Crowcroft (1957). Ovulation probably follows copulation and almost all females become pregnant shortly after first oestrus (Brambell 1935).

Period of gestation doubtful, between 13 and 19 days (Brambell 1935).

Embryo rate shows steady drop throughout season, first through decline in ova shed, later through increased foetal mortality, e.g. 7·7 embryos ($n=$ 16) in May, 6·7 ($n=6$) in June and 5·7 ($n=6$) in August (Crowcroft 1954b). Foetal mortalities of 21% in August and 18% in September have been reported (Tarkowski 1957).

Number of litters per season variable, probably up to five. At first most females conceive at post-partum oestrus, but later lactation dioestrus becomes more extended until breeding ceases in August or September.

The young are naked and blind at birth and weigh just under 0·5 g. They grow linearly to about 18th day when they weigh *c*. 7 g and the eyes begin to open. Weaning takes place at about 22 days. They disperse within a few weeks of weaning.

Normally do not breed until year following birth but a small proportion of females from first litters may become sexually mature in year of birth (Pucek 1960, Stein 1961).

POPULATION No animals normally survive beyond second autumn. Young animals quickly replace parent generation during summer when

FIGURE 16 Common shrew, juvenile. (Photo: G. Kinns)

the two generations can easily be distinguished by the paler colour, tufted tails and unworn teeth of the younger animals. It has been postulated that 'the annual summer mortality of old adults is the outcome of their inability to maintain a territory because of subordination to the individuals of the new generation' (Michielsen 1966).

Population densities estimated in a Dutch dune area varied from 18·5/hectare in autumn to 12·3 in spring (Michielsen 1966). Less precise estimates in British woodland suggest considerably higher densities, e.g. up to 49/ha (Crowcroft 1957).

Considerable variation from year to year but not so great as in rodents. Southern (1964) gave following catch rates (in 468 traps) for 100 hectares of woodland: winter 1948–9, <10; summer 1949, *c*. 60; most of 1950 and 1951, *c*. 10; autumn 1951, *c*. 40; winter 1951–2, *c*. 25; June 1952, 2. Life-tables for three cohorts of young animals were given by Michielsen (1966). One June cohort had fallen only to 80% of its size by the end of the year and to 50% by the following June. The following year the May/June cohort fell to 54% by September and 23% by the following June.

PREDATORS AND MORTALITY Main predators are owls, and common shrews are often the dominant prey species of barn owl in particular. In woodland constitute only *c*. 5% by weight in diet of tawny owl (Southern 1954). Rarely taken by stoats and weasels and, although frequently killed by domestic cats, they are rarely eaten. Adults are particularly exposed to predation when they are excluded from the more favourable ground by territorial young.

PARASITES AND DISEASE Most abundant fleas (shared only by other species of shrews) are *Doratopsylla dasycnema* and *Palaeopsylla soricis*. The large mole flea, *Hystrichopsylla talpae*, is less frequent whilst several rodent fleas are found occasionally. The fur mite *Labidophorus soricis* is frequent and nest mites such as *Euryparasitus emarginatus* and *Haemogamasus horridus* are commonly carried in the pelage. Larval ticks, e.g. of *Ixodes ricinus* and *I. trianguliceps*, are common. Randolph (1975) studied the seasonal distribution of *I. trianguliceps*.

A nematode, *Porrocaecum talpae*, is very common, coiled under the skin, the final hosts being owls.

RELATIONS WITH MAN Easy to trap, but die of starvation very readily unless traps visited every hour or so. In captivity thrive on diet of fresh meat or earthworms and can be kept on tinned dog food (Crowcroft 1957).

LITERATURE Crowcroft (1957)—a general account of shrews with the emphasis on this species in Britain.

AUTHOR FOR THIS SPECIES G. B. Corbet.

Pygmy shrew *Sorex minutus*

Sorex minutus Linnaeus, 1766; Barnaul, Western Siberia. *Sorex pygmaeus* Laxmann, 1769. *Sorex rusticus* Jenyns, 1838; near Cambridge, England. *Sorex rusticus hibernicus* Jenyns, 1838; Dublin, Ireland.
Lesser shrew.

RECOGNITION Smaller than common shrew but tail proportionally longer and thicker (Table 4). Lacks distinctively coloured flanks, and colour of back never so dark as in adult common shrews.

Unicuspid teeth distinctive, third being larger than or at least as large as second (smaller than second in common shrew). See Fig. 15.

DESCRIPTION No seasonal variation in colour, being a medium brown above, similar to juvenile pelage of common shrew, separated by a rather

FIGURE 17 Pygmy shrew, juvenile. (Photo: G. Kinns)

obscure dividing line from dirty white ventral pelage. Tail as in common shrew, becoming naked in second year. Body moults and seasonal changes in skull as in common shrew.

Teeth as in common shrew except for large size of third unicuspids. Chromosomes: $2n = 42$; F.N. $= 56$ (Meylan 1965).

DISTRIBUTION See Fig. 18. The whole of Europe except for the Mediterranean region, eastwards through Siberia to the Yenesei and in the mountains of central Asia south to the Himalayas.

Throughout the mainland of Britain and Ireland at all altitudes and very widespread on the smaller islands. Absent from the Shetlands, Scilly Islands and Channel Islands, but present on all other islands with an area in excess of 10 sq km and on the following smaller islands: Orkney, Flotta; Hebrides, South Rona, Pabay (Skye), Soay (Skye), Pabbay (Outer Hebrides), Scarba, Iona, Gigha, Sanda (Kintyre); Great Cumbrae, Ailsa Craig, Skomer, Lundy. Ireland, Tory Island, Aranmore, Inishkea, Cape Clear.

VARIATION Very little geographical variation described, and none between Britain and continent nor within British Isles. Albino and

FIGURE 18 Pygmy shrew: distribution.

cream-coloured animals rare; albinism of the tail-tip less frequent than in common shrew—2 out of 75 (Corbet 1963).

HABITAT Widespread in all types of habitat with plenty of ground cover. Relatively less abundant than common shrew in woodland, e.g. 4% pygmy in forest, 10–16% in grassland (Crowcroft 1957); 12% in woodland and wood-edge, 35% on dunes (Heydemann 1960).

BEHAVIOUR Much as in common shrew but movement and reactions even faster. When kept with common shrew avoids contact successfully (Crowcroft 1957). Does not burrow but uses runways of other species. More frequent alternation of rest and activity than in common shrew and relatively more active during the day.

Territorial behaviour as in common shrew but territories larger: means varied from 530–1860 m^2 in dunes in the Netherlands (Michielsen 1966, 1967). The same study showed that in winter this species spent about half of its time on the surface compared with only 20% for the common shrew. In Britain marking and recapture demonstrated ranges of 16–45 m with an average of 31 m (Shillito, unpubl.).

FOOD Similar to that of the common shrew but prefers smaller items (Pernetta 1973b). In captivity when offered choice of different woodlice chose more of the smaller *Trichoniscus pusillus* than did the common shrew (Crowcroft 1957). Experiments with litter (see under common shrew) showed a high proportion of woodlice, especially *Trichoniscus*, removed by pygmy shrew (Shillito, unpubl.). Like common shrew, tended to select spiders and beetles and reject springtails and insect larvae. Intake of food in captivity found to be 5·5–9 g wet weight/day or 3·1 Kcal/g body weight/day (Hawkins & Jewell 1962).

BREEDING Breed mainly from April to August of second year, producing several litters usually of about 4–7 young. Some young animals breed in first summer—in Poland up to 22% of breeding females were found to be young of the year (Pucek 1960).

Data on British animals mainly from Brambell & Hall (1937). First oestrus and ovulation apparently always followed by pregnancy but in some animals a lactation anoestrus occurs. Peak of breeding occurs in June. Gestation period uncertain, probably about same as lactation—about 22 days. Embryo number 2–8, mean of 31 was 6·2. Young take same time to weaning as common shrew but reach full weight more quickly: from 0·25 g at birth to *c.* 2·5 g at 14 days, retaining this weight until they begin to develop breeding condition.

POPULATION Annual turnover as in common shrew (Crowcroft 1954). Variable proportion breed in first year, probably correlated with availability of food (Pucek 1960, Stein 1961). Population density generally lower than in common shrew. In Netherlands mean annual production of young was found to be 15/hectare compared with 58 for common shrew; density decreased from 10·5/hectare in summer to 5/hectare in the following spring (Michielsen 1966, 1967).

PREDATORS AND MORTALITY Main predators are owls. Over a period of eight years pygmy shrews comprised 13% of shrews in pellets of tawny owl (Southern 1954). Higher frequencies occur in some collections of pellets of barn owl.

PARASITES AND DISEASE Both shrew fleas, *Palaeopsylla soricis* and *Doratopsylla dasycnema*, are regularly found in the pelage, other species less frequently. Mites and ticks as for common shrew.

RELATIONS WITH MAN As for common shrew.

AUTHOR FOR THIS SPECIES G. B. Corbet.

GENUS *Neomys*

A fairly distinctive genus of two species distinguished by almost black colour above, red-tipped teeth, presence of four pairs of upper unicuspids and smooth, unlobed first lower incisors. The British species is quite strongly aquatic with hair fringes on tail and hind feet, but in the other species, *N. anomalus*, found mainly in the montane forests of central and eastern Europe, these characters are less pronounced.

Water shrew *Neomys fodiens*

Sorex fodiens Pennant, 1771; Berlin, Germany. *Sorex aquaticus* Müller, 1776; France. *Sorex bicolor* Shaw, 1791; Oxford, England. *Sorex ciliatus* Sowerby, 1805; Norfolk, England. *Amphisorex pennanti* Gray, 1838; England. *Crossopus sowerbyi* Bonaparte, 1840.

RECOGNITION Distinguished from all other British shrews by black upper parts, large size and regular habit of swimming. In hand, fringe of silvery hairs on underside of tail and on margins of hind feet are distinctive (but other shrews have shorter fringes on feet).

Skull distinguished by absence of fifth unicuspid teeth, more strongly hooked upper incisors and absence of lobes on large lower incisors.

DESCRIPTION Upper surface slaty black, often with some white hairs
on ears. Underside pale grey with sharp line of demarcation, and with
a variable wash of yellow or brown in the mid-line. Tail dark brown
above, white below, with the hairs of the midventral line elongate and
stiff, forming a continuous keel. Similar fringes on margins of fore and
hind feet. Autumn and spring moults probably as in *Sorex araneus*; also
apparently a summer moult proceeding from head to tail like spring moult
of common shrew (Shillito 1960).

Flank glands are highly developed and fringed with white hairs only
in adult males, and are situated on the thorax, further forwards than in
Sorex.

The large first upper incisors have the anterior cusps very long and

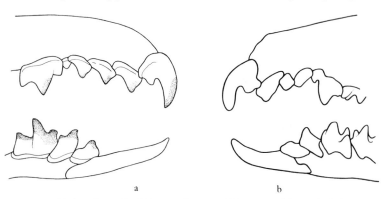

FIGURE 19 Anterior teeth of (a) water shrew; and (b) greater white-toothed shrew.

curved and the posterior cusps shorter than in other species. The large
lower incisors have the upper surface smooth, with only a single, ill-
defined lobe.

A vascular plexus in the interscapular adipose tissue resembles typical,
although poorly developed, retia mirabilia found in diving mammals
(Ivanova 1967).

Chromosomes: $2n = 52$; F.N. $= 92$? (Bovey 1949, Fredga & Levan
1969).

DISTRIBUTION See Fig. 20. The whole of Europe except for the Mediterranean region, eastwards to Lake Baikal and recurring on the Pacific
coast and Sakhalin.

Throughout mainland Britain but probably rather local in northern
Scotland. Absent from Ireland and many of the small islands but present
on the following and may have been overlooked on others: Hoy (Orkney),

Raasay, Skye, Pabay (Skye), Mull, South Shuna (Argyll), Garvellachs (all four main islands), Islay, Kerrera, Arran, Bute, Anglesey and Isle of Wight.

VARIATION British population not distinguishable from Continental. Colour of ventral pelage very variable, melanism being rather frequent. Few data available on insular populations but some may be distinctive, e.g. the ventral pelage is a very uniform pale grey on Shuna. White on ears and near eyes is frequent. Albinos occur rarely.

HABITAT Mainly by clear, unpolluted streams and ponds wherever there is cover. Especially abundant in watercress beds. In north-west Scotland frequent amongst boulders on rocky beaches. Also occur at considerable distance from water, often in woodland, rare specimens being encountered regularly and larger numbers, almost amounting to invasions, at sporadic intervals. Near Oxford found up to 3 km from water (H. N. Southern, unpubl.).

In Poland range extends into coniferous and deciduous woodland, in contrast to *Neomys anomalus* which remains by water in that area (Dehnel 1950).

BEHAVIOUR Semiaquatic. Propulsive power of toes and tail increased

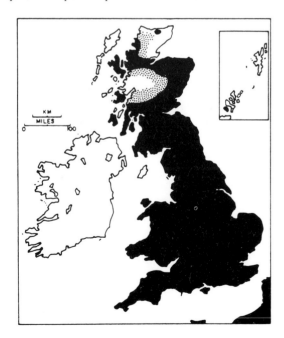

FIGURE 20 Water shrew: distribution.

by fringes of stiff erectile hairs. Air trapped in dense coat makes animal very buoyant; swims on surface of water and considerable effort required to dive and remain submerged. Although fairly water-repellent, fur does become wet and is usually cleaned on leaving the water or squeezed dry in passage through the narrow tunnels which are flattened in cross section. Tunnelling involves use of forefeet and nose for probing and loosening soil (Lorenz 1952, 1957, Crowcroft 1957). Extensive shallow burrow systems are excavated in banks with entrance above or below water level.

Active throughout 24 hours with one or two peaks of maximum activity. Daily rhythm regulated by light (Crowcroft 1957). Conflicting opinions about metabolic rate; no higher than that of mice (Hawkins *et al.* 1960, Hawkins & Jewell 1962) while the converse view was proposed by Tupikova (1949) and Gebczynska & Gebczynski (1965).

Although solitary, home ranges overlap. Evidence for nomadic existence and records of distances of 28–162 m travelled (Shillito 1963). Territorial in captivity; introduction of stranger provokes fighting accompanied by strident squeaking; resident usually victorious. Pugnacity eventually diminishes and they coexist, avoidance probably aided by utterance of long drawn-out squeaks (Bunn 1966).

Good spatial memory; strange areas explored cautiously but once developed routes are traversed at speed. Deviations in learned path thoroughly reinvestigated, while unnecessary detours only gradually eliminated.

Sensitive, mobile whiskers important for detecting prey when swimming. Olfactory sense well developed.

FOOD Feed on land and in water (Crowcroft 1957); prey carried ashore to eat (Lorenz 1952, Cranbrook 1959). Prey, usually attacked from behind, includes insects and other invertebrates, small fish and amphibians and may be larger than themselves. Caches of snail shells, partially eaten frogs and fish may be eating places and possibly food stores for future use (Buchalczyk & Pucek 1963, Shoczeń 1970). A shrew weighing 15·6 g consumed 18 g food per day (Tupikova 1949).

Venom produced by the submaxillary gland is thought to be contained in saliva and affects the nervous system and, to a lesser extent, the respiratory and vascular systems. It is effective when injected into small mammals, although no predatory behaviour towards the latter was observed in the laboratory. *N. anomalus* is probably not venomous (Pucek 1959).

BREEDING All data from captive specimens (Price 1953, Crowcroft 1957, Vogel 1972). Peak breeding season is May and June but extends from April to September. Generally breed in second year, though some females may do so in the first. Two or more litters produced each season, female often becoming pregnant at post-partum oestrus. Ovulation probably stimulated by coitus.

Gestation period 20–24 days, perhaps longer in lactating females. Average number of foetuses in late pregnancy is 6·8; maximum number is 11 but usually 3–8 nidicolous young produced, weighing over 1 g at birth. Dorsal pigment is apparent by 4th day, bicoloured by 7th, pelt developing by 10th. Escape reaction exhibited by 20th day and eyes open a couple of days later. Tooth eruption immediately precedes termination of lactation period of 27–37 days, at which time weight is about 10 g. Fur slightly lighter than that of adults.

POPULATION Maximum life-span is 14–19 months, death occurring in the second autumn and winter. Sex ratio is almost equal, 52% females to 48% males (Price 1953).

PREDATORS AND MORTALITY Carnivorous mammals, owls and fish are known predators. Found to form only 3% of the total number of shrews recovered from pellets of tawny owl (Southern 1954) and 4% of over 15000 shrews in pellets of barn owl from all parts of Britain (Glue 1974).

PARASITES AND DISEASE The usual shrew fleas, *Palaeopsylla soricis* and *Doratopsylla dasycneme*, are frequent and rodent fleas such as *Ctenophthalmus nobilis* occasionally occur. Non-specific ticks and mites occur as on other small mammals and fur mites, *Labidophorus* sp., have been found abundantly on animals from the Inner Hebrides (Corbet *et al.* 1968).

The following helminths have been recorded in Wales (Lewis 1968): the trematodes *Dicrocoelium soricis* and *Brachylaimus oesophagei*; the tapeworms *Choanotaenia crassiscolex* and *Hymenolepis singularis*; the nematode *Capillaria incrassata* and the acanthocephalan *Centrorhynchus aluconis*; also a protozoan, *Trypanosoma* sp. (Cox 1970).

RELATIONS WITH MAN In Czechoslovakia may act as a reservoir animal, with two species of *Sorex*, for *Pneumocystis carinii*, the causative agent of a group of infantile interstitial pneumonias affecting humans (Šebek & Rosický 1967).

Not very easy to keep in captivity (Lorenz 1952, 1957, Crowcroft 1957).

AUTHOR FOR THIS SPECIES P. D. Jenkins.

GENUS *Crocidura*
WHITE-TOOTHED SHREWS

A large homogeneous group distributed throughout the Ethiopian, Oriental and southern Palaearctic regions. Distinguished by unpigmented teeth, three upper unicuspids, long scattered hairs on the tail,

FIGURE 21 Lesser white-toothed shrew from the Scilly Isles. (Photo: H. N. Southern)

and more prominent ears than in *Sorex* or *Neomys*. Represented in the British Isles only on the Scilly and Channel Islands. The two species involved are rather difficult to distinguish but so far have not been found together on the same island. In Table 6 the more critical dental differences are placed first.

Greater white-toothed shrew *Crocidura russula*

Sorex russulus Hermann, 1780; near Strasbourg, France. *Crocidura russula peta* Montagu & Pickford, 1923; Guernsey, Channel Islands.

RECOGNITION Generally larger than *C. suaveolens* but absolutely separ-

TABLE 6 Identification of white-toothed shrews

	Greater white-toothed shrew	Lesser white-toothed shrew
Lenth of upper unicuspids (at cingula): labial length of large premolar	>1·3	<1·3
2nd unicuspid smaller than 3rd (in crown view)	Slightly	Markedly
Lingual part of large upper premolar	Larger	Smaller
Length of upper tooth row	7·7–8·5 mm	7·4–8·0 mm
Length of head and body	60–90 mm	50–75 mm
Length of hind feet	10·5–14 mm	10–13 mm

able only by the dental characters shown in Table 6. It is the only species of shrew on those Channel Islands on which it occurs.

DESCRIPTION Small, greyish-brown above, duller below. Paired lateral glands present in both sexes. Six inguinal mammae, buried in pelage when female is non-oestrous, thus sexing difficult. Males have subcaudal and lateral caudal glands which cause thickening of the tail (Niethammer 1962). Weight and histology of the submaxillary gland differs between males and females and pregnant and non-pregnant females (Raynaud 1964).

Chromosomes $2n=42$; F.N.$=52$ (Bovey 1949).

MEASUREMENTS See Table 6.

DISTRIBUTION Central and southern Europe, north to the Baltic, east to the Caucasus and possibly south-west Asia. Also on most Mediterranean islands and in North Africa.

In Britain known only on Alderney, Guernsey and Herm of the Channel Islands.

VARIATION Guernsey form no longer considered a distinct subspecies but variation between Alderney, Guernsey and continental populations has been demonstrated (Delany & Healy 1966).

HABITAT Fairly abundant in hedgerows and open ground. The tendency to live in and around buildings is reflected by the continental name of house shrew.

BEHAVIOUR Not very well investigated and only in captivity. Maximum activity early in night and at dawn with a secondary rhythm of about one hour, subject to varying conditions (Saint Girons 1959). Nest usually made of grass.

Rapidly acquire exact knowledge of environment mainly by tactile exploration, subsequent orientation by spatial memory. When exploring or disturbed, emit audible and ultrasonic squeaks, but although hearing is good, no evidence for echolocation (Grünwald 1969). Well developed olfaction; scent-mark but do not follow their own scent trails. Vision probably not very important.

FOOD Insects and other invertebrates, lizards and small rodents (Fons 1972). No evidence for potent venom in saliva (Bernard 1960).

BREEDING In Channel Islands breeding season extends from February to October (Bishop 1962). Remaining data are from captive animals (Vogel 1969, 1972, Fons 1972). Females reach sexual maturity in third month of life, slightly before the males. Female polyoestrous, showing post-partum oestrus but no evidence of delayed implantation. Milk has high protein content (10%) correlated with very rapid body growth (Hellwing 1973). Litters of 2–10 young, weighing 0·8–0·9 g, born after a gestation of 28–33 days. On 7th day begin to exhibit 'caravanning' behaviour in which the mother leads the young from the nest in line, each grasping the tail of the one in front (in wild probably only in response to disturbance). By 8th or 9th day eyes are open and pelage complete. Weaned at about 20–22 days.

Pairs established during the breeding period showed aggression to other individuals and the male showed a tendency to shelter the young (Vogel 1972).

POPULATION STRUCTURE During several years' study, young individuals appeared in June, predominated by August, overwintered as adults and only a few survived longer than $1\frac{1}{2}$ years (Bishop 1962). Average life-span in captivity 2–$2\frac{1}{2}$ years, longest 4 years. First- and second-year animals distinguishable by height of M_3 (Bishop & Delany 1963).

PREDATORS AND MORTALITY Predators include barn owl, tawny owl and weasel. Although killed by cats, probably not generally eaten.

PARASITES AND DISEASE The following fleas have been found on specimens from Guernsey: *Typhloceras poppei*, *Rhadinopsylla pentacantha*, *Ctenophthalmus nobilis*, *Nosopsyllus fasciatus* (the last also from Alderney). These are all primarily rodent fleas. A mite, *Myobia* (*Croci-*

durobia) *michaeli*, also occurs. Tapeworms of the genus *Hymenolepis* occur in Continental animals, so could be expected from the Channel Islands.

AUTHOR FOR THIS SPECIES P. D. Jenkins.

Lesser white-toothed shrew *Crocidura suaveolens*

Sorex suaveolens Pallas, 1811; Crimea, Russia. *Crocidura suaveolens cassiteridum* Hinton, 1924; uninhabited island, Isles of Scilly.
Scilly shrew.

RECOGNITION See Table 6 for differences between this and the greater white-toothed shrew. It is the only species of shrew on the islands on which it occurs except for Jersey where *Sorex araneus* occurs. The lesser white-toothed shrew is smaller, paler, with scattered long hairs on the tail and wholly white teeth.

DESCRIPTION Little seasonal variation in pelage; slightly longer and thicker in winter and in spring when ventral fur may be lighter coloured. Males tend to moult before females and some show successive moults. Spring moult usually begins on ventral surface of head, spreading dorsally and posteriorly. Autumn moult more rapid and proceeds in reverse direction, new fur appearing on posterior and moving anteriorly and ventrally. Tail glands absent.
 Chromosome numbers: $2n = 40$; F.N. $= 50$ (Meylan 1966, based on Continental animals).

MEASUREMENTS See Table 6.

DISTRIBUTION Central and southern Palaearctic, east to Korea. In Europe, north to central Poland, apparently absent from most of Spain and North-West France (van den Brink 1967), but present on offshore islands of Ouessant and Yeu.
 In the Channel Islands occurs on Jersey and Sark. In the Isles of Scilly found on all but some of the smaller islands (on St Mary's, St Martin's, Tresco, Bryher, St Agnes, Gugh, Samson, Tean and doubtfully on Annet).

VARIATION Animals from the Scilly Isles described as a distinct subspecies; subsequent evidence suggests this separation is invalid (Rood 1964). Populations from various Scilly Islands are more alike than those from Sark or Jersey, but, on the basis of skull and tooth-row lengths,

are intermediate in size between Sark populations which are the largest
and those from Jersey which are the smallest (Delany & Healy 1966).

Adults show seasonal variation in weight, reduction occurring in
autumn at end of breeding season.

HABITAT Found in most habitats affording adequate cover, commonly
in bracken and tall vegetation, also hedgebanks and woodland. Abundant
among sea-shore rocks on Bryher, St Mary's and St Martin's.

BEHAVIOUR All observations from captive Scilly Island specimens
(Rood 1965a, b), except those on home range.

Run rapidly in familiar environment, tunnel through leaf-litter and
climb well; tail partially prehensile. Active at regular intervals (one or
more per hour) during day and night with two peak periods in early morning and mid-afternoon. Feed during some part of most activity phases,
although juveniles tend to spend greater time in exploration. Diurnal
activity increases during summer months.

Males tend to have larger home ranges (average diameter 50 m) than
females (27 m) or juveniles, the latter appearing to move and enlarge their
ranges more than adults. (Spencer-Booth (1963) recorded smaller ranges
on Bryher.) Probably not very territorial, since ranges overlap, and in
captivity, while generally ignoring each other, share the same nests.

Males are dominant to females, and old to young. Threat behaviour,
in which head is raised and animal emits sharp squeak, leads usually to
retreat of one or both, rarely to a short scuffle. Other vocalisations include
a continuous soft 'twitter' when investigating or when slightly disturbed.

Hearing and touch acute, olfaction probably important, sight poorly
developed.

FOOD In captivity, total wet weight intake of food per day is close to
animal's body weight. Insects and other invertebrates preferred. Prey
orientated by shrew so that head is eaten first. In coastal habitats of the
Isles of Scilly shrews feed on amphipods, dipterous flies and adult beetles
(Spencer-Booth 1963. Pernetta 1973a). Fresh fish, meat and grain also
eaten. Feeding from everted rectum has been observed, as in common
shrew.

BREEDING Breeding season extends from early part of year to autumn;
tendency for decrease in testes size in late summer and autumn (Rood
1965a). Three to four litters produced per year, possibly more since a
captive female produced three litters in less than 3 months (Vasarhelyi
1929). Females and some males may breed in year of birth in the Isles
of Scilly.

Post-partum oestrus allows possibility of female simultaneously lactating and pregnant. Gestation period about 28 days; 1–6 young, weighing an average of 0·63 g shortly after birth. Lactation period lasts about 3 weeks, dorsal pelage developed within 9 days, eyes open by 10th, solid food taken after 15 days. Young carried by mouth and also 'caravanning' occurs from 8th day (Hanzák 1966).

POPULATION STRUCTURE Juveniles first observed in spring, form half the population in summer and are in the majority by autumn. They are short-lived, rarely surviving more than one winter. Although sex ratio may alter from year to year, Rood (1964) observed significantly more males than females in the population.

Population densities are greater on the Isles of Scilly than on the Channel Islands. On Jersey, where *Sorex araneus* is a possible competitor, neither species is very abundant (Bishop 1962). The height of the posterior cusp of M_1 has been used to determine age (Rood 1964).

PREDATORS AND MORTALITY Owls, foxes and weasels probably important on the Channel Islands. On the Isles of Scilly, possible predators include kestrels, domestic cats and perhaps rats.

PARASITES AND DISEASE Two rodent fleas, *Nosopsyllus fasciatus* and *Ctenophthalmus nobilis*, occur on shrews from the Isles of Scilly, the latter also on Sark specimens. Scilly animals are also parasitised by a mite *Myobia (Crocidurobia) blairi*, a tick *Ixodes dorriensmithi* (considered by some to be conspecific with *I. arvicolae*) and a digenean fluke *Maritrema* sp. A liver nematode was found in shrews on St Martins, especially those trapped near the shore (Pernetta 1973).

RELATIONS WITH MAN Apparently easier to keep and breed in captivity than species of *Sorex*.

AUTHOR FOR THIS SPECIES P. D. Jenkins.

Order Chiroptera
Bats

By R. E. STEBBINGS

Bats are the only mammals capable of true flight (Chiroptera=hand-wing). Structurally bats are little different from the typical mammal but with the obvious extension of finger bones to carry flight membranes (Figs. 22 and 23). The only other distinctive modification is the back-ward-bending knee. This arrangement, with the rearward-facing toes, facilitates landing and hanging head down. Apart from these two features which are common to all bats there are many modifications which are concerned with their mode of life. The most spectacular features are the ears and facial skin growths involved with echolocation. Additionally some species have tails within the interfemoral membrane while others have the tail projecting from the edge or from the upper surface of the membrane and still others have almost no tail nor membrane. Further details of structure and biology can be found in Vaughan (1972), Wimsatt (1970) and Yalden & Morris (1975).

Although there are systematic affinities between the Insectivora and Chiroptera little is known about bat evolution. There are a few well-pre-served bat fossils of early Eocene and Oligocene periods that are not greatly different from present-day microchiropterans.

About 900 species of bat are known, divided between two suborders. The Megachiroptera are represented by one family consisting of about 150 species distributed in the Old World tropics from Africa to the Pacific islands. These include the familiar flying foxes and all species feed pre-dominantly on vegetable diets, e.g. nuts, fruit, pollen, nectar. Micro-chiroptera include the other 18 families and are represented throughout the world, generally below the tree lines and excluding Arctic regions and some remote islands particularly in the Pacific. Various species occupy most of the available feeding niches, from fruit, pollen, nectar, fish-eaters and including carnivorous, sanguinivorous and insectivorous bats. The last are by far the most plentiful in number of species and prob-ably individuals. In cool temperate regions including Europe and the British Isles only insectivorous species occur. Two families are repre-sented in Britain, Rhinolophidae and Vespertilionidae. Rhinolophidae has two species of the genus *Rhinolophus* represented in the British Isles

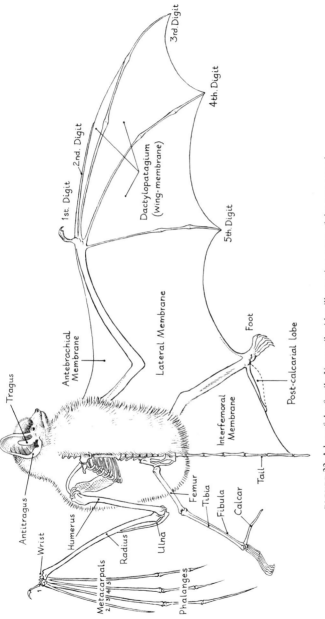

FIGURE 22 A bat of the family Vespertilionidae illustrating some of the terms used in the text.

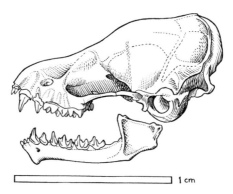

1 cm

FIGURE 23 The skull of a pipistrelle bat, *P. pipistrellus.*

and these are characterised by their noseleaves. These consist of a horse-shoe-shaped process around the nostrils surmounted by a vertical sella and lancet (Fig. 24). There is no tragus. Horseshoe bats always hang free by their toes and when torpid the wings envelop the body, with the tail downwards over the back. In this way the bat has some control over its body microclimate within the wings, and during wet weather dripping water does not wet the fur but instead runs over the membranes and drips off the wrists. Quadrupedal movement is very poor.

Seven genera of Vespertilionidae occur in the British Isles, *Barbastella*, *Eptesicus*, *Myotis*, *Nyctalus*, *Pipistrellus*, *Plecotus* and *Vespertilio*, although the last is a rare vagrant. Facial characters are simple and a prominent tragus is present in all species. These bats sometimes hang 'free' but more often they are found in crevices or tight in corners. Those hanging free hold wings at their sides although long-eared bats are occasionally found partially enveloped by wings. Most species are very agile quadrupedally.

Variations due to sex and age can cause confusion during the identification of species. Males are mostly smaller than females. Young bats tend to have dull greyish fur for the first 12 months. Maximum body size, in terms of bone length, is normally reached within 60 days from birth but maximum body weight is not attained generally until the third year. In England the maximum annual weight is reached in late October and the minimum in early May. Loss of weight during hibernation is usually about 23%. Maximum weights of individuals may be more than twice the minimum whereas linear dimensions rarely exceed 20% above minimal values.

Fifteen species are resident along the central south coast of England but only two or three reach the north of mainland Scotland while in Ireland seven or possibly eight species are found.

Bats roost in almost any position with protection from direct sunlight but most are found in hollow trees or buildings and some species occur in caves or tunnels during hibernation. Bats are creatures of habit and most seasonally occupy the same roost. During the course of a year an individual bat may occupy many roosts in sequence and these different positions may be within one cave or building or may be scattered several kilometres apart.

During hibernation most bats seek sheltered roosts buffered against rapid temperature fluctuations but with high humidities. Some species are gregarious while others are solitary. Individual species select differing temperature regimes generally with the range 0–10°C (Gaisler 1970) and as winter progresses lower roost temperatures are selected. Also the periods of continuous torpor shorten throughout hibernation. Torpid body temperature is close to ambient. Bats may fly at any time during winter and often in the day. Under favourable conditions feeding can occur but this may not be the primary cause of winter activity. While most bats roost on ceilings or walls of caves, some, particularly Daubenton's, are found in loose floor scree.

In summer females of all species seem to segregate into large nursery roosts consisting of pregnant bats, some non-breeders and immatures of both sexes. Adult males usually roost in small groups or singly away from the nurseries. They may be within the same building.

About an hour before sunset bats become active and in large colonies squeaking and chattering become intense just before emergence. On hot days colonies of some species can be located by these noises which can carry long distances.

Certain species (e.g. noctules) often leave their day roosts shortly after sunset while others (e.g. long-ears) wait until it is almost dark before emerging to feed. Duration and frequency of night activity depend on many factors and can be semi-continuous throughout the night or confined to a single feed for about one hour at the beginning of the night.

Exceptionally in summer, bats may not emerge at all, particularly if it is cold and windy. During the day, bats' body temperatures usually approximate to that of their surroundings which on a cool cloudy day may be 15°C or on a hot sunny day may be 40°C in a roof. Slate roofs often exceed this temperature on hot days and bats can be expected to seek cooler areas as well as actively cooling themselves.

All species are insectivorous but different species have differing feeding strategies. Most catch their prey during flight, sometimes in their mouth, but slow-motion film has shown that larger insects are often caught either in the interfemoral membrane or in a cupped wing. Some species eat their prey during flight while others tend to perch.

A few species (e.g. long-ears) specialise in searching vegetation, hovering to pick off resting insects. Others (e.g. horseshoes) are known to forage on the ground.

Bats make a variety of sounds under varying conditions. Some low-frequency chattering is usually heard at all times from active colonies and this becomes intense before emergence in the evening. These sounds have been little studied whereas echolocation emissions have received much attention. Despite this it remains unclear exactly how bats use their cries although many differing types of sounds have been described. (See Griffin 1958, Sales & Pye 1974.)

No species in Britain is known to migrate in the accepted sense, although some make regular movements of at least 25 km between summer and winter roosts.

Spermatogenesis takes place during the summer and copulation begins in the autumn. Copulation is promiscuous and active males are seen to mate intermittently throughout hibernation in caves. Females and males store sperm throughout winter and copulation can sometimes occur in the spring. Ovulation and fertilisation take place in April–May. Pregnant females may become torpid during adverse weather, and foetal development is slowed or halted as a result. Because of this, gestation periods may vary. In general they average about 50 days. Young, usually single in Britain, are born blind with the mother hanging head upward. Suckling usually begins immediately.

Young of Vespertilionidae are hairless, but those of Rhinolophidae have sparse down dorsally at birth. They are about 20% of the mother's weight at birth. Young are capable of flight at about 3 weeks but forearm growth lasts about 5 weeks. Females do not normally carry young during flight but may do so if disturbed in their roost. Some females attain sexual maturity (i.e. come into oestrus and mate) in their first, and most of the remainder in their second, autumn. In some species (e.g. the greater horseshoe) maturity is usually reached in the third year but even the fourth year is known. Spermatogenesis usually first occurs in the summer following birth.

Survival rate of females is usually higher than of males. Mean life span is usually 4–5 years and maximum longevity for both families is over 20 years.

There are no specialist predators of bats but opportunist owls, raptors, carnivores and small mammals have been known to eat bats.

During a recent Mammal Society survey (Racey & Stebbings 1972) it was found that there was evidence of population declines in bats. This was most evident for the greater horseshoe, whose range and numbers have declined substantially. Ringing or banding is known to have contributed to this decline partly because of the poor quality of early rings which caused damage to the bats. More important was the amount of disturbance caused during hibernation. This results in loss of fat and leads to premature death, particularly of immatures. Loss of caves as well as increased 'potholing' have contributed to declines, and pesticides may also be implicated.

Under the Protection of Wild Creatures legislation, 1975, it is an offence to mark bats without a licence and the greater horseshoe and mouse-eared bat are specially protected because they are endangered species in Britain.

In any proposed study it is recommended that the Mammal Society should be contacted since this will help prevent undue disturbance in areas where study is already in progress. The Society has specially designed rings (bands) which are well tried and cause no damage to bats if applied carefully. A licence is required before rings can be issued and the Society will advise a prospective worker on procedures. It is the responsibility of those who work on bats to ensure their continued survival.

The records of ectoparasites given in the accounts of the individual species are taken mainly from the following sources. Bugs (Cimicidae) from Usinger (1966); fleas from Smit (1957); nycteribiid flies from Theodor (1967); mites from Radford (1954), Rudnick (1960) and Evans & Till (1966); and ticks from Thompson (1963, 1968).

Key to the species of bats

1 { Nose leaf present; no tragus (Rhinolophidae) — See 2
{ Nose leaf absent; tragus present (Vespertilionidae) — See 3

2 { Large, forearm over 50 mm — **Greater horseshoe bat** (p. 76)
{ Small, forearm under 43 mm — **Lesser horseshoe bat** (p. 80)

3 { Ear bases joined over top of head — See 4
{ Ear bases widely separated — See 5

4 { Ears very long, over 28 mm — **Long-eared bats** (see note A below and p. 120)
{ Ears short, about 18 mm, triangular; fur blackish all over — **Barbastelle** (p. 118)

5 { Tragus short, rounded, broader than long — See 6
{ Tragus longer than broad — See 7

74   *Order Chiroptera*

$6\begin{cases}\text{Forearm over 48 mm} \\ \text{Forearm under 47 mm}\end{cases}$ 　　　　　Noctule (p. 108)
　　　　　　　　　　　　　　　　　　　Leisler's bat (p. 105)

$7\begin{cases}\text{No post-calcarial lobe; tragus pointed} & \text{See 8} \\ \text{Post-calcarial lobe prominent; tragus blunt; forearm under} \\ \quad\text{36 mm} & \text{Pipistrelle (p. 112)} \\ \text{Post-calcarial lobe slight; tragus blunt; forearm} \\ \quad\text{48–55 mm} & \text{Serotine (p. 102)}\end{cases}$

$8\begin{cases}\text{Very large, forearm over 57 mm} & \text{Mouse-eared bat (p. 94)} \\ \text{Smaller, forearm 31–45 mm} & \text{See 9}\end{cases}$

$9\begin{cases}\text{Ears long, 18–26 mm, reaching 6 mm beyond nose when laid} \\ \quad\text{forward} & \text{Bechstein's bat (p. 91)} \\ \text{Ears shorter, up to 17 mm} & \text{See 10}\end{cases}$

$10\begin{cases}\text{Ears 14–17 mm; edge of interfemoral membrane with fringe of} \\ \quad\text{bristles, 1 mm long} & \text{Natterer's bat (p. 89)} \\ \text{Ears shorter; edge of interfemoral membrane at most lightly} \\ \quad\text{hairy} & \text{See 11}\end{cases}$

$11\begin{cases}\text{Hindfoot more than half as long as shin; ear shortish, rounded,} \\ \quad\text{brown, outer margin of tragus convex} & \text{Daubenton's bat (p. 97)} \\ \text{Hindfoot less than half length of shin; ear more elongated, very} \\ \quad\text{dark brown, appearing black; outer margin of tragus straight or} \\ \quad\text{slightly concave} & \text{Whiskered/Brandt's bat (see note B below and pp. 84, 87)}\end{cases}$

NOTE A Long-eared bats (*Plecotus*). Separation of the two species can be very difficult since there is a large overlap of the most easily taken measurements. *P. austriacus* tends to be larger and grey but young *P. auritus* are also greyish. Face colour in *P. austriacus* is usually dark brown to black, in *P. auritus* pink to brown. In *P. austriacus* the first upper premolar is less than half the height of the second whereas in *P. auritus* it is more. Because of the morphological similarity between these two species diagnostic measurements are given in Table 7. Tragus width and upper canine length (from cingulum to tip) are the most diagnostic characters. No single character is diagnostic. *P. auritus* in central and northern England and in Scotland tend to be larger than those in the south. It seems unlikely that *P. austriacus* occurs north of a line from Bristol to London.

NOTE B Whiskered bat, *Myotis mystacinus*, and Brandt's bat, *M. brandti*. Field identification of these species is much more difficult than of *Plecotus*. No measurements are useful indicators of species, although *M. brandti* tends to be the larger. Males may be conclusively separated on

TABLE 7 Distinguishing characters of long-eared bats (common long-eared bat, *Plecotus auritus* and grey long-eared bat, *Plecotus austriacus*). These measurements (in mm) enable the majority of individuals to be identified but no single measurement is diagnostic

| | Males | | Females | |
	P. auritus	*P. austriacus*	*P. auritus*	*P. austriacus*
Forearm length	< 39·0	> 39·0	< 39·7	> 39·7
Thumb length	> 6·2	< 6·2	> 6·4	< 6·3
Fifth digit length	< 51·0	> 51·0	< 52·0	> 52·0
Wingspan	<265	>265	<270	>270
Tragus width	< 5·4	> 5·4	< 5·5	> 5·5
Tragus length	< 14·5	> 14·5	< 14·8	> 14·9
Foot length	> 7·2	< 7·2	> 7·5	< 7·5
Head and body length	< 44	> 45	< 45	> 45
Tail length	< 46	> 46	< 47	> 47
Total length	< 90	> 90	< 92	> 92
Upper canine length	< 1·7	> 1·7	< 1·8	> 1·8
Medial ear-flap width			< 4·2	> 4·2

the basis of the shape of the penis. In *M. mystacinus* the penis is thin and parallel-sided throughout, while in *M. brandti* it is distinctly club-shaped (distally) and generally thicker. Male and female *M. brandti* have an extra cusp on the third upper premolar, on the anterior inner angle, and this rises as high as or higher than the second upper premolar. In some *M. mystacinus* a cusp has been found but it is always lower than the second premolar. This latter tooth in *M. mystacinus* is very small and usually overlapped by the much larger first.

Adult *M. brandti* are usually a rich brown dorsally but immatures tend to appear grey brown like adult *M. mystacinus*.

FAMILY RHINOLOPHIDAE
GENUS *Rhinolophus*
HORSESHOE BATS

A large genus with many species in the tropics of the Old World. Five species reach Europe and two of these occur in Britain.

The muzzle bears a complex series of nose-leaves (Fig. 24) consisting of a lower *horseshoe* around the nostrils and a central plate or *sella* which is joined by a connecting process, flattened in the sagittal plane, to an upper triangular lobe or *lancet* with the free tip projecting upwards against the forehead. The ears are widely spaced, lack a tragus (see Vespertilionidae) but have the antitragus (*behind* the basal notch) enlarged.

The dental formula is

$$\frac{1.1.2.3}{2.1.3.3}.$$

The upper incisors are carried at the tips of very slender premaxillae which frequently become detached when skulls are cleaned.

Horseshoe bats roost mainly in caves during winter, often communally. They hang freely from the roof by the claws of their feet and sleep with their wings wrapped round the body and almost completely concealing it. In this they differ from all vespertilionid bats except that the long-eared bats sometimes adopt a similar but less extreme posture. Echolocation pulses are emitted through the nostrils, with mouth closed.

The two species found in Britain differ greatly in size and in the shape of parts of the nose-leaf.

Greater horseshoe bat *Rhinolophus ferrumequinum*

Vespertilio ferrum-equinum Schreber, 1774; France. *Vespertilio ferrum-equinum insulanus* Barrett-Hamilton, 1910; Cheddar, Somerset, England.

RECOGNITION Distinguished from all but lesser horseshoe by presence of nose-leaf and absence of tragus. Very much larger than lesser horseshoe (forearm over 50 mm), appearing the size of a clenched fist when hanging at rest. Shape of nose-leaf, especially the sella, also differs (Fig. 24).

The skull can be recognised by the loosely attached premaxillae and the large size (condylobasal length 20–22 mm).

DESCRIPTION A large bat with the upper parts medium to light brown, often with a reddish tinge, and the under parts greyish buff. Young animals, up to 12 months, are greyer above. Wing membranes thick and opaque.

Ears large, extending slightly beyond tip of muzzle when laid forwards. Nose-leaf about 14 mm high and 8 mm wide, lateral profile of connecting process (above sella) distinctive. Wings broad and rounded at tips. Chromosomes: $2n = 58$, F.N. $= 64$ (Capanna & Civitelli 1964, Dulić 1967).

MEASUREMENTS Head and body 58–68 mm; forearm 51–59 mm; wingspan 340–390 mm; ear 21–26 mm; weight varies from 13–34 g. In Gloucestershire adult females and males 29 g and 24 g respectively in

FIGURE 24 Greater horseshoe bat. (Photo. S. C. Bisserôt)

October falling to 19 g and 18 g in April. For juveniles the corresponding figures are 21 g and 20 g falling to 16 g and 15 g (Ransome 1968).

DISTRIBUTION See Fig. 25. Widespread throughout the southern part of the Palaearctic Region from Britain to Japan. The northern boundary runs through south Poland, Caucasus and Korea; the southern boundary from Morocco through Iran and the Himalayas.

In Britain confined to South-West England and South Wales, with isolated recent records in Hampshire and Surrey. There are many older records, up to about 1900, from Kent and the Isle of Wight, but it is probably extinct in these counties.

VARIATION Recognition of a British subspecies, *R. f. insulanus*, was based entirely on small size of wings and is quite invalid. Caubere *et al.* (1968) recorded apparent clines in Europe, the smallest being in North-West France and increasing in size southwards to the Mediterranean and eastwards to Roumania. In Dorset males are smaller than females. Forearm means 55·0 mm, range 52·0–57·8 ($n=57$) for males and 56·0 mm, range 53·5–58·6 ($n=79$) for females (author's data).

HABITAT Found hibernating mostly in large caves, mines and cellars during winter. In summer occur predominantly in large roof spaces and

barns where free access through open doorway is always possible. Largest
known roosts are in sheltered, well-wooded valleys.

BEHAVIOUR Flight heavy and butterfly-like with glides, often along
stream or river banks. Usually low but up to 13 m. Wings very broad
with rounded tips. Unable to crawl on flat surface, hence their roost requirement of access by flight. Always hang by their feet.

Summer. Emerge about 30 minutes after sunset for feeding, and activity
continues throughout night. Pregnant females form large nursery
colonies in which some non-breeding and juvenile females and immature
males also present. Young normally remain in roof when mothers go out
foraging. Adult males are found in small scattered groups. These bats
are almost always active except on very cold days when they become
torpid.

Nursing colonies are very noisy with continuous chattering. They are
also sensitive to the slightest disturbance, which makes observation difficult and causes colonies to desert roosts.

Winter. Essentially gregarious in hibernation, but the mechanism of
cluster formation is complex (Ransome 1968). Its main purpose may be
to 'buffer' ambient temperature fluctuations. The same area of cave roof

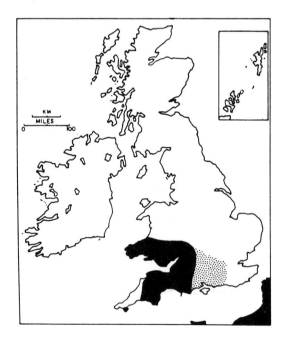

FIGURE 25 Greater
horseshoe bat:
distribution.

may be used for many years and large accumulations of faeces form beneath, often containing dead bats and insect remains. The temperature selected for hibernation varies due to many factors (Dulić 1963, Gaisler 1970, Ransome 1971) such as sex and age of bat, but generally 11°C preferred in October and 7°C in February. Frequency of arousal appears to be dependent upon temperature both inside and outside the hibernaculum (Ransome 1971). During winter flights, feeding and movements between roosts occur (Hooper & Hooper 1956, Ransome 1968). Most of the known movements are short, less than 8 km, but many movements of over 16 km have been recorded (Hooper & Hooper 1956, Ransome & Stebbings unpubl.). The longest movement of 64 km was recorded by Hooper & Hooper (1956). This bat made a return journey from place of banding with recapture at intervals of 7 months and 48 days respectively.

While in hibernation they are very sensitive to disturbance by noise (vibration) and torch light. Initial reaction is of a characteristic 'knees bend' in which the body is drawn up and the wings unfold slightly. If the stimulus is not too great the legs release and extend again a few minutes later. Some bats will then wake, a process which takes up to 50 minutes, while others apparently remain torpid.

FOOD Mainly flying insects, but some may be caught by bat landing on ground with outstretched wings. Dor beetles have been observed to be taken off cow-dung (Blackmore, unpubl.). Large prey is often taken to a perch, but most food is eaten on the wing.

BREEDING Copulation begins in late September and continues throughout the winter and probably until the spring. Sperm are stored during the winter in the uterus and oviducts. Occurrence of sperm in large vaginal plugs probably a fortuitous concomitant of the mechanism of plug formation (Racey 1975). Plugs may be voided soon after formation, and subsequent copulations can then occur (Ransome 1973). Ovulation and fertilisation takes place during April. In British Isles, blastocyst enters uterus third week in April (Matthews 1937). Single young born late June to early August, most around mid-July. Milk teeth said to be absorbed before birth but does not always happen. Young observed to fly short distances when about 22 days old, before being weaned. Lactation period unknown, but by mid-August most juveniles independent. Some segregation of sexes apparent in nursing colonies, where parous females usually accompanied by non-breeding immature females and immature males. They do not normally achieve sexual maturity until third autumn, although some females may come into oestrus one year earlier (Dinale 1964).

POPULATION STRUCTURE Little known. Sex ratio of bats in hibernation shows slight male bias (Hooper & Hooper 1956, Ransome 1968) but more or less unity at the weanling stage. In Dorset 40% were males ($n=$ 108, author's data). In Gloucestershire Ransome (1968) refound only 48% of juveniles and then showed that males were recaught at a lower frequency than females, demonstrating a probable higher survival rate for females. In Devon many bats have carried rings for over 15 years and one bat was recovered over 22 years after ringing (Hooper, unpubl.) (19 years quoted previously, Hooper & Hooper 1967). British population numbered about 800 in 1973 (author's data).

PREDATORS AND MORTALITY Both barn owls (*Tyto alba*) and tawny owls (*Strix aluco*) will roost in or near the entrances of caves, and bat bones have been recovered from pellets. Most mortality is thought to be caused by starvation, but disturbance by cavers may have reduced the survival rate.

PARASITES AND DISEASE Ectoparasites tend not to occur in high densities but a number of species are found regularly: the fly *Stylidia biarticulata*; the mites *Eyndhovenia euryalis*, *Paraperiglischrus rhinolophinus*, *Neomyobia rollinati* and *Macronyssus uncinatus*; and the tick *Ixodes vespertilionis*. The greater horseshoe is not considered the preferred host of *M. uncinatus*.

RELATIONS WITH MAN Difficult to maintain in captivity, but two have been successfully kept on a diet of mealworms (*Tenebrio*), moths and water. A male and female captured in February 1933 died after 643 and 671 days respectively (Blackmore 1964). Protected by Conservation of Wild Creatures and Wild Plants Act, 1975.

Lesser horseshoe bat *Rhinolophus hipposideros*

Vespertilio hipposideros Bechstein, 1800; France. *Vespertilio minutus* Montagu, 1808; Wiltshire, England.

RECOGNITION See greater horseshoe which it resembles in general form but is very small, delicate and of similar size to terminal part of human thumb. Forearm less than 43 mm. Skull similar to greater horseshoe but much smaller (condylo-basal length 14–16 mm).

DESCRIPTION A small bat with dark grey-brown fur dorsally (hairs with pale buff bases) and paler beneath. Young are much greyer for first 12 months. Wing membranes thin, glossy and translucent but dark. Ears relatively large, extending about 5 mm beyond tip of muzzle when laid

FIGURE 26 Lesser horseshoe bat. (Photo: S. C. Bisseröt)

forward. Noseleaf is less than 12 mm long and 8 mm wide and of distinctive shape (Fig. 26). Wings are broad and rounded at tips.

Chromosomes: $2n=56$, F.N.$=60$ (Capanna *et al.* 1967).

MEASUREMENTS Head and body 35–39 mm; forearm 36–40 mm; wingspan 225–250 mm; weight varies from about 5·3 g in October rising to 6·0 g in December and falling to 4·9 g in April (Hooper & Hooper 1956). Range of small number 4·0–9·0 g.

DISTRIBUTION See Fig. 27. South-western Palaearctic, from Ireland, Spain and Morocco east to Russian Turkestan and Kashmir. Northern boundary through Netherlands, Germany and South Poland, said to be withdrawing southwards in Germany (Feldman 1967).

In Britain range not clearly known but occurs mostly in South-West England and throughout Wales, northwards to Yorkshire, with three recent (1950s) records from South-East England. Also found in western Ireland.

VARIATION Recognition of British subspecies, *R. h. minutus*, was based on smaller size of forearm and is invalid. The existence of a cline from western France eastwards, with smallest bats in France (and Britain) and increasing through Czechoslovakia and Austria to Roumania, was demonstrated by Saint-Girons & Caubère (1966). Males are smaller than females: forearm mean 37·0 mm ($n=171$) for males and 38·0 mm ($n= 110$) for females (Saint-Girons & Caubere 1966).

HABITAT Essentially similar to the greater horseshoe, but often found in small tunnels hanging close to the ground in winter and also in small attics in summer. One colony was known in a large cedar tree in Somerset.

BEHAVIOUR Flight similar to greater horseshoe but lighter and more rapid wing beat with erratic turns and glides. Unable to crawl and hangs by its feet.

Summer. Emerges about 20 minutes after sunset and is active throughout the night. Large nursery colonies are formed by pregnant females where adult males not usually present.

Winter. Almost always solitary, although loose aggregations with intervening spaces of 20–50 cm not uncommon. Preferred temperatures in hibernation unknown in Britain, but found to be 7–8°C by experimentation (Harmata 1969b) and under natural conditions in Yugoslavia 5–9°C (Dulić 1963). Preference for the deeper, warmer parts of caves is shown (Hooper & Hooper 1956, Bezem *et al.* 1964). Little is known of movements but regular short movements from summer to winter roost of about

FIGURE 27 Lesser horseshoe bat: distribution.

3 km were recorded in Devon (Hooper & Hooper 1956). These authors recorded a maximum movement of 22 km. Bels (1952) has recorded the longest movement of 150 km for this species.

FOOD Small beetles, flies, moths and spiders are taken, but no detailed study has been made.

BREEDING Details of reproductive cycle given by Gaisler (1966a). In general similar to greater horseshoe, but some females become sexually mature in their first year although most do not until 2 years old. Ovulation occurs in April before vaginal plug is lost. Males attain maturity at the end of their first year. Sluiter (1960) calculated that Dutch lesser horseshoes produce a mean of 1·35 young per reproducing female and some breed in their first year.

POPULATION STRUCTURE Nothing known in Britain. Bezem *et al.* (1960) recorded the following results of a study of lesser horseshoes in hibernation. Adult survival rate of 0·567, which gives an estimated maximum life span of 8 years and mean longevity of 2·3 years. These figures appear to be too low as Gaisler (1966a) has found that the reproductive rate is not substantially higher than in other European species. Greatest longevity recorded in Britain 12 years (Hooper & Hooper 1956) and in Czechoslovakia over 18 years (Gaisler & Hanák 1969). Sex ratio in hibernation biased towards the males—58·6% (Hooper & Hooper 1956).

PARASITES AND DISEASE Few ectoparasites are known but the following have been found: the mites *Paraperiglischrus rhinolophinus*, *Macronyssus uncinatus* and *Neomyobia chiropteralis*; and the tick *Ixodes vespertilionis*.

RELATIONS WITH MAN Very difficult to maintain in captivity.

FAMILY VESPERTILIONIDAE
GENUS *Myotis**
MOUSE-EARED BATS

The largest genus of bats with representatives worldwide, except some of the remoter islands and in polar regions. Ten species occur in Europe and six of these are known to be resident in Britain.

The muzzle is narrow and unspecialised with nostrils opening outwards. Ears are well-spaced, longer than their width and all have an emargination on the outer margin. In most species this is inconspicuous.

* Synonyms: *Leuconoe, Selysius*

Tragus at least half as high as conch and mostly narrow and more or less pointed. No post-calcarial lobe. The dental formula is

$$\frac{2.1.3.3}{3.1.3.3}.$$

Myotis bats are very variable in their roost preferences but, apart from the largest members, are usually found in confined spaces such as tree holes and crevices in caves. The large species usually hang freely by their feet but hold their wings to their sides and not wrapped round the body. Echolocation pulses are emitted through the open mouth.

NOTE. In 1970 (Hanák, 1970, 1971) *Myotis mystacinus* in Europe was found to consist of two morphologically similar but distinct forms which are now generally treated as two species, *M. mystacinus* and *M. brandti*. Both species are recognised as existing throughout Europe and in Britain. Thus all data presented below under *M. mystacinus* might include *M. brandti*. Until we know the distributions of both species we cannot assess the likelihood of past results being referable to one species. Therefore each statement referable positively to *M. mystacinus* will be followed by (M). The *M. brandti* description is all positive.

Whiskered bat *Myotis mystacinus*

Vespertilio mystacinus Kuhl, 1819; Germany.

RECOGNITION Smallest of the *Myotis* but very similar to *M. brandti* and easily confused with *M. daubentoni*. Distinguished from latter by its small feet, very dark grey-black face, nostrils, ear and membranes, dark grey dorsal pelage and straight or concave outer margin of long pointed tragus (Fig. 28). Distinguished from *M. brandti* by its relatively longer tragus and more pointed ear. Males have thin parallel-sided penis.

The whiskered bat could also be confused with the larger, yellow-brown *M. emarginatus* which has not yet been found in Britain. This latter species has thick opaque membranes and a deeply angular notch slightly above the middle of the posterior edge of the ear.

Skull of *M. mystacinus* distinguished from *M. brandti* by lack of conspicuous cusp on anterior inner angle of upper P^3. This character is visible in the living animal viewed from the side and slightly forward of perpendicular to the maxilla.

DESCRIPTION Upper parts dark grey with lighter tips, under parts greyish white. Juveniles up to 12 months are often almost black. Membranes, face and ears usually very dark brown to black. Ears moderately long,

FIGURE 28 Whiskered bat. (Photo: S. C. Bisserôt)

narrow, extending 2 mm beyond muzzle when laid forward. Tragus a little more than half length of conch, anterior border straight and posterior border straight or slightly concave, narrowing to blunt point. Wings narrow and membranes almost translucent.

Chromosomes: $2n=44$, F.N. $=50$ (Bovey 1949), needs confirmation.

MEASUREMENTS Head and body 35–48 mm (M); forearm 30–37 mm (M); wingspan 210–240 mm (M); ear 14–15 mm (M); condylobasal length 12·0–13·5 mm (M); weight in hibernation 4–8 g.

DISTRIBUTION See Fig. 29. Uncertain due to confusion with *M. brandti*, but widespread in Europe and possibly also in Palaearctic Asia.

In Britain, positive records have been made from Devon, Dorset, Wiltshire and Sussex north to Yorkshire including Wales and Suffolk and it is probably found throughout England and Wales.

VARIATION In Czechoslovakia males smaller than females as shown by forearm lengths: for males 33·9 mm ($n=73$) and for females 34·6 mm ($n=86$) (Hanák 1971). In Britain males average 33·4 mm, range 32·0–35·3 mm ($n=36$) and females 33·7 mm, range 32·5–34·9 mm ($n=11$) (author's data).

HABITAT Found in wooded and open country. Roost in trees and buildings in summer and sometimes in caves in winter.

BEHAVIOUR Flight medium speed and fluttering, up to 20 m, often along a 'beat' over a hedgerow. Emerge early, often at sunset and probably remain active intermittently throughout night. Nyholm (1965) in Finland found two distinct periods of activity in summer—after sunset and before sunrise.

Summer. Adult females segregate from adult males to form large nursery colonies, often in buildings (M). Adult males seem to be solitary.

Winter. Found in caves, cellars, but probably also hibernate in trees and houses. They prefer cooler entrance regions of caves (M) (Bezem *et al.* 1964) and are more frequently found in caves during very cold weather (M). Always solitary but sometimes hang freely from roof and sometimes found in tight crevices (M).

Often seen flying during the day in winter and spring. Longest movement recorded is 1936 km (Krzanowski 1964).

FOOD Small insects and spiders which are sometimes picked off foliage.

BREEDING Some females achieve sexual maturity at 3 months, majority at 15 months (Sluiter 1954). Copulation observed in Dutch cave in

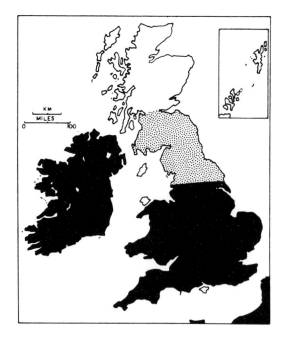

FIGURE 29
Whiskered bat:
distribution.

January (Nieuwenhoven 1956) and an increasing proportion found to be inseminated as hibernation progressed (Strelkov 1962).

POPULATION Sex ratio in hibernation usually shows male bias. In Suffolk 60·3% (*n* = 68) were males (Stebbings 1965) and in the Netherlands 61·7% (*n* = 1377) (Bels 1952). Gaisler (1966b) in Czechoslovakia similarly recorded 59·5% males (*n* = 42) for individually roosting bats but 93·0% (*n* = 213) for winter colonies. Bezem *et al.* (1960) have estimated several population parameters from studies in hibernacula. Adult survival rate was 0·752, giving a life span of 16 years and mean longevity of 4·0 years. In Surrey one was refound 19·5 years after banding (P. Morris unpubl.) and Heerdt & Sluiter (1961) refound a male over 18 years old in the Netherlands.

PREDATORS AND MORTALITY Several eaten during hibernation by mouse or shrew in caves in Suffolk (author's data).

PARASITES AND DISEASE The following ectoparasites have been recorded but prior to the discovery of *M. brandti*. Therefore these will need confirmation: the flea *Ischnopsyllus simplex*; the mites *Spinturnix myoti*, *Steatonyssus periblepharus* and *Neomyobia mystacinalis*.

RELATIONS WITH MAN Has been maintained in captivity for several months on diet of moths and beetles.

Brandt's bat *Myotis brandti*

Vespertilio brandti Eversmann, 1845; Russia.

RECOGNITION See *M. mystacinus*. Adult's upper pelage is a characteristic red-brown. Tragus is almost half the length of conch and has a more or less convex posterior margin.

DESCRIPTION A small bat closely resembling the whiskered. Adults red-brown above and buff beneath. Membranes, face and ears are dark red-brown. Young bats up to 12 months old are dark grey—almost identical to whiskered. Wing narrow and membranes translucent.

Ears shorter and squarer than whiskered, extending to tip of muzzle. Penis distinctly club-shaped.

MEASUREMENTS Head and body 37–48 mm; forearm 31–38 mm; wingspan 210–255 mm; ear 11–13 mm; condylobasal length 13·0–14·5 mm. In Devon 21 adult females measured: forearm mean 34·8 mm; wingspan mean 241·1 mm.

DISTRIBUTION See Fig. 30. Since its recognition it has been recorded from most European countries. In Britain positive records have been made in North Devon, Somerset, Wiltshire, Gloucestershire, Suffolk, Norfolk, Surrey, Kent, Staffordshire and Yorkshire.

HABITAT Found in wooded country in caves (winter) and buildings (summer).

BEHAVIOUR Flight similar to whiskered.

Summer. One nursery colony found in North Devon hanging from the roof apex of a hay loft in full daylight on 16th July consisted of 49 bats. Thirteen fully grown bats escaped and of the remainder 15 were recently born babies, 16 were lactating adult females and 5 were nulliparous females at least one year old.

Winter. Found in crevices further from entrance than whiskered, so may prefer warmer hibernation temperatures. Two winter movements recorded of 2·5 km in Suffolk.

POPULATION STRUCTURE Little known. Greatest longevity 13 years (author's data).

FIGURE 30 Brandt's bat: distribution.

FIGURE 31 Natterer's bat. (Photo: S. C. Bisserôt)

Natterer's bat *Myotis nattereri*

Vespertilio nattereri Kuhl, 1818; Germany.

RECOGNITION Distinguished from all other species by the presence of a conspicuous fringe of stiff hairs (1 mm in length) along the edge of the interfemoral membrane.

DESCRIPTION A medium-sized bat with upper parts light brown and under side very light buff or white. A clear line of demarcation exists from shoulder to ear. Juveniles light greyish brown for first year. Wing membranes mid-brown, face pink to light brown, ear shading from pink below to light brown distally.

Ear fairly narrow and long, extending 5 mm beyond tip of muzzle when laid forward. Tragus two-thirds length of ear, straight-sided, long and pointed. Wings broad but pointed.

MEASUREMENTS Head and body 40–50 mm; forearm 36–43 mm; wingspan 250–300 mm; ear 14–18 mm; condylobasal length 14–15 mm; weights in hibernation range from 7–12 g.

DISTRIBUTION See Fig. 32. Occurs throughout central and southern Palaearctic from Ireland to Japan and northwards to Finland.

In Britain widespread northwards to central Scotland and probably all of Ireland.

VARIATION Sexual dimorphism exists, females being larger. Mean forearm length 39·0 mm ($n=39$) males and 39·7 mm ($n=32$) females in Suffolk (author's data). Balcells (1956) in Spain recorded males 38·4 mm ($n=12$) and females 39·6 mm ($n=71$).

HABITAT Frequently found in open woodland and park areas; roosts in hollow trees, buildings and caves.

BEHAVIOUR Flight slow to medium up to 16 m, sometimes over water but more usually around trees. Bats flying at a slow speed under controlled conditions have their tails directed downwards and not held in line behind the body. This has been shown by high speed photographs by E. Hosking and S. C. Bisserôt.

Summer. Emerge soon after sunset and have several activity periods throughout the night. Emergence time seems to be related partially to light intensity but is also influenced by the maximum day temperature. Englander & Laufens (1968) have found that high day temperatures delay emergence, especially in the autumn. Laufens (1969) also found that in-

FIGURE 32 Natterer's bat: distribution.

dividual bats in a colony maintained their respective activity periods each day. Adult females form large nursery colonies in buildings.

Winter. Arrive into hibernation caves mostly during December and leave early March in Wiltshire and Suffolk (author's data). Egsbaek & Jensen (1963) also found Natterer's left Danish caves before Daubenton's. Harmata (1969b) has found Natterer's hibernating at temperatures of 8–14°C in autumn, falling to 6–10°C in winter. Bezem *et al.* (1964) record a preference for cool entrance areas and this applies in Wiltshire and Suffolk. Usually solitary but small groups not uncommon. Longest movement in Britain 4 km but in the Netherlands 62 km (Bels 1952).

FOOD Small insects, including moths, caught and eaten mostly in flight but some taken off foliage.

BREEDING Copulation observed during December in cave (Gilbert 1948, Gilbert & Stebbings 1958). Single young born in British Isles at end of June or early July.

POPULATION STRUCTURE Little known. Sex ratio in hibernation (Suffolk) 59·0% males ($n = 261$) (Stebbings 1965). In Denmark, Egsbaek & Jensen (1963) found 55·6% males ($n = 153$) and Bels (1952) recorded 59·5% ($n = 1556$). Greatest longevity in Britain over 12 years (Stebbings 1965) but Heerdt & Sluiter (1961) refound one banded 17 years previously.

PARASITES AND DISEASE Three ectoparasites are found commonly: the flea *Ischnopsyllus simplex*, and the mites *Spinturnix myoti* and *Macronyssus ellipticus*.

RELATIONS WITH MAN Has survived in captivity several months (Racey 1972).

Bechstein's bat *Myotis bechsteini*

Vespertilio bechsteinii Kuhl, 1818; Germany.

RECOGNITION Similar in general characters and size to *M. nattereri* but with relatively long ears, extending half their length beyond the tip of the muzzle when laid forward. Lacks fringe of hairs on interfemoral membrane.

DESCRIPTION A medium-sized bat with upper parts light brown and lower parts greyish buff to white. Wing membranes and ears opaque, mid to dark brown.

Ears separate and relatively the largest of all European bats except *Plecotus* spp., extending about 8 mm beyond the tip of the muzzle when laid forward. Tragus barely half the height of conch, narrow with posterior and anterior edges more or less straight. Wings broad and slightly pointed.

MEASUREMENTS Head and body 43–50 mm; forearm 38–45 mm (mean 40·9 mm) for males ($n=12$) in Dorset (author's data); wingspan 250–300 mm; ear 20–26 mm; condylobasal length 16–17 mm; weight 7–13 g.

DISTRIBUTION See Fig. 33. Occurs throughout Europe as far as the Caucasus but is very rare. Most records come from Germany.

In Britain very few authenticated records but has been recorded from Shropshire (1), Gloucestershire (1), Wiltshire (2), Somerset (1), Dorset (16), Devon (1), Hampshire and Isle of Wight (several old records), Sussex (1) and Berkshire (1).

HABITAT This species can be regarded as a forest bat that normally roosts in trees, both summer and winter. Of particular interest was the discovery of many Bechstein's bones in the excavations at Grimes Graves, Norfolk (Clarke 1963). These were about 3000–4000 years old, and at that time forests were extensive in eastern Britain.

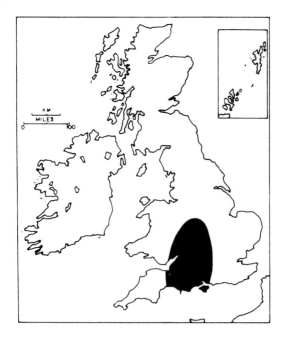

FIGURE 33
Bechstein's bat:
distribution.

BEHAVIOUR Flight slow, with wings held rather stiffly, up to 15 m but generally low. Emerges about 20 minutes after sunset.

Summer. Most often found in tree holes where either solitary males or small nursing colonies of adult females are found. Issel (1958) in Germany reported four nursing colonies using artificial roost boxes placed in conifer forest with 5, 16, 21 and 47 individuals. Harmata (1969a) in Poland found a small nursing colony of eight adults and two young in an ash tree on 25th July. In Dorset during August and September for several years a male roosted in a hole in a house roof. Three months after finding the dead remains of the first, another male was found occupying the same hole (Stebbings 1966a, 1968a).

Winter. Probably hibernates in trees but occasional records of solitary hibernators in caves where it usually hangs free from roof. Sometimes found in crevices but always hanging. Prefers cooler entrance areas.

FIGURE 34 Bechstein's bat in hibernation. (Photo: S. C. Bisseròt)

FOOD Probably mostly moths eaten in flight. In Dorset on 30 May a male caught a damsel fly (*Enallagma cyathigerum*) at midday (Stebbings 1968a). A bat, almost certainly of this species, watched at close quarters, flew round an oak tree for 20 minutes catching moths both on the wing and resting on leaves. One in captivity also picked moths off the walls of a room (Blackmore 1964).

POPULATION STRUCTURE Little known. Sex ratio in hibernation strongly biased to the males, 26 ♂ : 5 ♀ in Netherlands (Bels 1952) and 12 : 4 in Dorset (author's data). Greatest longevity 7 years (Stebbings 1968a).

PREDATORS AND MORTALITY One evidently eaten by a raptor (Stebbings 1968a).

PARASITES AND DISEASE The fly *Basilia nana* has been recorded.

RELATIONS WITH MAN One survived in captivity for 172 days and drank on the wing from a bath (Blackmore 1964).

Pond bat *Myotis dasycneme*

Vespertilio dasycneme Boie, 1825; Denmark.
No authenticated records from British Isles.

RECOGNITION In general form similar to *M. daubentoni* but much larger and relatively longer ears. Could be confused with *Eptesicus serotinus* but latter has post-calcarial lobe.

DESCRIPTION A medium-large bat with upper parts generally dark grey with pale yellow-brown tips. Under parts greyish white. Line of demarcation along side of neck well defined. Ears conspicuously long, extending 3–4 mm beyond tip of muzzle when laid forward and very dark brown. Tragus less than half height of conch, anterior border slightly concave and posterior border strongly convex. Tip blunt.

MEASUREMENTS Head and body 55–64 mm; forearm 43–49 mm; wingspan 300–330 mm; ear 16–18 mm; condylobasal length 16–17 mm; weights 10–20 g.

Mouse-eared bat *Myotis myotis*

Vespertilio myotis Borkhausen, 1797; Germany. *Vespertilio murinus* Schreber, 1774 (not of Linnaeus 1758). This name was almost universally used for this species throughout the nineteenth century.

RECOGNITION A very large bat (forearm over 57 mm) distinguished from noctule by its pointed tragus and lack of post-calcarial lobe.

DESCRIPTION Very large. Upper parts medium to light brown and under side greyish white with distinct line of demarcation along side of neck. Juveniles (sub-adults) up to 12 months are much greyer (Mazák 1965). Face almost bare, pinkish or brown. Ears and membranes brown, the latter thick, leathery and broad.

Ears large, extending about 5 mm beyond tip of muzzle when laid forward. Similar in actual size and form to those of *M. bechsteini*. Tragus about half the height of conch with both anterior and posterior sides more or less straight.

MEASUREMENTS Head and body 65–80 mm; forearm 57–68 mm; wingspan 365–450 mm; ear 20–28 mm; weight 20–45 g.

Chromosomes: $2n=44$, F.N.$=50$ (Bovey 1949), needs confirmation.

DISTRIBUTION Widespread throughout central and southern Palaearctic north to Baltic.

In Britain there were two old records, from London (pre-1850) and Cambridge (1888), but two recent colonisations have apparently taken place in Dorset and Sussex (Blackmore 1956, Phillips & Blackmore 1970).

The bat found in Cambridge, (University Museum of Zoology no. E.5762A.) has been attributed to the southern European *M. blythi* by Dr V. Aellen (pers. comm.). Another bat found as a complete skeleton at Furzebrook, Dorset in 1962 can also be assigned to this species on the basis of its very small size (forearm *c.* 54 mm). However, skull shape was not typical for *M. blythi* so there is still some doubt (author's data).

VARIATION Females are larger than males. Forearm lengths of sample from Sussex 59·9 mm ($n=10$) for males and 62·4 mm ($n=21$) for females (author's data).

HABITAT Said to frequent open, lightly wooded country. Roosts in buildings and caves in summer and winter.

BEHAVIOUR Emerges very late. Flight is slow, heavy and generally straight, medium height up to 20 m.

Summer. Males solitary or in small groups, usually roost in buildings with large roofs, and females form large nursery colonies in buildings or caves. Interchange between adjacent nursery colonies seems to occur frequently (Roer 1968). In the Netherlands, Bels (1952) caught 312 bats in a nursery cave roost consisting of 156 adult females, 121 juveniles and

35 adult males. The last may have been one year old and just reaching sexual maturity (Sluiter 1961). Nursing colonies in Czechoslovakia (Gaisler 1966b) comprised 86% adult females, 2% adult males and 12% immature ($n = 933$). Females visit solitary males for mating in the autumn (Gaisler & Hanák 1969). Topal (1966), watching summer egress and ingress times from a cave in Hungary, noted very late emergence when it was quite dark, and return an hour before sunrise, again when still dark. Weather conditions did not seem to influence emergence time.

Winter. Generally solitary but also found in small groups. Harmata (1969b) recorded hibernation thermopreferendum of 7–8°C. Bels (1952) stated that they prefer to hang free in high regions away from entrances but Bezem *et al.* (1964) found no preferences. Later Daan & Wichers (1968) and Dorgelo & Punt (1969) demonstrated distinct preferences for internal areas at beginning of winter, moving towards the entrance by spring. The few observations in Britain conform to this latter pattern and most have been found hanging in high exposed parts of tunnels. Movements of 3·5 km have been noted in Dorset but Gaisler & Hanák (1969) recorded regular movements of up to 200 km between summer and winter roosts. Greatest movement 260 km (Eisentraut 1937).

FOOD Mostly larger moths and beetles eaten in flight.

BREEDING Females achieve sexual maturity at 3 months of age (Sluiter & Bouman, 1951) and males at 15 months (Sluiter 1961). Gestation period 46–59 days (Sklenar 1963).

POPULATION STRUCTURE During hibernation in the Netherlands a sex ratio biased to the males—58% ($n = 2914$)—was found by Bels (1952), but Gaisler (1966b) in Czechoslovakia reported a predominance of females 55% ($n = 1251$). In Sussex 32% ($n = 31$) were females (author's data). Some statistics calculated for hibernating populations in the Netherlands by Bezem *et al.* (1960) gave a survival rate for adults of only 0·637. It was thought that mortality had been increased due to banding and disturbance as the population had declined considerably during the study. Greatest longevity recorded in Britain 14 years (Blackmore & Stebbings, unpubl.) but Pieper (1968) records a male caught over 18 years after banding.

PREDATORS AND MORTALITY In Poland apparently frequently taken by owls, notably barn owls (*Tyto alba*) (Harmata 1962, Ruprecht 1971).

PARASITES AND DISEASE The mites *Spinturnix myoti* and *Macronyssus ellipticus* occur on this host.

RELATIONS WITH MAN Has been maintained in captivity for up to two years. Protected by Conservation of Wild Creatures and Wild Plants Act, 1975.

Daubenton's bat *Myotis daubentoni*

Vespertilio daubentonii Kuhl, 1819; Germany. *Vespertilio aedilis* Jenyns, 1839; Durham, England. *Vespertilio daubentonii albus* Fitzinger, 1871; renaming of *aedilis* Jenyns.

RECOGNITION Distinguished from other species of *Myotis* by its small-medium size, posterior margin of tragus strongly convex (Fig. 35) and large feet. It has relatively the shortest ears of the genus.

DESCRIPTION Upper parts medium to dark brown and under side pale buffy-grey. Young bats tend to be paler for the first 12 months. Wing broader than that of whiskered bat and dark brown. Ears and face mid-brown.

Ear short, almost reaching tip of muzzle when laid forward. Tragus half the height of conch, straight anteriorly and convex posteriorly. Foot over half the length of tibia, conspicuously large. Chromosomes: $2n = 44$, F.N. $= 54$ in Poland (Fedyk & Fedyk 1970). $2n = 44$, F.N. $= 56$ in Russia (Strelkov & Volobuev 1969).

FIGURE 35 Daubenton's bat. (Photo: S. C. Bisserôt)

MEASUREMENTS Head and body 40–50 mm; forearm 33–39 mm; wingspan 230–270 mm; ear 8–12 mm; condylobasal length 13·0–14·0 mm; weight 6–12 g.

DISTRIBUTION See Fig. 36. Widespread through Palaearctic from Ireland to Japan, northwards to central Norway.
   In Britain widespread throughout England and Wales and north to Inverness, and probably throughout Ireland.

VARIATION Sexual dimorphism is evident in British populations. Mean forearm lengths for males 36·6 mm ($n=87$) and females 37·3 mm ($n=76$) measured in Suffolk, while in Inverness 37·3 mm ($n=37$) and 37·6 mm ($n=18$) were recorded (author's data).

HABITAT Preference for open wooded country where it roosts mostly in hollow trees and buildings in summer and, additionally, caves in winter.

BEHAVIOUR Flight steady but fairly fast and often along well-defined beats (Nyholm 1965), up to 16 m but more usually fairly low. Emerges about 30 minutes after sunset and is more or less active throughout night. Has been caught over water, but frequently occurs elsewhere. Other

FIGURE 36
Daubenton's bat:
distribution.

species when flying low over water adopt a similar vibrating flight characteristic. In the Thames valley pipistrelles have more often been recorded
over water with a bat detector than Daubenton's (Hooper, unpubl.).

Summer. Adult females form very large nursery colonies up to several
hundred in buildings.

Winter. Often found in caves where they are usually solitary but several
may be found together. Usually found in tight crevices, often horizontally
and sometimes with head uppermost. Also found to burrow into soft scree
in caves and mines (Egsbaek & Jensen 1963, Stebbings 1965, Roer &
Egsbaek 1966). It has been found in Suffolk that males arrive in hibernation caves before females in the autumn and leave before the females in
the spring (author's data). A similar situation has been found in Denmark
(Eliassen & Egsbaek 1963, Egsbaek & Jensen 1963). Bezem *et al.* (1964)
have found that Daubenton's prefer the warmer inner regions of caves
in the Netherlands; Daan & Wichers (1968) found equal preference is
shown in the autumn but by January most are found near the cool entrances. This has also been found in Dorset and Suffolk caves. Longest
movement recorded in Britain 3·5 km, but 215 km in Czechoslovakia
(Gaisler & Hanák 1969).

FOOD Mostly consists of small insects eaten during flight.

BREEDING Copulation observed in German cave in October; male hung
close behind female and apparently tried to stimulate her by biting neck
and back of head (Eisentraut 1949). Another pair, in Dutch cave, copu-
lated in February and attracted notice by loud squeaking (Nieuwenhoven
1956). Increasing proportion of females in Russia found to be inseminated as hibernation progressed (Strelkov 1962). In England often found
mating throughout the winter, the latest recorded date being 12th March
1974 (author's data).

POPULATION STRUCTURE Bezem *et al.* (1960) recorded an adult survival rate in a hibernating population of 0·800, giving an estimated life
span of 20 years and mean longevity of 5·0 years. The same authors confirmed the earlier findings of Bels (1952) that the sex ratio of bats hibernating in Dutch caves was 43·9% males ($n=920$). This contrasts with
60·7% ($n=2820$) males in Danish caves (Egsbaek & Jensen 1963) and
56·3% ($n=370$) in Suffolk (Stebbings 1965). Greatest longevity recorded
for this species was for a male recaught 18 years after banding in Suffolk
(Stebbings 1968c).

PREDATORS AND MORTALITY Several eaten during hibernation by
mouse or shrew in a cave in Suffolk (author's data). Similarly eaten *M.*

lucifugus in Canada were attributed to the deermouse *Peromyscus* (Fenton 1970).

PARASITES AND DISEASE Three ectoparasites occur frequently: the fly *Nycteribia kolenatii* and the mites *Spinturnix myoti* and *Macronyssus ellipticus*.

RELATIONS WITH MAN Survived several months in captivity fed on mealworms (Racey 1972).

Notched-eared bat *Myotis emarginatus*

Vespertilio emarginatus Geoffroy, 1806; France.

No authenticated record from British Isles, but one said to have been taken near Dover—see Barrett-Hamilton (1910–11).

RECOGNITION Similar in form to *M. mystacinus* but rather larger—similar to *M. nattereri*. Forearm 38–42 mm. Posterior margin of ear with distinct angular emargination slightly above middle (other *Myotis* have less distinct angular emargination). Ears and membranes relatively thick and opaque. Tragus pointed with straight anterior and posterior edges. Interfemoral membrane usually has a fringe of hairs but less conspicuous than in *M. nattereri*. Colour a distinctive yellowish-red dorsally.

GENUS *Vespertilio*

A small genus with only three representatives, in the northern and central Palaearctic, one throughout and the others in eastern Asia. The first is a vagrant to Britain.

Generally similar to *Eptesicus* but ears short and square, more like *Nyctalus*. The dental formula is

$$\frac{2.1.1.3}{3.1.2.3}.$$

Generally found in hollow trees and buildings but have occurred in caves. Rare animals through their range, consequently little is known about them.

Parti-coloured bat *Vespertilio murinus*

Vespertilio murinus L. 1758; Sweden (note that in the nineteenth century this name was erroneously but widely used for *Myotis myotis*). *Vespertilio discolor* Natterer, 1819.

RECOGNITION A medium-large sized bat with squarish ears, small bean-shaped tragus and distinctive bicoloured fur dorsally.

DESCRIPTION Hairs of upper parts with dark brown bases and white or cream-buff tips, giving a 'frosted' appearance. Under parts cream-buff; a clear demarcation along the side of the neck. Face, ears and membranes are very dark brown.

Ears short, slightly wider than high, and extending nearly to tip of muzzle when laid forward. Tragus short, bean-shaped, being concave along anterior margin and strongly convex posteriorly. Post-calcarial lobe present but indistinct. Wings are narrow and pointed. Membranes are thin.

MEASUREMENTS Head and body 55–64 mm; forearm 40–49 mm (mean 44·5 mm for males ($n = 17$)—Aellen 1962); wingspan 260–330 mm; ear height 15 mm; ear width 16 mm; condylobasal length 14·2–15·5 mm; weight 11–24 g.

DISTRIBUTION Little known but ranges from Scandinavia through central and eastern Europe to eastern Siberia. Only four authenticated records in Britain and these can be considered as vagrant: Plymouth and Yarmouth (early nineteenth century); Whalsey, Shetland, March 1927 (Ritchie 1927); North Sea 170 miles east of Berwick, June 1965 (Stansfield 1966). Strelkov (1969) recorded three long flights of 360, 800 and 850 km and regarded this species as being migratory.

GENUS *Eptesicus*

Like *Myotis* this is a very large genus distributed worldwide but with about a third fewer species. Two species are found in Europe and one in Britain.

Similar to *Vespertilio* but ears generally longer and widely spaced. Tragus short and blunt; post-calcarial lobe present. Wings are mostly broad. Dental formula is

$$\frac{2.1.1.3}{2.1.2.3}.$$

Occur in range of habitats but usually regarded as tree-hole species. Also found in buildings and rarely in caves.

One species in Britain, but *E. nilssoni* could possibly turn up. It is a small-medium bat about the size of *Plecotus auritus*.

FIGURE 37 Serotine. (Photo: S. C. Bissèròt)

Serotine *Eptesicus serotinus*

Vespertilio serotinus Schreber, 1774; France.

RECOGNITION A large dark brown bat, with post-calcarial lobe. Separated from *Nyctalus* by medium length, bluntly pointed tragus, longer ear, conspicuously large teeth, and free end to tail.

DESCRIPTION Upper parts very dark brown with sometimes lighter yellowish tips, under-parts generally paler but no distinct line along side of neck. Juveniles up to 12 months are very dark, almost black. Face, ear and membranes very dark brown-black.

Ears moderately long and extending two-thirds the distance from eye to tip of muzzle when laid forward. Tragus blunt-tipped, less than half the height of conch, with anterior border slightly concave and posterior edge slightly convex, thus being almost parallel-sided for two-thirds its length (Fig. 37). Muzzle has distinct glandular swellings. Wing broad with fairly thick opaque membranes. A small, ill-defined post-calcarial lobe is present and about 6 mm of free tail.

MEASUREMENTS Head and body 58–75 mm; forearm 48–55 mm;

wingspan 340–380 mm; ear 15–20 mm; condylobasal length 19–22 mm; weight 15–35 g.

DISTRIBUTION See Fig. 38. Widespread throughout central and south-ern Palaearctic, north to Denmark.

In Britain confined to south and east England within a line roughly from the Wash to the Severn estuary but appears to be absent from Devon and Cornwall. Absent from Ireland.

HABITAT Seems to prefer lightly wooded country and is basically a tree hole species, but is often found in buildings and rarely in caves.

BEHAVIOUR Bats roosting in colonies emerge 15–20 minutes after sunset but individually roosting bats seem to be very variable, from sunset to complete darkness. Observations on a marked male showed intermittent activity throughout the night. Flight is variable—straight and level upon emergence but with deep dives when feeding.

Summer. Females form large nursery colonies in trees and buildings. Adult males are usually solitary. In Czechoslovakia, Gaisler (1966b) recorded 33 adult females with 2 adult males and 2 sub-adults in colonies, and of individually roosting bats 16 adult males to 3 adult females.

Winter. Hibernates in buildings and trees in Britain. In western Europe

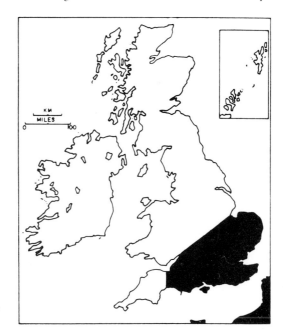

FIGURE 38 Serotine: distribution.

occasionally found in caves (Bels 1952, Harmata 1962) but in eastern Russia mostly found in caves, while further south in the Ukraine it seems to prefer buildings to caves (Strelkov 1969). Strelkov also notes that it is resistant to and prefers cold entrance parts of caves, and Harmata (1969b) in Poland records bats hibernating at temperatures of 0–6°C. Although regarded by Strelkov (1969) as a non-migratory bat, Topal (1956) in Hungary recorded a movement of 144 km.

FOOD Larger moths and beetles taken by preference, mostly caught and eaten in flight but sometimes bats land on foliage with wings outstretched to catch prey. Cranbrook (1964b) found them feeding with noctules on chafers (*Amphimallus solstitialis*). Chafers released into a room $4 \times 5 \times 3$ m high were immediately caught and eaten in flight. Ingestion took up to 100 seconds with only the elytra and some legs falling to the ground. Echolocation did not seem to be impaired while eating, although this was carried out in darkness (author's data).

BREEDING Maternal care, growth and development of young born in captivity from wild matings described by Kleiman (1969). Captive pairs remained in copulation for several hours, but this did not result in the birth of young (Racey & Kleiman 1970).

POPULATION STRUCTURE Little known. Greatest longevity of over 6 years recorded by Heerdt & Sluiter (1961) and Gaisler & Hanák (1969).

PARASITES AND DISEASE High densities of ectoparasites are found on this host in nursery roosts mainly of the following species: the flea *Ischnopsyllus intermedius*; and the mites *Spinturnix kolenatii*, *Ornithonyssus pipistrelli* and *Steatonyssus occidentalis*.

RELATIONS WITH MAN Has been kept in captivity for up to 3 years on basic diet of mealworms (*Tenebrio molitor* larvae) with calcium and vitamin added (Racey 1970).

GENUS *Nyctalus*

A small genus with about five species, found throughout the Palaearctic. Three species occur in Europe.

All members are characterised by the narrow, pointed wing (indicative of fast migratory flight), short, squarish ears and very short tragus, wider above than below.

Dental formula as for *Pipistrellus*,

$$\frac{2.1.2.3}{3.1.2.3}.$$

Skull broad.

Noctule bats are mostly confined to tree holes (often very high from the ground) throughout the year, but are occasionally found in buildings (not in caves but some in rock crevices). All species probably migratory—hence the only bat found in the Azores (*c.* 1600 km west of Portugal) is of this genus.

Two species found in Britain more or less distinguishable on size alone but coloration also different. *N. lasiopterus*, which has been found in Central Europe and France east to Russia, is similar to *N. noctula* but very much larger—forearm 64–69 mm, condylobasal length 22–23 mm.

Leisler's bat *Nyctalus leisleri*

Vespertilio leisleri Kuhl, 1818; Germany.

RECOGNITION Similar to the noctule but distinguished by its smaller size (forearm less than 48 mm) and distinctly bicoloured dorsal fur, basal zone of fur being very much darker than the tips. Skull can be recognised by its small size (condylobasal length 15–16 mm) and relatively small lower incisors.

DESCRIPTION A medium-large bat with upper parts dark golden or rufous brown with very dark brown bases to the hairs. Under parts lighter and slightly grey brown. Juveniles up to 12 months are a distinctive dark greyish-brown. Facial skin, ears and membranes very dark brown, sometimes blackish. Wings narrow and pointed with thick and opaque membranes. Ears short, reaching more than half-way to tip of muzzle when laid forward and relatively narrower than those of noctule, giving the appearance of being more pointed. Tragus very short as in the noctule. Prominent post-calcarial lobe is present. Chromosomes: $2n = 46$, F.N. = 54 (Fedyk & Fedyk 1970).

MEASUREMENTS Head and body 54–64 mm; forearm 39–47; wingspan 280–340 mm; ear 12–13 mm long and 8–10 mm wide; weight 11–20 g.

DISTRIBUTION See Fig. 40. Widespread in western Palaearctic north to Poland but rather uncommon in France and Iberia; present on Madeira and the Azores.

In Britain as elsewhere the very few records probably indicate the

FIGURE 39 Leisler's bat. (Photo: S. C. Bisserôt)

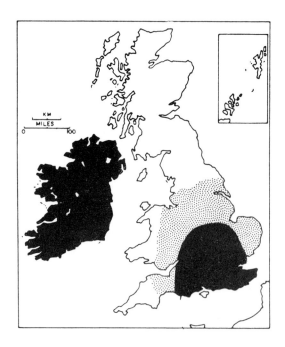

FIGURE 40 Leisler's
bat: distribution.

mode of life rather than rarity. All records bounded by Cheshire, York-shire south to Worcestershire and Kent. One, apparently vagrant, found in Shetland in July 1968 (Corbet 1970). In Ireland it appears to be fairly abundant.

VARIATION Forearms measured from a small number in Switzerland show females slightly larger than males. Mean 43·8 mm ($n = 11$) for males and 44·3 mm ($n = 14$) for females (Aellen 1962). In Ireland mean 43·8 mm ($n = 128$) for adult females and in Worcestershire 43·7 mm ($n = 8$) (author's data).

HABITAT Essentially a forest bat roosting in tree holes, but in Britain and Ireland has been found in buildings. Several recent records have been from central London.

BEHAVIOUR Flight straight and fairly fast with shallow dives, mostly at tree top level or higher.

Summer. Emerges early, at or soon after sunset. Moffat (1900) watching a small group roosting in a tree noted two nightly activity periods of about one hour each. The first began about 15 minutes after sunset and the second ended some 26 minutes before sunrise. Adult females segregate from males and form large nursery groups. One large colony of *c.* 400 in Co. Cork was studied and of 127 caught during three annual samples 104 were adult females and 23 were immature females. There were no immature males (author's data).

Winter. Nothing known but probably similar to noctule. It is probably a migratory species. Krzanowski (1960) recorded a flight of 418 km and the 25 specimens caught by Aellen (1962) in Switzerland were probably migrating. One was found dead on a glacier at 2600 m.

FOOD Medium to large insects eaten during flight. On the Azores Moore (1975) found them feeding during the day, probably due to lack of competition from birds.

BREEDING Probably similar to noctule.

POPULATION STRUCTURE Nothing known, but sex ratio of unweaned bats apparently unity ($n = 107$) (author's data).

PARASITES AND DISEASE The flea *Ischnopsyllus intermedius* has been recorded.

RELATIONS WITH MAN One survived in captivity 372 days (Blackmore 1964).

FIGURE 41 Noctule. (Photo: S. C. Bisserôt)

Noctule *Nyctalus noctula*

Vespertilio noctula Schreber, 1774; France. *Vespertilio magnus* Berkenhaut, 1789; Cambridge, England. *Vespertilio altivolans* White, 1789; Selborne, Hants, England.

RECOGNITION A large bat distinguished from all others except Leisler's by dark yellowish-brown fur with short ears and tragus wider above than below. Differs from Leisler's in having forearm generally over 48 mm and base of hairs not darker than tips.

DESCRIPTION Upper parts dark yellowish-brown; under parts similar but often slightly paler. Juveniles are slightly darker and usually dull. Face, ears and wing membranes dark brown.

Ears short, broad and reaching half-way between eye and tip of muzzle when laid forward. Tragus height more or less equal to width and broader at tip than at base. Muzzle broad with distinct glandular swellings and mouth with conspicuous buccal glands. Conspicuous post-calcarial lobe is present. Tip of tail barely emerges from interfemoral membrane. Wings narrow, pointed and membranes thick and opaque. Chromosomes: $2n = 42$, F.N. = 54 (Dulić *et al.* 1967).

MEASUREMENTS Head and body 70–82 mm; forearm 47–55 mm; wingspan 320–390 mm; ear 15–18 mm long and 14–17 mm wide; condylobasal length 17·6–19·0 mm; weight 15–40 g. Cranbrook & Barrett (1956) recorded the weight of eight individual males caught while feeding in June/July and later in October. They were $31·5 \pm 2·0$ g (28–34) and $35·0 \pm 1·9$ g (33–38) respectively.

VARIATION In Roumania females larger than males, as shown by their forearm lengths, 54·3 mm ($n = 145$) for females and 53·9 mm ($n = 83$) for males (Barbu & Sin 1968).

DISTRIBUTION See Fig. 42. Found throughout Palaearctic north to 60° latitude in Scandinavia.

In Britain found through England and probably all of Wales. There have been no recent records from Scotland and none from Ireland.

HABITAT Predominantly a tree and forest bat, it is found in all types of country and even roosts in isolated trees in suburban areas.

BEHAVIOUR Often emerges very early before sunset, but usually about 20 minutes after. It flies high (up to 160 m) directly to preferred feeding area, thence intermittent activity throughout the night. Flight straight and high with repeated deep dives—presumably chasing insects.

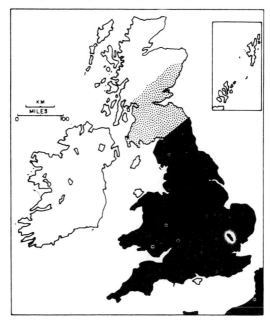

FIGURE 42 Noctule: distribution.

Summer. A number of tree holes in an area are successively used by a local population so that the number occupying one hole is constantly changing. This includes lactating females who must carry their young (Bels 1952, Heerdt & Sluiter 1965, Sluiter & Heerdt 1966). These authors found that segregation of the sexes apparently takes place at the end of hibernation, females forming nursery roosts which may contain over 100 bats, males being solitary or in small groups.

On hot afternoons roosting bats can be located by their loud squeaking noises, and on most evenings unless it is cold much noise precedes emergence. A dark brown streak down a tree of bat urine, tree sap, faeces, etc., always indicates a much-used hole. In the autumn individual males apparently occupy territorial 'mating roosts' between which females move. An individual male has been found with from 0–18 females over a period of several days (Sluiter & Heerdt 1966).

Winter. They form large colonies of up to 1000 (Strelkov 1969) in buildings and trees. Sexes are mixed but no consistent tendency for one to predominate. In a Dutch tree 56% were males ($n=152$) (Heerdt & Sluiter 1965) while in rock clefts in Roumania 36% were males ($n=228$) (Barbu & Sin 1968). Preferred temperatures for hibernation are unknown, but Mislin & Vischer (1942) found that noctules could remain alive at temperatutes of -4°C and that the metabolic rate is increased (producing heat) if the external temperature should fall further. In Roumania, Barbu & Sin (1968) found that with an ambient air temperature at -7°C the outer members of a cluster of 150 were at $+1^\circ$C and the centre was at $+2^\circ$C. Cranbrook (1964a) maintained a female in a room with temperatures fluctuating between 5–15°C throughout a winter and found that it would hibernate for periods of up to 16 days. It would seem that noctules are tolerant of widely varying temperatures in hibernation.

Many long distance migratory movements of between 500–1600 km have been recorded in eastern Europe especially (see Strelkov 1969), and they appear to move at the rate of 20–40 km per day. However, Sluiter & Heerdt (1966) in the Netherlands, although recording migrations of up to 900 km, found many hibernated close to their summer roosts. Therefore it seems likely that only some migrate in warm oceanic climates, while most spending their summer in Russia must migrate south in the winter.

Cranbrook & Barrett (1965) suggested that the foraging home range is about 1·5–2·5 km radius but recorded a maximum movement between two feeding sites of 5 km.

FOOD Mostly larger insects caught and eaten in flight. Cranbrook & Barrett (1965) caught two populations feeding on house crickets (*Acheta domestica*). The first bats arrived at about sunset but mostly left when dark, although increased activity was recorded again before sunrise. Although some noctules were caught while flying in light rain or thick mist, none was seen during heavy rain.

BREEDING Male sexual cycle described in detail by Racey (1974c). Only species of several kept in captivity by Racey & Kleiman (1970) to breed regularly in captivity. In captivity most copulations occur in September and October, but continue throughout winter. Individual males will mate several times with the same female. Sperm retains its fertilising capacity after storage by both male and female bats for up to 7 months (Racey 1973a). Gestation period 70–73 days (Eisentraut 1936). Single young born June and July; twins not uncommon. Ryberg (1947) records exceptional instance of triplets in Sweden and Bels (1952) reports another set in Holland. Some segregation of sexes apparent when females give birth to young, but mixed colonies are not uncommon towards end of July. Maternal care, growth and development of young in captivity described by Kleiman (1969).

POPULATION STRUCTURE Sex ratio at birth is equal (50·0% males, $n=$ 214, Bels, 1952). Cranbrook & Barrett (1965) caught slightly fewer males than females in feeding populations (47·6% males, $n=319$). Survival rates unknown but probably similar to *Myotis* spp. Greatest longevity eight years (Bels 1952).

PREDATORS AND MORTALITY Strelkov (1969) and Barbu & Sin (1968) record deaths due to prolonged frost and small numbers are killed during tree felling operations. Starlings drive out (and possibly kill) noctules from roost holes (Mason *et al.* 1972).

PARASITES AND DISEASE This host is often heavily infected with ecto-parasites especially the young in nursery roosts. The following species have been recorded: the bug *Cimex pipistrelli;* the fleas *Ischnopsyllus elongatus*, *I. intermedius* and *Nycteridopsylla eusarca ;* the mites *Spinturnix acuminatus*, *Macronyssus flavus* and '*Radfordia*' *noctulia*. One protozoan *Trypanosoma vespertilionis* has been found (Baker 1974).

RELATIONS WITH MAN A laboratory breeding stock has been main-tained for 4 years (Kleiman & Racey 1969, Racey 1970).

GENUS *Pipistrellus*

A large genus, second only to *Myotis*, with representatives worldwide with the apparent notable exception of South America. Four species occur in Europe; one is common in Britain but another has occurred once.

General characters similar to *Eptesicus* but with relatively shorter ears, shorter blunt tragus and post-calcarial lobe. Form robust as opposed to the slender, small *Myotis* with which some confusion may be experienced.

Dental formula is similar to *Nyctalus*,

$$\frac{2.1.2.3}{3.1.2.3}.$$

Pipistrelles are mostly found in trees and buildings throughout the year but occasionally also in rock crevices and caves, especially in eastern Europe. Usually roosts in very confined spaces in which very large numbers occur.

Due to individual variation, identification of the four European species by external characters is difficult, but is possible by means of comparison of teeth.

P. kuhli and *P. savii*, both found in southern Europe near the Mediterranean, can be separated from *P. pipistrellus* and *P. nathusii* by the anterior upper premolar not being visible from the outside.

Pipistrelle *Pipistrellus pipistrellus*

Vespertilio pipistrellus Schreber, 1774; France. *Vespertilio pygmaeus* Leach, 1825; Dartmoor, Devon, England.

RECOGNITION Small size (forearm less than 35 mm), short ears, short curved blunt tragus and a post-calcarial lobe separate this from all but other *Pipistrellus*. Separated from *P. nathusii* by its smaller size, short teeth and small anterior upper premolar, half hidden by the canine when viewed from the outside. Also lacks pale or white tips to dorsal hair.

DESCRIPTION Colours quite variable with local population differences evident. Upper parts medium to dark brown, dark orange to blackish. Some Scottish populations light grey-brown, others rufous. Under parts generally similar but paler. Juveniles up to 12 months are usually darker and often quite grey. Membranes, ear and face usually very dark brown.

Ear short and broad, extending nearly to tip of muzzle when laid forward. Tragus less than half the height of conch, anterior border concave, posterior almost equally convex, with rounded blunt tip. A post-calcarial lobe is present. Muzzle is short, and has glandular swellings. Membranes are opaque (cf. *Myotis mystacinus*). Wings fairly narrow. Chromosomes: $2n = 42$, F.N. $= 48$ (Bovey 1949), needs confirmation.

FIGURE 43 Pipistrelle. (Photo: P. Morris)

MEASUREMENTS Head and body 35–45 mm; forearm 28–35 mm; wingspan 190–250 mm; ear 8–11 mm; condylobasal length 11–12 mm; weight 3–8 g. Weights taken at beginning of August of bats emerging from nursery roost: means and range of adult females 5·19 g (4·24–5·81, $n=39$), juvenile females 4·30 g (2·93–5·15, $n=184$) and juvenile males 3·98 g (2·85–4·65, $n=203$) (Stebbings 1968b). At the end of hibernation males weigh about 3·7 g and females 3·9 g (Stebbings 1966). Lovett (1961) weighed bats caught while feeding between August and October and found females were 6·8 g (5·5–7·5, $n=90$) and males 6·3 g (5·5–7·5, $n=32$).

DISTRIBUTION See Fig. 44. Widespread throughout the western Palaearctic east to Kashmir and north to about latitude 68° in Scandinavia.

Common throughout British Isles including Ireland and some of the outer islands.

VARIATION Females are larger than males as shown by forearm means of a Dorset colony; 31·8 mm ($n=185$) for females and 30·9 mm ($n=204$) for males (Stebbings 1968b). Detailed study of adult female forearm size in Britain has shown a correlation between the June maximum temperature and forearm length (being a function of body size). Larger bats were found in cooler regions. Smallest bats 31·0 mm ($n=175$) in Wiltshire and Monmouth with larger animals in Devon 31·4 ($n=83$), Dorset 31·7 ($n=225$), Kent 32·2 mm ($n=50$), East Norfolk 32·5 mm ($n=152$), Wigtown 32·2 mm ($n=214$), Stirlingshire 32·0 mm ($n=412$) and Kincardineshire 32·2 mm ($n=85$). The largest were in east Lincolnshire, 32·9 mm ($n=75$). Of particular interest were those on the Isle of Rhum being only 31·2 ($n=18$) (Stebbings 1973). Apparently the reverse of small rodent variation in which the island populations are usually larger.

HABITAT Occurs in all types of habitat except highly exposed regions. Roosts usually in confined spaces but sometimes found sleeping on trees or walls. Frequently found flying over or near water and watermeadows.

BEHAVIOUR Emergence usually about 20 minutes after sunset (Church 1957) but time seems to vary throughout the season (Venables 1943). They fly intermittently through the night and sometimes return after sunrise. Flight fast and jerky, often high and along a beat.

Summer. Large nursing colonies are formed by the adult females, particularly in buildings. Numbers up to 1,000 may not be uncommon but

FIGURE 44
Pipistrelle:
distribution.

more usually up to 300. Numbers emerging from a given roost vary from day to day and it is probable that several roosts within an area are used successively. Much squeaking and shuffling precedes the emergence, and one or two bats usually leave roost some minutes before the main stream (Venables 1943, Stebbings 1968b). There is some evidence that weanlings emerge before adults, possibly because they have greater need for food.

During August and September in Czechoslovakia Palasthy & Gaisler (1965) and Hurka (1966) recorded sudden 'invasions' of roosts by up to 800 bats. These bats are probably changing from summer to winter roosts and transitory roosts are possibly used for mating.

Males are usually solitary or in small groups during the summer. However, in central Russia, Strelkov (1969) found no males and suggested they live further south where they are joined by females in autumn.

Winter. Hibernation spent mostly in buildings and trees in western Europe and roosts are not occupied until late November or December in England (Racey 1973c). While Hurka (1966) in Czechoslovakia recorded segregation of the sexes and some differentiation amongst age groups, Racey (1972) found all ages and sexes together in England. Flights during the winter are not uncommon and many are taken during the day. Hurka (1966) in Czechoslovakia recorded the temperatures beside hibernating bats in a building from November to January. They varied from -2 to $9°$C but averaged $3.5°$C. Racey (1974b) continuously recorded temperature close to hibernating bats in an Essex church from November to March. Temperature varied from $-5°$C to $12°$C with a median of $3.4°$C. Hurka (1966) and Gaisler (1966b) recording numbers of bats in hibernation, found respectively 44.4% ($n=1708$) and 42.2% ($n=211$) were males. However, Racey (1973a) found 57% were males ($n=797$) of bats found mostly in East Anglia. Hurka also found a predominance of sub-adults over juveniles and adults in the ratio $5:1:4$.

In 1962 Dumitresco & Orghidan (1963) explored an enormous limestone cave in Roumania and found large colonies of *P. pipistrellus*. Numbers estimated since total between 80 000–100 000 bats in hibernation. Buresch (1941) recorded a flight of 1150 km and Strelkov (1969) suggests that the bats hibernating in Roumania migrated and spend their summer in central Russia.

Longest movement in Britain 69 km of bat ringed at Bury St Edmunds, Suffolk in November and killed by a cat in October at Buxton, Norfolk (author's data).

FOOD Mostly small insects caught and eaten in flight but larger insects taken to a perch (Poulton 1929, Hayden & Kirkby 1954). A captive adult

female during winter consumed up to 1·66 g of food at one feed lasting
9–15 minutes (Stebbings 1966b). In captivity pregnant bats ate 3 g
Tenebrio/bat/day (Racey 1973b).

BREEDING Male sexual cycle studied in detail by Racey & Tam (1974).
Earliest inseminated female caught 23 September (Racey unpubl.) but
copulation also observed by Aubert (1963) in spring. Sperm retain their
fertilising capacity after storage in uterus for several months (Racey
1973a). Mechanism of sperm storage investigated by Racey (1975).
Ovulation and fertilisation occur in May. Methods of pregnancy diagnosis compared by Racey (1969), and palpation found to be accurate.
Gestation about 44 days (Deanesly & Warwick 1939) but may be
extended if adverse environmental conditions cause mother to become
torpid (Racey 1973b). Single young (occasional twins in British Isles)
born from third week June until second week July, with exceptionally
late births in early August. Criteria for assessment of reproductive status
given by Racey (1974a). Maternal care, growth and development of young
described by Kleiman (1969).

POPULATION STRUCTURE Little known. Sex ratio of weaned bats is
near unity (204 ♂♂ : 185 ♀♀, Stebbings 1968b). Greatest longevity in
Europe 8·5 years (Gaisler & Hanak 1969) but the only pipistrelle found
in the caves at Bury St Edmunds (Stebbings 1960) was killed by a cat
at Buxton, Norfolk, after 11 years.

PREDATORS AND MORTALITY Organochlorines, notably DDT, probably responsible for many deaths (Jefferies 1972). A small mustelid, probably a weasel, was eating pipistrelles in a house in Scotland (Stebbings
& Placido 1975).

PARASITES AND DISEASE This host is often very heavily infected with
ectoparasites (particularly mites) while in the nursery roosts and by many
species: the bug *Cimex pipistrelli*; the fleas *Ischnopsyllus octactenus* and
Nycteridopsylla longiceps; the mites *Spinturnix acuminatus, Macronyssus
kolenatii, M. uncinatus* (not preferred host), *Steatonyssus periblepharus,
Pteracarus pipistrellia, Acanthophthirius etheldredae,* and *Leptotrombidium
russicum* (Hutson 1964); and the tick *Argas vespertilionis.* Four endopara-
sitic protozoans are known: *Trypanosoma incertum, T. dionisii, Babesia
vesperuginis* and *Polychromophilus murinus* (Baker 1974).

RELATIONS WITH MAN Has been maintained in captivity for two years
and females have given birth and successfully weaned babies (Racey
1970). One female born in captivity subsequently mated and became
pregnant.

Nathusius' pipistrelle *Pipistrellus nathusii*
Vespertilio nathusii Keyserling & Blasius, 1839; Germany.

RECOGNITION Similar to *P. pipistrellus* but distinguished by its conspicuously longer, slender teeth and by the first upper premolar lying entirely in the tooth-row.

DESCRIPTION Slightly larger than *P. pipistrellus*. Upper parts dull yellow brown with basal fur much darker than mid-fur. Tips are usually very pale, giving a 'frosted' apppearance. Under parts quite pale grey brown. A more or less distinct line of demarcation is present along side of neck. Hair long and loose. Membranes, ears and face are dark brown. Wing is relatively broader than in *P. pipistrellus*. Proportion of fifth digit to forearm is 130% in *P. nathusii* and about 120% in *P. pipistrellus*.

Ear short and slightly narrower than *P. pipistrellus*. Tragus longer and parallel sided, ending in blunt tip. Chromosomes: $2n = 44$, F.N. $= 48$ (Bovey 1949), needs confirmation.

MEASUREMENTS (British specimen in brackets) Head and body 45–53 mm (50); forearm 32·0–35·1 mm (33·0); wingspan (242 mm); ear (11)–12·6 mm; weight (6·4 g).

DISTRIBUTION Unknown in detail but fairly common in eastern Europe and central Russia, north to Finland, south to South-East France. A few records in Netherlands and Denmark. Strelkov (1969) regards this species as highly migratory, with several records over 1000 km (longest 1600 km). One record from Britain, in Dorset, October 1969 (Stebbings 1970b).

GENUS *Barbastella*

A small genus, with two species represented in the Palaearctic. One occurs in Britain.

Dark to black bats with very broad triangular or squarish ears joined at the bases. Dental formula

$$\frac{2.1.2.3}{3.1.2.3},$$

as in *Nyctalus* and *Pipistrellus*.

Barbastelle bats are found in buildings and trees in summer and additionally in caves during very cold weather in winter. Generally considered rare but this may be due to the lack of observations in suitable habitat.

FIGURE 45 Barbastelle. (Photo: S. C. Bisseròt)

Barbastelle *Barbastella barbastellus*

Vespertilio barbastellus Schreber, 1774; France. *Barbastellus daubentonii* Bell, 1836; France.

RECOGNITION The black, short, broad ears joined across the forehead distinguish this from all other species.

DESCRIPTION A medium-sized bat with upper parts blackish brown and tips pale yellow or cream giving a frosted appearance. (Juveniles up to 12 months may not have these light tips.) Under parts grey-brown with paler tips. Face, ears and membranes very dark brown, almost black.

Ears almost as broad as long and extending 4 mm beyond tip of muzzle when laid forward. Tragus large, triangular and slightly more than half the height of conch. Muzzle is short, broad and glandular. Wings are broad and membranes thin. Chromosomes: $2n = 32$, F.N. $= 50$ (Capanna *et al.*, 1968).

MEASUREMENTS Head and body 40–52 mm; forearm 36–43 mm; wingspan 245–280 mm; ear 14–16 mm; condylobasal length 12·9–13·8 mm; weight 6–13 g.

DISTRIBUTION See Fig. 46. Occurs throughout Europe north to 60 latitude and east to central Russia.

Status is little known in Britain. It is probably to be found throughout England and possibly Wales, but recent records have mostly been confined south and east of a line from the Severn estuary to Sunderland.

VARIATION Males are smaller than females. Forearm means for males 38·8 mm ($n=26$) and for females 39·9 mm ($n=21$) (Aellen 1962).

Of 1002 examined in Czechoslovakia 2·1% (21) were partially albino. some with patches and others with flecks. Males were affected more than females, 17:4 (Palasthy 1968).

HABITAT Seems to prefer wooded river valleys but infrequently found. Mostly found in hollow trees and buildings but also hibernates in caves during very cold weather.

BEHAVIOUR Emergence time is rather variable, sometimes begins before sunset. Active intermittently throughout night. Flight generally low, often over water, tending to be heavy and fluttering. Flies faster when flying to feeding areas. It usually alights head up but sometimes turns somersault and hangs by its feet.

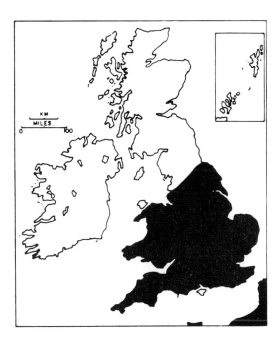

FIGURE 46
Barbastelle:
distribution.

Summer. Little known. Females segregate from males and form small nursery colonies. Males usually remain solitary.

Winter. In central Europe large numbers are sometimes found in hibernation but usually only in January and February when very cold. Harmata (1969b) recorded the mean experimental and naturally preferred temperatures in hibernation as 4·3°C and 4·0°C. Some prefer 0°C and are able to withstand much lower temperatures (reviewed by Harmata 1969b). Sex ratio in hibernation shows strong bias towards the males, 67·6% (n=641, Gaisler 1966b).

It is not known whether this species is stationary or migratory, but several medium-length movements up to 290 km have been recorded (Kepka 1960).

FOOD Little known but one watched for 50 minutes near Bath from just before sunset feeding on swarming dipterans 0–30 cm above mill pond, often dipping to the water, possibly drinking. After 30 minutes it rested on stone bridge for 3 minutes before resuming feeding (author's data).

POPULATION STRUCTURE No information. Abel (1967) recaptured two over 18 years after initial banding.

PARASITES AND DISEASE Little is known about the ectoparasites but two species are found: the flea *Ischnopsyllus hexactenus* and a mite *Neomyobia pantopus.*

RELATIONS WITH MAN Difficult to keep alive in captivity.

GENUS *Plecotus*
Long-eared bats

A small genus distributed throughout the Palaearctic from Ireland and northern Scandinavia to Japan. In the Nearctic several related species can be referred to this genus but are sometimes separated as *Corynorhinus.* Two species occur in Britain.

Until recently it was considered that there was only one species of *Plecotus* although a number of people during the past 150 years had described two forms. Bauer (1960) finally concluded these various forms could all be attributed to one of two distinct and often sympatric species, *P. auritus* and *P. austriacus.*

Distinguished from all other species by its enormous ears joined at inner bases. Form generally delicate. Prominent tragus which remains erect when ears are folded under wings during rest or in hibernation.

Dental formula

$$\frac{2.1.2.3}{3.1.3.3}.$$

Long-eared bats are mostly found roosting in buildings and trees but occasionally hibernate in caves, especially during cold weather. In hibernation wings usually folded loosely around body and legs held bent. Echolocation pulses are very weak (Hooper 1969) and are probably related to the mode of feeding, in which most food is sought and picked at rest off vegetation.

Common long-eared bat *Plecotus auritus*

Vespertilio auritus L. 1758; Sweden. *Plecotus brevimanus* Jenyns, 1829; Grunty Fen, Cambs, England.

RECOGNITION Distinguished from all other species except *P. austriacus* by its long ears (over 28 mm) which are three-quarters the length of head and body. Separated from *P. austriacus* by its generally smaller size (cf. Variation below), brown-buff fur, long slender thumb (generally over 6·2 mm), narrow tapering tragus and by the second upper premolar being more than half the height of the first. See Table 7, p. 75.

Note: In Britain *P. austriacus* may be confined to southern English counties.

DESCRIPTION A small to medium-sized bat. Upper parts usually a yellow-buff or light brown with under parts buff, yellowish brown, creamy or white (a brown exudation sometimes covers the fur and head regions— see Stebbings 1966c). An indistinct line of demarcation exists along side of neck. Juveniles up to six weeks are often dark greyish-brown and remain greyish-brown for twelve months. Wings broad, membranes thin and semi-transparent. Face generally mid to light brown, sometimes pinkish.

Ears very large and oval. Tragus almost half as high as conch, anterior border more or less straight and posterior border convex proximally and becoming straight or slightly concave distally. Rounded tip (Fig. 47). Thumb relatively long and slender. Upper canine small and rounded in section just below cingulum. Chromosomes: $2n = 32$, F.N. $= 54$ (Bovey 1949, Fedyk & Fedyk 1970).

MEASUREMENTS Head and body 37–48 mm; forearm 34–42 mm; wingspan 230–285 mm; ear 29–38 mm; condylobasal length 13–16 mm (thumb generally over 6·2 mm, tragus width generally less than 5·6 mm); weight 6–12 g. Weights were taken throughout several years in a Dorset

a

b

FIGURE 47 Common long-eared bat (a) alert, with ears erect; (b) asleep with ears folded under wing leaving erect traguses. (Photos: S. C. Bisseròt)

colony ($n=293$) Means for January 8·0 g, mid April 7·0 g, October 9·0 g. Males were 1·0 g less than females in October but only 0·5 g less in April (Stebbings 1970a). Hibernation weight loss of 22%.

DISTRIBUTION See Fig. 48. Distributed throughout the Palaearctic from Ireland to Japan north to 63° latitude in Scandinavia.

In British Isles probably occurs everywhere except perhaps exposed regions of North-West Scotland and the offshore islands.

VARIATIONS Females are larger than males. In Dorset mean forearm length 38·3 mm ($n=46$) for females and 37·5 mm ($n=38$) for males. In Suffolk 38·5 mm ($n=35$) and 37·6 mm ($n=32$) respectively. Females in Nottinghamshire were 39·3 mm ($n=31$) and females and males in Inverness were respectively 39·2 mm ($n=23$) and 38·2 mm ($n=28$). Thus there is a tendency for increase in size towards the north (author's data). In Czechoslovakia they are rather larger with females 40·2 mm ($n=58$) and males 39·5 mm ($n=37$) (Hurka 1971).

HABITAT Prefers sheltered, lightly wooded areas. Roosts in buildings and trees throughout the year but occasionally found in caves. In central and eastern Europe seems to be mainly confined to upland wooded areas (Piechocki 1966, Hanák 1969).

FIGURE 48 Common long-eared bat: distribution.

BEHAVIOUR Generally emerge late when dark but some emerge about 20 minutes after sunset especially in the north. Flight periods last approximately one hour initially, then intermittent flights throughout night but returning before dawn. Flight rather weak and fluttering, usually amongst trees, where they frequently hover with body inclined at about 30° to the horizontal (Norberg 1970).

Summer. In Dorset hibernation ends at the end of March. Females, with some immatures, segregate from adult males in June to form nursery roosts and after weaning of young rejoin the males in late August. Hibernation begins about mid-November (Stebbings 1970a). Observations in roof throughout 24 hours indicate that most of the time during daylight hours bats roost in confined spaces unless air temperature exceeds about 40°C, when they crawl and hang from rafters with wings partially spread. Air temperatures up to 59°C were experienced in roost (Stebbings 1966c). Normally, at about sunset, bats begin moving out of their day crevices and groom vigorously. Thirty minutes later the first flights take place within the roof and when dark they will fly out. Some bats spend up to 75 minutes grooming and taking short flights. First bats return 45 minutes later, fly around roof and groom. During cool evenings bats return directly to their day crevices but on warm nights they hang from beams digesting their food and then fly out again. By sunrise all bats are in their crevices (author's data).

Winter. Probably mostly hibernate in trees and buildings. During cold weather particularly, some occur in caves, where they prefer the cool entrance regions but are usually hanging in crevices (Bezem *et al.* 1964, Daan & Wichers 1968). Harmata (1969b) found individuals hibernating in temperatures from $-3\cdot5$ to $11°C$ with most at $6°C$, while specimens kept under experimental conditions occupied regions between 1 and $8°C$ with a mean of $6\cdot0°C$. In Dorset several have hibernated in bat roost boxes during frosty weather. One bat occupied a box for at least 107 days from October to February where outside temperatures fluctuated from $-5°C$ to $15°C$ (Stebbings 1974). Sex ratio in hibernation is more or less equal; 53% males ($n=283$, Bels 1952).

Movements have been rather short and many instances known of this species occupying the same roost throughout the year. Gaisler & Hanák (1969b), regarding it as a stationary species, record a movement of 42 km. But in November 1948 a group alighted on a boat 72 km north-east of Spurn Point, Yorkshire, having been watched arriving from the north-east. At dusk they continued towards England (A. Gutteridge, *in litt*). Likewise in October 1968 a young male was found dead on Smiths Knoll lightship, 50 km east of Great Yarmouth, Norfolk (Corbet 1970), and

Barrett-Hamilton (1910–11) gave two autumn records at offshore light-houses in Ireland.

FOOD Insects taken both in flight and more often from foliage. Small insects eaten in flight but some taken to temporary perch. In a study of remains found under roosts in four areas of Europe Roer (1969) concluded that noctuid moths form the main diet in summer.

BREEDING Increasing proportion of females found to be inseminated in Russia as hibernation progressed (Strelkov 1962). Moffat (1922) observed most mating activity in April and May in Ireland and in southern England at least some occurs in spring (Stebbings 1970a). Segregation of the sexes begins in early June with immature bats often remaining with pregnant females. No bats produce young in their first year in southern England and about 75% give birth to one young at two years. The remainder breed first in their third year. However, a proportion breeds every other year for the first 5 years then produce every year. One female was known to breed every year for 11 years (author's data). Males appear to become mature at 12 months.

POPULATION STRUCTURE Colony in Dorset consisted of 20 individuals which remained constant for ten years. Increment rate was 5 per year. Survival rate of 0·758 for females and 0·542 for males indicate life spans of 16 and 7 years respectively. With females surviving longer, the annual sex ratio remained constant at 39% males (Stebbings 1970a). Longevity of over 12 years recorded by Heerdt & Sluiter (1961), and over 13 years for a female in Dorset (author's data).

PREDATORS AND MORTALITY This species is often caught by cats (author's data) and owls (Ruprecht 1971).

PARASITES AND DISEASE Heavy infestations of ectoparasites are not normally encountered on this host but five species occur frequently: the fleas *Ischnopsyllus hexactenus* and, although not the preferred host, also *Nycteridopsylla longiceps*; and the mites *Spinturnix plecotina*, *Ornithonyssus pipistrelli* and *Neomyobia plecotia*.

RELATIONS WITH MAN Has been maintained in a laboratory for up to 18 months and females have given birth and weaned young (Racey 1970).

Grey long-eared bat *Plecotus austriacus*

Vespertilio auritus austriacus Fischer, 1829; Austria. *Plecotus auritus*, Jenyns, 1829.

FIGURE 49 Grey long-eared bat. (Photo: S. C. Bisserôt)

RECOGNITION Very similar to *P. auritus* but distinguished by its overall grey colour, dark brown to black face, small thumbs (generally less than 6·2 mm), slightly larger size, broad tragus, large upper canine which is angular in section above cingulum and by having a very small second upper premolar. This latter is less than half the height of the first upper premolar. See measurements in Table 7, p. 75.

DESCRIPTION A medium-sized bat with upper parts grey to dark grey, sometimes almost black, and under parts light grey with whitish tips. The bases of hairs both dorsally and ventrally are very dark, almost black. Face colours range from dark brown to black. Ears and membranes are dark brown.

Ears very large and broad. Tragus also is relatively broad with anterior edge more or less straight and posterior edge strongly convex in proximal half and concave distally (Fig. 49). Thumb short and relatively thick. Upper canines large and angular (Stebbings 1967). Chromosomes: $2n = 32$, F.N. $= 54$ (Fedyk & Fedyk 1971).

MEASUREMENTS Head and body 40–52 mm; forearm 38–43 mm; wingspan 255–300 mm; ear 30–38 mm; condylobasal length 15–17 mm; tragus width generally over 5·6 mm but usually about 6·0 mm; weight

7–14 g. Annual weight changes recorded in a Dorset colony ($n=299$) showed males 1·0 g lighter than females pre-hibernation and 0·8 g in the spring. Mean weights for January 10·0, April 8·0 and October 11·3 g. Hibernation weight loss 29% (Stebbings 1970a).

DISTRIBUTION See Fig. 50. Since its recognition (Bauer 1960) it has been found throughout central and southern Europe, north to Poland (latitude 53 N; Ruprecht, 1971) and east to the Himalayas. First recognised in England in 1963 (Corbet 1964) but has only been found in Dorset, Hampshire and Sussex (November 1976).

VARIATION Males are smaller than females. In Dorset colony forearm means for males 39·9 mm ($n=22$) and for females 41·1 mm ($n=35$) (author's data). In Czechoslovakia forearm means 39·8 mm ($n=131$) for males and 41·0 mm ($n=151$) for females (Hurka 1971).

HABITAT In England only known colony is in house roof in open, lightly wooded country. In central Europe seems to live almost exclusively in lowland cultivated valley areas with nursery roosts associated with villages and small towns (Hanák 1969).

BEHAVIOUR Little known. Emerges late and intermittently active throughout night.

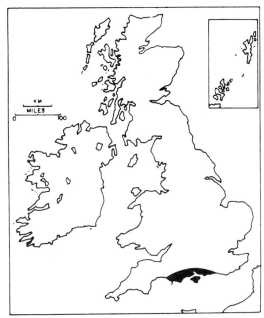

FIGURE 50 Grey long-eared bat: distribution.

Summer. In Dorset hibernation ends in March for females and April for males and sexual segregation occurs from June until September. Hibernation begins at the end of October. Adult males appear to be territorial, particularly in the autumn during the mating period (Stebbings 1970a).

Winter. In Dorset seems to be more active than *P. auritus* possibly due to unsuitable hibernation conditions. One found in a cave in Britain but in Europe generally hibernates deep in warm caves, hanging free or in exposed positions (Hurka 1971). Sex ratio is equal in hibernation sites. Regarded by Gaisler & Hanak (1969) as a non-migratory species but they recorded a maximum movement of 62 km. Migration is also suggested by an animal killed at a lightship 18 km south of Bognor Regis, Sussex on 10 September 1969 followed by one found dead in Bognor 11 days later (Corbet 1971).

FOOD Noctuid moths have been brought back to Dorset roost, but feeding behaviour unknown.

BREEDING Appears to be similar to *P. auritus* with females first breeding in their second and third years, and males reaching maturity after 12 months (Stebbings 1975).

POPULATION STRUCTURE Dorset colony consisted of over 22 in 1961 but crashed to 4 in the cold winter 1962–3. Numbers increased slightly thereafter. Survival rates for males and females averaged over ten years were 0·452 and 0·621 respectively, giving life expectations of 5 and 9 years. Sex ratio in the colony was highly biased with only 30% males (Stebbings 1970a). Greatest longevity in Britain 11 years and in Europe 12 years (Gaisler & Hanák 1969).

PREDATORS AND MORTALITY Owls are known to take some (Ruprecht 1971).

Order Lagomorpha
Lagomorphs

Lagomorphs are small herbivores, comprising the rabbits, hares and pikas. At one time the group was included in the order Rodentia as a suborder, named Duplicidentata, because of the presence of a small second pair of upper incisors behind the large, chisel-shaped first pair (there is also a third pair which only appears as rudiments in the milk dentition). The long gap (diastema) between incisors and cheek-teeth is a further character shared with rodents and also with other herbivorous groups like ruminants and kangaroos. In other respects lagomorphs are very distinctive. The cheek-teeth as well as the incisors are rootless and grow continuously; the naked rhinarium around the nostrils is covered by flaps of skin which can be retracted; there is a very large caecum with a spiral septum; and the tail is very short. They also indulge in a unique nutritional strategy known as refection. During the day very soft faecal pellets are produced and eaten, thereby passing most food twice through the alimentary canal before the production of hard fibrous faecal pellets.

There are two families, the Ochotonidae—the pikas of the mountains of Asia and western North America with short ears and legs—and the Leporidae including all the rabbits and hares.

FAMILY LEPORIDAE

RABBITS AND HARES

This worldwide family contains one large genus, *Lepus*, including the cursorial hares living mainly in open country, along with a number of small, highly localised genera of mainly burrowing 'rabbits', including *Oryctolagus*. The most prominent characters in the family are the long ears and long hind legs and feet. The dental formula is

$$\frac{2.0.3.3}{1.0.2.3}.$$

The characters of the three species in Britain are compared in Table 8, p. 131.

FIGURE 51 (a) Brown hare; (b) mountain hare (summer); (c) rabbit.

GENUS *Oryctolagus*

A monospecific genus clearly distinct from the hares (*Lepus*) but super-ficially very similar to other genera of rabbits such as the American *Sylvilagus* (cotton-tails).

Rabbit *Oryctolagus cuniculus*

Lepus cuniculus Linnaeus, 1758; Germany.
Coney, conyng (obsolete), cwningen (Welsh).

TABLE 8 Identification of lagomorphs

	Rabbit	Brown hare	Mountain hare
Overall colour	Yellowish brown	Yellowish brown	Greyish brown, sometimes white in winter
Upper surface of tail	Black	Black	White
Tips of ears	Brown	Black	Black
Length of ears from notch (mm)	60–70	90–105	60–80
Length of hind feet (mm)	75–95	130–155	125–170

RECOGNITION Smaller than brown and mountain hares; ears without black tips, and hind legs shorter in relation to body than in both species of hares. When running, the white underside of tail, and its position held close to the body, distinguish it from the hares. Skull distinguished from hares by bony palate being longer in relation to width of posterior nares, and by persistence of interparietal bone throughout life (Fig. 52).

SIGN Footprints in snow characterised by the long print of the hind legs and small round print of fore feet. Rarely walks, but sometimes intermittently when grazing. Progresses by leaps with one foreleg ahead of the other at slow speeds, but forelimbs tending to move together as speed increases. At high speed hind prints lie ahead of those of the forefeet. Jumping mode of progression reflected in their runs from cover, through and along fences and hedges and to their grazing areas. The depressions or jumps are 20 to 30 cm apart. Where rabbits are few, impressions of the jumps may be slight in short-grazed grass, and are best seen when angle of the sun is low or, if there are bare areas nearby, by smears of soil from rabbits' feet.

Fur frequently found on snags through fences, hedges, etc.; not so much black in hair fibres as in brown hare. Well-used burrows may be indicated by soil on jumps leading to burrows. Sometimes faeces on the soil heaps, and in spring and summer occasionally wet patches of urine on soil. Presence of rabbits also indicated by short-cropped grasses near to burrows or to surface cover, e.g. around bramble bushes and field headlands and banks; also growing cereals or root crops may be eaten at margin of fields. In winter, small trees, fallen branches or prunings may have evidence of rabbit toothmarks when bark eaten. Bark eaten, not stripped as with squirrels.

Droppings not always distinguishable from hares'—size and friability depend on grasses eaten. May be found in 'latrines', in scrapes (frequently two droppings only) or elsewhere. Distinguish from lamb faeces by absence of flat facets on surface. Small scrapes much in evidence in densely populated rabbit groups but also occurs where rabbits are few. Nesting burrows or 'stops' may be found, or lying up places as in short, fired, sheep-grazed gorse. Forms may be used more than once but not puddled by hind feet as frequently is the case with hares. Eye-shine pink. Numbers of rabbits difficult to judge by field signs except to the experienced eye. Taylor (1956) developed technique using faecal pellet counts to estimate numbers.

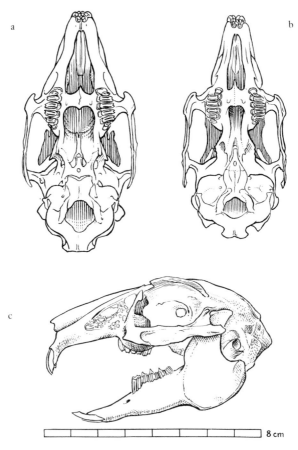

8 cm

FIGURE 52 Skulls of (a) brown hare; (b) and (c) rabbit. Note the very wide nasal passage in the hare.

DESCRIPTION Sexes alike but female (doe) smaller with narrower head; profile from ears to nose slightly less rounded than in male (buck). Coat colour greyish brown, but much variation from sandy yellow to grey. Guard hairs banded brown and black (or grey). Nape of neck (woolly fur) and scrotum reddish, underparts white or grey. Juveniles frequently with white star on forehead, not often seen in adults.

Moult once yearly; begins in March on face then spreads from back; growth of underfur not complete until October or November. (Sometimes moult in head region has similarities to fur replacement, in region of eyes, following recovery from myxomatosis.)

Ears long, not tipped with black. Nipples, five pairs, inguinal to pectoral region. Long black vibrissae. Feet furred—buff colour. Testes scrotal in adult in breeding season. Eyes with iris not so yellow as in hares, pupil round.

Lumbar region heavily muscled and mobile—much of power to hind limbs derived from lower back movements. Proximal epiphyseal closure of tibia used to distinguish adult from juvenile in live and dead animals (Taylor 1959). Chromosomes: $2n = 44$.

MEASUREMENTS Adult head and body up to 400 mm. Weight at birth 30–35 g, at weaning (3 weeks) c. 150 g, adult (i.e. when skeletal growth has ceased) 1200–2000 g. Stomach and intestines represent about 20% of live weight. Mean weight of paunched adult females about 10% less than males; some pregnant females may weigh up to 2200 g. Weekly weight gain from four weeks, 40–60 g.

DISTRIBUTION See Fig. 53. Originally in north-western Africa and Iberia but now through most of western Europe (but only in southern Scandinavia and absent from most of Italy and the Balkans). Introduced in Australia, New Zealand, USA, Chile and elsewhere.

Widespread in Britain and Ireland, up to the tree-line and on most small islands. In 1970, 59% of farm holdings had rabbits on cultivable land compared with 94% before the pandemic of myxomatosis in 1954.

Introduced to Britain late in the twelfth century to be kept in confinement and bred for fur and meat. Enclosed warrens soon became established in much of the lowlands but it is uncertain when rabbits became feral on a large scale. Their history in Britain has been described in detail by Sheail (1971).

VARIATION British form not distinguishable from Continental animals. Much variation in pelage in Britain, from light sandy colour to dark grey and totally melanic forms. Black forms not uncommon but albinos rare on mainland. On some islands albinos are common, e.g. about 2% albino on Skomer in 1953/62. Island populations often adulterated in past with introduced fancy strains, e.g. piebald, skewbald and long-haired forms may be common as on Skokholm and formerly on Inner Farne Island (rabbits now absent there). Island rabbits frequently smaller than mainland forms. Unconfirmed reports of rabbits on lighter sandy soils being lighter in colour than those on heavy loams. Flashes of white sometimes occur, most frequently on forelimbs and over shoulders.

HABITAT Most suitable habitats are areas of short grasses, either naturally occurring as on dry heaths and machairs or closely grazed agricultural pastures, with secure refuge (warrens, boulders or scrub) in close proximity to feeding areas. Home ranges are small—150 to 200 m radius— thus small pasture fields bounded by hedgebanks provide ideal habitat. Except in areas where erstwhile rabbit burrows exist, expanding rabbit colonies exploit areas of scrub or surface cover more readily than earth banks where ready-made cover is not immediately available. Warrens in open ground not now so common as formerly, partly because re-seeding (and ploughing) of pastures is becoming more widely practised and also because more widespread use of cyanide gas, awareness of potential for damage by rabbits, and better organised control have eliminated or pre-

FIGURE 53 Rabbit: distribution.

vented occupation of more readily accessible warrens. Suitability of habitat not the only feature determining abundance and distribution of rabbits at present time (see Population). Occurs up to tree line if land is well drained and suitable resting refuge available. Can make burrows equally well in sand, shale or chalk. Never abundant in large coniferous plantations, except on peripheral areas and along fire breaks and rides.

BEHAVIOUR Crepuscular and nocturnal, but diurnal if undisturbed. Range 150–200 m from warren (Southern 1940), but at low population densities there is evidence of movements up to 400 m. Active throughout most of night, tending to range further from burrows on dark nights, more timid in moonlight. Little information on dispersal, but subjective observations suggest that gregarious nature tends to militate against distant dispersal of juveniles. On Skokholm, in high density populations juveniles normally recaptured as adults within 200 m of initial place of capture, except when population density artificially reduced when immigration of juveniles from up to 800 m observed.

Use runs to and from feeding areas. Dislike getting belly fur wet in long grass, but venture forth on the roughest, wettest nights, keeping fur dry by shaking body. Inexplicably, however, fewer rabbits seen out on some nights, and times of emergence can be variable, even in areas where ground predators are absent. Communal alarm systems—thumping with hind foot, both above and below ground, and also erect posture on hind feet—seem to warn others of possible threat.

Social behaviour has been most extensively studied in Australia (Myers & Poole 1959, 1961 Mykytowycz 1958, 1959, 1960). Populations subdivided into groups with well-defined social hierarchical system. Dominant bucks and does occupy group territory, lower-ranking animals having smaller non-exclusive territories. Territoriality strongest in breeding season. Offspring of dominant doe tend to rank highly subsequently. Dominant does (in confined study groups) live and nest in the main warren but lowest-ranking does relegated to nesting in stops, or away from the warren. Territorial marking by subcutaneous 'chin' gland (Mykytowycz 1962, 1965) and by urine and anal glands via faeces (Mykytowycz 1966, Mykytowycz & Gambale 1969). Anal glands probably under some control since all faeces not 'pungent', and perhaps not all of territorial significance. Differences in reproductive performance observed between young (yearling) and older does, but may be regulated by social status as well as age. Subordinates, usually yearlings, have shorter breeding season than more dominant, usually older, animals, and higher occurrence of total loss of embryos. 'Density syndrome' postulated by Myers *et al.*

(1971) concomitant with rise in numbers or density, as a physiological response to spatial restriction on the individual.

Communication mainly olfactory, by faeces, urine and chin gland. Sexual status conveyed by inguinal gland (Mykytowycz 1967). Some visual signalling during reproductive and aggressive behaviour (Southern 1948). Alarm signalled visually by flashing of tail during high speed running, and acoustically by thumping with hind feet, above and below ground. Usually silent, but has distress and juvenile nestling calls. Tooth grinding may be of significance. Field of vision is 360° when head is held up.

FOOD Eat a wide range of herbage, selecting the more nutritious species. Greatly attracted by agricultural crops, including cereals, roots, pasture, horticultural crops and young trees. Marked biotic effect on natural vegetation: can convert ling heath to grassland (Farrow 1925) and by close cropping favour dwarf plant forms. Erect agricultural grasses are selected when not rank, and composition of pastures can be changed from predominantly cultivated species to wild grasses with creeping habits, mainly *Agrostis* and *Festuca*. *Holcus* is not favoured except when young in spring. Bark of many trees eaten but elder is avoided and used to grow commonly amongst hedgerow warrens.

Zonation of vegetation is produced by feeding close to burrows and erosion may be precipitated. Rabbits are responsible for short turf of downland which in the absence of intensive grazing turns to scrub. Annual weeds are encouraged by the disturbance of soil (Tansley 1939).

BREEDING Mainly from January to August when a succession of litters of up to seven young are produced at a minimum interval of about 30 days.

Proportion of pregnant females may be high in January. Time of onset considered by many to be determined by winter weather conditions but little real evidence except in very severe winters (e.g. 1963) when it may be retarded dramatically. In high density pre-myxomatosis populations season was from January/February to June, with about 5% of females pregnant in the other months. Season extended in post-myxomatosis low density populations, with some out-of-season breeding as formerly. Pre-myxomatosis breeding season lasted 15 to 17 weeks (Brambell 1942); post-myxomatosis (1958) 22 weeks or more (Lloyd 1963). High density Skokholm population, 10–12 weeks duration (Lloyd 1970). Males fecund some 6–8 weeks before does come into oestrus, in January/February.

Courtship involves chases and enuration (Southern 1948). Does will copulate frequently at oestrus and less frequently when pregnant. Ovulation is induced by copulation and there is therefore no short-term oestrous cycle. If unmated, a succession of ripe follicles is generated.

Gestation lasts *c*. 30 days, post-partum oestrus is normal and females are usually pregnant within 24 hours of parturition. No lactation anoestrus as is common in domestic rabbit. Number of ova shed increases at each pregnancy (within season) reaching peak in June and declining thereafter. Number of ova shed also related to body weight of doe.

Litter size usually 3–7, but seasonal mean variable according to environment. Brambell (1942, 1944) described massive pre-natal mortality of entire sets of embryos. Such total loss is characteristic of high-density populations (up to 60% litters lost), but occurs to a smaller degree in low-density populations. See also Watson (1957).

Young born in nests composed of grass or moss lined with belly fur. Nests found in main warrens and in separate small burrows (or stops) 1–2 m long. Occasionally may breed above ground in dense vegetation. Stops may be dug during pregnancy, or old blind burrows may be utilised—not used twice in same season. Nest lined with grass 2–8 days before parturition, with fur during last two days. One visit per night to suckle young, doe in nest for about five minutes only.

Young blind at birth and not heavily furred as in hares. Eyes open at about 7 days. Begin to emerge from stops or nests in many warrens at about 18 days, weaned by withdrawal of maternal attention at about 21 or 22 days and desert stops at 23 to 25 days. But evidence from Skokholm that sometimes some juveniles up to 6–7 weeks old have access to milk. Males fecund at about 4 months; females can breed at about $3\frac{1}{2}$ months at a weight of *c*. 830 g.

Productivity 10–11 live offspring per year in high-density populations (Brambell 1942), over 30 in 1958 (Lloyd 1963) and about 20 in many currently expanding low density populations. Pre-natal and post-natal sex ratios equal.

POPULATION STRUCTURE Very unstable in post-myxomatosis populations but little known about pre-1954 situation (see Southern 1940). Currently much may depend upon prevalence and virulence of myxomatosis combined with the effects of predation, rabbit control and agricultural practice. Reproductive productivity high but recruitment from 1965 to 1973 low in many groups of rabbits examined. Adult: juvenile ratio in November/December ranged from $1:0.8$ to $1:3.0$ with a mean *c*. $1:1.3$. Potential ratio *c*. $1:10$, thus mortality of 70–92% of young of the year. Surveys from 1961 to 1973 revealed that significant proportion of low density populations declined and disappeared locally, and others barely maintained their size over several years. In West Wales, 1960–5, about 30% of farm infestations were lost each year, and an equal number of new infestations occurred annually. Thus although in that period about 42% of holdings had rabbits in any year, 81% of holdings had had rabbits at some time during the period of survey. On Skokholm, in climax size populations, mortality rate of juveniles about 60% per annum, adult mortality about 30% per annum and 8% of breeding yearlings survive to six years of age. No details of longevity for mainland populations. Population densities highly variable, from less than 2 to perhaps 30 rabbits per hectare. Some indications in 1973 that high-density populations are becoming more common. Nationwide, rabbits in 1973 probably no more than 5% of former numbers. Heaviest populations now seem to be located in south and south-east England, but in Wales, at one time one of the highest density areas, rabbits are on the whole remarkably scarce, even 20 years after the first outbreak of myxomatosis.

PREDATORS AND MORTALITY Foxes, stoats, polecats and wild cats prey on all ages; badgers, buzzards, weasels and domestic cats on young animals. Predation by other species such as owls, great black-backed gull, raven and crow more occasional. In immediate pre-myxomatosis era unlikely that predation had significant impact on population size except possibly in marginal or less suitable habitats. Immediately post-myxomatosis, predators in many areas outnumbered rabbit, and with the exception of the stoat and buzzard, the status of which may have been affected to some degree by the comparative absence of rabbits, none was prey-specific on rabbits and all were able to exploit other prey or foods. Up to 1965, many of the more dense rabbit populations occurred on sporting estates where predator control was practised and also on islands where ground predators were absent. Evidence is accumulating that slow rate of increase of rabbits may be associated partly with predation. Breeding success of the buzzard was depressed in some areas for one to three years after myxomatosis and the number of stoats declined from 1958 to *c*. 1963, subsequently recovering. Causal relationship with rabbit abundance not clearly established however.

PARASITES AND DISEASE The flea *Spilopsyllus cuniculi* is specific to the rabbit and usually very abundant, especially on the ears. Reproduction of this flea is correlated with that of the rabbit through the reproductive hormones in the rabbit's blood (Mead-Briggs 1964). The sucking louse *Haemodipsus ventricosus* is regular. Two species of mites often found abundantly in the ears are larval harvest mites *Trombicula autumnalis* and mange mites *Psoroptes equi*. The sheep tick *Ixodes ricinus* is frequent.

The most common nematode is *Graphidium strigosum*, of which massive infestations are found in the stomach mucosa in dense populations, but no information, for Britain, on adverse affects. Other common nematodes are *Passaleurus ambiguus* and *Trichostrongylus retortaeformis*. Of tapeworms, two adult forms commonly found, but not known to have significant effect on survival of hosts, are *Cittotaenia denticulata* and *C. pectinata*. Others are *Andrya* sp. and *Hymenolepis* sp. The probably harmless larval form of *Taenia pisiformis* (bladderworm) is very common, but the large coenurus cyst of *Taenia serialis*, which can be highly incapacitating, is now less common. Adult forms of both are found in dogs and some wild carnivores. The sheep liver fluke *Fasciola hepatica* occurred in rabbits in pre-myxomatosis populations and rabbits may have been responsible for persistence of the fluke in some areas (E. L. Taylor, pers. comm.).

Diseases of significance to rabbit populations are myxomatosis and coccidiosis, but latter only in heavy density populations. Myxoma virus appeared in 1953 and spread throughout country in following two years. Virulence has since declined, most prevalent strains (1963) having virulence of 70–95% (Fenner & Chapple 1965). Disease now endemic and occurs annually in many populations. The vector is mainly the rabbit flea, *Spilopsyllus cuniculi*. On Skokholm, where there are no rabbit fleas, 2% of rabbits affected at all months from 1963 to 1971. Coccidiosis can cause high mortality among young rabbits—most prevalent and devastating where rabbit numbers high but effect can be very localised.

RELATIONS WITH MAN Considered to be one of the more important vertebrate pests of agriculture. Their potential to reach high population densities in many habitats makes their presence incompatible with good agricultural practice. In many areas one of the greatest boons to agriculture has been the comparative absence of rabbits since 1954. At one time rabbit trapping for food and fur was a considerable industry but now pursued mainly as a pest and for sport. Ability to recover to former numbers not to be underestimated.

The ancestor of the domestic rabbit.

LITERATURE Thompson & Worden (1956): a general monograph; Sheail (1971): a detailed account of their history in Britain.

AUTHOR FOR THIS H. G. Lloyd.

GENUS *Lepus*
HARES

The dominant genus of lagomorphs with about 20 species occupying open habitats through most of the world. Characterised by long ears, long hind legs and very large and wide nasal passage. They are fast runners, living in the open and never making more than very simple short burrows. The young are born above ground, fully furred and with eyes open.

The characters of the two species in Britain are contrasted in Table 8, p. 131.

Brown hare *Lepus capensis*
Lepus capensis Linnaeus, 1758; Cape of Good Hope. *Lepus europaeus* Pallas, 1778; Burgundy, France. *Lepus europaeus occidentalis* de Winton, 1898; Moorhampton, Herefordshire, England.

RECOGNITION From rabbit by longer, black-tipped ears, longer legs and loping gait. From mountain hare by longer ears, brighter yellowish brown colour and dark upper surface of tail.

Skull (Fig. 52) distinguishable from rabbit's by wide nasal passage and from mountain hare's by lesser curvature of upper incisors and position of muscle attachments on zygomatic arches.

SIGNS Trails may be obvious across grassland, and footprints are characteristic, with large elongated impressions of rear feet side by side and showing five toes in soft ground, and forefeet placed asymmetrically and leaving small almost round impressions of four toes. Track much larger than that of rabbit. Droppings about 1 cm in diameter, usually paler and more fibrous than those of rabbit, but not certainly distinguishable. Form a shallow depression in long grass, rushes, heather or scrub, not uncommonly in woodland.

DESCRIPTION General colour warmer brown than rabbit or mountain hare, underside white, cheeks, insides of limbs and feet yellowish or ruddy. Moult into dense, redder winter coat occurs in late summer or early autumn; sometimes hindquarters are partly or largely grey. Spring moult starts mid-February and goes on to June or July, i.e. almost to beginning of autumn moult. The spring moult starts along the back, proceeds down flanks and limbs to finish on the head. The autumn moult begins at the feet and legs and moves upwards, in reverse order to the spring moult (Hewson 1963). The ears are longer than the head and have an extensive

TABLE 9 Measurements of brown hares

	Adults from Norfolk (9♂, 10♀)*	
	Range	Mean
Head and body	520–595 mm	544 mm
Tail (with hairs)	85–120 mm	106 mm
Ear to notch	95–105 mm	99 mm
	Adults from Aberdeenshire†	
	31♂	26♀
Weight (mean)	3·54 kg	3·71 kg

* Barrett-Hamilton & Hinton 1911–21.
† Flux 1967.

black area at the tip, on the posterior/external surface. The tail has a bold black stripe on the upper surface but is otherwise white.

MEASUREMENTS See Table 9.

DISTRIBUTION See Fig. 54. If the Palaearctic forms are correctly associated with the African *L. capensis*, the range is one of the largest of any species of mammal. It occupies all the dry savanna, steppe and

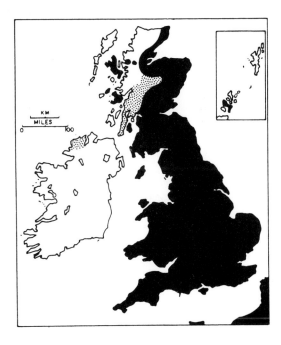

FIGURE 54 Brown hare: distribution.

semidesert zones of Africa, the whole of Europe south of (and below) the coniferous forest zone, and similar open and deciduous woodland habitats across Asia as far as central China. In southern Sweden and Finland it overlaps slightly, and in Siberia much more extensively with the northern *L. timidus*. It has been introduced to Australia, New Zealand, Chile and parts of North America.

In Britain it is widespread on low ground, but it is absent as a native species in Ireland and in the Hebrides and Shetlands. In Scotland it is present on farmland and rough grazings to the far north of the mainland, although absent from parts of the north-west. Its distribution on the smaller islands is greatly complicated by introductions and extinctions. It has been recorded since 1960 on Wight, Anglesey, Man, Arran, Mull, Luing, Coll, Skye and Orkney Mainland. It has been introduced to many other islands but has not always survived.

It has been introduced also to Ireland but has not spread widely there.

VARIATION The British form has been described as a subspecies (*occidentalis*) on the basis of darker colour, but assessment of its validity is complicated by introductions of animals from the continent.

Many abnormal colour variants have been recorded, the most frequent being a grey form of the winter pelage, probably caused by absence of the yellow and brown pigment but not of the black. Melanic, albino (entire or partial) and sandy coloured variants occur.

HABITAT Agricultural land including rough pasture up to the limit of cultivation, moorland usually within half a mile of farmland, woodland perhaps mainly for shelter rather than feeding. Less dependent upon long vegetation for cover than is mountain hare. At fringe of range may occupy habitat of mountain hare and vice versa when one or other species at low density (Lind 1963, Hewson 1974). Highest densities occur in plain country especially eastern counties and low uplands, e.g. chalk and limestone country. In the Peak District the range of the brown hare lies between 120 and 500 m mostly on grassland, while mountain hares were mostly seen between 300 and 550 m and on moorland (Yalden 1971).

BEHAVIOUR Long ears, large eyes, keen scent and long limbs are characteristic of an animal adapted to escaping from predators by running, but if disturbed by man will often crouch low to ground, ears flat against head. Inconspicuous when feeding at dusk; ears almost flat, body low and movement often one step at a time. May feed in daylight, particularly in spring, but mostly nocturnal. Average distance from day shelter to feeding grounds in North-East Scotland about 1·7 km (Hewson & Taylor

1968), but extent of home range uncertain. Pielowski (1972) gave 330 ha for Poland and densities of 50 hares to 100 ha. Little seasonal change in habitat. Normally solitary or during breeding season in pairs or small groups. Usually silent but loud scream when hurt or frightened, also low grunt.

FOOD Few systematic observations. Grass, particularly in May–June and after grass cutting; cereal crops in spring and early summer; turnip bulbs in winter, showing preferences for particular varieties (author's data). Andrzejewski & Pucek (1965) considered that feeding on farm crops—leaves of corn near ground, young leaves of root crops—not of economic importance in Poland. Tears strips of bark from young trees but less destructive than rabbit. Soft faeces produced during the day are re-ingested (Watson & Taylor 1955).

BREEDING No systematic account available of spectacular courtship and aggressive behaviour, which includes 'boxing', chasing, leaping and enurination (Boback 1954). Pregnant females found in north-east Scotland in 7–12 months of each of 13 consecutive years, usually 8–11 months. Incidence of pregnancy rose from 11% in January to over 90% in April and May, then declined to 11% in November and 4% in December. Embryo counts varied from means of 2·0 in January to maximum of 3·2 in May, and remained at 2·0 or more to October (Hewson & Taylor, 1975). Gestation period 42 days, probably 3–4 litters per year. Superfoetation uncommon, Lloyd (1968) finding one example in 69 pregnant females collected in Cambridgeshire. Andrzejewski & Pucek (1965) found embryonic losses of 50–80% in Poland. Young born fully furred, weighing about 110 g, and deposited in forms. They reach adult weight in about 240 days (Pielowski 1971a).

Breeding in year of birth was recorded by Flux (1967) in New Zealand, who also showed that the breeding seasons of *L. capensis* in New Zealand, Australia, Canada, Scotland and USSR are similar, starting soon after shortest day regardless of environmental conditions (Flux 1965).

POPULATION STRUCTURE Little information for Britain; Pielowski (1971b) considered hares in Poland had physiological life of up to 12–13 years, but only about 6% over $5\frac{1}{2}$ years old, and no males over 4 years. Andrzejewski & Pucek (1965) found about 34% under one year old in autumn population. These can be distinguished by notch at epiphysis of tibia or ulna up to about 8 months. Lloyd (1968) found that 23–30% of 91 females killed in Cambridgeshire in January–February 1965 were less than one year old.

Sex ratio normally near 1:1 in killed samples. Densities estimated at one hare to 2·4–5·5 ha in Poland (Petrusewicz 1970); in England one to 4 ha (Rothschild & Marsh 1956), and one to 2–3 ha (Lloyd 1968). Numbers thought to have increased following reduction of rabbits by myxomatosis, but Andersen (1957) showed an overall increase in hares killed in 63 districts of Denmark from 1903 to 1943, and a tendency towards peak numbers at about 9-yearly intervals.

PREDATORS AND MORTALITY Little information on predation. Fox is likeliest predator, but leverets could be taken by domestic cat, buzzard or stoat. Mortality due to coccidiosis in young (Rieck 1956).

PARASITES AND DISEASE Rabbit fleas, *Spilopsyllus cuniculi*, occur commonly as do sheep ticks, *Ixodes ricinus*, and the sucking louse *Haemodipus lyriocephalus*.

In a survey of animals from the Berkshire Downs nematodes of the genus *Trichostrongylus* were present in all stomachs with the nematode *Graphidium strigosum* in 63% and the tapeworm *Cittotaenia* sp. in 37% of small intestines (Irvin 1970).

RELATIONS WITH MAN Esteemed as a game animal, for shooting and coursing, over many years but more recently destroyed as a pest of agriculture and of little sporting value. Carcases becoming more valuable and status as sporting animal may change. Extent of damage to farm crops uncertain. Easily reared in captivity.

LITERATURE Eabry (1969): an extensive bibliography.

AUTHOR FOR THIS SPECIES R. Hewson.

Mountain hare *Lepus timidus*

Lepus timidus Linnaeus, 1758, Upsala, Sweden. *Lepus variabilis* Pallas, 1778. *Lepus hibernicus* Bell, 1837; Ireland. *Lepus timidus lutescens* Barrett-Hamilton, 1900; Donobate, Co. Dublin, Ireland. *Lepus timidus scoticus* Hilzheimer, 1906; N. Scotland.
Blue hare, varying hare, Arctic hare, Irish hare.

RECOGNITION In summer coat distinguishable from brown hare by shorter ears, greyer coat and absence of black top to the tail. In winter white or in transitional pelage.

SIGN Moves through heather on conspicuous trails, which usually lie up and down hill and are maintained by the hares biting off heather tips. Track not distinguishable from that of brown hare although hind feet

FIGURE 55 Mountain hare in November but retaining summer pelage. (Photo: A. Tewnion)

in winter, being heavily furred, leave unexpectedly large impression in snow. Droppings about 1 cm in diameter, brown or grey-green, fibrous. Form usually in long old heather, with stems up to 6 mm bitten through.

DESCRIPTION Smaller, stockier animal than brown hare, with shorter ears. In summer and autumn coat dusky brown, with grey-blue underfur showing through particularly at flanks. Moults three times each year; brown to brown (early June–mid September), brown to white (mid October–early February, although main moult finishes in December), and white to brown (mid February–late May). Some hares, particularly late leverets, do not whiten fully (Hewson 1958). Rate of moulting in spring influenced by altitude and temperature (Watson 1963). Irish race much redder and in winter moults only to a piebald coat or may not whiten at all.

MEASUREMENTS See Tables 10 and 11.

DISTRIBUTION See Fig. 57. Tundra and boreal forest zones throughout the Palaearctic and the tundra zone of North America (*L. t. arcticus*) and Greenland (*L. t. groenlandicus*). Isolates in the Alps (*L. t. varronis*) and on Hokkaido (*L. t. ainu*).

In the British Isles indigenous in the Highlands of Scotland and in

TABLE 10 Measurements of mountain hares (from Barrett-Hamilton & Hinton 1911–21)

	Scotland (*n*=45) Range	Mean	Ireland (*n*=27) Range	Mean
Head and body (mm)	457–545	502	521–559	545
Tail (without hairs) (mm)	43–80	60	65–83	74
Hind feet (with claws) (mm)	127–155	142	149–168	156
Ear (to notch) (mm)	63–80	70	69–81	75
Weight (kg)	(see Table 11)		2·7–3·6	3·2

Ireland. Most numerous on grouse moors in North-East Scotland, where heather management for grouse favours hares also (Hewson 1954). Uncommon on arctic-alpine ground in west Scotland and low moors in western Ireland and even scarcer on low moors in west Scotland (Watson

FIGURE 56 Mountain hare in winter pelage. (Photo: A. Tewnion)

TABLE 11 Weights of mountain hares in North-East Scotland (Hewson 1968)

	Adult males		Adult females	
	Mean	*n*	Mean	*n*
Autumn/winter	2·7 kg	69	2·9 kg	59
Spring/summer	2·6 kg	102	3·1 kg	104
	First winter animals about 0·3 kg less than adults			

& Hewson 1973). Introduced, mostly during the nineteenth century, to Shetland, Orkney, Outer Hebrides, Skye, Raasay, Scalpay, Eigg (now extinct), Mull, Islay (now extinct) and Jura. The Scottish Lowlands were colonised from introductions into Ayrshire and elsewhere about the middle of the nineteenth century, and the Pennine areas of south Yorkshire and Derbyshire from introductions there about 1880. In North Wales few mountain hares remain from introductions near Bangor about 1885. Yalden (1971) found that in recent years the area occupied by mountain hares in the Peak District may be decreasing.

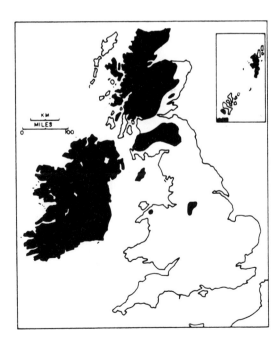

FIGURE 57 Mountain hare: distribution.

VARIATION The population in Ireland represents a distinctive sub-species, *L. t. hibernicus*, characterised by the russet colour of the pelage and the absence of complete winter whitening. They are larger on average than Scottish animals (Table 10) but are comparable in size to many continental forms.

The Scottish form, *L. t. scoticus*, is generally considered to be sub-specifically distinct from continental animals on the basis of its small size (occipito-nasal length of skull 83–89 mm in Scotland, usually over 89 mm on the Continent).

In South-West Scotland the descendants of Irish hares introduced about 1923 were still noticeably redder, and thirty years later had moulted less completely than the Scottish race from the same locality. Yellowish variety not uncommon in both races and black animals are recorded from time to time in part of Caithness.

HABITAT Heather moorland and the arctic/alpine zone of Scottish mountains. Feeds mostly on heather but also on upland pastures and occasionally on farm crops. Form, or day resting place at burrow entrance, usually in upper part of home range, feeding grounds lower. In North-West and West Scotland mountain hares frequent dry rocky hilltops, sheltering in boulder fields. Irish race occupies lower ground in absence of brown hare, and in the Peak District (Yalden 1971) mountain hares are confined to *Calluna-Eriophorum* moorland between 300 m and 550 m.

BEHAVIOUR Less timid than brown hare. Move to feeding grounds about dusk and return after dawn, but will graze in daylight before rain or during snow. May feed close to other hares on small patches of short heather, or with brown hares and rabbits in upland pastures. Home range 20–28 ha and overlapping; similar for adults and juveniles of both sexes (Hewson 1974). Flux (1970) gave daytime ranges of 16 ha for adult males and 10 ha for adult females. No evidence of dispersal of marked juvenile or adult hares. On hilly ground home range is long and narrow, lying up and down hill. Hares sit tight in heather in summer (moulting?) but move to open faces in winter and spring and become more wary. Some move to higher ground in summer (Flux 1970). Dig short simple burrows *c.* 2 m long or take over rabbit burrow; function of these is unknown and hares usually sit at entrance and run away if disturbed. Small leverets readily escape into burrows, though most young probably born above ground. Adults usually solitary or in pairs but groups occur in breeding season and at feeding places.

FOOD Mainly heather *Calluna vulgaris*, in winter 90% and from April to October about 50%, with cotton grass *Eriophorum* spp. and grasses. Short young heather is preferred and may become overgrazed, when hares will feed on *Erica* spp. and old heather. Heath rush (*Juncus squarrosus*), bilberry (*Vaccinium myrtillus*) and deer sedge (*Tricophorum caespitosum*) are minor constituents of diet of hares on heather moorland. During deep or ice-crusted snow hares eat gorse (*Ulex europaeus*), soft rush (*Juncus effusus*), and bark and twigs of willow (*Salix* spp.), rowan (*Sorbus aucuparia*), juniper (*Juniperus communis*), and occasionally birch *Betula* spp. In stormy weather, groups of up to 40 may gather in sheltered places to feed (Hewson 1962, 1964). Refection occurs from 09·00 h to 16·00 h and about 200 hard pellets are excreted daily (Flux 1970).

BREEDING Courtship behaviour more subdued than that of brown hare, with one or more males following a female at a slow lope. When female halts, male approaches and may be struck at or chased by female. Mating rarely seen, but Flux (1970) saw two cases in each of which 7 hares, including 5 males, were involved. However hares often in pairs during breeding season. Males fecund by end January, females pregnant February–August, rarely September or later. Three litters likely but four theoretically possible, with 6–7 young produced per female annually (Hewson 1970). Flux (1970) found mean number of embryos per female was 2·1, average number of litters 2·6, and total prenatal mortality estimated at 47%. No record of hares breeding in the year of their birth. On a moor with much young, nutritious heather hares bred earlier and had bigger litters than on a moor not so well managed (Hewson 1970).

POPULATION STRUCTURE Up to 50% of leverets in autumn. Age structure on study area in North-East Scotland varied according to population phase. At high numbers and subsequent decline 75% of adults and 84% of leverets died within a year of marking. At low numbers and during increase more three-year-old adults were caught than two-year-old, and 30% of leverets were recovered in the third to seventh year after marking. Oldest hares were at least 9 years. Sex ratio did not vary significantly during population changes (Hewson 1974). Most numerous on eastern grouse moors reaching 2·45 hares/ha (Watson *et al.* 1973). Uncommon on west Scottish moors and Irish bogs, one hare to 80 ha (Watson & Hewson 1973). Population fluctuations often long-term but regular cycle uncertain.

PREDATORS AND MORTALITY Fox is main predator (over two-thirds of kills) but wild cats and golden eagles kill adults and so occasionally do stoats. Nesting hen harriers take leverets up to 20 days old; buzzards also take older leverets (Flux 1970, Hewson 1974).

PARASITES AND DISEASE Ticks (*Ixodes ricinus*), rabbit fleas (*Spilopsyllus cuniculi*) and the sucking louse (*Haemodipsus lyriocephalus*) occur but the frequency of infestation is unknown.

Fourteen mountain hares from Banffshire had the nematode worm *Graphidium strigosum* in 21% of stomachs and *Trichostrongylus* sp. in 100%. The tapeworm *Cittotaenia* sp. was present in 29% of small intestines (Irvin 1970).

RELATIONS WITH MAN Killed in large numbers as pest on heather moorland, and until recently carcases of little value. Breeds successfully in captivity in Sweden but has proved difficult to keep alive in hutches and runs in Britain.

AUTHOR FOR THIS SPECIES R. Hewson.

Order Rodentia
Rodents

This is the largest order of mammals with about 1500 species worldwide, the majority mouse- or rat-sized. They occupy all terrestrial and fresh-water habitats and many species are individually very abundant.

The most striking morphological characteristic of rodents is the form of the teeth. The incisors are reduced to a single pair above and below. They grow continuously from open roots and have chisel-shaped cutting edges. The lower ones in particular occupy extremely long sockets that may extend back almost to the articulation of the jaw. There is a long gap (diastema), without canines, between the incisors and the cheek-teeth which number from 3 to 5 in each row. The way in which the jaw muscles are modified for gnawing varies greatly from group to group and influences the overall shape of the skull. The majority of rodents are seed-eaters but some are insectivorous, many are herbivorous and some are very versatile omnivores.

Fifteen species are present in Britain of which at least six have been introduced by man. They are classified in five families to which could be added one more for the extinct beaver. The characters of the extant families are tabulated in Table 12. All these characters do not apply consistently to exotic species.

FAMILY CASTORIDAE
GENUS *Castor*

Contains only the beavers, of which there are one or two species according to whether the Old and New World forms are considered conspecific or not.

Beaver *Castor fiber*

Castor fiber Linnaeus, 1758; Sweden.

Extinct in Britain but survives in parts of Europe, western and central Siberia and in North America although the American form is sometimes treated as a distinct species.

TABLE 12 The principal characteristics of the families of rodents

	Sciuridae squirrels	Gliridae dormice	Muridae rats & mice	Cricetidae voles	Capromyidae coypu
Length of head and body (mm)	200–300	60–180	60–250	80–220	400–600
Tail: length relative to head and body	80–90%	80–90%	80–120%	25–60%	70–80%
Tail: shape	Bushy	Bushy	Almost naked	Almost naked	Almost naked
Cheek teeth: number in each row above/below	5/4	4/4	3/3	3/3	4/4
Cheek-teeth: shape	Low-crowned, cusped	Low-crowned, transverse ridges	Low-crowned, cusped	High-crowned, alternating prisms, $\pm$ roots	High-crowned, transverse ridges
Habitat	Woodland, arboreal	Woodland, shrubs	Woodland, scrub, commensal	Open ground, aquatic	Aquatic

Subfossil remains abundant in Britain, especially in the peat of the Fens and East Anglia. Historical records suggest that it survived in Wales as late as the end of the twelfth century and perhaps later in Scotland. Apparently never occurred in Ireland.

FAMILY SCIURIDAE
SQUIRRELS

The squirrels are one of the larger families of rodents with about 50 genera and well over two hundred species, on all continents except Australasia and Antarctica. The nocturnal flying squirrels, mostly in the Oriental Region, form a clearly defined subfamily (Petauristinae). The remainder are diurnal (subfamily Sciurinae) and predominantly tree squirrels, but other ground-burrowing types, with intermediate tree-climbing forms like chipmunks, include many species of strictly ter-restrial ground squirrels, like marmots and sousliks. Some burrowing species hibernate but tree squirrels do not.

Squirrels are characterised by relatively unspecialised teeth and jaw muscles compared with other rodents. There are one or two premolars in each toothrow in addition to three molars.

GENUS *Sciurus*

Contains three Palaearctic species and up to fifty species in North and South America (depending whether certain New World species are included in the genus). In Britain the indigenous red squirrel and the introduced grey squirrel are very closely related and, although they are frequently placed in separate subgenera, there is no justification for separating the grey squirrel into genus *Neosciurus*. The genus is fairly typical

FIGURE 58 Grey squirrel (left) and red squirrel (right).

of tree squirrels, and several other large genera such as *Callosciurus* in South East Asia and *Heliosciurus* in Africa, do not differ greatly from *Sciurus*.

Red squirrel *Sciurus vulgaris*

Sciurus vulgaris Linnaeus, 1758; Upsala, Sweden. *Sciurus vulgaris leucourus* Kerr, 1792; England.
Common squirrel, brown squirrel, light-tailed squirrel, con, skug, and numerous dialect variants of squirrel. Note: the red squirrel of North America is in a different genus, *Tamiasciurus hudsonicus*.

RECOGNITION (Fig. 58) Arboreal with large bushy tail. Upper parts are relatively uniform brown which may vary between individuals from

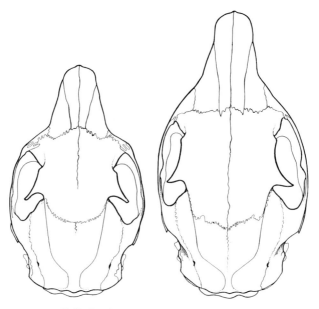

FIGURE 59 Skulls of red squirrel (left) and grey squirrel (right).

FIGURE 60 Cones of Scots pine stripped by red squirrels. (Photo: A. M. Tittensor)

deep brown through rich chestnut to pale greyish brown. Ear tufts prominent in winter coat only. Grey squirrel, which is larger, may show some reddish brown but only quite exceptionally so uniformly as in red squirrel. Skull shorter (under 55 mm) but relatively deeper than grey squirrel, with smaller nasal bones (Fig. 59).

SIGN Obvious signs are compact leaf-nests (dreys), usually built near trunk of conifer, and feeding remains on forest floor (Fig. 60). These consist of stripped cores and scattered scales of cones (birds splay and split scales leaving very ragged sign rather than clean-cut edges left by squirrels), split shells or husks of mast (in halves or larger clean-cut holes than mice or dormice), cut tree shoots and buds, strips of bud scales, toothmarks on fungi (incisor marks larger than mice and voles, and unlike ragged bird pecks or slimy irregular holes of slugs). Also stripped bark on conifer trunks, often in long spiral twists.

Tracks between tree bases show widely separated print sets, usually with no tail scuffing; prints show four distinct claws on forefeet but five on hindfeet and are about 3 cm wide. Sometimes chipped and scratched bark on tree trunks. Droppings variable, but relatively small and widely scattered; urine often confined to localised sites which may have social significance.

DESCRIPTION In British Isles summer coat chestnut red above, ear tufts sparse and pale or absent, tail hairs thin and ranging from red brown through buff to creamy white. Winter coat thicker, brownish grey above, ear tufts long, thick and brown, tail hairs dense and blackish becoming dark brown. White underparts distinct from back colour. Sexes alike in colouring. Juveniles similar but more intense red; moult from nestling to appropriate seasonal coat after weaning. Body fur moults spring and autumn, but ear tufts and tail hairs only once, before autumn moult; timing variable. Moult proceeds front to back in spring but in reverse direction in autumn. Whole winter coat becomes progressively paler, interrupted by spring moult in the case of the body fur, but ear tufts and tail hairs (from tip forwards) continue to bleach, producing some individuals with white eartufts and tails from June onwards. Differences in rate and extent of bleaching, and in timing of moult, cause considerable and continuously changing individual variation, quite apart from any influence of foreign stock.

Body shows adaptations for climbing and leaping; bones are relatively light and hind limbs disproportionately long and heavy. Feet plantigrade; all toes long except fore-thumbs which are reduced to small tubercles. Long curved claws give good grip and ability to hang by only one or two claws. Tail well developed, aiding balance as well as having an expressive use; hairs controlled by muscles which enable them to be fluffed or flattened (Barrett-Hamilton & Hinton 1910–21). Fluffed tail, spread limbs, and loose skin on flanks help sustain height when leaping.

Sexes differ by distance between genital opening and anus (close in females but about 1 cm apart in males). Testes usually abdominal in autumn but retractable at any time; baculum can be used to determine age (Degn 1973). Male reproductive organs described by Grosz (1905); accessory glands enlarge seasonally. Vulva obviously swollen at oestrus; 4 pairs of nipples (difficult to find in immature females).

Skull described in detail by Barrett-Hamilton & Hinton (1910–21); in comparison with grey squirrel has condylo-basal length under 50 mm, nasals under 16 mm, cranium deeper, and post-orbital processes longer and narrower. Full tooth formula:

$$\frac{1.0.2.3}{1.0.1.3}.$$

Incisors grow continuously; upper first premolar is a peg-like vestige, the remaining upper cheek-teeth with prominent inner cusps and transverse ridges, lower with large concavities. Teeth erupt from 3 weeks onwards, incisors first, and first dentition is complete soon after 10 weeks; deciduous teeth are limited to lower and second upper premolars which are shed from 16 weeks onwards. Wear of cheek-teeth (Kiris 1937) and growth of cementum (Lemnell 1973) can be used to determine age, as can weight of eye-lens (Karpukhin & Karpukhina 1971, Degn 1973, Lemnell 1973) and epiphyseal fusion of long bones (Degn 1973, Lemnell 1973). Skeleton illustrated by Shorten (1962b).

Chromosomes: $2n = 40$ (material from Hokkaido: Hsu & Benirschke 1970).

MEASUREMENTS Marginally smaller than some continental subspecies. Head and body about 205 to 220 mm (range 180 to 240 mm) and tail about 170 to 180 mm (range 140 to 195 mm), depending on method used; hind foot without claws averages 54 to 56 mm (range 49 to 63 mm). Condylo-basal length between 44 and 48 mm and nasal length 13 to 16 mm (Miller 1912). Juveniles first active away from drey at 80 or 90 g (7 or 8 weeks) and independent around 100 to 150 g (10 to 16 weeks), reaching adult weight in 6 or 7 months. No significant weight difference between sexes of adults. Data from East Scotland: males 279 g (range 230–340 g, $n = 323$), females 278 g (range 220–355 g, $n = 244$) (author's data); and from East Anglia: males 300 g (range 260–435 g, $n = 58$), females 296 g (range 260–345 g, $n = 70$) (Shorten & Courtier, unpubl.). Regional variation probably insignificant compared with differences between seasons and years; lightest late winter and spring, heaviest late summer and autumn. Emaciated female down to 195 g and large male up to 480 g recorded. Weight is no criterion of pregnancy, thus female of 445 g was not pregnant.

DISTRIBUTION See Fig. 61. Throughout wooded parts of Eurasia, from Mediterranean in Balkans to northern Scandinavia and from Spain eastwards through USSR to North China, Korea and Hokkaido. Replaced in rest of Japan by *S. lis* and from Caucasus and Asia Minor to Iran by *S. anomalus*.

Formerly throughout mainland Britain and Ireland where trees available, but range has been contracting since 1940's and now absent from most of central southern England. Still common in parts of East Anglia, North Wales, northern England, and widespread in Scotland (but absent from far north and central Lowlands) and Ireland. Present on Jersey, Isle of Wight, Brownsea Island, Anglesey, Arran and possibly Skye.

Numbers have undergone considerable long-term fluctuations within historic times. Extinct in Ireland and southern Scotland by early eighteenth century, and close to extinction in Scottish Highlands during late eighteenth and early nineteenth centuries (Moffat 1938, Harvie-Brown

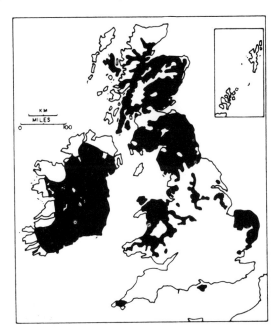

FIGURE 61 Red squirrel: distribution.

1880–81). No contemporary scarcity known in England and Wales, but such may have happened before written records. Reintroduced to Scotland (mainly from England) at 10 or more sites between 1772 and 1872 (Harvie-Brown 1880–81) and to Ireland (from England) at about 10 sites between 1815 and 1856 (Barrington 1880). Period of superabundance throughout British Isles from about 1860, reaching a peak between 1890 and 1900, followed shortly by extensive decline. Partial recovery by 1930, but lost considerable ground during 1940's and at a slower rate to the present, becoming extinct over large areas of England and Wales except for small pockets. However recent expansion in North West Scotland. Declines are largely independent of influence from grey squirrel and main cause probably widespread habitat destruction; epidemic disease may have accelerated losses but unlikely to be fundamental cause. However, their return over large areas apparently prevented by presence of grey squirrels.

VARIATION Endemic British and Irish race, *S. v. leucourus*, clearly definable by progressive bleaching of ear tufts and tail, and lack of dark phase. No evidence of geographical variation within Britain, apart from confusion due to introduced forms, but considerable individual colour variation. True melanism (including underside) extremely rare in Britain if it occurs. Sporadic albinism plus parti-coloured intermediates occur in endemic and continental races. All-red form, including underside, reported in Germany.

Over 40 subspecies, not all valid, listed by Ellerman & Morrison-Scott (1951); races predominantly dimorphic with red and dark brown (or blackish) phases, plus a range of intermediates, freely interbreeding; detailed hair structure and pigmentation described by Lühring (1928). Relative proportion of phases varies geographically, connected with habitat characteristics and altitude, but stable at any one site (Voipio 1969). Dimorphic races introduced to Britain include *S. v. vulgaris* (=*varius*) from Scandinavia and *S. v. fuscoater* (=*russus*) from western Europe (distribution and characteristics in Sidorowicz 1958, 1961); former introduced to Perthshire in 1793 (Harvie-Brown 1880–81 and flea evidence), and latter probably to Lothians about 1860 and Epping Forest about 1910 (Harvie-Brown 1880–81; Shorten 1954). Dark-coloured phases also reported elsewhere in Britain (for example by Clegg 1970) presumably introduced continental forms causing locally greater colour variation.

HABITAT Most abundant in large blocks (50 hectares upwards) of mature conifer forest including dense plantations. Endemic race particularly adapted to native Scots pine which provides main foods and cover, but some introduced conifers are suitable substitutes; pine produces most reliable seed crop, drey sites and continuous aerial canopy when between 25 and 80 years old. Less abundant in small conifer woods, overmature conifer, and mixed woods containing a significant proportion of conifer. Overflows into pure hardwood (especially beech) or sparsely wooded areas when numerous, but these provide less stable food supply. Immature woodland of all types used for foraging rather than residence.

BEHAVIOUR Gait on ground a series of short leaps or runs on an erratic course, tail held out behind; frequent pauses, and in alert position rears up on hind limbs, tail flat along ground, ears erect and obvious sniffing. Climbs trees rapidly with tail aiding balance and shows great agility when jumping; descends more jerkily head first. Evades detection by moving to far side of trunk, or remains motionless, pressed flat to bark. Able to swim.

Diurnal. Activity starts within $\frac{1}{2}$ hour each side of sunrise; main peak for 3 or 4 hours after dawn, with sporadic activity throughout day, and lesser peak for 2 or 3 hours before dusk. In winter, with shorter day length, two peaks merge to concentrate activity around midday (author's data). High wind, heavy rain or snow inhibit activity; availability and type of food supply also influence routine. Rest in drey or on secluded branch; no hibernation and unable to live more than a few days without food. Dreys compact, spherical (about 30 cm diameter) and normally built next to main trunk of pine, spruce or larch; only exceptionally below 3 m and usually above 8 m. Outer frame usually of conifer twigs, with needles when fresh; central cavity (12 to 16 cm diameter) lined with grass, moss, and other soft material (Abe 1967, Tittensor 1970). Hollow trees (dens) used, but less important in Britain.

Overlapping home ranges show considerable variation in size and shape; three-dimensional with height important. In East Scotland mean trap-revealed range in Scots pine habitat was $470 \times 285 \times 15$ m (29 sampled), with little difference between sexes (author's data); in Sweden male summer activity radius of 107 m reducing to 61 m or less in winter, by radio telemetry (Lemnell 1970), and in Japan 500×55 m by observation (Abe 1967). Summer and autumn movement of juveniles before taking up residence. Dreys apparently placed anywhere within home range, and do not show the regular dispersion expected for a territorial mammal. Density of 12 dreys per hectare, in present or recent use, found in pine woodland, suggesting several dreys per squirrel (author's data).

Much non-sexual agonistic behaviour throughout year, usually involving 2 or 3 males, and high speed chasing, biting of tails and screaming.

Probably hierarchical social structure, with dominant males consistently heavier, longer-lived and with larger ranges (author's data).

Vocal communication, consisting of a chucking call with answering sounds, can be heard throughout year; 'chuck' varies from soft to loud, also explosive 'wrruhh' sound, and various moans and teeth chattering. Young emit shrill piping call. Vocal sounds are accompanied by equivalent body posture; harsh aggressive 'chuck' associated with vigorous tail flicking and foot stamping. Eibl-Eibesfeldt (1951) described postures associated with courtship, aggressive and defensive behaviour. Possibility of scent marking but no evidence.

Eye with exceptional focussing power and wide-angled vision but poor colour discrimination; blind spot a slender horizontal stripe above centre to give minimum interference with vertical objects and clear upward vision. Hearing not exceptional, but smell acute. Several groups of tactile hairs, most prominent on juveniles.

FOOD Granivorous herbivore. Wide range of foods acceptable, but tree seed or mast, assorted tree foliage, and fungi are basic diet items; list and seasonal preferences in Tittensor (1975). Native Scots pine is major food source in main habitat, providing seed from cones, leaf and flower buds, shoots and needles, pollen from male flowers, and sappy tissue under bark; staple diet for 11 or 12 months of year is pine seed, starting on green cones in midsummer, continuing on brown cones through winter, until seed shed following spring or early summer—mainly eaten in canopy during autumn and winter, but forced increasingly to forage on ground through spring to summer as crop depletes (author's data). Usually an early summer gap of a few weeks (variable between years and localities) between successive crops, when alternative foods become important; also when cone crop partly or completely fails large quantities of other foods sought. Similar range of food taken from alternative conifers (including larches, spruces, other pines and Douglas fir) and mast, buds, shoots, leaves, pollen and galls from numerous hardwoods (including beech, oak, sweet chestnut, sycamore, hazel and hawthorn), plus berries, seeds, pollen, leaves, roots, bulbs and tubers from assorted small shrubs and non-woody plants. Ascomycete and basidiomycete fungi (hyphae and fruiting bodies) are most important non-arboreal item of diet. Small amount of animal matter taken, including eggs, young and adults of insects and birds. Soil ingested for roughage or minerals; incisors trimmed on bark, bones and stones (which may also provide calcium). Water requirements obtained from food or dew, but may seek standing water in hot weather.

Food items detected by smell, then mouthed before selection. Attached foods gnawed free and carried in mouth to feeding site near centre of tree canopy; if picked up from ground, often taken to raised stump or into canopy to eat. Foods held and rotated by forefeet, while squatting or hanging. Cone scales gnawed off from base to expose seeds, seedwings discarded. In Scots pine forest over half of active period and much energy are spent feeding, utilising some 100 to 150 cones per day and taking about 3 minutes per cone; cones each contain an average of 30 seeds, weighing between 0·1 to 0·2 g in total, and representing a daily consumption of about 5% of body weight (author's data). Hazel nuts and other mast dealt with as for grey squirrel. Main purpose of bark stripping is to obtain sappy tissue below, and most prevalent at time of early summer gap; bark gnawed off and dropped, and pulled back in spiral twists by forefeet, while tissue below is consumed. May also have some social significance, and it has been suggested that it is a behavioural trait caused by stress; strips sometimes used in drey construction.

Large-scale food stores (caches) in hollow trees or dreys exceptional; haphazard storage of mast, singly or in small groups, in ground, tree hollows and clefts, and dreys is a response to food surplus. Fungi stored in tree clefts or hung on twigs. Cones not normally buried when they are readily available on trees throughout the winter. Relocation of stored food as for grey squirrel; an adaptation much more important in severe climates of East Europe and Asia.

BREEDING Males fecund most of the year, normally with only a short non-active period from August to October (Delost 1966); females polyoestrous, with no post-partum oestrus until young partially weaned (about 10 weeks after first conception), usually sexually active by January, but variable. Length and success of breeding season influenced by preceding food availability and weather. Courtship occurs during first half of year; lengthy process with close contact display and slow motion chasing leading up to mating (Eibl-Eibesfeldt 1951) and apparently polygamous. Pregnancies found between December and September (Rowlands 1938, Shorten 1962c), but two main periods in British Isles giving spring (January/March) and summer (May/July) litters. Mature females capable of producing two litters, yearling females one litter per season. Gestation about 36 to 42 days (38 days observed by Eibl-Eibesfeldt 1951). Litter size averages 3, normal range 1 to 6, occasionally more (mean 3·2, $n = 81$—Shorten & Courtier, unpubl.), with summer litters (mean 3·6) larger than spring (mean 3·0) but poorer survival. Some uterine loss, and even higher losses during weaning. Breeding drey lined with exceptionally thick layer of soft material (Tittensor 1970); if litter disturbed, young may be carried in female's mouth to alternative nest. Lactation 7 to 10 weeks; male apparently takes no part in raising young.

Young blind, deaf and naked at birth, weighing 10 to 15 g (Eibl-Ebesfeldt 1951, Frank 1952). Pigment appears on back, with hairs emerging at 8 to 9 days, giving thin downy covering by 13 days, and dense coat at 19 days. Lower incisors erupt at 20 to 25 days, eyes open at 28 to 32 days (weight about 50 g) and upper incisors erupt at 37 to 41 days. Begin exploration and eating solids at 7 weeks, and weaned at 8 to 10 weeks as cheek-teeth develop. By 16 weeks nestling coat replaced by seasonal pelage. Maternal protective behaviour extends beyond weaning period. Young sometimes capable of breeding at 6 months, but normally at least 10 to 12 months.

POPULATION In favourable pine woodland habitat minimum densities of 0·8 squirrels per hectare in East Scotland (author's data) and 0·5 squirrels per hectare in East Anglia (Shorten 1962b) have been recorded. Sex ratio variable, seasonally biased by method of data collection, but approximates to 1 : 1, with periodic excess of one sex. Autumn recruitment to exploited populations in USSR found to be 300 to 400% per year after good seed crops but only 75% after poor crops (Kiris 1937). Recruitment to the following year's adult breeding stock of an unexploited population in East Scotland found to be 20 to 40% per year, well below reproductive potential, with greatest contribution from spring litters; complete population turnover period estimated at minimum of 4 to 5 years (author's data). Population increases from January to July, falling again during autumn. Considerable short-term fluctuations between years, following abundance of conifer seeds (Formosov 1933, Lampio 1952).

In captivity live to at least 10 years; at least 5 years recorded in wild. Tooth-wear suggests an age-class of over 6 years (Kiris 1937). Young squirrels that survived to leave the drey in unexploited population in E. Scotland had a mean expectation of life of about 3 years (author's data).

PREDATORS AND MORTALITY Relatively little predation on adults, due to arboreal habit; can form significant part of diet of wildcat and pine marten but area of overlap restricted in Britain. Stoats can climb and occasionally prey on the young. Greatest risk on ground, especially young, and predation recorded by fox, domestic dog and cat, golden eagle, buzzard, goshawk and some other raptors and owls. Intraspecific aggression and conflicts with grey squirrel occasionally results in death. A few deaths result from natural accident—drowning, forest fire, tree falls—but starvation prevalent after failure of cone crop, associated with mass migration (especially northern Eurasia) and high incidence of parasites, disease and predation. Man, apart from control and road mortality, has greatest effect by altering or destroying habitat.

PARASITES AND DISEASE Flea *Monopsyllus sciurorum* specific to red squirrel and common throughout British Isles, while flea *Orchopeas howardi*, introduced with the grey squirrel from North America, is sometimes found (Shorten 1954b, Blackmore & Owen 1968); *Tarsopsylla octodecimdentata*, a red squirrel nest flea, found over most of Eurasia including Scandinavia, is known only from a small area of North East Scotland, and almost certainly introduced with *S. v. vulgaris* to Dunkeld in 1793 (George, unpubl.). Ticks and mites non-specific; most frequent tick is *Ixodes ricinus*, and mite of genus *Sarcoptes* is possibly associated with mange disease. Sucking lice include *Enderleinellus nitzchi* and *Neohaematopinus sciuri*.

Non-pathogenic ringworm fungus, *Microsporum cookei*, has been found (English 1971). Mange or scab disease causes epidemics described by Edwards (1962); viral agent has been isolated (Vizoso *et al.* 1964, Vizoso 1968). Enteritis, and coccidiosis caused by protozoan *Eimeria*, known. Shock disease, associated with hypoglycaemia and caused by exposure or fear, usually results in death.

RELATIONS WITH MAN Regarded by many as aesthetically attractive and in need of conservation as part of our native forest fauna; present decline is however a regional rather than national problem. No short-term solution is available, but long-term forestry planning for conservation should concentrate on main coniferous habitat; favourable habitat can be provided by growing a continuous succession of mature Scots pine (or suitable introduced substitute conifers) over a large and continuous area, with progressive thinning rather than clear-felling, and keeping the hardwood content low (Tittensor 1975).

Forestry pest potentially of economic importance; serious damage caused during superabundance in late nineteenth century, and numerous enough at present to cause timber damage to conifers in East Scotland, northern England and East Anglia. Strips bark as part of normal feeding behaviour from main trunk, usually within 4 or 5 metres of leading shoot, particularly on Scots pine, but also European larch, lodgepole pine and Norway spruce (Shorten 1957); other tree species occasionally attacked. Complete girdling rare, results in top die-back and windsnap; normally wounds heal over, leaving timber calluses. Removal of buds and shoots can cause growth distortion in young plantations, while cone utilisation can be a nuisance in seed orchards. Occasional damage to cereal crops, orchards and soft fruit. Control by cage trapping or shooting, immediately before and during damage period. Not regarded as a resource in Britain but in parts of Europe and Asia provides sport, food and pelts.

Difficult to tame in captivity when adult and high death rate results, but easily handled when reared from young. If kept in small cages requires opportunity to exercise; can be bred in larger outdoor cages, with raised nest boxes and branches provided.

LITERATURE Shorten (1954b)—monograph on biology and history of both squirrels; Shorten (1962b)—popular, well illustrated account; Shorten (1962c)—summary of biology and history of both squirrels; Tittensor (1975)—recent account of biology.

AUTHOR FOR THIS SPECIES A. M. Tittensor.

Grey squirrel *Sciurus carolinensis*

Sciurus carolinensis Gmelin, 1788; Carolina, USA. *Neosciurus carolinensis*.
Sciurus leucotis Gapper, 1830; Ontario, Canada.
American grey squirrel, eastern gray squirrel (in North America).
Note: western gray squirrel is *S. griseus*.

RECOGNITION (Fig. 58) Arboreal with large bushy tail. Upper parts grey with yellowish brown along back, with chestnut on flanks and limbs in summer, but only quite exceptionally uniform brown. Brown ear tufts present in winter but very rarely prominent. Red squirrel, which is smaller, may be ashy grey in winter but ear tufts prominent, and brown on legs and tail. Fat dormouse, which is also arboreal but much smaller, has dark stripes on legs and is nocturnal. Skull longer (to 65 mm) but relatively shallower than red squirrel, with larger nasal bones (Fig. 59).

SIGN Large leaf-nests (dreys) untidy and more obvious than those of red squirrel, often built away from main trunk and in hardwoods, but summer platform nests and tree hollows (dens) are also used. Feeding remains indistinguishable from those of red squirrel, consisting of split shells or husks of mast (in halves or with larger clean-cut holes), stripped cone cores and scales, cut tree shoots and buds, strips of bud scales, toothmarks on fungi. Also stripped bark on trunks of hardwoods, with shredded bark lying at tree base, and gnawed marker points on lower trunks and branches (described by Taylor 1968).

Tracks between tree bases as for red squirrel, with similar print size.

Chipped and scratched bark more obvious on smooth trunks. Droppings variable, cylindrical or round, and widely scattered; urine used for scent-marking by both sexes.

DESCRIPTION Summer coat short and sleek, brownish grey above with a chestnut streak along flanks, on feet and often on the outer edge of limbs; ears relatively hairless, without white backs or tufts; tail hairs thin with indistinct white fringe. Winter coat silvery grey above with yellowish brown on head and as a mid-dorsal stripe but limbs and feet grey; ears white behind with short brown tufts (usually inconspicuous), tail dark grey distinctly fringed with white. White underparts distinct from back colour. Sexes alike in colouring. Juveniles usually greyer than summer coat but some browner; moult from nestling to appropriate seasonal coat after weaning. Body fur moults in spring (usually March/May) and autumn (usually September/November), but ear tufts and tail hairs only once, before autumn moult (usually July/August); lactating females delay moult. Moult proceeds front to back in spring but reverse direction in autumn, and takes up to 6 weeks. Pelage characteristics of the winter coat (Barrier & Barkalow 1967) and tail (Sharp 1958) can be used to separate age classes.

Body shows same adaptations for climbing and leaping as red squirrel; although only about one-third longer, it is twice the body weight of the native species. Sexes differ by distance between genital opening and anus (see red squirrel). Testes abdominal in autumn but retractable at any time; baculum can be used to determine age (Kirkpatrick & Barnett 1957). Male reproductive organs described by Allanson (1933), with accessory glands enlarging seasonally (Hoffman & Kirkpatrick 1956); female by Deanesly & Parkes (1933). Vulva obviously swollen at oestrus; 4 pairs of nipples (difficult to find in immature females).

Skull, compared with red squirrel, has condylo-basal length up to 56 mm, nasals over 17 mm, cranium shallower, and post-orbital process shorter and stouter. Tooth formula and development as for red squirrel, and similar in appearance; wear of cheek-teeth, can be used to determine age (Shorten 1954b), as can weight of eye lens (Fisher & Perry 1970) and epiphyseal fusion of long bones (Petrides 1951, Carson 1961). Skeleton (illustrated by Shorten 1962a) has dorsal spines of vertebrae more pronounced than red squirrel.

MEASUREMENTS Intermediate between *S. c. carolinensis* and *S. c. leucotis*. Head and body about 250 to 265 mm (range 230–300 mm) and tail about 210 to 220 mm (range 195–240 mm), depending on method used; hind foot without claws over 60 mm. Juveniles first active away from drey at 150 or 200 g (7 or 8 weeks) and independent around 250 to 350 g (10 to 16 weeks), reaching full adult weight in 6 or 7 months. No significant weight difference between adult sexes. Data from southern England: males 512 g (range 350–705 g, $n=32$), females 515 g (range 400–700 g, $n=27$) (Allanson 1933, Deanesly & Parkes 1933). No evidence of regional variation but considerable difference between seasons and years; lightest in late winter and spring, heaviest in autumn. Weights up to 800 g recorded; weight is no criterion of pregnancy, thus female of 700 g was not pregnant.

DISTRIBUTION See Fig. 62 Hardwood forests of eastern North America, from Florida to Great Lakes and St Lawrence, and west to Prairies. Closely related species *S. griseus* on Pacific coast and *S. arizonensis* in Arizona.

Possible occurrence in North Wales around 1830, but present populations from introductions at about 30 sites between 1876 and 1929 in England and Wales (originally from USA), 3 sites between 1892 and 1920 in Scotland (from Canada), and 1 site during 1913 in Ireland (from England) (Middleton 1930, 1931). Also introduced to South Africa about 1905 (Davis 1950). Most rapid spread in England and Wales during 1920s, with temporary check in early 1930s, accompanied by

FIGURE 62 Grey squirrel: distribution.

epidemic disease; spread continued more slowly to present, with different centres coalescing during 1950s. Now throughout England and Wales where trees available, except North Norfolk, Lake District, Northumberland and North Durham. Scottish population separate, confined mainly to central Lowlands but slow spread into Peeblesshire and up Tay valley. In Ireland largely confined to central counties. Absent from offshore islands.

VARIATION Up to 6 subspecies recognised in North America (Hall & Kelson 1959); pelage characteristics in Britain intermediate between *S. c. carolinensis* and *S. c. leucotis*, with tufted ears in winter coat nearer latter race. Body hairs, many of which are banded with different colours, are not grey but shades of black, white and brown; some geographical differences in frequency of occurrence of colour variants. Dark melanic phase, and intermediates, common in parts of North America especially within range of *S. c. leucotis*, and locally predominant over typical grey phase before man altered woodland habitat; rare in Britain but full and partial melanics reported in Bucks, Beds, Herts and West Cambs probably from black squirrels introduced at Woburn. Albinos rarer in North America but most frequent within range of *S. c. carolinensis*; in Britain relatively common in Kent, Sussex and Surrey. Erythristic forms, with red-brown backs, known in South East England, but rarely reported because of confusion with red squirrel.

HABITAT In North America typically dense hardwood forests, particularly oak, hickory and walnut but also enters southern edge of conifer belt. In Britain most abundant in mature hardwood or mixed woodlands (with at least 25% hardwood) of 10 hectares upwards, containing a variety of tree and shrub species particularly oak, but also beech, sweet chestnut and hazel. Less abundant but still numerous where woodlands smaller or immature, but overmature trees provide useful den hollows; also where trees are scattered as in hedgerows, urban parks and gardens. Found in pure conifer woodland where hardwoods are available nearby.

BEHAVIOUR Gait on ground, climbing and leaping ability as for red squirrel, but less hesitant on ground, achieving speeds up to 18 mph, with bounds of 1 to 2 m. Able to swim

Diurnal. Similar activity pattern to red squirrel, beginning before sunrise, especially in winter, and ending well before sunset; main peak for 4 or 5 hours after dawn, with sporadic activity through the day, and a minor peak towards dusk (Taylor, unpubl.). Permanent dreys fairly compact and spherical, while temporary summer dreys are platform-like;

built in a wide variety of hardwood and conifer trees, particularly oak (Shorten 1951, Brown & Twigg 1965), either by main trunk or in branches. Outer frame typically of hardwood twigs, often with persistent leaves; central cavity lined with grass, dry leaves, moss and other soft material. Drey construction in USA described by Fitzwater & Frank (1944). Dry tree hollows, such as in oak and beech, used for dens; cavity hollowed out inside, and entrance constantly gnawed to maintain hole 7 to 10 cm diameter.

Overlapping home ranges show considerable variation in size and shape; males extend range in breeding season and again in August, while females extend range during September (Taylor, unpubl.). In southern England observed range in hardwood habitat was 1·5 ha for males and 0·5 ha for females (Taylor 1966); mean maximum distances for males of 310 to 480 m and females 130 to 260 m (Taylor 1966, Taylor *et al.* 1971). In North America male range also greater than female's, but home range varies from below 1 ha (Flyger 1960, Pack *et al.* 1967) up to 20 ha (Robinson & Cowan 1954) with mean maximum distance of under 100 to 340 m. Movements of juveniles before taking up residence, especially in summer and autumn; movements over 1 km rare but up to 3 km have been recorded (Taylor *et al.* 1971).

Much agonistic behaviour throughout year, involving high speed chases as well as dominant and submissive signals (Taylor 1966). Hierarchical social structure, especially apparent at food concentrations, involving both sexes (Taylor 1966, Pack *et al.* 1967).

Vocal communication consists of scolding 'chuck-chuck-charee' (often quite lengthy), low 'tuk-tuk', and various moans and teeth-chattering. Expressive body postures, often accompanying vocal sounds, including tail flicking and foot stamping. Olfactory signals by scent marking with urine at marker points (Taylor 1968).

Senses as for red squirrel; eyes show dark adapted threshold similar to that of man and probably have a pure-cone retina (Arden & Silver 1962).

FOOD Granivorous herbivore. Detailed study of food habits in North America (Nixon *et al.* 1968) showed important items were mast of hickory, beech and oak, followed by walnut, green matter and fungi. In Britain wide range of foods acceptable, but tree mast or seed, assorted tree foliage, and fungi are basic items of diet; list and seasonal preferences in Middleton (1930) and Shorten (1962a, c). Oak is major food source in favoured habitat, supplemented by beech, sweet chestnut and hazel, providing mast, leaf and flower buds, shoots and leaves, pollen from cat-

kins, and sappy tissue under bark (particularly beech). Most active foraging on ground during autumn and winter when fallen mast is eaten,
buried or dug up, moving increasingly into canopy through spring to
summer as alternative foods sought; food most varied mid-summer. Also
eats fruits, buds, shoots, leaves, and sappy tissue of elm, maple, sycamore
and hornbeam, plus seed and pollen from pine and larch cones. In addition, berries, seeds, pollen, leaves, roots, bulbs and tubers from assorted
small shrubs and non-woody plants, fungi, and a small amount of animal
matter including eggs, young and adults of insects and birds. Soil ingested
for roughage or minerals; incisors trimmed on bones and stones, possibly
to obtain calcium. Water requirements obtained from food or dew, but
may seek standing water in hot weather.

Food selection and method of feeding as for red squirrel. Hazel nuts
nibbled at one end until lower incisors inserted to prise off pieces of
shell; skilled adult can rapidly nick and split in half lengthways. Selection
of sound nuts also improves with experience (Lloyd 1968). Softer shells
of other mast split with ease, and cones dealt with as by red squirrel.
May eat 60 to 80 g of mast per day; energy requirements for basic maintenance of a 500 g adult calculated at about 137 kcal/day of metabolisable
energy but normally activity 30% above this (Ludwick *et al.* 1969). Main
purpose of bark stripping is to obtain sappy tissue below, for nutrients
or liquid, but bark gnawing also has social significance (Taylor 1968);
strips sometimes used in drey construction.

Surplus mast buried, singly or in small groups, in ground (2 to 5 cm
in soil), tree hollows and clefts, and dreys. Acorns, chestnuts and hazel
nuts may survive to following spring, and beech nuts until summer.
Memory may be used to remember general area of storage, but location
of buried nuts is by scent and requires damp conditions. Because mast
falls from canopy during autumn and size of crop is very variable, buried
food is much more important in hardwood habitat than in conifer woodland.

BREEDING In North America two main breeding periods, with
quiescent period for males of about 2 months during early autumn (Kirkpatrick & Hoffman 1960). In Britain some males fecund every month
in some years but individuals undergo quiescence (Allanson 1933,
Shorten 1962c); females polyoestrous, with no post-partum oestrus, and
normally anoestrous between September and December. Length and
success of breeding season influenced by preceding food availability and
weather (Nixon & McClain 1969). Courtship involves chasing and display, leading up to mating (Shorten 1954b) and apparently polygamous.

Pregnancies normally found between January and July (Deanesly & Parkes 1933, Shorten 1951), with early or late litters found in some years, but two main periods in British Isles giving spring (January/March) and summer (May/July) litters. Mature females capable of producing two litters, yearlings one litter per season. Observed gestation between 42 and 45 days. Litter size averages 3, range 1 to 7, exceptionally 8 (Barkalow 1967) (mean 3·5, $n = 33$—Deanesly & Parkes 1933; mean 2·9, $n = 203$—Shorten 1951), with summer litters (mean 3·2) larger than spring (mean 2·5) but poorer survival. Up to 25% uterine losses, and further loss during weaning. Breeding drey lined with exceptionally thick layer of soft material (Shorten 1954b); if litter disturbed may be carried in female's mouth to alternative nest. Lactation 7 to 10 weeks; male apparently takes no part in raising young.

Young blind, deaf and naked at birth, weighing 13 to 17 g (Shorten 1951, Uhlig 1955). Pigment appears on back, with hairs emerging at 10 days, giving thin downy covering by 14 days, and dense coat at 20 days. Lower incisors erupt around 21 days, ears open at 25 to 28 days, eyes open and upper incisors erupt around 28 to 35 days (weight about 90 g). Begin exploration and eating solids at 7 weeks, and weaned at 8 to 10 weeks as cheek-teeth develop. Between about 13 and 16 weeks, nestling coat replaced by seasonal pelage, and dispersal starts soon after. Young sometimes capable of breeding at 6 or 7 months, but normally at least 10 to 12 months (Smith & Barkalow 1967).

POPULATION In favourable hardwood habitat densities from 1 to 13 squirrels per hectare, varying with season and year, in Britain and North America. Sex ratio variable, seasonally biased by method of collecting data, but approximates to 1 : 1, with periodic excess of one sex. Recruitment to the adult breeding stock of an unexploited population in North America found to be about 40% per year, with a calculated 15% of juveniles dispersing out of the population; complete population turnover period estimated at over 6 years (Barkalow *et al.* 1970). Compared with an unexploited population, Mosby (1969) in North America found average annual mortality slightly higher in an exploited population (48% of population compared with 42%) but natural losses were reduced to 10% of population; recruitment to adult breeding population was about 35 to 40% (6 year average), complete population turnover period in excess of 6 years. Population increases through spring to June, with minor autumn peak. Considerable short-term fluctuations between years, following abundance of mast crops (Shorten & Courtier 1955, Smith & Barkalow 1967).

In captivity live exceptionally up to 20 years; known to live 8 or 9 years in wild, but under 1% survive beyond 6 years. Mean expectation of life at birth is about 1 year (Barkalow *et al.* 1970), but rises considerably to 2 or more years for young that survive to leave the drey (Mosby 1969).

PREDATORS AND MORTALITY Relatively little predation on adults, due to arboreal habit. Stoats can climb and occasionally prey on the young. Greatest risk on ground, especially for young, and predation recorded by fox, domestic cat and dog, and some raptors and owls. Intraspecific aggression occasionally results in death. A few deaths result from natural accident—drowning, forest fire, tree falls—but starvation prevalent after failure of mast crop, associated with mass migrations (expecially in North America) and high incidence of parasites, disease and predation. Man is an important predator by control, and to a lesser extent by road mortality, but has greatest effect by altering or destroying habitat.

PARASITES AND DISEASE Flea *Orchopeas howardi* specific to grey squirrel, and introduced with it from North America, common throughout Britain and possibly Ireland; red squirrel flea *Monopsyllus sciurorum* is sometimes found (Freeman 1941, Shorten 1954b); occasionally others such as rabbit flea *Spilopsyllus cuniculi*. Ticks and mites nonspecific; most frequent tick is *Ixodes ricinus*, and mite of genus *Sarcoptes* is possibly associated with mange disease. Harvest mite larvae *Trombicula autumnalis* attack head and underparts during summer. Suckling lice include *Enderleinellus longiceps*, *Neohaematopinus sciurinus* and *Hoplopleura sciuricola* (Blackmore & Owen 1968); lice are most numerous ectoparasites, especially on head, back and legs (Parker & Holliman 1972). Fauna of drey given by Twigg (1966). Grey squirrels can carry foot and mouth disease virus (Capel-Edwards 1971) and leptospires (Twigg & Cuerden 1966).

Mange or scab disease causes epidemics; not known if the virus is the same as for red squirrel. Also coccidiosis caused by protozoan *Eimeria*. Shock disease, associated with hypoglycaemia and caused by exposure or fear, usually results in death (Guthrie *et al.* 1967), and is possibly more frequent in low-ranking squirrels (Pack *et al.* 1967).

RELATIONS WITH MAN Controversial mammal, regarded by many as a disastrous pest but by some town dwellers as an attractive asset. Forestry pest of considerable economic importance; serious timber damage caused to hardwoods over most of its range. Strips bark as part of normal feeding behaviour from any portion of main trunk or larger branches, particularly of beech and sycamore, but also a wide range of other hardwoods and some conifers (Shorten 1957); also gnaws on lower trunks as part of social behaviour and enlarges holes for den construction. Girdling leading to severe damage and die-back quite frequent. Removal of buds and shoots can cause growth distortion. Locally serious damage to cereal crops, orchards and soft fruits, as well as a nuisance to game interests, gardeners and householders. Control by cage trapping, spring trapping, poison baiting and shooting immediately before and during period of damage (Rowe 1973). Not regarded as a resource in Britain but in North America it is a highly prized game animal and provides food and pelts.

Illegal to import and release or keep grey squirrels in captivity in Britain without licence from Ministry of Agriculture or Secretary of State for Scotland.

LITERATURE Middleton (1931)—popular account of introduction, early distribution and habits; Shorten (1954b)—monograph on biology and history of both squirrels; Shorten (1962a)—popular, well illustrated account; Shorten (1962c)—summary of biology and history of both squirrels; Anon (1962)—brief account of habits, damage and control.

AUTHOR FOR THIS SPECIES A. M. Tittensor.

FAMILY CRICETIDAE
SUBFAMILY MICROTINAE
VOLES AND LEMMINGS

The microtine rodents form a large, clearly defined group which is usually treated as a subfamily of the Cricetidae (along with other subfamilies including the hamsters, gerbils and New World mice) but is sometimes treated as a separate family, the Microtidae. They are the dominant herbivorous rodents throughout the non-arid parts of the Holarctic region and are characterised especially by the very high-crowned cheek-teeth, which are usually rootless and continue to grow throughout life. The cusp-pattern of the molars is worn off immediately the teeth erupt, revealing a complex prismatic pattern composed of areas of softer dentine surrounded by walls of hard enamel. These patterns are very characteristic of the species.

Compared with mice, voles have a rather long shaggy coat, blunt nose, small eyes and ears, short legs and short tail (under 75% of head and body).

There are about 20 genera of microtines of which three occur in Britain (Table 13). A fourth, the American *Ondatra*, is dealt with briefly since it was at one time established in the wild here. It is very much larger than *Arvicola* (head and body up to 400 mm, hind feet 65–80 mm) and has the tail laterally compressed.

TABLE 13 Principal characters of the genera of voles

	Clethrionomys	*Microtus*	*Arvicola*
Colour of back	Chestnut	Brown	Brown or black
Tail: head and body	40–60%	25–40%	60–70%
Length of hind feet (mm)	15–20	16–21	27–37
Length of upper molar row (mm)	5·0–6·4	5·8–7·0	8·5–11·0
Molars develop roots	Yes	No	No
External angles of molars	Rounded	Pointed	Pointed

GENUS *Clethrionomys*

Contains about five species in Eurasia and North America, in woodland and tundra habitats. Differ from most other voles in that the molar teeth become rooted and are therefore less adapted to tough vegetation.

The common North American species, *C. gapperi*, is similar to *C. glareolus*, the only species in Britain, and may perhaps be conspecific as is suggested by cytological evidence (Matthey 1956). Two other species, *C. rufocanus* and *C. rutilus*, occur in northern Europe.

Bank vole *Clethrionomys glareolus*

Mus glareolus Schreber, 1780; Island of Lolland, Denmark. *Hypudaeus hercynicus* Mehlis, 1831; Harz Mts., Germany. *Evotomys hercynicus britannicus* Miller, 1900; Basingstoke, Hampshire, England. *Evotomys skomerensis* Barrett-Hamilton, 1903; Skomer Island, Pembrokeshire, Wales. *Evotomys alstoni* Barrett-Hamilton & Hinton, 1913; Tobermory, Mull, Scotland. *Evotomys caesarius* Miller, 1908; St Helier, Jersey, Channel Islands. *Evotomys erica* Barrett-Hamilton & Hinton, 1913; Island of Raasay, Inner Hebrides, Scotland.
Red-backed vole.

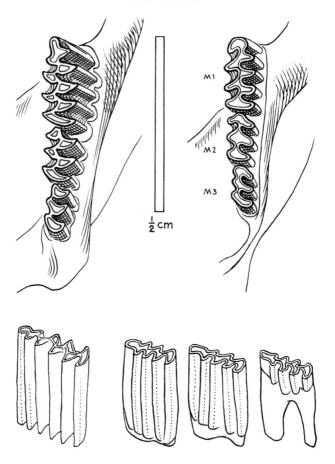

FIGURE 63 Above. Left lower tooth-row of field vole (left) and bank vole (right) showing the sharper angles and longer first tooth of the former. Below. Right lower first molar of field vole (left) and bank vole (remainder). Note the absence of roots in the field vole and the presence of roots, lengthening with age, in the bank vole.

RECOGNITION Distinguished from field vole (and much larger water vole) by rich, reddish brown upper surface, but young animals more greyish and easily confused. The tail longer (half head and body) and ears more prominent.

Skull less angular than that of field vole; molar teeth have more rounded edges and if extracted show signs of rooting unless the animal is quite young.

SIGN Droppings rounded in section, up to four times diameter in length;

FIGURE 64 Bank vole. (Photo: G. Kinns)

distinguished from those of the wood mouse by their smaller diameter and from those of the field vole by the absence of a green coloration (but this depends on the foods eaten by the two species). Colour often brown to black and they may be found in small groups. Make runways above ground in suitable habitats and are active burrowers, the tunnels being centred on a nest at 2–10 cm depth (von Wrangel 1939). Nest in woodland made of leaves, moss and feathers; in grassland of grass and moss; there is a definite entrance/exit. Breeding nests may be below or above ground in tree trunks, etc. (von Wrangel 1939). Nest building may be encouraged by placing corrugated iron, uralite, etc. on the ground. Food stores may be found within the tunnel system.

DESCRIPTION Chestnut red upper surface often grades into grey on the flanks; the ventral surface may be silvery-grey to creamy-buff. Juveniles are grey-brown before the first moult (post-juvenile moult) to longer and denser fur; this takes place between weeks 4 and 6 (Kaikusalo 1972). Moulting is predominantly sublateral (ventral to dorsal) with some older animals showing a diffuse moult; a cephalo-sacral moult is rare (Zejda

& Mazák 1965). Adults were observed to moult throughout the year with peaks in spring and autumn. The post-juvenile moult leads to the seasonal moult of spring or autumn.

Molar roots are not formed until *c.* 2–3 months old; the growth of

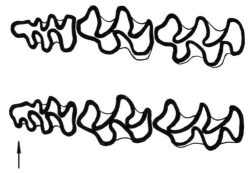

FIGURE 65 Upper right molars of bank vole showing (above) the simple and (below) the complex variant of the inner margin of the 3rd (posterior) tooth.

FIGURE 66 Bank vole (left) and field vole (right).

these roots (often those of the first upper or lower molar) may be used as an indicator of age (Hyvärinen & Heikura 1971) but growth rate varies with season (Lowe 1971, Zejda 1971). The changes in root development with age have also been followed in the second upper molar (Tupikova, Sidorova & Konovalova 1968). Before the roots form, the growth of the constriction of the crown to form the 'neck' may be used to indicate different developmental stages (Smyth 1966).

The baculum consists of a proximal stalk and three distal processes; differences in length and width may be used to distinguish sexually mature males from immature ones (Artimo 1964); however there is much regional variation.

Os coxae (Brown & Twigg 1969) show graded phases in development and sexual dimorphism based on male pubertal changes and female parturition changes. Males have a shorter pubis and a convex posterior margin contrasting with a longer pubis and a slightly concave posterior margin in females. The thinning and lengthening of the pubis, accompanied by total resorption of the symphysial region, 'the hook', in multiparous females is most striking. The remodelling of the pubic symphysis is under hormonal control (Zarrow & Wilson 1963).

Placental scars show as prominent dark spots on the uterine horns (Brambell & Rowlands 1936) and corpora lutea in the ovary are seen as pink/white spheres. In large males there may be an area of enlarged sebaceous glands on the flanks (Lehmann 1962a).

Chromosomes: $2n = 56$, F.N. $= 56$ (Matthey 1956).

MEASUREMENTS Variable: late summer generation overwinters at about 90 mm (head and body) and increases with onset of breeding in next spring to 100–110 mm; first generation may grow to full size in same year and breed (Bureau of Animal Population, Oxford, unpubl. records). Weight increases with breeding condition (Zejda 1965) and decreases after breeding and during the winter (Tanton 1969, Kaikusalo 1972). Minimum weight during the winter is often reached during February (Flowerdew 1973).

DISTRIBUTION See Fig. 67. Whole of Europe except tundra and Mediterranean lowlands, and eastwards to Lake Baikal.

Throughout mainland Britain, and on the islands of Handa, Raasay, Mull, Bute, Anglesey, Ramsey, Skomer, Isle of Wight, Jersey. Also in south-western Ireland where first discovered in 1964; by 1971 had been confirmed in Co. Limerick and a large part of Cos. Cork and Kerry, and in small areas of southern Clare and Tipperary (Fairley 1971a). The Irish population is almost certainly a recent introduction, but origin unknown. Population on Raasay, Skomer, Ramsey and Jersey very likely to be earlier introductions (Corbet 1961).

VARIATION Five subspecies can be recognised as in Table 14. Mainland form originally separated from continental on basis of smaller size and brighter colour but large series do not allow this to be upheld (Corbet 1964). Clinal variation on mainland involves size and shape of M^3; northern and especially highland populations are larger and have a more complex M^3. M^3 is everywhere individually variable and a strictly local and temporary example of a population with predominantly complex M^3 has been recorded in Perthshire (Corbet 1963a, 1975). Mainland and island races will interbreed (Steven 1955).

Pale sandy mutants occur rarely (von Lehmann 1962b), albino and melanic forms very rare. Albinism of the tail tip is rare (0.8% in Britain; Corbet 1963b). Most island forms are larger; Skomer animals are 30% heavier than the mainland form (Coutts & Rowlands 1969).

In Europe there is a clinal variation in the length of the mandibular tooth row, increasing from south-west to north-east (Kowalski 1970).

HABITAT Abundant in deciduous woodland and scrub; also along banks and hedges, usually in thick cover. They do not move far into fields (Pollard & Relton 1970) although grassland is sometimes a good habitat (Chitty & Phipps 1966). There is a definite preference for thick cover (Southern & Lowe 1968), but they are not infrequent on open ground with a high herb layer or cover from banks or walls. In coniferous wood-

FIGURE 67 Bank vole: distribution.

TABLE 14 Subspecies of the bank vole, *Clethrionomys glareolus*

	C. g. glareolus	C. g. caesarius	C. g. skomerensis	C. g. alstoni	C. g. erica
Range	Mainland, etc.	Jersey	Skomer	Mull	Raasay
Dorsal colour (winter)	Dull	Dull	**Bright**	Dull	Dull
Ventral wash (winter)	Buff	Buff	**Cream**	Buff	Buff
Hind feet	**Small** (<17·8)	Large (>17·8)	Large (>17·8)	Large (>17·8)	Large (>17·8)
Condylobasal length of skull (adults, spring)	**Small** (<24·2)	Large (>24·2)	Large (>24·2)	Large (>24·2)	Large (>24·2)
M³	Simple	Complex	Complex	Simple	Complex
Nasal bones: shape of posterior halves	Tapering	Tapering	**Parallel-sided**	Tapering	Tapering
Anterior palatal foramina: width as % of length	Narrow (<30%)	**Wide** (>30%)	Narrow (<30%)	Medium (*c.* 30%)	Narrow (<30%)

land they are most numerous in stands 6–30 years old (Birkan 1968). Local distribution changes with seasonal alteration in ground cover (Kikkawa 1964). Extends up to 850 m in scree in Scotland. On a lake island in Poland humid plant associations are preferred to dry associations and old adults occupy the preferred habitats in greatest numbers; an increase in density causes the population (notably the younger animals) to occupy the less favourable dry habitats (Bock 1972).

BEHAVIOUR Usually run in a hurried fashion but will jump if startled. Agile climbers: in Czechoslovakia 16% (mostly males) of the ground catch were also caught in trees (Holišová 1969). Active throughout the 24 hours but with more nocturnal activity in summer (Miller 1955, Kikkawa 1964). Under conditions of 12 hours light : 12 hours dark in the laboratory there is still a change from predominantly nocturnal activity to predominantly diurnal activity over the year (Erkinaro 1972). The time spent resting or sleeping amounts to 62% of the day and other activities in the laboratory such as being alert, grooming, feeding and exploration, each account for up to 15% of the day (Ashby 1972).

Size of home range varies from 0·05–0·73 ha (Brown 1966). Trapping results (Crawley 1969) show that in woodland the average area of the home range of males is 0·20 ha and of females 0·14 ha; males move more widely than females and movement is greater in summer than in winter. Home range size will vary with habitat, population density, age etc. In woodland, dispersal was observed in most males and half the females weighing less than 13 g; in the adults about 6% of the males and 2% of the females do so (Watts 1970a).

Large males often showed dominance in aggressive encounters near a baited trap but similar sized voles did not always exhibit a constant social relationship; subordinates were chased from the bait and would spend only a few seconds inside the trap whereas dominants would remain there for a few minutes (Kikkawa 1964). The agonistic behaviour is similar to that of other myomorphs with attacking, defensive and escape elements (Johst 1969). Voice chattering and squeaking similar to field vole but not used as often. Ultrasounds are emitted (apparently by the male during genital sniffing, attempted and successful mating and audible squeaks are also emitted when the litter is removed (Sales 1972). Ultrasounds produced by the young initiate retrieval by the female and the intensity of the sound varies with the temperature to which the young are exposed (Okon 1972). The odours of the urine, faeces and body are probably important in communications; it has been demonstrated that they can distinguish between the odour of their own and another subspecies, and that males prefer the odours of closely related females (Godfrey 1958). The eyes are insensitive to red light.

FOOD Almost wholly herbivorous (Watts 1968). Fleshy fruits and seeds with a soft testa are eaten when available; the leaves of woody plants are preferred to those of herbs, and dead leaves are eaten in winter. Other food items include fungi, moss, roots, flowers, grass, insects and worms. The young eat less seed than adults. In Sweden and Poland feeding habits are similar but without the emphasis on dead leaves (Hansson 1971a, Zemanec 1972). Hazel nuts are opened with a clean-edged hole (East 1965) and only the flesh of rose hips is eaten (Eldridge 1969). They are known to eat the cocoons of forest moths (e.g. *Bupalus piniarius*) (Kulicke 1963). In some winters they will strip the bark of elder bushes and eat the cambium below (Southern 1970b). Refection has been observed in the nest (Ashby 1972). When daylength is reduced from 12 to 8 hours food is stored (Miller 1955). The greatest daily energy demands are required by the lactating female (Kaczmarski 1966).

BREEDING Length of season and breeding success vary greatly. Breeding usually starts in April and ends by September/October, but in some years it continues until December or does not stop at all; this is related to the abundance of seed food (Smyth 1966, Flowerdew 1973). The experimental addition of food may bring forward the start of breeding by 2–3 weeks (Watts 1970b); mild temperatures may have a similar effect (Zejda 1962, Kaikusalo 1972). High density conditions will bring forward the end of the breeding season (Corbet 1964, Bergstedt 1965). The Skomer form has a very short breeding season lasting from May to September (Jewell 1966a). The late-born young remain non-parous through the winter and the testes of adult males regress; in the spring there is a rapid increase in testis weight (Rowlands 1936).

In the laboratory females are induced ovulators (Clarke *et al.* 1970) and may become pregnant by $4\frac{1}{2}$ weeks of age; the development of the ovary from birth to maturity is slower than in the field vole (Peters & Clarke 1974). Females may become pregnant post-partum but if they do not conceive at this time they do not become pregnant until after lactation (Clarke, Hellwing & Greig, unpublished). Experiments with successive matings of females suggest that strange males can block pregnancy but that soon afterwards mating can take place again (Clarke & Clulow 1973). Such successive matings induce a series of sets of ovulations and corpora lutea which would explain the observations that bank voles show a number of sets of corpora lutea at the start of the breeding season (Brambell & Rowlands 1936, Coutts & Rowlands 1969). Embryo number rises

and falls through the season; mean for England 4·1 with a sex-ratio of
1 : 1 (Brambell & Rowlands 1936). In winter embryo numbers are smaller
(Smyth 1966, Zedja 1962). Gestation 17–18 days prolonged to 19–22 days
during lactation; sometimes up to 30 days (Bujalska & Ryszkowski 1966).
Lactation usually lasts for 18 days. Pregnancies reach a peak between
May and July and in a 9 month season probably 4–5 are possible (Saint-
Girons 1972).

Virgin females caged with males, and allowed visual, tactile, auditory
and olfactory communication, showed fresh corpora lutea in the ovaries,
whereas those caged in the absence of males showed none. The females
caged with males also showed heavier uteri and ovaries with larger graafian
follicles (Clarke & Clulow 1973). Thus in the absence of coitus males
can cause ovarian follicular growth and in some cases ovulation. (This
is similar to the 'Whitten effect' observed in the house mouse.)

Island populations exhibit delayed maturity compared with mainland
ones (Jewell 1966a, Mazurkiewicz 1972); the number of breeding females
on a Polish island has been shown to remain relatively constant whatever
the population density (Bujalska 1970).

Young are born *c.* 2 g, weaned at about $2\frac{1}{2}$ weeks. Incisors are partially
erupted at birth, molars erupt during first $4-4\frac{1}{2}$ weeks (Mazák 1963). At
birth they are naked and blind, the dorsal skin darkens at *c.* 3 days,
juvenile pelage appears between days 4–10 and the eyes open at *c.* 12
days. Early growth in the laboratory varies with the number in the litter
and the temperature (Pearson 1962); in the field, growth is retarded if
no dispersal is allowed (Mazurkiewicz 1972). Thermoregulation is
usually fully developed by 16–19 days (Okon 1972).

POPULATION STRUCTURE The overwintering population (young born
in the latter part of the previous year and a few parous adults) grow
rapidly in spring and produce the first generation, which will in turn produce a second generation during the summer. The later born young grow
slowly without reaching sexual maturity in the year of their birth and
form the bulk of the overwintering population (Crawley 1970). Winter
breeding will alter this sequence of events (Newson 1963). Length of life
very variable; at high density in Poland (average of 16/ha) mean length
of life was 2·2 months; at low density (average of 4/ha) it was 3·2 months
(Bobek 1969) (calculated from molar root growth). In the field individual
animals may be followed for 18 months or more; in the laboratory survival
to 40 months is known (Godfrey 1958).

Annual fluctuations: typically high numbers in late summer and
autumn declining through the winter and reaching a trough in April–

May, then increasing during the summer (Crawley 1970). There is much variation on this theme so that numbers may remain high in the winter and spring and decline during the summer and autumn; the extent of the summer and autumn increase varies greatly (Newson 1963, Southern 1970a). Numbers tend to increase from winter to summer after winter breeding (Southern 1970a). In English woodland there is little evidence of cyclic fluctuations (Southern 1970b), but nevertheless increases and decreases may be dramatic. Outbreaks are known in Norway (Wildhagen 1952) and Germany (Stein 1956) and 'crashes' in numbers have been observed (Corbet 1964).

Densities in woodland probably 12–74/ha according to season and amount of favourable habitat. On Skomer Island they reach 210/ha even when the estimate is corrected for edge effect (Fullagar *et al.* 1963). In Czechoslovakia a high density of 72/ha caused breeding to stop (Zejda 1961). In Britain numbers are generally more stable than are those of the field vole.

PREDATORS AND MORTALITY Taken by most birds of prey and carnivores, but usually in small numbers by species that hunt open ground: tawny owls and weasels probably most important (Southern 1954, King 1971). On Skomer Island barn owls take a large proportion of juveniles and only a few adults, probably by hunting in the thinner cover (Brown & Twigg 1971).

Heavy animals survive better at high density in Germany (Stein 1956). When the mast crop is good, overwinter survival is good (Bergstedt 1965). Survival in winter is usually better than during the breeding season (Newson 1963, Crawley 1970). The survival of unweaned and juvenile bank voles in Poland (in nest boxes placed in the field) until first capture varies from 47% over 39 days and 61% over 39 days in nestlings marked in May, to 56% over 59 days in nestlings marked in June (Ryszkowski & Truskowski 1970). Some decreases in the survival of young are presumed to be the result of intraspecific or possibly interspecific strife (with *Microtus*) (Chitty & Phipps 1966).

PARASITES Ectoparasite records and distributions were reviewed by Blackmore & Owen (1968) and the fleas also by Smit (1957). The following are the principal ectoparasites recorded from bank voles in Wytham Woods, near Oxford (O'Donnell 1971).

Fleas: *Ctenophthalmus nobilis, Megabothris turbidus, Malareus peniciliger* and *Hystrichopsylla talpae* all common, *Peromyscopsylla silvatica* and *Megabothris walkeri* rare; Acarina: the mites *Haemogamasus nidi, H. pontiger, Listrophorus leuckarti* and *Trombicula autumnalis* and the tick *Ixodes trianguliceps* (see Randolph (1975) for seasonal occurrence of the last species). It should be noted that the species of ectoparasites found will vary with season annd location. The harvest mites are common in autumn and are very noticeable on the shoulders of bank voles that have lost a leg (Smyth 1965).

The Helminth parasites include the following (Elton *et al.* 1931, Lewis & Twigg 1972):

Cestodes:

Catenotaenia lobata (small intestine), *C. pusilla* (small intestine), *Paranoplocephala blanchardi* (small intestine), *Cysticercis taeniae taeniaeformis* (liver), *Taenia tenuicollis* (liver);

Trematodes:

Corrigia vitta (pancreas and duodenum);

Nematodes:

Capillaria muris-sylvatici (stomach), *Nematospiroides dubius* (small intestine), *Syphacia obvelata* (caecum), *Heligomosmoides glareoli* (small intestine), and *Aspicularis tetraptera* (small intestine).

The orbital fluid frequently contains many larval nematodes, possibly of a species of *Rhabditis* (H. Trapido, pers. comm.)

Ringworm fungi are common (English 1969). Infection with the spirochaete bacterium *Leptospira* is widespread; highest infection rates are found in the smallest weight groups. In a sample of 151 from Surrey, 26·3% of males and 11·6% of females were infected; the incidence of infection increases with the wetness of the habitat (Twigg, Cuerden & Hughes 1968). Fifteen species of parasitic protozoa have been recorded (Cox 1970).

RELATIONS WITH MAN On the Continent it is known as an occasional forestry pest, not only eating seeds and seedlings, but barking small trees, especially larch and elder, up to 5 m (von Wrangel 1939). Similar records in Britain in winter between 1958 and 1960 (Keeler 1961). The lead content of bank voles has been shown to increase to $1·81 \pm 0·61$ ppm wet weight near main roads compared with $1·50 \pm 0·17$ in woodland and arable sites (Jeffries & French 1972). Easily takes to captivity and breeds freely, though some individuals remain very wild. Skomer form remarkable for its docility. Usual diet in captivity, hay, oats, etc., slows down development of molar roots.

AUTHOR FOR THIS SPECIES J. R. Flowerdew.

GENUS *Microtus*

A large genus with about 50 species distributed throughout the Palaearctic and Nearctic regions (more if the closely similar *Pitymys* is included). The species are superficially very similar, being small with rather long, soft pelage, usually greyish or yellowish brown, short ears and rather short tail. They are the dominant herbivorous rodents in many habitats and have sharply angled, rootless molar teeth.

Only one species, *M. agrestis*, occurs on the British mainland, but another, *M. arvalis*, possibly introduced, occurs on the Orkney Islands and on Guernsey. The only clear-cut difference is in the shape of the second upper molars (Fig. 68).

Species of *Microtus* were well represented in the Pleistocene in Britain. The most abundant species in deposits from the Last Glaciation is *M. oeconomus*. This now has a northern and eastern distribution in Europe and has not been found living in Britain, but subfossil remains have been recorded from as late as the Bronze Age on the Scilly Islands (Pernetta & Handford 1970).

Field vole *Microtus agrestis*

Mus agrestis Linnaeus, 1761; Upsala, Sweden. *Arvicola hirta* Bellamy, 1839; Yealmpton, Devon, *Arvicola neglectus* Jenyns, 1841; Megarnie, Perthshire, *Arvicola britannicus* de Sélys Longchamps, 1847; England. *Microtus agrestis exsul* Miller, 1908; N. Uist, Outer Hebrides. *Microtus agrestoides* Hinton, 1910; Grays Thurrock, Essex; Pleistocene. *Microtus agrestis mial* Barrett-Hamilton & Hinton, 1913; Island of Eigg, Inner Hebrides. *Microtus agrestis luch* Barrett-Hamilton & Hinton, 1913; Island of Muck, Inner Hebrides. *Microtus agrestis macgillivrayi* Barrett-Hamilton & Hinton, 1913; Island of Islay, Inner Hebrides. *Microtus agrestis fiona* Montagu, 1922; Island of Gigha, Inner Hebrides.

Short-tailed vole, short-tailed field mouse.

RECOGNITION A small, greyish brown vole, with small ears and eyes, a blunt snout and short tail. The colour of the back varies from greyish to yellowish brown but never shows the deep chestnut colour of the bank vole. Young water voles may be very similar but have larger hind feet (over 21 mm) and relatively longer tails (see Fig. 66).

The skull is recognised by the sharply angled prisms of the cheek-teeth which remain rootless. The molar tooth-row never exceeds 7 mm. The additional postero-medial loop on M^2 is the most clear-cut difference between this species and *Microtus arvalis*.

SIGN Their presence can be detected by well-formed runways at ground level amongst dense cover. Recent use is indicated by the presence of green, oval droppings and small mounds of short, nibbled grass leaves or stems.

DESCRIPTION Greyish brown above, usully pure grey below but sometimes tinged with buff. No sexual dimorphism; juveniles darker grey than adults. No seasonal colour change, but summer and winter coats show structural differences. The summer coat is sparser, with coarser guard hairs and fewer fine hairs than the dense winter coat. In southern England there are a number of moults each year. Overwintered animals begin their

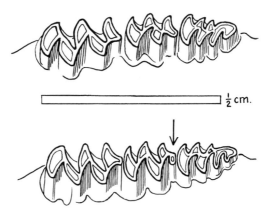

FIGURE 68 Left upper molars of field vole (below) and Orkney vole (above). The arrow indicates the additional postero-internal lobe on the 2nd tooth that is characteristic of *Microtus agrestis*.

spring moult in February and animals born during the summer have a succession of moults, ultimately producing an adult coat. This is replaced during the autumn moult, which is completed by October/November. No hair growth occurs during December and January. Adrenal, thyroid and sex hormones are involved in the regulation of moult (Al-Khateeb & Johnson 1971).

The molar teeth remain open-rooted throughout life and the column is continually renewed from the base of the tooth as it is worn away at the top. Distinguishable from the molars of the bank vole by the sharp angles on the grinding surface and the presence of a fifth loop of enamel on M^2.

Chromosomes: $2n = 50$. Sex chromosomes very large: X is 14 microns long, Y is 8 microns long (Hansen-Melander 1964a, 1964b).

MEASUREMENTS Wide variations in weights of animals, according to sex, age, season and population phase. In length, adults (head plus body) vary from *c*. 90–115 mm with a tail of *c*. 31–46 mm. Voles born into a population during late summer maintain a weight of about 17 g during winter. Weight increase begins in March in males and April in females (in southern England), reaching June maxima of 35–40 g and about 30 g respectively. The weights of adult females during the breeding season are much more variable than those of males, depending on reproductive condition. Those few adults that survive into a second winter are some 6–8 g heavier than those in their first. More details in Chitty (1952), Evans (1973). Northern forms tend to be larger.

DISTRIBUTION See Fig. 69. One of the most abundant and widespread voles of the Western Palaearctic. Found from the Arctic coast south to the Pyrenees and Alps, and eastwards to the River Lena and Lake Baikal. Its ecological replacement in the steppes of Asia and European Russia is *M. socialis*. *M. arvalis*, which does not occur on mainland Britain, has a similar range and ecology to *M. agrestis*, but is more southerly and absent from tundra and most of the taiga.

It is the only species of *Microtus* on the British mainland where it is

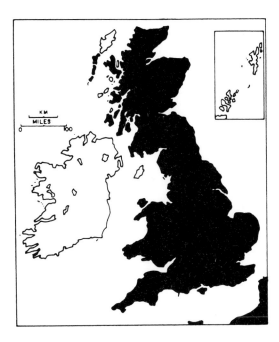

FIGURE 69 Field vole: distribution.

ubiquitous. It occurs on most of the Hebridean islands, but is absent from the following: Lewis, Barra, some Inner Hebrides (S. Rona, Raasay, Rhum, Colonsay, Pabay, Soay), Orkney (where it is replaced by the larger *M. arvalis orcadensis*) and Shetland. Also absent from Ireland, Isle of Man, Lundy, Scillies and the Channel Islands (replaced in Guernsey, by *M. arvalis sarnius*).

It is well represented in British fossil sites from the penultimate (Wolstonian) glaciation onwards (Kowalski & Sutcliffe 1976).

VARIATION The British form is not clearly distinguishable from continental populations, its separation as a subspecies, *hirtus*, having been based only on average differences of colour and size that are overshadowed by clinal variation within Britain.

Within the British mainland there is an increase in size and darkening of colour towards the north, the largest and darkest animals being in the Scottish Highlands. A fourth inner ridge on M^1 is variable in all populations but increases in size and frequency towards the north with a more marked increase in Scotland between the central Highlands and the north-west Highlands. It also increases significantly with altitude (Corbet 1960).

Hebridean animals mostly resemble those from western mainland of Scotland in size and colour. M^1 is mainly complex (as in north-west Highlands) in the Outer Hebrides and on Skye, Scalpay, Eigg, Luing and Islay; but simpler (as in central Highlands) on Muck, Mull, Jura, Scarba, Lismore, Gigha, Arran and Bute. The only insular form that possibly justifies recognition as a subspecies is that on Islay (*M. a. macgillivrayi*) characterised by very dark greyish brown ventral pelage (and consistently complex M^1) (Corbet, unpubl.).

Berry & Searle (1963) described 25 skeletal variants (involving skull, vertebrae, girdles and long bones), found with different frequencies in two widely separated populations.

Reported mutants in coat colour include Agouti (main alternatives black or black and tan), Pink-eye (normal pigmentation or red eye and pale coat) and Piebald (normal or white spotting on coat) (Robinson 1970). Piebalds and pale coated forms occasionally found; albinos rare and melanics very rare.

There is a widespread polymorphism for the presence or absence of a serum esterase (E^1), controlled by four autosomal alleles (Semeonoff & Robertson 1968). At high population densities, animals lacking the enzyme activity (E^1 negative genotype) increase in frequency, but appear to be less well adapted to winter conditions than E^1 positive genotypes, which survive better in normal winters. Thus, a selective balance maintains the polymorphism. The species is also polymorphic for other enzymes (Russel & Semeonoff 1967).

HABITAT In Britain, mainly rough, ungrazed grassland, including young forestry plantations with a lush growth of grass. Low density populations in marginal habitats, such as woodlands, hedgerow, blanket bog, dunes, scree and moorland, to over 1300 m in the Cairngorms. A detailed account of habitat preferences in Swedish populations was given by Hansson (1971b), who suggested that the species appears in open field habitats mainly in regions lacking other *Microtus* species with which it might compete, e.g. *M. oeconomus* and *M. arvalis*.

BEHAVIOUR Active throughout twenty-four hours. Davis (1933) showed in the laboratory that greatest activity occurred at night. Brown (1956a), from trapping results, found peaks at sunrise and sunset. Home range estimated from trapping as 975 m^2, with most animals moving less than 27 m (Brown 1956b). Use of a Geiger counter gave home range as 198 m^2 (Godfrey 1954).

In captivity, both adult males and pregnant or nursing females show vigorous aggression towards other voles, and young, unweaned animals (about 9 days old) can perform effective retaliatory gestures. Within a group, one animal (usually male) emerges as dominant. Captive females frequently eat their new-born young. Detailed account of aggressive behaviour by Clarke (1956).

They maintain a detailed knowledge of their home range by regular exploratory activity, which occurs in familiar surroundings as well as in new situations (Shillito 1963). A strange object elicits a 'new object reaction', in which the sense of smell is most important, supplemented by tactile information from the vibrissae. Sight and sound are also used.

Vocal communication is conspicuous, encounters between animals often being accompanied by loud chattering. As in other rodents, olfactory cues are probably important in communication. Faecal deposits in runways may have territorial function, at least in adult males in which both rectal and preputial glands are highly developed.

FOOD Herbivorous, feeding primarily on green leaves and stems of grasses (Godfrey 1953, Evans 1973), though some dicotyledons are also eaten. In Sweden, Hansson (1971b) found an increase in consumption of dicotyledons during mid-summer, with some grass seed taken in addition. In winter, in northern Finland, Kalela (1962) found that bark was eaten in addition to herbaceous plants and grasses. Ferns (1970) found three caddis fly larvae (probably the terrestrial *Enoicyla pusilla*) in the stomach of a dead female vole.

BREEDING A succession of litters of about 4–6 young is produced from spring to late autumn. Animals born at the beginning of the season usually reproduce in the same year.

Photoperiod is important in timing the onset of gonad maturation (Baker & Ranson 1932). It is possible to distinguish, in winter populations, between regressed individuals (i.e. those which have been sexually mature in the previous breeding season) and inhibited individuals (late-born young which have remained sexually immature) (Clarke & Forsythe 1964). In southern England, testis growth begins in February and maximum testis weight is reached in May (Evans 1973). Maturation of the ovary also commences in February, females becoming fully perforate in about April, when first litters are produced. Last litters usually born in September. Females construct nests, often at the base of grass tussocks. Number of embryos between three and seven, reaching maximum in June. Females normally polyoestrous, with 3- to 4-day cycle, continuing during lactation (H. Chitty 1957). Young weigh about 2 g at birth; weaning 14 to 28 days. Females become sexually mature at 3 weeks (12 g) and may mate at 6 weeks. Sex ratio approximately equal.

In the laboratory, Clarke & Kennedy (1967) showed that short photoperiod, but not low temperature, inhibits sexual development or causes sexually mature females to regress (decrease in weight of ovaries and pituitary). There appears to be a threshold photoperiod of 12 to 14 hours, above which sexual development is much more rapid than below it (Breed & Clarke 1970). Changing day-length is probably a more important stimulus than a given, fixed photoperiod, but decreasing day length is not always efficient in stopping breeding, which occasionally continues throughout winter (Smyth 1966).

POPULATION Overwintering population consists almost entirely of animals born during previous summer, mainly from July litters onwards (e.g. Chitty & Phipps 1966). These may be regressed or sexually immature, and those that survive the winter form the breeding population of the following spring. Few survive into a second autumn. In the laboratory, Leslie & Ranson (1940) found the average expectation of life at birth to be $7\frac{1}{2}$ months and, from life table data, that only 2·3% of their original population would be alive after 15 months.

Population density shows non-annual fluctuations, with a periodicity of three to five years between maximum densities. Amplitude of fluctuation (between maximum and minimum densities) very variable. Declines can occur among relatively sparse overwintered populations (Chitty & Chitty 1962) or continue throughout the breeding season (Godfrey 1955). Changes in population density are associated with other diagnostic features, e.g. variations in mean adult body weights, differences in survival rates between animals of different sex, age class and genotype (Chitty 1952, Semeonoff & Robertson 1968). More obvious explanations (weather, disease, parasites, predation, quantitative food deficiency, migration) can be eliminated (Chitty 1952, 1960, Chitty & Phipps 1966). Chitty's current hypothesis of self-regulation involves a behavioural polymorphism in which less aggressive genotypes (which are however more resistant to local mortality factors such as weather, disease, poor quality food) are selected for during the phase of increase. However, at high densities they are at a selective disadvantage because they are less tolerant of crowding than more aggressive genotypes. As the latter are now favoured, density begins to fall (due to elimination of other animals and wider spacing of those which remain). At low densities, less aggressive genotypes (selected for resistance to other mortality factors), which survive and multiply at the highest rates, once again increase until a peak density is reached. This may be expected to vary from one habitat, and one population, to another. Detailed accounts by Chitty (1967, 1970), Krebs & Myers (1974) and general review by Tapper (1976).

PREDATORS AND MORTALITY Preyed upon by many birds including: heron, kestrel, buzzard, eagle, harriers, barn owl, tawny owl, long- and short-eared owls, little owls (Southern 1954, Glue 1970). Mammalian predators include: fox (Lever 1959), stoat, weasel, polecat, pine-marten (Lockie 1961), wild cat (Lindemann 1953). Although predators increase during vole 'plagues' (Elton 1942, Lockie 1955), they probably exert little effective control on vole numbers (Chitty 1938). Pearson (1966) suggested that carnivores have a rôle in microtine cycles, by keeping prey numbers at a low level for an appreciable period, once they have declined from peak density.

PARASITES AND DISEASE The most abundant fleas in the pelage are normally *Ctenophthalmus nobilis*, *Malareus penicilliger*, *Megabothris walkeri*, *M. rectangulatus*, *Peromyscopsylla silvatica* and *Hystrichopsylla talpae* (Elton 1942, George & Corbet 1959). All these species are more abundant on the field vole than on other species of mammals. Up to seven species of larval fleas have been found in nests (Cotton 1970).

The sucking louse *Hoplopleura acanthopus* is frequent and is shared only by other species of *Microtus*. Larval ticks, especially *Ixodes ricinus*, are usually abundant (Randolph (1975) has studied the seasonal distribution of *I. trianguliceps*), as are many species of mites such as *Trombicula autumnalis*, *Eulaelaps stabularis*, *Laelaps hilaris* and *Haemogamasus nidi*. These are not host specific, but hair mites, *Listrophorus leuckarti*, looking like rows of white beads on individual hairs, are more specific.

The human ringworm fungus, *Trichophyton persicolor*, occurs in wild populations, with a 25% infection rate in voles from Berkshire (English 1966, English & Southern 1967).

Several genera of Protozoa are regularly encountered, as follows (data from Elton 1942, and Cox 1970).

Gut:
Entamoeba sp. (non-pathogenic); intestinal flagellates, including the genera *Chilomastix*, *Hexamita*, *Giardia*, *Trichomonas* (non-pathogenic); the coccidian *Eimeria falciformis* (responsible for enteritis).

Blood (Baker, Chitty & Phipps 1963):
Hepatozoon microti (in leucocytes and infecting lungs and liver); *Babesia microti* (transmitted by ticks); *Trypanosoma microti* (see Molyneux 1969).

Brain:
Frenkelia microti and possibly *Toxoplasma gondii* (Tadros 1968).

Striped muscle:
Sarcocystis sp.

Nematodes, trematodes and cestodes all recorded from the gut (Elton *et al.* 1931, Lewis 1968). *Leptospira* bacteria—the causative agent of leptospirosis in man—was isolated by Broom & Coghlan (1958). Twigg & Cuerdon (1966) found the following infection rates in natural vole populations: Derbyshire—20·7%; Surrey—33·3%. The animals carried antibodies to *Leptospira*, but no living organisms were found. *Mycobacterium tuberculosis* was isolated from a naturally infected vole by Wells (1937) and is the cause of endemic tuberculosis in wild populations.

H. Trapido (pers. comm.) recorded larval rhabditid nematodes in the orbital fluid of *c* 50% of a sample of voles.

RELATIONS WITH MAN A full historical account of vole plagues and associated events has been given by Elton (1942). At high densities they can cause considerable damage to grassland, by destruction of vegetation, and in young plantations (Elton 1942, Charles 1956); they are not, however, climbers. In arable land, they have been held responsible for damage to cereal crops, by cutting through the cereal stem close to the ground and eating the stem and leaves (as with natural grasses). This type of damage, however, is rare and slight compared with that caused by other species.

The field vole is a possible source of infection of ringworm (English 1966) and jaundice (leptospirosis).

It is a useful laboratory animal (Chitty 1957). Wells' discovery roused clinical interest in *Mycobacterium tuberculosis* from voles as a means of protecting man against TB. In 1949, the Medical Research Council mounted a trial, comparing it with BCG vaccine, but it was never used for widespread inoculation. There has been a recent suggestion that its use be reconsidered (Anon 1969).

LITERATURE Very scattered, with nothing approaching a monographic treatment available.

AUTHOR FOR THIS SPECIES Dianne Evans.

Orkney/Guernsey vole *Microtus arvalis*

Mus arvalis Pallas, 1779; Germany. *Microtus sarnius* Miller, 1909; St Martins, Guernsey, Channel Islands. *Microtus orcadensis* Millais, 1904; Pomona (= Mainland), Orkney. *Microtus orcadensis sandayensis* Millais, 1905; Island of Sanday, Orkney. *Microtus orcadensis westrae* Miller, 1908; Island of Westray, Orkney. *Microtus orcadensis ronaldshaiensis* Hinton, 1913; Island of South Ronaldsay, Orkney. *Microtus orcadensis rousaiensis* Hinton, 1913; Island of Rousay, Orkney.
Orkney vole, Guernsey vole, 'common vole' (on Continent), cuttick (Orkney).

RECOGNITION The British forms are the only voles on their respective islands. As a species, it can be safely distinguished from *M. agrestis* only by the teeth, M^2 lacking a terminal, inward-facing loop (see Fig. 68).

SIGN As for field vole. The runways are especially conspicuous on the Orkney Islands.

DISTRIBUTION Throughout Europe south of Baltic (but not in Denmark) and eastwards to Iran and the Altai Mts.

In British Isles confined to Guernsey and to the Orkney Islands (Mainland, Westray, Sanday, South Ronaldsay and Rousay). There are strong reasons for believing these to be due to human introduction, perhaps from Iberia (Corbet 1961).

Subfossil finds on Orkney suggest that it has been present on the main island for at least 4000 years (specimens in British Museum). From Guernsey a 'late Pleistocene' specimen has been reported (Morrison-Scott 1938), but there was no evidence of dating beyond the fact that it was in a stalagmite collected in 1830.

Pleistocene forms from mainland Britain, named as *M. corneri*, have been considered to be fore-runners of the Orkney and Guernsey forms, but it is probable that many British fossil records of *M. arvalis* really refer to *M. oeconomus*, and the history of true *M. arvalis* in Britain remains obscure (Kowalski & Sutcliffe 1976).

VARIATION The form on Guernsey can be considered a well differenti- ated subspecies, *M. a. sarnius*. The Orkney forms are also distinctive as a group but the relationship between the forms on the separate islands needs clarification. These have each been described as subspecies but it has been shown that those on Westray and Sanday cannot be clearly separated, although together they can be distinguished from animals on Mainland (Turner 1965). The characters of the subspecies are detailed

TABLE 15 Subspecies of *Microtus arvalis*

	M. a. orcadensis	*M. a. sandayensis*	*M. a. sarnius*
Range	Orkney Mainland, probably also Rousay and S. Ronaldsay	Sanday and Westray (Orkney)	Guernsey
Dorsal colour	Dark	Light	Light
Ventral colour	Strongly suffused with orange-buff	Lightly suffused with creamy buff	Pure grey
M_1—anterior outer groove	Deep	Shallow	Deep

in Table 15. Study of epigenetic polymorphism shows that the Guernsey form is very close to the continental, but the Orkney forms are distinctive (Berry & Rose 1975).

Black individuals occur regularly in Orkney and appear to be particu- larly frequent in certain localities. Albinos are very rare.

HABITAT As in field vole. In Orkney it occupies a wide range of habitats including marsh, heather, grass and growing crops (Hewson 1951, Turner 1965), but unlike the Continental form it does not inhabit short pasture or arable land. Runway systems do not extend beyond the mar- gins of fields and grass parks. They extend to an altitude of 200 m on Orkney Mainland.

BEHAVIOUR Generally similar to that of field vole. In Orkney they are active by day and night. Most animals enter traps at night but in the laboratory the peak of activity occurs during the day. The runways radiate from a bank or raised area of ground where possible. Where the ground permits the nest is subterranean, at the end of a short network of tunnels. Runs are found in the long grass of marginal and uncultivated ground. They extend up to 6 m from the nest. Occupied nests may be within 3 m of each other along grassy banks between fields. When surprised in a run, an animal will quickly escape but if caught in the open it appears lost and unsure.

In captivity they settle down quickly and readily live in groups provided only one male is present. New individuals introduced into a colony are killed. Nursing females readily allow young to be inspected and other voles are not repelled.

FOOD As for field vole. Roots of the rush *Juncus squarrosus* are favoured.

BREEDING As in field vole. On Guernsey early breeding has been recorded with mating in February and young of the year difficult to distinguish from adults by August (Bishop & Delany 1963). Number of foetuses in eight pregnant females ranged from 2 to 5, mean 3·3.

Mean litter size in 508 births of captive Orkney animals was 2·7 (Leslie *et al.* 1955).

Crosses producing fertile young have been made between animals from Orkney and Guernsey (Crowcroft & Godfrey 1962) and between Orkney and Germany (Zimmermann 1959).

POPULATION Often quite dense in Orkney, but does not appear to fluctuate to same extent as *M. agrestis*. In laboratory conditions mean expectation of life about 1·6 years, longer than field vole under similar conditions. Since litter rate is smaller than in field vole, population turnover is slower which may partly account for greater stability of numbers (Leslie *et al.* 1955).

PREDATORS In Orkney forms the principal diet of hen harriers and short-eared owls, and a large number are taken by cats.

PARASITES The flea *Malaraeus penicilliger* (a characteristic flea of *M. agrestis* in mainland Britain) occurs on *M. arvalis* in Orkney.

RELATIONS WITH MAN Easily kept in captivity (see Chitty 1957). In Orkney they enter hay and oat stacks and grain stores, but they remain at the bottom of a stack and do little damage.

AUTHOR FOR THIS SPECIES G. B. Corbet and S. J. Wallis based on the first edition account by H. N. Southern.

GENUS *Arvicola*

A Palaearctic genus of two species, rather closely related to *Microtus*. They differ in their large size, longer tail and more prominent glandular regions on the flanks. The cheek-teeth remain unrooted, as in *Microtus*, with a pattern of prisms resembling the simpler patterns found in *Microtus*, e.g. in *M. oeconomus*. Like *Microtus* they are adapted to feeding on tough vegetation including grass.

The number of species has been controversial, but recent work supports the view that there are only two species, *A. terrestris* with a wide distribution and *A. sapidus* in France and Spain (Reichstein 1963, Corbet *et al.* 1970).

FIGURE 70 Water vole.

Water vole *Arvicola terrestris*

Mus terrestris Linnaeus, 1758; Upsala, Sweden. *Mus amphibius* Linnaeus, 1758; England. *Arvicola ater* Macgillivray, 1832; Aberdeen (preoccupied by *Hypudaeus terrestris β ater* Billberg, 1827). *Arvicola amphibius reta* Miller, 1910 (substitute for *ater*). *Arvicola amphibius brigantium* Thomas, 1928; Huddersfield, Yorkshire.
Water rat.

RECOGNITION A rat-sized vole about 200 mm long with rather shaggy pelage which is usually brown but may be black, especially in North Scotland. Distinguished from rats by shorter tail (half to three-quarters head and body), shorter ears and shorter muzzle. An expert swimmer and diver, but note that the common rat is also very frequently seen swimming. The young leave the nest when only about half grown and are then very similar to field voles, but the tail and hind feet are longer.

The skull is easily recognised by the prismatic cheek-teeth, similar to those of the smaller voles but much larger (tooth-row always over 8 mm, even when newly erupted, compared with maximum of 7 mm in other British voles).

SIGN Presence in an area characterised by latrine sites, at which most of the droppings are deposited. Droppings perfectly cylindrical, 10–12 mm long, and khaki to light green in colour. In spring presence is disclosed by tangled masses of white inner pith from rushes deposited on bank. Holes may be below, or even considerably above the water level. Holes leading to nursing chambers plugged with grass and mud, and are often in the centre of a closely grazed circle of 15–20 cm radius.

DESCRIPTION The structure is not noticeably modified in spite of the aquatic habits. The form is as in other voles with short, chubby face, small eyes, and ears that just project beyond the fur. The front feet have four toes and the hind five, without webs. The tail is terete and well haired, and varies from 55 to 70% of the length of head and body. The pelage is a uniform brown above and a lighter brown or brownish grey below. The guard hairs are oval in cross-section without grooves. A scent organ is visible on each flank in the form of an oval area of almost naked skin, present in both sexes from the age of three weeks. Most conspicuous in adult males but not always so. Cycle of glandular activity follows testis cycle in male.

The skull is robust and angular. The cheek-teeth are similar in pattern

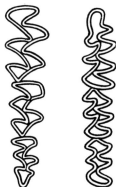

FIGURE 71 Right upper (on left) and left lower (on right) molar teeth of water vole.

to those of *Microtus arvalis*, except that the posterior end of M^3 and the anterior end of M_1 are simpler. Temporal ridges are well developed and meet in the interorbital region in fully grown animals.

Chromosomes: $2n = 36$ (Matthey 1956) (based on only one British animal, from Edinburgh).

MEASUREMENTS See Table 16. Since young animals are only about half grown when they leave the nest the range of size in active animals is very great. Those included in Table 16, from a variety of localities throughout Britain, are adults with the interorbital ridges of the skull fused or within a millimetre of each other.

TABLE 16 Measurements of water voles in Britain

	Males ($n = 20$)		Females ($n = 20$)	
	Mean	Range	Mean	Range
Head and body (mm)	191	163–221	182	142–220
Tail (mm)	120	98–140	114	95–133
Hind foot (mm)	32·0	29–37	32·0	27–36
Condylobasal length of skull (mm)	41·5	39·0–44·4	40·8	37·2–42·5

DISTRIBUTION See Fig. 72. Whole of Europe except for western and southern France, Iberia, southern Italy and Greece; and extending into Asia as far as the River Lena, Lake Baikal and the mountains of central Asia.

Throughout mainland of Britain, but probably very local in the northern and western Highlands of Scotland, and in general confined to low ground. Absent from Ireland and most of the small islands, but present on the Isle of Wight, Anglesey and on Eilean Gamhna and Eilean Creagach, two small islets near the entrance of Loch Melfort, Argyll.

Abundant fossils show presence in Britain during both glacial and interglacial periods since the end of the penultimate interglacial.

VARIATION British subspecies, *A. t. amphibius*, is very doubtfully distinguishable from *A. t. terrestris* of Scandinavia, being very slightly larger. With condylobasal length of skull as a measure of size, 88% of a sample of 76 Scandinavian skulls are less than 40·5 mm, whilst 82% of 65 British skulls exceed 40·5 mm

Within Britain, the most obvious regional variation is in colour, most animals in north and north-western Scotland being completely black. But little is known of the position and extent of the transitional zone, and black individuals occur sporadically in lowland populations, with an area of local abundance in Cambridgeshire and Norfolk. The black form has been considered a distinct subspecies, *A. t. reta*, but this has little validity in view of the indefinite boundary and the absence of any other distinguishing characters.

The angle of projection of the upper incisors is variable, especially in northern England, but there is no evidence of a discrete subspecies with projecting (pro-odont) teeth as supposed by Thomas (1928) in describing *A. t. brigantium*.

Size varies regionally to a slight extent, animals in North Scotland being rather smaller than those farther south.

The form on Eilean Gamhna, Argyll, is moderately distinctive, characterised especially by shortness of the molar tooth-row which is usually under 9·2 mm, and a tendency to simplification of the prismatic pattern of the molars.

Albinism of the tail-tip and of the crown is more frequent than in most other British mammals.

HABITAT Mainly on well vegetated banks of lowland rivers, ponds, canals and drainage ditches. In central Europe the species is less aquatic,

FIGURE 72 Water vole: distribution.

burrowing like moles in pasture, and this habit is found in some areas in Britain, e.g. on Read's Island in the Humber Estuary (Southern & Crowcroft 1956), Caistor, Lincolnshire (R. A. Davis, unpubl.) and on Eilean Gamhna, Argyll (Corbet 1966).

BEHAVIOUR Move clumsily on dry land, though surprisingly agile among rushes. Excellent swimmer and diver; latter asset normally used only as a defence measure. In agreement with van Wijngaarden (1954), Stoddart (1969) showed that voles are more active during the day than at night, and that males are more active than females at all times, but especially so during the night. Juveniles of both sexes take individual ranges from age of three weeks. Males more likely to remain in these ranges for life than females who appear to shift range quite frequently and usually immediately prior to parturition. Individual ranges often linear. Difference between range lengths of males and females is significant (males c. 130 m, females c. 77 m). Latrines situated at extremities of individual range (Stoddart 1970). Not known to hibernate though in cold, snowy weather males are more active above ground than females (author's data).

When frightened, utter rasping 'crick-crick', otherwise usually silent. Scent communication highly developed. Odorous secretion produced by lateral flank organ transferred by scratching and stamping action of hind feet to the latrine site during defaecation (Frank 1956)—hence the latrines seem to serve a social function. Cycle of scent production echoes testis cycle, and laboratory experiments verify that, in both sexes, the scent organ is stimulated into activity by the presence in the blood of androgens and oestrogens (Stoddart 1972). Sight poor but hearing acute.

FOOD Diet consists chiefly of grasses, although when available certain dicotyledonous plants may be taken. In Czechoslovakia 31 species of plants have been recorded in the diet, with juveniles having a more varied diet (less reeds and rhizomes) than adults (Holišová 1970); in the Netherlands 28 species have been reported (van Wijngaarden 1954).

Some authenticated records of carnivorous habit, e.g. eating dead perch under semi-natural conditions (Fig. 73 and Ryder 1962).

When feeding exhibit characteristic hunch-backed attitude; fore paws used to push rushes and grasses, often end-on, into the mouth. Wasteful feeders; spring and summer feeding places identified by deep carpet of discarded morsels. Some evidence of food storage in late autumn, when grasses are laid along floors of tunnels.

BREEDING Nests usually below ground, but in marshy regions may be

FIGURE 73 A young water vole eating a dead perch. (Photo: G. Kinns)

FIGURE 74 Nest of water vole on surface of ground amongst sedge. (Photo: G. Kinns)

built at base of rushes. Closely woven ball of rushes, 20–25 cm diameter, lined with shredded inner pith from rushes. Males fecund February, first conceptions unusual before late March in England, late April in northern Scotland. Gestation 20–22 days (van Wijngaarden 1954). Van Wijngaarden gave embryo rate as 4·1 to 5·6 embryos per pregnancy ($n=116$); in Britain (northern Scotland) the rate appears to be higher, varying between 6·0 and 6·7 embryos per pregnancy ($n=32$) (Stoddart 1971). Perry (1943) observed an intermediate rate of 5·7 with the number of corpora lutea being 6·4 ($n=18$). Litter size in Britain is not definitely known, but probably about 5. Losses from immediately pre-parturition until about 3 weeks old are high: 64·3% and 86·1% in two successive years during a population study in Aberdeenshire (Stoddart 1971).

At birth young weigh about 5·0 g, and increase by 1·0 g per day for the first 7 days, then 1·2 g per day for the second week. Born naked with eyes closed. Fully furred by 5 days; eyes open at 8 days. Weaned at 14 days and apparently settled in population by 3–4 weeks. Rapid development is necessitated by post-partum oestrus, resulting in second litter being born 22 days after first.

Mean number of pregnancies per year per adult female varies between 1·5 and 2·3. In European Russia 4 litters per female per year is not unusual (Panteleyeev 1968). Young born in the first litter of the year stand a greatly enhanced chance of surviving until the following breeding season compared with late-born young. In contrast to the continent of Europe and Asia, young voles must pass through one winter before they can breed (Scotland, and usually so in England) (Stoddart 1971).

POPULATION STRUCTURE At the start of the breeding season (March/April) two age classes present, but the older of these has disappeared by June or July, by which time the young of the year are readily found above ground. It is most unusual to find animals entering or surviving their third winter. In captivity water voles may live for up to 5 years. Mean longevity under natural conditions is 5·4 months.

Populations usually stable, although an annual increase of density is observed with the establishment of young in the population. Lowest numbers are observed immediately prior to the breeding season. Non-cyclic species, though populations in Britain appear to suffer setbacks in years with severe winters.

Little known about social structure of populations. New areas can be colonised by only one pregnant female—no other class of individual in the population has been observed to undertake dispersal movements (Stoddart 1970). Such a system allows the establishment of family-based demes. Whole families reputed to fight off intruders, but so far unsubstantiated. Retention of individual range for life usual amongst males, females may shift up to three times.

Social integration most probably based on a complex system of range tenure, but laboratory observations suggest the involvement also of some sort of dominance hierarchy. Sex ratio at start of breeding season approximately unity, shifting to 1·7 males per female by September. Return to unity by next breeding season effected by increased mortality, probably through predation, of males during winter (Stoddart 1971).

PREDATORS AND MORTALITY Van Wijngaarden (1954) listed many species of mammal and bird predators. Pike (*Esox lucius*) also known to take them. In northern Scotland, it only rarely inhabits rivers and streams that harbour common rats (*Rattus norvegicus*). In general, it appears to lose ground to this species. Most important mammalian predators in Britain are the stoat and the mink.

PARASITES AND DISEASE Healthy adults carry few fleas (mostly *Ctenophthalmus nobilis* and *Hystrichopsylla talpae*) and mites, but up to 1500 lice (*Polyplax spinigera*). In late summer ticks (mostly *Ixodes ricinus* and *I. trianguliceps*) can be observed at the edge of the ears. Kalabukhov (1937) reported that in central USSR a total of 31 species of parasites were found in and on *A. terrestris*—13 species of fleas, lice and ticks, 17 species of intestinal and one species of blood parasite. Tularaemia is frequently associated with water voles, the bacillus responsible (*B. tularense*) being transmitted by various blood-sucking arthropods. No cases have been recorded in Britain, but frequent outbreaks occur amongst humans in central USSR. Recent reports (Dumaeva *et al.* 1967) have confirmed the presence of *Listeria monocytogenes* in voles from the USSR forest tundra zone. Listeriosis in man has been linked with infectious mononucleosis and meningo-encephalitis. This pathogen has not been isolated from British specimens.

RELATIONS WITH MAN Economically inert in Britain, though isolated damage to canal and dam banks is reported. Considerable pest in Holland (van Wijngaarden 1954) where gross damage to flower bulbs is sustained during late autumn and winter. Formerly a pest of the osier industry, and currently one of the cricket bat industry. Pelts used commercially in central USSR and Siberia, but processing costly owing to the necessary removal of lateral flank organs.

LITERATURE Van Wijngaarden (1954)—detailed study of biology and pest problem in Holland. Panteleyeev (1968)—comprehensive account of central Asian status of the genus *Arvicola*. Stoddart (1970) population study in Scotland. Stoddart (1971)—population, breeding and survival. Holišová (1970)—food in central Europe. Airoldi & Meylan (1974)—a comprehensive bibliography of works on *Arvicola* published in Europe (except Russia) from 1900 to 1972.

AUTHOR FOR THIS SPECIES D. M. Stoddart.

GENUS *Ondatra*

Contains only the North American musk rats, generally placed in two species.

Musk rat *Ondatra zibethicus*

Castor zibethicus Linnaeus, 1766; Eastern Canada.

Introduced, extinct.

This large American relative of the voles became established in the wild in Britain about 1930 as a result of escapes from fur farms, but it was successfully exterminated by 1937 and has not reappeared. It has however become well established in parts of continental Europe and (by deliberate introduction) in the USSR. In Britain it occupied considerable areas in central Scotland (especially in the valley of the River Earn) and in the upper Severn Valley in Shropshire, with lesser colonies in Surrey and Sussex. There was also a small colony in Ireland.

The musk rat is considerably larger than the water vole (head and body up to 350 mm) and has the tail laterally compressed. Ecologically it closely resembles the aquatic forms of the water vole. The fur is known commercially as musquash.

For details of the species in Britain in the 1930s see Warwick (1934, 1940).

FAMILY MURIDAE
MICE AND RATS

This family contains a very large number of genera and species of rats and mice, mainly in tropical Africa, Asia and Australasia. Only two genera, *Apodemus* and *Micromys*, are predominantly Palaearctic, but representatives of two others, *Mus* and *Rattus*, have become worldwide in association with man. Wherever they occur murids are generally the dominant small rodents in woodland and forest, but many species are adapted to more open habitats.

The six species in Britain are fairly typical representatives. Compared with voles, they have long tails (at least 80% of head and body), rather pointed muzzles, large eyes, large rounded ears (least so in the harvest mouse), sleek pelage and rather long hind legs and feet. The cheek-teeth (three in each row) are low-crowned with the cusps arranged in three longitudinal rows.

Four genera are represented (Table 17).

TABLE 17 Principal characters of the genera of mice and rats

	Micromys	*Mus*	*Apodemus*	*Rattus*
Length of head and body (mm)	50–70	70–90	80–130	150–270
Length of hind feet (mm)	13–16	16–19	19–26	30–45
Length of ear (mm)	8–9	12–15	15–19	20–25
Yellow spot on chest	No	No	Yes	No
Length of upper molar row (mm)	2·6–2·8	2·9–3·4	3·7–4·6	6·4–8·0
Upper incisors notched	No	Yes	No	No
No. of roots of M^1	5	3	4 (or 5)	5

GENUS *Apodemus*

This genus contains the dominant mice of the Palaearctic Region, with about ten species, only two of which occur in Britain. They both have large ears and eyes; the dorsal pelage is dark brown mixed with yellow which is prominent on the flanks; the ventral fur is pale grey. The tail is darker above than below and lightly haired; it is as long as the head and body. The wearing surface of each upper incisor is not notched (cf. house mouse) and the first upper molar usually has four roots with corresponding alveoli (Fig. 77). The first and second upper molars each have three cusps on the inner side.

The genus is replaced in woodland habitats in North America by *Peromyscus* (a cricetid) which shows a remarkable convergence in appearance and ecology.

In Britain the two species, the wood mouse, *A. sylvaticus* and the yellow-necked mouse, *A. flavicollis*, are clearly distinct, but in parts of continental Europe they are so similar that they have been suspected of interbreeding although this has not been proved (Niethammer 1969). Of the differences detailed in Table 18 only the chest-spot and the colour of

TABLE 18 Characters of mice of the genus *Apodemus*

	Wood mouse	Yellow-necked mouse
Yellow marking on chest	A narrow longitudinal streak, or absent	A broad collar making contact with the dark dorsal colour
Colour of underparts	Pale grey	Very pale grey
Length of hind feet, without claws	19–23 mm	23–26 mm
Anterior-posterior thickness of upper incisors	1·10–1·30 mm	1·45–1·65 mm

Skulls with the thickness of the upper incisors measuring about 1·35–1·40 mm should be treated as unidentifiable unless the molars are heavily worn, in which case they will be old wood mice, or, particularly unworn, in which case they will be young yellow-necks.

the ventral pelage of the adults are sufficiently clear-cut to allow individuals to be identified without doubt. The measurements given for *A. sylvaticus* refer to mainland English animals, i.e. from the areas where both species occur. On many small islands *A. sylvaticus* is as large as *A. flavicollis*.

Wood mouse *Apodemus sylvaticus*

Mus sylvaticus Linnaeus, 1758; Upsala, Sweden. *Mus intermedius* Bellamy, 1839; Devon. *Mus hebridensis* de Winton, 1895; Uig, Lewis, Outer Hebrides. *Mus hirtensis* Barrett-Hamilton, 1899; St Kilda, Outer Hebrides. *Mus sylvaticus celticus* Barrett-Hamilton, 1900; Caragh Lake, Co Kerry, Ireland. *Mus sylvaticus fridariensis* Kinnear, 1906; Fair Isle, Shetland. *Apodemus sylvaticus butei* Hinton, 1914; Mountstuart, Isle of Bute, Firth of Clyde. *Apodemus hebridensis hamiltoni* Hinton, 1914; Island of Rhum, Inner Hebrides. *Apodemus hebridensis cumbrae* Hinton, 1914; Great Cumbrae Island, Firth of Clyde. *Apodemus hebridensis maclean* Hinton, 1914; Tobermory, Isle of Mull, Inner Hebrides. *Apodemus hebridensis fiolagan* Hinton, 1914; Island of Arran, Firth of Clyde. *Apodemus fridariensis granti* Hinton, 1914; Mid Yell, Shetland. *Apodemus fridariensis thuleo* Hinton, 1919; Foula, Shetland. *Apodemus hebridensis tirae* Montagu, 1923; Island of Tiree, Inner Hebrides. *Apodemus hebridensis tural* Montagu, 1923; Island of Islay, Inner Hebrides. *Apodemus hebridensis ghia* Montagu, 1923; Island of Gigha, Inner Hebrides.

FIGURE 75 The four species of mice found in Britain: (a) yellow-necked mouse, (b) wood mouse, (c) harvest mouse, (d) house mouse.

Apodemus hebridensis larus Montagu, 1923; Island of Jura, Inner Hebrides. *Apodemus hebridensis nesiticus* Warwick, 1940; Island of Mingulay, Outer Hebrides.
Long-tailed field mouse.

RECOGNITION In Britain the small size or even absence of the chest spot is sufficient to distinguish adults from yellow-necked mice. In both species the chest spot is more obscure in juveniles with dark pelage but it can be detected. Dark juveniles are more easily confused with house mice but the larger ears, eyes and hind feet are distinctive and they lack the characteristic smell of house mice.

SIGN Droppings larger than those of house mouse, rather rounded in section; may be pale but darken rapidly. Use a complex system of underground runways with food stores. Nests usually underground, constructed of leaves and/or finely shredded grass. The weight, volume, number of leaves and depth increase in winter (with decrease in temperature) (Dufour 1972). Use platforms above ground such as old birds' nests for feeding places. Longworth traps may be found, particularly in autumn and winter, with twigs, leaves, stones and other debris stuffed in the entrance.

DESCRIPTION Some adults show much brighter yellow on the flanks whereas juveniles are very grey with very little yellow. The chest spot (if present) is visible in the greyish ventral fur of the juvenile. Old animals often look lighter, even sandy, in colour. Mature males have prominent

FIGURE 76 Wood mouse. (Photo: G. Kinns)

testes and the posterior scrotal skin shows black pigmentation with short white hairs.

Moult varies between localities. Juvenile coat obvious by two weeks of age with post-juvenile moult during weeks 5–9; pattern sublateral (ventral to dorsal), then most adults have only a patchy moult with no seasonality (Fullagar 1967). However, in another British study (Rood 1965) no adults (except one) moulted between March and July and extensive black pigment (moulting) was seen in skins from August to January. In France a spring and autumn moult have been described, mainly of

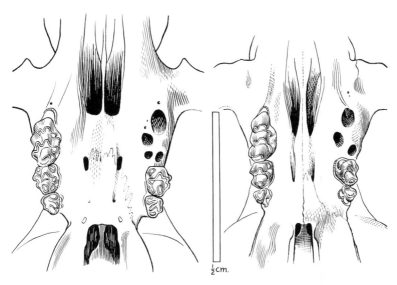

FIGURE 77 Palate and upper molars of wood mouse (left) and house mouse (right) with the left M^1 removed.

the sublateral type, and moulting was observed to take place during most of the year (Saint Girons 1967).

The first upper molar usually has four roots, but five are found in Corsican and Sardinian populations (Kahmann 1969). The number of cusps on the maxillary tooth-row visible from the side may be used as a criterion of age (Delany & Davis 1961). As the animal gets older its teeth become worn so that the 12 cusps seen in juveniles are gradually reduced in number. There is little sexual dimorphism in cranial characteristics except in some island populations (Hedges 1969). Os coxae shows marked sexual dimorphism in adults (Brown & Twigg 1969). Males show a more or less straight or slightly convex posterior margin (descending ramus of ischium and ascending ramus of pubis) and females have a strongly sinuous outline with a concavity above and a convexity below.

Reproductive tracts usually regress or do not develop in late autumn and winter. Vesicular glands lag behind testes in development (Baker 1930). Placental scars (brown/black spots on the uterine wall) are easily seen when present. Corpora lutea appear as large pink or cream spots in the ovary. Sub-caudal sebaceous glands hypertrophied in males over 19 g, undeveloped in females (Flowerdew 1971a).

Chromosomes: $2n=48$ (all acrocentric); X chromosome is largest in males and forms the largest pair in females (Kral 1970). Karyotype indistinguishable from that of yellow-necked mouse.

MEASUREMENTS See Table 19.

TABLE 19 External measurements of adult wood mice from Perthshire

| | Male | | | Female | | |
	Mean	Range	n	Mean	Range	n
Head and body	93·6 mm	86–103	20	91·0 mm	81–103	13
Tail	83·2 mm	74–95	20	82·0 mm	71–93	13
Hind feet	22·0 mm	20·8–23·0	20	21·6 mm	20·2–22·8	13
Ear	15·9 mm	14·7–17·8	17	16·1 mm	14·6–17·3	13
Weight	19·1 g	13–27	20	17·8 g	13–24	13

DISTRIBUTION See Fig. 78. The woodland and steppe zones of the western Palaearctic, but not extending far into coniferous zone. Throughout Europe except for northern Scandinavia; east to the Altai and Himalayas; south to northern Arabia and North Africa. Present in Iceland and on most of the Mediterranean islands.

Ubiquitous in Britain and Ireland except on very open mountain areas. Widespread on the small islands. Absent only from some very small islands, e.g. Lundy, Isle of May, North Rona, and from the Scillies other than Tresco and St Marys (but subfossil finds from Nornour—Pernetta & Handford 1970).

Probably introduced by man to Ireland and many of the smaller islands (Corbet 1961), those on some of the Hebrides and northern isles probably from Scandinavia (Berry 1969).

VARIATION British and Irish mainland animals not clearly distinguishable from the continental form. Many subspecies have been described from small islands (see synonymy above) but most of these were based on characters of colour and size that have subsequently proved to overlap widely with other populations. It seems likely that no insular form is sufficiently distinguishable from *all* other forms to justify designation as subspecies. In general, island forms are large (the largest being on Rhum, St Kilda and Fair Isle). On some islands a large proportion of individuals have the underside heavily washed with buff—this occurs especially on the Channel Isles, St Kilda and Lewis. Variation in size and pelage was reviewed by Delany (1970).

Gross variation on the British mainland is slight but has been studied in great detail along with the insular forms, e.g. by Delany & Healy (1964), Berry, Evans & Sennitt (1967), Hedges (1969), Delany (1970), Berry (1969, 1970a, 1973).

Variation with time has been demonstrated in the St Kilda population between 1910–19 and 1948–67. In contrast samples from Lewis and Harris (Outer Hebrides) collected 45 years apart did not differ significantly (Berry 1970).

Albinism of the tail tip occurs in $3 \cdot 1\%$ of the population (Corbet 1963). Gross variants of the pelage are exceedingly rare but silver-grey and melanistic forms are known.

FIGURE 78 Wood mouse: distribution.

HABITAT Very varied, wherever there is cover in the form of trees, shrubs or, sometimes, rocks. It is the characteristic small rodent of woodland, living in runways in and below the litter. Occupies areas with less ground cover than the bank vole and often shows no particular preference for any particular habitat type in mixed deciduous woodland (Southern & Lowe 1968). However a preference for habitats with bracken and bramble as opposed to deciduous trees with a shrub layer, has been noted (Corke 1971) and bracken/bramble is avoided when bank voles are at high density (Corke 1974). Common in hedgerows and fields (Pollard & Relton 1970, Jeffries *et al.* 1973, Corke 1974), gardens and sometimes grass and heather, especially if field voles are absent. In Ireland, despite lack of field voles, more caught in heather, grass and bracken than in grass (Fairley 1967). Rarely above the tree line on high moors and scree except where stone walls or buildings give cover, but recorded up to 1300 m (Corbet 1960). In the absence of human occupation they will successfully compete with house mice in buildings and this probably caused the extinction of the latter on St Kilda (Berry & Tricker 1969).

BEHAVIOUR Locomotion rapid, either scurrying or leaping, unless cautiously investigating when slow deliberate steps are taken. When exploring may adopt an upright position, standing on hind legs and pointing nose upward. Lethargic movement noted in winter during hypothermia (Morris 1968).

Activity in the laboratory predominantly nocturnal with dusk and dawn peaks in winter, changing to a single peak in summer (Miller 1955). Males significantly more active than females (Gelmroth 1970). Most active on dark nights and inhibited even by moonlight.

Captures at different points during the night indicated that movement is not only to a single feeding point and the nest may be left for two hours or more (Kikkawa 1964). The outward and return journey may be along the same route; published home ranges vary from 0·0016–2·4 ha (Brown 1966). Home range size in woodland 2250 m² for males (from trapping) and 1817 m² for females but it is possible that not all of the ranges were covered by the trapping grid (Crawley 1969); many ranges overlap. Juvenile home range increases with sexual development whereas juveniles not maturing (in autumn) remain in a small range (Randolph 1973). Movement increases in summer and decreases in winter (Miller 1958); males may move over large distances (Kikkawa 1964, Jewell 1966b) but little dispersal of adults within woodland (Watts 1970a). Movement out of woodland into other habitats noted in spring and summer (Kikkawa 1964, Brown 1969, Corke 1971, author's data). Homing sure from 336 m; from 663 m half of mice returned (Hacker & Pearson 1951).

Social organisation (Brown 1966, 1969) based on group with dominant male controlling area of 1·6–2·4 ha within which subordinate males and females live; many young are probably forced to disperse. Females defend breeding ranges and presumed subordinates often move to feeding grounds in groups; little overt aggression seen in summer. Observation at a baiting point revealed no aggression in winter (Kikkawa 1964); however, in the laboratory some adult males will fight vigorously on occasion (Flowerdew 1971b). Resident adults will cause immigrating adults to disperse, and in the laboratory established males and females will isolate or kill strange juveniles (Flowerdew 1974). In an indoor enclosure containing two adult males and two adult females long periods of amicable behaviour interspersed with agonistic behaviour were observed (Bovet 1972); also 'asocial' times when activity was asynchronous and 'social' times when activity coincided.

Ultrasounds are produced by young up to 24 days and initiate retrieving behaviour in lactating females (Sewell 1970, Okon 1972). Audible squeaks and ultrasound (70 kHz pulses) emitted during agonistic encounters (Sewell 1968) and when exploring a new cage. Ultrasounds are also emitted by males during genital sniffing of female, attempted and successful mating and after disturbance of the nest (Sales 1972). Low temperatures initiate ultrasonic calling of young (Okon 1972). Scent from urine and body secretions probably important in chemical communication. The eyes are insensitive to red light (Brown 1969).

FOOD Mainly seedlings, buds, fruits, nuts, snails and arthropods. In English deciduous woodland the major foods in autumn and winter are tree seeds and when these are scarce in spring and early summer they turn to arthropods (larval Lepidoptera and centipedes) or to buds and the young shoots of green plants (Watts 1968). The young eat less seed and a greater variety of foods than adults. Fungi, moss, fruits, bark, galls, dead leaves and earthworms have also been recorded.

In Sweden earthworms are taken to a greater extent in spring and summer than at other times, and bark is more common in winter and spring than in summer and autumn, otherwise the results were similar to those in England (Hansson 1971a). Molluscs, grass, rushes, sedges, ferns and root-hairs were rare. Hazel nut shells opened with a hole surrounded by toothmarks (cf. bank vole which leaves no mark on the surface (East 1965)). The carpels of rose hips are eaten but the flesh is discarded (Eldridge 1969), whereas the bank vole eats the flesh and discards the carpels. Grain is manipulated with fore paws and typical coarse dust of 'kibblings' left behind, as with house mice but not with voles. Snails are opened by biting through the shell away from the spire.

BREEDING Males are fecund in March and pregnancies occur in April, reaching a peak in July or August and declining by October (Baker 1930). Breeding seasons in island populations are shorter (Jewell 1966a). A good seed crop in woodland prolongs the breeding season or allows it to continue throughout the winter (Smyth 1966, Hansson 1971, Louarn & Schmitt 1972). Early breeding is related to high weight in February (Flowerdew 1973) but is known to occur without abundant seed (Fairley & Comerton 1972). Additional food in spring will advance the start of breeding (Watts 1970b) and increase weight (Flowerdew 1972).

Gestation 25–26 days. Mean number of embryos 5·5 rising to 6 at the height of the breeding season and declining to below 5; counts of corpora lutea indicate that early in the season some eggs fail to be fertilised, later, fewer eggs are ovulated (Baker 1930). In winter, litter sizes are probably small (Smyth 1966). Some sets of embryos show evidence of resorption (Pelikán 1967, Fairley 1970b). In the field a maximum of four pregnancies was recorded from 2 out of 34 females followed during one breeding season (Flowerdew 1971b). Females may be pregnant at 12 g and conception at post-partum oestrus is regular (Lowe 1957). In summer males may be fecund at 15 g but late-born young remain immature until the following spring. The sex-ratio of litters born in captivity is approximately equal but live traps show seasonal changes in sex-ratio, often catching more males in winter and spring (Crawley 1970).

The young are born naked and blind, weighing between 1 and 2 g. The grey-brown juvenile coat appears dorsally at *c.* 6 days and then the white ventral fur follows in a day or so. The incisors erupt at *c.* 13 days, the tail and hind feet darken dorsally at *c.* 14 days and the eyes open at *c.* 16 days. The young are weaned by *c.* 18 days. Growth in the laboratory and in the field shows much variation (Flowerdew 1972).

POPULATION In spring the population consists of young born late in the last breeding season and a few adults from the previous year. Fewer young are caught in the spring and early summer than would be expected from recorded pregnancies (Tanton 1965, Watts 1969). Most over-wintered animals disappear by autumn. A good food supply increases winter density (Hansson 1971a, Flowerdew 1972, Louarn & Schmitt 1972). The mean expectation of life from weaning (in summer) ranges from 14·2 weeks with supplementary food to 8·4 weeks without (Flowerdew 1972). Maximum age in the wild probably 18–20 months (Roben 1969); longer in captivity.

The increase in numbers as a result of breeding is most notable from July to October, reaching a peak in September–October or even February according to length of breeding season. Numbers decline to a trough in March–April. The low level of numbers is often relatively stable through the summer and the timing of the increase is density-dependent, being the main regulatory factor (high-density—late increase; low-density—early increase) (Watts 1969). Removal of adult males brings forward the time of the increase (Flowerdew 1974). There is no evidence of cyclical fluctuations although the annual sequence sometimes breaks down (Southern 1970a). Densities vary from 0·25–100/ha.

PREDATORS AND MORTALITY The following birds and mammals are known to include wood mice in their diet: fox, weasel, stoat, badger, marten, domestic cat, long-eared owl, barn owl, short-eared owl, tawny owl, little owl and kestrel (Glue 1970, Fairley 1972). In Ireland the wood mouse forms about 70% of the diet of the long-eared owl whereas in Britain the field vole is also available and the wood mouse accounts for 25–50% of the prey (Fairley 1972). In English woodland the wood mouse makes up 30% of the prey of the tawny owl and when both the wood mouse and bank vole are scarce the owls show a reduction in the number of pairs breeding; exceptionally none breeds at all (Southern 1970b).

Experiments have indicated that the survival of juveniles and over-wintered adults in summer is improved by a good food supply (Flowerdew 1972). The removal of adult males also increases juvenile survival (Flowerdew 1974). In general, survival is better in winter than in summer and a good food supply in autumn leads to good overwinter survival (Bergstedt 1965, Watts 1969). Survival decreases in the spring, probably as a result of intraspecific strife, dispersal and increased predation.

PARASITES AND DISEASE The commonest ectoparasites found on wood mice in deciduous woodland near Oxford are as follows (O'Donnell 1971).

Fleas: *Ctenophthalmus nobilis* (common), *Peromyscopsylla silvatica*, *Megabothris walkeri*, *M. turbidus*, *Malareus penicilliger*, *Hystrichopsylla talpae* (all rare); lice: *Polyplax serrata* (common); mites: *Laelaps agilis*, *Eulaelaps stabularis*, *Radfordia lemina*, *Trombicula autumnalis* (all common); tick: *Ixodes trianguliceps* (common). See Randolph (1975) for a study of the last species.

There is however considerable variation throughout the country and according to season. For example, the flea *Megabothris walkeri* is dominant in western Scotland and is mutually exclusive on the Scottish mainland with *M. rectangulartus* (Corbet *et al*. 1968). The occurrence and distribution of ectoparasites on Irish wood mice was reviewed by Fairley (1972). The parasitic beetle *Leptinus testaceus* is common in the pelage and is specific to the wood mouse.

Endoparasites are numerous and include the following (position of infection, when known, given in brackets). Cestodes: *Catenotaenia pusilla* (small and large intestine), *C. lobata* (small intestine), *Paranoplocephala* sp., *Hymenolepis muris-sylvatici* (large intestine). *Taenia taeniaeformis* (small intestine); trematodes: *Brachylaimus recurvum* (small intestine), *Corrigia vitta* (interlobiary canals of pancreas and duodenum), *Maritrema apodemicum* (small intestine); nematodes: *Capillaria hepatica* (liver), *C. muris-sylvatici* (small and large intestine), *Nematospiroides dubius* (duodenum and small intestine), *Syphacia stroma* (small and large intestine), *Aspicularis tetraptera*, and an accidental acanthocephalan, *Centrorhynchus aluconis* (Elton *et al*. 1931, Lewis & Twigg 1972). H. Trapido (pers. comm.) records in *c*. 10% of mice larval rhabditid nematodes in the orbital fluid.

Ringworm fungi are widespread (English 1969). A sample tested for infection with a tuberculosis condition (*Mycobacterium tuberculosis* var. *muris*) showed a positive result in 2·3% (Wells 1946). Infection with the spirochaete bacterium *Leptospira* (many serotypes) increases with age (Twigg, Cuerden & Hughes 1968) and with the water content of the soil (Lewis & Twigg 1972). In Surrey 64 out of 248 showed evidence of infection with leptospires (Twigg 1973). Sixteen species of parasitic protozoa have been recorded (Cox 1970), also louping ill virus, a sheep disease (Varma & Page 1966).

RELATIONS WITH MAN Will sometimes enter houses but more usually found in outhouses and sheds. It is believed that cereals are grazed but the fact is disputed (Pollard & Relton 1970). They are easily maintained in captivity but breeding is not certain; they never become really tame and always demand some skill in handling. If one is picked up by any part of the tail, other than the base, the skin sloughs off and the exposed caudal vertebrae eventually drop off.

Increased lead content of wood mice living near main roads has been reported: $1·66 \pm 0·20$ ppm wet weight compared with $1·14 \pm 0·08$ in woodland and arable sites (Jeffries & French 1972). Animals inhabiting both the field edge and the open field surface fed on dressed grain immediately it was drilled. Mean whole-body load of dieldrin increased 68 times and that of mercury increased 11 times; some levels were high enough to cause mortality (Jeffries *et al*. 1973).

LITERATURE The most comprehensive review of the biology of the species is that of Fairley (1972) which deals mainly with the Irish literature.

AUTHOR FOR THIS SPECIES J. R. Flowerdew; with acknowledgements to T. G. O'Donnell for providing the list of ectoparasites and Dr G. B. Corbet for information on synonomy and measurements.

Yellow-necked mouse *Apodemus flavicollis*

Mus flavicollis Melchior, 1834; Sielland, Denmark. *Mus sylvaticus wintoni* Barrett-Hamilton, 1900; Graftonbury, Herefordshire.

RECOGNITION In Britain the yellow collar appears to be consistently well developed and allows easy separation from the wood mouse (and other mice). The upper parts are a rather richer reddish brown than in the wood mouse and the tail is usually longer than the head and body (Saint Girons 1957) and proportionately thicker at the base than in the wood mouse. The yellow collar (suffused by grey) is visible in mice in juvenile pelage. Adult mice are on average 1·5 times the weight of a wood mouse. When handled they bite more readily and squeak more vociferously than do wood mice. Skulls difficult to distinguish from those of wood mice—see Table 18 (p. 206).

SIGN As wood mouse.

DESCRIPTION As in wood mouse except for those characteristics mentioned under 'recognition' and 'measurements'.

MEASUREMENTS Weights: females 27·4 g ($n=56$, range 10·0–44·0); males 29·0 g ($n=66$, range 11·0–42·0) (Corke 1974).

DISTRIBUTION See Fig. 79. Throughout most of Europe, extending further north in Scandinavia than the wood mouse but elsewhere more restricted; east only to the Urals and Caucasus, south to north Spain and central Italy.

In Britain restricted to southern England and Wales, and absent from large areas within that range, e.g. from most of the Southwest and the Midlands.

A single specimen in the British Museum came from Riding Mill, Northumberland some time before 1911 but the continued presence of the species there has not been confirmed.

VARIATION The extent of the chest-spot is very variable in continental

Europe, being reduced especially in the south and east (Ursin 1956).
British animals are not distinguishable from the more north-western continental ones. Their recognition as a distinct subspecies on the basis of
darker underparts and larger chest-spot (Miller 1912) cannot be upheld.
There is little obvious variation within the British population.

HABITAT In the British Isles occurs mainly in woods, also in hedgerows
and field edges but is less likely to colonise the central area of crop fields
than is the wood mouse. Often found in rural gardens and homes but
does not extend so far into urban areas as does the wood mouse. Always
found with wood mice and is usually less common than that species. For
example in Essex woods, where both species occur, between a quarter
and a fifth of all the *Apodemus* are *A. flavicollis* (Corke & Harris 1974),
although sometimes a much higher propertion of yellow-necked mice
occurs (Montgomery 1976). Does not show the avoidance of the more
open areas of woodland that wood mice sometimes do (Corke 1970) which
may be explained by the latter's greater selection of areas of cover (Hoffmeyer 1973). There is some evidence that the most favoured habitats
are woodland areas in low-lying regions where arable farming predominates (Corke 1974).

Continental authors working in eastern Europe mostly indicate habitat

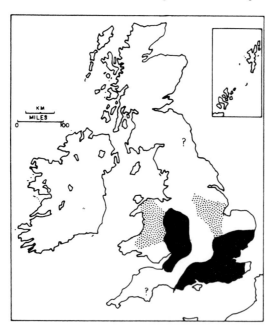

FIGURE 79 Yellow-
necked mouse:
distribuion.

divergence between the two *Apodemus* species (e.g. Grodzinski 1959). Yellow-necked mice are more truly woodland animals, while wood mice occupy field and scrub. It is also claimed that in France (Saint Girons 1966, 1967) and Norway (Collett 1911–12) there is a vertical zonation with the yellow-necked mouse occurring at higher altitudes than the wood mouse. This is the reverse of the situation in Britain.

BEHAVIOUR Locomotion and nocturnal activity as in wood mouse. The home range is probably larger than for the wood mouse, although this is based on a relative measure of range lengths rather than direct measures of range size. In a trapping study the sex ratio was much nearer unity than is usually found with wood mice. This is probably because both sexes are equally active and so equally exposed to capture (Corke 1974).

There is evidence of great climbing powers by yellow-necked mice in Poland (Borowski 1963) and if this also applies in Britain it may explain why this species is more adept at entering houses than the wood mouse.

FOOD This has not been studied in Britain but it seems probable that the range of food items is similar to that of the wood mouse.

BREEDING In Czechoslavakia the breeding season was found to be closely similar to that of *A. sylvaticus* but with a lower number of pregnancies per female (4·38) and a smaller number of embryos per pregnancy (5·04) than in the wood mouse (Pelikan 1966).

In Britain there is some evidence of a slightly shorter breeding season than for the wood mouse (Corke 1974).

POPULATION The annual population cycle is very similar in both *Apodemus* species. Because the yellow-necked mice show less tendency to disperse into non-woodland breeding habitats, the summer population does not decline quite so markedly and recruitment to the woodland population starts slightly earlier than in the wood mouse.

PREDATORS AND MORTALITY Presumably the same as the wood mouse but there is little evidence for this since *Apodemus* remains are difficult to identify specifically in predator guts, droppings or pellets.

PARASITES AND DISEASE Not investigated in Britain.

RELATIONS WITH MAN Comes into country houses more often than wood mice, where it may cause annoyance and damage in lofts and apple stores, etc. Less likely to damage field crops than wood mice. Can be bred in captivity but does not become tame easily.

AUTHOR FOR THIS SPECIES D. Corke.

GENUS *Micromys*

Contains a single species.

Harvest Mouse *Micromys minutus*

Mus minutus Pallas, 1771; Volga, USSR. *Mus soricinus* Hermann, 1780; Strasbourg, France. *Mus tricetus* Boddaert, 1785; Hampshire, England. *Mus minimus* White, 1789; Selborne, Hampshire. *Micromys messorius* Kerr, 1792; Hampshire.
Dwarf mouse, red mouse, red ranny.

RECOGNITION The smallest British rodent, weighing only 6 g when adult. Easily distinguished from other murids by the blunt muzzle and small hairy ear, reminiscent of a vole's. Tail similar in length to the head and body, tip very prehensile. The tail does not strip when handled. Sexually mature animals have a russet orange dorsal pelage and are pure white ventrally. Newly independent juveniles have a grey brown pelage similar to that of house mice but are easily distinguishable both by their small size (*c.* 4 g as opposed to *c.* 7 g) and by the prehensile tail.

The skull is easily distinguished from other murids by the relative shortness of the rostrum and the long braincase. Distinguished from small house mouse skulls by having five roots in the first upper molar, three in the lower, no notch in the upper incisors and the molar tooth rows less than 3 mm in length.

SIGN The only British mouse that builds its breeding nests well above ground level, in the stalk zone of vegetation. The height depends on the vegetation, 30–60 cm being normal. The nest, usually made of grass leaves, is almost spherical up to 10 cm in diameter and built within the grass tussocks or amongst other densely growing vegetation such as cereals, rushes, herbs or brambles. When newly constructed the nests are difficult to find, but in early winter the brown withered grass balls stand out more clearly.

Unless present in very large numbers, there is no other obvious sign of their presence, and damage to cereal ears is rarely noticeable.

DESCRIPTION A small slender delicate rodent. The hind legs are not conspicuously large as in wood mice—the hind feet are 12–16 mm in length and are more slender than in the house mouse. The outer toes of the hind feet are adapted to the climbing habit by a slight separation.

The small pubescent ears have a large triangular meatus, unlike other British murids. The tail is weakly bi-coloured and sparsely haired.

The dorsal pelage of adults consists of long dark guard hairs overlying

FIGURE 80 Harvest mouse and nest. (Photo: G. Kinns)

the finer russet orange contour hairs. The ventral fur remains white in winter whilst the dorsal pelage is dark orange brown. Juvenile animals have an overall grey/brown pelage but soon start to moult, from the haunches forward, into the adult phase. They thus become bi-coloured dorsally for a period. The ano-genital distance is the best guide for determining the sex of individuals, though for recently independent juveniles this is difficult.

Adult breeding males tend to have a far thicker penis than non-breeding males. Breeding females have four pairs of nipples. Lactating females are often pregnant.

The width of the brain-case is similar to that of the zygomatic breadth, 8·6–9·6 mm. The distance from the upper border of the infra-orbital foramen to tip of nasal bone is less than a third of the distance to the posterior border of occiput. The first molar of the upper jaw has 5 roots and that of the lower jaw 3. The upper incisor has no notch (cf. Fig. 83) Fragments from owl pellets can be identified with certainty by these features. The post-cranial skeleton is very delicate.

MEASUREMENTS See Table 17, p. 205. Weight is about 0·7 g at birth, 3·5 g as juvenile, 6 g as adult, with pregnant females up to 15 g.

DISTRIBUTION See Fig. 81. Much of the Palaearctic Region from France to Siberia and Korea, with insular populations at both ends of the range, in Britain and Japan. In central Europe from Denmark to Italy.

In Britain the distribution appears to have become more limited within this century. Reports from Angus, Fife and Perth in 1800s have not recently been repeated. Most abundant south of a line from Humber to

FIGURE 81 Harvest mouse: distribution.

Bristol Channel but recent records have confirmed its presence in Cheshire, Wales, Yorkshire and as far north as Durham and Edinburgh. Not present in Ireland. The distribution, though local, may be more widespread than commonly thought.

VARIATION Study of geographical variation on the continent has been confused by the protracted winter moult from juvenile to adult pelage when animals with bicoloured dorsal pelage are common.

Individual variation is mainly related to age, season, moult and breeding condition. At one week old the average weight of two nestlings may vary by the factor of two, but such discrepancies disappear as adult weight is reached. Russian animals are larger than British, being over twice the weight. Melanistic and albino forms have not been observed in the wild but individuals with white patches have been found.

HABITAT Favours areas of tall, dense vegetation. The breeding nests are the obvious sign of satisfactory conditions and these may be found in long grass, reedbeds, rushes, grassy hedgerows, ditches and bramble patches, cereals (with some aversion to barley) and some legume crops. In areas of modern agriculture, field headlands and rough grass banks act as a refuge and a reservoir during the winter. Large-scale movements are necessary in areas of water meadows and salt marshes, where flooding occurs. Harvest mice have been recorded from young plantations but captures in mature woodland may represent overspill from adjoining areas. Ungrazed meadows cut once annually may contain considerable numbers.

With the dying back of vegetation in winter the animal appears to alter its habitat from a stalk zone dweller and is found using other small mammal runway systems. There is no evidence for the formation of 'winter underground colonies' in the open habitats, though concentrations do occur in ricks.

BEHAVIOUR An extremely active animal whose small size allows it to climb and feed in the stalk zone. When undisturbed, the mouse moves quietly amongst the vegetation, carefully testing the strength of the stems. A frightened animal either 'freezes' or attempts to escape by rapid leaps through the stalks.

In captivity, activity rhythms have been investigated. Cross (1970) found that well fed animals on short daylength became nocturnal. Smirnov (1957) considered them crepuscular. There has so far been only one study of British harvest mice populations in the wild, but data gathered from trapping suggest the species is more nocturnal during the summer and diurnal during winter (author's data). Other observations of a captive breeding stock show that they may be active throughout the 24 hours.

In undisturbed habitats, harvest mice appear to be sedentary animals for much of the year, staying within an area of 0·04–0·06 hectares. There is considerable movement of juveniles during the autumn and adults may move up to 100 m in spring when the populations are apparently lowest. There is considerable overlap of home ranges for much of the year, especially for males (trap-revealed data only) (Trout 1976).

Isolated reports of a social colony structure cannot be substantiated in the field. In the laboratory, high densities of non-breeding animals live agreeably, but on lowering the density, one animal becomes dominant and may attack others. Mated females drive away the male, but consecutive litters have been raised successfully in captivity where the male remained in the same cage throughout. In captivity the female may actually consume a disturbed litter in contrast to most other rodents that simply mutilate the young.

Audible signals between individuals in the field are rare, but have been reported during courtship, mating and when density is high. Blind youngsters often squeak audibly when disturbed, and it is possible that ultrasonic communication occurs in the young. There are no published works concerning olfactory communication.

Hearing is very acute, the animals reacting sharply to any rustling or scraping sound. Aided by the prehensile tail, these mice have an excellent sense of balance and judgement concerning the strength of single stems of foliage. Visual acuity is poor, but mice will detect sudden changes in silhouette from several metres.

FOOD Reputedly an insect and seed eater, but little published data on animals living in natural surroundings, i.e. not in ricks. Certainly takes hard and soft bodied insects, but eats many fruits, seeds and berries. In early spring grass shoots are probably eaten when other food is scarce. Takes grain from cereal heads, often eating it well above ground level and leaving characteristic sickle-shaped remains. In captivity will chase moths and flies to eat.

BREEDING There is little literature concerning breeding in Britain though a certain amount has been published from Germany and USSR. For captive British mice Trout (1976) found a gestation period of 17–19 days, litter size 1–7 (mean 4·8) from 86 litters. A post-partum oestrus occurs and up to 8 litters may be produced by a single female, though in the wild 3 is probably the maximum. Mated females lose the vaginal plug quickly. In England the breeding season extends from late May until October or even December (S. Harris, unpubl.) depending on the weather. Several nests of dead, blind young have been found in early November (Trout 1976) and Sleptsov (1947) indicated great mortality of nestlings in USSR during adverse autumn weather. Early literature gave litter sizes of 5–12 and though wild litters are often larger than those from captive animals, in Britain eight is the maximum found in recent years.

Construction of the breeding nests has been described by several authors (Sleptsov 1947, Piechocki 1958, Frank 1957). Aerial nests are built in late pregnancy by the female. Long almost intact leaves still attached to the plant stalks are arranged to form a hammock and the outer framework. The main walls are formed of grass blades slit longitudinally and woven into a springy ball, 8–10 cm in diameter. The central chamber is lined with shorter shredded lengths. Usually the entrance hole is kept closed during the first week of the youngsters' life but there is at least one obvious entrance spot. Reports of entry and exit from any part of the nest are incorrect.

In captivity birth usually occurs in early morning, but this may not be so in the wild. In captivity, the young weigh 0·65–0·8 g at birth. Subsequent growth is extremely rapid. By the 4th day, light brown down begins to cover the back. This becomes thicker and a dark line becomes apparent dorsally. The belly is white by the 8th and 9th days, when the eyes usually open (2·5–3·5 g). The position of the nipples is easily seen at this age.

The young begin to leave the nest and explore at 11 days. The nest rapidly acquires a battered look, entrance holes remaining unclosed even at night.

By the 14th day a new moult to a grey/brown is nearly complete and the young are capable of feeding themselves. If the mother is pregnant, the young are often chased out of the nest area on day 15 or 16. Kastle (1953), Smirnov (1959) and Frank (1957) gave very detailed descriptions of development, but it should be remembered that some authors have used foster mothers for their litters and that central European and Russian animals are distinctly larger than British ones. These factors will affect the rate of development in terms of body weight, as will the difference between laboratory and field situations.

POPULATION STRUCTURE On the basis of tooth wear, Kubik (1952) suggested that the maximum life span in the wild is 18 months. Data from a wild population in Britain however suggest that very few animals survive 6 months: 30% of animals marked as juvenile survived 6 weeks, 10% survived 18 weeks from first capture (Trout 1976). In captivity, several instances of non-breeding individuals living 5 years have been reported.

Cycles of abundance occur, populations of 200+/ha being followed by several years of low numbers. Local populations fluctuate seasonally. The peak numbers occur during November and fall steeply in Feburary/March. Live trapping appears to become ineffective during early and mid-summer due either to a behavioural change perhaps associated with breeding or to a very low density of animals. A huge surge of juveniles is recruited into the population in September and October. Breeding adults are removed from the population very rapidly after the termination of the breeding season up to four generations of mice may reproduce within one breeding season.

PREDATORS AND MORTALITY Harvest mice are taken by a wide variety of vertebrates; the carnivores and bird predators include mustelids, owls, hawks, corvids and even pheasants (Sleptsov 1947). Being active throughout the twenty-four hours, they are liable to predation by both nocturnal and diurnal animals. Most published work on predator food shows harvest mice to form less than 1% of the diet; but a study of the food of several barn owls in West Sussex, where harvest mice are common, has shown a seasonal cycle of occurrence of harvest mice in pellets varying from maximum 65% in November down to less than 1% in June/July. Adverse weather towards the end of the breeding season causes the death of many young mice, but February is the month with the greatest mortality rate (as revealed by trapping). Changes in habitat management and modern methods of agriculture have doubtless caused a great reduction in abundance; combine harvesting, insecticide spraying, stubble burning and hedge clearing being major factors.

PARASITES AND DISEASE Sleptsov (1947) and Mohr (1950) give lists of ectoparasites, but state that there are no specific species. Several species of flea, the tick *Ixodes trianguliceps* and a number of mites may be found in the short fur. Rowe (1961) found few ectoparasites on British specimens. A few cases of infection by helminths have been reported (Frank 1959). Klets (1936) has shown the harvest mouse to be susceptible to experimental infection by plague, tularemia, pneumococcus, anthrax, Friedlander's pneumobacilli; and there are reports that it might be susceptible to tuberculosis. The protozoans *Babesia microti* and a trypanosome have been recorded (Cox 1970) as intestinal parasites.

RELATIONS WITH MAN There are no official reports of harvest mice causing damage in Britain; however, Sleptsov (1947) gave several instances of plague numbers of this species causing damage in USSR. Even in Britain, the harvest mouse may be the most abundant small mammal species in some localities so presumably some damage could be attributable to them. Rowe (1964) found large numbers in unthreshed ricks during the winter and Trout (1976) recorded trapped population of up to 270/ha in grassland.

Harvest mice are very easy to keep in captivity, requiring little specialized attention. There have been sporadic reports of breeding in captivity, but it is only recently that the continuous breeding success described by Kastle (1953) and Frank (1957) in Germany have been repeated with British specimens. Diet does not seem to be an important factor in captive breeding.

LITERATURE Piechocki (1958)—a monograph in German. Knight (1963)—a popular account.

AUTHOR FOR THIS SPECIES R. Trout.

GENUS *Mus*

A moderately large genus mainly in the Oriental Region and in Africa, although the African species (and some Oriental ones) are sometimes separated as a genus *Leggada*. One species, *M. musculus*, is worldwide. Closely related to *Rattus* and distinguished mainly by dental characters, especially the distorted shape of the first upper molars and the very reduced third molars.

House mouse *Mus musculus*

Mus musculus Linnaeus, 1758; Upsala, Sweden. *Mus domesticus* Rutty, 1772; Dublin. *Mus musculus* var. *nudo-plicatus* Gaskoin, 1856; Taplow, Bucks, England. *Mus muralis* Barrett-Hamilton, 1899; St Kilda. *Mus musculus jamesoni* Krausse, 1921; North Bull Island, Dublin Bay, Ireland.

RECOGNITION Dull greyish brown colour is distinctive but note that juveniles of wood mouse and yellow-necked mouse are very grey. Tail is thicker and more prominently scaly than that of other mice. In the hand, the notched upper incisors (in side view) are distinctive. This also distinguishes isolated skulls as do the 3-rooted first upper molars and the very small third upper molars.

SIGN Presence revealed by faeces, runways, footprints, smears, hole scrapes, partially eaten food particles and damage. Faeces often concen-

FIGURE 82 House mouse. (Photo: G. Kinns)

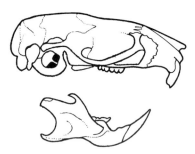

FIGURE 83 Skull of house mouse. Note the characteristic notch in the upper incisor.

trated in favoured places; similar to those of the wood mouse but smaller (about 7 mm long). Runways and footprints discernible along regular routes through dusty places and finely divided foods. Small mounds, 'urinating pillars', consisting of faeces, dirt, grease and urine sometimes found in habitual places. Dirty black smears often present along well-travelled runways. Loop smears similar to but smaller than those attributable to ship rats may be found at roof height around joists. Occasionally toothmarks evident on damaged commodities. Characteristic 'stale' smell.

DESCRIPTION Pelage a rather uniform greyish brown above and usually only slightly lighter below, but occasionally much paler grey below. Eyes and ears smaller than in wood mouse. Skin of tail does not readily slip off as in wood mouse.

Upper incisors with a distinct notch on the wearing surface when seen from the side. M^1 with the first lamina of cusps greatly distorted, M^1 with only three roots. M^3 rudimentary.

Chromosome number: usually $2n=40$, all telocentric or acrocentric, but Robertsonian fusions giving rise to $2n=38$ reported from Switzerland. (Another Swiss form, *poschiavinus*, has $2n=26$ and may be specifically distinct.)

MEASUREMENTS See Table 17, p. 205.

DISTRIBUTION See Fig. 84. Now worldwide through introduction by man, original range probably in the steppe zone of the southern Palaearctic and perhaps including the Mediterranean region.

Widespread throughout British Isles and Ireland wherever there is human habitation and including practically all inhabited small islands. Present in Britain at least since the pre-Roman Iron Age, the earliest well stratified find in an archaeological site being from a site of that age at Gussage All Saints, Dorset (specimen in British Museum).

FIGURE 84 House mouse: distribution.

VARIATION Extremely variable—in general small, white-bellied, short-tailed forms occur outdoors in areas that could be the original range, e.g. in the steppes of central Asia and in parts of the Mediterranean coast. Commensal forms tend to be larger and darker with longer tails, but the two forms may occur side by side and the ecological and genetical relationships are obscure. Subspecies in Britain, *M. m. domesticus*, characterised by dark belly, also occurs in western Europe but is replaced in eastern Europe and Scandinavia by *M. m. musculus*.

In Britain two insular races have been described. *M. m. muralis*, formerly on Hirta, St Kilda, became extinct after the human population left the island in 1930, probably due to inability to compete successfully with the wood mouse (Berry & Tricker 1969). It was characterised by large size and paler belly, and can be considered a moderately distinctive subspecies. On North Bull Island in Dublin Bay a pale form was described as *M. m. jamesoni* but is probably not clearly distinguishable from pale forms elsewhere. White-bellied individuals occur sporadically elsewhere—those in Ireland have been called *M. m. orientalis* (an invalid name of a North African form) by O'Mahony (1935) but these should be considered as individual variants of *M. m. domesticus* (Fairley 1971b).

Skeletal variation throughout Britain has been described by Berry (1963, 1964) and can provide a measure of genetic affinity between populations. Biochemical polymorphism has been extensively studied in other parts of the world (see for example Selander 1970, Berry & Murphy 1970). The physical basis and genetics of variation in coat colour have been reviewed by Deol (1970).

HABITAT Common in a wide range of urban habitats—in houses, shops, factories, warehouses and mills; also recorded in cold stores and coal mines. In rural areas present in farm buildings, granaries, poultry-houses, piggeries, refuse tips, hedgerows. Also found in open fields in arable country but less abundant than wood mice in mainland hedgerows.

BEHAVIOUR Excellent sense of balance and running and climbing ability, moving up wooden and brick walls, cables, etc., without much difficulty. Jump well and swim capably. Characteristically often stand on hind legs and 'smell the air'. Show positive 'new object reaction', initial cautious behaviour followed by rapid and thorough investigation.

Mainly nocturnal but not completely so, particularly when food is scarce or when populations are dense and subject to little disturbance.

Home range largely determined by the availability of food and cover. In indoor habitats where food and cover are co-incident foraging range normally small (5 m²) and can overlap with other mice (Chitty & Southern 1954, Young *et al.* 1950). Feral mice tend to have a far less localised range and may be semi-nomadic (Caldwell 1964, Berry & Jakobson 1974); movements on arable land can be much influenced by farming practice (Rowe *et al.* 1963).

Growing populations rapidly exploit unoccupied areas and nearby premises. Little movement between stacks of food once each stack is occupied. In late autumn and winter movements away from fields and hedgerows into cover of farm and suburban premises tend to occur. In the spring minor movements in the reverse direction from farm buildings into fields have been recorded. Occasionally increase to plague proportions especially in areas where there is reduced inter-specific competition, and mass migration may result (Chitty & Southern 1954, Elton 1942, Newsome 1969).

Confined unrelated adult males fight and the outcome is the establishment of a social order with a single male dominating others of lesser rank (Mackintosh & Grant 1966). Aggressive behaviour less intense in small family groups but the adult members attack introduced strange mice of either sex (Rowe & Redfern 1969). At moderate densities aggressive behaviour increases and males will live with one or more females in territories which they defend vigorously (Crowcroft 1955). At high densities surplus live in subordinate state without territory or breeding (Crowcroft & Rowe 1963). Indoor populations of free-living mice appear to be similarly socially organised through territorial behaviour (Anderson 1965). Fighting observed in dense corn-rick populations (Rowe *et al.* 1963) and between individuals of different populations occupying the same building (Brown 1953).

Voice a high squeak, frequently heard. So-called 'singing' mice due to inflammation of lungs. Subordinate often rears up and squeals when attacked. Lactating female responds to ultrasonic sounds of infant mice. Ability to recognise landmarks by scent. Evidence that family groups have a characteristic smell and that communication is largely by scent. Adults and juveniles of either sex readily detect the unfamiliar smell of strangers.

Clear vision improbable but respond readily to different light intensities and to sudden movement at close quarters. Sense of hearing acute and sensitive to any sudden noise and to high frequency sounds. Sense of smell and taste important in locating and discerning the palatability of foods and of touch in the recognition of landmarks away from the nest.

FOOD In urban areas eat many of the same foods as man (average adult daily intake 3–4 g). Cereal foodstuffs constitute much of the diet but fat and protein foods also consumed. Green foods and fruit of secondary attractiveness. Unlikely substances such as plaster, soap and glue taken on occasion. Basic diet sometimes supplemented with insect food. Essentially a diffuse, light, sporadic feeder with two main feeding periods, at dusk and before dawn, interspersed with shorter feeding bursts, but there is considerable individual variation in feeding behaviour.

In open fields diet closely related to food availability. Cereals regularly taken in arable country and grass and weed seeds in grassland. Lepidopterous and coleopterous larvae also taken and occasionally plant roots and stems (Whitaker 1966). Worms, arthropods and fungi are minor food items. Can exist on very little water and intake largely regulated by moisture content of food and external temperature. On dry food prolonged water deficiency can result in lowered fertility.

BREEDING Continuous in most urban habitats producing between 5 and 10 litters of about 4–8 young per year.

Will breed in complete darkness, and fertility largely unaffected by low temperatures provided food supply and nesting material are adequate. Ovulation spontaneous (oestrous cycle 4–6 days) and copulation leaves vaginal plug which persists for 18 to 24 hours. Gestation 19 to 20 days; fertilisation can occur at post-partum oestrus and implantation is then delayed 2 to 16 days. Loss of embryos after implantation small (c. 5%). Young weaned at 18 to 20 days; average litter size 5–6. Young born in well-built substantial nest made from available material, e.g. shredded grass, leaves, paper, sacking, string and insulation lining. Females tend to share a communal nest when nesting sites are limited, nesting material is scarce or the population density is high. New-born weighs c. 1 g, has eyes and ears closed and is hairless except for short vibrissae. Fully furred at 14 days with eyes and ears open and incisor teeth erupted. Infant mice sometimes involuntarily dragged away from the nest clinging to nipples of mother, but first voluntary excursions normally occur towards the end of the third week when young begin to take solid food. At weaning reaches almost two-thirds of normally attained adult length; young mature rapidly (females fecund at c. 7·5 g, males at c. 10 g).

Breeding rates in different habitats studied by Laurie (1946a); range from 10·2 litters per female per year in ricks to 5·5 in urban premises. In confinement fecundity found to be lowered in both sexes at moderate densities and, at very high densities reproduction ceased.

POPULATION STRUCTURE Live in groups which increase rapidly, but may be eliminated as quickly. Consequently they are opportunistic in colonisation, and apparently able to tolerate a considerable amount of inbreeding. Natural populations develop a territorial structure with males defending an area of variable size (depending on food availability). These territories may persist for several generations in commensal populations, but undergo a considerable amount of mixing in outdoor animals (Berry & Jakobson 1974).

PREDATORS A number of natural enemies, both birds of prey (notably the barn owl) and predatory mammals (weasel, stoat), but unlikely that they act as a serious brake on well-established feral populations. The domestic cat probably most important in intercepting individual mice between buildings or moving into cover from fields; its value in curbing thriving mouse populations is over-estimated. In many of its habitats the mouse has virtually no predators apart from man and the common rat which is known to prey upon mice to some extent although both species are commonly found living in the same habitat.

PARASITES AND DISEASE Common ectoparasites are the flea *Nosopsyllus fasciatus* and the sucking louse *Polyplax serrata*. Capable of transmitting several dangerous diseases to man but subject of scant investigation in Britain and incidence documented elsewhere (Cameron 1949). Human cases of rat-bite fever, tularaemia and murine and scrub typhus have been linked with the mouse; so has rickettsial pox, the symptoms closely resembling chicken pox, and the organism responsible has been isolated from humans and the blood sucking mite, *Allodermanyssus sanguineus*, recovered from mice. A recent study in an endemic area of leptospirosis showed that the mouse can be a major carrier of the disease (Minette 1964). Favus, a skin disease caused by the fungus, *Achorion quickeanum*, and a virus infection known as lymphocytic choriomeningitis can be contracted through close contact with infected mice. Important potential carrier of bacteria of the *Salmonella* group causing food poisoning diseases. Also serves as host of intestinal parasites such as the two small tapeworms *Hymenolepis nana* and *H. diminuta* transmissible to man.

RELATIONS WITH MAN Long-standing pest but information on actual losses scanty. Estimated damage caused to grain stacks up to 16%. Most serious damage caused to stockpiled food; often only partially eaten so that more food can be destroyed or rendered unfit through contamination than is actually consumed. Also responsible for 'invisible' losses often as a result of nest building activity e.g. re-bagging of spilled food, repair of insulating materials. Known to attack unprotected electrical wiring and create fire hazard. Of public health importance because of its close association with human settlements and disease carrying potential.

Can be maintained and bred easily in captivity; laboratory strains much used in a wide range of experimental work.

LITERATURE Crowcroft (1966)—a detailed and entertaining account of studies of house mice in grain stores. Green (1966)—a comprehensive reference work on the laboratory mouse. Berry (1970b)—a general account with special reference to life-history and population structure under out-door conditions.

AUTHOR FOR THIS SPECIES F.P. Rowe, with acknowledgement to R. J. Berry for comment and additions.

GENUS *Rattus*
RATS

A large genus with numerous species in the Oriental Region and also in Australasia. Many African species have been included, but these are now generally excluded (in the genera *Praomys*, *Aethomys*, etc.). A few

FIGURE 85 Ship rat (above) and common rat (below). Note the longer ears, sleeker fur and longer, thinner tail of the ship rat.

species have become widely spread by association with man and two of these occur in Britain.

Synonym: *Epimys*.

The more clear-cut differences between the two species are listed in Table 20. The smaller size and more slender build of the ship rat is apparent to anyone already familiar with the common rat, but identification can be tricky and any observation of ship rats away from their normal limited haunts should be confirmed by careful examination of specimens whenever possible. Colour is too variable to be of much assistance.

TABLE 20. Distinguishing characters of adult rats

	Common rat	Ship rat
Length of head and body (mm)	Up to 280	Up to 240
Tail: head and body	80–100%	100–130%
Colour of tail	Dark above, light below	Uniformly dark
Length of hind feet (mm)	40–44	30–38
Length of ear (mm)	20–22	24–27
Condylobasal length of skull (mm)	43–54	38–43
Temporal ridges on either side of brain-case	Straight and almost parallel	Curved

Ship rat *Rattus rattus*

Mus rattus Linnaeus, 1758; Sweden. *Mus alexandrinus* Desmarest, 1819; Egypt. *Musculus frugivorus* Rafinesque, 1814; Sicily.

Black rat, roof rat, alexandrine rat.

RECOGNITION Very similar in appearance to common rat, but relatively larger eyes and ears, and longer, thinner, unicoloured tail serve to distinguish it at close quarters. In the hand, ears can be seen to be thinner and almost hairless compared with common rat's rather furry ears. Guard hairs on back and flanks and vibrissae proportionately very much longer than those of common rat giving animal a somewhat spiky appearance when seen against a light background. Black coloration of fur not diagnostic, since a proportion of common rats are black and many ship rats are brown. Skull very similar to that of common rat; may be distinguished by flask-shaped outline of cranium (Fig. 86) and smaller, lighter construction.

SIGN In buildings leaves dark, greasy smears in places where fur frequently brushes walls etc. Smears similar to those of common rat except that 'loop smears' (i.e. those left beneath joists or other obstructions under which rats pass) are broken instead of continuous. This characteristic appears diagnostic. Footprints indistinguishable from those of common rat. Out of doors, may make burrows similar to those of common rat, and even occasionally runways, although these are rarely pronounced. In tropics and sub-tropics frequently builds nests, similar to squirrel dreys, in trees.

Droppings, which average about 9 mm in length, tend to be smaller than those of common rat, having rounded rather than pointed ends. In large samples (over 50), droppings of the two species can be distinguished with 95% confidence on the basis of the relationship between length (L)

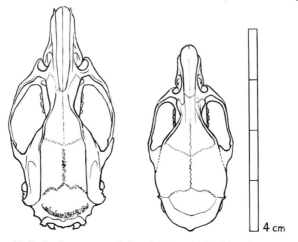

FIGURE 86 Skulls of common rat (left) and ship rat (right). Note the more rounded brain-case and temporal ridges of the ship rat.

and diameter (D), those of ship rat being proportionately thinner. If D/L is between 0·31 and 0·37 the likelihood is that the droppings are those of ship rat; if D/L is between 0·42 and 0·46 they are of common rat (R. A. Davis and B. D. Rennison, personal communication).

DESCRIPTION Fur typically grey-brown above and pale grey beneath, but may also be completely black, or grey-brown above and dark grey or creamy white beneath. In the last colour form there is usually a fairly sharp demarcation between the belly and flanks, whereas in other colour forms gradation occurs. Number of nipples variable, but often 2 pairs axillary and 3 pairs inguinal. Pollex absent from fore feet, otherwise all toes present and clawed. Tail uniformly dark and usually as long as or longer than head and body.

FIGURE 87 Ship rat grooming tail. (Photo: G. Kinns)

M^1 large in relation to other molars. Incisors not normally notched. Chromosomes: $2n=42$.

MEASUREMENTS Growth may continue throughout life; head and body of old individuals may reach as much as 240 mm and tail up to 260 mm. Weight may reach 280 g but adults usually weigh 150–200 g. Males generally larger than females.

DISTRIBUTION See Fig. 88. Probably originated in South East Asia, but development of commensal habit led to early spread along ancient trade routes to Europe and thence to rest of world. Present day distribution includes urban areas throughout tropics and sub-tropics extending to many small villages and even remote farms, but does not live away from buildings except on islands where there are few or no indigenous competitors, e.g. in Caribbean and Pacific. Occurs in many towns in temperate regions, but tends to be restricted to ports in cooler temperate areas.

In Britain, date of introduction uncertain, but probably about eleventh century AD. Used to be widespread but now largely replaced by common rat. Has managed to hold on in seaports longer than elsewhere; in 1956, occurred in most major ports and some inland towns (Bentley 1959), whereas by 1961 occurred only in major seaports (Bentley 1964, Corbet

1971). Later incomplete information indicates disappearance from Welsh ports and from ports on north-east coasts of England and further contractions of range in London where it occurs mainly in Southwark (E. J. Wilson and P. Wilson, per. comm.). Colonies may occasionally develop in unexpected places following accidental translocation of individuals by road or rail. Present on the island of Lundy in 1970 but numbers probably falling (Perrin & Gurnell 1971) and probably still exists on Alderney and Sark, and Westray in Orkney. Also present on Shiant Islands, off Skye. Contraction of range in mainland Britain probably partly due to habit of living only within buildings, making it more vulnerable to rodent control measures than common rat.

VARIATION The colour of the pelage is polymorphic in most populations, the three forms being all black (*rattus* type), brown with grey belly (*alexandrinus* type) and brown with creamy white belly (*frugivorus* type). The frequencies of the morphs vary geographically and in different habitats, black usually being dominant in urban areas and the others in rural areas, but they do not constitute geographically definable subspecies. Geographical variation in this and related species was described on a world-wide basis by Schwarz & Schwarz (1967).

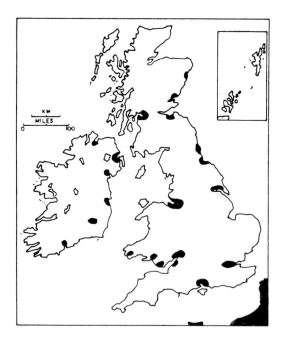

FIGURE 88 Ship rat: distribution (1960's).

In London, 56% were black form, 24% white-bellied, 18% grey-bellied and 2% intermediate (Watson 1950), but proportions fluctuate.

HABITAT In Britain, mainly restricted to dockside warehouses, food-processing plants, etc., but may also occur in supermarkets, restaurants and modern department stores. Does not live out of doors in towns. Favours buildings with cavity walls, wall panelling and false ceilings where it can move unseen. Occupies rocks and cliffs on Shiants, Lundy and Channel Islands where it is also said to live in trees (Baal 1949).

BEHAVIOUR Gait similar to that of common rat but tends to move much more rapidly. Typically, sprints along ledges, overhead pipes or beams and then pauses motionless at a vantage point before sprinting again. An extremely agile climber; able to cope equally with thin wire (vertical or horizontal), brickwork and vertical pipes, provided they are sited against a wall. In presence of common rat, tends to occupy upper floors of buildings, but is otherwise found from basement to roof. Can swim, but unlike common rat does not often enter water voluntarily. Almost exclusively nocturnal in urban environments. Senses similar to those of common rat, but does not exhibit such marked avoidance of unfamiliar objects placed in environment. Very little known about social behaviour.

FOOD Catholic in taste, although often more vegetarian than common rat, and notably partial to fruit. Most agricultural crops eaten including cereals and, in the tropics, sugar cane, coconuts and cocoa. Apparently enjoys chillies. On Lundy, stomachs contained more vegetable matter and fewer animal remains than those of common rat.

BREEDING Females sexually mature at about 90 g. Average litter size recorded as 6·9 on shore and 7·5 on ships in port of London (Watson 1950). Number of embryos correlated with body weight of female. Intra-uterine mortality 25% in London. Most breeding in London mid-March to mid-November. Litter rate about 3–5 per year. Gestation period 21 days (Kenneth & Ritchie 1953).

POPULATION Densities vary greatly with environment. Watson (1951) found 5–12/ha in scrubland in Cyprus whereas Leslie & Davis (1939) estimated 52/ha in a residential area of Freetown, Sierra Leone. Turnover is fast, annual mortality being of the order of 91–97% (Davis 1953).

PREDATORS In urban situations domestic cat is probably chief predator, but in agricultural and natural environments outside British Isles ship rats are fair game to most small mammalian, avian and reptilian predators. It has frequently been said that common rats will fight with and kill ship rats, and Barnett (1958) has shown that this is indeed the case in confined colonies. However, the two species are sympatric over much of their range (including Lundy) and it is doubtful whether the common rat under natural conditions ever preys significantly on ship rats. Replacement of the latter species by the larger common rat in many temperate regions is probably due to the common rat's greater ability to withstand cold and to hunt for food under adverse conditions. In the tropics the ship rat is well able to hold its own.

PARASITES AND DISEASE Under popular name of 'black rat' has been associated in people's minds for centuries with the Black Death (bubonic plague), and was responsible for transmitting the catastrophic outbreaks of the disease that occurred in Europe in the Middle Ages. But common rat can also act as vector, and both species are highly susceptible to the disease and therefore, strictly speaking do not constitute reservoirs. The true reservoirs are certain species of wild rodent that are comparatively resistant to plague. Ship rats appear to carry the same diseases and parasites as common rats.

RELATIONS WITH MAN Has developed marked ability to live in close association with man; much better adapted to living in buildings than common rat and consequently a more important urban pest in many areas. Often occurs in residential areas of tropical towns, living within the houses, and has been known to gnaw the soles of the inmates' feet while they slept. Damage and fouling in stored foodstuffs very widespread. A serious pest of agriculture on islands (notably in Pacific and Caribbean, but also Cyprus and elsewhere) attacking most crops, but particularly coconuts, sugar cane and cocoa. An important vector of plague and typhus, principally in the East.

AUTHOR FOR THIS SPECIES K. D. Taylor.

Common rat *Rattus norvegicus*

Mus norvegicus Berkenhout, 1769; Great Britain. *Mus decumanus* Pallas, 1779. *Mus hibernicus* Thompson, 1837; Rathfriland, Co Down, Ireland. Brown rat, Norway rat, sewer rat.

RECOGNITION Large size, relatively pointed muzzle and long scaly tail (a little shorter than head and body length) preclude confusion with mice, voles and squirrels. Hind feet of young much heavier and a little longer than those of adult mice (over 27 mm as opposed to 22–25 mm for *Apodemus*) and tail relatively much thicker. Distinguished from ship rat by relatively smaller eyes and smaller ears which are finely furred compared with the almost hairless ears of ship rat; tail relatively shorter and thicker than that of ship rat and usually dark coloured above and pale beneath, against the ship rat's uniformly dark tail. Skull very similar to that of ship rat but somewhat heavier; supraorbital ridges tend to be less divergent over cranium than those of ship rat (Fig. 86).

SIGN Burrows generally 65–90 mm in diameter, often situated on sloping ground—banks or the sides of ditches, or beneath some form of cover such as flat stones, logs or tree roots. Earth dug from burrows remains in a heap close to the entrance. Characteristic pathways (runs) may show as slight linear depressions in grass or other low vegetation or as well-worn trails of bare, trampled earth. They may be 50–100 mm wide, and are continuous (rabbit runs are discontinuous, showing as a series of depressions in grass). Runs in buildings show as dark, greasy smears on wood or brickwork. Droppings average 12 mm long, often tapering to a point at one or both ends; frequently deposited in groups (ship rat droppings are rather thinner, usually have rounded ends and tend to be deposited singly; those of water voles smaller, with rounded ends and smooth textured). Footprints in soft mud sometimes, and in snow frequently, accompanied by tail swipes.

DESCRIPTION Fur of adults somewhat shaggy, grey-brown above and pale grey beneath (but albinos and melanics may occur). Fur of juveniles from weaning to about 3 months (up to 100 g body weight) shorter, sleeker and greyer than that of adults. Clear moult patterns sometimes evident in animals reaching maturity. No sexual difference in pelage, and external genitalia may appear similar in young, but small hairless area behind vaginal papilla serves to identify females. Number of nipples variable, but often 3 pairs axillary and 3 pairs inguinal. Pollex absent from fore feet otherwise all toes present and clawed. Tail usually shorter than head and body.

M^1 large in relation to other molars. Incisors not normally notched. Chromosomes: $2n=42$.

MEASUREMENTS Head and body about 110 mm at weaning increasing to 280 mm or more. Condylobasal length of skull up to 54 mm in large adults. Body weight from 40 g of weanlings to 500 g or even 600 g in exceptional cases. Males tend to be larger than females. Growth may occur throughout normal life span of 1–2 years.

DISTRIBUTION See Fig. 90. Occurs in urban areas throughout most of the world except in low altitude inland towns in the mainland tropics

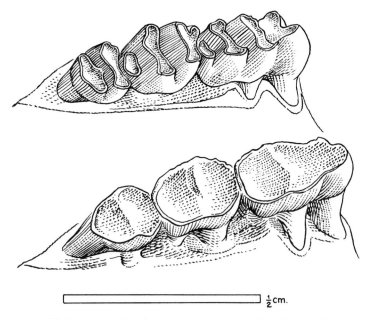

$\frac{1}{2}$cm.

FIGURE 89 Left lower molars of common rat, slightly worn (above) and heavily worn (below). Anterior tooth on right.

FIGURE 90 Common rat: distribution.

and sub-tropics (Africa, Asia, South America). Occurs in cultivated land and away from human habitation only in temperate regions and tropical islands where there are no or few indigenous competitors. Commonly occurs in riverbank habitats up to 70 km from human settlements in eastern USSR (Khamaganov 1972).

Found in all parts of the British Isles except possibly in some of the more exposed mountain regions and on some of the smaller off-shore islands (but present on the majority of small islands). Spread across Europe and into the British Isles during the eighteenth century largely replacing the ship rat which had been present for many hundreds of years. Exact date of introduction to Britain uncertain but thought to have been around 1728–29 (Barrett-Hamilton & Hinton 1910–21) in shipping from Russia. Arrival in Norway considerably later and the assumption, perpetuated in the specific name '*norvegicus*'. that it came to Britain from Norway erroneous. Spread in Scotland slow: described in 1855 as 'recently introduced' in some remote areas (Matheson 1962). Still replacing ship rat in parts of United States as late as 1951 (Ecke 1954) and to present day in Israel (Gratz 1973).

VARIATION Little variation over vast geographical range. Albinism rare; melanics may comprise 1–2% of some populations (Watson 1944, Becker 1952), or rarely 20% (Smith 1958).

HABITAT Typically found associated with farms, refuse tips, sewers and warehouses but occurs in hedgerows around cereal crops, principally in summer and autumn, and root crops (particularly sugar beet) all the year round. Prefers areas with dense ground cover close to water. Free living populations often occur in coastal habitats, particularly salt marshes; whereas on islands (e.g. Isle of Man, Rhum, Lundy) free-living population may occupy grassland as well as all types of coast line.

BEHAVIOUR Gait a fast trot along familiar runs but may amble slowly, rocking body from side to side while searching for food. Will progress by repeated high bounds if chased over unfamiliar ground. Swims and dives well. Mainly nocturnal but may become diurnal in undisturbed situations, especially when nights are frosty. Peak activity generally at onset of darkness and again around 3 a.m. until dawn (Chitty 1954).

Home range very variable. Generally chooses to live near food source when range may be only 12 m (Davis *et al.* 1948), but runs have been traced for 400 m in farmland. No clearly defined annual rhythm in urban situations. In agricultural land tends to live in fields in summer and autumn but not in winter and spring. Probably increased random movement at end of autumn results in influx into farm buildings at this time of year. Many hearsay reports of mass movement of rats, but no evidence of any regular movement of this type.

Colonies typically develop from a pair or single pregnant female. Social relationships harmonious within small colonies and intruders repelled vigorously—even killed if escape prevented. Dominance structure develops as population density increases with high-ranking individuals taking up favoured positions close to food source (Calhoun 1962). Low ranking individuals may be forced to feed while dominants are inactive, e.g. during daylight. Offspring of low ranking females have comparatively low survival. Large colonies more tolerant of intruders—presumably because individual recognition within the colony tends to break down as numbers increase (Telle 1966).

Vocalisations include shrill squeaks and squeals uttered during scuffles between individuals and a repeated 'grunt-squeak' uttered by cornered or restrained rats. Under certain social situations rats occasionally emit a drawn-out whine, almost too high for the human ear to detect. Nestlings communicate with their mother by ultra-sonic squeaks. 'Colony smell' may be transferred from rat to rat by physical contact. Typically, two individuals meet and sniff noses momentarily then one passes beneath the belly and raised hind leg of the other before both rats continue on their way: behaviour described by Barnett (1963) as 'crawling under'. Senses of hearing and smell acute, sight relatively poor. Mainly uses hearing to detect danger but sight sufficiently good to detect movement of potential predator. Disturbed by torch light at night, eye reflects dull red; use of red filter on torch has little effect on degree of disturbance. Shows intimate knowledge of environment and reacts suspiciously to any change. Unfamiliar objects placed within environment may be avoided for 48 hours or so (Shorten 1954a, Barnett 1963).

FOOD Prefers protein-rich or starch-rich foods, typically cereals, but will eat almost anything. In urban environment, meat, fish, bones and even soap and candles are eaten. In agricultural land cereals and root crops are most commonly eaten but brassicas may be attacked in the absence of more sustaining food. Many weed seeds are also eaten, e.g. dock (*Rumex*) and goose foot (*Chenopodium*), also invertebrates such as earthworms. Sea-shore colonies may feed on rice grass, *Spartina* (Drummond 1960) or crustaceans, principally crabs (*Carcinus*) and sandhoppers (Amphipoda). Particles of food are typically picked up in the mouth and carried to a safe spot to be eaten. Food is sometimes held in the fore paws while it is gnawed. Repeated journeys are often made from a vantage point to the food source to pick up a small item of food such as a wheat grain. Large items of food such as an apple or crab are carried in the mouth with the head held high and the animal progressing in high leaps to keep its burden clear of the ground. Larger items of food may be dragged towards safe cover. No evidence of large scale hoarding of food. New food sources approached with caution and during first few days may only be sampled.

BREEDING May be continuous in an unchanging environment with good food source; in these circumstances around 30% females pregnant throughout year (Leslie, Venables & Venables 1952). In less favourable habitats breeding may take place mainly in summer and autumn. There is often a post partum oestrus but females rarely produce more than 5 litters per year. Litter size related to size of mother, e.g. 6 at 150 g, and 11 at 500 g; average litter size 7–8. Gestation 21–24 days; young born naked and blind; eyes open at six days; weaned at about 3 weeks; females mature at about 115 g (11 weeks).

POPULATION STRUCTURE Very dense populations composed mostly of young individuals may develop in favourable environments such as

FIGURE 91 Common rat with nestlings. (Photo: G. Kinns)

refuse tips. Thus of 185 rats caught on a refuse tip in November, 120 (65%) weighed 110 g or less. By the following January none of the 42 rats caught was under 115 g. Mortality of young in the nest and just after emergence in saturated populations was reckoned by Davis (1953) to be 99% per annum, and adult mortality may be over 90% per annum. Few rats therefore live for more than a year. Populations tend to be high in autumn and early winter and low in spring.

PREDATORS Young rats are fair game to most predatory animals but the aggressive nature of large rats may deter the smaller predators such as weasels and owls. Established populations less vulnerable to predation than rats on the move. Cats may prevent reinvasion of farm buildings by rats but cannot eliminate an established population (Elton 1953). Rat remains occurred in 13% of fox stomachs examined by Lever *et al.* (1957).

PARASITES AND DISEASE Common ectoparasites found on 444 rats mainly from London were the mites *Laelaps echidninus* (24%) and *Haematopinus spinulosus* (11%). The tape worms *Hymenolepis diminuta* and *H. longior* were found in respectively 28% and 25% of the rats. *Trypanosoma lewisi* was found in 19% (Balfour 1922).

Leptospirosis is possibly the most common disease transmissible to man that is carried by rats in Britain. Kidney examination showed 23% infected with leptospires in 1922 (Balfour 1922) and 43% infected in 1958 (Broom 1958). The gut parasite, *Salmonella*, which causes food poisoning in man is also commonly found in rats. Other diseases carried by rats in Britain are lymphocytic choriomeningitis and toxoplasmosis: common rats transmit plague and typhus in some parts of the world but they are probably not as important vectors as ship rats because they tend to live outside rather than inside houses.

RELATIONS WITH MAN Success and spread all over the world due to development of ability to live in close association with man. Noted as a pest of crops and stored foodstuff. Losses due to consumption of stored wheat by rats shown to be small compared with losses resulting from damage to the bags containing the wheat (Barnett 1951). Contamination of foodstuff intended for human consumption with excreta and hairs important economically in most developed countries of the world (e.g. Dykstra 1954). Very important as vector of some human diseases, particularly leptospirosis amongst rice field workers in Spain and Italy (Babudieri 1953) and canefield workers in Pacific and Caribbean islands.

On the credit side, has served man for many decades as a laboratory animal. Laboratory rats are docile and respond to regular handling. Captive wild rats, even if hand reared from very young, become jumpy and difficult to handle at an early age.

LITERATURE Matheson (1962)—a general, illustrated account.

AUTHOR FOR THE SPECIES K. D. Taylor.

FAMILY GLIRIDAE
DORMICE

A small but distinctive family with seven genera, mostly monospecific, in the Palaearctic Region and Africa. Compared with the small murid and cricetid rodents, dormice tend to occupy more specialised habitats. They occur at lower density, have a lower breeding potential and spend the winter in hibernation. In Britain there is one native and one introduced species, belonging to separate genera. Their characters are contrasted in Table 21.

TABLE 21 Characters of dormice

	Common dormouse	Fat dormouse
Length of head and body	60–90 mm	130–180 mm
Length of hind feet	15–18 mm	24–34 mm
Colour of pelage	Orange-brown	Grey or greyish brown
Tail	Slightly bushy	Very bushy

GENUS *Glis*

A monospecific genus.

Fat dormouse *Glis glis*

Sciurus glis Linnaeus, 1766; Germany.
Edible dormouse, squirrel-tailed dormouse, seven-sleeper.

RECOGNITION Very different from common dormouse, being about twice the size and lacking any suggestion of orange in the pelage. More easily confused with grey squirrel but much smaller. Small hind feet (under 35 mm) distinguish it from a young grey squirrel of equal size.

DESCRIPTION Pelage of upper parts a rather uniform greyish brown except for dark rings round the eyes and slightly darker stripes on the outsides of the legs. White below. The tail is somewhat flattened in the horizontal plane, with a median parting of hair below. It is easily damaged and short-tailed animals are frequent. Mammae: 6 pairs extending from thorax to groin.

The cheek-teeth (four in each row above and below) are transversely ridged but with many fewer ridges than in the common dormouse.

MEASUREMENTS Head and body of adult up to 175 mm, mean *c*. 150 mm; tail up to 150 mm, mean *c*. 125 mm; weight up to 185 g, mean *c*. 140 g.

DISTRIBUTION See Fig. 93. Widespread in southern and eastern Europe and east to Iran, but absent from most of Iberia, northern France, the Low Countries, Denmark and Scandinavia.

Not indigenous in Britain but introduced to England at Tring, Hertfordshire in 1902 from where it has spread to only a very limited extent in the Chiltern Hills, west at least as far as the Bledlow Ridge (SU 79) and east to Potters Bar (TL 02). Distribution up to 1951 described in detail by Thompson (1953).

HABITAT Mainly mature deciduous woodland but also in orchards and gardens. Unlike the common dormouse it does not require a dense shrub layer.

BEHAVIOUR A very agile climber spending most of its life in the canopy of trees but readily entering lofts of houses. Entirely nocturnal, spending day in a tree hole or in a nest built in a fork close to the trunk, not out on a limb as is common in squirrels.

Hibernation usually from October to April, in a tree-hole or a cavity amongst roots, sometimes in the roof of a building. Loss of weight during hibernation may be 35–50% (Vietinghoff-Riesch 1960). Home range *c*. 100 m in diameter, young may disperse up to 1 km.

Voice: a variety of squeaking and snuffling noises.

FOOD All kinds of fruit, nuts, buds, bark (e.g. of willow and plum), insects, fungi and occasionally the eggs and nestlings of birds. Apples are eaten avidly in autumn and are often taken from stores in buildings. Does not store food.

BREEDING From Vietinghoff-Riesch 1960. One litter, usually of 4 or 5 young, is produced in mid-summer. In Germany breeding starts mid-June and ends in August. Litter size varies from 2 to 7 and the yearly

FIGURE 92 Common dormouse (above) and fat dormouse (below), to same scale.

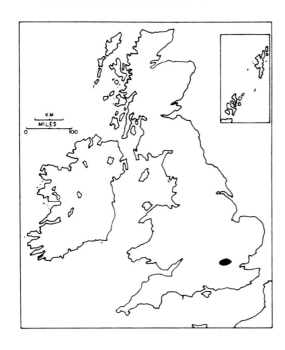

FIGURE 93 Fat
dormouse:
distribution.

mean litter size may vary from 2·0 to 6·4. Probably do not breed until after their second winter.

POPULATION Density fluctuates widely in Europe, from 0·2 to 4/ha. Mark-recapture study by Vietinghoff-Riesch (1955) showed population composed of 73% 1 to 2-year-old animals, 18% 3-year, 4% 4-year, 3% 5-year and 2% older. Sex ratio about 50% except in years of population decline when females predominate. Said not to breed until 2 years old.

PREDATORS AND MORTALITY Tawny owls probably most important but also stoats, weasels and cats.

PARASITES AND DISEASE The sucking louse *Schizophthirius gliris* is found on the Continent but does not appear to have been recorded from British animals.

RELATIONS WITH MAN In classical times were a favourite food of the Romans who fattened them for the table in special jars called gliraria. At times a serious pest to fruit crops on the Continent but only serious damage reported in England has been the barking of conifers in a plantation (Thompson & Platt 1964). Their presence in attics frequently causes complaint—Chiltern District Council Public Health Department trap about 30 per year as a result of complaints.

LITERATURE Vietinghoff-Riesch (1960)—a monograph in German.

AUTHOR FOR THIS SPECIES G. B. Corbet.

Common dormouse *Muscardinus avellanarius*

Mus avellanarius Linnaeus, 1758; Sweden. *Muscardinus avellanarius anglicus* Barrett-Hamilton, 1900; Bedford Purlieus, Thornhaugh, Northamptonshire.
Hazel dormouse, sleeper, dory mouse.

RECOGNITION Bushy tail is distinctive amongst mouse-sized animals. Very small size and bright orange-brown pelage make it very different from the fat dormouse.

   Skull is easily distinguished by four cheek-teeth in each row, the large ones with a unique pattern of numerous transverse ridges.

SIGN Best located by searching for nests and especially signs of honeysuckle bark having been stripped in fine shreds for nest building in the shrub layer. (Grey squirrels and rabbits will also strip bark but more coarsely and generally high or at ground level.) Nests are most distinctive when above ground, generally amongst dense undergrowth or in the cleft of a sapling. Up to 15 cm in diameter, commonly made entirely of honey-suckle bark but grass, moss and leaves also used. Distinguished from birds' nests by lack of a clearly defined entrance hole. The structure is woven to surround the animal—only a few species of birds make domed nests, in particular the wren, sometimes found in similar situations, but then entrance hole is distinct and reinforced below with dry grass or fibres.

DESCRIPTION Upper parts and tail uniform orange-brown, underside pale buff with pure white on throat, sometimes extending back as a narrow line to belly. Pelage of juveniles greyer but little difference between summer and winter coat. Moult to winter pelage in October.

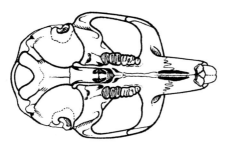

FIGURE 94 Skull of common dormouse from below.

Muzzle short, vibrissae very long, up to 30 mm. Feet slender, prehensile and capable of much movement at wrist and ankle, front with four digits, hind with four plus a vestigial hallux. Scent glands ventral to anus in both sexes (Hrabe 1971).

Dental formula

$$\frac{1.0.1.3}{1.0.1.3},$$

premolars small, molars large, rooted, with multiple transverse ridges.

MEASUREMENTS Head and body of young animals in autumn 68–79 mm (8 in British Museum), of adults in summer about 80–85 mm. Tail 57–68 mm. Weight 23–43 g, heaviest just prior to hibernation (Rabus 1881).

DISTRIBUTION See Fig. 95. Europe from the Mediterranean to the Baltic (but not Iberia nor Denmark) and east to the Volga and Asia Minor.

In Britain confined to England and Wales; absent from Ireland. Widespread but local in suitable habitats from mid-Wales, Leicestershire and

Suffolk southwards. Apparently scarce further north and likely to have declined in the northern English counties. Records in nineteenth century from as far north as Carlyle and the Tyne.

VARIATION Description of a distinctive British race, *anglicus*, was based on supposedly brighter colour but was discredited by Miller (1912). White tail-tip not uncommon, frequency probably about 10%. Albinos recorded but rare.

HABITAT Deciduous woodland with secondary growth and scrub, especially where there are trees with edible seed, e.g. hazel, sweet chestnut, beech. Frequently in coppice, sometimes in species-rich hedgerows. Much of its activity takes place above ground level in the protection of the shrub layer.

BEHAVIOUR An agile climber spending much time above ground. Strictly nocturnal except on rare occasions. In summer usually occupy nests above ground, up to 5 m high (Schulze 1970) but more often in the shrub layer within a metre of the ground. Sometimes in bird nest-boxes. In the Forest of Dean many have been found in nest-boxes 3–3.5 m high on oaks, including six in one box on 7 October (Holland 1967). Breeding nest about 15 cm diameter; newly independent young

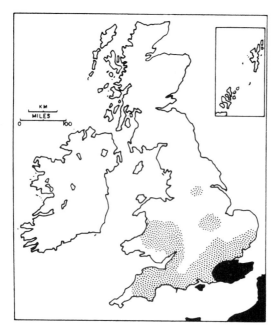

FIGURE 95
Common dormouse:
distribution.

FIGURE 96 Common dormouse in hibernating attitude. (Photo: V. Almy)

make smaller nests, up to 10 cm, often grouped only a few metres apart (Hurrell 1962).

Movement of marked animals in Germany recorded up to 1600 m for males and 700 m for females but most appeared to remain close to point of first capture (Schulze 1970).

Hibernate in nests that are usually at or below ground level, occasionally above. Hibernation usually lasts from October to April but observations in captivity suggest that it is not normally continuous, with several days of activity alternating with several weeks of sleep (Hurrell 1962). Hibernation studied in detail by Eisentraut (1930). Onset appears to be induced by environmental temperature remaining below 15°C. Body temperature controlled during hibernation and does not fall below 0°C. Fully awake when body temperature reaches 31–32°C, normal temperature 34–38°C.

Generally silent but shrill squeaking noises have been recorded during chases in captivity (Hurrell 1962). Mewing and purring sounds also heard and hibernating animals may produce a wheezing sound (E. Hurrell, in litt.).

FIGURE 97 Hazel nuts opened by (a) common dormouse, (b) wood mouse and (c) bank vole. Note the smooth inner edge of the hole in the case of the dormouse. (Photo: G. Barbour)

FOOD Primarily nuts, fruit and berries. Probably also buds and some insects in spring and early summer but little definite information. Chestnuts, acorns and hazelnuts important prior to hibernation. Hazelnuts opened by gnawing a smooth, round hole, whereas wood mice and bank voles show marks of lower incisors left radially on cut surface of hole (E. Hurrell, unpubl.). In captivity fruit and sunflower seeds are accepted but not grain.

BREEDING Breed first in year following birth, producing one or two litters per year, each of about four young.

On Continent two main peaks of births, in late June/early July and in late July/early August (Sidorowicz 1959). Young may be found from May to September and exceptionally October.

Gestation period 22–24 days. Litter size (in Germany) 2–7, mean 3·7 (Wachtendorf 1951). Earlier litters larger than later ones. Sidorowicz (1959) believed at least two litters per year was normal in Poland; Wachtendorf (1951) considered one per year was normal in Germany.

Young blind at birth, pelage well developed by 13 days, eyes open at 18 days, begin to leave nest at 30 days and are independent by 40 days (Wachtendorf 1951). First pelage grey, moulted at about 18 days, second pelage more like adult but duller and greyer.

POPULATION No estimates of absolute density available. Probably much lower density than wood mice and bank vole even in good habitat, but density relative to other rodents difficult to determine because the above-ground activity of dormice makes them more difficult to trap. Hurrell (1962) reported three dormice out of 1500 'mice' caught on an anemone farm in Devon. On Continent may exceptionally be so abundant after a good mast crop as to cause serious damage to young trees (Kindler 1946).

Ratio of young to adult in autumn in Poland was found to be 51 : 41 in 1957 and 19 : 36 in 1958 (Sidorowicz 1959).

Longevity up to 6 years in captivity, 4 years recorded in marked animals in wild (Schulze 1970). Ridges on molar teeth more or less worn away by third year suggesting that few survive beyond that age (Lozan 1961).

PREDATORS AND MORTALITY Predation by birds probably very low compared to wood mice and bank voles. Rarely found in owl pellets.

Most mortality probably occurs during hibernation, by starvation or by predation, e.g. by foxes, badgers, weasels and corvids—dormice have been seen to be dropped by crows and magpies.

PARASITES AND DISEASE The louse *Schizophthirius pleurophaeus* is shared with other species of dormice. The follicle mite *Demodex muscardini* appears to be specific.

RELATIONS WITH MAN A harmless species, vulnerable to local extinction owing to loss of its specialised habitat.

LITERATURE Hurrell (1962)—a general, illustrated account.

AUTHOR FOR THIS SPECIES G. B. Corbet.

FAMILY HYSTRICIDAE
PORCUPINES

Porcupines of the genus *Hystrix* have escaped from captivity on several occasions and have bred at liberty on at least one of these occasions. Since they are potentially destructive to both agricultural and forestry crops, known escapes are investigated by the Ministry of Agriculture and the Forestry Commission with a view to extermination, and no widespread colonisations have taken place. In Devon a pair of Hodgson's porcupine, *Hystrix hodgsoni*, a species from southern China and the Himalayas, escaped in 1969 and four animals were accounted for by 1974—two dead and two live-trapped. In Staffordshire a pair of crested porcupines, probably *Hystrix cristata* from northern Africa, escaped in 1972 and caused considerable damage to larch trees but there has been no sign of them since 1974.

FAMILY CAPROMYIDAE

A small family of caviomorph rodents, i.e. related to guinea pigs, agoutis, etc. It includes three genera of 'hutias' confined to the West Indies (and others recently extinct) and one, containing only the coypu, in southern South America. The last is sometimes separated from the hutias in a distinct family, Myocastoridae.

GENUS *Myocastor*

Contains only one species, the coypu.

Coypu *Myocastor coypus*

Mus coypus Molina, 1782; River Maipo, Chile.
Nutria.

RECOGNITION Adults unmistakable by large size: full-grown males frequently over 7 kg, non-pregnant females about a kilo lighter. Superficially rat-like with tapering cylindrical tail but nose blunt with widely spaced nostrils and hind feet webbed; anterior surface of incisors orange; large infra-orbital foramen in robust, flared zygomatic arch.

SIGN Footprints distinctive, those of adult hind foot up to 15 cm long; five claw marks on fore and hind foot and web mark often visible on latter. Shallow tail scrape, up to 2 cm wide, sometimes occurs. Droppings long, cylindrical, often slightly curved with fine longitudinal striations; scattered on banks or floating in water; from 2×7 mm at two weeks to 11×70 mm at full adult size. Small flat nests common at ditch edges: about 30 cm diameter and 2–5 cm deep, composed of dead large monocotyledonous leaves. Large nests up to 1 m high recorded in Russia and Poland, very uncommon in East Anglia. Burrows in banks of ditches common; entrance half submerged, diameter 20 cm. Often several metres deep with exit holes in level ground beyond bank. One explored in Argentina was complex, with nest cavities, and was over 6 m deep (Sierra de Soriano 1960). Commonly under roots of trees or bushes at water's edge. Ledges, often about 40×25 cm, half way down banks intensively used, probably as grooming stations. Runs, bare of vegetation when intensively used, 15 cm wide leading from regularly used 'climb-outs' at water's edge to complex network away from bank.

FIGURE 98 Coypu.

Paired crescentic incisor marks on food items (roots, leaf blades, etc.) up to 17 mm wide.

DESCRIPTION Adapted for semi-aquatic existence: webbed hind feet, valvular nostrils, underfur that remains dry during submersion. Long powerful claws on forefeet used for grooming, holding food and excavating burrows and food.

Soft grey underfur (the commercially used 'nutria'), in adults 2 cm deep and dense on ventral surface, 2·5 cm and less dense on back. Glossy brown and yellow-brown guard hair, 3·5 cm long and sparse on lower surface; 8 cm and dense on back.

8–10 mammary glands in two rows along the dorso-lateral body line; female sits in upright position while suckling young. Position of glands usually regarded as adaptation to semi-aquatic habit but there is a more likely explanation in terms of the hydrodynamics of the female's body by Arvy (1974). Young fully furred and active at birth with functional incisors and premolars.

Males have large anal gland lying ventral to rectum; weight averages 12·2 g (S.D.: 4·1); extruded during marking. Female gland smaller: 4·1 g (S.D.: 1·3). Genital systems have been described by Hillemann *et al.* (1958).

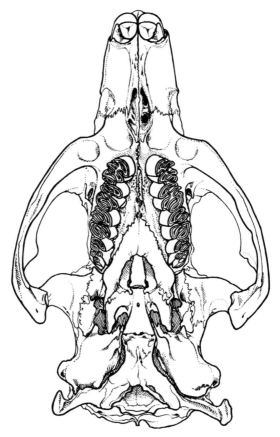

FIGURE 99 Skull of coypu from below.

Tooth formula

$$\frac{1 . 0 . 1 . 3}{1 . 0 . 1 . 3},$$

incisors larger in full-grown males (upper 15 mm wide) than in females (12 mm). Anterior enamel deep orange in males and deep orange to yellow in females. Pre-molar and molars wear to uniformly flat grinding surface with complex infundibular pattern which changes as attrition proceeds.

MEASUREMENTS (Table 22) Newson (1966) gave newborn weight of 175–332 g but juveniles, in good condition, are frequently up to 60 g lighter than this. Asymptotic weight attained at about 100 weeks (author's data). Full-grown males slightly but significantly larger than females.

TABLE 22 Measurements of adult coypus over 100 weeks old (author's data)

	Males (n=82)		Females (n=99)	
	Mean	s.d.	Mean	s.d.
Total weight (kg)	6·70	0·79	6·36	1·16
Weight after evisceration (kg)	5·82	0·72	5·05	0·66
Total length (mm)	995	45	980	40
Length of head and body (mm)	603	29	593	28
Length of hind feet (without claws) (mm)	136	4	130	4

VARIATION Five subspecies have been recognised in South America (Osgood 1943), of which *M. c. bonariensis* Geoffroy is the most widespread (Argentina, Uruguay, Paraguay, southern Brazil) and is the one the British animals most closely resemble.

Some variation in coat colour in England: yellow-dun animals were regularly trapped in one area of Norfolk (TG 40) during 1970–71 but have not occurred since.

DISTRIBUTION See Fig 100. Originally confined to South America: Bolivia, southern tip of Brazil, Paraguay, Uruguay, Argentina, central and southern Chile.

Feral populations from escapes and introductions in North America (mainly Louisiana), USSR, Kenya, Israel, continental Europe and England; population in West Germany has grown rapidly over past 7 years and expanded into Limburg province in southern Holland. French population expanding in Camargue and Loire valley.

Wild coypus reported over much of southern and eastern England in 1930s and 1940s. A colony persisted in Buckinghamshire (now Berkshire) until 1954 (Norris 1967) when it disappeared. Otherwise largely confined to East Anglia. Initially confined to Yare Valley, Norfolk, then expanded to Bure Valley (Laurie 1946b). Rare after severe winter of 1946/47. By late 1950s had consolidated range in Norfolk and Suffolk and expanded to surrounding counties. Intensive trapping and severe winter of

1962/63 eliminated outlying colonies and by mid-1963 coypus were again confined to 6000 km² area of Norfolk and East Suffolk. In spite of increasing population in early 1970s this range remained similar up to 1975.

HABITAT Majority of East Anglian population in extensive fen, reed swamp and other marshland communities of Norfolk east of Norwich and of East Suffolk and on the extensive grazing marshes (over 200 km²) of east Norfolk and north-east Suffolk. The brackish grazing marshes of north Norfolk support moderate population densities. Dykes with their associated aquatic and semi-aquatic plant communities are an important component of the habitat; banks provide optimum burrowing sites. Over most of Norfolk west of Norwich coypus are in limited areas of marshland or in dyke systems near rivers. Coypus never penetrated, in large numbers, into the fens of Lincolnshire because of intensive dyke cleaning and lack of pasture.

BEHAVIOUR Most commonly used gait is a walk which appears awkward as the large webbed hind feet are retracted. When alarmed first changes to fast walk then breaks into bounding gallop in which hind feet make contact outside and in front of fore feet contact point.

Swims with alternate propulsive thrusts of hind legs and rapid

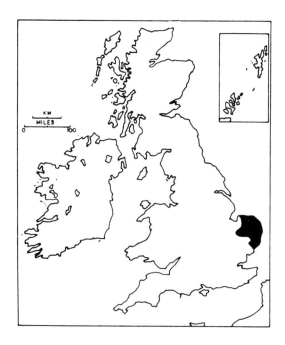

FIGURE 100 Coypu: distribution.

paddling movements of fore legs. Dives silently or, when alarmed, with loud splash (possible alarm signal function). Can lie immobile under water with legs outstretched for several minutes: probably anti-predator behaviour.

Three main periods of activity in captivity at Norwich each of 3–5 hours; one at dusk, one around midnight and one before dawn. Generally inactive throughout daylight hours with intermittent grooming and regular coprophagy (author's data). In wild, rest on nests or in burrows during the day.

Behaviour little studied at motor pattern level; some agonistic and body care behaviours described by Sierra de Soriano (1961). Several authors have mentioned extensive and prolonged grooming behaviour using the teeth, fore feet and hind feet.

Few reliable published observations on social organisation. Ryszkowski (1966) concluded that coypus were essentially non-gregarious but data were obtained from high-density enclosed population. Warketin (1968) mentioned colonial habit with alpha female and alpha male; male subordinate to female except during mating; rest of colony equally subordinate to these two. Research in Norfolk suggests a clan structure based on female lineage. Female offspring established ranges partially overlapping that of mother so that clan progressively expands around 'clan matriarch'. Little intra-clan agonistic behaviour: members often feed and move together. Alpha males have large ranges which sometimes include more than one clan; ranges of adjacent alpha males probably spatially exclusive at any one time. Post-pubertal males excluded from clan by aggression of older clan females and the alpha male; set up range in peripheral area of alpha male's range or emigrate. Records by Norris (1967) of a migratory class of young males are consistent with these observations (author's data).

Home ranges of clan adult females are about 2–4 ha in a 7 ha study enclosure of mixed habitat and those of alpha males 3–5 ha. Ranges on grazing marshes are considerably larger than in fen/reed swamp habitats: some male ranges on grazing marsh up to 120 ha.

FOOD Entirely herbivorous except for occasional feeding on fresh water mussels.

Coypus in East Anglia have complex but ordered pattern of plant utilisation. Different species and parts of plants (e.g. basal meristem) eaten at predictable time of year. Only leaf blade of pasture grasses eaten throughout year. Grass very important constituent of diet hence success of coypus on extensive grazing marshes of east Norfolk and north-east Suffolk.

In spring wide range of sprouting plants eaten; some selection for parts, e.g. basal meristem of the tufted sedge (*Carex elata*). More selective pattern through summer, e.g. heavy utilisation of basal meristems of burr-reed (*Sparganium erectum*) and the great pond sedge (*Carex riparia*), rest of plant usually discarded. In autumn diet augmented by fruits of various kinds, e.g. seed pods of water lily. In winter most important food source are roots and rhizomes often excavated to considerable depths; again selective: rhizomes of reed mace (*Typha*) are a favourite (Gosling 1974).

Complex feeding strategy allows utilisation of a wide range of crops. Can graze cereals in spring and eat mature seed heads in late summer; also brassicas and root crops, especially sugar beet.

Chemical analysis suggests that these feeding patterns are linked with seasonal variation in food quality; e.g. frequency of feeding on the leaves of the reed (*Phragmites communis*), highest from mid-summer to autumn, is correlated with carbohydrate content. Coypus thus appear to feed adaptively in their novel environment.

Food items held in one or both forefeet while animal sits supported on hind feet. Large items held on ground until small enough to pick up. High food items, e.g. seed head of mature wheat, pulled down with forefeet or stem bitten through first. Basal meristems eaten after shallow digging using forefeet and biting through shoot below ground level. Deep excavations, sometimes over 20 cm for roots and rhizomes, employ claws of forefeet.

BREEDING Coypus breed throughout the year in East Anglia. 1–13 embryos implant but partial resorptions reduce mean litter size to 5·3 at birth; mean size of first litters significantly smaller than of later litters. Gestation 127–138 days, i.e. $4\frac{1}{2}$ months (Newson 1966).

Prenatal embryo losses are high: Newson (1966) estimated a total loss between implantation and birth of 50–60%. Loss divided between deaths of individual embryos, which is more likely in larger litters and occurs mainly between weeks 5–10 of pregnancy, resorption of entire litters (about 28% in week 6) and abortion of entire litters (about 27% in week 13). Recent research has shown higher prenatal losses in years when the population is in poor condition as a consequence of adverse climate and poor food supply (author's data).

Conception occurs uniformly throughout the year but the distribution of total resorptions and abortions, dictated by environmental factors, results in varying frequencies of births: usually more births in the last half of the year following good summer and autumn conditions; more rarely a spring birth peak when older females manage to maintain pregnancies over the winter. Lactation is for 6–10 weeks although juveniles have been experimentally weaned at 5 days (Newson 1966).

POPULATION Anecdotal information only about English population up to early 1960s. After original escapes in early 1930s population grew slowly; 193 killed in Norfolk between 1943 and 1945 (Laurie 1946b). Population greatly reduced by 1946 winter, then grew to peak in late fifties and up to 1962. Norris (1967) estimated that there were 200 000 in 1962. During a period of intense trapping organised by the Ministry of Agriculture, Fisheries and Food the severe winter of 1962 reduced the population by 80–90%. Colder than average winters and continued trapping kept the population low and declining up to 1969. From 1970 to 1976 winters were average or mild, with low juvenile mortality, and 1971, 1972 and 1975 were years of very successful breeding. Numbers rose sharply from *c*. 1600 in 1970 to *c*. 8500 in 1973. Increases in the trapping force to 15 men in 1973 and 18 men in 1975 slowed, then stopped population growth after a maximum of *c*. 12 000 in late 1975. Simulation model prediction indicates a reduction to less than 3000 by spring 1978 if current trapping intensity maintained (author's data).

Population from 1963 to 1976 well below carrying capacity of habitat. Probably limited by variation in reproductive success and juvenile survivorship which are linked with variation in climate and food supply. Adults limited by trapping: comparison of survivorship curves from the wild population and an uncontrolled study population show higher mortality rate in wild with very few survivors over 2·5 years; survivorship in study population is 20% at same age. Physiological longevity is variously quoted in the literature from 5 to 12 years; 6–8 is probably nearer the truth.

PREDATORS AND MORTALITY No systematic study of predation in East Anglia. Predation by stoat, dogs and marsh harrier observed. Remains of coypus seen in heron pellets and fox faeces. Probably only large dogs kill full-size adults; several instances known of dogs incurring severe lacerations from the incisors of coypus during predation attempts. Young juveniles subjectively appear vulnerable and are probably taken by a number of predators including owls, hawks, weasels, domestic cat and pike.

Probably considerable juvenile mortality ultimately related to food supply and climate. Juveniles become thin at 8–10 weeks during weaning and many probably die then. Proximity of peak birth period (September–

December) to winter is non-adaptive in this respect. Weaned juveniles must experience difficulty in excavating roots and rhizomes, the main winter food source, particularly in frozen ground. Many unweaned juveniles undoubtedly die from starvation and exposure when their mothers are killed during control operations.

Few adults die from exposure/starvation although their fat reserves are reduced even during mild winters (Gosling 1974). Exception to this in severe winters: British coypu population has experienced three: 1939/40, 1946/47 and 1962/63. Anecdotal information indicates great reduction during second and in third drop in numbers trapped suggested 80–90% mortality (Norris 1967). Dying animals were emaciated; proximate cause of death in some cases was *Pasteurella pseudotuberculosis.*

Great majority of adult deaths from trapping by Coypu Control operators. Very few approach physiological longevity (see 'Population' section).

Aliev (1966) has listed the numerous predators of coypus in the USSR.

PARASITES AND DISEASE The ectoparasites of East Anglian coypus were surveyed by Newson & Holmes (1968). Of 1861 coypus examined 63% were infested by the host-specific louse *Pitrufquenia coypus*, which is the only ectoparasite recorded in South America (Marelli 1932). Of 2578 coypus 74 (2·9%) carried ticks: 34 were *Ixodes ricinus*, 39 *I. arvicolae*, 1 *I. hexagonus* and 2 *I. trianguliceps*. Fleas, mites and other ectoparasites were very rare.

A variable proportion, sometimes up to 50%, infected by liver fluke, *Fasciola hepatica*; coypus can thus act as alternative host for fluke and also be an agent in its spread (Holmes 1962). Other helminths identified are the fluke *Dicrocoelium dendriticum*, the tapeworm *Taenia serialis* and the nematode *Strongyloides papillosus*. A number of species of *Eimeria* (coccidian protozoans) have been identified in coypu faeces.

Serological tests showed that 81% of a sample of 70 wild coypus in Italy carried leptospire antibodies. A small percentage of coypus in Norfolk are infected with *Pasteurella pseudotuberculosis.*

RELATIONS WITH MAN Status in various countries ranges from protected rarity to pest. Utilised for fur and meat in some parts of natural and introduced range.

Probably long history of utilisation by man in South America. Hunting for fur at beginning of last century led to rarity status and protection by the Argentine dictator Rosas. As a result numbers increased dramatically until 'a mysterious malady fell on them from which they quickly perished becoming almost extinct' (Allen 1942). Nowadays protected in many areas but poaching has reduced numbers and range. Extensive fur farming in Argentina and considerable export of fur, then breeding stock in late 1920s and 1930s. Farms set up in many areas including North America, Europe and the USSR. Deliberate introductions particularly in the USSR although the animals die in hard weather except when trapped and kept under cover during the winter. Coypus were kept in captivity and semi-captivity in France from the late nineteenth century but until recently feral populations have been small: probably attributable to 'la chasse' which emphasises the vulnerability of coypu populations when heavily preyed upon by man.

First coypus brought to England in about 1929. Fifty fur farms established; moderately profitable but decrease in value of fur led to closure of all by 1939. After initial attempts at control in the 1940s the attitude to feral coypus was of cautious optimism; some positive benefits from clearing dykes and broads by feeding activities. In late fifties damage to dyke banks and river walls, through burrowing, to agricultural crops and the indigenous flora led, in 1962, to inclusion of coypus in list of species in the Destructive Imported Animals Act. Systematic control started in 1962 with a campaign organised by the Ministry of Agriculture, Fisheries and Food; 40 461 killed by end of 1965 (Norris 1967). Since then annual numbers killed have been: 1890(1966), 1628(1967), 1583(1968), 1026(1969), 1145(1970), 2196(1971), 3243(1972), 8303(1973), 10 239(1974), 12 096(1975). Control entirely by use of cage traps; trapped animals shot. Control operations are currently the responsibility of an independent consortium, 'Coypu Control', which is financed by contributions from Drainage Boards, the River Authority and the Government.

LITERATURE The history and biology of the East Anglian population described by Laurie (1946b), Davis (1963), Ellis (1965), Newson (1966), Norris (1967) and Gosling (1974). Extensive literature on feral populations in North America and the USSR.

AUTHOR FOR THIS SPECIES L. M. Gosling.

Order Cetacea
Whales, dolphins and porpoises

BY P. E. PURVES*

A very distinctive order including whales, dolphins and porpoises. Cetaceans are entirely aquatic, being born, feeding, reproducing, sleeping and dying in the water. Prolonged accidental stranding on beaches usually results in death.

Anatomy and physiology essentially mammalian but with profound modifications for adaptation to an aquatic life. These are as follows.

External form Generally 'streamlined' with absence of hind limbs and protuberances such as ear pinnae and external genitalia. Front limbs modified to form flippers with fingers enclosed in a common integument. No well-defined neck. Nostrils or 'blowhole' situated near the top of the head except in the sperm whale. In toothed cetaceans there is great hypertrophy of the upper lip to form a bulbous mass of fat referred to as the 'melon'. Integument of back frequently raised to form a triangular dorsal fin. Lateral expansion of integument of the tail to form a pair of large, fibrous 'flukes', the main external organs of propulsion.

Skin Epidermis perfectly smooth and attached to the dermis by parallel dermal ridges orientated in the average direction of the water flow over the body. No sweat glands nor hair follicles. Small isolated vibrissae on head and lower jaws of baleen whales, but found only in the young of toothed whales and confined to the snout.

In baleen whales skin at lateral margins of palate developed ventrad into a system of long, triangular horny plates set approximately at right-angles to the long axis of the mouth. The plates are for the most part smooth but their lingual edges are frayed out into fringes of bristles. The whole system of plates and their fringes acts as a sieve to strain from the sea water the planktonic animals on which these whales feed. Dermal layer of fat hypertrophied into a thick layer of heat-insulating blubber.

Muscles Panniculus carnosus heavily developed on the flanks, chest and abdomen obliterating the transverse contours of the underlying muscles thus maintaining the streamlined shape. Pectoral and abdominal muscles

---

*Based on the account in the 1st edition by F. C. Fraser.

approximating in shape to those of terrestrial mammals. Muscles of fore-arm and fingers degenerate. Dorsal spinal muscles greatly augmented in bulk and in adults fused into a single propulsive unit stretching from occiput to tail. Intrinsic muscles of thorax and neck greatly shortened and thickened to assist in rapid breathing. Muscles of hind limbs absent except for the psoas which is fused to the pubococcigeus and acts in flexion of the tail. Differential development of epaxial and hypaxial loco-motor muscles indicates that propulsive action is mainly on upstroke of tail. Nasal muscles greatly enlarged for rapid dilation of the blowhole and nostrils.

Skeleton Modification of the skeleton mainly concerned with alteration in relative proportion of its various parts. Neck vertebrae greatly flattened anteroposteriorly and frequently fused into a single mass. Thoracic verte-brae often reduced in number. Lumbar vertebrae generally increased in number, being augmented by unfused elements of a sacrum. Tail verte-brae heavily developed with enlarged mobile chevron bones for attachment of tendons. All vertebrae extremely simplified but having high neural spines and wide transverse processes for attachment of large, locomotor muscles. Pelvis generally reduced to two small bones repre-senting ischium. In some baleen whales vestiges of thigh and shin bones also present. Ribs in baleen whales loosely connected to vertebrae and sternum. Ribs more normal in toothed whales and connected to sternum by fully ossified 'sternal ribs'. Bones of flippers include those normally found in mammalian fore limbs but flattened in conformance with paddle-like form. Finger bones may be greatly increased in numbers with elongation of the flipper. No collar bone.

Skull in large whales up to 40% of body length. Upper jaw bones flat-tened dorsoventrally with obliteration of anterior nasal canals and turbi-nals. Nasal bones shortened and compressed against cranium revealing posterior nasal canals from above. Nasal area in toothed whales asym-metrically developed. Much overlapping of bones on upper surface of skull in toothed whales and on under surface in baleen whales. Brain-case enlarged and expanded laterally. No bony air sinuses but equivalent areas in toothed whales occupied by saccular extensions of middle ear cavity. Ear bones separated from skull. Lower jaws simplified with only vestiges of vertical processes. No teeth in baleen whales except in foetus. In toothed whales they may be very numerous in upper and lower jaws or found only in lower jaw and sometimes reduced to a single pair. They are usually conical in shape and single-rooted.

Vascular system Characterised by elaborate networks of blood vessels between muscles in thorax and abdomen, mainly concerned with free mobility of muscles and internal organs under a semi-rigid integument, but may have other important functions. Large venous plexuses in association with saccular extensions of middle-ear cavity concerned with regulation of air pressure in middle ear at various depths (Fraser & Purves 1960). Internal carotid artery reduced in function, blood supply to brain taking place through large spinal meningeal arteries situated in neural canal. Peripheral circulation adapted for alternative conservation or reduction of bodily heat. Blood temperature and composition similar to that of terrestrial mammals but many more red blood corpuscles.

Nervous system Exceptionally large convoluted brain sometimes proportionally equal to that in man. Cerebral hemispheres overlap the laterally expanded cerebellum. Olfactory bulbs and nerves rudimentary in baleen whales, absent in toothed whales. Trigeminal and acoustic nerves very large, consistent with enhanced auditory and tactile senses. The roots and cortical centres of these nerves also unusually large. Cervical and brachial plexuses well developed but iliac plexus rudimentary consistent with absence of hind limbs. Cross linking of post-thoracic spinal nerves for coordination of tail movements.

Respiration Oxygenation of blood by succession of brief emergences at water surface when blowhole is dilated and inhalation occurs. This usually followed by a period of deeper submergence (sounding) during which the lungs are evacuated. The 'blow' is produced by forceful release of compressed air from bronchi and tidal air passages after deep diving. Blowhole sealed by elastic recoil of tissues and inflation of pneumatic chambers in upper nostrils. Glottis greatly elongated and protruded into nasopharynx forming continuous air passage from blowhole to lungs. Surrounded by a powerful palatopharyngeal sphincter muscle preventing escape of air through the mouth. Construction of glottis indicates that it produces the echolocating pulses that have been recorded from most cetaceans. Trachea, bronchi and bronchials in cetaceans surrounded by incomplete cartilaginous rings and a vascular mucous membrane allowing considerable contraction of the lumen. Pulmonary air chambers (alveoli) of lungs guarded by small sphincter muscles are confined to the peripheral layers of lungs, the main body consisting of elastic tissue. This arrangement allows for more complete exchange of pulmonary air than in terrestrial mammals.

Digestive system Owing to intranarial position of epiglottis the pharynx is divided into a double passage. Large salivary glands. Short oesophagus leads into muscular, nonglandular fore stomach where food is retained and comminuted. Finely ground food passes through narrow aperture into main digestive stomach which is thick-walled and highly glandular. Main stomach leads into pyloric stomach which may be divided into as many as five compartments interconnected by small apertures. The following somewhat dilated duodenum receives the pancreatic and hepatic ducts which are frequently joined together. There is no gall bladder. The rest of the intestine is exceptionally long, uniform in diameter and thick walled, suggesting strong peristaltic action. No caecum nor appendix. Faeces fluid and finely divided.

Urinogenital system Kidneys very large and composed of a great number of separate renules each with its own branch of renal artery, vein and ureter. Bladder very small and muscular. Testes always internal and suspended below and posterior to kidneys. Retractor penis causes penis to be pulled into a complete loop. Ovaries almost covered by Fallopian funnels. Uterus bicornuate. Internal surface of vagina transversely folded. Mammary teats concealed in slits on either side of genital opening except during lactation.

Senses Eyes functional and apparently equally effective in and out of water. Spherical, non-adjustable lens. Exceptionally thick sclera to maintain lenticular shape of optic cavity. Ear adapted for hearing under water. Ear cartilage entirely internal and forming narrow tube leading to flattened triangular eardrum (tympanic ligament). In baleen whales ear tube is closed beneath the blubber. Internal lumen in baleen whales filled by

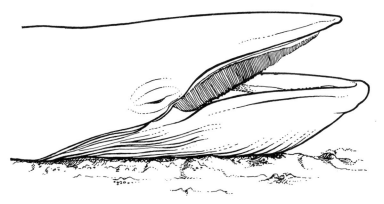

FIGURE 101 Head of a stranded lesser rorqual with the mouth opened to show the series of baleen blades attached to the upper jaw.

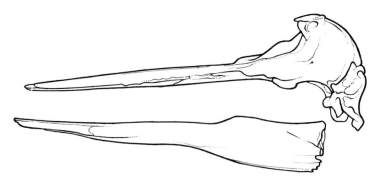

FIGURE 102 Skull of Sowerby's whale.

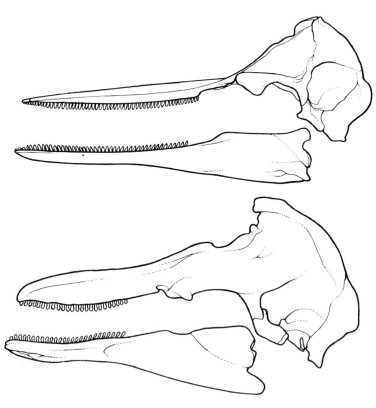

FIGURE 103 Skulls of common dolphin (above) and porpoise (below). Note the flattened, spade-shaped teeth of the porpoise.

conical plug of keratin. Auditory ossicles and cochlea adapted for receipt of ultrasonic vibrations. Middle ear cavities adapted to rapid changes in hydrostatic pressure. Rich trigeminal nerve supply to forehead indicates highly tactile sense in this region. No sense of smell in toothed whales and rudimentary in baleen whales. Gustatory sense enhanced. Skin sensitivity normal.

Whales are classified in two suborders as follows: (1) Mysticeti (baleen or whalebone whales) which have no teeth but a system of horny plates for straining plankton as described above. They are mostly large (10–30 m) have a double blowhole and symmetrical skull. The Mysticeti are divided into three families, two of which occur in British waters. (2) Odontoceti (toothed whales) varying in size from sperm down to porpoises and characterized by possessing teeth, a single blowhole and asymmetrical skull. Divided into six families of which five have been recorded round our coasts.

The records of British cetaceans in the following accounts have been compiled almost entirely from records of animals stranded on the coasts of the United Kingdom since 1913. In a statute enacted in the fourteenth century *De Praerogativa Regis* the sovereign's entitlement to whales and dolphins stranded on, or caught near the British coasts was established and these have since been designated *Fishes Royal*. Strandings of royal fishes are reported to H.M. Receivers of Wreck by coastguards and others, primarily in connection with disposal of the carcases.

A former Keeper of Zoology and later Director of the British Museum (Natural History), Sir Sidney Harmer, saw the potential zoological application of the Receiver's concern with royal fishes. At the request of the Trustees of the British Museum instructions to Receivers were issued in 1912 to send reports of strandings of cetaceans to the Museum. The first Report on Cetacea stranded on the British coasts covering the year 1912 was published in 1914 (Harmer 1914). Since 1913 an approximate total of 1800 strandings have been reported with an average of about 30 per year involving 22 different species.

The seasonal distribution and frequency of stranding of the various species may be found in the Reports on Cetacea published by the British Museum (Harmer 1927, Fraser 1934, 1946, 1953, 1974). More recently the Mammal Society has formed a Cetacea Group to organize observation of sightings of cetaceans at sea (Evans, in press). The causes of stranding are still a matter of conjecture.

The most comprehensive account of the cetaceans of the northern hemisphere, covering many aspects of their biology, is that of Tomilin (1967).

Key to stranded cetaceans (adapted from that in Fraser 1974)

1 { Whalebone present on palate; teeth absent; lower jaw very wide, its halves arched outwards . . . . . (whalebone whales) — See 2
Whalebone absent; teeth present, though sometimes concealed beneath the gum; lower jaw narrow, at least in front . (toothed whales) — See 7

2 { Lower surface of throat not grooved; no back fin; mouth and upper border of lower lip much arched; whalebone blades long, up to 2·7 m . . . . **Black right whale** (p. 275)
Lower surface of throat with numerous parallel grooves . . . See 3

3 { Flippers extremely long, nearly one-third the length of the animal, sometimes white externally, with a scalloped lower margin . . **Humpback** (p. 276)
Flippers much less than one-third the total length, not scalloped below . . . . (rorquals) See 4

4 { Whalebone yellowish white, slate-coloured or both . . . . See 5
Whalebone black or nearly black . . . . See 6

5 { Size, up to 21 m; whalebone yellow and slate-coloured, except at the front of the right side where it is white; its hairy fringes white or yellowish; tail-flukes white below . . **Common rorqual** (p. 279)
Size, up to 9 m; whalebone and its hairy fringes all white or yellowish; a white region on outer side of flipper . . **Lesser rorqual** (p. 280)

6 { Size, up to 26 m; whalebone very black, with coarse black hairs . . . . **Blue whale** (p. 283)
Size, up to 15 m; whalebone mostly dark, with very fine, white, curling, silky hairs; tail-flukes not white below . . . **Sei whale** (p. 282)

7 { Tip of lower jaw well behind front end of head . . . . See 8
Lower and upper jaws of approximately equal length . . . See 9

8 { Size that of a large whale (to 18 m); many large teeth in lower jaw; upper jaw toothless or with a few irregular vestigial teeth, smaller than in lower jaw; head one-third total body length; no well defined dorsal fin . . . . **Sperm whale** (p. 285)
Size much less (to about 3 m); slender, elongated, recurved teeth in lower jaw, absent in upper jaw; head one-sixth total body length; well defined dorsal fin . . . . **Pigmy sperm whale** (p. 287)

9 { Back-fin absent. . . . . See 10
Back-fin present . . . . See 11

10 { Head short, with prominent 'forehead'; colour greyish, with black spots or mottlings; either without visible teeth (females), or with a tusk-like tooth, up to 2·5 m long, spirally twisted, projecting forwards from the front of the upper jaw (males), exceptionally with two spiral tusks . . . . **Narwhal** (p. 293)
Colour, white all over (greyish-brown in young individuals); 8–10 pairs of teeth in each jaw . . . . . . **White whale** (p. 292)

11 { Teeth confined to the lower jaw, or apparently absent . . . See 12
     Teeth in both jaws . . . . See 16

12 { Back-fin large, near middle of body; teeth, 2–7 pairs, at front end of
       lower jaw . . . . **Risso's dolphin** (p. 301)
       Back-fin considerably behind middle of body; front end of jaws narrow;
       two grooves on throat . . . . See 13

13 { Size large, up to 9 m; distance from tip of snout to blowhole one-fifth
       to one-seventh the total length; 'forehead' very prominent; teeth
       (one or two pairs) at tip of lower jaw, usually concealed . .
                                         Bottle-nosed whale (p. 288)
       Distance from tip of snout to blowhole less than one-seventh the total
       length . . . . See 14

14 { Size large, up to 8 m; distance from tip of snout to blowhole one-
       tenth to one-eighth the total length; 'forehead' not specially
       prominent; teeth, one pair at tip of lower jaw, massive in males
       (diameter 25 mm), concealed in females . . **Cuvier's whale** (p. 289)
       Size smaller, not exceeding 6 m; beak long . . . . See 15

15 { Length about 4·5 m; colour mostly black, usually with white marks;
       one pair of teeth at middle of lower jaw, conspicious and triangular
       in males, concealed in females . . . **Sowerby's whale** (p. 290)
       Size rather larger; colour not satisfactorily known, one pair of teeth at 15
       tip of lower jaw, conspicuous and flattened sideways in males, con-
       cealed in females . . . . . **True's beaked whale** (p. 291)

16 { Size large, up to 9 m in adults; teeth, 8–13 pairs in each jaw . . See 17
     Seldom exceeding 3·6 m, usually less than 2·7 m; teeth not more than
       13 mm in diameter, more than 15 pairs . . . . . See 19

17 { 'Forehead' greatly swollen, overhanging the tip of the very short beak;
       flippers narrow, about one-fifth of the total length; colour black, with
       only a small amount of white on lower surface; teeth, 8–12 pairs in
       each jaw, less than 13 mm in diameter . . . **Pilot whale** (p. 299)
       'Forehead' not prominent, teeth, 10–13 pairs in each jaw, at least 19 mm
       in diameter . . . . See 18

18 { Colour conspicuously black and white (or yellow); flippers broad, not
       pointed; teeth about 25 mm in diameter, roughly oval in cross-
       section . . . . **Killer whale** (p. 296)
       Colour black all over; flippers narrow and pointed; teeth circular in
       cross-section . . . . **False killer whale** (p. 298)

19 { Size up to 1·7 m; teeth about 21–24 pairs in each jaw, flattened
       sideways, with spade-shaped crowns; beak not distinguish-
       able . . . . **Common porpoise** (p. 295)
       Size larger, teeth conical, the crowns not flattened sideways; beak
       distinct . . . . See 20

20 { Length up to 3·6 m; beak about 7·5 cm long in middle line; teeth large,
       20–25 pairs in each jaw; diameter 13–19 mm . . . .
                                         Bottle-nosed dolphin (p. 305)
       Teeth not exceeding 6 mm in diameter . . . . . . See 21

21 { Beak about 5 cm long in middle line; length up to 3 mm . . . See 22
   { Beak up to 15 cm in middle line; teeth, 40–50 pairs in each jaw, about 2 mm in diameter; length up to 2.1 m . . . . . See 23

22 { Upper lip white; dark colour of flippers continuous with that of body, their lower margin not much curved; teeth, about 25 pairs in each jaw, diameter 6 mm . . . . . **White-beaked dolphin** (p. 302)
   { Upper lip black; flippers, with strongly curved lower margin, arising from white part of body, usually connected with dark part by a narrow dark streak; a conspicuous white region on each side, behind the back-fin; teeth, 30–40 pairs in each jaw, diameter 5 mm . .
   White-sided dolphin (p. 303)

23 { A well-marked, narrow dark band of pigment extending from the eye along the flank and curving down to the vent, with a subsidiary branch in the region of the flipper insertion **Blue-white dolphin** (p. 306)
   { This band wanting, but an arrangement of yellowish, white and dark bands on the sides of the body . . . **Common dolphin** (p. 308)

Suborder Mysticeti
Baleen whales

This group, including most of the large whales, comprises two families, Balaenidae and Balaenopteridae, dealt with here, along with a third, Eschrichtiidae, containing only the Californian grey whale, *Eschrichtius gibbosus*. Subfossil remains of the last have been found in England and elsewhere in Western Europe but it is not known when it became extinct in the Atlantic.

FAMILY BALAENIDAE
RIGHT WHALES

A family of three species, of which one has occurred in British waters. Compared with the rorquals (Balaenopteridae) right whales are slow swimmers with very large heads, highly arched upper jaws with very long baleen, no grooves on the throat, no dorsal fin and broad rounded flippers.

GENUS *Balaena*

Includes the Greenland right whale or bowhead and the black right whales. The latter are sometimes placed in a separate genus *Eubalaena*. There are three forms of black right whale which are variably treated as separate species or as races of a single species. Only one of these has occurred in British waters.

Black right whale *Balaena glacialis*

Balaena glacialis Müller, 1776; North Cape, Norway. *Balaena britannica* Gray, 1870; Dorset, England.
Biscayan whale, nordcaper.

RECOGNITION Arched head with horny excrescence or 'bonnet' at tip of snout. Double 'blow' on exhalation. Totally black, no dorsal fin. Rectangular alisphenoid bones.

DESCRIPTION Large head 25% of body length. Generally all black but occasionally with white patches on belly. No grooves on throat. No dorsal

FIGURE 104 Black right whale.

fin. Prominent lower lips. Rounded flippers. All-black baleen blades up to 3 m in length. Bonnet and mouth generally infested with barnacles and whale lice. Eye placed low on head. Mammary slits on either side of genital aperture in female. Size difference between male and female unknown.

MEASUREMENTS Length up to 18·5 m. Weight estimated *c.* 40–50 tonnes. Length of skull up to 5 m.

DISTRIBUTION Probably world-wide in Northern Hemisphere. Formerly abundant in North Atlantic, Bay of Biscay and southern parts of Arctic seas; now much rarer. No British strandings since 1913 when systematic recording started. Sixty-seven landed at Scottish whaling stations between 1908 and 1914, mostly caught to the west of the Outer Hebrides and mostly inside the edge of the Continental shelf (Thompson 1928). Peak numbers were taken in June.

VARIATION Claimed by Gray (1864) to be conspecific with the southern

right whale *Balaena australis*, but a specific difference has been demonstrated by Muller (1954).

BEHAVIOUR Slow swimmer, not more than six knots and easily caught.
Strong protective instinct for young. Formerly aggregated in large herds
but now widely dispersed, in small, family groups. Acute sense of hearing.
A great number of underwater sounds have been recorded (Cummings
et al. 1972).

FOOD Small, swarming crustaceans, mainly *Meganyctiphanes norvegica*
and other related forms. Lower jaws and lips rotated outwards to allow
sea water to pass into mouth. Lower jaws and lips then rotated inwards
and tongue raised to force water out between baleen blades leaving food
residue on lingual fringes of baleen plates.

PREDATORS Known to be attacked and killed by packs of killer whales.
Mortality rate unknown.

PARASITES Heavily infested with barnacles *Coronula biscayensis* and
whale lice, especially *Cyanus ovalis*, which is particularly abundant on the
'bonnet'.

RELATIONS WITH MAN Nearly hunted to extinction but now totally
protected and increasing in numbers.

FAMILY BALAENOPTERIDAE

The largest family of baleen whales, comprising the humpback (*Megaptera*) and the rorquals (*Balaenoptera*).

GENUS *Megaptera*

Contains a single species, *M. novaeangliae*.

Humpback whale *Megaptera novaeangliae*

Balaena Novae Angliae Borowski, 1781; New England, USA. *Balaena
boops* Fabricius, 1780 (not of Linnaeus, 1758); Greenland. *Balaena
nodosa* Bonnaterre, 1789; New England. *Balaena longimana* Rudolphi,
1832; Germany. *Megaptera longimana moorei* Gray, 1866; Estuary of
Dee, Cheshire.

RECOGNITION The blow is a short, broad jet distinctive to whalers.

Strongly arched back when diving (sounding) with flukes appearing clear of the water. Conspicuous black and white pigmentation, extremely long flippers. Skull does not differ markedly from that of rorquals although proportionally broader.

DESCRIPTION General form stout. Very long flippers one quarter to a third of the body length with the leading edges marked by a row of swellings corresponding in position to the interphalangeal cartilages. Snout short, broad with parallel rows of small humps (associated with tactile vibrissae). Similar humps along sides of lower jaw. Dorsal fin at commencement of hinder third of body, small, variable in shape and set on low hump. Posterior margin of flukes with notch in middle and irregularly scalloped. Throat grooves fewer in number (20 to 36) and more widely spaced than in rorquals. Barnacles and whale lice very common on body,

FIGURE 105 Humpback whale.

particularly on head and flippers. Back black, belly white but distribution of pigment very variable. Under surface of flippers white but lack of pigment may also occur very extensively on upper surface. Under surface of flukes white. Baleen up to 1 metre in length, 300–400 plates each side. Colour nearly black with labial fringes of same colour. Occasionally some anterior blades white.

MEASUREMENTS Length up to 15 m. Weight at 12·4 m, 31 tonnes.

DISTRIBUTION World wide. In British Isles no records of stranding in recent years but caught off the Hebrides and west coast of Ireland early in present century. Migratory route west of Ireland and Faroes. Most captures from the Scottish whaling stations were in July and August (Thompson 1928).

One was killed in the Tay Estuary in 1884.

VARIATION Distribution of black and white pigment very variable but not associated with subspecific nor clinal variation.

BEHAVIOUR Slow swimmer, not more than ten knots and easily caught. Capable of a great variety of swimming movements, breaching clear of the water, rolling over and over, side swimming and 'lob-tailing'.

Migratory routes between polar seas and subtropical coasts very direct and well known by whalers. Consequently heavily exploited in past. Formerly aggregated in large schools but now widely dispersed. A great variety of vocalisations have been recorded which may travel 100 km or more under water (Payne 1970).

FOOD Planktonic crustaceans (krill), small swarming fish, exceptionally cod and accidentally cormorants. Lower jaws rotate outwards and muscles underlying throat grooves relax to allow water to enter mouth. Water is squeezed out between baleen blades by contraction of muscles and throat grooves thus trapping planktonic animals on lingual fringes of baleen blades.

BREEDING Sexually mature at 10–12 years. Period of gestation 10 months. Laction 6 months or longer. Breed every two years (Simons & Weston 1958).

POPULATION STRUCTURE Apparent annual mortality rate 12%; longevity 60 years.

PREDATORS Has been known to be attacked by packs of killer whales.

PARASITES Heavily infested with barnacles, *Coronula* and *Conchoderma* spp. and by whale lice, *Cyamus* spp.

RELATIONS WITH MAN Greatly reduced in numbers by whaling but now totally protected.

GENUS *Balaenoptera*

RORQUALS

Whales belonging to this genus distinguished from humpback by flipper length being much less than one third of total body length and not irregularly outlined. Trailing edge of tail without serrations. Grooves on throat and chest more numerous, averaging 85 to 90. Five species, of which four are widely distributed and have been recorded in British waters.

Common rorqual *Balaenoptera physalus*

Balaena physalus Linnaeus, 1758; Spitzbergen. *Balaena sulcata* Neill, 1811; Firth of Forth. *Balaenoptera tenuirostris* Sweeting, 1840; Dorset. *Physalus duguidii* Heddle, 1856; Orkney.
Fin whale, finback, herring hog.

RECOGNITION The second largest of the whales, females up to 24 m in length. Tend to congregate in schools. Slate grey. Does not generally show tail flukes when diving. Vertical blow narrowly conical in shape before dispersal. On ventral surface of skull, squamosal does not make contact with palatine as in blue whale.

DESCRIPTION General form slender in relation to length. Margins of mouth forming an acute angle. Slight concavity of floor of mouth when not feeding. Dorsal fin at commencement of hinder third of body,

FIGURE 106 Common rorqual.

moderately high with concave trailing edge. Flippers about one seventh body length. Throat grooves about 85–95 ending posterior to maximum cross-section of body. Asymmetry of lower-jaw colour diagnostic of species. External surface of right lower lip white, that of left pigmented. Pigmentation of tongue also asymmetrical. General body colour grey above, white below including lower surface of flukes and inner surfaces of flippers (cf. sei whale). Largest blades of baleen *c.* 1 m. Blades on right side of palate usually white for 75–100 cm from front end. Remaining blades of right side and all of left slaty grey alternating with longitudinal yellowish bands. All labial fringes white.

MEASUREMENTS Length up to 24·5 m but 18 to 21 m more usual in females. Males average 1 m shorter than females. Calves at birth *c.* 6·7 m. Weight at 20·8 m 53 tonnes.

DISTRIBUTION World-wide in subtropical and sub-polar regions. Migratory, the smaller northern hemisphere race passes British coast on way northward in early spring and southward in autumn. Not uncommon in British waters but less frequently stranded now than earlier in the present century. Hunted up to 1922 from whaling stations off west coast of Ireland and Hebrides.

VARIATION Northern hemisphere animals average *c*. 1 m smaller than those of southern hemisphere.

BEHAVIOUR Inclined to congregate in large schools. Very fast swimmer, up to 30 knots. Undergoes regular migrations from subtropical waters where it breeds in winter to subarctic regions to feed in summer. Low pitched (20 cycle) pulses have been recorded as well as high pitched squeaks which may have communication content (Schevill *et al.* 1964, Perkins 1966).

FOOD Planktonic crustaceans, small herring, 'sild'. Method of feeding as in humpback.

BREEDING Sexually mature at 8–12 years, probably reduced in age in recent years. Period of gestation *c*. 1 year. One or two calves produced every two years. Lactation *c*. 6 months. (Purves & Mountford 1959, Laws 1961, Lockyer 1972).

POPULATION STRUCTURE Only known from whaling catch statistics, including all ages from 6–80 years. Maximum life-span unknown. Age distribution of catch shows fluctuations in juvenile mortality from year to year.

PREDATORS AND MORTALITY Age structure shows annual average adult natural mortality rate of *c*. 10% per year. Probably attacked by killer-whales but no records.

PARASITES AND DISEASE External parasites, e.g. the copepod crustacean *Penella* sp. and the barnacle *Coronula* sp., only occur in warmer waters and are lost in polar regions.

RELATIONS WITH MAN Heavily exploited by whaling and reduced in numbers, but may recover under existing international whaling regulations.

Lesser rorqual *Balaenoptera acutorostrata*

Balaenoptera acutorostrata Lacepède, 1804; Cherbourg, France.
Minke whale, little piked whale.

RECOGNITION The smallest of the baleen whales in British waters. Blow inconspicuous, tail does not normally break surface. Skull triangular in shape with straight rather than curved lateral borders to rostrum.

DESCRIPTION Commonest rorqual in British waters. General form similar to fin whale but head smaller in relation to body length and with sharply pointed snout. Flippers one-eighth of body length, relatively short and narrow. Throat grooves *c.* 50 in number. Small dorsal fin at commencement of hinder third of body. Colour dark grey to black above, pure white below. Outer surface of flippers black with white band across greatest width, distinctive of species. Baleen blades all white with labial fringes of fine texture.

MEASUREMENTS Length up to 9 m. Newborn calves *c.* 2·8 m. Weight at 4·9 m 1250 kg.

FIGURE 107 Lesser rorqual.

DISTRIBUTION World-wide. Found all round British Isles but more frequently stranded on west coast.

VARIATION Southern hemisphere form lacks white band across flippers.

BEHAVIOUR Migrates between higher and lower latitudes associated respectively with feeding and breeding. Distribution of stranding suggests migration route to and from North Sea by west coast and round north of Scotland.

FOOD Diet varied. Herring and krill favoured. Cod and other gadoid fish also taken.

BREEDING Pairing January to May. Gestation *c.* 10 months, sexually mature 6–8 years. Most often simultaneously lactating and pregnant, producing one calf each year (Ohsumi *et al.* 1970).

POPULATION STRUCTURE Small, family groups and sometimes larger aggregations of which age-structure is as yet unknown. Life span unknown.

PREDATORS Sometimes attacked by killer whales.

PARASITES AND DISEASE Ectoparasites rare but the crustaceans *Penella balaenopterae* are found embedded in the skin, especially near the urinogenital opening.

RELATION WITH MAN There has been a Norwegian coastal fishery of this species for many years but more recently it has become the target of pelagic whalers and requires conservation.

Sei whale *Balaenoptera borealis*

Balaenoptera borealis Lesson, 1828; Germany.
Rudolphi's rorqual.

FIGURE 108 Sei whale.

RECOGNITION Blow low and inconspicuous, showing much less of head and body than other rorquals. Baleen blades black with fine, white fringes on labial borders. Skull larger but similar in shape to lesser rorqual.

DESCRIPTION General form less slender but otherwise resembling fin whale. Margins of snout forming an acute angle. Fin at commencement of hinder third of body, relatively larger than in blue and fin whale of similar length. Posterior margin of flukes with median notch. Throat grooves fewer (40 to 60) and shorter (ending some distance in front of navel) than in blue and fin whales. A few vibrissae on upper and lower jaws. General colour, including dorsal surface of flukes and under surface of flippers, bluish grey varying in shade, lighter grey on under surface. White area in ventral groove region, very variable in extent, not usually extending to chin or beyond posterior limit of ventral grooves. Under surface of flukes and flippers pigmented like upper surface of body.

MEASUREMENTS Length up to 18·3 m but usually about 15 m. Newborn calf *c.* 4·5 m.

DISTRIBUTION World-wide but not very abundant in British seas. More common on western seaboard.

BEHAVIOUR Very fast swimmer, up to 30 knots. Has often been seen to leap clear of the water. Migrate to high latitudes for a month or so during summer but remain in warmer water during most of the year. Northerly route includes western coast of Britain where most abundant in June. Formerly aggregated into very large schools, up to thousands, but now much more widely dispersed due to whaling operations.

FOOD Planktonic crustaceans (krill) and the copepod *Calanus finmarchicus*. Does not turn on its side when feeding as has frequently been observed in humpback and fin whales.

BREEDING Gestation *c.* 1 year. Sexual maturity 8–9 years. Lactation about 5 months. Produces one calf every two years.

POPULATION STRUCTURE Age structure indicates mortality of 8% per year with probable fluctuation in juvenile mortality. Longevity 60–70 years.

RELATIONS WITH MAN Heavily exploited by whaling industry but according to some authorities not in immediate danger of extinction.

Blue whale *Balaenoptera musculus*

Balaena musculus Linnaeus, 1758; Firth of Forth, Scotland. *Physalus (Rorqualus) sibbaldii* Gray, 1847; Yorkshire coast, England. Sibbald's rorqual.

FIGURE 109 Blue whale.

RECOGNITION Largest whale, with high, distinctive blow and dark blue colour. Does not show tail flukes when sounding. In skull the only rorqual in which squamosal makes contact with palatine (Fraser & Purves 1960).

DESCRIPTION Largest and heaviest existing mammal with broad snout and large head up to 25% of body length. Dark blue colour over most of body but with numerous irregularly spaced small white areas on sides and belly. Under surface of flippers white extending to upper leading edge at extremity. Dorsal fin small and placed more posteriorly than in other rorquals. Throat grooves 70 to 120 extending more than half way towards tail. Baleen blades short, very wide and jet black including labial fringes.

MEASUREMENTS Length may reach 30·5 m but usually not over 28 m. Males smaller, 24 m. Weight at 27 m, 120 tonnes.

DISTRIBUTION World-wide and formerly not uncommon off west coast of Ireland and Scotland but now very rare.

VARIATION The existence of a pygmy race or separate species, *B. brevicauda*, has been alleged but has not been confirmed.

BEHAVIOUR Very fast swimmer, up to 30 knots. Two distinctive populations in southern and northern hemispheres migrating to polar regions in summer to feed and to subtropics in winter to breed. Formerly forming very large herds but now widely dispersed and extremely rare. High and low pitched communication signals have been recorded (Beamish & Mitchell 1971). Very acute sense of hearing and easily scared by noise.

FOOD Almost exclusively planktonic crustaceans.

BREEDING Sexually mature at 8 to 10 years. Period of gestation 12 months. Weaning 6 to 7 months. One or more rarely two calves born every two years.

POPULATION STRUCTURE Not enough data available but evidence indicates similar to fin whale with annual mortality 10–12% per year, longevity *c*. 80 years. Catch curves indicate fluctuating juvenile mortality rate (Mackintosh & Wheeler 1929).

PREDATORS Said to have been attacked by packs of killer whales.

PARASITES The copepod crustacean *Penella balaenopterae* is found embedded in the skin and a commensal crustacean, *Balaenophilus unisetus*, is found on the baleen.

RELATIONS WITH MAN Nearly brought to extinction by whaling operations but now totally protected.

Suborder Odontoceti
Toothed whales

FAMILY PHYSETERIDAE

Contains two genera, *Physeter* the sperm whale, and *Kogia* the pygmy sperm whale, both of which have been stranded on the British coasts.

GENUS *Physeter*

Contains only one species.

Sperm whale *Physeter catodon*

Physeter catodon Linnaeus, 1758; Orkney. *Physeter macrocephalus* Linnaeus, 1758.
Pot-head, cachalot.

FIGURE 110 Sperm whale (adult male).

RECOGNITION Large blunt head with conspicuous forwardly projecting 'blow' from anterior of snout in distinction from that of all other whales in which it emerges from top of head. Numerous large teeth in lower jaw only. Skull with high occipital crest and in general form shaped like a chariot.

DESCRIPTION Largest of all the toothed cetaceans. Head one third of total body length, with single blowhole placed at left anterior limit of snout. Front of head nearly flat, rounding off to top and sides, tapering ventrally towards anterior end of lower jaw. Lower jaw not extending to anterior limit of head and very narrow, the two rami being fused together for most of their length. Thirty large teeth on each side of lower jaw. Small teeth in upper jaw concealed below the gums. Flippers rounded. Dorsal fin ill-defined and succeeded posteriorly by four or five smaller humps. Hinder end of tail with posterior notch. On the flanks skin irregularly corrugated. A few short furrows in throat region. General colour dark grey to black, lightening somewhat to sides. Very light grey to white on belly, varying greatly in extent. White usually in region of upper and lower lips. Head and anterior part of body generally marked by numerous scratches and circular scars said to be inflicted by the tentacles of giant squid which forms the main diet. The pointed extremities of the lower teeth fit into sockets on the sides of the palate when the mouth is closed. Disproportionate size of head due to development of a large sac of fat, the spermaceti organ, unique to the Physeteridae.

MEASUREMENTS Length of male to about 18·5 m, female to 9 m. Newborn calf 3·7 to 3·9 m. Weight at 18 m, 52 tonnes.

DISTRIBUTION World-wide in tropical and subtropical waters but single males occur in polar waters. Those stranded on the British coasts have all been males.

BEHAVIOUR Relatively slow swimmer, rarely exceeding 6 knots, but can exceed this when attacked. Oxygenation of lungs occurs by a series of spouts, about 40 times in 7 to 10 minutes, before diving for about half to one hour to depths exceeding 1000 m. Navigation and food-finding by the emission of echolocating sound pulses (SONAR) (Worthington & Schevill 1957). Generally docile but will attack whaling vessels when wounded.

FOOD Almost entirely large squids but large fish may be swallowed accidentally.

BREEDING Polygamous. Sexual maturity at 9 to 10 years, gestation *c.* 16 months. Lactation *c.* 6 months. Sex ratio at birth 50%.

POPULATION STRUCTURE Dominant male accompanied by a variable number of females and immature males. Old males solitary. Age structure indicates 6% annual mortality rate. Longevity about 60 years.

RELATIONS WITH MAN Especially valuable to whaling industry for waxy spermaceti, blubber, meat for fertiliser and ambergris sometimes found in intestine. Whaling is mainly from shore stations and the species is thought not to be in immediate danger of extinction (Gambell 1972).

GENUS *Kogia*

Contains two forms which may or may not be conspecific.

Pygmy sperm whale *Kogia breviceps*

Physeter breviceps Blainville, 1838; South Africa.

RECOGNITION No data available for recognition at sea. Resembles sperm whale in having numerous teeth in lower jaw only. Exceedingly small mouth placed ventrally, much posterior to anterior limit of upper jaw like that of a shark. Skull resembling that of miniature sperm whale, with similar marked asymmetry of bony nares.

DESCRIPTION The head is only one sixth of the body length as opposed to one third in the sperm whale. The blowhole is situated on top of the head as in most other odontocetes. The rest of the body resembles that of a common porpoise with well developed dorsal fin and rounded flippers. Colour similar to that of sperm whale. Possesses miniature spermaceti organ in same relative position as in sperm whale. The teeth, of which

FIGURE 111 Pygmy sperm whale.

there are 9 to 14 pairs in the lower jaw, are slender, sharp and strongly recurved backwards like those in some sharks.

MEASUREMENTS Length up to 3·5 m.

DISTRIBUTION World-wide in tropical, subtropical and temperate waters. No British records but one was stranded on the coast of Co. Clare, Ireland, in 1966 (Fraser 1974).

FOOD Cuttlefish.

BREEDING Two females stranded in December of 1924 and 1925 respectively contained foetuses of approximately the same length which may indicate a restricted breeding season.

POPULATION STRUCTURE No data available but there have been semi-mass strandings on the coast of New Zealand and Japan.

RELATIONS WITH MAN Like most other small cetaceans in the coastal waters of Japan, the pygmy sperm whale has occurred in local fish-markets of that country. Otherwise there is no important commercial fishery of this species.

FAMILY ZIPHIIDAE
BEAKED WHALES

Whales belonging to this family are medium in size, 4·5 to 9 m in length, with well-defined, more or less elongated snout and triangular dorsal fin situated at commencement of hindmost third of body. Tail without well-defined notch in middle of hinder margin. Two throat grooves diverging posteriorly. Single crescentic blowhole concave towards snout and rather larger than in most toothed whales. Three genera are represented in British waters.

GENUS *Hyperoodon*

World-wide. Two species, one confined to Southern Ocean.

Bottle-nosed whale *Hyperoodon ampullatus*

Balaena ampullata Forster, 1770; Maldon, Essex, England. *Delphinus bidentatus* Bonnaterre, 1789; R. Thames. *Delphinus diodon* Lacepède, 1804; R. Thames. *Delphinus hunteri* Desmarest, 1822; R. Thames. *Hyperoodon bidens* Fleming, 1828; Essex. *Hyperoodon latifrons* Gray, 1846; Orkney.
Bottle-head, flounders-head.

FIGURE 112 Bottle-nosed whale.

RECOGNITION Large, bulbous head and short snout. Small flippers. Only two teeth at tip of lower jaw in males, no teeth visible in mouth of females. No central notch in tail flukes. Solid bony maxillary crests on rostrum becoming larger and heavier with age.

DESCRIPTION The largest of the British beaked whales, distinguished from other members of the family by large, almost spherical shape of the head and short snout *c*. 15 to 17·5 cm in length. Colour varying from slate grey in young to black in adult. Slightly lighter shade on belly. Old males assume a lighter almost brown colour. Teeth up to 45 mm in length, 19 mm in diameter. Minute vestigial teeth embedded in gums of upper and lower jaws. Males larger than females.

MEASUREMENTS Length of male up to 9 m, female to 7·5 m. Newborn calf *c*. 3 m. Weight at 6·6 m, 2900 kg.

DISTRIBUTION World-wide in Northern Hemisphere. Most abundant in Arctic Ocean and fairly common round British coasts.

BEHAVIOUR Occurs in small schools of up to a dozen. Believed to undertake migrations to high latitudes in summer, and southward to temperate waters in winter passing British Isles where strandings commonest in late autumn and winter. Deep diving ability said to equal that of the sperm whale. Emits echolocating sound pulses.

FOOD Chiefly cuttlefish but sometimes herring.

BREEDING Size difference between males and females indicates probable polygamous behaviour.

RELATIONS WITH MAN Hunted from Norwegian shore stations.

GENUS *Ziphius*

Cuvier's whale *Ziphius cavirostris*

Ziphius cavirostris Cuvier, 1823; Mouth of Rhône, France. Goose-beaked whale.

RECOGNITION Data on recognition at sea not available. Distinguished from bottle-nosed whale by absence of bulbous forehead, but similar in having only a pair of teeth at tip of lower jaw in males. Skull without bony maxillary crests on rostrum.

FIGURE 113 Cuvier's whale.

DESCRIPTION General form rather robust. Head with snout passing without conspicuous differentiation into forehead. Flippers and back fin not distinguishable from those of bottle-nosed whale. Distance from snout to blowhole less than in the bottle-nose. Colour blue-black on back, slightly paler on belly. Whole head including lower jaw and part of front end of body cream-white separated from dark skin of rest of body by an oblique line passing from front end of dorsal fin to angle of lower jaw.

Two teeth in male, conical in shape 57 mm long and *c*. 32 mm in diameter.

MEASUREMENTS Length up to 7·9 m.

DISTRIBUTION World-wide. British strandings on west coast of England, Scotland and Ireland suggests approach from Atlantic to British Isles.

FOOD Cuttlefish.

RELATIONS WITH MAN Fished off the coast of Japan.

GENUS *Mesoplodon*

Sowerby's whale *Mesoplodon bidens*

Physeter bidens Sowerby, 1804; Moray, Scotland.

RECOGNITION No data on recognition at sea. Long slender beak with single large triangular tooth on each side at mid-point of lower jaw in male. Smaller and hidden beneath gum in female.

FIGURE 114 Sowerby's whale.

DESCRIPTION Slender beak passing without conspicuous differentiation into low forehead. Body laterally compressed. Small, narrow flippers; flukes without central notch. Colour all black above and slightly paler on belly. Juveniles slate grey. Males have numerous elongated, unpigmented scars on flanks due to intra-specific fighting.

MEASUREMENTS Length up to 4·9 m.

DISTRIBUTION A North Atlantic whale known from specimens found on New England coast in America and western European seaboard. Many British strandings.

BEHAVIOUR Extremely fast swimmer and obviously mainly pelagic. A young specimen kept in a large dolphinarium for a few hours broke its beak on the side-walls through lack of manoeuvrability. Echolocating sound pulses were recorded from this specimen. A specimen stranded alive was reported as lowing like a cow.

FOOD Exclusively cuttlefish. Oral musculature indicates a suctorial action when feeding.

POPULATION STRUCTURE Probably single family groups. In 1971 a female accompanied by a calf was stranded on the coast of Belgium and on the same day a large male came ashore on the east coast of England. It is probable that all three were members of the same family.

RELATIONS WITH MAN Nowhere sufficiently abundant to be hunted.

True's beaked whale *Mesoplodon mirus*

Mesoplodon mirum True, 1913; North Carolina, USA.

RECOGNITION No data on recognition at sea. Very similar but slightly larger than Sowerby's whale. Single pair of teeth situated at extreme tip of lower jaw in males and directed forward. Concealed below the gum in female.

FIGURE 115 True's beaked whale.

DESCRIPTION Body slender, laterally compressed, tail stock particularly so. Flippers, dorsal fin and flukes similar to Sowerby's whale. Teeth flattened, oval in cross section, 25×13 mm.

MEASUREMENTS Length about 5·2 m.

DISTRIBUTION One of the least known of cetaceans. Six known strandings, two on the American coast (North Carolina and New England), four from British waters (three Irish, one Outer Hebrides).

FAMILY MONODONTIDAE

Contains two genera only, both monospecific and together meriting distinctive superfamily rank.

GENUS *Delphinapterus*

White whale *Delphinapterus leucas*

Delphinus leucas Pallas, 1776; Mouth of River Ob, Siberia. Beluga.

RECOGNITION Generally seen in large or small schools and all members except juveniles pure white. Upper profile of skull slightly convex rather than concave as in all other odontocetes except narwhal but distinguished from latter by having teeth in both upper and lower jaws.

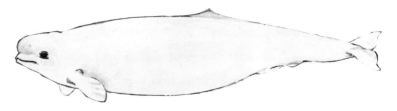

FIGURE 116 White whale.

DESCRIPTION Head bulbous and not produced into a beak. Slight suggestion of a neck. No back fin. Flippers broad, moderately large and rounded. Flukes with central notch and obliquely truncated lobes. Head small in relation to body. Body rather robust. Pure white or cream colour specifically diagnostic. The grey colour of calf may lead to confusion with narwhal. Eight to ten teeth in each of upper and lower jaws, *c*. 60 mm in diameter. Males larger than females.

MEASUREMENTS Length usually 3·7 to 4·3 m.

DISTRIBUTION Entire Arctic Ocean, rarely penetrating more temperate waters. Very few records of occurrence in British waters. One stranding since 1913, in River Forth 25 miles above Forth Bridge.

BEHAVIOUR Relatively slow swimmer, not more than 6 knots. Shallow diver. Migration seems to be confined to seasonal limits of sea ice. Occurs in open ocean but also known to ascend rivers for considerable distances.

Social structure complex, showing polygamous and monogamous behaviour. Segregation of males from females out of breeding season. Very vocal, emitting a great variety of yelps, whistles and echolocating clicks. Hearing very acute.

FOOD Mainly squid but cod, herring and salmon also taken.

BREEDING Sexually mature at 4–5 years. Gestation 12 months, lactation 6 months (Sergeant 1973).

POPULATION STRUCTURE Proportion of males to females varies according to breeding season. Average age 20–25 years, maximum 40 years.

PREDATORS Frequently attacked by killer whales. Average annual mortality 12%.

RELATIONS WITH MAN Has been heavily exploited commercially for 'porpoise-hide', meat and blubber for food of animals and man. One of the first cetaceans to be kept in an aquarium, at Brighton in 1878.

GENUS *Monodon*

Narwhal *Monodon monoceros*

Monodon monoceros Linnaeus, 1758; Arctic seas.

RECOGNITION Occurring in small or large schools of which all male members carry a long tusk similar in shape to that of the mythical unicorn. Skull similar to that of white whale but having no teeth in lower jaw.

DESCRIPTION No beak. Bulbous forehead, inconspicuous low ridge in

FIGURE 117 Narwhal. Female above, male below.

normal position of back fin. Flippers short and rounded. Flukes with central notch and slightly convex trailing edges. Colour mottled grey, lighter on sides and belly. Juveniles darker due to absence of mottling. Extension of left incisor tooth of male into a spirally marked tusk up to 2·5 m long. Occasionally both incisors are thus elongated. In female, tusks embedded in bone of rostrum and not erupted.

MEASUREMENTS Length up to 4·9 m.

DISTRIBUTION As with white whale, entire Arctic Ocean, occasionally penetrating temperate waters. Very few British strandings, the latest being two in the Thames Estuary in 1949.

BEHAVIOUR Gregarious and fast swimming. Congregate in large numbers at holes in sea ice (known to Greenlanders as savssats) keeping these open by head butting. Emits echolocating clicks and communication whistles.

FOOD Cuttlefish, fishes and crustaceans.

BREEDING Few data available. Presence of tusk only in male indicates intraspecific fighting and therefore polygamous behaviour.

RELATIONS WITH MAN Hunted by Eskimoes for blubber, meat and ivory. Tusks now very valuable in world markets.

FAMILY PHOCOENIDAE

True porpoises, never more than 2 m in length and all having flattened spade-shaped teeth. Divided into two genera *Phocoena* and *Neophocaena*. Only one species (of *Phocoena*) occurs in British waters.

GENUS *Phocoena*

Common porpoise *Phocoena phocoena*

Delphinus phocoena Linnaeus, 1758; Swedish Seas. *Delphinus ventricosus* Lacepède, 1804; R. Thames. *Phocoena tuberculifera* Gray, 1865; Margate, Kent.

FIGURE 118 Common porpoise

RECOGNITION Smallest British cetacean, not more than 2 m in length, occurring in small or very large schools in coastal waters. Does not normally leap clear of water as do dolphins. Short blunt head, no snout or 'beak'. Upper and lower jaws containing spade-shaped as opposed to conical teeth.

DESCRIPTION General form short, stout and robust. No beak. Low receding forehead. Back fin triangular, at middle of body. Flippers roughly oval in outline. Central notch in tail flukes. Considerable variation in colour. Back black, belly white, varying amount of grey on sides. Dark streak from mouth to flipper. Upper and lower jaws, chin, flippers and flukes black. Teeth 22 to 27 upper and lower on each side, spade-shaped.

MEASUREMENTS Length 1·8 m. Newborn calf *c*. 76 cm. Weight at 1·5 m, 59 kg.

DISTRIBUTION Widely distributed in coastal waters of North Atlantic including Baltic, White, North and Greenland seas. Commonest British cetacean, found on all parts of the coast.

BEHAVIOUR Slow swimmer, not normally leaping from water. Adults with calves assemble in coastal waters on both sides of North Atlantic from July to October but breeding locality unknown. Experiments have shown echo-locating capability to be extremely accurate. Hearing very acute. Frequently die of shock when lifted from deep water but docile when taken from shallow water. Easily scared by noise.

FOOD Herring, sole, whiting, crustaceans and cuttlefish.

BREEDING Gestation 11 months, sexual maturity at 3 to 4 years. Single calf born July onwards (Fisher & Harrison 1970).

POPULATION STRUCTURE Sex ratio 1:1. All ages up to 15 years have been recorded.

PREDATORS Killer whales and sharks.

PARASITES Circular lesions frequently occur on skin, attributed to lamprey.

RELATIONS WITH MAN Frequently caught in mackerel nets and used commercially for mink farms in Canada. Formerly a commercial fishery in Baltic and coast of Holland. Herded by slapping surface of water with sticks.

FAMILY DELPHINIDAE

Contains the great majority of all cetaceans. World-wide and divided into 15 genera, 8 of which are known in British waters.

GENUS *Orcinus*

Containing only one species.

Killer whale *Orcinus orca*

Delphinus orca Linnaeus, 1758; European seas.
Grampus.

RECOGNITION High, triangular dorsal fin of males, striking black and white pattern, noisy explosive 'blow'. Teeth large, pointed and anteroposteriorly compressed; 10–13 each side upper and lower jaws; 25–30 mm diameter.

DESCRIPTION Powerfully built, robust. No beak. Forehead receding. Back fin in middle of body; moderate in height in females and young with concave trailing edge. In adult males, very high, up to 1·8 m, short-based and triangular. Flippers rounded in form and disproportionately large in old males. Flukes with posterior median notch, also disproportionately large in old males. Black back, white belly. Lens-shaped white patch behind eye. Lobe of white extending from belly on to flanks between dorsal fin and tail. Grey 'saddle' behind dorsal fin. Flippers

FIGURE 119 Killer whale.

black, flukes black above, white below. Teeth 10 to 13 upper and lower on each side.

MEASUREMENTS Length of males to 9·2 m, of females to 4·6 m. New-born calf *c*. 2·1 m.

DISTRIBUTION World-wide and fairly common in British waters.

BEHAVIOUR Very fast swimmer, up to 35 knots. Solitary or gregarious with no particular migratory habits. Often gathering in large packs to attack and kill large whales. Apparently docile and inoffensive to man. Intelligent and easily tamed as a display animal in aquaria.

FOOD Whales, dolphins, porpoises, seals, penguins and large fish, especially salmon.

BREEDING Gestation 12 months. Young believed to be born at end of year. Great sexual dimorphism indicates strongly polygamous behaviour.

POPULATION STRUCTURE Small family groups or large packs according to hunting behaviour—all ages up to and probably in excess of 40 years.

RELATIONS WITH MAN Often hunted by whale ships on voyages to and from whaling grounds. Said to have assisted in the herding of humpback whales. Now used extensively as performing animal in dolphinaria.

GENUS *Pseudorca*

Contains a single species.

False killer whale *Pseudorca crassidens*

Phocaena crassidens Owen, 1846; Lincolnshire Fens (subfossil).

RECOGNITION All black, form slender. No beak. Rounded snout projecting beyond extremity of lower jaw. Falcate dorsal fin with no difference between males and females. In small or very large schools, very fast swimmer. Skull with large teeth somewhat smaller proportionately than those of killer whale and circular in cross-section, 9–11 each side of upper and lower jaws, 25 mm diameter.

FIGURE 120 False killer whale.

DESCRIPTION General form slender in relation to length. Bulbous snout with no beak. In adults back fin anterior to mid-point of body, of moderate height and strongly concave on posterior border. Flippers one tenth of body length (cf. pilot whale), tapering rapidly from very broad to narrow. Concave at extremity of leading edge. Colour predominantly black but frequently having white borders to upper and lower lips, and a faint grey patch on chest (cf. pilot whale). Teeth 9–11 on each side of upper and lower jaws. Diameter 25 mm, circular in cross-section (cf. killer whale).

MEASUREMENTS Length of male to 5·6 m, of female to 5·0 m. Weight at 5·3 m, 1700 kg.

DISTRIBUTION World-wide except in polar regions. In British waters known only from a small number of mass strandings: in 1927 (*c.* 150 at Dornoch Firth, Scotland); 1934 (*c.* 25 in Angus, Yorkshire and Lincolnshire); 1935 (*c.* 75 in South Wales).

BEHAVIOUR Very fast swimmer, up to 30 knots. Although small groups have been observed in Mediterranean and elsewhere, they are predominantly pelagic, following the main ocean currents of the world in very large schools. Characterised by becoming stranded en masse at widely separated intervals—apparently even in prehistoric times. Larger size of males indicates polygamous behaviour.

FOOD Cuttlefish, cod. Has been seen chasing shoals of tuna and was the main predator of the Japanese long-line tuna fishery.

BREEDING Sexual maturity at 8–10 years. Gestation 13 months, lactation 6 months, gives birth every 3 years.

POPULATION STRUCTURE Age structure indicates fairly high immature mortality rate. In schools, adult animals predominate. Longevity 30–40 years. Sporadic occurrence of mass stranding might indicate cyclic changes in population numbers.

PARASITES Scars caused by shark-suckers (*Remora*), a commensal fish, are frequently found on the body.

RELATIONS WITH MAN No important commercial fishery but often occurring in fish markets of Japan. Kept as display and performing animal in many dolphinaria.

GENUS *Globicephala*

At least three species, possibly more.

Pilot whale *Globicephala melaena*

Delphinus melas Traill, 1809; Scapa Bay, Orkney.
Blackfish, caaing whale, pothead whale.

RECOGNITION Usually seen in small schools, up to 20. Long, slender body and bulbous, almost spherical head. Skull similar in shape but differing from that of killer and false killer by having much smaller teeth, less than 13 mm diameter, 8–10 each side at front of upper and lower jaws.

DESCRIPTION Long, slender body except in old males which are larger than females. Spherical, bulbous head with small beak. Back fin low, strongly recurved posteriorly and placed slightly anterior to centre of back. Flippers very long, up to one fifth of body length (cf. false killer). Colour all black except for conspicuous white throat patch extending tail-wards for variable length. Hinder margin of flukes with central notch. Males up to 1 m larger than females.

FIGURE 121 Pilot whale.

MEASUREMENTS Length up to 5 m in females and to 6 m in males. Weight at 4 m 830 kg and at 6 m, 2900 kg.

DISTRIBUTION North Atlantic and North Pacific. Very frequently stranded on British coasts, sometimes en masse.

BEHAVIOUR According to most authorities relatively slow swimmer, 6–7 knots, but according to one author a school maintained 22 knots for several days. Undertakes regular annual migrations between temperate and sub-polar regions. Large size difference between males and females suggests promiscuous or polygamous behaviour. Echo-navigational clicks and communicational whistles have been recorded (Evans 1966). When observed in the open sea, schools average about 20 individuals but when stranded naturally may exceed 200.

FOOD Cuttlefish, including *Ommatostrephes*, *Architeuthis* and *Toderodes* spp.

BREEDING Pairing in warmer waters, calves born at higher latitudes. Females sexually mature at 6–7 years, males 12 years. Period of gestation 16 months, lactation 22 months. Young born every three to four years.

POPULATION STRUCTURE Sex ratio 40% males out of breeding season. All ages up to 50 years have been estimated.

RELATIONS WITH MAN Highly organized drives have been carried out for centuries in the Faeroes and still continue. Until recently extensive fishery in Canada. The species takes well to captivity and can be trained.

GENUS *Grampus*

Contains only one species.

Risso's dolphin *Grampus griseus*

Delphinus griseus Cuvier, 1812; Brest, France. *Grampus cuvieri* Gray, 1846; Isle of Wight, England.

FIGURE 122 Risso's dolphin.

RECOGNITION Usually seen in small family groups round British coasts but these are sometimes aggregated into large schools in other localities. Bulbous head, greyish colour with numerous, white parallel scars on flanks (probably tooth marks). No teeth in upper jaw, 2–7 but usually 4 on each side at tip of lower jaw.

DESCRIPTION Body rather stout for length. Bulbous head with no beak. Dorsal fin at mid-length of body, high, backwardly sloped with posterior margin pronouncedly concave. Median notch on trailing edge of tail. Flippers rather long, tapering acutely, one sixth of body length. Colour in general grey, lighter on head, darker on sides. Invariably marked with intersecting, parallel, white scars, probably tooth marks indicating intraspecific fighting. Belly may be white, fins and tail black. Upper jaw normally toothless.

MEASUREMENTS Length to 4 m. Weight at 3·4 m, 343 kg.

DISTRIBUTION World-wide except in polar regions. Stranding fairly common on west and south coasts of British Isles.

BEHAVIOUR Very little known. The famous Pelorus Jack that escorted ships through Cook Strait, New Zealand, for 32 years is said to have been a Risso's dolphin. Will often remain in vertical posture with head and flippers out of water for several seconds and then dive steeply, showing tail.

FOOD Exclusively cuttlefish.

BREEDING Little information. Captures in the English Channel suggest that birth takes place in winter and spring (e.g. Fraser 1937). Sightings usually in small family groups, suggesting monogamous behaviour. Hybridisation with bottle-nosed dolphins has been suspected (Fraser 1940).

RELATIONS WITH MAN Not easily kept in captivity. Very aggressive towards man and other dolphins in aquaria.

GENUS *Lagenorhynchus*

A widespread genus with many species, two of which occur in British waters.

White-beaked dolphin *Lagenorhynchus albirostris*

Lagenorhynchus albirostris Gray, 1846; Great Yarmouth, England.

RECOGNITION Usually in large schools. Short but conspicuous white snout. Fairly large dorsal fin. Often leaps clear of water revealing white on sides and belly. Skull distinguished from that of white-sided dolphin by having fewer and larger teeth, 22–25 each side upper and lower jaws,

FIGURE 123 White-beaked dolphin.

c. 6 mm diameter. A bridge of bone, stretching from pterygoid to squamosal, frequently lost during maceration.

DESCRIPTION General form stoutish. Distinct but short beak, *c.* 5 cm. Forehead receding. Back fin prominent at mid-body length, tip pointing tailwards, distinct concavity in hinder margin. Flippers tapering to rounded tip, broad at insertion. Tail stock with transverse width much less than depth. Flukes notched in middle posteriorly. Beak white; forehead and back to at least behind back fin very dark to black; longitudinal light areas on sides which may approximate or meet behind back fin. Darkly pigmented region on sides behind flippers extending well on to belly. Throat and belly white as far as posterior of vent. Tail stock, flukes and flippers black. Dark streak stretching from angle of mouth to flipper insertion, above which a speckled region.

MEASUREMENTS Length *c.* 3·1 m. Newborn calves *c.* 1·2 m. Weight at 2·3 m, 216 kg, at 2·8 m, 305 kg.

DISTRIBUTION North Atlantic, Baltic, North Sea, Greenland, south to Portugal on east, Massachusetts on west.
   A northern species in British waters, more frequent in North Sea than on west or south coasts. Frequently stranded.

VARIATION Considerable variation in distribution of black pigment within school. Some members do not have white beaks.

BEHAVIOUR Very gregarious, and seasonal sightings and strandings indicate annual migration between temperate and sub-polar waters.

FOOD Herring, cod, whiting.

BREEDING Calves born after middle of year, no further data available.

RELATIONS WITH MAN Not hunted commercially and not yet kept in captivity as with the related *L. obliquidens.*

White-sided dolphin *Lagenorhynchus acutus*

Delphinus (Grampus) acutus Gray, 1828; ?Faeroes.

RECOGNITION Similar in shape and head profile to white-beaked dolphin but without white beak. When leaping clear of water reveals distinctive, light brown, oblique patch on flanks in addition to white belly. Not seen in large schools off coast of British Isles, but said to aggregate in large numbers off coast of Norway. Teeth more numerous and smaller than in white-beaked dolphin, 30–40 each side upper and lower jaws, *c*. 5 mm diameter. No bony bridge between pterygoid and squamosal in skull.

DESCRIPTION General form robust. Distinct beak, *c*. 5 cm long. Receding forehead. Prominent back fin in mid-body length, tip projecting tailward, concave hinder border. Tail stock laterally compressed and strongly keeled. Snout, top of head and back black, belly white, pigmentation on sides not extending so far ventrally as in white-beaked dolphin, so that flippers inserted in unpigmented region. Narrow dark streak from mouth to flipper insertion. Flippers, flukes and chin dark. Broad, oblique, elongated patch of light brown on flanks from level of back fin to hinder end of tail-stock distinctive of species.

FIGURE 124 White-sided dolphin.

MEASUREMENTS Length 2·7 to 3·0 m.

DISTRIBUTION North Atlantic including Greenland seas, American coast to Cape Cod, north-western European coasts especially off Norway. Orkney, Shetland and occasionally as far south as North Devon and Sligo on Atlantic seaboard. Fewer sightings and strandings on British coasts than of white-beaked dolphin.

BEHAVIOUR Migratory between temperate and sub-polar regions. Occurrence indicates probable segregation into smaller groups during breeding season in south, and aggregation into larger schools during northern summer season.

FOOD Herring, cod, whiting.

BREEDING Gestation about 10 months; birth in spring before mid-summer.

RELATIONS WITH MAN No commercial fishery.

GENUS *Tursiops*

A widely distributed genus with three or four species, one of which is recorded from British waters.

Bottle-nosed dolphin *Tursiops truncatus*

Delphinus truncatus Montagu, 1821; River Dart, Devon, England.

RECOGNITION Usually seen in small schools off British coasts but sometimes in large schools in other localities. Slate grey or light brown; prominent beak and dorsal fin. Skull with 22–25 teeth each side upper and lower jaws, diameter 10–13 mm.

FIGURE 125 Bottle-nosed dolphin.

DESCRIPTION General form robust. Forehead low, receding. Back fin prominent, backwardly inclined, concave hinder margin. Distinct beak, lower jaw protrudes beyond tip of snout. Colour slate grey or light brown, quickly turning to much darker colour upon stranding. Streak of lighter colour stretching from insertion of beak to blowhole. Throat and belly white or pale pink. Flippers broad, triangular and very mobile. Flippers and flukes same colour as back.

MEASUREMENTS Length to 3·7 m. Weight at 3·4 m, 394 kg.

DISTRIBUTION Widely distributed in North Atlantic, West African, Mediterranean and English coastal waters chiefly south and west. Next in abundance to common porpoises and frequently seen in English Channel.

VARIATION Smaller varieties occur in most of the temperate waters of the world, all of which have been given different specific status but mostly differing in external pigmentation only.

BEHAVIOUR Capable of short bursts of speed, up to 20 knots, but generally slower than smaller dolphins. Congregate into small mixed schools during breeding season but later sexes segregate. North Atlantic population appears to be migratory, occurring in British waters mainly during summer months. When pursued, dives and comes up astern of ship. Large variety of echolocation clicks and whistles which have been intensively studied. Attentive and helpful towards young and wounded.

FOOD Wide variety of fishes and cuttlefish.

BREEDING Incidence of births show two peaks during spring and autumn in Californian species (*T. gilli*), but probably only one in summer months in British species. Sexual maturity at *c*. 12 years in both sexes. Period of gestation 12–13 months.

POPULATION STRUCTURE Equal numbers of males and females of all ages up to 30 years. Evidence of a hierarchical social structure (Dudok van Heal, unpubl.).

PARASITES Frequently infested with nematode worms in middle ear and other cavities. Oval or circular scars on skin caused by lampreys or remoras.

RELATIONS WITH MAN The best known and most widely exhibited of all the dolphins in aquaria. Highly intelligent and friendly with man. Wild specimens often known to associate with bathers and yachtsmen. Most of the cetacean behavioural experiments have been carried out with this species.

GENUS *Stenella*

A genus widely distributed, mainly in warmer waters, but taxonomy still confused.

Blue-white dolphin *Stenella caeruleoalbus*

Delphinus caeruleo-albus Meyen, 1833; east coast of South America. *Delphinus styx* Gray, 1846; South Africa. *Delphinus euphrosyne* Gray, 1846. Euphrosyne dolphin, Meyen's dolphin.

RECOGNITION A small, swift dolphin with conspicuous beak. Frequently leaps from water showing blue-black back, white belly and flanks with distinctive black stripe running from position of eye to three-quarters length of body. No yellow pigment as in common dolphin.

Skull lacking deep palatal grooves of the common dolphin. Teeth 43 to 50 each side upper and lower. Diameter *c*. 3 mm.

DESCRIPTION General form slender. Elongated beak (to *c*. 13 cm), well defined from forehead, which is low and receding. Back fin of moderate height, hind margin concave, tip tailwardly projecting. Tail stock without pronounced keeling, rather slender. Flukes with notch in middle of hind border. Flippers tapering, lower border shallowly concave, upper convex proximally, concave distally. Back dark, white on belly and lower part of flanks. Characteristic narrow stripe from eye along side to vent giving off branches, two from eye to base of flipper, another obliquely ventrally behind flipper level. Flippers and flukes darkly pigmented; former inserted in white region. Adult females slightly larger than males.

FIGURE 126 Blue-white dolphin.

MEASUREMENTS Length to 2·5 m. Weight at 1·7 m, 55 kg.

DISTRIBUTION World-wide in tropical and temperate waters. Uncommon round British coasts—only three strandings known, all in extreme south-west.

VARIATION Non-specific colour variations demonstrated by Fraser & Noble (1970).

BEHAVIOUR Often seen in association with schools of common dolphins with which it is frequently confused. Schools numbering several thousand individuals consisting of this species alone have been caught off Japan. Only locally migratory, probably following shoals of fish.

FOOD Mainly fish, also cuttlefish. One specimen was found to contain 876 otoliths of *Trisopterus minutus* (poor-cod).

BREEDING Sexual maturity at 9 years in both sexes. Gestation 12 months, lactation 15 months. Parturition every three years. Breeding season varies with locality of schools.

POPULATION STRUCTURE Variable, mixed schools of mature and immature males and females have been caught during breeding season. Some schools consist entirely of immature animals. Some evidence of segregation of sexes out of breeding season. All ages up to 25 years.

RELATIONS WITH MAN Fished in large numbers off coast of Japan and in Solomon Islands. Kept in captivity in dolphinaria. Often depicted in ancient Greek and Roman art.

GENUS *Delphinus*

Two species, one of which is confined to the tropics.

Common dolphin *Delphinus delphis*

Delphinus delphis Linnaeus, 1758; European seas.

RECOGNITION A small swift dolphin with conspicuous snout or beak, usually seen in large schools. Frequently leaps clear of water revealing bow-shaped, yellow and white intersecting patches of colour on flanks. One of the most brightly pigmented dolphins. Very inquisitive, swimming alongside and in front of ships.

FIGURE 127 Common dolphin.

Skull with two deep, parallel grooves on underside of rostrum. 40 to 50 teeth each side, upper and lower jaw, diameter 3 mm.

DESCRIPTION General form slender. Elongated beak 11 to 12 cm with chevron shaped groove separating it from low, receding forehead. Dorsal fin of moderate height, tailwardly directed tip, concave posterior margin. Flukes with notch at middle of hinder margin. No pronounced keeling of tail stock. Lower margin of flipper convex, upper convex proximally, concave distally. Although, when dead, back very dark to black, in life impression of dark brown coloration. Belly white. Complicated pattern of alternating light and dark bands on flanks. Two waves of yellow and white intersecting at level of dorsal fin diagnostic of species. Dark circle round eye extended into line along side of forehead. Tapering band from base of flipper to side of lower jaw.

MEASUREMENTS Length to 2·4 m. Weight at 2 m, 114 kg.

DISTRIBUTION World-wide in temperate and tropical waters. In British waters more abundant in south and west. Less frequently in North Sea. Ranks about equally with bottle-nosed dolphin in number of strandings.

BEHAVIOUR Distinctive schooling patterns have been observed during migration. Loose oval pattern or in column. Random distribution when feeding. Diurnal movement facing sun during day, resting at night. Split into separate groups when pursued and reassemble later. Mixed schools with equal numbers of males and females. Attentive and helpful to young and wounded. Large variety of echolocation clicks and communication whistles. Synchronised blowing and sounding.

FOOD Herring, pilchard, mackerel, cuttlefish and octopus.

BREEDING Few data except for Black Sea population where mating takes place mainly in second half of year with peak in September, gestation period is about 10 months and births occur mainly in summer and autumn with peak in July (Tomilin 1957).

POPULATION STRUCTURE Behavioural evidence of hierarchical system. Mixed schools of all ages up to 30 years.

PREDATORS AND MORTALITY Stranded specimens frequently show deep scars and lacerations suggesting attacks by sharks.

PARASITES Internal organs sometimes heavily infested with nematode worms. Whale lice and barnacles, *Xenobalanus globicipites*, have been observed on some specimens.

RELATIONS WITH MAN Has been kept in captivity but does not train easily.

Order Carnivora
Carnivores

This order includes most of the truly carnivorous mammals, i.e. predators feeding predominantly on vertebrate prey. All the species in Britain are indeed carnivorous except for the badger. The pinnipedes (seals, sealions) are sometimes included in the order Carnivora but more often in recent classifications they are treated as a separate order and that course is followed here.

Carnivores vary enormously in outward form, from the tiny sinuous weasels to the heavy lumbering bears. The dentition is characterised by enlarged conical canine teeth and by the specialisation of one upper and one lower cheek-teeth on each side (P^4 and M_1) for cutting and shearing—the carnassial teeth. The articulation of the jaw allows little movement other than direct opening and closing. Most species have a characteristic technique of hunting—pouncing and snapping with the long jaws in the case of the fox; pouncing and striking with the paws and sharp, retractile claws in the cat; fast pursuit in confined spaces in the case of the weasel and stoat. But most carnivores are very adaptable with regard to the species of prey taken, being able to concentrate on species that are temporarily or locally abundant.

Eight indigenous species occur in Britain; a further two (wolf and brown bear) have been exterminated in historic times whilst one introduction, the American mink, is well established. Most of the native species have suffered severely from exploitation for fur and persecution in the interests of game preservation. However all but the otter are now either widespread or expanding their range.

Our carnivores belong to four families (if the extinct bear is included): Canidae (fox, wolf), Ursidae (bears), Mustelidae (weasel, marten, badger, otter, etc.) and Felidae (cats). However if they are well seen all species are individually distinctive and easily recognised by superficial appearance. Any problems of identification arise within the Mustelidae and are dealt with under that family.

FAMILY CANIDAE
DOGS

A clear-cut family with a worldwide distribution and about 38 species including the wolves, jackals and foxes. In general they are long-legged and cursorial, hunting their prey largely by sight and mainly in open country. The muzzle is long and the canine and carnassial teeth well developed. Now represented in Britain only by the fox (and domestic dogs) but formerly also by the wolf.

GENUS *Canis*

Besides the wolf this genus includes three species of jackal, the Simian fox and the American coyote. Compared with foxes they tend to be larger, more social and more diurnal.

Wolf *Canis lupus*

Canis lupus Linnaeus, 1758; Sweden.

Extinct in Britain and Ireland but surviving in small numbers in Continental Europe and more abundantly across Palaearctic Asia and northern North America. The wolf was exterminated in England and Wales probably about 1500, but it survived in Scotland until about 1740 and in Ireland until about 1770 (Harting 1880). Wolves are versatile animals but they are adapted particularly for hunting in packs by daylight, cooperating to run down large prey such as deer in fairly open country.

GENUS *Vulpes*

A widespread genus comprising about 12 species of foxes, distributed throughout the Northern Hemisphere and in southern Africa. Most are adapted to open habitats—the sole species in Britain probably frequents woodland to a greater extent than any other.

Fox *Vulpes vulpes*

Canis vulpes Linnaeus, 1758; Sweden. *Canis crucigera* Bechstein, 1789; Germany.
Tod.

RECOGNITION Too well known to warrant detailed description. Conspicuous characters are the erect black-backed ears, slender muzzle and long horizontally held bushy tail, the white muzzle, bib of throat and tail tip, and the black socks and ears. Skull dog-like but narrower, with more sharply pointed, prominent, slender canine teeth; the concavity of the upper surfaces of the post-orbital processes distinguishes it readily from that of dog.

FIGURE 128 Fox.

SIGN Prints of four toes on fore and hind feet readily observed in mud or snow. Typically print is more oval in shape than in most small dogs, with the two centrally placed toes extending well ahead of others. When walking and trotting, overprinting of fore prints by hind feet usually occurs, and may sometimes give mistaken impression of five toes being in contact with ground. The prints of a trotting fox form a straighter line than those of a dog (not infallible identification sign). Runs through hedges smaller than those of badger, and larger than brown hare without the jump pattern of latter. Regular passage through hedges, rusty fences, bramble patches, under chestnut palings etc., can usually be determined by hairs adhering to snags.

Faeces variable according to food—if much indigestible remnant (e.g. fur or feather) usually pointed and may be linked together by hairs; length 5–20 cm. When fresh usually black with characteristic odour. Faeces containing fur or feather may persist for several months after smaller inclusions have been leached. In absence of indigestible hard parts, faeces may be indistinguishable from dogs', except, if fresh, by odour. Faeces deposited often on prominent objects—stones, fallen branches, molehills. Scent stations, where drops of urine have been sprinkled on prominent

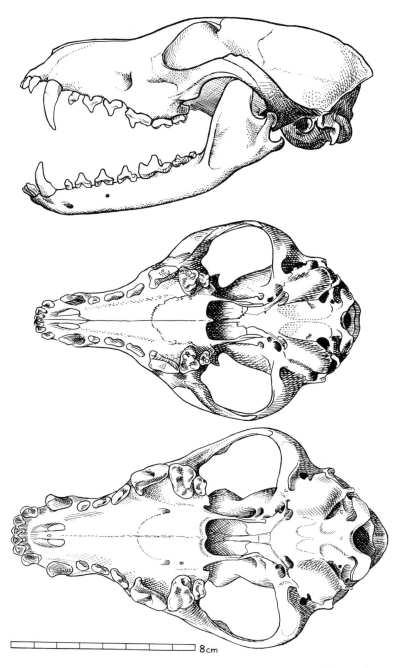

FIGURE 129 Skulls of fox (top and centre) and dog (bottom). Note the wider muzzle and more crowded teeth in the dog.

objects (even long stalks of grass), can be detected by smell. At all times of year wind-borne characteristic smell of fox may be detected but apparently not by all individuals. Vocal calls—usually after dark but sometimes in daylight at the rut—will indicate presence of foxes. Occupancy of den by cubs indicated by unconsumed food remnants inside and outside den. In winter, many earths or disused rabbit burrows may be 'cleaned out' with fresh soil in evidence—not always indicative of occupancy, but of presence of foxes in the vicinity. Cached food items— buried singly—may sometimes be found; often buried very conspicuously. Primary wing feathers sheared close to bases are indicative of fox. Manner of killing and subsequent treatment often characteristic—e.g. in lambs, teeth marks over shoulder and crushed cervical vertebrae; lambs and poultry often decapitated, heads sometimes buried. Fox eyes highly reflective—blue/white when viewed head-on, but pink at lower intensity, if not looking directly at light source. Difficult to distinguish from eye shine of domestic cat. Can be seen at 400 m with car spotlight.

DESCRIPTION Overall colour yellow/brown but much variation from sandy colour to (rarely) henna red. Guard hairs composed of black, yellow/brown, and white bands, but much variation in proportions of these according to parts of body. Under-fur grey. The backs of ears, socks, sometimes the entire leading edge of the limb, and a stripe from eye to muzzle, black; lips and nose dark brown; the belly may be white or grey (no age distinction). The tail is less colourful than the shoulder and back, often tipped with white. Mandible, upper lips and throat white. White flecking may occur throughout pelage, even in juveniles. Pads naked, but much interdigital fur. Penis and scrotum held closer to body than in dogs; scrotum covered with cream coloured hair. Eyes yellow; pupil, when contracted, a vertical slit.

Difficult to separate sexes in the field; light-coloured fur over scrotum best feature. Body size subjective and not reliable, but frontal silhouette of head and ears has been used (Burrows 1968). Belly fur of both dog and vixen assumes pinkish tinge in March–April. Four pairs of nipples. Moult once a year but prolonged, from late spring to autumn. Under-fur lost first.

Skull of adult males and females differentiated in about 70% of cases by prominent sagittal ridge in male. Juvenile skulls (up to 10 months of age) resemble female skulls in this respect. Churcher (1960) described temporal sequence of closure of cranial sutures which can be used for age determination up to about 6 years.

Five digits on forefeet (4 in contact with ground); 4 on hind, no dew claws. Scent glands in anal sacs and on upper surface of tail. Urine probably a vehicle for scent secretions. Merocrine sweat glands in foot pads. Apocrine and sebaceous glands elsewhere in skin. Testes scrotal at all times; Cowper's gland and seminal vesicles absent; prostate not large. Primitive bicornuate uterus with direct continuity between two horns; ovaries in bursa; placenta zonary, endotheliochorial, with prominent lateral haematomata. Embryos can be sexed at 45 days. Swelling of vulva at oestrus. Corpora lutea large and persistent throughout pregnancy.[&]

Chromosomes: diploid number variable, 35–40, most frequently 38. Variation due to number of microchromosomes, ranging from 1 to 6 (Buckton & Cunningham 1971).

MEASUREMENTS See Table 23.

TABLE 23 Measurements of foxes from lowland England (from Hattingh 1956)

	Males		Females	
	Mean	*n*	Mean	*n*
Head and body	67 cm	37	63 cm	36
Tail	41 cm	37	38 cm	36
Weight	6·7 kg	33	5·4 kg	29

DISTRIBUTION See Fig. 130. Most of Palaearctic Region north to Arctic coast; south to Vietnam, Central India, Arabia and North Africa; east to Sakhalin and Japan. North America south to New Mexico and northern Florida.

Almost ubiquitous on British mainland and in Ireland; absent or uncommon until recently in many parts of Norfolk, and coastal areas of Aberdeenshire, Nairn and Moray (Hewson & Kolb 1973). Becoming more abundant in urban areas. Occurs at over 1300 m in Cairngorms. Absent from all Scottish islands except Skye (present some years on Scalpay). Absent Anglesey until 1962. Absent from Isle of Man, Scilly Isles and Channel Isles.

Introduced from Britain to eastern USA in mid-eighteenth century, to Australia about 1850.

VARIATION Confused by introductions but no good evidence of discrete races on continent nor of clear-cut differences between British and continental forms. Northern animals in Europe and North America have larger white tip to tail than southern animals. Very dark foxes occur in

Britain but not completely melanic forms as in North America and in
Scandinavia following introduction. A darker band of richer colour along
and over shoulders is variable, seen as a cross in prepared skins. 'Cross
foxes' are partial melanic forms with this feature—absent Britain.

In Britain, hill foxes of Westmorland said to be larger than lowland
foxes, but opposite tendency in Wales. Larger in Scotland and Northern
Ireland than in England (Kolb & Hewson 1974).

Sporadic individuals lack guard hairs locally or completely, giving
affected areas a woolly appearance ('scorched' or 'Samson' foxes).

HABITAT Most abundant in fragmentary habitats offering wide variety
of cover and food, but also found on large expanses of hill land, sand
dune areas and suburbs. Small woodlands, especially conifer, afford good
shelter; large coniferous plantations are good habitat while ground
vegetation remains, but not highly desirable later except to provide
shelter on the periphery whence foxes foray to other areas for food. If
adequate surface cover is available, foxes do not seek holes or rock dens,
except in breeding season. A highly adaptable, unspecialised, versatile
species.

BEHAVIOUR Most frequent gait a trot at about 6–10 km/hour. Swims
well.

FIGURE 130 Fox:
distribution.

Juveniles disperse October to January inclusive, males further than females. In hill and fringe areas of mid-Wales average distances dispersed were 14 km for males and 6·5 km for females. In Pembrokeshire, where density was high, dispersal distances were less. Dispersal behaviour variable. Stimulus to dispersal not known, but observation of behaviour of radio-tracked foxes suggests that hunting with hounds may have some influence. Some move swiftly from origin to area of settlement, others in intermittent movements and sometimes returning near to area of origin. Little information on territory for Britain. In North America Sargeant (1972) described non-overlapping territories for family groups from April to August. In mid-Wales ranges determined by radio-tracking varied from 2·5 to 15 km², females usually having the smaller ranges, up to 5 km². Ranges may be much smaller in richer habitats. Range or territory boundary marked by scent—by urine in both sexes (Tembrock 1957) and perianal gland secretions, but little unequivocal information.

Mainly nocturnal and crepuscular, but may also be active during daylight, especially in autumn. Emerge at dusk, and in summer will remain active for many hours after dawn. Nocturnal activity not greatly influenced by weather conditions. Activity varies according to human presence and activity. Mainly surface dwelling where cover is abundant; in such areas may seek refuge underground after heavy prolonged rainfall and in early part of cubbing season. Where no natural surface cover, will seek refuge in holes, rocks, or beneath garden sheds, electricity transformers, etc. Earths may be self-excavated or enlarged disused rabbit burrows or abandoned badger sets. Will bolt readily from holes and, except in urban areas, will move with cubs to another earth at slightest disturbance by man or dogs.

Hierarchical system in wild described by Vincent (1958) in Alaska but little information for Britain. Males monogamous in captivity—possibly mainly so in wild although there is much evidence of two vixens in a family group. Pooling of two litters frequently affirmed. Communication is visual, auditory and olfactory. Visual signalling described by Tembrock (1958a, 1958b) and Fox (1971). Some chemical components of anal gland secretions described by Albone & Perry (1976). Twenty-eight different calls have been identified by Tembrock (1958, 1963). Most common vocal period is from one to three hours after sunset. Most common calls are intermittent high-pitched barks, usually in groups of two to four, and a hoarse wailing bark. In the breeding season screaming interspersed with a chatter, not unlike the alarm note of a jay, may be heard. Aggressive behaviour described by Vincent (1958).

FOOD An opportunist feeder and predator on small animals (Southern

& Watson 1941, Lever 1959). The numbers of small rodents taken seem to reflect preference or ease of capture rather than relative abundance; field voles taken more readily than bank voles which in turn preferred to wood mice. Rabbits, now fewer in number than formerly, occur relatively more frequently in diet than when they were abundant nationally before myxomatosis arrived in 1954. Englund (1965) considered this to be the case in Sweden also. Shuns feeding on shrews, moles, toads and slugs, but will kill shrews and moles and sometimes eat them. Earthworms a frequent prey in some habitats.

Stomach and scat analyses may be misleading if only frequency of occurrence is considered, also size of prey may give biased results, e.g. evidence of lamb may occur in stomach or faecal analyses long after the bulk of the carcase has been eaten, because bones, skin and other remnants may be returned to and picked at or chewed. One fibre of sheep wool in stomach must be distinguished from a stomach-full of mutton since wool, or other hairs, may be eaten accidentally when taking beetles lying beneath a long-cleaned carcase. Feeding tests on captive foxes by Scott (1941) and Lockie (1959) showed that most food items are identifiable in faeces.

A skilful scavenger in rural and urban areas, taking sheep and cattle afterbirths, myxomatous rabbits, the edible contents of refuse and litter bins, spent salmon, bird food, etc. Small mammals taken throughout the year, small birds more frequent in spring and summer; carrion and scavenged foods in winter and early spring in rural areas; insects in summer; fruit and berries in summer and autumn. Take lambs and poultry. No information on viability of lambs taken in Britain, but frequently a missing lamb is less than 24 hours old and is a twin. Losses of ducks and geese on farms now relatively more important than poultry losses due to new methods of poultry husbandry. Food requirement about 500 g food daily. Surplus killing of lambs, poultry and colonial nesting birds not uncommon. Caches food surplus to requirements.

BREEDING A single litter of usually four or five young is produced in spring.

Males are seasonally fecund with a peak in December, January and February, but some fecund males in November and March in Britain. Onset of breeding later with increasing latitudes. Females have a single oestrous period lasting 3 weeks but fertilisation possible during only 3 days. Mating takes place night or day and the pair are locked in coitus for up to half an hour. The gestation period is 52/53 days.

Mean number of corpora lutea 5·7 (Wales), 5·5 (Kent), range 1–11. Mean litter size at birth, calculated from last ten days of gestation, 4·7 (Wales), 5·4 (Kent), range 1–10. Proportion of vixens sterile (non-fecund, non-mated, sterile matings, resorptions and abortion) varies from 10 to 22·5% in Wales. In Sweden sometimes as high as 80% (Englund 1970). Pseudo-pregnancy lasts 40 days, sometimes with milk in glands. Placental scars are persistent, and can sometimes be discerned one or two pregnancies later (except in pregnant and immediately postparous uteri).

Lactation lasts about 6 weeks. Cubs furred but blind at birth, weighing 100–130 g. No nest. Vixen is in attendance in daytime and much of night for about 3 weeks, thereafter she lies up elsewhere in daytime. Some evidence that male brings food to vixen during the period immediately after parturition. Cubs begin weaning on regurgitated food at about 4–5 weeks, fully weaned at 6–7 weeks. Growth rate about 50 g per day from 4 to 10 weeks. See Lloyd & England (1973).

POPULATION STRUCTURE Probably much variation according to habitat. Males predominate in all large samples; 54% males in Wales (15,000 foxes taken by several methods). Age structure mid-Wales in January–March: *c.* 1 year old, 60%; 2, 24%; 3, 10%; 4, 4%; 5, 2%; 6, 1%. Pembrokeshire different: 1 year old, 43%; 2, 23%; 3, 13%; 4, 11%; 5, 3%; 6, 4%. Adult to yearling ratios (Jan–March) in these two areas were 1:1·44 and 1:0·75 respectively. On Isle of Skye, where much fox control is exerted, ratio was 1:2·03 in 1969 and 1970. According to age determination using annulation of the cement of the teeth, foxes survive in wild to over 10 years.

No good data on population densities in different habitats. Lockie (1964) suggested 1 pair per 40 km² in Scottish hill land. Empirical estimate for mid-Wales is one breeding pair per 1·2–4·8 km² for Pembrokeshire, one pair per 0·4–0·8 km² in places. Number of foxes killed in a small area in late autumn/early winter does not represent population density, e.g. in Pembrokeshire over 8 weeks in winter on 3·2 km² an average of 1 fox per 4 ha was killed, 40% were (itinerant) juveniles. Recovery rates of tagged cubs very high in some areas, e.g. 43% in mid-Wales. Some urban populations thought to be of high density, but estimates highly subjective. At least 50,000 foxes of all ages killed annually in Britain, but could be more than 80,000.

Population level in the main is probably only slightly depressed by control, but locally there can be an appreciable reduction in number of breeding pairs of foxes, a loss that may be compensated by higher survival rates of cubs and juveniles. If the number known to be killed annually reflects the population density, there is evidence of aperiodic fluctuation in numbers (Fairley 1969a, 1969b, Hewson & Kolb 1973) and a trend towards increase from 1953 to 1970.

PARASITES AND DISEASES Most fleas recorded are stragglers but perhaps fox may be normal host to *Ctenocephalides canis*. Ticks, *Ixodes ricinus* (adults) and *I. hexagonus* (adults and juveniles), occur commonly and *I. canisuga* has also been recorded. The louse *Trichodectes vulpis* is specific to the fox and *T. melis* occurs as a straggler from badgers. Of mites *Sarcoptes scabei* is common in some years; *Notoedres* sp. also occur less frequently. Both can be highly debilitating, frequently predisposing death. The pentastomid *Linguatula serrata* is also found, but rarely.

About 17 species of trematodes have been recorded and about 8 of nematodes. *Toxocara canis* is sometimes seriously debilitating in cubs. About 9 species of tapeworms have been recorded in British Isles. Apart from *Echinococcus granulosus* there is some uncertainty as to whether or not all those found ever reach maturity in the gut of foxes. See Williams (1976).

Subject to wide variety of diseases and disorders; only one disease, rabies, has significant impact on population density, with up to 70% reduction—happily not yet present in Britain. Sarcoptic mange epizootics in past have also been devastating. Highly susceptible to pesticide accumulation in tissue, being at top of food chain. Large-scale local mortality from this cause occurred in 1959–61. Transmits rabies, possibly *Echinococcus* infections of sheep and possibly mange in dogs. May be a mechanical carrier of infection of some domestic animal diseases.

RELATIONS WITH MAN Uncomfortable in the main. Unwelcomed by gamekeepers, most shepherds, and by naturalists in areas of ground-nesting bird colonies. Bitter–sweet relationship with hunts. Disliked by some suburban dwellers, welcomed by others. The only mammal for which a part-paid Government bounty is offered in sheep-rearing areas through medium of Fox Destruction Societies, in England, Wales, Scotland and Northern Ireland. Increasing value of pelt (£12–£15 in 1976) is a new incentive to kill foxes. Widely admired for tenacity of life and ability to survive under adversity. In North America and Continental Europe the fox is the primary target in rabies control schemes, otherwise of little significance in zoonosis.

LITERATURE Vesey-Fitzgerald (1965), Burrows (1968): popular accounts of foxes in Britain. Lloyd (1968)—control.

AUTHOR FOR THIS SPECIES H. G. Lloyd.

FAMILY URSIDAE

GENUS *Ursus*

Brown bear *Ursus arctos*

Ursus arctos Linnaeus, 1758; Sweden.

Extinct in Britain and Ireland but still present in small numbers in parts of western Europe and more abundantly across Palaearctic Asia and in western North America. The history of the brown bear in Britain is confused by the practice of bear-baiting and the undoubted importation of captive animals for that purpose. It is probable that they were extinct or at least very rare by the tenth century (Harting 1880), although it is possible that they may have survived in the less populous parts of the country to a later date. They were hunted for sport, fur and food and were trapped alive for the sport of baiting, when tethered animals were set upon by dogs.

FAMILY MUSTELIDAE
WEASELS, etc.

One of the largest families of carnivores, found throughout the world except for Australasia. The dominant family of small carnivores in the north temperate region but outnumbered by the Viverridae (mongooses, etc.) in the tropics of the Old World. Most species are fairly small with long slender bodies and short legs and constitute the subfamily Mustelinae; other subfamilies are the Melinae (badgers), Lutrinae (otters), Mellivorinae (honey badger) and Mephitinae (skunks), the last two not represented in Britain or Europe.

The jaws of mustelids are intermediate in relative length between those of dogs and cats, and the dental formula is also intermediate, being

$$\frac{3 . 1 . 3 - 4 . 1}{3 . 1 . 3 - 4 . 2}$$

All species have prominent scent glands adjacent to the anus and the smell is sometimes pungent, as in the polecat.

Four genera are represented in Britain, three of them each with one species (*Martes*—marten, *Meles*—badger and *Lutra*—otter), the other with four. The characters of the genera are given in Table 24.

TABLE 24 Some characters of the genera of Mustelidae

	Martes	*Mustela*	*Meles*	*Lutra*
Upper teeth	3.1.4.1	3.1.3.1	3.1.4.1	3.1.4.1
Lower teeth	3.1.4.2	3.1.3.2	3.1.4.2	3.1.3.2
Upper carnassial teeth	Long and narrow	Long and narrow	Small and triangular	Large and triangular
Upper molar (last upper tooth)	Transversely elongate	Transversely elongate	Large and square	Transversely elongate
Toes	Unwebbed	Unwebbed	Unwebbed	Webbed
Tail	Long and bushy	Moderately long	Short	Long and tapering

FIGURE 131 (a) Pine marten, (b) polecat, (c) stoat and (d) weasel.

Subfamily Mustelinae

GENUS *Martes*
MARTENS

A genus of eight species, in the Palaearctic and Nearctic, with one extending to India. *M. martes* in northern Europe is replaced by the sable, *M. zibellina*, in Siberia and by the American marten, *M. americana*, in North America. The beech marten (or stone marten), *M. foina*, is a more southern species overlapping extensively with the pine marten in Europe. Last century it was commonly believed to occur also in Britain, but there is, in fact, no evidence that it has ever occurred here.

Martens are agile, mainly arboreal animals with a longer muzzle, and more teeth, than species of *Mustela*: dental formula

$$\frac{3.1.4.1}{3.1.4.2}.$$

Most species provide valuable pelts for the fur trade.

Pine marten *Martes martes*

Mustela martes Linnaeus, 1758; Upsala, Sweden.
Marten cat, sweet mart.

RECOGNITION Rarely seen in good light. In trees much larger and longer in the body than squirrels. On the ground could be confused only with polecat, polecat-ferret or mink. Marten is larger with prominent pale throat, projecting ears and very bushy tail.

Skull distinguishable from that of all other mustelids (except sometimes the badger) by having four pairs of premolars above and below.

SIGN Footprints rounded, cat-like: large pad with five toes set clear in an arc. Claws do not show unless on very soft ground. Stride when bounding 60–90 cm, prints in groups of two: when running, prints linear. Scats deposited in regular latrines, often in conspicuous places, e.g. boulder, log in trail; 4–12 cm long (Lockie 1961); dark and coiled, hair and feather remains bound together with mucus.

DESCRIPTION A strikingly beautiful, graceful animal, the size of a large cat but distinctively mustelid in shape of head and ears, and length of body. Tail long, bushy; legs longer in proportion than in terrestrial *Mustela*; feet hairy. Coat rich chocolate brown, with undivided creamy-

FIGURE 132(a) Pine marten (Photo: G. Kinns)

FIGURE 132(b) Pine martens on a bird table (Photo: Lady McKissock)

orange throat patch, variable in size; no sharply distinct white belly as in stoat and weasel; ear rounded, with pale edges, over 40 mm long.

Juvenile pelage soft, woolly and lighter brown, moulting to darker pelage in first winter. Complete moult only once yearly, in spring, beginning on legs and ending on back; winter fur begins to grow in September and is prime by mid-October (Hurrell, unpubl.).

Males about 12% larger than females, sexes otherwise similar (Lampio 1951). Abdominal scent gland (Hall 1926) as well as usual mustelid circum-anal glands.

Skull of typical mustelid form, with upper jaw less than half total length of skull. Five upper cheek-teeth, canines directly in line with cheek-teeth. Milk teeth fully erupted by 7 weeks, completely replaced by 4 months (Stubbe 1968, in Germany), carnassials last to be replaced (Mazák 1963).

Adaptation to climbing reflected in broad scapulae and powerful, highly differentiated muscles of forelimbs; long tail for balancing; well developed claws and long legs.

Chromosomes: $2n = 38$ (Robinson 1972).

MEASUREMENTS See Table 25. Craniometric analyses of the genus have been published by Anderson (1970) in relation to taxonomy and by Mal'dzhyunaite and Ryabov (see King 1975c) in relation to age determination.

TABLE 25 Measurements of pine martens (range and size of sample (*n*))

	Britain and Ireland—B.M.(N.H.)		USSR—Heptner *et al.* (1967)	
	Male	Female	Male	Female
Head and body (mm)	441–507 (3)	430–439 (2)	405–473 (93)	365–420 (102)
Tail (mm)	205–241 (3)	202–225 (2)	185–228 (104)	170–210 (100)
Weight (g)	1049–1418 (3)		670–1050 (59)	484–850 (49)

DISTRIBUTION See Fig. 133. Europe from the northern edge of the coniferous forest to the fringe of the Mediterranean region; eastwards to the R. Yenesei, beyond which it is replaced by the sable, *M. zibellina* (but boundary may have moved eastwards due to exploitation of sable).

Formerly widespread on mainland of Britain and Ireland and on some smaller islands including Wight, Jura and Lewis. Now restricted to Scottish Highlands, Lake District, Wales and Ireland. Scattered recent records elsewhere (Cheviots, Ayrshire, Yorkshire), which may represent overlooked remnants of the former range or may be recent colonisations

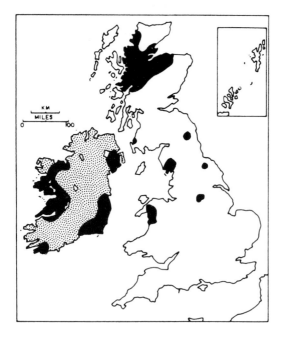

FIGURE 133 Pine marten : distribution.

or undocumented introductions. At its greatest reduction in Scotland, probably restricted to north-west of the Great Glen, but since the 1920's it has spread considerably, helped to some extent by new coniferous plantations (Lockie 1964).

Extinct in South East England by about 1850 and in northern England and southern Scotland soon after 1900 (for detailed account see Millais 1905).

VARIATION No evidence of difference between British and Continental populations nor of regional variation within British Isles. Considerable variation in size on Continent, being largest in Denmark and the Caucasus and smallest in central Russia (Reinwaldt & Erkinaro 1959, Anderson 1970).

Intensity and extent of yellow throat patch are variable, but this cannot adequately be judged on preserved skins since the colour fades and old skins can easily be mistaken for beech martens, *M. foina*, in which the throat patch is pure white.

HABITAT Mainly woodland, though, when pressed, may survive on bare rocky hills as in Sutherland. Reafforestation only partly benefited marten in Scotland (Lockie 1964). Variations in density in different kinds of forest associated with carrying capacity and prey at different stages in seral succession. Russian survey of 1953 showed 0·6 marten per 1000 ha in young plantations, 2·8 per 1000 ha in woods of intermediate age, and 3·7 per 1000 ha in mature plantations (Aspisov 1959). If present, martens prefer deciduous or mixed forest to pure stands of conifer: in Caucasus, spruce forest selected (Yurgenson 1939).

BEHAVIOUR Extremely agile climber, can run very fast over short distance, swims rarely. Climbs squirrel-fashion by embracing tree and ascending by series of upward jerks. Can fall on all fours unharmed from up to 20 m (Hurrell 1968). Downhill leap of 4·3 m noted in snow (F. Chard, unpubl.). Less arboreal than usually believed: usually hunt on ground, easily tracked and trapped (Yazan 1970). Nyholm (1970) followed 1880 km of marten trails in Finland, of which 0·1% was in trees.

In Finland mainly nocturnal, being susceptible to attack from golden eagle if out by day (10 cases 1958–68) (Nyholm 1970). Of 20 sight records in Scotland, 5 by day, 4 by night, 11 within 2 hours of sunrise or sunset (Lockie 1961, and unpubl.). Hurrell (1968) noted that tame martens climbed less confidently at night.

Nest in rocky crevice, hole in peat or river bank, tree hole, disused nest of squirrel or bird or even in nest boxes placed for owls. Recorded in woodpecker hole by Millais (1905). Normally use several dens scattered throughout home range.

Dulkeit (1929) stated that 'hunting plot' in Europe averaged 5–23 km². The size of the 'hunting plot', or total territory, primarily dependent upon food supply, is also influenced by number of enemies and competitors, etc. Exceptionally, winter range may reach 30 km² but when food abundant, individuals remained on less than 130 ha, once only 16 ha. Yurgenson (1939) found, in European Russia, normal range 5–10 km² depending on ecological characteristics and food reserves of area: range of activity in one day $\frac{1}{2}$–$\frac{1}{3}$ of total, and average daily travel 6–7 km. Males and females lived in pairs on adjoining territories. In Finland trails of resident marten distinguishable in snow: residents covered 8·6–10 km per hunting trip, non-residents 16–65 km in a night: alternation of different hunting areas by residents confirmed (Nyholm 1970). Home range in Britain not known, but it is asserted that martens travel from den to den round mountain massif many miles in circumference (Hurrell, unpubl.).

No data on social behaviour in Britain. In America marten territories not actively defended, although antisocial behaviour noted. Some ranges very stable with same boundaries for years (Hawley & Newby 1957). Branches are marked with scent from abdominal gland; young animals begin to deposit scent marks at about 4 months old (Habermehl & Röttcher 1967). Usually solitary, hunting alone (Nyholm 1970).

Usually silent. Call note sounds like 'tok-tok-tok'. When slightly alarmed, deep 'huffy' growl, emphatically repeated with long-drawn-out moan. When angry or fighting, high-pitched squeal or scream, the noise most often heard from wild marten. Further vocabulary includes grunts and chattering, and in mating season female makes clucking noise as she deposits scentmarks; during copulation both sexes purr and growl. Call of lost cub like tearing of cloth, or call of snipe (combined observations of Markley & Bassett, 1942 and H. G. Hurrell in first edition).

FOOD Varies greatly according to habitat, season and availability. In Scotland rodents and small birds are main constituents of diet at all seasons (Lockie 1961). Bird prey included high proportion of tits, wrens and tree creepers. 90% of small rodents were field voles, a much larger proportion than in trapped samples at the same place. Beetles, caterpillars, carrion, birds' eggs, fish and berries were also eaten seasonally.

In Sweden and Finland main food is red squirrel (Höglund 1960, Nyholm 1970). In Russia eggs of grouse are eaten in some numbers (Yurgensen 1951).

Observations on North American marten show similar range but often with a preference for microtine rodents (e.g. Cowan & Mackay 1950). Usually hunt by following trails and attacking roosting sites (Nyholm 1970). Daily intake reckoned to be about 10% body weight (Schmidt 1943) or up to *c*. 160 g (Novikov 1956).

Tame martens have been observed to kill frogs, rabbits, rats, bumble bees and cockchafers (Hurrell, unpubl.). They usually ignore slugs but occasionally eat them after dragging them about with the fore paws to remove slime.

BREEDING Mating in late summer, single litter of about 3 born in March or April.

Most information from captive animals, mainly of American marten. Oestrus occurs in July and August when female shows prominent swelling of the vulva and frequently sets scent and urinates.

In copulation, male drags female about by the scruff, and both sexes purr and growl. Usually occurs on the ground (but has been observed in trees—Siefke 1960) and lasts 15–75 minutes, usually over 1 hour. Individual females mate several times and are highly promiscuous. Oldest fertile female recorded was 9 years (Markley & Bassett 1942).

Implantation of blastocysts delayed until about January, controlled by photoperiod (Pearson & Enders 1944). Period of gestation from implantation less than 28 days in American marten (Jonkel & Weckwerth 1963).

Litter size usually 3 (in captive pine marten)—range of 41 litters was 2 to 5 (Schmidt 1943). Weight at birth about 28 g (in American marten: Markley & Bassett 1942), pelage white or grey. Young soon develop glandular structure on neck, which may reach 3·0–3·3 per cent of body weight by 15 days but then declines and disappears by 6 weeks (Petskoi & Kolpovsky 1970). Soft, woolly brown pelage developed by 3 weeks. Eyes open at 32–38 days (King 1975c), Habermehl & Röttcher 1967). Eruption of milk teeth begins about 3 weeks in Germany according to Habermehl & Röttcher (1967) but 4–5 weeks in Russia (Ryabov, in King 1975c). Weaned at 6–7 weeks and begin to emerge from den about 8 weeks but lactation may continue for 2–2½ months (Tumanov 1972). Not fully independent until about 6 months.

Weight at 4 weeks about 200 g, sex difference apparent from 8 weeks— at 12 weeks males are 950–1150 g and females 800–900 g; at 6 months males *c*. 1700 g, females *c*. 1350 g (Habermehl & Röttcher 1967). Both sexes reach adult weight in first summer.

POPULATION STRUCTURE Techniques of age determination have been developed using closure of sutures, wear of teeth, development of sagittal crest and of baculum (Yurgensen 1956, Mal'dzhyunaite in King 1975c, Anderson 1970). Trapped samples usually show similar proportion of sexes or slight preponderance of males.

Maximum longevity in wild about 17 or 18 years (Yurgensen 1956). The age structure in a population in Lithuania was found to be as follows (Mal'dzhyunaite in King 1975c).

	0–1 year	1–3 years	over 3 years
males	36%	23%	41%
females	48%	31%	20%
Total	45%	29%	26%

Estimates of population density in Europe have ranged from 1 marten per 82 ha to 1 per 10 km^2 (Stubbe 1968, Goethe 1964). No evidence of periodic fluctuation in density.

PREDATORS AND MORTALITY Predation, other than by man, probably not significant but reported to be taken by golden eagle in Finland (Nyholm 1970).

PARASITES AND DISEASE The biting louse *Trichodectes salfii* is recorded from the Continent.

The nematode *Skrjabingylus nasicola*, which infests the nasal cavity, occurs frequently in Russia, being found in up to 90% of young animals (under 1 year) and up to 50% of animals over 3 years (King 1975c); mean 5% in Scandinavia (Hansson 1970). A lungworm, *Filaroides* sp., is also frequent in Russia.

RELATIONS WITH MAN Formerly hunted for sport in Britain (Millais 1905) and as vermin (Lockie 1964, Steele-Elliot 1936). It is no longer hunted in Britain, although it is not legally protected.

Still important fur resource in Canada and Russia, despite decrease in catch to 1/6 of that of 1920's (de Vos 1952).

Breeding of marten in captivity for fur on a commercial scale generally unsuccessful owing to late maturing, small litter size, and difficulty of getting them to breed.

AUTHOR FOR THIS SPECIES C. M. King.

GENUS *Mustela*

In its wider sense, as used here, this genus contains about 15 species and is represented throughout the Northern Hemisphere. Three species, stoat, weasel and polecat, are native to Britain whilst a fourth, American mink, has been introduced. To these must be added one feral domestic form, the ferret. The polecat and mink are sometimes separated from the stoat and weasel in distinct genera, *Putorius* and *Lutreola* respectively. Although this may seem reasonable when considering the species represented in Britain, such a separation has very little basis when the entire genus is considered. The distinguishing characters of the four species are given in Table 26.

TABLE 26 The characters of the species of *Mustela*

	Weasel *M. nivalis*	Stoat *M. erminea*	Polecat *M. putorius*	Mink *M. vison*
Colour of upper parts	Reddish-brown	Reddish-brown	Dark brown	Dark brown
Colour of under parts	White	White	Brown	Brown
Colour of tail	Uniform	Black-tipped	Uniform	Uniform
Length of head and body (mm)	170–230	240–310	320–440	350–400
Length of tail (mm)	20–70	95–140	130–190	130–150
Greatest length of skull (mm)	32–42	42–53	58–71	60–72
Width of post-orbital constriction (mm)	7–9	9–12	16–18	10–13

Stoat *Mustela erminea*

Mustela erminea Linnaeus, 1758; Sweden. *Putorius hibernicus* Thomas & Barrett-Hamilton, 1895; Enniskillen, Co. Fermanagh, Ireland. *Putorius ermineus stabilis* Barrett-Hamilton, 1904; Blandford, Dorset. *Putorius erminea ricinae* Miller, 1907; Islay House, Isle of Islay, Inner Hebrides.
Clubtail, royal hunter, hob, white weasel, stot; whittret (Scotland), weasel (Ireland), ermine.

RECOGNITION Black tip to tail is distinctive at all times: most similar species is weasel, which is smaller, with a relatively shorter tail. See Fig. 131 (p. 322).

Skull distinguishable from that of weasel only by larger size (greatest length over 42 mm, lower jaw over 22 mm), but there is a slight overlap.

SIGN Tracks of hind feet usually register in those of fore feet; sometimes 'tripled', leaving three imprints rather than a pair. Footprints of male average 62 mm, of females 46 mm. Droppings dark and irregularly elongated, about 4–8 cm long, with characteristic twists of fur at each end, often piled up in den (Fitzgerald 1972).

DESCRIPTION Summer pelage brown above, yellowish white below, dividing line usually sharp and straight. Two moults a year, in spring and autumn. Spring moult slow, progressing from head across back to belly; autumn moult is swift, progressing in reverse direction (Soest & Bree 1969, Fog 1969). Winter pelage in north of range entirely white except for black tip of tail ('ermine' condition); further south, brown but denser and sometimes paler than in summer. Across narrow zone where both types occur various halfway stages can be observed; here females more often found in full ermine than males (America: Hall 1951, Yorkshire: Flintoff 1935b).

Good correlation between mean winter climate and proportions of stoats turning white, but colour change influenced only secondarily by temperature (Rothschild 1944, Rust 1962). Moult progress primarily controlled by daylength and (in autumn) by withdrawal of sex hormones (Rust 1965); perhaps also by change in activity in spring (Bäumler 1973). Histology of moult and colour change illustrated by Schwalbe (1893).

MEASUREMENTS See Table 27. Males about 50% larger than females. In Britain males grow to *c.* 260 g by July and reach adult weight of *c.* 320 g by following spring; females grow faster, reaching *c.* 190 g by July and adult weight (*c.* 220 g) by following spring (Deanesly 1935). British race largest: mean weights of adult males from other European countries range 208–283 g; Russia 134–191 g; North America 56–206 g (Fog 1969, Soest & Bree 1970, Heptner *et al.*, 1967, Hall 1951).

TABLE 27 External measurements and weights of stoats

	Male			Female			Source
Britain (winter and spring)	Mean	Range	*n*	Mean	Range	*n*	
Head and body (mm)	297	275–312	4	264	242–292	8	Flintoff (1935a)
Tail (mm)	110·5	95–127	4	117	95–140	8	Flintoff (1935a)
Weight (g) (Jan–July only)	321	200–445	204	213	140–280	99	Deanesly (1935)
Ireland (all year)							
Head and body	252·2	240–274	24	212·4	184–260	16	Fairley (1971)
Tail	85·3	72–104	24	65·3	57–73	16	Fairley (1971)
Weight	233	112–292	39	120	74–160	19	Fairley (1971)

DISTRIBUTION See Fig. 134. Eurasia and North America from Arctic coasts south to Pyrenees, Alps, Kashmir, Japan, California and Virginia. Introduced from Britain to New Zealand. Absent from Mediterranean lowlands.

Throughout British mainland and Ireland at all altitudes, and on most of the larger islands including Shetland mainland (introduced), Skye, Mull, Islay, Jura, Man, Anglesey, Wight, Jersey and Guernsey. Absent from Orkney, the Outer Hebrides and from most of the smaller islands.

VARIATION British and continental forms once separated (larger size, darker dorsal colour in British subspecies), but differences not now considered significant, and British mainland population designated as *M. e. erminea* by Dadd (1970).

Irish form, *M. e. hibernica*, differs from the British in average smaller size (see Table 27), dark upper lip, dark margins of ears, white below restricted to a narrow line except between the legs (Dadd 1970). The mammae are not more numerous as has often been stated (Fairley 1971).

The form on Islay and Jura, *M. e. ricinae*, has been considered subspecifically distinct (average smaller size, small differences in cranial proportions), but this is dubious.

FIGURE 134 Stoat: distribution.

Winter whitening is normal in northern Scotland, abnormal in southern England, but variation in its incidence has not been precisely mapped.

Intraspecific and individual (age) variation of skulls very thoroughly investigated in Russia for economic assessment of ermine catch (see King 1975c: 39–54, 155–78). 'Bergmann's Rule' does not apply to variation in Russian stoat skulls (Petrov 1962).

HABITAT Very wide range of habitats, from lowland agricultural country, marsh and woodland to moorland and mountains. Distribution of stoats closely related to cover and potential food supplies (Vaisfeld 1972).

BEHAVIOUR Usual gait bounding; average length of each bound (measured from tracks in snow) given by Nyholm (in King 1975c) as 56 cm for male and 30 cm for female, and by Heptner *et al.* (1967) as varying from 30 to 100 cm.

Swims readily and well (eye-witness account for closely related *M. frenata* given by Davis 1942); once encountered over 1 mile from land (Anon. 1949). Climbs well, even to very considerable heights; sometimes poked out of squirrel dreys.

Active both day and night in wild, with seasonal changes in rhythm (Bäumler 1973). Structure of retina suggests good vision, possibly with colour perception (Gewalt 1959). Family may hunt together into autumn, and, since families can be large, reports arise of stoats hunting in packs. Characteristically very curious, and can be drawn near to observer, especially if rabbit squeal is imitated. Usually silent, but can produce range of sounds similar to weasel (Gossow 1970).

Sexes usually live separately, except while young are being reared, when male may help provide food (observations on stoat families in wild by Osgood 1936 and Müller 1970). Size of territory varies with density of prey. In a young Forestry Commission plantation in Scotland where density of prey (field voles) was 110–540/ha, one male stoat occupied *c.* 20·2 ha (measured by livetrapping) (Lockie 1966). Abroad, winter ranges have been estimated by snow tracking: Finland, male 34 ha ($n=17$, range 29 to 40 ha), female 7·4 ha ($n=46$, range 4 to 17 ha) (King 1975c); Russia, male 20·5 ha ($n=11$, range 4·2 to 49 ha), female 7·1 ha ($n=28$, range 0·2 to 42·3 ha) (Zharkov in King 1975c); Russia, male 43 ha ($n=7$, range 17–117 ha), female 45 ha ($n=6$, range 11–124 ha) (Vaisfeld 1972). In different regions of Russia, stoat territories may vary from 10–200 ha, according to habitat and food supplies, and tend to increase in size towards the end of winter (Nasimovich 1949, Heptner *et al.* 1967). These large living territories divided into a number of smaller hunting areas, up to *c*. 10 ha each, visited for a few days in turn. When foraging, usually work along hedgerows, stone walls and stream banks, following regularly revisited routes (Musgrove 1951, King 1975c). Intrusions into a neighbouring territory occur only in absence of owner (Vaisfeld 1972). Distance travelled in one hunt averages *c*. 1–3 km but may be up to 8 km (Nasimovich 1949, Vaisfeld 1972). Dens may be in a hollow tree, rock crevice or burrow (often commandeered from prey animals) and territory may contain several, used in turn.

Strong musky scent emitted from anal glands when alarmed; scats impregnated with this scent assumed to constitute territorial markers (Lockie 1966, Stubbe 1972).

F O O D Until myxomatosis arrived, rabbit was staple food in British Isles; subsequently, stoats have been readjusting to different circumstances. An analysis of 116 guts and 3 scats from various parts of Britain produced 168 prey items, principally birds (33%), lagomorphs (28%) and small rodents (22%) (Day 1968). In Ireland 29 guts contained 45% birds, 34% lagomorphs, 17% small rodents (Fairley 1971). Generally, food mainly mammals of rabbit/water vole size or less, of whatever species locally available, though not necessarily in direct proportion to availability. Favoured prey may be especially selected, e.g. in America fat hibernating jumping mice (*Zapus*) taken from their subnivean nests (Northcott 1971); shrews usually avoided, though two studies in America found them in 20% or more of diet (Aldous & Mannweiler 1942, Hamilton 1933).

When food short, stoats may turn to secondary foods. Osgood (1936) watched a pair carrying earthworms to young, and in New Zealand, (voles and shrews absent) stoats eat many rats, large insects and carrion opossums (*c*. 1500 guts analysed) (author's data). During a vole crash in Lapland, only 8% of 83 scats contained voles, remainder mostly juniper fruit and berries (71%), with some insects, birds, lizards and frogs (Nasimovich 1949).

Daily food requirements calculated by Day (1963) as: males, 57 g/day (23% body wt), females 33 g/day (14%) (minimum estimates). From extensive records of captive colony, Müller (1970) calculated males required 19–32% of body weight and females 23–27% of body weight per day. Elongate shape allows pursuit of prey into small holes, but at high cost in energetic inefficiency (Brown & Lasiewski 1972).

Prey followed largely by scent: a hare twice observed to throw off pursuit by sideways leap to break trail (Murie 1935, Ward 1936). Notable that a single rabbit will be relentlessly followed through a colony whose other members continue to feed. Pursued rabbit often observed to act in panic-stricken way and to lie down squealing at approach of stoat (Forsyth 1967). Birds sometimes attracted by stoat 'dancing', and one may be pounced upon (Humphries 1962). Kill always made by bite at back of neck (Wüstehube 1960, Gossow 1970, Hewson & Healing 1971). Large prey gripped at nape, enfolded by forelegs and scratched with hind claws. If blood extrudes from wound, stoat will lick it first before beginning to eat, which may have given rise to false idea that mustelids suck blood of prey.

BREEDING Stoats mate in summer, but implantation is delayed until the following spring, when a single litter of about 6–12 is born.

Males become sexually mature in spring following year of birth. Weight of baculum remains at 20–30 mg until February, when it increases by about 100%. Male stoat has well-defined fertile season, mid-May to mid-August. Seasonal changes in production of testosterone, with peaks in March and June/July. Young females become sexually mature in year of birth and mate with older males (even unweaned females of 5 weeks can have fertile matings—Müller 1970). Ovulation always induced. During delay (when blastocysts lie free in the uterus, about 280 days) corpora lutea remain small and sexual activity declines. Implantation occurs in March of following year; subsequent gestation lasts 21–28 days (Deanesly 1935, 1943, Müller 1970, Gulamhusein 1972).

Mean ovulation rate 10, range 6–17 (Gulamhusein 1972). Embryo rate 9 ($n = 12$, range 6–13, Deanesly 1935). Gulamhusein (1972) also observed embryo rate of 9 ($n = 17$) but 25% of these females contained some embryos being resorbed. Litter rate in USA 6·4 ($n = 9$, range 4–9, Hamilton 1933); in Germany 5·8 ($n = 9$, range 4–9, Müller 1970); in Russia 8·7 (range 2–18, Heptner *et al.* 1967). Sex ratio at birth 1 : 1 (Müller 1970), but trapping normally produces an excess (about 60–65%) of males.

Growth and development of young described by Hamilton (1933), East & Lockie (1965), Müller (1970). Young born April or May with coat of fine white hair, and while still blind have prominent brown mane on neck, presumably where carried by female. Eyes open 5–6 weeks (females first), black tail-tip appears 6–7 weeks. Milk teeth erupt at about 3 weeks, weaned by 5 weeks. Lactation lasts 7–12 weeks, but solid food taken from 4 weeks on. Permanent carnassials P^4 and M_1 are last in place. At 3 months typical prey-killing behaviour pattern fully developed but young can kill inexpertly at *c.* 10 weeks (Gossow 1970).

POPULATION British stoat populations severely reduced by the loss of rabbits due to first outbreaks of myxomatosis, 1953–56. Numbers caught annually on 1600 ha in Hampshire were 136–302 in 1947–53, 13–58 afterwards (Anon. 1960); on 9200 ha in Norfolk, annual kill was 419–1137 in 1903–54, 40–257 in 1955–68 (Harrison, unpubl.). Less drastic variations normal, especially if prey species also variable, but generally numbers rather more stable than weasel (Nasimovich 1949). Capable of startling population increase if introduced into favourable habitat: 9 multiplied to 180 in 3 years on Terschelling Island, Holland (van Wijngaarden & Bruijns 1961).

Age determination by skull characters, development of lateral supra-sesamoid tubercle of femur, and baculum (Soest & Bree 1970), relative width of tooth pulp cavity (King 1975c), or wear of teeth (Stroganov 1937).

Majority (60–90%) of any sample composed of young of the year. Turnover of population rapid (3–5 years), average individual life-span short, *c*. 1–1·5 years (Kopin in King 1975c). Maximum age attained in wild about 7 years (Stroganov 1937, Soest & Bree 1970).

PREDATORS AND MORTALITY Recorded killed by hawks, owls and larger carnivores, and mortality from predation could be significant (Latham 1952, Powell 1973). In Britain, probably most important predator is man, but stoats can learn to avoid traps (Cahn 1936).

PARASITES AND DISEASE Fleas are scarce and are normally rodent fleas acquired from their prey. The biting louse *Trichodectes ermineae* is specific to the stoat.

Rate of infestation of the nasal passage by the nematode *Skrjabingylus nasicola* in Britain varies from 17% (*n* = 12, Lewis 1967) to 31% (*n* = 46, Soest *et al*. 1972); generally 20–50% on large samples in continental Europe (Hansson 1970, Vik 1955). Obligate intermediate hosts are terrestrial snails, but theory that shrews act as carrier hosts (Hansson 1967) not applicable in New Zealand, where infection rates may be at least as high as in Europe—up to about 30% in some populations (King 1974). Infestation adversely affects numbers, skull size, body weight and fertility (Popov 1943, Heptner *et al*. 1967, Soest *et al*. 1972).

RELATIONS WITH MAN In Britain, because of potential predation upon game birds and poultry, regarded as vermin, and regularly trapped or shot by gamekeepers. A single individual in a pen or enclosure can cause great damage, killing far in excess of requirements (Hewson & Healing 1971). However, probably stoats threaten game only during short period of breeding, and during rest of year offset this by destruction of rabbits, rats, mice and voles.

In Arctic North America and Russia ermine pelts commercially valuable and harvested in very large but declining numbers. When kept in captivity rather timid and less aggressive than weasel (J. D. Lockie, unpubl.).

AUTHOR FOR THIS SPECIES C. M. King.

Weasel *Mustela nivalis*

Mustela nivalis Linnaeus, 1766; Vesterbotten, Sweden. *Mustela vulgaris* Erxleben, 1777.
Kine, cane, beale, rassel, mousehunter; whittret (Scotland), bronwen (Wales).

RECOGNITION Very small size and long slender body distinguish it from all other species except stoat. Tail of weasel very short and lacks any terminal black tuft.

Skull recognisable by its very small size (total length under 42 mm, jaw under 22 mm) but there is a little overlap with that of stoat.

SIGN Droppings similar to those of stoat but smaller, about 3–6 cm long (sketch in Lockie 1961); sometimes accumulate in large numbers in dens.

DESCRIPTION Colour similar to that of stoat, variable from deep rusty brown to light sandy tan; lacks straight line between brown upper parts and white underparts of stoat, and often has spots and blotches of brown on belly. This pattern allows recognition of individuals (Linn & Day 1966). Tail relatively short and without black tip. Males about 10% larger than females. Moults twice a year, as stoat, and in northern continental parts of range turns white in winter (Heptner *et al.* 1967); southern limit of white forms further north than stoat, and only rare records for British Isles. (See Fig. 131, p. 322).

Chromosomes: $2n=42$ (Robinson 1972).

MEASUREMENTS Highly variable. Differential rate of growth between first and second litter young is most probable explanation for persistence of stories about a dwarf species of weasel in Europe. See Table 28.

DISTRIBUTION See Fig. 135. Throughout most of the Palaearctic Region and much of North America, from the Arctic coasts south to North Africa, Afghanistan, southern China, Nebraska and Missouri. Introduced to New Zealand.

Throughout mainland Britain but absent from Ireland. Generally absent from the small islands but present on Skye, Anglesey and Wight.

VARIATION Considerable geographical variation, particularly in size,

TABLE 28 Measurements of weasels

Locality	Source		Weight (g)				Head and body (mm)				Tail (mm)			
			n	Mean	s.d.	Range	n	Mean	s.d.	Range	n	Mean	s.d.	Range
Aberdeenshire†	Moors (1974)	♂	194	129	27	73–202	54	210	10	185–229	54	50	4	39–58
		♀	22	62	7	52–74	8	174	4	167–180	8	37	3	34–42
Wigtownshire	King (1971)	♂	30	131	24	72–174	31	210	10	180–225	24	44	5	33–57
		♀	3	55	—	53–57	3	173	—	168–181	3	28	—	18–36
Northumberland	King (1971)	♂	38	122	26	80–189	38	209	12	183–226	38	46	6	35–60
		♀	14	61	10	47–77	15	181	4	169–185	15	40	6	29–54
Berkshire†	King (1971)	♂	262	112	17	55–138	13	214	9	202–229	13	46	8	36–59
		♀	38	63	7	50–77	5	177	1	176–179	5	40	4	34–44
Hertfordshire	Walker (1972)*	♂	26	117	—	109–125	27	205	—	194–216	27	47	—	42–52
		♀	10	69	—	56–82	12	177	—	171–183	12	39	—	34–44
Sussex	King (1971)	♂	104	106	19	68–161	34	204	10	175–219	34	44	5	32–55
		♀	61	63	7	45–80	21	180	5	172–192	20	40	3	32–44
Devonshire	Day (1963)	♂	25	95	—	71–115								
General	Hill (1939)	♂	162	115	—	70–170	46	202	—	175–220	46	60	—	40–75
(mostly Wales)	Deanesly (1944)	♀	36	59	—	35–90	12	178	—	165–190	12	50	—	40–65

*Gives medians, not means.

†Weights of live animals, measurements of carcases. Figs include juveniles and pregnant females.

which increases from north to south of Continent by 2–3 times; in Britain, largest weasels in north (Table 28). Especially small forms in the Alps, in eastern Siberia and North America. Recent studies do not support proposal that these small forms can be considered specifically distinct (e.g. as *M. minuta* in Europe: Beaucournu & Grulich 1968).

British form not distinguishable from Continental: geographical variability within Britain can be seen from Table 28. Variation in size in British populations has led to widespread popular belief in second, smaller species 'miniver', or 'finger weasel'), but no specimens of this form have been produced.

HABITAT Very varied, from lowland farming country and woodland up to moorlands and mountains, though overall population density may differ markedly between habitats. Broadly, found wherever there are voles and mice. In severe climates, woodlands preferred to open ground in winter (Nasimovich 1949). In farmland, weasels generally restricted to hedgerows, stone dykes, fence-lines and other cover (Moors 1974).

BEHAVIOUR Moves much like stoat, but length of bounds only 12–32 cm. Uses own regular hunting routes and, unlike stoat, can follow along tracks and burrows of voles and mice and penetrate cornricks in-

FIGURE 135 Weasel: distribution.

fested with mice. Occasionally caught in mole traps. Frequently seen standing upright on hind legs investigating surroundings.

Apparently active day and night in the wild: weasels enter traps at any time though more during the day (King 1975b, Moors 1974), but often show more or less strong nocturnal preference in captivity (Kavanau 1969, Linn unpubl.) and are easily influenced by feeding regime (Price 1971).

Sexes remain separate and have their own territories; those of females very much smaller than of males. Size of territory varies with density of prey: in a young Forestry Commission plantation in Scotland, where density of prey (field voles) was 110–540/ha, range of males was 1–5 ha (Lockie 1966); in mature deciduous woodland near Oxford where density of prey (bank voles and wood mice) was 21–39/ha, range of males was 7–15 ha (King 1975b). Winter ranges of 5 males in farmland in Aberdeenshire were 9–16 ha, and summer ranges of 3 males were 10–25 ha; ranges of 2 females were about 7 ha (Moors 1974). Whole territory hunted regularly and can be covered rapidly: movement of 1·3 km in 55 minutes noted by Moors (1974). The above estimates calculated by trapping: in colder climates, ranges of males, estimated from snow tracking, vary from 0·8 ha in Iowa (Polderboer 1942) and 1·7 ha in Finland (King 1975c) to 10 ha in Russia (Heptner *et al.* 1967). Distance travelled in one night's hunting varied between 1·5 and 2·5 km in the Kola Peninsula, Lapland (Nasimovich 1949). Dens were not permanent, though in other places nests have been found thickly lined with accumulated fur of prey (Criddle 1947). Territories presumably marked out by deposition of scats tainted with scent from anal glands (Lockie 1966, Stubbe 1972).

Voice described and analysed by Huff & Price (1968) and Gossow (1970). Four basic sounds: two threatening, a guttural hiss when slightly alarmed and a short, screaming bark or chirp when provoked; a shrill, defensive squeal; and an excited, high-pitched trilling during friendly encounters between mates or between mother and young. Vision is good (Herter 1939). General behaviour described by Goethe (1950, 1964).

FOOD Specialist in small mammals, especially voles; takes relatively small range of prey, the principal species varying with habitat. Day (1968), investigating 91 gut contents and 25 scats from various parts of Britain, found 55% small rodents (mainly field voles), 19% rabbits, 15% birds, 3% rats and 2% insectivores. Guts of 28 weasels from two estates in Hertfordshire (woodland, pasture and arable) contained 71% small rodents (mainly wood mice), 14% rats, 3% rabbits, 11% birds and no insectivores (Walker 1972). In woodland near Oxford 250 scats, collected

1968–70, contained 78% small rodents, 22% birds, 0·4% rabbits, no rats, 0·4% moles but no shrews: staple diet was bank voles, with a large number of birds and eggs taken in spring (King 1971). Moors (1974) analysed 189 scats, collected in farmland near Aberdeen, which contained 70% small rodents (mainly field voles), no rats, 13% rabbits, 2·5% shrews and 15% birds: bank voles were present, but rarely eaten.

Similar data from other parts of range, but one 30-year study in Arctic Russia found shrews in 6% of 258 scats and stomachs along with 77% rodents and 5% birds (King 1975c); in Sweden water voles made up 16% of the food of weasels in a woodland in Scania along with 12% lagomorphs, 9% bank voles, 46% field voles, 10% wood mice, 1% shrews and 2% birds (Erlinge 1975).

Often raid bird nestboxes (Sherell 1953) and may have a marked effect on these bird populations (Krebs 1971, Ferns 1974). Acceptable prey species taken according to availability, which may vary with place and season. In 1968–70, 89 guts from Sussex contained 81% small rodents, 12% birds, 6% rabbits, while 54 guts from Northumberland contained 51% small rodents, 16% birds and 33% rabbits (King 1971): in Aberdeenshire, wood mice comprised 4% of diet of farmland weasels in spring, 33% after harvest (Moors 1974). When introduced to islands where voles are absent, weasels have not thriven: quickly died out on Terschelling, Netherlands (van Wijngaarden & Bruijns 1961) and survive only at low densities in New Zealand (Marshall 1963).

Day (1963) measured daily food consumption and found, on average, males ate 33 g/day (27% of body weight) and females 23 g/day (30% of body weight) although Moors (1974) found this varied with the diet and season. Short (1961) calculated that one male ate 1 g food per hour; timed passage of dyed mouse through gut averaged 3–4 hours. Assimilation was 74–83% efficient, in inverse proportion to the amount of hair and bone in food (Moors 1974).

Prey killed by bite at back of neck: behaviour patterns involved have been extensively analysed (e.g. Goethe 1964, Gossow 1970).

BREEDING One or two litters, each of usually 4–6 young, born each season. No delayed implantation; early born young females can breed in their first summer.

Males fecund from February to October, though early stages of spermatogenesis present throughout winter (Hill 1939). In females, anoestrus lasts September to February, and pregnancies may occur at any time between March and August (Deanesly 1944). In America and in Germany, breeding season ill-defined; pregnancies recorded in most months of year (Hall 1951, Pohl 1910). Breeding rate presumably adjustable to fluctuations in food supply. Probable that ovulation occurs only on stimulus of copulation.

In Britain, majority of young weasels born April–May; smaller numbers may be produced July–August by variable proportions of adults having second litters and by precocious first year females. Gestation period 34–37 days (Heidt 1970, Hartman 1964), overall mean number of young per litter 5·4 (based on 258 young in 48 litters, recorded throughout the species' range: figures collected by author). Mean of 17 of the above litters that were from Britain, 6·2 young, range 4–8. Mean number of corpora lutea 7·1 (32 pregnancies, range 4–11: Deanesly 1944).

Mating behaviour and development of young in captivity described in detail by East & Lockie (1964, 1965), Hartman (1964) and Heidt (1970). Deciduous teeth erupt at 2–3 weeks; weaned at 3–4 weeks, but lactation may last to 12 weeks. Eyes open at *c.* 4 weeks (females first), permanent dentition completed at 10 weeks, and family groups break up *c.* 9–12 weeks. Young kill efficiently by 8 weeks. Birth weight *c.* 1·5 g, increasing to adult weight in 12–16 weeks.

Sex ratio of newborn young 1:1. Young of spring litter grow quickly: (males reach 70–90 g, females 50–55 g at 2 months), and by August (*c.* 4 months) both sexes can be sexually mature. Young of second litter grow more slowly and do not mature until following spring. 'Minivers', or small weasels, may represent these late-born young (Corbet 1966).

POPULATION Sex ratio in trapped samples normally very uneven. Proportion males recorded in collections in Britain 73% (*n* 446, Deanesly 1944), 86% (*n*=154, Lockie 1966), 71% (*n*=171, King 1971), 78% (*n*=83, Walker 1972), 69% (*n*=78, Moors 1974). No evidence of differential mortality between sexes, so this is more likely due to trap shyness of females, and/or the much larger territories of males giving them a higher chance of being caught (King 1975a).

Numbers fluctuate with abundance of mice and voles, and vary over wider range than those of stoat. Immediate effect of first myxomatosis dramatic: in 1957–58, a year of mouse and vole abundance throughout southern Britain, there were record catches of weasels on game estates (Anon 1960, Jefferies & Pendlebury 1968). Long term effect was to reverse pre-myxomatosis ratio of weasels to stoats trapped (Craster 1970, Hewson 1972). Correlation between numbers of rodents and of weasels has been demonstrated (Nasimovich 1949, Rubina 1960, Erlinge 1974).

Greatest part of population at any one time composed of young-of-the-year, e.g. 68–86%, mean 75% in different British populations

($n = 171$, King 1971); or, if animals over 6 months old only are counted, 53% ($n = 154$, Lockie 1966). Mean expectation of life at independence, on British keepered estates, less than one year. Turnover of population very rapid; in four samples, mean mortality of first year weasels 63%, of second year 96%. Maximum age attained in wild about 3 years; only about 1 in 80–90 young survive to over 2 years old in wild, but can live up to 10 years in captivity. Among undisturbed populations these figures are probably underestimates (King 1971).

Age can be determined approximately in living animals by wear of canine teeth (Lockie 1966); in skulls, by development of post-orbital constriction. The post-orbital width is greater than the inter-orbital up to 3 months, about equal to it up to 6 months, and thereafter increasingly narrower. Rate of change decreases after 9–12 months but continues slowly throughout life. If baculum and date collected are also available, age can be estimated at least to the season of birth or closer. Layering in periosteal bone of jaws is not reliable indicator of age in weasels. Nasal sutures are indistinguishable by 6 months old (King 1971).

PREDATORS AND MORTALITY Hawks, owls, foxes and stoats will kill occasional weasel, although outcome of encounter not always unfavourable for weasel (Burnham 1970). Often recorded killed by domestic cats. McCabe (1949) noted inverse correlation between numbers of mink and weasels caught in two winters (in America). In Britain, man is most important predator, but even at most concentrated trapping pressure, many fewer are caught than can be replaced.

PARASITES AND DISEASE The biting louse *Trichodectes mustelae* is specific to the weasel. No specific flea, but species found on weasels in Wytham, Berks and Newburgh, Aberdeenshire, include the small rodent fleas *Megabothris walkeri*, *Ctenophthalmus nobilis*, *Hystrichopsylla talpae*, *Malaraeus penicilliger*, *Rhadinopsylla pentacantha*, *Megabothris turbidus* and *Peromyscopsylla spectabilis*; the specific mole fleas *Ctenophthalmus bisoctodentatus* and *Palaeopsylla minor*; and the bird flea *Dasypsyllus gallinulae* (King in press, a, Mardon & Moors in press).

Incidence of the nematode parasite *Skrjabingylus nasicola* in nasal sinuses may be high: in different British populations, infestation rates observed range from 43% (Walker 1972) to 88% (Lewis 1967), even 100% (King in press, b). The worms cause considerable contortion of frontal bones (Lewis 1967). but no adverse effect on body size, weight, fatness nor mortality detectable in sample of 614 British weasels (King in press, b).

RELATIONS WITH MAN Regarded widely as vermin, yet Linn (1962) showed that a family of weasels could account for *c.* 2000 mice and voles in a year. Local people attributed Scottish vole plague of 1892 to widespread removal of weasels for exportation to New Zealand (Harting 1894). Council for Nature's Code of Practice for management of predatory mammals in Britain (1973) recommends that no control is normally needed. Can make excellent pets (Brodman 1952, Drabble 1956).

AUTHOR FOR THIS SPECIES C. M. King.

Polecat *Mustela putorius*

Mustela putorius Linnaeus, 1758; Sweden. *Putorius vulgaris* Griffith, 1827. *Putorius foetidus* Gray, 1843. *Putorius putorius anglius* Pocock, 1936; Llangammarch, Breconshire, Wales. *Putorius putorius caledoniae* Tetley, 1939; Lochinvar, Sutherland, Scotland.
Foulmarten, foulmart, foumart, fitchet, fitch (in fur trade), ffwlbart (Welsh).

FIGURE 136 Heads of wild Welsh polecat (left) and polecat-ferret (right).

RECOGNITION Distinguished from mink by creamy wool over much of body, and guard hairs either dark (summer) or light and dark (winter); and by white facial band and ear-margins; from escaped ferrets by (usually) much darker appearance and more restricted white facial band. Some feral ferrets and recent ferret/polecat hybrids probably indistinguishable on external features.

Skull distinguished from mink by greater absolute and proportional width of post-orbital constriction which measures 15 mm or more in the polecat and less than 15 mm in the mink. Absolute separation from ferret and ferret/polecat hybrids difficult for single skulls but can be done with about 95% accuracy (Walton, unpubl.; see also Ashton & Thomson 1955, Ashton 1955).

SIGN Road casualties occur frequently in areas where the animal is common, especially in autumn when many young are killed. Often caught in traps set for grey squirrels, stoats, mink and rabbits. Footprints are rarely seen and may be confused with mink in areas where both species occur.

Droppings are a useful guide to presence, often found around farm buildings where polecats have taken up residence. When fresh they are usually black with much fur and fragments of small bones, but they tend to vary in colour according to the diet. Individual droppings can be up to 70 mm long and 5 mm wide, often twisted and with tapering ends. Mink droppings may be mistaken for polecat but almost always contain some small fish bones, never observed in polecat.

DESCRIPTION Typical mustelid build—long sinuous body, relatively short legs, blunt face and small, rounded ears. The distinctive white facial marks first appear about the ninth week of life, firstly as two white patches between the eyes and ears which elongate towards the jaw angle as the animal grows older. In autumn the patches elongate across the forehead, sometimes joining completely, more often separated by a grizzled area. Below they may join up with the patch beneath the chin; thus, a complete ring is sometimes present.

Juveniles have reached adult body dimensions by the autumn of the year in which they are born. Then they acquire a winter coat, dense buff wool over most of the body but dark grey over shoulders, rump, limbs and tail, and many guard hairs, each pigmented for only the distal half, giving a very light appearance to the body.

This coat is moulted in May–June when the animal reverts to the juvenile pattern of face patches, completely pigmented guard hairs and sparser wool. The sexes are alike except for size.

Dental formula

$$\frac{3\,.\,1\,.\,3\,.\,1}{3\,.\,1\,.\,3\,.\,2}$$

in the adult, preceded by

$$\frac{3\,.\,1\,.\,3}{3\,.\,1\,.\,3}$$

in the deciduous set which is replaced from the seventh week of life (Murr 1933 for ferret). A proportion of adult skulls have supernumerary teeth perhaps due to recent addition of ferret genes (Bateman 1970).

Juvenile skulls differ from adults in their pear-shaped cranium which results in them having a greater cranial capacity than adults; several measurements of breadth are greater in juveniles. The surface of the bone in the juvenile skull is rough and gritty to the touch with poorly developed crests and obvious sutures. By contrast, the adult skull has a smooth shiny appearance with marked crests and most of the sutures obliterated (Walton 1968a).

The stink-glands are paired spherical bodies about the size of large peas which secrete a foetid musk of creamy consistency. These glands open on to the perineum and the musk may be extruded deliberately when the animal is marking objects by 'setting scent'; or, apparently, as a reflex act if the animal is frightened or enraged.

Females in heat show an enlarged and engorged vulva. Nipples are difficult to locate in non-lactating animals: the maximum number appears to be about 10. In the male, the testes are evident externally from January to about July. There is a baculum (penis bone) whose weight and shape can be used to separate juveniles from adults from July through to January (Walton 1968c).

TABLE 29 Measurements of polecats in Britain

	Males			Females		
	Mean	Range	*n*	Mean	Range	*n*
Head and body (mm)	380	305–460	45	335	290–355	12
Tail (mm)	140		45	125		12
Hind foot (mm)	57		48	54		11
Weight (g)	987	502–1522	46	623	442–800	9
Condylobasal length of skull (mm)	67·0		31	60·4		7
Zygomatic breadth (mm)	41·4		25	34·8		7
Minimum frontal breadth (mm) (= post-orbital constriction)	16·5		31	15·8		7

MEASUREMENTS See Table 29. Minimum measurements included in the table are for animals that were very young but had, nevertheless, left the nest. The body weight shows seasonal variation, in males at least, being at a maximum in March. There is a marked sexual dimorphism, the males being considerably larger than the females.

DISTRIBUTION See Fig. 137. In Europe from the Atlantic coast to the Urals, north to south-east Norway, south Finland and Sweden, south to the Mediterranean and the Black Sea. Eastward it is replaced by the steppe-polecat, *M. eversmanni*, with considerable overlap in eastern Europe and European Russia.

Despite the much repeated statements of Cabrera (1932), does not appear to occur in Africa (Owen 1964). Introduced to New Zealand.

In Britain, widespread up to nineteenth century but gradually exterminated over most of country. Apparently never present in Ireland. Last records for Scotland in 1907 (Tetley 1939). Gone from north-west and south-west England by mid-1930's. Apparently always plentiful in mid-Wales and Herefordshire at least. Now present in all Welsh counties, except Anglesey, as well as Herefordshire, Gloucestershire and Shropshire as a result of expansion from mid-Wales in 1950's (Walton 1964, 1968b). Records from outside this area need checking carefully because of confusion with feral ferrets. Introductions and escapes from wildlife parks probable in future.

VARIATION Some average differences in dimensions between British and continental samples (Walton 1968a). A British sub-species, *angliae*, supposedly distinguishable from continental form by failure of the frontal band to turn completely white in winter (Pocock 1936) shown to be invalid (Poole 1964).

An erythristic variety occurs in Britain, the 'red polecat', in which the black pigment of the hairs is replaced by a reddish-brown one. Records of red polecats were collated by Matheson (1963). There does not appear

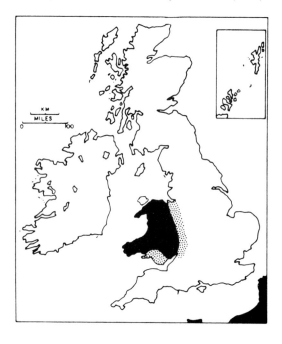

FIGURE 137 Polecat: distribution.

to be any mention of this variety from anywhere else in the polecat's range.

Flare-shaped extensions of the white chin patch on to the black of the throat are sometimes found, as are white tips to the normally black paws. Since these features are frequently seen in dark forms of the ferret it seems likely that they have been acquired from crossing in the wild with escaped ferrets. Only a small proportion of skins show these characters (Walton 1968a).

HABITAT In Britain occupies a variety of habitats, e.g. woodland, farmland, marsh, river banks, sand-dunes, forest plantations, generally in thinly populated areas. Often associated with farm buildings and houses on the edge of settlements. Less common on high ground in mountainous areas (although once recorded at 920 m), but frequents river valleys and lower ground. In Europe it occurs continuously in woodland and wooded steppe and sporadically in steppe; but human settlements and river valleys affect this distribution. Dense forest masses are not utilised; these form the northern and eastern boundaries (Heptner 1964). A recent decline in Denmark has been attributed to a loss of habitat by drainage (Jensen & Jensen 1972).

BEHAVIOUR Very poorly known in wild animals. Most observations made on captive animals.

Normally walk with the body almost level and the head low, sniffing at the ground. When moving at a pace faster than a walk the back is repeatedly arched giving a sinuous appearance to the gait. They climb rarely and avoid swimming.

Mainly active at night but many reports of polecats hunting during the day as well. Almost nothing known of home range, long distance movements or social structure in the wild. Fighting between wild polecats has been observed, possibly territorial between males as described for captive animals (Poole 1967).

Polecats make a variety of sounds whose function is little understood. Both young and old animals make chattering sounds in relaxed situations. Adults often scream when frightened or enraged.

The stink glands are used for setting scent on objects, presumably to mark territory as in other mustelids (Eibl-Eibesfeldt 1955).

Hearing and smell largely used in hunting. Eyesight in daytime not good but better at night.

FOOD Completely carnivorous, taking a wide variety of prey as available. In Britain this includes the brown hare, rabbit, voles, mice and hedgehog;

birds; common frog and lizard; and a variety of invertebrates including insect larvae and earthworms. The most frequently found were mammals and frogs. Presence of blowfly eggs and larvae suggests that some food is taken as carrion. Mammal prey is often in the form of several young animals, presumably from a nest (Walton 1968a). In Europe they are reported to eat fish as well (Ognev 1935).

Living mammalian prey is killed by a neck bite which is instinctive but only partly developed in young animals and must be perfected by practice (Eibl-Eibesfeldt 1955, 1956). See also Kratochvil (1952).

BREEDING Begin to breed in year following that of birth, with usually one litter of about 5–10 young per year.

Males become sexually mature at the beginning of the year following birth. They have abundant sperm present in the testes from March to May inclusive and some present for a month on either side of this period. Females begin to come into heat from about the end of March (Walton, 1968a). By contrast in north-west Russia according to Danilov & Rusakov (1969) polecats were found in spring 'which obviously were not taking part in multiplication'. It was concluded that 'some of the animals become sexually mature in the second year of life at the age of 22–23 months'.

Mating behaviour is quite vigorous, the male grasping the female by the neck and dragging her about (Eibl-Eibesfeldt 1955). Presumably this acts as a stimulus to ovulation, which is induced. Copulation is prolonged—up to an hour. Gestation takes about 42 days and is direct (Herter 1959).

Nothing is known of the period from impregnation to birth in wild polecats. Litters in nest occasionally found but usually next observed occurrence is the appearance of families of young polecats. Earliest recorded on 20 July estimated to be 60 days old, placing birth date in May. Regression of testes and finding of non-pregnant females in July/August suggest one annual litter is usual (Walton 1968a). No pregnant females found in this study but post-breeding animals had numbers of used nipples from 6–9. Number surviving to weaning less than this suggests.

Development of young polecats described by Habermehl & Röttcher (1967) (summarising several previous authors). At birth the young weigh 9–10 g and have a head and body length of 55–70 mm and tail length of 14–15 mm. Eyelids and ears closed. The eyes open at the beginning of the fifth week of life, at which time litter mates of both sexes are roughly equal in size. Subsequently males grow faster than females.

At birth young are covered with a fine, silky white hair. This is gradually replaced with a darker coat, except for the muzzle and ear-tips, during the third to fourth week of life. This new coat consists largely of under-fur giving the animal a woolly appearance; the sparse guard hairs are pigmented from tip to base making the coat appear dark.

The development of the milk teeth and their replacement is described in detail by Habermehl & Röttcher (1967).

POPULATION STRUCTURE Very little known. Life expectation of males at birth, from ratio of juveniles to adults after breeding, calculated as 8·1 months. High mortality of juveniles in first year of life occurs August to October. Adult sex ratio, found as 4 males to 1 female, must be heavily biassed due to behavioural differences (Walton 1968a). Some evidence, however, that males exceed females at birth (Herter 1959). Life spans of 8–10 and 14 years in captivity have been given by various authors but unlikely in the wild where 4–5 years seems more probable as upper limit.

Monthly fluctuations in numbers of animals recorded in Britain prob-ably influenced by changes in behaviour, e.g. females seem to become more secretive during the breeding season. On edge of range, e.g. Fin-land, numbers apparently much influenced by hard winters (Kalela 1940, 1948, 1952).

PREDATORS AND MORTALITY Polecats sometimes killed by dogs. Otherwise man is the chief predator. In Britain the proportion of animals killed by various means where the cause of death was known was found to be about 90% by road traffic and trapping, 10% by dogs, shooting, snares and other causes. Latter includes animals apparently diseased; and some poisoned by anti-coagulant poisons used against rats (perhaps secondary poisoning) (Walton 1968a).

PARASITES AND DISEASE No specific fleas; those found are stragglers from prey and other mammals, e.g. *Archaeopsylla erinacei*, *Nosopsyllus fasciatus* and others. About a quarter of a sample examined had ticks, mainly *Ixodes hexagonus*, but also some *I. canisuga* (Walton & Page 1970).

The cestode *Taenia tenuicollis* and the nematodes *Molineus patens* and *Skrjabingylus nasicola* were also found, the last being a parasite of the nasal and ethmoid sinuses (Lewis 1967). Abscesses of the head and jaw region have been recorded (Walton 1968a).

RELATIONS WITH MAN Long regarded as vermin and still trapped as such by many estates. Once hunted for sport with hounds, in Wales at least (Forrest 1907). Still hunted by sportsmen in Europe (e.g. Jensen & Jensen 1972, Kalela 1948). Large numbers once caught in Britain for fur trade. Ritchie (1920) gave details for Scotland. Several tens of thousands of pelts still imported annually into Britain for auction to the fur trade in various countries.

Takes well to captivity if captured when young. 'Polecats' in zoos and wildlife parks are usually hybrids with ferrets.

AUTHOR FOR THIS SPECIES K. C. Walton.

Ferret *Mustela furo*

Mustela furo Linnaeus, 1758; 'Africa'.

TAXONOMIC STATUS A domesticated form of rather complex status. It has been bred since Roman times at least (mentioned by Strabo in the first century BC). It is derived either from the polecat, *M. putorius*, with which it is fully interfertile, or from the steppe polecat, *M. eversmanni*, which it resembles most closely in the form of the skull. These two wild forms have been considered conspecific, but current opinion in eastern Europe and Russia, where their ranges appear to overlap, is that they are good species. In view of this uncertainty it is best to treat the domesticated ferret provisionally as if it were a distinct species. The situation is further complicated by the habit of producing 'fitch ferrets' or 'polecat ferrets' by crossing true ferrets with wild polecats. (See Fig. 136.)

RECOGNITION Darkest forms may be indistinguishable externally from polecat, but generally pelage is either albino or like that of polecat but lighter, with more extensive white on face and throat.

Skull has more distinct post-orbital constriction than in the polecat, minimum frontal breadth being usually less than 15 mm.

SIGN As polecat.

DESCRIPTION As polecat except for pelage and skull as described above under 'Recognition'. Chromosome number: $2n=40$ (Matthey, 1958).

DISTRIBUTION Since ferrets are widely kept, escaped animals may be encountered anywhere and make it difficult to detect well established feral populations. However, these appear to exist on the Isle of Man, Anglesey, in Renfrew and in parts of Yorkshire. Such a colony once existed on the island of Mull (Tetley 1945) and animals may still be there although 1951 was the last year that one was recorded. Other Scottish islands, however, seem to have thriving colonies, including

Lewis (Cuthbert, unpubl.), Arran (Gibson 1970b) and Bute (Gibson 1970a).

They are widespread in New Zealand.

VARIATION Feral populations very variable in pelage but little information available on whether long-standing colonies develop greater uniformity (but this has happened in New Zealand). Supernumerary teeth are not unusual.

HABITAT Little information. On Mull mainly in open moorland.

AUTHOR FOR THIS SPECIES K. C. Walton

FIGURE 138 Mink.

Mink *Mustela vison*

Mustela vison Schreber, 1777; eastern Canada.

RECOGNITION Medium-size mustelid, dark chocolate brown. Usually a white chin patch. Tail slightly bushy.

SIGN Footprints distinctive, with 5 claw marks; smaller than otter and more splayed than polecat or pine marten. Usually a tail drag, and hind-foot tracks in front of or superimposed on those of the front feet. Seen mainly by anglers, keepers and others frequenting rivers.

DESCRIPTION Dark brown, appearing almost black, in standard wild state. Dark guard hairs protrude through grey-brown underfur. White spots, patches and sometimes only a few white hairs at chin, throat and on ventral surface. In captivity mink have been bred in a variety of colours: Aleutian, Palomino, Pastel, Pearl, Platinum, Topaz, many shades of brown, dark, medium and pale greys, white, and white marked with black. Offspring of escaped mink vary in colour but most approximate to the wild type.

Dental formula

$$\frac{3.1.3.1}{3.1.3.2}.$$

Chromosomes: $2n = 30$ (Venge 1973).

MEASUREMENTS A male ranch mink may attain 3 kg but a male in the wild seldom exceeds 1·8 kg or 66 cm from nose to tail tip. Males are about twice the weight of females.

DISTRIBUTION See Fig. 139. N. America, spreading over most of Canada and USA except Arctic islands and south-west parts of USA, absent from Mexico. Kept on fur ranches in many parts of the world and escaped animals have built up wild populations, e.g. in Iceland, Norway, Sweden, Finland, Denmark and Britain. Since 1933, over 16 000 released in USSR, mainly east of the Urals (Pavlov 1970); large populations are now available for hunting and a total of 240 000 skins have been purchased.

In British Isles fur farms were first established in 1929; escaped animals living ferally were recorded from then onwards. Breeding in the wild was first noted in 1956 on the upper reaches of the river Teign in Devon. Mink are now known to be present almost throughout England,

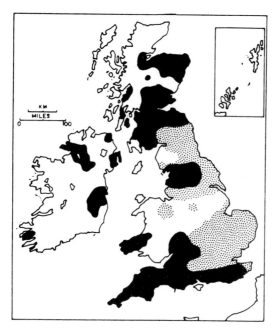

FIGURE 139 Mink: distribution.

Scotland and Wales (compared with 4 counties in England, 2 in Scotland and 1 in Wales in 1961). Similar history in Ireland, but still less widespread there.

VARIATION See under Description.

HABITAT Usually found near rivers and lakes and on marshes. When lakes freeze they seek open water and may live in tunnels beneath snow.

BEHAVIOUR Males mainly nocturnal at all seasons; their level of activity is directly related to increasing length of night and decreasing temperature (Gerell 1970). A female was found to be less active during pregnancy and much more active when suckling, when she was mainly diurnal. Radio-tagged mink ranged between 1 and 11 km. Mink tolerate most conditions of weather. They are more terrestrial than otters but swim well, having partly webbed feet, and climb with agility. They do not hibernate. They are very silent except during the mating season when both sexes make purring noises; shriek when alarmed.

FOOD Mink are facultative predators with catholic food habits; they eat what is freely available. In much of North America, and some parts of USSR, muskrats (*Ondatra zibethicus*) are abundant and a basic mink food. In Sweden there are seasonal variations of diet; crayfish (*Astacus astacus*) are eaten mostly in the summer, fish in winter and spring, birds most frequently during migration and breeding seasons, while rodents are a variable source of food owing to the marked fluctuations in their numbers. In Britain there is little doubt that birds, especially moorhen and coot, mammals such as young rabbits, voles and rats, and fish are the main constituents of mink food. The occasional predation on poultry and young game birds attracts public attention and it is rather surprising that freshwater fishery interests appear to have been relatively little disturbed by mink. Studies by Akande (1972) showed fish, especially Salmonidae, to be important in mink diet in Scotland, while Day & Linn (1972) found mammals and birds to be of greater importance in England and Wales.

BREEDING Domestic mink mate between late February and early April but under free-living conditions this may be affected by environmental factors. In captivity Stevenson (1959) recorded that first-year and older males become sexually active in February; females have some four oestrous cycles between late February and early April, each lasting 7–10 days. Ovulation occurs only after copulation (or artificial stimulus such as handling) but there is much variation in the interval before implanta-

FIGURE 140 Mink. (Photo: Ministry of Agriculture, Fisheries and Food)

tion, minimum period of 'gestation' being 39 days, average 45-52 days and maximum of 76 days recorded.

The normal litter is 5-6 but larger numbers (up to 17) found. Data for USA confirm (Enders 1952). Stevenson noted great consistency in ranch-living mink all over the world, breeding conditions being attained *c.* 100 days after shortest day on both sides of the equator. Pregnant wild mink have been found in Britain during April. Parties of adults with from 2 to 6 young have been seen in June, July and August. Dens have been found in tree trunks, holes and crevices among stones. The young are weaned after 8 weeks, attain adult size in about 4 months and can breed the following year.

POPULATION STRUCTURE Little known. Up to 1961 the total of wild mink known to be caught in Britain was 128; over 7000 catches were recorded during the decade 1961-70 and about a thousand a year have been caught subsequently; the population is still expanding its range.

PREDATORS AND MORTALITY There is interaction between mink and otter and Erlinge (1972) found an inverse correlation between densities of otter and mink in Sweden, attributed to habitat preference and specific interference. He inferred that otters may attack mink and referred to reports of mink remains in otter scats. In Britain man is main predator; otter hounds have killed some mink, especially in Devon and Cumbria.

RELATIONS WITH MAN Relatively easy to rear in captivity and high financial returns ensure popularity on fur farms.

The killing by mink of poultry, game birds and wild, domestic and ornamental waterfowl, tame pigeons, kittens and puppies causes concern periodically. The impact of mink on native fauna deserves more study, especially their interaction with some prey species such as the moorhen, potential competitors—otter, polecat and stoat—and predators such as the fox and buzzard.

LITERATURE Clark (1970): an account of mink in Yorkshire and Lancashire; Cuthbert (1973): origin and distribution in Scotland; Deane & O'Gorman (1969): origin and distribution in Ireland; Thompson (1971): a general account.

AUTHOR FOR THIS SPECIES H. V. Thompson.

SUBFAMILY MELINAE

GENUS *Meles*

The Palaearctic badger is the only member of this genus. Other badgers are very distinctive and are placed in separate genera—*Taxidea* (North America), *Arctonyx* and *Melogale* (South East Asia).

Badger *Meles meles*

Ursus meles Linnaeus 1758; Upsala, Sweden. *Meles taxus* Boddaert, 1785. *Meles meles britannicus* Satunin, 1906; England.
Brock, grey—pate, bawson, baget.

RECOGNITION Unlike any other British mammal in having a white head with a conspicuous dark stripe on either side which includes the eye region. Skull of adult has prominent interparietal ridge, prominent canines and flattened molars (see Fig. 142).

SIGN Sets easily recognised by the diameter of the tunnels—at least 20 cm (often much greater at the entrance) and the large spoil heaps outside in which hay, bracken or other plant debris is incorporated. (An earth dug by a fox contains no plant matter in the spoil heap.) Paths leading from a set are often well marked and may be followed for long distances; where they cross hedge banks they are very conspicuous. Hairs often get caught in the lowest strand of barbed wire where a badger path passes under it. Footprints typical, showing five toes and broad impression of fused plantar pads; the large claw-marks show up well in soft ground. Droppings are placed in shallow pits which are not covered after use. Pits are usually found near a set, but also occur at strategic places near the perimeter of the home range. Droppings looser than those of dog, but consistency depends on the food eaten; they always appear muddy when earthworms have been eaten. Beetle elytra and corn husks are conspicuous at certain seasons.

FIGURE 141 Badger.

DESCRIPTION Appears grey from a distance owing to the colour of the individual guard hairs which in dorsal and lateral regions are light at the base and tip with a dark patch between, near to the tip. Legs and underside of body are covered by uniformly dark hairs which are often very sparse on the ventral surface. The underfur is thick in winter and pale in colour. Hair colour shows a good deal of variation, the light areas ranging from white through cream to sandy yellow and the dark part from black through reddish brown to gingery (erythristic). Head white with conspicuous dark stripe on either side from the ears surrounding the eyes and ending 1 cm from nose. There is a single prolonged moult lasting most of the summer (Novikov 1956).

Snout is flexible and muscular, an aid to probing and digging. Eyes small, ears short and tipped with white. Body somewhat wedge-shaped, legs short and very powerful for digging. Feet digitigrade with five toes on each foot with specially large claws on the front feet.

Skull with prominent interparietal ridge which starts growth at 10 months, and may reach a height of 15 mm in old animals. Lower jaw articulates in such a way that in the adult dislocation is impossible without fracturing the skull.

Sexes difficult to distinguish, but typically the boar has a broader head, thicker neck and a rather pointed narrow white tail. The sow is sleeker and has a broader and greyer tail. However, the tail is not always a reliable distinguishing feature on its own. In the male the penis is forward and lies retracted in a pouch. The female has three pairs of nipples. Both sexes have musk glands just below the root of the tail.

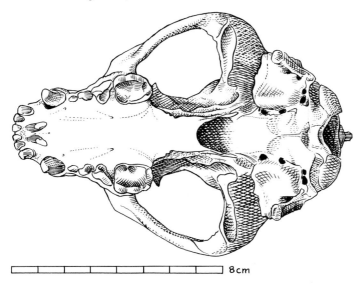

8 cm

FIGURE 142 Skull of badger. Note the large, flat-crowned and rectangular last molars.

Dental formula of the functional teeth

$$\frac{3.1.3.1}{3.1.3.2}$$

but an additional minute vestigial premolar (P_1) may occur just behind one or more of the canines; they are more usually found in the lower jaw. The dentition is well suited for an omnivorous diet: the incisors are small and chisel-like, the canines are prominent, there are no conspicuous carnassial teeth and the molars are considerably flattened for grinding. Deciduous teeth are

$$\frac{3.1.3}{3.1.3},$$

sometimes with additional first premolars as in the permanent dentition. The incisors are sometimes reduced in number and I_1 and I_2 often never penetrate the gums—an adaptation for suckling.

The gut is longer than that of the fox (intestine 5·18–5·22 m); there is no caecum.

MEASUREMENTS See Table 30. The wide range of weights is mainly due to the accumulation of fat in late summer and autumn giving maximum weights during the Oct.–Jan. period. Minimum weights occur in the period March–May when surplus fat has been used up. Greatest weight changes occur in adult sows probably because of the long lactation: September–February, average 12·2 kg (22), March–May, average 8·8 kg (25). Average weight attained by cubs in their first year, 8·9 kg (14).

TABLE 30 Measurements of badgers over one year old from South West England

	Males			Females		
	Mean	Range	n	Mean	Range	n
Head and body (mm)	753	686–803	31	724	673–787	31
Tail (mm)	150	127–178	31	150	114–190	31
Weight (kg)	11·6	9·1–16·7	33	10·1	6·5–13·9	84
Condylobasal length of skull (mm)						
(M. Hancox, unpubl.)	120	116–130	28	119	111–125	26

DISTRIBUTION See Fig. 143. Widely distributed throughout Europe including some of the Mediterranean islands and across Asia to Japan. The northern limit is roughly a line just south of the Arctic Circle and the southern limit, the Himalayas.

Present in every county in England, Wales and Ireland and in most of Scotland. In England, rarest in the flat lands of East Anglia and most common in the southern, south-western and western counties. Medium/ high densities occur in Yorkshire, Derbyshire and the more northern counties. In Wales they occur commonly in the south and west and in Denbighshire, but detailed information is lacking for mid-Wales. In Scotland they are widely distributed and fairly common in the southern counties with lower densities in the Highlands. Common in most parts of Ireland. Absent from islands round Britain except Anglesey and Wight.

Fossil remains go back in Britain approximately 250 000 years, but in

Europe they have been found in deposits from the Early Middle Pleistocene, possibly a million years ago (Kurtén 1968).

VARIATION Many sub-species have been named, but it is improbable
that more than ten are valid. These have been divided into two main
groups relating to Western and Eurasian complexes (Ognev 1931). There
appears to be a reduction in average size in island populations and towards
the north. Albinos occur sporadically.

HABITAT Badgers make their sets in a wide variety of places including
woodland, scrub, hedgerows, quarries, sea cliffs, moorland and open
fields, and occasionally in embankments, iron-age forts, mines, natural
caves, coal tips, rubbish dumps and under buildings. The Badger Survey
carried out by the Mammal Society (Neal 1972) showed that there was
a marked preference for deciduous woodland and copses (56%) and
hedgerows and scrub (13%), only 9% being in open fields. The favourable factors influencing choice were the presence of adequate cover, soil
which was well drained and easy to dig, little disturbance by man or his
animals, and a plentiful and varied food supply nearby at all seasons of
the year. The latter is assured where deciduous woodland, pasture and
arable occur within the home range. Low-lying marshy areas are avoided.
Breeding sets are known up to 590 m in Britain.

FIGURE 143 Badger:
distribution.

FIGURE 144 Badger: foraging. (Photo: Hans Kruuk)

BEHAVIOUR When on its travels a badger moves at an ambling trot, head down, with its hind quarters swaying from side to side; it pauses frequently to listen. When alarmed its pace is considerable. Badgers often clamber on tree trunks and occasionally climb trees gripping the bark like a bear. They swim efficiently, but usually avoid having to do so if possible.

Mainly crepuscular and noctural except in remote parts. Emergence from the set is usually around dusk, but this varies according to sex, age, season and environmental conditions such as light intensity and nearness to habitation. Factors discussed by Lloyd (1968). Emergence usually before dusk May–August, usually after dusk at other times. Emergence much less regular November–February. Times of emergence and return have been recorded mechanically (Moysey 1959). Winter activity reduced, especially in December, but no true hibernation. Can go without food for long periods and may remain below ground for many days at a time, but even in coldest spells some badgers are about.

Home range varies in extent according to the closely related factors of food supply and population density; tentative conclusions are that in good badger country it is in the order of 1 km² (Hancox, unpubl.). Feeding areas of neighbouring groups overlap somewhat. The perimeter of the home range is often marked by dung pits. There is evidence of more extensive movements, especially by boars in late winter and early spring.

The social structure is not known precisely, but several families often share the same home range and occupy collectively or separately the various sets within it. Little is known about hierarchy within the social group except that a dominant boar is present who will set upon and may badly maul strange badgers that intrude.

Sub-caudal glands secrete a yellowish oily liquid with a characteristic odour. Badgers of the same social group set scent on each other, on objects in the vicinity of the set, when travelling along regularly used routes and persistently when in unfamiliar country as a means of finding the way back. Anal glands are also present which secrete a very powerful musky odour as a result of fright or other emotion.

Communication by scent appears to be important for territory marking, for individual recognition (Burke 1963) and for detecting when sows are in oestrus. Vocal means of communication are also used.

Cubs make high-pitched whickering when tiny and loud squeals if danger threatens. When older they make 'puppy noises' when playing. Adults utter a deep growl of warning followed by a staccato bark if other animals approach too near when feeding. Sow makes a single note like the cry of a moorhen. At mating season the boar uses deep throaty 'purring' noises, and when excited they are prolonged and become higher in pitch. Sow uses a much quieter 'purring' noise when small cubs are near her. Screaming occurs especially between January and April. Its significance is still doubtful, but it may be territorial as it occurs more often in places of high population density.

The senses of smell and hearing are very acute, but eyesight is poor. Cubs are extremely short-sighted and adults use their eyes mainly for detecting movement.

The set is a complex labyrinth of tunnels and chambers, often with many entrances. Tunnels may go into a hillside up to 100 m, but typically 10–20 m; they may be at several levels. Plans of excavated tunnels were given by Likhachev (1956). The chambers are lined with heaps of bedding brought in on dry nights. Bedding may consist of grass, straw, bracken, leaves and moss. 20–30 bundles may be brought in on a single night. The collecting of bedding may occur at any time of year, but especially January–May and August–October. Periodically old bedding is discarded and in winter, bedding may be aired near the entrance on sunny mornings. Apart from using dung pits, defaecation may also occur below ground in side chambers.

FOOD Badgers are truly omnivorous, the diet depending upon availability. Animal matter includes many small mammals (especially their young) including rabbits, rats, mice, voles, shrews, moles and hedgehogs; amphibians, slugs, snails, earthworms, wasp grubs, beetles and other large insects. Poultry is taken occasionally, but not typically; lamb killing is extremely rare, but still-born lambs are taken occasionally. Carrion is eaten including dead birds, especially in winter.

Vegetable food includes underground storage organs of woodland plants, fruits of all kinds from windfall apples, pears and plums to acorns, hazel nuts, beech mast, bilberries, raspberries and blackberries. Green food, especially clover and grass (Bradbury, K., unpubl.) is eaten particularly in the winter. Corn, mainly oats and wheat, are important items of diet in some parts (Barker, G., unpubl.).

The most important single item of diet is the earthworm which is preferred to any other food when available. In south-west England 75% of stomach contents analysed contained earthworms and 65% nothing but earthworms.

Andersen (1955) concluded for Denmark that the major items of diet were oats (July–August), earthworms (most of the year but especially spring and autumn), amphibians (summer), bumble bees and wasps (July–August), small mammals, especially voles and shrews (May–July).

Skoog (1970) showed that badgers in Sweden had a very similar diet to those in Denmark, but in Sweden there was a lower frequency of shrews, insects and amphibians, while berries, especially bilberries and raspberries, were of much greater importance. Figures from Russia (Likhachev 1956) are very similar.

Badgers typically forage individually, although cubs after weaning may keep somewhere near their mother. Most prolonged foraging—up to 10 hours away from the set—occurs in the autumn (Moysey 1959). Pasture and arable mainly chosen for foraging on mild, damp nights because earthworms available.

BREEDING A single litter of usually 1–4 cubs is born each year, normally mid-January–mid-March.

The reproductive cycle is complex and unusual. In Britain mating may occur in every month from February–October but is not necessarily followed by fertilisation. The main mating period is February–May when copulation is prolonged (15 minutes or more); fertilisation usually occurs during this period. Copulation stimulates ovulation (Notini 1948). Mating also occurs quite commonly during the July–September period involving sows in which earlier matings have not resulted in fertilisation and younger females coming into oestrus for the first time. There is a long period of delay before implantation of the blastocyst (3–9 months). Implantation typically occurs in December. Short duration copulations (up to 2 minutes) may occur at any time throughout the mating season and it is possible for a sow during the period of delay to undergo periods of secondary oestrus when she will receive the male. These pairings may result in further ovulations and hence an increase in the number of corpora, but the original blastocysts persist and no further fertilisation takes place (Neal & Harrison 1958). Canivenc (1966) found that a post-parturient ovulation was normal in France and that fertilisation usually followed.

Cubs are usually born below ground. Litter size 1–5, the last being unusual; most reports of high numbers are due to two families living together. Data from embryos give average of 3·1 per litter; numbers deduced from observations on families seen above ground in south-west England averaged 2·3 (50 families)—9 singles, 23 twins, 11 triplets, 7 quadruplets.

Cubs remain below ground about 8 weeks. Weaning starts at about 12 weeks, but some suckling may continue up to 4 months. During weaning the sow regurgitates semi-digested food (Notini 1948, Ashby E., unpubl.). Cubs live with the sow at least until the autumn and often over the first winter. Female cubs usually mature in southern England when 12–15 months old—in captivity even earlier, suggesting that food is a factor. Male cubs are not usually mature until 2 years old.

POPULATION STRUCTURE Largest number of badgers in a single social group (not necessarily in a single set) occurs between May and September and could consist of adult males, adult females of which up to two may have cubs, female cubs of the previous year (probably mated) and, exceptionally, male cubs of the previous year. The total at this time of year may be as many as 15. Sex ratio approx. 1:1.

The population density in typical badger country commonly reaches 12 adults per 1000 ha, but in smaller areas where conditions are very favourable much higher densities are possible, e.g. 34 (Hancox 1973), 56 (Stirling & Harper 1969).

Sows normally breed every year, but there is some evidence that a season may be missed occasionally and possibly some sows may breed every other year (van Wijngaarden & Peppel 1964, Paget 1970).

Badgers probably live at least 15 years. A sow in captivity regularly came into oestrus up to the age of 14 (Murray 1970).

Mortality rates are greatest during the first 8 weeks of life when 26% loss has been recorded (Neal & Harrison 1958). Hancox (1973) has shown through a study of 140 skulls that high mortality also occurs during the few months following weaning and also during the second year, especially the period following the cubs' first winter. He calculated that only 35% survived their first three years, but having done so, the majority could then be expected to reach a good age.

PREDATORS AND MORTALITY Adults have few natural enemies in Britain apart from man. They may occasionally be killed by hounds, and territorial fights may sometimes result in death. It is not unusual for young cubs to be killed by dogs or by a jealous vixen; occasionally they may be killed by a boar badger.

PARASITES AND DISEASES External parasites include the louse, *Trichodectes melis* (very common); fleas, *Paracerus melis* (specific and very common), *Pulex irritans* (occasional) and *Chaetopsylla trichosa* (occasional); ticks, *Ixodes hexagonus* (common), *I. canisuga* (common), *I. ricinus* (occasional), *I. melicola* (rare) and *I. reduvius* (rare) (Arthur 1963, Thompson 1961).

Badgers also suffer from various diseases including anthrax, enteritis, tuberculosis, pneumonia, leptospirosis, osteomyelitis and rabies.

RELATIONS WITH MAN The badger is of little economic importance (Council for Nature 1972). With medium densities they do little harm and some good. In places of high density when near habitation poultry killing may sometimes be a nuisance especially in spring, but this is usually confined to individuals which acquire the habit. Rolling in corn and eating grain occur to a variable extent in different parts, but loss as a result is seldom enough to matter. Foresters welcome badgers as they destroy many small rodents, wasps' nests and other pests. They may force up wire netting round plantations and let rabbits in, but this problem can be solved by the introduction of badger gates (King 1958). Game bird eggs are occasionally eaten, but losses are insignificant. Vast numbers of birds are raised without trouble in many places where badgers are common.

Badger baiting, badger digging for sport, the gassing of badgers and any unauthorised killing or taking of badgers is now illegal (Badgers Act 1973). It is also an offence to keep them as pets if obtained after January 1974.

LITERATURE Neal (1948, 1977)—comprehensive monographs. Paget & Middleton (1974).

AUTHOR FOR THIS SPECIES E. G. Neal.

SUBFAMILY LUTRINAE

GENUS *Lutra*

Of the fifteen or so species of otters, constituting the subfamily Lutrinae, about half belong to the genus *Lutra*. These have a worldwide distribution and can be considered the typical, fish-eating river otters, contrasting with the clawless otters (*Aonyx* and *Amblonyx*) which feed on crabs and molluscs and the very distinctive sea otter (*Enhydra*). There is only one species in Britain and Europe.

FIGURE 145 Otter.

Otter *Lutra lutra*

Mustela lutra Linnaeus, 1758; Sweden. *Lutra vulgaris* Erxleben, 1777. *Lutra roensis* Ogilby, 1834; Roe Mills, near Newton Limavaddy, Londonderry, Ireland.

RECOGNITION In water, distinguishable from mink and aquatic rodents by large size, flattened head and long, tapering tail, very thick at base. A large V-wake is usually produced. Swimming movements are not jerky like those of aquatic rodents or mink.

Skull distinguishable from those of all other mustelids by large size, narrow post-orbital constriction and five upper cheek-teeth on each side

SIGN Footprints—'seals'—show four or five webbed toes on each foot, with claw marks; stride about 36 cm at walk, 50 cm at gallop and 80–100 cm when bounding. Droppings—'spraints'—deposited at regular places, often on top of prominent rock or scraped-up mound of soil or grass; black, mucilaginous and very musky when fresh; contain mostly scales and bones of fish and shells of molluscs and crustaceans. Regular feeding places recognisable by food remains; may also establish runways, hauling-out places, and rolling places (Erlinge 1967a).

DESCRIPTION Body elongate, legs short, head flat with small ears and broad muzzle with prominent whiskers. Tail long and tapering evenly from a thick base. Feet webbed, five digits on each. Pelage appears glossy when wet ('spiky' after animal has shaken itself). Dense underfur remains dry when animal is in water. Colour uniform brown except for paler throat. Only one extended moult per year (Novikov 1956). Scent glands situated at either side of the anus—described by Stubbe (1969). Mammae 2 or 3 pairs.
    Dental formula

$$\frac{3 \cdot 1 \cdot 4 \cdot 1}{3 \cdot 1 \cdot 4 \cdot 2}.$$

Wear on teeth not usually apparent until third year of life (Stubbe 1969). Articulation of skeleton allows sinuous movement and 'boneless' appearance. Full development of skull not until over 2 years old (Stubbe 1969). Jaw hinged to move in one plane only.

MEASUREMENTS See Table 31. Measurements of 95 Danish animals were given by Jensen (1964). Exceptional animals up to 23 kg and 180 cm have been recorded (Harris 1968).

DISTRIBUTION See Fig. 147. Entire Palaearctic Region wherever there is water, from Ireland to Japan and from Arctic coast to North Africa; also in Oriental Region as far as Ceylon and Java, overlapping with *Lutrogale perspicillata*, *Lutra sumatrana* and *Amblonyx cinerea*.

TABLE 31 Measurements of otters in Britain (from Stephens 1957). (Presumed adults only, over 4·5 kg)

	Males			Females		
	Mean	Range	*n*	Mean	Range	*n*
Total length (cm)	119	96–136	23	104	94–112	12
Tail (cm)	43	36–47	10	39	35–42	4
Weight (kg)	10·3	5·5–16·8	12	7·4	6·4–12·3	7

Widespread throughout Britain and Ireland, including all the small islands. Individuals may travel great distances, making local distribution difficult to study, but there is probably no longer a resident population in some of the more industrial areas of the English Midlands where pollution of rivers is severe (Anon. 1969).

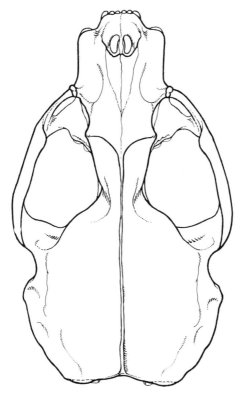

FIGURE 146 Skull of otter. The post-orbital waist in the adult is narrower than in the skull of any other British carnivore.

VARIATION Irish population can probably be recognised as a distinct subspecies (*L. l. roensis*) on the basis of darker colour, especially above, and lesser extent of white on the throat (Dadd 1970).

Occasional albinism occurs but melanism is very rare (Harris 1968).

HABITAT Lakes, rivers, streams, marshes, but capable of long overland journeys between watersheds. In coastal areas of western Britain, France and Scandinavia may alternate between marine and freshwater habitats (Duplaix-Hall 1971). Dependence on water makes otters vulnerable to interference from river control structures, human recreational activities, water pollution etc.

BEHAVIOUR On land move with typical mustelid bounding gait, rather heavy-footed but over short distances as fast as a man. In water, fore paws are used when swimming on the surface and in turning; under water swim by dorso-ventral flexion, top speed *c*. 10–12 km/h, and can travel at least 400 m under water without surfacing. Diving accompanied by brachycardia, duration of dive usually less than 1 minute but may be up to 4 minutes when alarmed (Duplaix-Hall unpubl.). Movement not impeded by snow or bad weather; habit of snow-sliding is well known. Often stands upright on hind-legs weasel-fashion (Harris 1968, pl. 15) and has been trained to dive head first from at least 3 m (Hurrell 1968).

Usually nocturnal, especially in disturbed habitats. Hurrell (1968) described automatic device used to record activity of wild otters. Lie up during day in burrows, drains, hollow trees and reedbeds.

Home range and movements calculated by Erlinge (1967a, 1968a) from snow-tracking in Sweden. Individual ranges well defined; size and location determined by topography and access to open water, also to lesser extent by food supply and population density. Male ranges *c*. 15 km diameter (*c*. 35–40 km circumference), female-with-young family groups

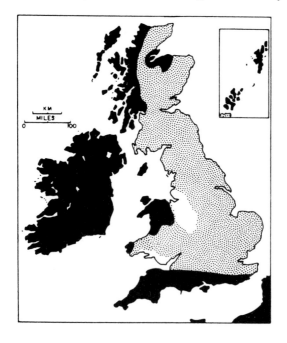

FIGURE 147 Otter: distribution.

c. 7 km diameter. Movements of adult males much influenced by presence and social status of neighbouring males. Distance travelled per night *c.* 3–4 km for family groups, increasing with growth of cubs; 9–10 km for adult males; very great variation on different nights. Travels follow recognisable patterns, visiting sprainting sites and favoured hunting areas more frequently than other areas and at regular intervals; also seasonal variation in extent of use of range. Territorial behaviour shown by signal activity and dispersion of individuals of same sex. Territories maintained by threatening signals and avoidance. Function in males mainly sexual, with conflict at overlapping zones; family groups occupy isolated areas, important as secure feeding areas. Cubs share mother's territory for about 12 months. No hibernation, but seasonal variation in activity; cover longer distances in spring and autumn than in summer and winter.

Mainly solitary, but definite hierarchy among resident males. Size and location of territory depends on position on scale; peripheral ground occupied by sub-dominant individuals. Females with cubs are avoided by other otters. Non-territorial males, and females without cubs, behave as temporary residents or transients (Erlinge 1968a). Behaviour patterns in captivity studied by Duplaix-Hall (1972a, 1972b, 1975).

Range of vocalisations noted, all except first known only from tame otters. Contact note, of adults, a short chirp or longer piercing whistle (*c.* 1 sec. duration); of cubs, piping and whickering; when apprehensive a drawn-out moan or low threatening growl; when startled, an explosive 'hah!'; in appeasement a low-pitched twitter (Harris 1968, Duplaix-Hall 1972b). Communication also by scent. Sprainting activity clearly correlated with territoriality and population density; intense scratching and signalling occurs at overlaps of adjacent ranges. One such boundary zone had 30–40 sprainting sites in regular use along 1 km stream, but at times of low density, previously well-used sites became overgrown with grass (Erlinge 1968a).

Hearing acute on land but ears (and nostrils) closed under water. Eyes remain open and vision below surface probably excellent. Vibrissae may assist hunting in clouded water.

FOOD Great controversy over alleged damage to fishing interests: most food studies undertaken to determine extent of feeding on game fish, especially Salmonidae, but general conclusion is that otters are unselective, catching fish in inverse proportion to their ability to escape (Erlinge 1968b, Ryder 1955). In certain circumstances large numbers of Salmonidae are taken, but these are usually very small specimens (Stephens 1957, Fairley & Wilson 1972) and otters probably live at too low a density to have any effect on numbers. Some authors have suggested that predation by otters may benefit trout by removing less desirable (usually slower-moving) competitive and 'noxious' fish (Ryder 1955) or by destroying eels which eat trout spawn (Harris 1968). In captivity, a young animal ate 5·5–9·0 kg of food per week (Stephens 1957). Table 32 summarises main results of food investigations. In coastal marshes in Norfolk stickle-backs were estimated to comprise 55% of the diet and eels 25% (Weir & Banister 1972). Literature (including field observations and scattered

TABLE 32 Analyses of the food of otters (percentage frequency of occurrence)

Locality Material Author	Britain 294 guts/scats Stephens (1957)	S. Sweden 14 615 scats Erlinge (1967b)	N. Ireland 74 scats Fairley & Wilson (1972)	W. Ireland 29 guts Fairley (1972)
Fish (general)	50	67		
Salmonids	21		81	14
Cyprinids	11		7	7
Sticklebacks	7			3
Eels	18		9	66
Percids	3		15	34
Pike			1	17
Amphibians	8	8	9	28
Crayfish	3	13		10
Birds	11	9	7	3
Mammals	10	1		
Insects	2	2		14
Worms				14

accounts) up to about 1966 collected and extensively quoted by Harris (1968).

In general, otters live almost entirely on fish, crustaceans and aquatic insects; diet may include small proportions of birds and mammals. Feeding patterns reflect availability and vulnerability of prey species, and so show marked local and seasonal variations: no preferences could be demonstrated and predation had no effect on fish or crayfish populations (Erlinge 1967b). Many minor food groups constitute fair proportion of total; small items also taken. Feeding habits of mink and otter overlap (by c. 60–70%), as both exploit most easily available prey; some competition for food in winter, but mink took more birds and mammals (24% and 10%) than otters (6% and 0·2%), and tend to take smaller fish—

30% of fish taken by otter exceeded maximum size taken by mink (Erlinge 1969, 1972). In coastal waters crabs and dogfish are taken.

Feeding behaviour of tame otters described by Stephens (1957), Harris (1968), Duplaix-Hall (1975) and, in wild, Rowbottom (1969); active hunters, seeking in mud and under stones, catching prey in the mouth but using front paws in subsequent handling. Remains of given food item begin to appear in scats *c.* 1 hour after ingestion (Liers 1951). Food is not stored. Adverse weather conditions (snow, freezing temperatures) do not affect foraging (Field 1970); tend to follow familiar routes, same on ice in winter as by water in summer, and to return regularly to favoured feeding places (Erlinge 1967a).

BREEDING Breeding occurs at any time of year without delayed implantation. (This contrasts with the North American otter in which delayed implantation is the rule.) In Britain 134 reports of cubs whose age could be estimated gave even distribution of births through all seasons (Stephens 1957). Similar in Sweden (Erlinge 1967a, 1968a) but late winter and early spring probably main rutting season, as in Germany (Stubbe 1969) and Denmark (Jensen 1964), since pairs most often observed travelling together then. Meeting of animals in heat presumably facilitated by sprainting signals. Limited data from Ireland indicate that males are fecund for at least greater part of year (Fairley 1972).

Gestation about 62 days (Stephens 1957, Stubbe 1969, Asdell 1964) but apparently no histological search has been made for delayed blasto-cysts. Most accounts give 2–3 young per litter, exceptionally 4 or 5 (Harris 1968). Born in 'holt' or breeding den lined with reeds, grass and moss, and reared (in wild) entirely be female. Family groups stay together for about a year, disbanding in spring or summer (Erlinge 1967a); hence possibility that females breed only every second year, at least in Sweden (Erlinge 1968a). Female usually stated to breed first at 2 years old (e.g. Erlinge 1968a) but mature at $1\frac{1}{2}$ years according to Stubbe (1969). Sex ratio of young 1 : 1. Orphan cubs have often been brought up in captivity (Stephens 1957), but breeding of captive European otters is less common (Wayre 1972).

At birth young are mouse-grey, finely furred or velvety, blind, tooth-less, *c.* 15 cm long and squeak loudly. They crawl at 12–19 days, open eyes at 31–34 days, eat solid food at 49 days though still suckling at 69 days. First enter water about 72 days. (Records of two litters bred in captivity—Wayre 1972.) Weights at 36 days, 647 g and 591 g (females) and 1·54 kg (male); at 75 days the two females were 998 g and 716 g. Stephens gave growth curves for 2 cubs (male and female) for 15 months;

male grew from 1·4 kg to 7·7 kg and was still apparently increasing, the female from 0·9 kg to 5·4 kg. Females have been observed teaching young to swim at 2–3 months old when adult waterproof coat has been grown (Harris 1968). Permanent molars begin to erupt at about 8 weeks (Neal 1962).

POPULATION STRUCTURE Recognition of young animals has been based upon the baculum (Jensen 1964), the shape of the skull, which does not reach its mature form until about two years, and tooth wear (Stubbe 1969). Relative proportions of categories vary according to classification method. In living otters in wild, Erlinge (1968a) estimated young of the year at 25–38% of total in different years. Estimates of proportion under 2 years old range in different populations from 32–41% (Bree 1968) to 73% (Stubbe 1969). Variation probably due to use of different techniques or trap selection. Notable that as expected, proportion of young generally low by comparison with smaller mustelids. Expectation of life in captivity up to 20 years in North American otter.

Varied diet, plentiful prey and long life expectancy indicate population likely to be fairly stable. Hunting figures from Britain and Continent (at least, until recently) confirm this. Density never high; in Britain normal considered 1 per 10 km of stream; in southern Sweden, in optimum habitat, 1 per 4–5 km stream, or 1 per km² or less (Erlinge 1968a). Hunting records show populations stable this century up to 1957, although they have decreased considerably since then in some areas especially in the south and west: in north-west England and Scotland numbers changed little and otters still considered plentiful (Anon. 1969). Likewise in Ireland (Fairley 1972). Recently slight increases in some areas reported, considered due to improved control of pesticide pollution of river water.

MORTALITY No predators in Britain other than man. Have been accidentally drowned in nets, lobster pots and coypu traps, and are shot by fishing interests. Little indication of causes of natural mortality. Much influenced by water pollution and interference from people engaged in aquatic sports, also river control schemes. Decrease after severe winter of 1962–63 reported. Otter hunters report no significant decrease due to culling between 1900 and 1937 (Anon 1969).

PARASITES AND DISEASE The biting louse *Lutridia exilis* is specific to otters and occurs in Britain. Ticks are frequent, e.g. *Ixodes ricinus*. Endoparasites were listed by Stephens (1957). In captivity otters have been reported to suffer from dental abscesses, canine distemper and pneumonia (Harris 1968, Duplaix-Hall 1972a, 1975).

RELATIONS WITH MAN Formerly killed for fur and to protect fishing interests, but low density ensures that neither value of fur nor damage to fishing is commercially important in Britain. Otter hunting with hounds is carried out, with about twelve hunts covering most of England, Wales and southern Scotland. Statistics of finds and kills were given by Hewer (1974).

LITERATURE Harris (1968): a detailed compilation dealing with all species of otters and with a very extensive bibliography. Stephens (1957): the most comprehensive account of otters in Britain.

AUTHOR FOR THIS SPECIES C. M. King.

FAMILY FELIDAE

The cat family, comprising the 'big cats' in the genus *Panthera*, the cheetah (*Acinonyx jubatus*), and the 'small cats' (including however the puma), which are variously classified in a single genus *Felis* or in a number of separate genera. Cats are characterised especially by their powerful paws with retractile claws and very short muzzles with reduced number of cheek-teeth. Dental formula

$$\frac{3.1.2\text{--}3.1}{3.1.2.\ \ 1}$$

GENUS *Felis*

In its most restricted sense includes about four species of cats in Eurasia and Africa but many more are frequently included. The domestic cat was derived from *F. silvestris*, probably originally from the North African race *F. s. lybica*. More or less feral cats of domestic origin occur throughout the country and must have an important impact on the ecology of other mammals but very little has been recorded about them.

Wild cat *Felis silvestris*

Felis (*Catus*) *silvestris* Schreber, 1777; Germany. *Felis grampia* Miller, 1907; Invermoriston district, Inverness, Scotland.

RECOGNITION Typically larger than domestic cat and with crossstriped coat; short, thick, bushy tail with blunt black tip.

FIGURE 148 Wild cat (top) and domestic cat (bottom). Note the bushy, truncated tail of the wild cat. Some domestic tabbies are completely striped but most show some blotchy markings as shown here.

SIGN Footprints circular with three-lobed pad-mark and four toe-marks, the same as domestic cat, only larger. Droppings compact, cylindrical, about 15 mm in diameter and 40–80 mm long, having pointed ends and with few large bone fragments. Not generally buried, in contrast to the domestic cat. Kills of larger mammals and birds are neatly defleshed with few broken bones. Rarely seen by daylight.

DESCRIPTION There would be no problem in identifying wild cats were it not for the fact that feral domestic cats tend to revert to the tabby form. Diagnostic differences between the two have been described in detail by

Suminski (1962) from a study of wild, domestic and North African cats. The basic coat colour of wild cats is buff/grey. On this there are black or grey stripes, running across the body, sometimes broken up into irregular blotches. They meet in the middle to form a longitudinal, dorsal stripe which does not extend into the tail. Four narrow stripes run between the ears and on to the forehead, four or five thicker transverse stripes across the legs. The hair on the tail is thick and long, giving it a typical blunt, round-ended appearance. The tip is black and there are from three to five complete rings in front of it. The tail is less than half

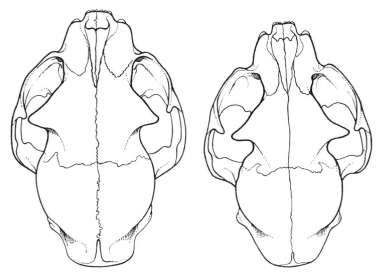

FIGURE 149 Skulls of wild cat (left) and domestic cat (right).

the head/body length. There are often white patches on the throat and between the hind legs, and black spots on the belly.

The commonest form of tabby has a blotched coat with broad dark markings. Striped tabbies generally have more stripes than a typical wild cat, particularly on the legs. The dorsal stripe extends into the tail and fuses with the black tail bands, which are thicker and more numerous. The tail is long in proportion to the body and tapers to a point. White patches are common, particularly on the feet. The basic colour of the coat is more variable, and the fur is shorter and sleeker than in a wild cat.

Skull larger and more robust than that of the domestic cat, with a number of distinctions in detail. The clearest of these are in the structure of the frontal region. In the wild cat the medial junction of the nasals and frontals is in one plane, whereas in the domestic cat it is in a pit, and the hindmost tips of the nasals in the wild cat project further back relative to the ends of the maxillae than in the domestic cat. Wild cat skulls are also completely separable from those of domestic cats by an index of cranial volume and overall length (Schauenberg 1969). The gut of the domestic cat is longer than that of the wild cat, over 200 cm as compared with 150 cm or less (Haltenorth 1957).

Both sexes and juveniles have the same markings. Females are on average smaller than males but can be distinguished only by the external genitalia. Moult undescribed.

Tooth formula:

$$\frac{3 . 1 . 3 . 1}{3 . 1 . 2 . 1},$$

with the first upper premolars vestigial, sometimes absent, and typical cat development of the canines and carnassials. Basic anatomy the same as the domestic cat.

Chromosomes: not known. However domestic cat and all other Northern Hemisphere cats so far examined have $2n = 38$.

MEASUREMENTS See Table 33. These are considerably smaller than the published figures for German specimens, but similar as regards weight to French wild cats (Condé & Schauenberg 1971). Condylobasal length about 92 mm for males and 89 for females.

TABLE 33 Measurements of Scottish wild cats

	Kirk & Wagstaffe (1943) 1919–1939 102 males	Author's data 1958–1973	
		26 males	16 females
Head and body	589 mm (365–653)	564 mm (515–650)	543 mm (507–595)
Tail	315 mm (210–342)	307 mm (235–356)	293 mm (240–360)
Hind feet	138 mm (127–147)	134 mm (115–147)	126 mm (105–140)
Weight	5·1 kg (3·0–6·9)	4·7 kg (3·5–7·1)	3·9 kg (2·5–5·6)

DISTRIBUTION See Fig. 150. From British Isles eastwards through central and southern Europe to Asia Minor and Caucasus. Some recent authors have followed Haltenorth (1953) in including what were originally considered as a number of separate species of North Hemisphere cats as variants of the one species and in this sense the distribution includes much of Africa, central Asia and China.

Formerly found throughout Britain but not Ireland. Deforestation and persecution have reduced its range and it is now restricted to the Scottish Highlands. The last recorded wild cat in the Borders was killed in 1849, and within 25 years it was virtually extinct in all areas of Scotland south of the Great Glen (Ritchie 1920). However after World War I it started to increase in numbers and began to extend its range. Wild cats were firmly re-established in Argyll, Perth and West Aberdeenshire by 1946 (Taylor 1946) and in Moray, Nairn and Angus by 1960 (Jenkins 1962). Increase and movement into Banffshire from 1930 onwards has been documented by Hewson (1967). More recently there have been records from south of the Highland boundary (Corbet 1971) and the species is probably now re-establishing itself in the Border area.

VARIATION The British subspecies, *F. s. grampia*, was distinguished from central European *F. s. silvestris* by darker general colour and more pronounced black markings. However these characters were considered to separate some of the southern European races, and are also variable within the Scottish population. Description of the normal variation within the population is considerably confused by hybridisation of wild cats with feral domestic cats. Suminski (1962) drew up an extensive list of colouring and cranial characters from which he attempted to measure

FIGURE 150 Wild cat: distribution.

the proportion of characters in a specimen that are typical wild cat as against those that have come in from hybridisation. From an examination of 35 skulls he stated that the average Scottish wild cat is 66% pure, as compared to an average for Europe of 63% (the highest degree of purity being in cats from Poland—73%, and the lowest from the Swiss and French Alps—44%). Hybridisation may also be indicated by a reduction in the size of wild cats as suggested by a comparison of older measurements with modern ones (Table 33). On a comparison of limb bones Ritchie (1920) suggested that wild cats in Neolithic times were considerably larger than those in Scotland at present, but this is probably part of a more general evolutionary trend (Kurtén 1965).

HABITAT High woodland, the border of forested and hill ground and grouse moors, but mainly below 500 m in Scotland. In Germany winters in dense woodland and uses it as a refuge in summer (de Leuw 1957). Not found above 2000 m in Europe, and only secondarily driven into mountainous ground as a result of persecution (Haltenorth 1953).

BEHAVIOUR Most of this section taken from de Leuw (1957). Hunt either solitarily or as a pair. Home range 60 to 70 ha, defended by male, organised into system of tracks, resting places and claw sharpening trees. Latter may be method of marking range by secretion from foot glands, in addition to droppings and urine. In hard winters and during rut activity may extend beyond range.

Activity nocturnal with peaks at dusk and dawn but also controlled by weather since they tend to lie up during rain. Usually move about on ground but can climb and swim well. In sunshine frequently lie out in favourite places basking and in summer will hunt during day. Most frequently seen during autumn when they hunt hard and lay up fat for winter.

Hunting often organised in circuit, moving around areas where food is abundant. Method is by stalking or lying in wait and leaping on prey. Vision and hearing keen; scent subordinate. Large prey usually have head torn off and may be left with only brains eaten. Smaller prey often taken off to store, though more often eaten where killed. Domestic cats' habit of bringing back live prey and playing with it unknown in wild cat.

Usual call a short 'mau'; deep growl when angry. When at ease or bringing food to kittens a penetrating purr. Screams noisily. Dens made among rocks, under tree stumps, and occasionally in large birds' nests.

FOOD Of 18 stomachs examined from North East Scotland, 14 contained lagomorph remains (both rabbit and mountain hare included), 5 small rodents (wood mice and field voles) and 4 birds (Hewson & Kolb unpubl.). It is probable that in West and North West Scotland rodents feature to a greater extent in the diet. All European food studies so far published show small rodents to be the main food. For instance Condé *et al.* (1972) found that 92% of stomachs of French wild cats contained voles and 25% mice.

BREEDING In captive animals the period of sexual activity in the male ranges from the end of December to the end of June (Condé & Schauenberg 1969). The female comes into oestrus in the British Isles in the first half of March (Matthews 1941) and is receptive for 5 to 6 days (Condé & Schauenberg). Haltenorth (1957) gave period of gestation as 63 days, and Condé & Schauenberg as 66 days, compared with 58 days for the domestic cat. Most litters are born in May. Haltenorth stated that it is typical of the species for there to be only one litter per year, but Matthews has reported a second litter in August, and possibly even a third in the autumn for Scottish wild cats, and two litters in a year have also been reported for French cats by Condé & Schauenberg. However this may be the result of hybridisation. The most frequent litter size is 4, but it can vary from 1 to 8 (Condé & Schauenberg). Sex ratio in litters is equal, but not known for adult population. Trapped samples show a strong bias towards males.

At 4 to 5 weeks kittens emerge and play with mother; at 10 to 12 weeks they go out hunting with her and the den is frequently moved near to hunting grounds. Weaned at *c.* 4 months and family breaks up at 5 months (Lindemann 1955). At 10 months they are fully grown though further slight growth is made up to 2 years. Sexual maturity attained the year after birth.

POPULATION STRUCTURE Practically nothing known. Matthews (1941) examined a sample of 25 of which 5 were juveniles (unfused epiphyses), 9 'sub-adults' (partly fused epiphyses) and 11 adults, and suggested heavy juvenile mortality. The mortality rate of young in zoos is high, many dying between 2 and 4 months (Condé & Schauenberg 1969). De Leuw (1957) noted corpses found in hard weather, presumably from starvation.

RELATIONS WITH MAN Regarded as vermin, particularly on grouse moors, and an appreciable number killed each year during fox control operations, though killing is much less severe than during the nineteenth century. Has been kept and bred in a number of zoos, and also as a household pet, but even when tamed young remain intractable.

LITERATURE Two monographs in German on taxonomy and habits: Haltenorth (1953) and de Leuw (1957). No recent, detailed accounts in English.

AUTHOR FOR THIS SPECIES H. H. Kolb.

Order Pinnipedia
Seals etc.

BY W. N. BONNER

The seals and their relatives constitute a very clearly definable group that is sometimes included as a suborder in the order Carnivora, but is more often in recent classifications treated as a distinct order. There are three families: Otariidae, including the fur seals and sea-lions, not found in British waters; Phocidae, the true seals; and Odobenidae, including the walrus. Only two species of seal are regularly found in British waters but four others, and the walrus, are occasional vagrants from the Arctic.

All pinnipedes are carnivorous. They are highly adapted to aquatic life, the hind limbs being modified as propulsive flippers, but they come ashore (or on to ice) to give birth.

FAMILY PHOCIDAE
SEALS

Seals have the body streamlined and elongated, without a pronounced neck-constriction, covered in short coarse hair with very sparse or no underfur. The young are typically born in woolly natal coat differing in colour from adults. Hind limbs principal means of propulsion in sea, but not used on land; all digits bearing claws, but more pronounced on fore limb. Head often described as dog-like; external ear pinna very small and almost invisible; post-canine teeth typically multicuspidate.

Two sub-families: Phocinae, northern seals, comprising genera *Phoca*, *Halichoerus*, *Cystophora* and *Erignathus* (Burns & Fay 1970), all of which have been recorded from British waters, circumboreal in Arctic, Atlantic and Pacific Oceans with some adjacent seas and lakes; and Monachinae, Antarctic seals of Southern Ocean, monk seals of Mediterranean, Caribbean and Hawaiian seas, and elephant seals of sub-Antarctic and western North America.

The two species resident in Britain belong to different genera but can be difficult to distinguish in the water. The differences are detailed in Table 34.

The vagrant species are distinctive as adults but juveniles are much

TABLE 34 Identification of common and grey seals

	Common seal *Phoca vitulina*	Grey seal *Halichoerus grypus*
Size (nose to tip of flipper)	Up to 1·7 m	Up to 2·45 m
Spots	Small and numerous	Larger and fewer
Head	Small, crown rounded, concave 'bridge' between nose and forehead	Large, crown rather flat, no 'bridge'
Nostrils	Form V, touching below	Parallel and separated below
Post-canine teeth	Clearly tricuspid	Single-cusped, or with additional rudimentary cusps

more difficult to identify and are the ones most likely to wander south into British waters—see under the individual species for their characteristics.

GENUS *Phoca*

In addition to *P. vitulina*, the common seal, this genus includes *P. largha* from the north-west Pacific and three further taxa which have sometimes been regarded as of generic rank. These are *P. fasciata*, also known as *Histriophoca fasciata*, from the Bering Sea and Sea of Okhotsk; *P. groenlandica*, also known as *Pagophilus groenlandicus*, from the North Atlantic and Arctic seas; and *P. hispida*, also known as *Pusa hispida*, circumpolar from southern ice-edge to pole and in Baltic Sea, together with the closely allied forms *P. sibirica*, from Lake Baikal, and *P. caspica*, from the Caspian Sea. *P. groenlandica* and *P. hispida* have been reported from British coasts and are dealt with under 'Vagrant Seals' (p. 403).

Common seal *Phoca vitulina*

Phoca vitulina Linnaeus, 1758; Gulf of Bothnia, Baltic.
Spotted seal; sand seal; selchie (selkie) (Northern Isles); black seal, tangfish (obsolete, Shetland); harbour (harbor) seal (usual in North America); ranger (Newfoundland and usual in fur-trade). Both species of seals are called selchie or selkie in northern Scotland.

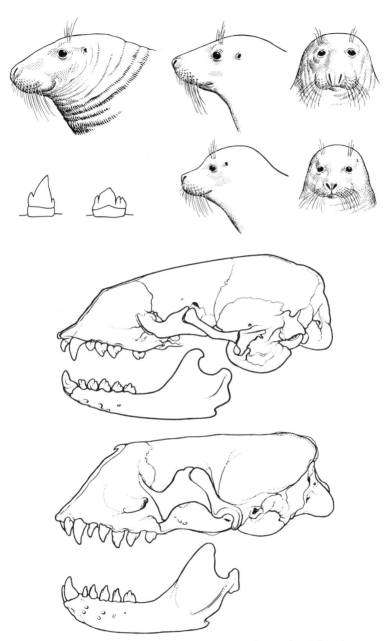

FIGURE 151 Heads of (top) grey seal (bull on left, cow in centre) and (lower) common seal. Note the concave forehead and closely adjacent nostrils in the common seal. Also lower post-canine teeth of grey seal (left) and common seal (right). Skulls of grey seal (lower) and common seal (upper). Not to same scale: condylobasal lengths; grey seal c. 270 mm, common seal c. 230 mm.

RECOGNITION Difficult to distinguish from grey seal, particularly in water (Fig. 151). When hauled out often adopt characteristic 'head up–tail up' attitude. Colour black to grey to sandy-brown, though animals may appear white to silvery at a distance when dry; spots small and numerous; head small in relation to body (cf. grey seal) and top of head rounded; nostrils at V angle and almost touching below (Wynne-Edwards 1954) (Fig. 151).

Post-canine teeth (except 1st) much longer than broad and clearly tricuspid, posterior cusps often subdivided; interorbital region of skull slender; palate anteriorly flat.

SIGN On suitable substrates leave clear tracks (Fig. 154), width variable, adults 55–75 cm, pups 30–45 cm. New-born pups leave scratch marks from long nails. Generally defaecate in water but droppings sometimes found on sandbanks, more rarely on rocks; dog-like, irregularly rounded, 2–3 cm diameter, brown or rarely grey. Occasionally fish bones or shell fragments recognisable. Have been known to vomit up small fish (e.g. sand eels) at basking places.

DESCRIPTION Colour and pattern very variable. Basically a mottle of dark spots on a lighter ground; in dorsal region spots coalesce to give a pale interrupted reticulation on a dark ground; there may be a black dorsal stripe. Coat fades to a brownish tinge prior to moult in late summer. Males generally darker than females. Pups born in first adult pelage, very rarely in white foetal coat.

Adult males distinguished from females only by heavier build, particularly in neck region where scarring may be apparent. Sex of juveniles indistinguishable in field.

Fore limbs paddle or wing-like; digits 1 and 2 subequal, others shorter in order, all digits bound together in common integuments, nails present on all. Hind limb fan-like, digits 1 and 5 subequal, 2, 3 and 4 shorter; joined by interdigital webs.

Two nipples present in both sexes. Testes inguinal, penile aperture inconspicuous. In female, vulva and anus in common furrow, hence easy to confuse sexes on cursory inspection. Ovaries ovulate alternately; uterus bicornuate, vaginal orifice internal, connected to vulva by a urogenital sinus.

Teeth

$$i\,\frac{3}{2}\,c\,\frac{1}{1}\,pc\,\frac{5}{5}.$$

Milk teeth usually resorbed or discarded before birth and permanent dentition erupted at, or shortly after, birth. Cheek teeth much longer

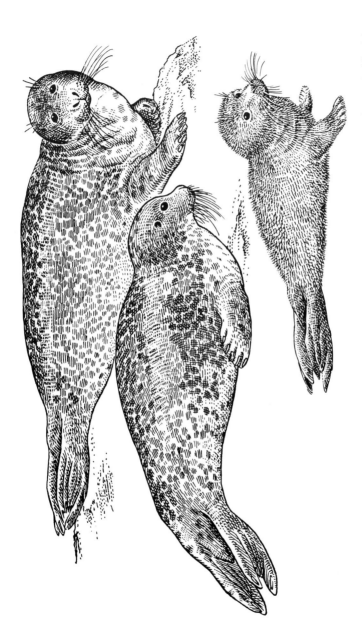

TABLE 35 Measurements of common seals

	Males			Females	
	Range	n		Range	n
Nose to tail	130–161 cm	26		120–155 cm	26
Nose to tip of flippers	150–185 cm			140–175 cm	
Weight	55–105 kg	22		45–87·5 kg	19
Length at birth			70–97 cm		
Weight at birth			9–11 kg		

than broad and set obliquely in jaw. Anterior part of palate shallow, posterior palatal foramen enters palate on maxilla, posterior border of palate ⌒ shaped. Tendency for lacunae to be present in basioccipital and exoccipitals. Nasals extend beyond posterior margin of maxillae.

Chromosomes: $2n = 32$ (material from Alaska, described by Fay *et al.* 1967).

MEASUREMENTS See Table 35.

DISTRIBUTION See Fig. 153. Coasts of North Pacific and North Atlantic. In Europe found around the coast of Iceland (Hook 1961), where

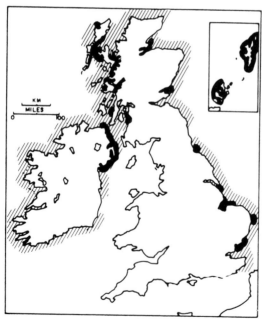

FIGURE 153 Common seal: distribution. Breeding areas shown in black. Ireland poorly recorded; probably breeding areas on west coast.

Arnlaugsson (1973) estimated 28 000 seals; in Norway south from Fin-mark, population about 4000 in early 1960's (Øynes 1964, 1966), now probably far less; sparsely in Baltic south of Stockholm, more abundantly in Denmark and German Frisian coast (1250 in 1974, Summers *et al.* in press); in Netherlands, Wadden Sea 1450 in 1968, 500 in 1974 (Sum-mers *et al.* in press); Rhine Delta, about 100. Sporadic occurrence on Channel coast and Biscay to as far south as Portugal (King 1964).

In British Isles largest single colony in Wash, numbering about 5500–6600 (Bonner 1976); smaller groups on sandbanks off East Anglia, Lin-colnshire and in Humber Estuary. Very occasionally seen as vagrants in south coast estuaries. On Scottish east coast in Firths of Forth, Tay, Dornoch and Moray, population unknown but probably not more than 850–1050. Shetland had population of about 1800 in 1971 (Bonner *et al.* 1973) and Orkney about 2800. Many small groups on west coast of Scot-land and Hebrides, probably minimum of 2600 seals in this area. Total for Great Britain about 13 000–16 400.

In Ireland 1250 estimated by Lockley (1966a), majority on shallow eastern and north-east coast; Venables & Venables (1960) recorded about 350 in Northern Ireland. Breeding probably more widespread than shown in Fig. 153.

VARIATION Pups from Wash have much paler coats than those from Scotland. Skins from Wash may entirely lack spotting on ventral surface (Dunbar (1949) pointed out a similar difference in *P. vitulina* pups from Arctic and maritime Canada.)

HABITAT Generally in shallow, sheltered waters, sea lochs and around island archipelagos. The characteristic seal of sandbanks, mud-banks and estuaries (e.g. Wash, Abertay Sands). In such situations use banks that allow immediate access to deep water for ease of escape. Haul out at highest point and follow water as tide recedes, leaving characteristic tracks. May occur in very large groups, up to 300 (rarely 500). In Shetland, Orkney, Western Isles off west coast of Scotland found on shores of small islands (e.g. Holm of Elsness, Orkney; Hascosay, Shetland); in remote sea lochs (Loch Teacuis, Argyll); or isolated skerries (Ve Skerries Shetland). Rarely in groups larger than 20–40 (exception—Mousa in Shetland where more than 100 may be seen together on occasion).

At Scroby Sands (Norfolk) mixed haul-outs of common and grey seals occur. In other regions where both species occur together haul-outs usu-ally separate.

BEHAVIOUR Locomotion in sea by side-to-side sweeps of hind flippers;

FIGURE 154 Aerial view of common seals on a sandbank in the Wash. Note the tracks
left in the sand. (Photo: Seals Research Division, IMER)

fore limbs used only for manœuvring or very slow progression, as in all
Phocidae. Common seals frequently 'porpoise', jumping repeatedly clear
of water, significance possibly sexual display. On land move by characteristic body-hitching, with forelimbs on ground, hind limbs trailing or held
together and lifted clear of ground. Can hitch forward with fore limbs
folded against sides or may progress in this way with one flank against
ground.

   Largely sedentary with individuals returning to same rock or bank day
after day; may move to other sites in bad weather. Juveniles range more
widely; recoveries of Wash-tagged pups in France, Belgium and Holland
(Bonner & Witthames 1974). Extent of feeding range unknown; no
known migratory movements. No obvious social system but gregarious

nature implies some interaction. Reports of dominant males keeping watch over hauled-out groups unsubstantiated.

Very silent seals, but grunts and low moans as well as coughing occasionally heard. Pups call to mothers with high-pitched 'waa-waa'. Scent characteristic, but not so marked as that of grey seal. Diurnal, feed during daylight high tides (Havinga 1933) but in Shetland low-water haul out, high water feeding irrespective of daylight (Venables & Venables 1955). Adults dive 7–30 min, pups less (Harrison, pers. comm.).

Vision good in both air and water but, because accommodation in air requires a stenopaic pupil, vision less effective in low light intensities in air (Walls 1942, Jamieson & Fisher 1972). As sensitive to waterborne sound as terrestrial mammals to airborne sound; sensitivity not as good in air as in water but still quite good; auditory range to 180 KHz; directional hearing in both media (Møhl 1968). Sense of smell acute.

FOOD Predominantly fish. Gadoids were most abundant fish type from stomachs taken in Scotland (Rae 1968). Flounders constituted 30%, whiting 17% and herring 17% by weight in seals from Dutch waters (Havinga 1933). Sergeant (1951) reported 92% by weight of molluscs, mainly whelks, in stomachs from Wash, but this may be misleading (Bonner 1972). Young seals may eat considerable quantities of shrimps. Daily

FIGURE 155 Common seals in the water. Note the short muzzle and closely approximated nostrils. (Photo: Seals Research Division, IMER)

food requirement not known but estimated at 5–8 kg/day for adults. Large fish brought to the surface to be broken up and swallowed. Often seen eating salmon or sea trout in this manner. May attack fish trapped in nets (herring, salmon especially). Occasionally take birds (ducks, gulls).

BREEDING No observable social organisation during breeding season. Monogamous or promiscuous. Adult females bear single young each year in midsummer (twin foetuses reported by Rae 1969). Birth season: Wash,

FIGURE 156 Common seal cow and pup. (Photo: Seals Research Division, IMER)

mid-June to 7 July; Shetland, 14 June to 5 July (Venables & Venables 1955); Orkney, early June to mid-July. Early pups (e.g. May) known for all areas. Birth takes place on temporarily exposed sandbanks, rocks or weed-covered shores, sometimes in water. Pup can swim and dive efficiently from birth; closely attended by mother who will allow pup to climb on her shoulders when tired, or will push it beneath surface when danger threatens. Cows suckle either on land or in water. Lactation 4–6 weeks, data scanty. No special segregation of breeding and non-breeding animals or males and females during pupping season. No observed territoriality but cows defend area around pup when ashore (J. F. Watkins pers. comm.).

Pupping followed by moult in August or early September when first copulation seen in Shetland. Venables & Venables (1957) record only fully-moulted seals seen pairing. Harrison (1963) reported copulation in the Wash in late July or early August, before moult of majority of seals. This observation not repeated, but copulation below water surface difficult to detect in estuarine environment.

Implantation of blastocyst delayed, duration of delay not established, but implantation probably in November–December. Venables & Venables (1955, 1957) recorded sexual play sometimes resulting in copulation during May and June in Shetland and speculated it might involve young or subadult animals.

POPULATION Little information for British seals. Harrison (1960) suggested sexual maturity reached later than age 3, more likely 5–6. Bigg (1969), with British Columbian *P. vitulina*, found 20% females mature at 2, 38% at 3, 34% at 4 and 8% at 5; males between 3 and 6, mostly 5; 80% of females age 2–7 pregnant and 97% of older females. Sex ratio approximately unity. Longevity; males about 20, females about 30 years.

PREDATORS Many records (but not from British waters) of common seals found in stomachs of killer whales, but not likely to be a significant controlling factor. No other known naturally occurring predators.

PARASITES AND DISEASE The louse *Echinophthirius horridus* is widespread and may occur in astonishingly large numbers. Lung worms *Otostrongylus circumlitus* and *Parafilaroides gymnurus* are frequent and recognised as a serious cause of mortality in Netherlands seals. Heartworms *Skrjabinaria spirocauda* also occur. Microfilaria in blood may be associated with these worms. Stomach nematodes *Contracaecum osculatum* and *Terranova* (*Porrocaeum*) *decipiens* are almost universal (for a further discussion of the latter species see p. 402 (Grey seal—Relations with man)). Acanthocephalan worm *Corynosoma strumosum* found in posterior part of ileum and large intestine. Cestodes, mostly *Diphyllobothrium* spp., and trematodes recorded from both gut and liver (see Bonner 1972). An epizootic occurred in Shetland in the 1920's (Bonner 1972) but no bacteriology has been described.

RELATIONS WITH MAN Locally regarded as a pest of fisheries, particularly in relation to set nets (Rae 1960). Less of a problem than the grey seal. Several commercial salmon fishing companies pay bounties for the killing of common seals at their nets. Local hunting for skins in Shetland (Tickell 1970, Bonner *et al.* 1973), Orkney, west coast of Scotland and some Scottish east coast estuaries. Larger scale hunting in Wash where an average of about 550 pups taken annually in last decade.

Protected in a close season from 1 June to 31 August by Conservation of Seals Act 1970 in Great Britain, during which period seals can be killed only under licence. Unprotected in Northern Ireland or the Irish Republic.

GENUS *Halichoerus*

This genus contains only the grey seal.

Grey seal *Halichoerus grypus*

Phoca grypus Fabricius, 1791; Greenland.
Atlantic seal; great seal, ron mor (Gaelic); haaf-fish (obsolete, Shetland); horse head (Canada).

RECOGNITION Colour very variable and not useful as field character. Spots, when distinguishable, larger and less numerous than in common seal. Head large and muzzle high, giving a 'Roman nose' or equine appearance to face; top of head flattish. Head shape of young grey seals similar to that of common seals. Nostrils almost parallel and separated below (Wynne-Edwards 1954) (Fig. 151).

Postcanine teeth large, usually with single conical cusp; secondary cusps when present insignificant. Interorbital region of skull wide, snout high, so that axis of nasals approximately parallel to tooth row. Anterior part of palate deeply concave.

SIGN Droppings dog-like, 4–4·5 cm diameter, brown or sometimes putty-coloured. Regular hauling rocks may show traces of shed hair, particularly in spring. Characteristic odour. Rarely occur on sandy beaches but when they do leave tracks similar to those of common seal, but wider.

DESCRIPTION Marked sexual dimorphism. Apart from generally darker tone of back, which shades into lighter belly (more noticeable in cows) there are two tones in colour pattern, a lighter and darker. In males the darker tone is more extensive, forming a continuous back-ground with lighter patches; in females lighter tone continuous with darker patches (Hewer & Backhouse 1959). Colour may vary from almost black (in some bulls) to almost uniform fawn (in yearlings near moult). A reddish or orange coloration of head, neck, belly and flippers occurs in animals from Hebrides (Hook 1960, Backhouse & Hewer 1960). Cows moult

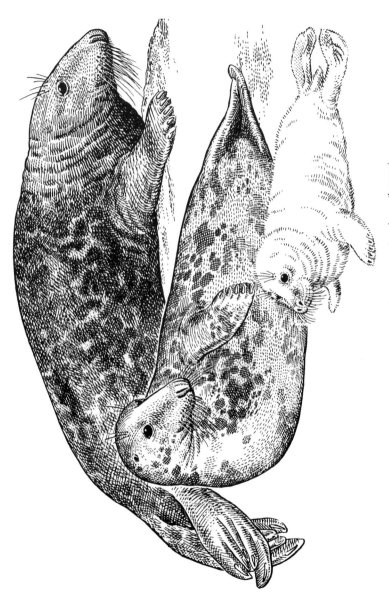

FIGURE 157 Grey seals: bull (top), cow (centre) and pup (bottom).

FIGURE 158 Bull grey seal. Note the long muzzle and straight profile. (Photo: Seals Research Division, IMER)

January to March, bulls March to May. Pups born in white natal fur, shed in 2–3 weeks. Next moult after about 15 months. Melanistic moulted pups occur at Farne Islands, less frequently Orkney, Hebrides, North Rona, Pembrokeshire.

Adult male much larger than female, with heavy neck and shoulders always showing much scarring. Bull profile convex, muzzle wide and heavy; cow profile flat, muzzle more slender (Fig. 158).

Other characters much as common seal, but note long slender claws on fore flipper of grey seal.

Teeth

$$i\,\frac{3}{2}\ c\,\frac{1}{1}\ pc\,\frac{5}{5}\ (often\ \frac{6}{5}).$$

Milk teeth shed before birth and permanent dentition erupts shortly after. Postcanines large and strong, some nearly circular in cross-section, each with single conical cusp (Fig. 151); secondary cusps usually only on 5th upper and 4th or 5th lower pc, insignificant; 1st upper pc pushed medially out of line in old animals. Posterior margin of palate evenly rounded, posterior palatal foramen opens on palatines, anterior part of palate strongly concave. Posterior margin of nasals approximately level with that of maxilla. Interorbital region wide. Most striking feature of cranium is elevated frontonasal region and very wide nasal openings.

MEASUREMENTS See Table 36.

TABLE 36 Measurements of grey seals

	Males				Females			
	Range	Mean	s.d.	*n*	Range	Mean	s.d.	*n*
Nose to tail (cm)	195–230	207·3	9·5	25	165–195	179·6	7·4	25
Nose to tip of flippers (cm)	210–245				195–220			
Weight (kg)	170–310	233·0	37·6	25	105–186	154·6	24·1	25
Length at birth (cm)				90–105				
Weight at birth (kg)				14·5				

DISTRIBUTION Reviewed by Smith (1966). Population estimates mostly very approximate. Confined to North Atlantic Ocean, North Sea and Baltic Sea. In west found in Gulf of St Lawrence, coasts of Newfoundland and Nova Scotia, with northern limit at Hebron in Labrador and southern at Nantucket. In north-eastern Atlantic round Iceland and Faroes (3000–6000); in Norway from Møre northwards to North Cape (2000); small group (1000–2000) on Murman coast; very small group (20) in Brittany; majority (about 46 000) round coasts of British Isles (see below for details). In Baltic population probably not exceeding 5000 ice-

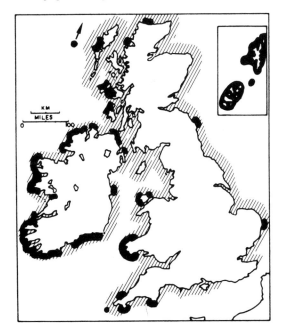

FIGURE 159 Grey seal: distribution. Black: breeding colonies; cross-hatched: other occurrence. Arrow indicates breeding colony in N. Rona. (just off map)

breeding grey seals. Previously in Denmark but now extinct as breeding species.

Breeding distribution in Britain and Ireland as follows (most totals derived from pup-counts $\times 3.5$). Scilly Isles, Cornish coasts, Pembrokeshire (particularly Ramsey), Cardigan coast, Caernarvon coast, Bardsey, Anglesey, Isle of Man (south west group 2800–3150); Hebrides, both Inner and Outer, particularly Monachs, Shillay and Gasker (20 475); North Rona (8000–9000); Orkney (12 600); Shetland (3000); Scottish north and east coasts (350); Farne Islands, Northumberland (5800); small groups in Humber, Wash and at Scroby Sands, Norfolk (200).

Ireland; Clare Island, Great Saltee, Lambay Island and probably elsewhere on west and south-west coasts (1000).

HABITAT The typical seal of exposed rocky coasts and caves, but now also found in many other localities including estuaries (e.g. Welsh Dee) and at sand banks (e.g. Scroby Sands). Largest breeding aggregations on offshore islands (e.g. Farne Islands) where seals may spread over entire top of island (e.g. Gasker) or ascend to considerable heights (e.g. 80 m at North Rona). Smaller groups in sheltered coves (e.g. Holm of Fara, Orkney) or on fringing beaches (e.g. South Ronaldsay, Orkney); very small groups often in sea caves (e.g. north Cornish coast and west coast of Ireland). Breeding areas rarely used by non-breeding assemblies which are most often on tidal rocks or reefs. Both breeding and non-breeding haul-outs may number several hundred animals.

BEHAVIOUR Locomotion as common seal but not seen to porpoise and makes more use of foreflippers when clambering over rocks.

Less sedentary than common seal with dispersal from breeding sites once season over (but less marked at Farne Islands and in sparsely populated areas). Evidence from branded animals of return to rookery of birth for breeding. Experienced breeding females may return to same spot year after year. Wide dispersal of pups from birth sites (e.g. Rona-marked pups recovered in Iceland, Ireland, Shetland; Farne-marked pups from Faroes, Minch, Norway, Denmark and Holland; Ramsey-marked pups from Biscay coast). No known migratory movements, but a general drift back to breeding sites in late summer. Extensive coastal wanderings often undertaken by young animals, e.g. along southern coast of England where breeding does not occur.

Social organisation confined to breeding animals.

Characteristically vocal, particularly females. Pups make high bleat when hungry, hiss and snarl when frightened; cows hiss, hoot and snarl, bulls similar but much deeper and can produce throbbing note from back of throat. Most vocal in breeding season but non-breeding groups often produce musical moans audible at some distance. Scent very character-istic and clings to regular hauling sites.

Feeding rhythm matched to tides. Activity at breeding sites same day and night, except in Pembrokeshire where cows leave beaches at night and join bulls in sea.

Senses probably as common seal but few data. Many records of blind grey seals in good condition so can evidently hunt without use of eyes (vibrissae perhaps important tactile receptors). Make much use of olfac-tory sense in identifying pups or investigating unfamiliar situations.

FOOD Like common seal a generalised fish-feeder. Rae (1968) found fish in 90% of stomachs with identifiable food; gadoids and salmonids most important groups and predation at salmon nets an important economic factor. Perhaps tend to eat larger fish than common seal, and flat fish and herrings less important. Grey seals eat considerable quantities of cephalopods, rarely found in common seals. Occasionally take birds swimming on surface of sea. Daily food requirement estimated at 7·5–12·5 kg/day, though probably do not feed every day. Individual seal seen to kill 13 salmon in 1 hour but to eat only part of them (Rae 1960). Neither sex feeds whilst breeding, cows fast about 3 weeks, bulls perhaps twice as long.

BREEDING Over most of the range form polygynous breeding aggrega-tions with definite social organisation. In Baltic Sea and Gulf of St Law-rence may breed in small family groups on ice but elsewhere on land. In British Isles cows produce single pup (twin foetuses reported by Rae 1969) in September–October (November at Farne Islands; December at Scroby Sands). Spring pups between March and May reported from Pembroke (Backhouse & Hewer 1957) and Cornwall; not known else-where in British Isles.

Prebreeding assembly usually in groups of separate sexes though with bulls predominating, at breeding grounds or nearby haul-out sites. Bulls acquire territory either on land or in sea bordering breeding beach. Cows enter territory but are not actively gathered by bulls. No special site selec-tion for births, but usually above high-water mark, less often between tide marks. Pups fed at 5–6 hour intervals for 16–21 days, average weight increases 1·8 kg/day (Coulson 1959). Milk contains 67% solids, 53% fat (Matthews 1950). Pups weigh 14 kg at birth and reach 41–45 kg (up to 54·5 kg) at weaning. Apart from feeding, little maternal care and cows readily desert pups. Pup recognition depends on topographical position, voice and scent.

FIGURE 160 Grey seal pups in breeding colony, Orkney. (Photo: Seals Research Division, IMER)

System breaks down on disturbance and cows may feed pups not their own, but doubtful if these thrive (Fogden 1971). Oestrous cows mated by bulls in whose territories they are. After matings, cows desert pups. Hickling (1962) described precopulatory behaviour, but overt courtship not usual. Cow may be mated several times by one or more bulls. At big rookeries such as North Rona bull may have average of 7·5 cows (Anderson *et al.* 1975), maximum 20. Bulls remain at breeding sites for up to 8 weeks. Many differences in breeding behaviour, largely related to topography (Hewer 1960, Fogden 1971).

Suspension of development (delay of implantation) of 102 days; attachment of embryo between 10 February and 4 March for Orkney and Shetland seals (Hewer & Backhouse 1968). Occasional sexual activity in spring (not to be explained by failure to delay implantation) noted in Pembrokeshire (Backhouse & Hewer 1957, Backhouse 1960).

POPULATION About half females sexually mature at age 4, rest at age 5 (but up to 9 in some crowded colonies, Platt *et al.* 1974); males sexually mature at 6, socially mature at 8–10 (Hewer 1964). Males rarely exceed 20, females 35, but can reach 46 years (Bonner 1971). Sex ratio at birth unity but males predominate early in breeding season, females later (Coulson & Hickling 1961). Mortality of pups on breeding grounds mainly from desertion and subsequent starvation, reaching over 20% at North Rona and Farne Islands, locally as high as 35%. Perhaps 60% of all pups born in crowded rookeries fail to reach age 1. Causes of adult mortality not known. Grey seals have increased very markedly in last half century in British Isles. Farne island population, for example, nearly doubled in decade 1960–70 (Bonner & Hickling 1971); Hebrides also show increase at similar rate. Many islets deserted by man, e.g. St Kilda, now used as breeding sites. Grey seals in Canadian waters also increasing. Perhaps associated with lessening of pressure from human hunters.

FIGURE 161 Grey seal cow and 2-day old pup. (Photo: Seals Research Division, IMER)

PREDATORS Killer whales seen to attack grey seals but reaction of seals to killers varies from panic to indifference. Owing to rarity of killers unlikely to be important controlling factor. No other known naturally occurring predators.

PARASITES AND DISEASE Probably essentially similar to common seal. Louse *Echinophthirius horridus* less common, as is lungworm *Otostrongylus circumlitus*. Mite *Orthohalarachne halichoeri* common on nasal mucosa and in trachea (Hewer, pers. comm.). Nematodes *Contracaecum osculatum*, *Terranova decipiens* and *Anisakis simplex* nearly always found in stomach (see below). List of Acanthocephala, Cestoda and Trematoda in Bonner (1971). Variety of organisms isolated from infected pups including *Pasturella multocida*, *P. haemolytica*, *Escherichia coli*, *Corynebacterium* sp., *Neisseria* sp., *Pseudomonas aeruginosa*, *Staphylococcus albus* and alpha- and beta-haemolytic streptococci. Perhaps many of these normally present as commensals (Bonner 1970). Uterine carcinoma reported (Mawdesley-Thomas & Bonner 1971).

RELATIONS WITH MAN Grey seals are a serious pest to fisheries, particularly when salmon are taken in set nets as on the east coast of Scotland from Caithness to the Tweed. Some netsmen maintain a rifleman to shoot seals at nets. Previously salmon kelts packed with strychnine were used for poisoning seals but this is now illegal. Seals eat salmon trapped in nets and also catch and eat wild salmon. From 5–15% of Scottish coastal salmon catch bear claw-marks attributed to grey seals (Rae & Shearer 1965). Gill nets set for cod, ground nets set for cod, lythe, saithe and hake, and long lines set for cod, are also affected by seal predation, particularly grey seals.

Besides direct damage to fish and gear, seals present another fisheries problem. The nematode *Terranova decipiens*, whose adult stage lives in the stomach of both grey and common seals, has its final larval stage ('cod-worm') in gadoid fish. Increase in proportion of wormy cod has been correlated with increasing numbers of grey seals (Rae 1968). Although cod-worm not known to be capable of affecting man, and certain to be destroyed by cooking, the presence of worms in fish may prejudice the public against cod as a food. Another nematode from seals, *Anisakis simplex*, has larvae which infest herrings. This worm is found also in porpoises and other cetaceans. Ingestion by man of raw or lightly-cured fish containing the larvae of *Anisakis* may result in the larvae penetrating the gastric or intestinal mucosa causing inflamed lesions and producing the zoonosis known as anisakiasis (van Thiel 1962).

In an attempt to reduce damage to fisheries Department of Agriculture

& Fisheries for Scotland authorised in 1961 the killing of 750 grey seal pups per year in Orkney to try to reduce total population there by 25% of its 1961 value. So far (1975), little effect on breeding population. Similar culls of pups in Farne Islands in mid-1960's. Orkney pup crop taken by licensed private hunters who sell the skins. Not as good quality as common seal pup skins and market uncertain. Some pups taken in Shetland and Hebrides by skin hunters. In 1972 owners of Farne Islands killed 600 adult cows and 130 bulls in attempt to lessen damage to soil and vegetation of islands by seals and improve the general condition of the seals during breeding season (Bonner & Hickling 1974). A further cull was carried out in the autumn of 1975.

Grey seals protected in Great Britain during a close season from 1 September to 31 December by Conservation of Seals Act 1970, and for same period by Grey Seal Protection Act 1932 in Northern Ireland. During close season seals can be killed only under licence. Unprotected in Irish Republic.

LITERATURE For accounts of both species see Hewer (1974), Matthews (1952) and Lockley (1966b); Bonner (1972) for review and Bonner (1976) for stock structure; Hickling (1962) for grey seals at Farne Islands.

VAGRANT SEALS

Ringed seal *Phoca hispida*

Phoca hispida Schreber, 1775; Greenland and Labrador. *Pusa hispida*.

This is a circumboreal species found from near the ice-edge to the pole, in the Baltic and in some fresh-water lakes. Occasional records from Scotland (e.g. Aberdeen Bay, 1901), but possibly more frequent in Shetland where a skin was obtained in the mid-1960's.

Adults 135–140 cm nose to tail, 90 kg weight, little difference between the sexes. Very similar in shape and colouring to common seal, but perhaps generally darker. Ground colour pale grey with numerous black spots; many spots surrounded by ring-shaped lighter areas but on back the dark spots may run together. (Common seals may also occasionally show ring-markings.)

Dentition weaker than in common seal and mandibular teeth always aligned with axis of jaw; inner side of mandible between middle postcanines concave (cf. common seal, where convex).

FIGURE 162 Vagrant pinnipedes: (a) ringed seal, (b) harp seal, (c) hooded seal, (d) bearded seal (e) walrus. Note that these are all adults—young animals are less distinctive. Not in same scale.

Ringed seals produce their pups in snow lairs from March to April. They feed on a variety of pelagic crustaceans and small fish.

Harp seal *Phoca groenlandica*

Phoca groenlandica Erxleben, 1777; Greenland and Newfoundland. *Pagophilus groenlandicus.*

The harp seal is a highly migratory species being nowhere resident the whole year. There are three breeding regions: (1) off the north-east coast of Newfoundland and in the Gulf of St Lawrence; (2) in the Greenland Sea around Jan Mayen; (3) in the White Sea. Breeding occurs in spring and in the summer the seals migrate, those from the first region moving to the west Greenland coast and the Canadian eastern Arctic; those from Jan Mayen moving to the east Greenland coast and the seas west of Svalbard; while those breeding in the White Sea move to around Novaya Zemlya. There are occasional records from Scotland and two adults were taken in the Severn in 1836. The reduction of the Jan Mayen stock (which might be expected to provide the British vagrants) has probably lessened the chance of further records.

Adults of both sexes 183 cm nose to tail, 181 kg weight. Easily recognisable by dark face and broad dark band starting on shoulders, dividing and spreading over flanks to form two roughly harp-shaped patches (whence name). In males the ground colour is nearly white and the band nearly black; in females there is much less contrast. Juvenile animals (and some adults) are covered with dark spots or blotches.

Harp seals breed on ice floes in the pack. They feed on pelagic Crustacea such as *Thysanoessa* and *Themisto* and fish, notably capelin (*Mallotus*).

GENUS *Erignathus*

Bearded seal *Erignathus barbatus*

Phoca barbata Erxleben, 1777; North Atlantic Ocean.

This is a circumboreal species usually found in shallow waters on the European, Asiatic and North American coasts and associated islands. It is not a migratory seal. Isolated stragglers have been reported from Scotland, Norfolk (1892) and the northern coast of France.

Adult male 285 cm nose to tail, 397 kg; female slightly smaller. Colour mostly uniform grey but brownish on top of head and down middle of back. Third digit on fore flipper slightly longer than the others, giving a square-ended appearance to the flipper (Canadian name—'square-flipper'). Very numerous mystacial vibrissae (hence vernacular and Latin names). Four nipples distinguish the bearded seal from all other seals, except the monk seals.

Dentition very weak. Teeth in adults loose-rooted and may be worn down or entirely missing. Post-canines widely spaced.

Bearded seals produce their young on ice-floes in April or May. They feed on bottom-living organisms, particularly molluscs.

GENUS *Cystophora*

Hooded seal *Cystophora cristata*

Phoca cristata Erxleben, 1777; Southern Greenland and Newfoundland.

The hooded seal is usually found in heavy ice in deep waters of the Arctic regions of the Atlantic. Occasional stragglers reach the British Isles, one being recorded as far south as the River Orwell in Suffolk.

Adult males 350 cm nose to tail, 410 kg; females 300 cm. Ground colour grey but lighter on sides and belly. Many light spots scattered over body, often coalescing to form pale rings round larger patches on back. Females generally less strongly marked than males. Well-developed claws are present on all digits. In male there is a nasal crest or hood on the top of the head which can be inflated to form a conspicuous bladder.

Dentition distinguishable from all other seals which might be found in British waters by presence of only one incisor on each side of the lower jaw. Post-canines peg-like and widely spaced.

Hooded seals produce their pups in March and April. They feed on a variety of fish and molluscs.

FAMILY ODOBENIDAE

GENUS *Odobenus*

Walrus *Odobenus rosmarus*

Phoca rosmarus Linnaeus, 1758; Arctic Ocean.

The walrus is found in shallow water round Arctic coasts. The nearest breeding stock in the European Arctic is at Svalbard (Spitsbergen) where walruses are now increasing again. There are many records of the walrus in the British Isles (perhaps because it is so easily recognised), ranging from one seen in the Thames in 1456 to one on the shore at Aberdeen in 1954.

The walrus is unmistakable and a description perhaps superfluous. Adult males 365 cm nose to tail, 1270 kg; females 300 cm, 850 kg. Skin greyish or reddish, nearly naked in old animals but covered with short brown hair in young ones. See Fig. 162 (e).

Dentition unique. The upper canines form a pair of massive tusks (more slender in females), while the remaining teeth (upper: incisor 3 and 3 post-canines; lower: canine and 3 post-canines) all reduced to flattened pads of dentine.

The young are born in May, usually on sea-ice. The food of the walrus consists mainly of clams, which are excavated from the sea-bottom at depths of up to 40 fathoms. Some walrus adopt a habit of feeding on ringed and young hooded seals.

ACKNOWLEDGEMENTS Many people assisted with this section on pinnipedes. In particular I should like to thank K. M. Backhouse, R. W. Burton, S. C. L. Fogden, R. J. Harrison, the late H. R. Hewer, Grace Hickling, the late Oliver Hock, C. F. Summers, R. W. Vaughan, L. S. V. Venables and J. F. Watkins.

Order Perissodactyla

The 'odd-toed ungulates', i.e. the horses, rhinoceroses and tapirs. No wild representatives in the British Isles at present or during the historic period, but the early history of horses in Britain is somewhat controversial.

FAMILY EQUIDAE

GENUS *Equus*

Horse *Equus*

Wild horses were present in Britain during the last glaciation and as late as the Boreal phase of the post-glacial period (i.e. around 7000–10 000 years ago), but there is no good evidence that they survived beyond that time. Domesticated horses have been present since the Neolithic period (about 5000 years ago).

There are no truly feral populations at present. Several primitive breeds live in a semi-wild state, e.g. in the New Forest (Hampshire), Dartmoor and Exmoor (Devon), Wales, the Lake District, Northumberland, Shetland, the Hebrides and western Ireland. It is frequently claimed that some or all of these are the direct descendants of indigenous wild horses but there is no evidence to support this and they are much more likely to be descended from domesticated stock brought to Britain at any time since the Neolithic period.

Order Artiodactyla
Even-toed ungulates

This order includes the great majority of the large, herbivorous mammals of the world, amounting to about 160 species. All are predominantly terrestrial and cursorial, with long slender legs. (Even the one that least fits that description, the hippopotamus, nevertheless comes ashore to feed and can produce a fair turn of speed.) The main common feature is the structure of the feet—the 2nd and 3rd digits are equally developed, with the axis of the leg passing between and the remaining digits are reduced to a variable degree. In other respects they are very diverse and three suborders are recognised: Suiformes, containing the pigs, peccaries and hippopotamuses; Tylopoda, containing the camels and llamas; and Ruminantia, containing the great majority of species, namely the giraffes, deer, cattle, antelopes etc. Only the last is now represented in Britain but the Suiformes need mention to deal with the extinct wild boar.

Suborder Suiformes

FAMILY SUIDAE

GENUS *Sus*

Wild boar *Sus scrofa*

Sus scrofa Linnaeus, 1758; Germany.
Extinct in Britain.

The wild boar was formerly widespread in Britain, but has never occurred in Ireland. It became extinct in England during the seventeenth century. Subsequent attempts at reintroduction were mainly in enclosed parks but no feral populations have survived. The wild boar is a species primarily of deciduous woodland and survives in much of Europe and Asia. It is the ancestor of the domestic pig but it is unlikely that the present domestic stock of pigs in Britain owes much to domestication of local wild boars.

Suborder Ruminantia
Ruminants

The ruminants are characterised especially by the presence of a complex, four-chambered stomach and the habit of ruminating or chewing the cud. Food, usually herbage, is stored in the first chamber of the stomach, the rumen, undergoes bacterial decomposition in the second chamber, the reticulum, is then regurgitated for further mastication before being again swallowed and passing into the third chamber, the omasum and finally into the fourth or true stomach, the abomasum, where acid digestion begins. The dentition is also specialised with no upper incisors, the food being cropped by the lower incisors (apparently four pairs since the lower canines are incisiform) pressing against a horny pad on the upper jaw. The cheek-teeth are high-crowned with crescentic ridges of enamel— 'selenodont'. Dental formula

$$\frac{0.0-1.3.3}{3.1.\quad 3.3}.$$

The two principal families, Cervidae and Bovidae, are distinguished especially by the presence of antlers and horns respectively. Antlers are solid and bony and are cast and renewed annually; horns consist of horny sheaths on a bony core and are not shed.

FAMILY CERVIDAE
DEER

A large family with about 50 species represented throughout Eurasia and the Americas. All but two monospecific genera (*Moschus* and *Hydropotes*) have antlers and these are confined to males with one exception (*Rangifer*). Only two species, red deer and roe, are indigenous in Britain, but a further four species are now feral. Two others, the elk *Alces alces* and the reindeer *Rangifer tarandus*, were present in Britain in the early post-glacial period but probably became extinct before Roman times. Domesticated reindeer have been introduced in the Cairngorms but are carefully managed and cannot be described as feral.

The six wild species represent five genera. The characters of all six are detailed in Table 37. Detailed distribution maps of all species of deer in Britain and Ireland, covering the period 1967–72, were published by Clarke (1974).

TABLE 37 Some characters of the six species of deer now at large in Britain

	Red	Sika	Fallow	Roe	Muntjac	Water deer
Max. shoulder height (cm)	120	85	100	75	50	60
Antlers (males only)	+	+	+	+	+	0
Tusk-like upper canines in males	0	0	0	0	+	+
Adult pelage spotted in summer	0	+	+	0	0	0
Visible tail	+	+	+	0	+	+
Upper surface of tail	Brown	White	Black stripe		Brown	Brown
Frontal skin glands	0	0	0	+	+	0
Metatarsal skin glands	+	+	+	+	0	0

GENUS *Cervus*

The largest genus of deer, best represented in the Oriental Region but with one species, *C. elaphus*, found through much of the Palaearctic and in North America. This, the red deer, is the only indigenous species in Britain but another, the sika *C. nippon*, has been introduced. The characters of all deer in Britain are compared in Table 37.

Red deer *Cervus elaphus*

Cervus elaphus Linnaeus, 1758; Southern Sweden. *Cervus elaphus scoticus* Lönnberg, 1906; Glenquoich Forest, Inverness-shire, Scotland.

RECOGNITION The only large, generally red to brown deer without spots in Britain. Pale rump patch extends dorsally to include the tail. Tail shorter than ear.

Skull with well developed upper canines; condylo-basal length, with only permanent teeth present, greater than 280 mm.

SIGN Droppings black, sometimes adherent, about 1·5 cm in diameter. Tree saplings (5–10 cm diam. breast height) frayed by stags with their antlers between 60–120 cm from the ground in August and September. Bark stripped from trees, particularly conifers, up to 2 m from the ground in winter and spring. Wallows, not always wet, in use from April to October.

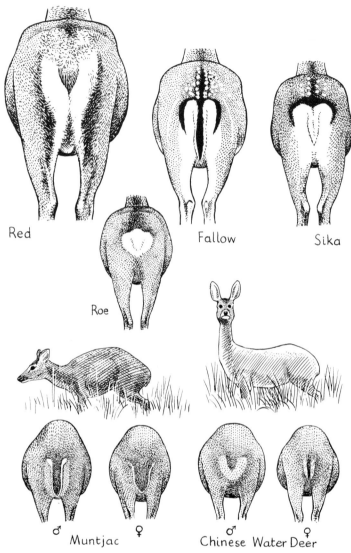

Red   Fallow   Sika

Roe

♂ Muntjac ♀   ♂ Chinese Water Deer ♀

FIGURE 163 Rump patterns of deer and characteristic profiles of muntjac and water deer.

DESCRIPTION In summer, coat short, thin and variable in colour, usually predominantly red, sometimes dark brown or yellow, rarely grey or off-white. In winter, coat longer and thicker, usually brown, but may be almost black, grey, reddish brown, yellow or again rarely off-white.

Inguinal region white or creamy yellow. Rump usually white below the tail, pale yellow or orange above, sometimes pale yellow or orange-brown below and orange or darker brown above, sometimes bordered with black, particularly down the thighs, tapering to a point above each hock. Hair covering metatarsal or hock glands similar in colour to surrounding hair or of lighter shades of brown to buff. A dark line sometimes present down the length of the neck and back, rarely extending to the tip of the tail. Occasionally a single row of lighter coloured spots visible either side of

FIGURE 164 Red deer hind and stag.

back, rarely with additional spots on flanks. Belly usually off-white or grey, sometimes dark grey or black. After the rut all stags have dark brown to black stained hair on the belly and this is retained until moulted in the following spring. Tail *c.* 15 cm long or 20 cm including hair, colour same as upper rump above and usually white beneath. In September stag develops a mane which persists until the following spring.

Moult starts towards the end of April in the older deer, in May for the majority and in June for deer in poor condition. Winter coat begins to develop in September and is complete by November for all deer except those in poor condition. Coat of stag longer but not as thick as hind's.

Primary follicles of both sexes of greater diameter than those of other mammals sampled (Carter 1965).

Calves variable, usually brown or reddish brown flecked with white spots on neck, back and flanks; sometimes almost black, red, orange, yellow, grey or off-white and exceptionally not spotted. As the hairs of the first coat grow and fall out the spots become less pronounced, usually not visible after two months. The second coat resembles the adult's winter coat, though softer and fluffier, and persists until the following May.

Deciduous upper canines small and pointed, replaced in second year by larger pear-shaped teeth or 'tushes'. Lower canines, both deciduous and permanent, incisiform and not separated from incisors. First premolar absent (Riney 1951). The three deciduous cheek teeth in each jaw, shed at the end of the second year, differ from permanent premolars in that instead of one cusp the third lower premolar has three cusps and the second and third upper premolars have two cusps each. Permanent molars all bicuspid except the third lower which usually has three cusps. With the exception of the first cheek tooth (P_2), all the premolars and molars after eruption move forward in the jaw throughout life and continue to erupt as crowns wear down with age. Wear and structure of teeth probably best means of estimating age (Lowe 1967, Mitchell 1967).

Stags generally develop antlers on pedicles arising from their frontal bones. On the European continent and in southern England, male calves may develop pedicles at eight months (Dzieciolowski 1969b, Raesfeld 1964); in Scotland, generally not before ten months and not visible in the field before twelve months. These first antlers of the yearling males may be no more than partly developed pedicles beneath hair-covered skin, more often develop as simple spikes. Under park conditions these simple antlers may fork at the top (Matthews 1952). Thereafter development in subsequent years is variable, some stags remain as knobbers (hummels), others develop larger and more complicated antlers with age (Lowe 1971). Sixteen points (tines) usually the maximum for the British race in the wild, average mature stag carries an eight-point head. Antlers cast mainly in March and April, but may vary with season in some districts (Watson 1971). Old stags and those in best condition cast first, yearlings seldom casting before June and occasionally delaying until August or September. New antlers in velvet begin to grow at once, those of the earliest to cast reaching their maximum size by early July and cleaning by the end of the same month. Most stags clean their antlers in August, but again the younger classes are later, yearlings not cleaning before September, more often October and sometimes not before December (author's data).

FIGURE 165 Red deer stag with antlers in velvet but probably fully grown. (Photo: G. Kinns)

Chromosomes: $2n=68$. Autosomes: 2 metacentrics, 64 acrocentrics. Sex chromosomes: X acrocentric, Y small metacentric (Hsu & Benirschke 1969).

MEASUREMENTS Largest British species. Height at withers over curves for a stag on Rhum up to 122 cm, length from nose to tip of tail over curves up to 201 cm. Hinds on Rhum up to 114 cm at withers and 180 cm in length (author's data). Condylobasal lengths of adult skulls of British subspecies range between 300–340 mm for stags and 280–335 mm for

FIGURE 166 Red deer stag shedding velvet. (Photo: G. Kinns)

hinds, and are small compared with Eastern European and Oriental races with stags reaching 470 mm and hinds exceeding 400 mm.

Weight very variable; average mature stag on Rhum *c.* 85 kg (56–132 kg), average mature hind *c.* 58 kg (38–77 kg) (all less alimentary tracts, Lowe 1971). Elsewhere in Scotland and Ireland body weights similar but stags in optimum habitats may exceed 190 kg, 178 kg in England (Whitehead 1960), and over 255 kg in Eastern European woodland (Baillie-Grohman 1896).

Antlers of mature stags also variable, average *c.* 71 cm in length (max. 91 cm), possess 4–5 tines on each antler (max. 9) and weigh 1·4 kg as a pair (max. 3·0 kg) on Rhum (*n* = 153, author's data). Elsewhere probably heavier and larger, but there are no recent records of native stags even in English woodland with antlers exceeding 94 cm in length, or possessing more than 9 tines on either antler. Stags in Eastern Europe have been recorded with antlers in excess of 130 cm in length, with many more tines and weighing more than 12 kg (Raesfeld 1964). The largest pair of antlers known, with a small fragment of skull bone, weighed 19 kg (Baillie-Grohman 1896).

DISTRIBUTION See Fig. 167. Throughout the Palaearctic Region from Ireland and the Scottish Hebrides to Manchuria, and from just south of the Arctic Circle in Norway (lat. 65°N) to the Himalayas and North Africa (Tunisian–Algerian border, lat. 33°N). Introduced in USA, Argentina, Australia and New Zealand.

The British race confined to Scotland, North West England and probably South West Ireland (Lowe & Gardiner 1974). Feral populations of park breeds established in Somerset and Devon, Hampshire, Surrey and Sussex (Ashdown Forest), Thetford Chase in East Anglia, Essex and Suffolk, North Staffordshire (The Roches), Cheshire, West Yorkshire and Durham. In Donegal of unknown origin. Presence in Wicklow uncertain, may all be hybrids (*C. elaphus* × *C. nippon*) (Harrington 1973). Present on the following islands: Arran, Bute, Islay, Jura, Scarba, Seil, Mull, Rhum, Skye, Scalpay and Raasay; in the Outer Hebrides, present on North Uist, Pabbay, Harris and Lewis.

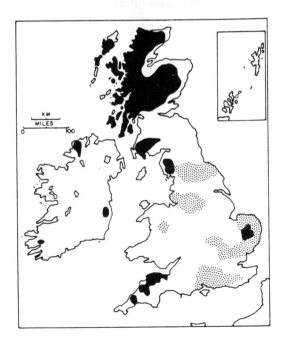

FIGURE 167 Red deer: distribution.

VARIATION Seventeen subspecies listed by Ellerman & Morrison-Scott (1955). Mainly distinguished on the characteristics of their antlers and pelage. British subspecies *scoticus* distinguished from the others by Lönnberg (1906) on the basis of skull measurements. The two stags' skulls examined had certain measurements in common with the Norwegian *atlanticus* and others with the Swedish *elaphus*, and, therefore, could not be included with either. Lowe & Gardiner (1974) concluded that none of the measurements commonly taken of a skull supports the concept of subspeciation in red deer. However, the race native to Britain can be distinguished clearly from deer selectively bred in parks and now feral in many parts of the country on the basis of their respective skull shapes.

HABITAT Inhabits a great range of habitats from above the tree-line on mountains to low lying plains. Found in forest, grassland, moorland and desert scrubland, preferring transition zone between forests and savannah. In Britain, most abundant on moorland and upland grassland in the Scottish Highlands.

BEHAVIOUR Gait most frequently a slow stride, otherwise a steady trot or a gallop for short distances after being disturbed or chased. When suddenly frightened, will often move off with a series of stiff-legged jumps, bouncing off all four feet each time, probably to advertise the presence of danger to other deer. When passing through undergrowth in woodland, the head is lowered, and the antlers of the stags are carried horizontally on either side of the body. If disturbed frequently, both sexes may lie down or 'clap' in thick cover (bracken, bramble, long grass etc.) rather than leave the area. Swim well.

Most active at dawn and dusk. In the Highlands deer ascend the hills early each morning and spend the day resting, ruminating or feeding fitfully, descending to their main grazing areas again each evening. Deer in woodlands also crepuscular but spend the hours of daylight under cover of trees, emerging in the evenings to feed in adjacent fields. Both make and then use paths when moving from one area to another; these often become general highways for other mammals including man.

Home ranges variable in shape but, on Rhum, approximately of the same size, about 400 ha for a hind and 800 ha for a stag (Lowe 1966, Youngson 1967). Elsewhere in Scotland distances between summering and wintering grounds often greater, but home ranges not necessarily larger. Size of home ranges of woodland deer not known.

In the Highlands in summer deer tend to congregate on hills or moors above the treeline having followed the flushing of the new growth of vegetation from the lower grazings where it began in the spring. In winter the deer descend to the lower grasslands, moors or woods, which provide both food and shelter. When these are inadequate damage to adjacent forestry and farm crops is likely to occur.

Social structure well developed and based on a matriarchal system (Darling 1937) but varies with habitat. In Scotland deer tend to congregate in herds of varying size, e.g. 9 on Rhum, 40 in eastern uplands (Lowe 1966). Herds of more than 600 head have been recorded in parts of the central Highlands. Apart from immature animals, sexes usually segregated. In woodland, groups seldom more than family parties and sexes probably always segregated (Eygenraam 1963, Ahlén 1965) except during the rut. In the Highlands, different classes exploit grazings at different altitudes. In winter mature stags generally found on slopes with southern aspect with breeding hinds higher up the glens. The highest grazings available are exploited mainly by young and yeld hinds with yearlings. In summer mature stags occupy the highest positions on the hill with the other classes distributed below them in the same order as before (Lowe 1966). Where woodland is available, hinds generally occupy the central parts of the most favoured areas with the stags distributed around the periphery in areas of suitable cover.

Communication by various means. Alarm usually signalled by a short sharp bark or series of barks by hinds, occasionally by stags, also by bouncing gait already described. When suspicious, head is held high and legs, especially forelegs, are each in turn raised and lowered stiffly, slowly and jerkily whilst the animal turns to one side and then the other on exposed ground, drawing attention to the source of its suspicion. Most characteristic sound made by red deer is the well-known 'roaring' made by stags during the rut. The pattern, intensity and pitch of the roar varies considerably between stags and for each stag depending on the stage reached during the rut. Towards the end of their rutting behaviour most stags end each roar with a series of coughs. In summer, hinds occasionally bellow, often mistaken for the early roaring of stags. Hinds may also give an extended nasal call when seeking their calves, and the latter occasionally bleat. If attacked, a calf will give a long and piercing scream which carries a great distance. Flight from danger also communicated by the light-coloured rump patches of moving deer, particularly pronounced in calves. Scent, produced by hinds in oestrus, appears to be perceptible only at short range and may be tasted rather than smelt. Importance of other scents from metatarsal, tail and lachrymal glands not understood. Sense of smell highly sensitive and discriminating. Sight and hearing also acute.

FOOD When available, grasses, sedges and rushes are the most important food throughout the year, comprising half the total consumption (Jensen 1968). Dwarf shrubs, particularly heather, next most important food, conifers and holly important in winter. Other foods include shoots and leaves of deciduous trees and bushes, herbs, lichens, ferns, mushrooms and the bark of trees, particularly conifers. In woodland, food consists mainly of shoots of trees and shrubs (82%); grasses and sedges less important, amounting to less than 20% of diet (Dzieciolowski 1969a). In Britain can browse shoots and leaves up to *c*. 180 cm by rearing up on their hind legs; stags sometimes then use their antlers as well in winter to break off branches of holly and yew up to *c*. 240 cm from the ground (author's data).

BREEDING Stags fecund from the time their antlers are fully developed in velvet until their antlers are cast. Only in the month of June are no stags fecund. Incidence of rut in Europe variable: August to October. In Britain main rut usually three weeks, end of September to mid-October. Larger stags move to areas favoured by hinds and round up as many as they can hold and defend them against other stags. During the rut both stags in possession and those challenging them appear darker in colour due to frequent wallowing in wet peat or mud. They also roar constantly to advertise their presence, particularly at night when they cannot be seen. Immature stags and even some yearlings fecund but have little opportunity to mate.

Most hinds fertile in third year, some in second year (normal in southern England) and exceptionally in first year (Daniel 1963). Generally conceive at first oestrus. Oestrus cycle $18·3 \pm 1·7$ days (Guinness *et al.* 1971). Gestation about 8 months, 236 days on Rhum from date of maximum rutting activity to date on which largest number of hinds calved, over a period of nine years (author's data). May be shorter in captivity: 227 and 229 days recorded for two yearlings calving for the first time (Lincoln *et al.* 1970), and $231 \pm 4·5$ days ($n = 13$) observed by Guinness *et al.* (1971) for penned deer. Peak day of calving 31 May on Rhum, half the calves born by 6 June.

Births observed from third week May to second week October. Normally single calf born though twins have been recorded. At birth, weight variable, in Scotland males average 6·7 kg, females 6·4 kg, range 3·2–10·4 kg (Mitchell 1971). Sex ratio about equal. First suckled within half an hour of birth and normally from a standing position. Calves lie up between feeds for most of their first 7–10 days, thereafter accompany their mothers more often and particularly in the evenings until 3–4 weeks

FIGURE 168 Newly born calf of red deer. (Photo: G. Kinns)

of age, after which their routine activities do not differ from the adults. Generally suckled in Scotland for 8–10 months, occasionally 17 months if the mother becomes yeld (not pregnant). Replacement of milk teeth begins in 14th to 15th month and is not completed before 25th to 26th month (Lowe 1967). Physical maturity not attained before the 7th year (Lowe 1971).

POPULATION Little known of red deer population dynamics in woodland or in England. In Scotland life tables available only for the deer on Rhum (Lowe 1969). When cropped fully, annual mortality among calves was low (10% of stags and 7% of hinds). Natural mortality among adults averaged little more than 3% for either sex, but increased after the ninth year for both sexes. Maximum longevity probably 20 years, mean expectation of life probably 5–6 years.

Adult sex ratio variable, depending on management. Average

1 stag: 1·6 hinds in Scotland revealed by large scale survey during 1953–59 (Lowe 1961); probably nearer 1 stag: 1·3 hinds if errors, arising from trying to classify deer over long distances, are corrected. Census method probably accurate to within 3%; described by Lowe (1969). No accurate census method yet devised for deer in woodland.

Density very variable. Averaged 13 deer/km² in survey, maximum of 77 deer/km² on some deer forests in Scotland.

PREDATORS AND MORTALITY Small numbers of newly born and young calves killed by eagles and foxes. Adults have no natural predators except man; some accidentally killed by cars and lorries. Occasionally killed in avalanches in snow, by lightning and in fights during the rut. Most mortality due to starvation. Calves losing their mothers rarely survive, and old deer with well worn cheek-teeth, being unable to ruminate efficiently, usually die during hard winters (Lowe 1969).

PARASITES AND DISEASE Of the oestrid flies, *Hypoderma diana* (warble fly) may also parasitise cattle, but *Cephanomyia auribarbis* (nasal bot fly) and the hippoboscid, *Lipoptena cervi* (ked) are commoner and specific to deer. Lice (*Damalinia* sp.) and the sheep tick (*Ixodes ricinus*) are the only other common ectoparasites.

Of the endoparasites, the nematodes specific to, and most commonly found in deer (A. M. Dunn 1969 & in litt.), include *Spiculopteragia asymmetrica, Haemonchus contortus, Trichostrongylus askivali, T. retortaeformis, T. vitrinus, Nematodirus battus, Capillaria* sp., *Oesophagostomum sikae, Trichuris* sp., *Rinadia mathevossiani, Ostertagia mossi* and *Apteragia quadrispiculata. Trichostrongylus capricola* is shared with goats. Other species, shared with cattle, sheep or goats and commonly present in the small intestine, include *Cooperia pectinata, Nematodirus filicollis, Oesophagostomum venulosum, Oe. radiatum, Ostertagia ostertagi, O. circumcincta* and the tape worm, *Moniezia benedeni*. Sometimes *Cysticercus tenuicollis*, which becomes *Taenia hydatigena* in the dog, may be found in the peritoneum.

The lung worm *Dictyocaulus viviparus*, which causes 'husk', and is shared with cattle, is also common. Two flukes may also occur, the liver fluke, *Fasciola hepatica* which is common, and the rumen flukes, *Paramphistomum* spp. which are rare. None of these parasites has been found to place an undue burden on its host (Dunn 1969).

The most common diseases carried by red deer are louping-ill and tick-borne fever (rickettsial disease), from neither of which deer appear to suffer.

RELATIONS WITH MAN Deer have always been important in art and mythology, and their antlers have been used to make implements and ornaments throughout history. In the Middle Ages the export of hides from red and roe deer formed an important revenue. Stalking and hunting, the sport of kings, became of great economic importance in the nineteenth and early twentieth centuries. After the 1939/45 war and until recently, less fashionable, and uncontrolled herds came into conflict with hill farming and forestry. Recently, with increases in price of venison, deer forest management policies have been reviewed and deer have again become an important asset. Attempts are also being made to farm deer.

LITERATURE General information may be found in Evans (1890), Millais (1897), Ritchie (1920), Cameron (1923), Ross (1925) and Lowe (1961).

AUTHOR FOR THIS SPECIES V. P. W. Lowe.

Sika deer *Cervus nippon*

Cervus nippon Temminck, 1838; Japan.

RECOGNITION Medium-sized deer; in summer, coat generally chestnut red with straw to white spots; in winter, greyish brown with no or only faint spots. Rump patch white, bordered by black above and heart shaped. Tail all white above or with thin black line down part of dorsal

FIGURE 169 Sika deer, hind and stag.

surface, tail tip hangs about 5 cm below rump patch when standing. Fur of metatarsal or hock gland white (winter) or pale buff (summer).

Skull distinguished by having short pointed rostrum. Maxillary canines present. Condylo basal length of skulls with only permanent teeth present 200–290 mm, only rarely exceeding 280 mm. In stags, brow tines arise at less than 90° angle with main beams of antlers.

SIGN Droppings black and similar to those of fallow deer. Presence also revealed by footprints, cast antlers and hair in the spring, as well as by frayed saplings, but all need careful comparison with those of other species of deer. Voice characteristic, and whistle of stags during the rut, will confirm presence of the species.

DESCRIPTION In summer coat short, bright chestnut red with variable number of straw to white spots, arranged roughly in rows. Most distinct row down either side of a dark dorsal line. Stags usually darker than hinds. Underparts fawn or grey, except for inguinal region which is white.

In winter, coat longer and thicker, hinds light brown or grey, stags darker grey to black. Spots absent or faint, most often persisting on either side of dorsal stripe. Rump patch white and heart-shaped, bordered by black above and on either side, can be extended to twice its normal area when erected in times of alarm.

Tail white, about 12 cm long (17 cm including hairs) often with thin black streak on mid-dorsal surface. Hair covering metatarsal or hock gland white in winter, pale buff in summer, twice as long as short dark grey or brown hair surrounding it. In both sexes there is a lighter U-shaped area of hair between the eyes enhancing the slightly raised anterior margins of the frontals. Tips of ears rounded. Internally, ears not pigmented, but covered by white fur except for one black thumb print on lower edge of each ear. Antler velvet black or with rust red patches on beams, originally described by Lydekker (1898) as '. . . of a bright chestnut red, with black tips . . .', but not found with velvet of this colour today in Britain. In September, stags develop dark brown or black manes which persist throughout subsequent winter months. Moult starts in May but varies with age and condition as in red deer. Winter coat begins to develop in September and is complete by early November.

Calves usually brown flecked with white spots. Rump patch small, fawn coloured, not surrounded by black border until end of second month (Horwood & Masters 1970). After three months calf pelage replaced by grey winter coat.

Tooth formula

$$\frac{0.1.3.3}{3.1.3.3}$$

Small deciduous upper canines replaced in second year by larger, but still small, pear-shaped teeth. Milk teeth and the timing and order of their replacement similar to red deer, completed by end of second year.

Male calves start to grow pedicles at 6–7 months, and generally produce short simple spikes in second year. In third year larger stags average six point heads with brow, trez and unbranched top to main beam of each antler. Thereafter some stags develop an extra tine from the inner side of the beam near each top to become 8-pointers. Rarely, more tines may be added up to a maximum of eleven (Whitehead 1964), but bez tines are absent. Mature stags probably average 6–8 points (Horwood & Masters 1970). As a rule antlers are distinguishable from those of red deer in three respects: (1) they have a pronounced keel on the main beam between the brow and trez tines; (2) the brow tine branches from the main beam at less than 90° from it; (3) the top forks of 8-pointers face forwards and not towards each other. Antlers cast mainly in April. New antlers covered with black skin, with occasional patches coloured red; hair short, fine and silvery. Most stags clean velvet from antlers in August or early September.

Chromosomes: $2n = 67$. Autosomes: 3 metacentrics, 62 acrocentrics. Sex chromosomes: X acrocentric, Y small metacentric (Gustavsson & Sundt 1968).

MEASUREMENTS In Dorset average height at shoulder of adult males 81 cm, of females 73 cm; average length from nose to tail of males 149 cm, of females 134 cm (Horwood 1971).

Condylobasal lengths of adult skulls of Japanese race, *C. n. nippon*: males 235–290 mm, females 209–245 mm.

Average weight in Dorset: males 63·9 kg; females 41·2 kg (Horwood 1971).

Antlers of mature stags shorter than those of red deer, majority probably 30 to 50 cm in length, occasionally may reach 65 cm (Whitehead 1964). Circumference of beam 8 to 10 cm.

DISTRIBUTION See Fig. 170. Occurs on many of the Japanese islands, on Taiwan and in countries on the continent of Asia within the east Palaearctic Region. Introduced into New Zealand, USA, Britain and Ireland, and widely on the continent of Europe.

In England feral herds established in Dorset, Hampshire and West Yorkshire. In Scotland found in Argyll, Caithness, Fife, Inverness-shire, Peeblesshire, Ross and Sutherland, and in Ireland established in Co. Dublin, Kerry and Wicklow. Also on the island of Lundy.

VARIATION Seven subspecies listed by Ellerman & Morrison-Scott (1955). Differences separating the four subspecies on the mainland of China and adjacent countries not clear, but those and that on Taiwan readily distinguishable from the two Japanese island races. Since so many of the Asiatic mainland group (see Imaizumi 1970) are similar to individuals arising in red deer X sika deer hybrid populations, e.g. Wicklow (Ireland) and south eastern area of the Lake District (England), and have similar skulls, Lowe & Gardiner (1975) have concluded all may be hybrids of great antiquity from deer parks, only the two island forms belonging to the true species.

HABITAT Prefers deciduous or mixed woodland on damp or poorly drained soils with dense undergrowth of rhododendron, blackthorn, hazel, bramble or other shrubs. Seen in parties in fields, on open grassland or moorland only in the vicinity of woodland. Coniferous forests favoured in early stages before being thinned.

BEHAVIOUR Gait similar to red deer, and has same stiff-legged bouncing action when alarmed. At the same time, white hairs of rump patch erected, thus producing both a visual and audible signal to other deer. Can swim quite well.

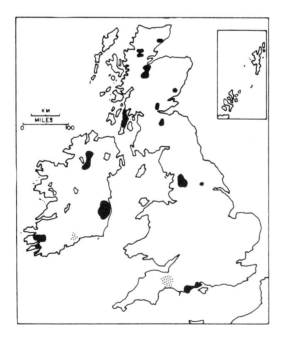

FIGURE 170 Sika deer: distribution.

Most active at dawn and dusk, moving out of cover in the evenings to graze in fields or on open moorland, and back into cover early each morning.

Home ranges vary with topography and situation; average size not known, nor the changes in seasonal use and requirements of them.

Social structure similar to that of red deer in woodland habitats. Hinds generally in small, mainly family, groups, congregating into herds when feeding away from cover at night. Stags usually single or in small groups; largest groups observed in late winter and spring. Unlike red deer, master stag tolerates subordinates of same sex in his territory during the rut (Horwood & Masters 1970).

Various means of communication used but few of them really understood. Soft nasal whine, frequently repeated, often heard from hinds with calves. When alarmed, in addition to flaring of rump patch and stiff-legged gait (like red deer), call often made resembling cross between a short sharp whistle and a squeal. Stags sometimes make a whistle which becomes louder as it reaches its highest pitch and then becomes more muted as it tails off. During the rut the stag's voice resembles the noise produced by a gate hung on unoiled and rusty hinges swinging in the wind, but, as the rut progresses the call becomes less whistle-like and instead becomes more of a hoarse shriek with some similarity to the intake of breath by a donkey and ends with a grunting roar. Each call rises and falls in pitch and is repeated three of four times, after which the stag remains silent for perhaps a quarter of an hour or more. Hinds may also give a short low bleat or grunt if in season (Horwood & Masters 1970).

Secretions from lachrymal and metatarsal glands, particularly during the rut, can be considerable, but importance of scent produced not understood. Sight and hearing acute; olfactory sense perhaps best developed.

FOOD Like red deer, sika are probably grazers rather than browsers, feeding principally on grasses and sedges. Ivy, holly, conifers and heather probably important in winter. Known to eat acorns, chestnuts and fungi, also to strip bark from trees and browse young shoots.

BREEDING Rut starts end of September, reaches a peak in first half October and is all but finished by the end of that month. Also, like red deer, polygamous. Stags stated by some authors to mark out and defend a territory (Bromley 1956, Kiddie 1962) within which each has a rutting 'stand' (Horwood & Masters 1970) or 'platform' (Bromley 1956) where mating takes place. Nearly all hinds fecund in second year, but pregnant calves not uncommon in Dorset (Chapman & Horwood 1968). Oestrous cycle not yet determined. Gestation about eight months as in red deer.

Most calves born end May and during June; exceptionally calves may be born as early as mid April and as late as December. Single births appear to be the rule. In Dorset calves weigh about 3 kg at birth (Harris & Duff 1970), and, between feeds, lie concealed most of the time for their first 3 weeks of life. Calves suckled for 8–10 months, but start grazing before the end of 1st month (Horwood 1971). Replacement of milk teeth probably begins in 12th month and is complete by 24th month. Physical maturity in Dorset probably attained by 4th year (Horwood 1971).

POPULATION Population dynamics not yet investigated. Maximum longevity probably more than 15 years (Harris & Duff 1970). Adult sex ratio not determined; foetal sex ratio 90 males : 100 females ($n = 57$, Horwood & Masters 1970). No method for censusing an entire population yet developed, hence no information on density.

PREDATORS AND MORTALITY Apart from accidental deaths due to cars, lorries and fences, adults have no natural predators other than man. Young calves sometimes killed by foxes and stray dogs.

PARASITES AND DISEASE The hippoboscid fly, *Lipoptena cervi*, has been found on sika. Lice (*Damalinia* sp.) and the sheep tick (*Ixodes ricinus*) are the only other common ectoparasites.

Round worms recorded, that are specific to deer, include *Spiculopteragia asymmetrica*, *Rinadia mathevossiani*, *Ashworthius sidemi*, *Oesophagostommum sikae*, *Schulzinema miroljubovi*, *Elaphostrongylus panticola*, *Pygarginema cervi*, *Wehrdikmansia cervipedis*, *W. flexuosa* and *Artionema altaica*. Many other species occur that are shared with domestic stock. All the cestodes, *Moniezia benedeni*, *Taenia hydatigena* (larva) and *Echinococcus granulosus* (larva), have domestic animals as their prime hosts. Also true of the trematodes, *Fasciola hepatica*, *Dicrocoelium dendriticum*, *Eurytrema pancreaticum*, and *Paramphistomum cervi* (Dunn 1969). None of these has been shown to be of any importance as a natural mortality factor. No diseases recorded.

RELATIONS WITH MAN Sika have increased their numbers considerably in recent years, particularly in Scotland and Ireland, but are, as yet, of little economic importance. Tendency to hybridise with red deer will need to be watched carefully as more of the red deer range becomes colonised by sika deer in the future.

LITERATURE General information may be found in Harris & Duff (1970), Horwood & Masters (1970), Horwood (1971) and Whitehead (1964).

AUTHOR FOR THIS SPECIES V. P. W. Lowe.

GENUS *Dama*

Marginally distinct from *Cervus* and sometimes included in that genus. Contains a single species, or two if the Persian form *mesopotamica* is treated as a distinct species. The latter is now limited to a very small area of south-west Iran and the original relationship to the main population of *D. dama* is unknown.

FIGURE 171 Fallow deer, doe and buck.

Fallow deer *Dama dama*

Cervus dama Linnaeus, 1758; Sweden (introduced).
Buck (male), doe (female) and fawn (immature).

RECOGNITION Many colour varieties ranging from nearly white to nearly black. The most common summer coat is reddish fawn with white spots along flanks and back, with a black vertebral stripe extending along dorsal surface of longish (*c.* 16–19 cm) tail. Winter coat most commonly greyish fawn, spots far less distinct. In some areas one colour variety predominates, e.g. black in Epping Forest.

SIGN Presence in area often suggested by cloven footprints and droppings, but former difficult to distinguish with certainty from other species of deer, sheep and goats. Size of prints varies considerably with age, condition and behaviour of animal. Droppings of adults characteristically shiny black pellets, cylindrical, with one end usually pointed and the other indented (*c.* 16×11 mm in males, *c.* 15×8 mm in females). Frayed trees and hair on fences also indicate presence.

DESCRIPTION Summer coat most commonly rich fawn with many prominent white spots on flanks and back. Black vertebral stripe. Tail black on top and white underneath, quite different to that of sika deer which is predominantly white. Tail surrounded by white rump patch which is bordered by black, curved, almost heart-shaped line. Winter coat duller grey-brown and spots scarcely detectable. A paler variety, lacking all black markings, retains spots in winter. Many colour varieties from nearly white (unspotted) to nearly black (very slightly dappled). Total albinos very rare. Hair over metatarsal gland lighter but similar colour to adjacent hair.

Male has prominent tuft of hair from penis sheath which is visible from about 3 months old and female has tuft of long hairs (*c.* 12 cm) immediately below the vulva. Testes scrotal. Two pairs of nipples in both sexes.

FIGURE 172 Fallow deer: young bucks showing little palmation of the antlers. (Photo: G. Kinns)

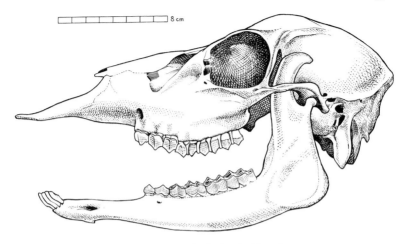

FIGURE 173 Skull of a female fallow deer.

Lactating female has prominent udder. Ears prominent, eyes relatively large, dew claws present. Scent glands suborbital, rear interdigital and metatarsal directly below hock. In addition, bucks have a scent gland associated with the penis sheath.

Pelage of newly born similar to adult summer coat. Numerous colour varieties from pale, unspotted sandy (becomes nearly white when mature) to nearly black (dappled). First winter coat similar to adults.

Moulting occurs in May–June and late September–October in southern England (Chapman & Chapman 1969b).

Antler size very variable, depending on age, condition and genotype. Pedicles usually first noticed from 7–12 months and antlers from 15 months. First antlers vary from small knobs (3 cm) to spikes (15 cm). Size increases with age and, when fully developed, antlers have broad palmate area which distinguishes fallow from other species of deer. Palmation may occur in third year but usually later (Chapman & Chapman 1975). Antlers cast April–June, older animals casting before younger ones; regrown and clean of velvet August–September, younger animals cleaning before older ones (Riney 1954).

Tooth formula usually

$$\frac{0.0.3.3}{3.1.3.3}.$$

Incisors and incisiform canine are spatulate, first incisor twice as wide as others. One or two incisiform teeth may be absent. Large diastema between canine and premolars.

Deciduous teeth usually

$$\frac{0\,.\,0\,.\,3\,.\,0}{3\,.\,1\,.\,3\,.\,0}.$$

One or two incisiform teeth may be absent and one or two upper canine teeth may be present (Chapman & Chapman 1969a, 1973). Deciduous P_2 and P_3 and permanent P_{2-4} lophodont whereas deciduous P_4 and M_{1-3} selenodont. All lower molariform teeth quadritubercular, each with two roots, except M_3 and deciduous P_4 which are sextubercular each with three roots. Molariform teeth hypsodont, erupting throughout life, and, except P_2, undergoing well-defined mesial drift. Molar rows in mandibles closer together than in maxilla and diverge distally in slightly curved 'V'. Mandibular tooth eruption occurs by 5–6 months (M_1), 9–12 (I_1), 13–16 (M_2, I_2), 17–20 (I_3, C), 21–24 (M_3, P_4, P_3), 25–26 months (P_2) and can be used for age estimation (Chapman & Chapman 1970a).

Skull described by Flerov (1952). Mandibles fully developed about 3 years. Skeleton unremarkable. Proximal parts of splint bones present on fore legs, the plesiometacarpalian condition.

Uterus bicornuate with paired pea-size ovaries. Cotyledonary placenta described by Harrison & Hyett (1954) and Hamilton *et al.* (1960). Annual changes in weight and histology of testes described by Chapman & Chapman (1970b). Accessory glands comprise seminal vesicles, ampullae of ductus deferens and peri-urethral glands. Compact prostate and bulbo-urethral glands absent. Gall bladder absent. Skin structure described by Jenkinson (1972) and circumanal and circumgenital glands by Frankenberger (1957).

Chromosomes $2n = 68$, F.N. $= 70$ (Gustavsson & Sundt 1968, Wurster & Benirschke 1967). Haemoglobin types described by Maughan & Williams (1967).

MEASUREMENTS Height at withers: male 90–95 cm, female slightly smaller; length about 170 cm. Antlers: length up to about 76 cm, inside span up to about 70 cm (Whitehead 1964).

For cranial measurements and weights see Table 38.

DISTRIBUTION See Fig. 174. Original range probably in Mediterranean zone of Europe and from Asia Minor to Iran. Now widespread by introduction in Western Europe north to about 60°N. Also introduced to parts of Africa, Australasia, North and South America (see Chapman & Chapman 1975).

No indisputable records from Roman or earlier archaeological sites in Britain in spite of abundant remains of other deer. Fallow deer of similar size to present day animals occurred in Britain in the last interglacial. Reintroduced to Britain in the Middle Ages, most probably by the Normans. Introductions from Europe have occurred since then. Descendants of original herds still living wild in Cannock Chase, Epping Forest and

TABLE 38 Cranial measurements and weights of fallow deer. Cranial—adults (park and wild) from England and Scotland; weights—S.E. England

	Male			Female		
	Mean	Range	*n*	Mean	Range	*n*
Greatest length of skull (mm)	263	241–283	47	247	231–267	46
Zygomatic width (mm)	127	115–140	69	109	102–118	54
Palatal length (mm)	101	93–117	71	98	88–106	54
Maxillary tooth-row (mean of both sides) (mm)	81	73–88	71	78	68–85	55
Length of mandible (mm)	200	185–216	68	191	175–203	49
Live weight of newly born, park (kg)	4·6	2·5–5·9	51	4·4	2·5–5·5	42
Weight of adult, entire carcase, park (kg)	72	51–94	17	43	37–56	37
Ditto, wild (kg)	67	46–80	20	44	35–52	15

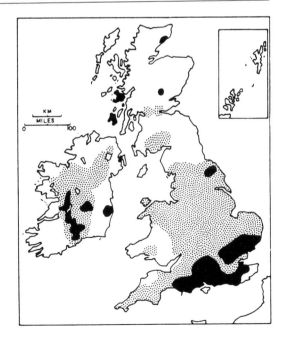

FIGURE 174 Fallow deer: distribution.

the New Forest. Widely kept in parks and present distribution largely result of escapes. Recorded from most English counties, several Scottish counties and the islands of Islay, Mull and Scarba, most Welsh counties and most Irish counties. Precise distribution imperfectly known (see Whitehead 1964).

VARIATION No subspecies recorded other than the larger and probably conspecific form *mesopotamica* in Iran. Numerous colour varieties (see above under DESCRIPTION). A long-haired variety occurs in Mortimer Forest, Shropshire (Springthorpe 1969), but many deer have long, sparse hairs scattered over body.

Variation of mandibular size discussed by Chapman & Chapman (1969c). One of two mandibular incisiform teeth (deciduous and permanent) may be absent. Incidence variable, 20 out of 107 deer (18·7%) recorded in one locality. One or two upper canine teeth may be present at birth but usually are lost at an early age; recorded in 17 out of 68 deer (25%) (Chapman & Chapman 1969a, 1973).

HABITAT Deciduous, coniferous or mixed woodland, preferably with thick undergrowth. Small areas of rank vegetation and waste land and fields if undisturbed even though close to human habitation. In Scotland, the stage of development of a forest affects the distribution of fallow deer in that area more than competition between them and red and roe deer (Batcheler 1960).

BEHAVIOUR Gait usually a walk but when alarmed will bound stiff-legged on all four feet (pronk), stop, look round and stare and then run away. Jump well but usually go under or through a fence or hedge rather than over. During day lie up in vegetation that affords cover where they ruminate and drowse. If disturbed move off quickly and quietly. At dusk they move to rides and neighbouring fields to feed. Diurnal in undisturbed areas, often graze and ruminate and lie in sun in fields during the day. Older males mainly nocturnal and rarely seen except at height of rut when often appear oblivious of man's presence.

Home ranges of males and females may be separate, coincide or overlap, and size depends on season, food, cover and disturbance, that of the males being smaller than that of the females (Heidemann 1973). Form groups which are 'permeable' and 'open' for most of the year. Adult males leave area occupied by females and young in December–March and return about August–September for rut. Male group made up of individuals whereas female group based on mothers and young. Young males may stay with female group for first 20 months and then leave area but may return for rut. Young females may remain with female group into which they were born. Group leadership by adults and generally of passive type. Female groups rarely large (*c.* 20–30) and usually led, in single file, by adult female.

Territorial behaviour appears to be limited to males in rut and possibly to females during period of parturition (Chapman & Chapman 1975, Gilbert & Hailman 1966, Heidemann 1973, Puttick 1972).

Usually silent for much of year. When rutting, male repeatedly makes a deep, loud, belching noise called 'groaning'. Female, when suspicious of danger, especially when near young, gives a short bark, sometimes repeated 2–3 times. Female may bleat or whicker when pursued by male. Fawns, up to 6 months or so, bleat when looking for or running with female and when worried by male during rut. Little known of non-vocal communication; when disturbed, frequently stamp a foot. Rear interdigital glands active within few weeks of birth and throughout year in both sexes; odour of rancid butter. Pungent scents deposited on ground and trees by males in rut may act as pheromone.

Orientation chiefly by sight. Large, movable ears give acute hearing. Sense of smell also important.

FOOD Diet affected by relative abundance of preferred foods. Sweet grasses (e.g. species of *Agrostis*, *Festuca* and *Poa*) and the rushes *Juncus bulbosus* and *J. squamosus* feature in diet throughout year and form bulk of food from spring to autumn. New foliage of many deciduous trees freely taken. When plentiful, acorns and beech mast form bulk of autumn and early winter food. Sweet chestnuts, crab apples, hips and blackberries also eaten. Bramble, rose, ivy, holly and foliage and bark of felled conifers are important winter foods as are heather and bilberry. Fungi, male fern, mosses and seed heads of certain grasses occasionally taken in large amounts. Certain plants, although common, little used, e.g. grasses *Molinia* sp., *Deschampsia caespitosa*, *Agrostis setacea*; bracken and gorse.

Numerous factors affect feeding behaviour including weather, disturbance, cover and availability of food. Feeding occurs throughout 24 hours, but night feeding probably more important at most times of year. Appears to be no significant difference in diet of male group or female group utilising the same areas. Male may stop feeding at height of rut. Rarely drink (Jackson 1974).

BREEDING Rutting season in autumn, followed by birth of single fawns in following June.

Rutting, often in traditional areas and usually under trees, occurs in latter half of October and early November, although later matings do occur. Time of tremendous activity for males. Rutting areas marked by scrapes (30–300 cm diam.) in leaf litter, grass or soil which often has characteristic 'rutty buck' odour (see Chapman 1975). Antlers used to fray and thrash young trees and bushes, and to plaster urine-soaked soil on the flanks. Noisy challenging and fighting and some rounding up of females occurs.

Males attain puberty at 7–14 months but social hierarchy in herd may prevent mating. Spermatozoa present from August to March or April, spermatogenesis reaching a peak in October–November. Antler development related to sexual cycle: casting and regrowth are in spring and summer when bucks sexually quiescent. Velvet shed late summer–early autumn when spermatogenesis increasing. Cycle described by Chapman & Chapman (1970b) and Chapman (1972).

Female polyoestrous, breeding first at 16 months and then annually; gestation $229 \pm 2 \cdot 7$ days (Prell 1938). Single fawn born in June although occasionally recorded as late as November. Twins rare, 2 out of 270 (0·8%) uteri containing foetuses. Sex ratio of 145 foetuses, 110 males to 100 females; 154 newly born fawns, 130 males to 100 females (Chapman & Chapman 1975).

Lactation may last up to 9 months or more and yearling fawns may suckle with fawn of the year. Ovulation and foetal development discussed by Armstrong *et al.* (1969).

Fawns suckle and can walk within a few hours of birth. Can run well by 24 hours but usually remain hidden and 'freeze' to avoid detection. Following mother by 2 weeks. Growth and development, as indicated by mandibular size, discussed by Chapman & Chapman (1970a).

POPULATION STRUCTURE Age structure of population unknown. Longevity unknown. Live at least 10 years in Richmond Park, London, and almost certainly much longer than this.

One deer per 6–8 ha throughout year increasing to 1 per 4 ha in the rut has been recorded in Essex. In some areas seasonal movement of adult males to and from rutting areas (Chapman & Chapman 1975). Heidemann (1973) recorded 1 deer per 12 ha throughout the year.

PREDATORS AND MORTALITY No predators except man although foxes may take weak fawns. Heavy mortality in first year. Of 87 wild deer (45 males, 42 females) killed in Essex and in Epping Forest, 21% of males and 21% of females were less than 1 year; and 42% of males and 29% of females were less than 2 years. Of 115 deer (57 males, 58 females) killed accidentally or died in Richmond Park, 58% of males and 45% of females were less than 1 year (Chapman & Chapman 1975).

PARASITES AND DISEASE Lice (*Damalinia tibialis*) are often numerous on debilitated animals and keds (*Lipoptena cervi*) and ticks (*Ixodes ricinus*) have also been recorded (Thompson 1964). Infection with lice greatest in late winter, spring and early summer whereas infection with keds greatest in autumn and early winter (Chapman & Chapman 1975).

Tapeworms, round worms and flukes recorded from fallow deer in Britain and listed by Anon. (1931), Batty & Chapman (1970) and Dunn (1969). Numbers of parasites usually low and much below those common in domestic stock. Rumen protozoa described by Prins & Geelen (1971).

Little information available but wild deer appear generally free from diseases. Tuberculosis, Johne's disease, pseudotuberculosis (*Corynebacterium*) and brucellosis mentioned by McDiarmid (1962) and tumours by Jennings (1969). Bone lesions similar to 'ring bone' recorded in 12 (50%) and damaged bones in 11 (46%) of deer from Epping Forest (Chapman & Chapman 1969b). Abscess in jaw with erosion of bone not uncommon in older animals.

RELATIONS WITH MAN Still hunted and has been from time immemorial. Carcases used for food and adornment. May cause damage to forestry, agriculture and horticulture. Widely kept in deer parks and zoological collections.

LITERATURE General information may be found in Cadman (1966), Chapman & Chapman (1970c, 1975) and Ueckermann & Hansen (1968)— a general account in German.

AUTHOR FOR THIS SPECIES D. I. Chapman.

GENUS *Capreolus*

A distinctive genus containing a single species, the roe deer.

Roe deer *Capreolus capreolus*

Cervus capreolus Linnaeus, 1758; Sweden. *Capreolus capreolus thotti* Lönnberg, 1910; Craigellachie, Morayshire, Scotland.
Buck (male), doe (female) and fawn or kid (immature).

RECOGNITION A small deer which appears almost tail-less although females have an anal tuft of hair. The black nose and white chin are distinctive. When alarmed, the hairs of the rump patch or speculum can be erected to form a 'powder puff'. Sika deer also display in this way but can be distinguished by their long tail and larger size. The coat of roe varies from sandy to bright reddish brown with paler underparts in summer, and from greyish brown to almost black, changing gradually to buff or white on the belly, in winter.

SIGN Presence in area often suggested by cloven footprints and droppings but difficult to distinguish with certainty from other species of deer, pigs, sheep and goats. Size of prints varies with sex, age, condition and gait of animal. Droppings of adults are shiny, black, cylindrical pellets, one end usually pointed and the other indented (*c.* 14 × 8 mm). Frayed trees, scrapes and hair on fences also indicate presence of deer.

FIGURE 175 Roe deer doe and buck

DESCRIPTION *Adult.* Summer coat usually a bright reddish brown with paler underparts and a pale buff rump patch, but some variation occurs. The area around the nostrils and extending to the corners of the mouth is black whereas the chin and a small area immediately below each nostril are white. Above the black nostril area, a white rim is sometimes present and this may extend along the nose. The rump patch of the female is white whereas that of the male is yellow-buff and less conspicuous. Winter coat is thick and dense and varies from greyish brown to almost black, merging with a white or fawn-coloured belly and a distinctive white or light buff rump patch, kidney-shaped in males and an inverted heart shape in females. One or two white throat patches may be present. There is no undercoat and only the distal portion of each hair is coloured. The tail is usually minute but may be up to about 7 cm in length. Testes scrotal. Two pairs of nipples in both sexes. Lactating female has prominent udder. Ears prominent, eyes large, dew claws present. Scent glands: well-marked metatarsal on outer side of hind leg just below hock, rear interdigital and suborbital (see Holmes 1974). In addition, males have glandular area between and in front of pedicles (Schumacher 1936).

Fawn Pelage of newly born is sandy brown strongly flecked with black and with white spots on the sides and flanks and a row of spots on either side of the back. Face similar to that of adult. Spots become fawn-

FIGURE 176 Roe deer buck with antlers in velvet. (Photo: G. Kinns)

coloured, start to fade at about six weeks and have disappeared by the time the fawn has attained its first, adult winter pelage about October. Moulting occurs from mid-March to end of May and from September to mid-October in southern England (Prior 1968).

Antlers rugose and rarely exceed 30 cm in length. Pedicles usually first noticed about 3–4 months and antlers by about 8–9 months although these are not fully grown until one year old. Some fawns grow 'button' antlers, which are cast in the middle of their first winter (*c.* 8 months), followed by normal spike antlers (see Chapman 1975). First antlers may be simple spikes up to 10 cm in length, or have forward-pointing tines or, less commonly, have forward- and rear-pointing tines making six in all. By two years, males usually have both the forward and the rear pointing tines, which are typical for the species.

Antlers cast in southern England from late October to December, older animals usually casting before younger ones; regrown and velvet usually shed in April, but young deer may still have antlers in velvet in June (Prior 1968).

Deciduous teeth usually

$$\frac{0.0.3.0}{3.1.3.0}$$

and permanent teeth

$$\frac{0.0.3.3}{3.1.3.3}$$

although upper canine(s) occasionally present. Incisors and incisiform canines are spatulate, first incisor twice as wide as others. Large diastema between lower canines and premolars.

Lower deciduous P_2 and P_3 and permanent P_{2-4} are lophodont whereas deciduous P_4 and M_{1-3} are selenodont. All lower molariform teeth quadritubercular except M_3 and deciduous P_4 which are sextubercular. Molariform teeth hypsodont, erupting throughout life and, except P_2, undergoing well-defined mesial drift. Molar rows in mandibles closer together than in maxilla and former diverge distally in slightly curved 'V'.

Order of eruption of mandibular teeth and the age at which this occurs is uncertain. In Dorset, Prior (1968) considered that the *average* age at which roe attain a permanent set of teeth is 8 months whereas in German roe tooth eruption is: 2 months (M_1), 5–6 months (I_1, M_2), 7–9 months (I_2), 9–11 months (I_3), 10–12 months (C), 11–14 months (M_3), and 12–15 months (P_{2-4}) (Rieck 1974).

Annual growth layers in the tooth cementum used for age estimation and considered more reliable than that based on tooth wear for roe deer in Thetford Chase, Norfolk (Aitken 1975a).

Excellent illustrated account of anatomy given by Hofmann & Geiger (1974).

Skull described by Flerov (1952). Skeleton unremarkable, distal parts of splint bones present on fore legs, the teleometacarpalian condition.

Uterus bicornuate with paired ovaries. Cotyledonary placenta described by Hamilton, Harrison & Young (1966). Gall bladder absent. Skin structure described by Jenkinson (1972) and circumanal and circumgenital glands by Frankenberger (1957). Scent gland on forehead of males is most active in spring and summer (Schumacher 1936).

Chromosomes $2n=70$, F.N.$=72$ (Amrud & Nes 1966, Gustavsson & Sundt 1968). Haemoglobin types described by Maughan & Williams (1967).

MEASUREMENTS Adult size attained at about 16 months. Shoulder height of German roe: males 64–67 cm ($n=888$), females 63–67 cm ($n=639$). Nose to rump length: males 106–112 cm ($n=864$), females 106–112 cm ($n=639$) (Stubbe 1966). Shoulder height of British roe probably similar.

Mean weight of deer from southern England: adult males in summer 26 kg ($n=71$), adult females in winter 24 kg ($n=60$), male fawns in winter 16 kg ($n=8$), female fawns in winter 16 kg ($n=16$) (Prior 1968). Mean weight of males from Inverness-shire, Scotland 25 kg, range 18–29 kg ($n=18$) (Prior 1968). Body size appears to be related most directly to density of deer; the largest animals being those from areas of lower deer density, poorer soil fertility, lower ratios of agricultural land to forest and lower ratios of perimeter to total forest area (Klein & Strandgaard 1972).

Antler size very variable depending on age, condition, locality and genotype. Sizes of antlers from 19 roe from southern England and recorded in the *Trophy-Catalogue of the World Exhibition of Hunting*, Budapest 1971, were: mean length of both antlers 26·2 cm (range 22·0–34·0 cm) and mean inside span 12·2 cm (range 9·0–16·6 cm). Many antlers never reach these record sizes.

DISTRIBUTION See Fig. 177. Indigenous in Britain (but not in Ireland) and in the Palaearctic Region. Although common in England in medieval times, it became extinct, except near the borders with Scotland, by the early eighteenth century. Deer of unknown origin were introduced to Milton Abbas, Dorset, in 1800 and deer from Germany were introduced to the Breckland of East Anglia about 1884. These and other introductions and escapes have resulted in roe now being present in southern England from Sussex and Surrey in the east to Cornwall and Gloucestershire in the west, and in Essex, Norfolk and Suffolk. Common also in the Lake District and the Border Forest in Northumberland, and in parts of Lancashire and Yorkshire as far south as Leeds. Still increasing its range in England. Believed to be absent from Wales. Common in Scotland, being present in every county and on the islands of Bute, Islay and Seil. Introduced to Ireland but now extinct. Detailed distribution in Britain given by Whitehead (1964).

VARIATION Three subspecies recorded in Continental range but of doubtful validity. Colour varieties are uncommon although in some areas of Scotland, particularly Galloway, and in northern England, there is a tendency to melanism which is most noticeable in the winter coat. Melanistic roe occur in eastern Holland and western Germany but there the summer coat is also black. Albino and parti-coloured animals reported, but extremely rare.

Males that fail to shed velvet from antlers, which are not then cast, are known as perruques. Roe appear most prone of deer species to this condition which results from inadequate levels of androgens such as may

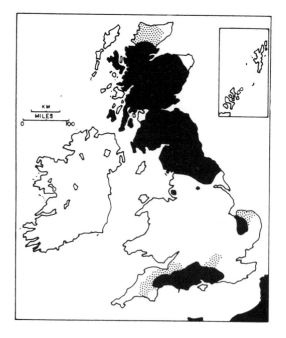

FIGURE 177 Roe deer. distribution.

occur when testes are damaged, removed or remain in the abdominal cavity (cryptorchidism) (Chapman 1975).

Females may also sport antlers which vary from small velvet-covered knobs to typical hard structures. Again, roe appear most prone of the deer species to this condition. The true sex, however, of many of these so-called females is unknown. Most females with poorly developed antlers, which remain in velvet, probably are females with some hormonal inbalance. Females with either well-developed antlers in velvet or clean, hard antlers are probably true hermaphrodites or male pseudo-hermaphrodites (Chapman 1975).

One or two upper canine teeth occasionally present.

HABITAT Occur in a wide variety of woodland habitats, both coniferous and deciduous, providing there is plenty of cover. Can also be seen along woodland edges and in fields. In East Anglia, for example, they occur in the coniferous woods of Breckland and in marshy reed beds on the edges. In Scotland, may be found on open moorland where there is deep heather but prefer woodland.

BEHAVIOUR Remain in cover during the day, coming into the open to feed at dawn and dusk but diurnal in undisturbed areas. Gait usually the walk. When alarmed, run away, bounding over the vegetation with rump patch flared, often uttering a characteristic bark. If disturbed, may slip away quietly and unseen. Not known to pronk.

Rings consisting of a well-trodden track are made around a natural feature such as a bush or a tree stump. Used by males, females and fawns particularly in July and August but significance remains obscure.

Social organisation lies between the solitary and the gregarious. Males exhibit aggressive behaviour such as chasing, barking, anointing and fraying of vegetation, in order to acquire and defend territories which are held from April to August. Fraying by non-territorial males may be due to frustration. Fighting not uncommon, sometimes with fatal results. Roe are unusual in that territorial behaviour is not confined to the period of the rut. Topographic features such as woodland rides or streams frequently appear to act as territorial boundaries. Home ranges of territorial males, which include their territories, are usually retained from year to year and, in Dorset, average 7·4 ha. Home ranges of non-territorial males in Dorset average 15·0 ha and are rarely retained for more than a year, the animals either acquiring a territory or emigrating in the spring when in their second or third year. Home ranges of females in Dorset average 7·1 ha, overlap considerably and are retained from year to year. The home range of a female may overlap the territories of two or three males, or the home ranges of one to three females may coincide with the territory of a male. Females also emigrate in their second or third year but the mechanism by which the number of females is regulated is unclear (Bramley 1970a, b, Cumming 1966, Holmes 1974, Prior 1968, Strand-gaard 1972). The idea of male and female pairing for life is now dis-counted. Territorial behaviour of female limited to time of parturition (Espmark 1969, Kurt 1968).

Usually solitary or in small groups of male, female and young but deer may congregate to form 'herds' in winter. Herds may be predo-minantly either females and young or males, up to about 30 animals hav-ing been seen in a single field. Rank order of males in winter is linear, a fall in rank occurring when antlers are cast and a rise occurring when antlers are cleaned of velvet. Dominance of adult males is related to dis-tance from summer territory, the greater the distance the less dominant the animal. Rank in females is less marked but related to arrival at feeding area, the earliest arrivals being the most dominant (Geiger & Krämer 1974).

Both sexes utter a bark that is repeated several times. Males also bark as part of territorial behaviour and make rasping noises particularly when courting. Females in season utter a high-pitched cry, which is emulated by hunters in order to attract males. Fawns squeak or bleat, apparently to keep contact with adults (see Holmes 1974).

Little known about non-vocal communication. Stamping of feet occurs when alarmed and as part of territorial behaviour. Scent glands on fore-head and near eyes used to anoint vegetation probably to delineate terri-tories. Interdigital and metatarsal glands active throughout year (Holmes 1974).

Orientation chiefly by sight. Large, moveable ear pinnae give acute hearing. Sense of smell also important.

Relationship with red and fallow deer investigated by Batcheler (1966).

FOOD Predominantly browsing animals although they graze in fields to a certain extent. In Dorset, major food throughout year is bramble. Broadleaved trees such as ash, hazel and oak are important in summer. Grasses, herbs and conifers form a minor part of the diet, but are impor-tant in some months. In Scotland, main winter foods include heather, grasses, spruce, bilberry and hazel twigs (Hosey 1974).

Feeding behaviour affected by many factors including season, disturb-ance, cover, availability of food and weather. Feeding occurs in short periods and occupies 8–10 hours per day usually from dusk to dawn un-less undisturbed, when they feed during the day (Prior 1968). Males do not stop feeding during the rut. Non-territorial males feed at different times from territorial males according to Robertson (1967).

BREEDING Rutting occurs from mid-July to mid-August. A period of erotic behaviour known as the 'false rut' occurs in early October but its purpose is obscure. Fawns born from April to July but the majority from mid-May to mid-June (Rieck 1955). Rutting area forms part of male's territory and is marked by scraping the soil with the feet, fraying vegetation with antlers and anointing vegetation with scent. Males restless and bark frequently.

Males probably attain puberty by 14 months and may mate with females coming into season late. Spermatozoa present from mid-May to mid-November, the testes being least active in January. Antler development related to sexual cycle, casting and regrowth occurring when animal sexually quiescent and velvet shed when spermatogenesis recommences (Short & Mann 1966).

It is uncertain whether female is mono- or polyoestrous: a partial resurgence of rutting activity in the second half of August suggests they may be polyoestrous. Breed first at 14 months and then annually. The only artiodactyl known to exhibit delayed implantation. After fertilisation the blastocyst increases slightly in size but remains free in the uterus from August to late December or early January when rapid embryonic growth and implantation occurs, probably as a result of increased activity of endometrial glands in the uterus (Aitken 1974, 1975b, Aitken *et al.* 1972, Short & Hay 1966). About 75% of adult females carry twin foetuses which may be of the same or opposite sex. About 20% of females carry single foetuses and 5% carry triplets but this varies with locality and season (Chapman & Chapman 1971).

Lactation may last throughout the winter (Holmes 1974). Fawns suckle and can walk within a few hours of birth. Fawns are left alone and usually remain hidden and 'freeze' to avoid detection for several days after birth. By 2–3 months fawns follow and remain with their dams (Espmark 1969).

POPULATION STRUCTURE Age structure of a Danish population of 213 animals that were exterminated is given in Table 39 (Andersen 1953). Longevity unknown but wild animals estimated to be 12 years of age have been recorded. Mean ages of the deer studied by Strandgaard (1972) at Kalo in Denmark were; males 2·1 years, females 3·5 years and *all* deer 2·9 years. Detailed discussion of problems involved in estimating population size and structure given by Strandgaard (1972).

Densities vary seasonally, 1 deer per 4 ha being recorded in the spring in Dorset for an unmanaged population (Prior 1968). Much higher

TABLE 39 Age structure, as percentage of population, of 231 roe deer at Kalo, Denmark (Andersen 1953)

	Fawn	1–2	2–3	3–4	4–5	5–6	6–7	7–8	8–9
				Age in years					
Male	21·1	8·0	6·1	2·8	2·8	0·9	0·9	0	0
Female	21·6	11·3	9·9	5·2	3·3	2·8	0·9	1·4	0·9
Total	42·7	19·3	16·0	8·0	6·1	3·7	1·8	1·4	0·9

densities recorded in winter when deer congregate on feeding grounds and territorial behaviour is at a minimum.

PREDATORS AND MORTALITY Man is the main predator, the effect of other predatory species in Britain being unknown. Heavy mortality in first year in Dorset; the potential annual increase is 90% of the number of adult deer whereas the actual increase is approximately 35%. Much of this loss is believed to be due to parasitic pneumonia caused by lungworm (*Dictylocaulus* sp.) although predation by foxes may be important (Prior 1968). In Scotland, male fawn mortality in a severe winter is greater than that of female fawns. Roe are killed in road accidents, particularly males from April to August (Holmes 1974).

PARASITES AND DISEASES Keds (*Lipoptena cervi*), lice (*Damalinia meyeri*) and ticks (*Ixodes ricinus*) all recorded from roe in Britain (Thompson 1964). In Dorset, ticks and keds are the commonest ectoparasites, greatest numbers of keds being found during the summer. Lice are rarely found (Prior 1968).

Cestodes, trematodes and nematodes have been recorded from roe, Dunn (1969) listing 74 species. Rumen protozoa (*Entodinium* sp.) described by Prins & Geelan (1971) but total numbers far fewer than in fallow and red deer. Wild roe in Britain appear generally free of disease but little precise information available (see Prior 1968).

RELATIONS WITH MAN Still hunted and has been from prehistoric times; carcases used for food. Causes damage to forestry, agriculture and horticulture. Management based on fact rather than empiricism now becoming widespread (see Chapman 1974, Prior 1968, Robertson 1967, Strandgaard 1972).

LITERATURE General information may be found in Holmes (1974), Prior (1968) and Tegner (1951).

AUTHOR FOR THIS SPECIES D. I. Chapman.

GENUS *Muntiacus*

A very distinctive genus of about five species in South East Asia. Two species have frequently been kept in captivity and one of these is now established in the wild in Britain. Distinguished by simple, backward-pointing antlers and tusk-like canines in males.

Muntjac *Muntiacus reevesi*

Cervus reevesi Ogilby, 1839; Kwangtung, South China.
Chinese muntjac, barking deer.

RECOGNITION Small brown deer with rounded back. Tail ginger with white underside, prominent in flight. Males carry simple antlers (60 mm) with occasional brow tine, on bony pedicles (*c.* 68 mm) growing from frontal bones in line of skull.

Skull notable by prominent pits for suborbital gland, larger in male (31 × 28 mm) than in female (27 × 22 mm); also by presence of upper canines, long and tusk-like (20 mm) in males, short (5 mm) in females.

SIGN Slots small and delicate (the inequality of the cleaves that has been described is not constant). Droppings are black and shiny with rounded facets, striations and a single peak. They can be passed as an intact accumulate (crottie).

DESCRIPTION Glossy chestnut colour. Individual hairs banded, with dark tips, giving speckled appearance at close quarters. Antlered male has dark brown stripes delineating medial sides of pedicles. Nape stripe present in females, not constant in males. Ears *c.* 80 mm, rounded with lighter fringes, dark brown backs, inside largely bare with variable light hairs and brown pigmentation most marked at periphery and lower third.

In field males look stockier, with thicker necks, than females and show more orange on head, shoulders and antler pedicles.

Under parts lighter, almost white in juveniles, greyer and browner in males and with increasing age. Chin lighter to white, and with irregular lighter throat patch. Legs with darker brown lateral lines and with irregular light patches above hooves. Tail ginger above and white below with white on inside of haunch, which is normally covered by tail but displayed in flight.

Moult in April to lighter summer coat. Replaced by duller winter coat in October and November.

Antlers cast in May or June, regrown by October–November. Growth of pedicle starts at 4 months in young male. Animals may be seen in velvet

FIGURE 178 Muntjac buck. (Photo: M. Clark)

in winter but those examined have proved to be juveniles growing their first head.

Upper canines present, up to 20 mm long in males. Lower canines present but small.

Chromosomes: $2n = 46$.

MEASUREMENTS Height at withers up to 48 cm in males and 45 cm in females. Mean weights 13·7 kg in males ($n=26$) and 11·8 kg in females ($n=26$). Sexual dimorphism reflected in thickness of neck: mean circumference 327 mm in males ($n=18$) and 255 mm in females ($n=17$).

DISTRIBUTION See Fig. 179. Mountains of southern China and possibly also on Taiwan.

Has become established in the wild in much of South East England as a result of escapes from deer parks, mainly from Woburn, Bedfordshire where it was introduced about 1900. Much of the expansion has been since 1950 and it is continuing to spread.

VARIATION Males can appear very dark, particularly in winter. Occasionally light coloured individuals are seen, bordering on yellow. Some animals have scattered white speckling or white patches.

HABITAT Deciduous or mixed woodland. Dense cover obligatory for successful establishment, e.g. bramble brakes or woods in thicket stage. Less suitable habitats colonised by juveniles.

BEHAVIOUR Usual gait a pottering walk. A swinging trot if moving faster on open ground. Under pressure can move very fast and outjump most dogs.

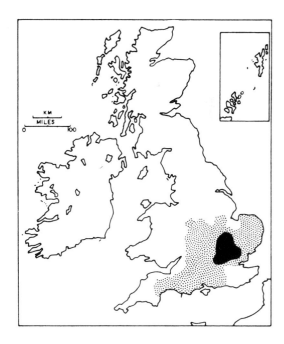

FIGURE 179 Muntjac: distribution.

Can be active by day or night, but most constantly seen in the evening, appearing about an hour before dusk.

Home range constant for does, which will occupy same area for years. Bucks appear to occupy larger ranges with perhaps several does. Small shoots are frayed with lower teeth and scented with glands as territorial markers (Clark 1968).

Social structure is based on the family unit of buck and doe living in an association based on regular olfactory contact, hence importance of suborbital, frontal and interdigital glands. Para-urethral glands are present and also appear to have a scent function (Dansie & Williams 1973).

There is no metatarsal gland.

Muntjac bark, most commonly during the post-partum oestrus. Single barks emitted every 4 to 5 seconds and continuing for long periods up to 45 minutes. Males emit a click when alarmed. All animals squeak, particularly the young and adults during sexual play. Fawns have a penetrating recurrent squeak emitted at same frequency as bark ('fawn lost' cry) audible up to 200 m. All animals have a very loud distress call if seriously injured or caught. Their hearing is acute. The eyes are large and well adapted to nocturnal vision. Their olfactory sense appears to be their most acute and important.

FOOD Browse on bramble, ivy and tree seedlings. Also graze and make use of fruits—crab apples, acorns, sweet chestnuts, horse chestnuts, blackberries.

BREEDING No clear seasonal pattern. One fawn per birth.

Does become mature at about 10 months, at a weight of $c.$ 8 kg. Gestation period 7 months. Uterus bicornuate, symmetrical at birth but later right cornu enlarged and contains most pregnancies (84%) (Chapman & Dansie 1969, 1970). Post-partum oestrus and copulation at 2–3 days after parturition, associated with considerable sexual activity, chasing and vulva-licking by buck and barking by doe.

Fawn weighs about 1 kg at birth and is chestnut with buff spots. Suckled for about 3 months; fawn will attempt longer but is discouraged by doe. Juvenile spots start to fade at 6 weeks and are lost by 3–4 months. Fawn gains up to $\frac{1}{2}$ kg/week. Remains with mother until next fawn dropped and occasionally associates after this.

POPULATION Population based on presence of mature pair holding a territory and producing continuous succession of young. These juveniles are displaced to surrounding suitable territories which are colonised if available. If already occupied, attempts to hold unsuitable and exposed habitats resulting in predation and loss.

Single animals known to live 12–14 years. Individuals known to hold territories in the wild up to 4 years.

PREDATORS AND MORTALITY Cause of death in a series of 168: motor car, 68; shot, 58; dog, 7; drowned, 4; fawning, 4; senility, 2; various, 13; unknown, 12. Fawns are taken by dogs, foxes and cats. Road deaths commonest in December, January and February.

PARASITES AND DISEASE One species of biting louse, *Damalinia indica*, and one of sucking louse, *Solenopotes muntiacus*, are present on most animals (Clay 1966).

Liver flukes, nematodes and the intestinal protozoa *Eimeria* have been recorded (Nelson 1966). *Pasteurella pseudotuberculosis* has been isolated from one animal.

RELATIONS WITH MAN Unimportant economically either as a crop or because of damage. Forestry damage limited to seedling browse. No evidence of agricultural damage. Unfenced gardens susceptible to browsing of plants. Not at present a trophy beast. Appears to be a harmless introduction.

Adult animals taken in wild do not settle well in captivity. Young animals do very well and breed freely.

AUTHOR FOR THIS SPECIES O. Dansie.

GENUS *Hydropotes*

A distinctive genus with a single species, notable as one of the two species of deer without antlers.

Chinese water deer *Hydropotes inermis*

Hydropotes inermis Swinhoe, 1870; Yangtze River, China.

RECOGNITION Slightly larger than muntjac with paler, sandy colour and large rounded ears. No antlers but long upper canines of adult male, up to 80 mm, may be visible in field.

SIGN Slot large and not so neat as that of muntjac.

DESCRIPTION Pelage long, hairs buff with dark tips giving speckled effect at close range. Tail same colour as body without prominent

FIGURE 180 Water deer buck. Note the wide rounded ears and protruding tusks.
(Photo: M. Clark)

speculum (rump patch). Winter pelage darker than summer but other-wise similar. Fawns have light spots distributed in parallel lines.

MEASUREMENTS Height at withers up to 60 cm in males, 55 cm in females. Weight 11·4–13·6 kg in males, 9·0–11·4 kg in females.

DISTRIBUTION See Fig. 181. Yangtze Valley in central China and in north-eastern China and Korea.

In Britain established in the wild only in a limited area in Bedfordshire and some adjacent counties as a result of escapes from Woburn Park where they were introduced about 1900. Only established outside Woburn within last 40 years. Occasional reports away from this area probably refer to escapes since the species is kept in a number of zoos.

HABITAT Grassland and adjoining cover, lying up in long grass, thistles etc. In China inhabits swampy country.

BEHAVIOUR Very few observations of wild animals. Active at dawn and dusk. Males display aggressive behaviour in captivity and appear to hold territories in the wild.

Males utter a whistling call during the rut and a bark has been recorded. Alarm call a scream like that of a wounded hare.

FOOD Mainly grass. Also takes vegetables and root crops.

BREEDING Rut takes place in December, fawns born late May and early June. Litter size unusually large for deer, up to five or six in China (Hamilton 1871) but usually fewer in park conditions in Britain. Of 12 pregnant deer examined by Middleton (1937) 75% carried twins and 25% either triplets or quadruplets. Puberty in females occurs at about 6 months, gestation 180–210 days.

RELATIONS WITH MAN Not yet sufficiently numerous in the wild to cause significant damage. Easily kept and bred in captivity.

AUTHOR FOR THIS SPECIES O. Dansie.

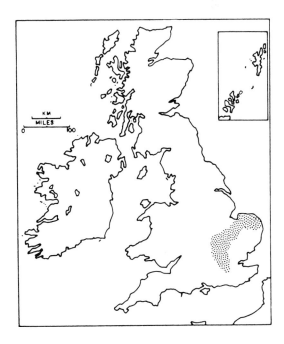

FIGURE 181 Water deer: distribution.

GENUS *Rangifer*

Reindeer *Rangifer tarandus*

Cervus tarandus Linnaeus, 1758; Swedish Lapland.

Reindeer occurred in Britain during the last glacial period. There is no good evidence from subfossil finds for their survival into the post-glacial period. A reference in the Orkney Saga to the hunting of reindeer in Caithness in the twelfth century is often interpreted as evidence of their survival in Scotland to that date. However in view of alternative explanations—confusion with red deer, introduction of reindeer by the Vikings—this cannot be considered conclusive.

Domesticated reindeer were introduced to the Cairngorms in Scotland in 1952 and survive there as a managed herd.

FAMILY BOVIDAE

The largest family of ungulates, containing the cattle, antelopes, goats, sheep, etc. The only species with any claim to have been indigenous in Britain in the postglacial period is the wild ox or urus, but domesticated cattle, sheep and goats have been present since the Neolithic period and have at various times given rise to feral populations. The most distinctive characteristic of bovids is the presence of horns, consisting of permanent horny sheaths on bony cores developed from the frontal bones of the skull. They may be present in both sexes, as in wild oxen, goats and sheep or only in males. (Domestic breeds may lack horns in one or both sexes.)

GENUS *Bos*

Contains the wild oxen of Eurasia, including the Asiatic gaur, banteng and yak in addition to the urus. The last is extinct as a wild species but is the ancestor of most domestic cattle.

Urus or wild ox *Bos primigenius*

Bos primigenius Bojanus, 1827.
Extinct everywhere as a wild species.

The wild ox of Europe and western Asia, the ancestor of domestic cattle, became extinct in the seventeenth century, the last survivors being in Poland. It undoubtedly occurred in Britain (but not in Ireland) in post-glacial times, but there is no good evidence of its survival beyond the Bronze Age (e.g. at Littleport, Cambridgeshire). Historical references to 'wild cattle' are just as likely to refer to feral domestic cattle, although the survival of the wild species into the historic period cannot be ruled out.

White cattle *Bos* (domestic)

No cattle are truly feral in Britain today but several herds of primitive white cattle now kept in parks are believed to have survived with relatively little change since mediaeval times. The best documented and most pure-bred herd is that at Chillingham in Northumberland. They are white with reddish brown ears and black muzzle, hooves and horn-tips. Other herds exist at Cadzow (Lanarkshire), Vaynol (Carnaervonshire), Dynevor (Carmarthenshire) and Woburn (Bedfordshire), the last having been moved there from Chartley (Staffordshire) in 1905. A detailed account of these herds was given by Whitehead (1953).

GENUS *Capra*

A genus of four or five species ranging from the Mediterranean region to the mountains of central Asia. One of these, *C. aegagrus*, is the ancestor of the domestic goat. There is no evidence that it or any other species of *Capra* has ever been native in Britain but feral domestic goats are well established in some areas and are generally referred to as 'wild goats'.

Feral goat *Capra* (domestic)

Capra *hircus* Linnaeus, 1758. The domestic goat of Sweden.

(The use of formal binomial names for domesticated forms leads to many difficulties and is best avoided.)

DESCRIPTION Vary in colour from pure white (with unpigmented horns and hooves) to self-coloured black, dark brown, light brown or grey. Self-coloured goats are less common than piebald and skewbald animals, however, and in animals of mixed colour there is a tendency for the forequarters, particularly in the males, to be darker than the hindquarters. Horns vary in shape from the backward sweep, as in the ancestral *C. aegagrus*, to the more common outward spreading form. The horns grow in length annually, and do not reach the lengths found in the wild species, despite published statements to the contrary.

The difference in appearance between feral goat and modern domestic goat is striking; the former is typically small and shaggy while the large, improved dairy goat is normally short-haired. The modern goat may weigh more than twice as much as his feral counterpart. This difference in appearance has led to talk of 'reversion' to a 'wild type'; there is no evidence at all for this phenomenon occurring in feral herds and it is quite clear that the mediaeval ancestors of the feral goat were equally small and equally shaggy.

FIGURE 182 Feral goat.

There are two easily recognisable characters that can be used to assess the 'purity' of a feral herd. Many modern goats possess a small dangling appendage called a tassel at each side of the throat. As tassels seem not to have occurred in Britain before modern goat breeding commenced, it can be taken that the presence of tassels in some individuals of a feral herd indicates that there has been some degree of intrusion of genetic material from the improved breeds. Similarly, the gene for hornlessness was introduced to Britain with the new milking strains, and thus if hornless goats are noted in a feral herd, some impurity may be suspected.

MEASUREMENTS Mature males normally weigh between 27 and 45 kg; females between 25 and 35 kg. Kids at birth may weigh 2·0 to 2·7 kg. Span of horns (tip to tip) depends on horn form but can reach 75 cm normally, with one of 115 cm recorded. Horn length along the curve depends on age: old males may attain 75 cm and there is a record of 95·2 cm. Female horns are smaller, reaching just over 30 cm.

DISTRIBUTION See Fig. 183. Present range of ancestral wild goats is from Greece through Asia Minor to Baluchistan. The domestic goat was imported into Britain in Neolithic times and is not native to Britain. Feral goats from this domestic stock occur in several parts of the Western Highlands of Scotland, some Hebridean islands, Holy Island (Arran), Galloway and the Cheviot Hills. In 1968 it was estimated that there were about 60 different populations of feral goats in Scotland, with a total of almost 4000 animals. One of these populations, in the Galloway Hills, was thought to consist of over 1000 goats (Greig 1969). This herd has since been considerably reduced by the Forestry Commission.

England has a few small groups on the Kielder Forest fells, and there are herds in Central and North Wales (Rhinogs, the Douallt–Rhobell, Fawr–Foel Dhu area south-west of Bala Lake, the Moelwyns and the Glyder range in Snowdonia). In Ulster, herds are said to exist on Rathlin

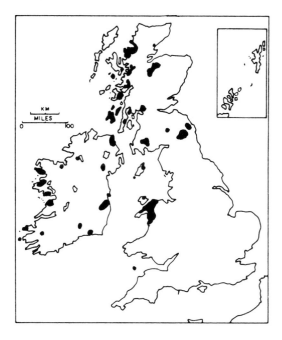

FIGURE 183 Feral goat: distribution.

Island, Fairhead, and Garron Plateau (Co. Antrim), on some islands of Lower Lough Erne (Co. Fermanagh) and in Co. Armagh. In Eire there are reports of herds at Malin Head (Co. Donegal), Rocky Valley near Dublin, Ross Island (Co. Killarney), Dingle Peninsula (Co. Kerry) and Knockroe (Co. Waterford).

Most British goat herds exist on the sufferance of landowners and farmers and could be easily exterminated; indeed, more than the 60 existing populations have become extinct in Scotland this century, some through natural catastrophe and some through the deliberate policy of a landowner. There is at present no legal protection for the feral goat.

HISTORY Modern British dairy-goat breeding commenced in the last quarter of the nineteenth century and to a large extent the basic stock was imported from Switzerland and the Middle East. The value of the new breeds was soon noted by goat owners and by the late 1930's the original domestic goat of Britain had all but disappeared in domestication, through crossing with animals of the new, more productive breeds. Fortunately, however, various feral herds remained, particularly in Scotland, and they are now the sole surviving examples of the unimproved British domestic goat. Most of the 60 Scottish populations are of the unimproved type but there are at least six herds of largely 'improved' modern stock, which have been established this century. Some of the 'primitive' feral herds have been established deliberately for sentimental or sporting reasons, but the majority owe their survival to the belief many sheep farmers hold, that goats on a sheep farm perform useful functions.

HABITAT Mainly on open, rocky hillsides and moorland, at all altitudes from sea-level to over 1000 m. Association with rocky areas is influenced by attitude of sheep farmers who like their feral goats to keep sheep away from rocks by eating the less accessible vegetation.

BREEDING One, occasionally two, young in late winter or spring, following an autumn rutting season.

Outside the breeding season the sexes tend to be separated, but males may be found with female/kid parties at any time of the year. The rut is promiscuous and there is no harem formation as found in the red deer. Fighting is rarely serious between males as hierarchy will normally be established prior to the rut, but all males participate in the pursuit of females and even young billies can succeed in mating. ('Master billies' and exiled defeated patriarchs are figments of popular writers' imaginations.) The rutting period varies considerably and is believed to be related to latitude, as the 'trigger' for the breeding season is light-induced. In the north of Scotland the rut is well under way by mid-August and in Wales and the south of Scotland it is two months later.

The gestation period is five months and births occur in mid-January in the north and March/April in the south. Singletons are normal but twins do occur, especially under good nutritional conditions. Female kids can conceive before they are a year old but may be two or three months behind the parturition peak of the mature nannies.

RELATIONS WITH MAN The bad reputation of the goat is probably un-justified in British conditions. The populations are easily managed as the goats can be stalked with ease, and, on suitable ground, can be rounded up by sheepdogs. Goats and trees do not mix, but the same can be said for deer. The greatest danger to the feral goat is genetic contamination. It is a unique animal, and any misguided dilution of its genetic make-up by the addition of improved goats to any herd, would not only be bad conservation, but could be positively damaging to the existing gene pool in that unsuitable genetic factors, reducing hardiness for example, might be introduced.

LITERATURE Whitehead (1972)—a detailed account of feral goats in Britain.

AUTHOR FOR THIS SPECIES J. C. Greig.

GENUS *Ovis*
SHEEP

Wild sheep occur in mountain habitats from Asia Minor and some Medi-terranean islands through central Asia to north-eastern Siberia and west-ern North America. Domestic sheep probably arose from *O. ammon* in western Asia. No wild sheep have occurred in Britain in post-glacial times but domestic sheep have been present since the Neolithic and one truly feral herd of primitive sheep deserves inclusion here.

Feral sheep *Ovis* (domestic)

The only ancient sheep of Britain that are living in a truly feral state are the Soay sheep on the islands of St Kilda. They are primitive domestic sheep, but the time of their introduction to St Kilda is not known. They survived only on the island of Soay, but in 1932 were introduced to the largest St Kildan island, Hirta.

DESCRIPTION The Soay sheep exhibit two colour phases, dark brown and fawn. Both types show a coat pattern that is reminiscent of the wild mouflon, with white belly, colour pattern on the legs, and lighter hairs round the eyes and on the chin. 'Self-coloured' types, without this patterning, also occur in the population. The males carry heavy, curving, horns that show distinct annual growth zones. The females may have small horns or be hornless. Flocks of Soay sheep have been bred in mainland parks for a long time and some fanciers have selected for the dark type with horned females. A few fawn flocks have also been selected and maintained. Adult rams weigh about 36 kg and ewes about 25 kg.

FIGURE 184 Soay sheep, ram.

BEHAVIOUR Females live in home-range groups that stay within the home range of 40 ha or so. Ewe lambs are usually recruited to their dam's group. Ram lambs leave and join, or form, separate groups of rams. These are sedentary for most of the year but disperse widely during the rut. In winter almost all the hours of daylight are spent grazing, but in summer much time, especially before noon, is spent lying and cudding. At night the sheep take shelter (in the dry-stone and turf cleits on Hirta). They show regular patterns of daily movement and form numerous sheep paths.

FOOD The sheep favour the *Holcus–Agrostis–Festuca* pastures of the glens and cliff ledges but use the heather heathland of higher ground in late summer and early winter.

BREEDING Oestrus occurs in the first two weeks of November and is highly synchronised throughout the population. Lambs are born in mid-April. Singletons are most frequent but twins are common. Many ewes conceive in their first autumn (at 6–7 months old) but have poor success in rearing their lambs. The rams disperse widely in the rut forming an 'open society' in which a well developed linear hierarchy is displayed. Rams high in the hierarchy have greater success in mating ewes in oestrus than those lower down. Ram lambs join in chasing ewes but have no success in siring them.

POPULATION Between 1952 and 1973 the total number of sheep on Hirta (638 ha) fluctuated markedly from year to year showing periodic die-offs. Maximum and minimum numbers (counted in May/June and including the surviving lambs of the year) have been 1783 and 610. The survival rate of rams is less than that of ewes. In the adult population the sex ratio is about 1 ram to 4 ewes. Most deaths occur in February and March when the nutritional value of the pastures is below the maintenance requirements of the sheep. During the rut in the autumn the rams spend much less time feeding than the ewes and this is a major factor pre-disposing them to higher mortality in late winter.

RELATIONS WITH MAN On Hirta and Soay the sheep are timid but inquisitive. They flee when approached within a few hundred yards. They scatter when worked with a sheep dog and cannot be rounded up in this way.

LITERATURE Jewell, Milner & Boyd (1974)—the results of a ten-year study on Hirta.

AUTHOR FOR THIS SPECIES P. A. Jewell.

Glossary

This glossary includes words used in the text that are not to be found in the *Concise Oxford Dictionary* or that are not adequately defined in the sense used here.

Agonistic Competitive (behaviour).

Alveolus The socket or cavity in a jaw bone occupied by the root or roots of a tooth.

Anoestrus A state of quiescence of the sexual organs in the female, seasonal or between oestrous cycles.

Apocrine glands Secretory glands in which the cells themselves constitute part of the secretion, as in sebaceous and mammary glands.

Baculum The bone found in the penis of some mammals, also known as the *os penis*.

Blastocyst A stage in the development of a fertilized egg after cell-division has begun but before firm attachment to the wall of the uterus. Development may be delayed for a considerable time at this stage.

Brachycardia Having a very slow heart-beat, e.g. during hibernation.

Calcar A cartilaginous or bony rod arising from the ankle of a bat, supporting the trailing edge of the tail membrane (Fig. 22, p. 69).

Carnassials The teeth of carnivores that are specialized for shearing flesh—the last upper premolars and the first lower molars.

Chromosomes The thread-like elements in the nucleus of a cell, carrying the genetic material. The number is usually characteristic of a species and is expressed as the *Diploid number* (2n), being the number in normal somatic (as distinct from reproductive) cells. Each chromosome may consist of one or two arms and the number of arms may be more constant in a species than the number of chromosomes. It is called the *Fundamental number* (FN, or, following the French version, NF).

Cline A kind of geographical variation within a species where there is a gradual and progressive change in one or more characters over a large area. The rate of change is not always constant and areas of more abrupt change may demarcate subspecies.

Cohort In analysing age-structure and longevity in a population a cohort is a group simultaneously recruited to the population whose subsequent fate is followed through.

Condylobasal length One of the most frequently used measures of the length of a skull, from the occipital condyles behind to the anterior points of the premaxillary bones in front.

Diastema A natural gap in a row of teeth, especially that between the incisors and the premolars or molars when canines are absent.

Dioestrus Sexual quiescence between two oestrous cycles.

Drey A squirrel's nest.

Epiphyses The terminal parts of a long bone or vertebra that ossify separately from the main shaft of the bone and only become fully fused with it on reaching adult size. The degree of fusion can sometimes be used to estimate age.

Erythrism A condition of the pelage in which red pigment (phaeomelanin) predominates due usually to absence of the black pigment (eumelanin).

Holarctic Region The biogeographical region comprising the Nearctic Region (North America) and the Palaearctic Region (northern Eurasia).

Home range The area normally utilized by an individual animal.

Hypsodont Of teeth, high-crowned (in extreme cases ever-growing) and therefore able to withstand considerable wear by abrasion.

Karyotype The set of chromosomes in a cell, especially when arranged in sequence for description.

Kinaesthetic Sensitive to one's own movement or position.

Leptospire A spirochaete bacterium causing the disease leptospirosis affecting especially the liver and kidneys of many species of mammals.

Life span The maximum age to which an animal can live (= physiological longevity).

Longevity Mean longevity is the average age lived by members of a population under natural conditions. Often given as 'expectation of further life.'

Lophodont Of a tooth, with the cusps elongated to form narrow ridges.

Merocrine glands Those in which the secretory cells remain intact during secretion as in most sweat glands (cf. apocrine).

Molar The posterior chewing teeth that are not represented by precursors in the milk dentition.

Nearctic Region The biogeographical region comprising North America.

Palaearctic Region The biogeographical region comprising Europe, North Africa and Asia north of the Himalayas.

Pc Postcanine (teeth)—all those behind the canines.

Pelage The hairy coat of a mammal (cf. plumage).

Pheromone An aromatic secretion that has a specific effect on another animal of the same species.

Polyoestrous Having a number of oestrous cycles per year or per breeding season.

Polymorphic In genetics, describing a population in which a number of discrete variants of one character are found in considerable numbers (as distinct from one uniform condition with rare variants).

Post-partum, post-parturient Immediately after birth (but referring to the mother, not the offspring).

Refection The habit of an animal eating its own faeces as a normal nutritional stratagem.

Rostrum The anterior part of a skull, in front of the orbits (i.e. the skeleton of the muzzle).

Selenodont Of teeth, with a crown pattern of longitudinal, crescentic ridges.

Stenopaic Of an eye, with a narrow slit-like pupil.

Sympatric Of two species, with overlapping ranges.

Tragus A lobe developed from the lower rim of the ear, extending upwards across the conch (especially developed in many bats).

Unicuspid Of teeth, having a single cusp or biting point (especially the simple conical teeth in the upper jaws of shrews).

Vibrissae Whiskers, i.e. specialised sensory hairs, usually best developed on the face but also found on other parts of the body.

Bibliographies

INTRODUCTION

ANDERSON S. & JONES J.K. (1967) *Recent mammals of the world: a synopsis of families*. New York, Ronald Press.

ARTHUR D.R. (1963) *British ticks*. London, Butterworth.

ASDELL S.A. (1964) *Patterns of mammalian reproduction*. 2nd ed. Cornell University Press.

AUSTIN C.R. & SHORT R.V. (eds) (1972) *Reproduction in mammals* (5 vols). Cambridge, University Press.

BANG P. & DAHLSTROM P. (1974) *Animal tracks and signs*. London, Collins.

BARRETT-HAMILTON G.E.H. & HINTON M.A.C. (1910–21) *A history of British mammals*. London, Gurney & Jackson.

BERRY R.J. & SOUTHERN H.N. (eds) (1970) Variation in mammalian populations. *Symp. zool. Soc. Lond.* no. **26**.

BRINK F.H. VAN DEN (1967) *A field guide to the mammals of Britain and Europe*. London, Collins.

CRICHTON M. (1974) *Provisional atlas of amphibians, reptiles and mammals in Ireland*. Dublin, An Foras Forbartha.

CRICHTON M. (no date) *Provisional distribution maps of amphibians, reptiles and mammals in Ireland*. Dublin, Folens An Foras Forbartha.

CORBET G.B. (1971) Provisional distribution maps of British mammals. *Mammal Rev.* **1**, 95–142.

CORBET G.B. (in press) *The mammals of the Palaearctic Region: a taxonomic review*. London, British Museum (Nat. Hist.).

COX F.E.G. (1970) Parasitic protozoa of British wild mammals. *Mammal Rev.* **1**, 1–28.

DAY M.G. (1968) Food habits of British stoats (*Mustela erminea*) and weasels (*Mustela nivalis*). *J. Zool., Lond.* **155**, 485–97.

ELLERMAN J.R. & MORRISON-SCOTT T.C.S. (1951) *Checklist of Palaearctic and Indian mammals*. London, British Museum (Nat. Hist.).

EVANS G.O., SHEALS J.G. & MACFARLANE D. (1961) *The terrestrial acari of the British Isles*. London, British Museum (Nat. Hist.).

EWER R. F. (1968) *Ethology of mammals*. London, Elek Science.

FAIRLEY J.S. (1972) *Irish wild mammals: a guide to the literature*. Galway, published by the author.

FERNS P.N. (1967) The classification of animal habitats. *Bull. Mammal Soc.* **28**, 10–14.

GEORGE R.S. (1974) *Provisional atlas of the insects of the British Isles part 4 Siphonaptera— fleas*. Huntingdon, Biological Records Centre.

GLUE D.E. (1967) Prey taken by the Barn Owl in England and Wales. *Bird Study* **14**, 169–83.

GLUE D.E. (1974) Food of the barn owl in Britain and Ireland. *Bird Study* **21**, 200–10.

HOPKINS G.H.E. (1949) The host-associations of the lice of mammals. *Proc. zool. Soc. Lond.* **119**, 387–604.

KURTÉN B. (1968) *Pleistocene mammals of Europe.* London, Weidenfeld & Nicolson.

LAWRENCE M.J. & BROWN R.W. (1973) *Mammals of Britain, their tracks, trails and signs.* London, Blandford.

MILLER G.S. (1912) *Catalogue of the mammals of western Europe.* London, British Museum (Nat. Hist.).

NIETHAMMER J. & KRAPP F. (in press) *Handbuch der Säugetiere Europas.* Wiesbaden, Akad. Verlagsgesell.

OGNEV S.I. (1928–50) [*Mammals of the USSR and adjacent countries*] Moscow, Acad. Sci. USSR. (English translations, 1962–63, Jerusalem, Israel Program for Scientific Translations.)

OVENDEN D., ARNOLD E.N. & CORBET G.B. (in press) *The wild animals of Britain and Europe.* London, Collins.

SIMPSON G.G. (1945) The principles of classification and a classification of mammals. *Bull. Am. Mus. nat. Hist.* **85**, i–xvi, 1–350.

SMIT F.G.A.M. (1957a) The recorded distribution and hosts of Siphonaptera in Britain. *Ent. Gaz.* **8**, 45–75.

SMIT F.G.A.M. (1957b) Siphonaptera. *Handbooks for the identification of British insects* 1(16), 1–200. London, Royal Entomological Society.

SOUTHERN H.N. (1954) Tawny owls and their prey. *Ibis* **96**, 384–410.

WALKER E.P. (1975) *Mammals of the world,* 3 vols. (3rd edn) Baltimore, Johns Hopkins Press.

MARSUPIALS AND INSECTIVORES

BERNARD J. (1960) A propos de l'action prédatrice des Soricidae sur les petits rongeurs. *Säugetierk. Mitt.* **8**, 25–7.

BIELAK T. & PUCEK Z. (1960) Seasonal changes in the brain weight of the common shrew (*Sorex araneus araneus* Linnaeus, 1758). *Acta theriol.* **3**, 297–300.

BISHOP I.R. (1962) *Studies on the life histories, ecology and systematics of small mammals inhabiting the Channel Islands.* M.Sc. thesis, University of Southampton.

BISHOP I.R. & DELANY M.J. (1963a) The ecological distribution of small mammals in the Channel Islands. *Mammalia* **27**, 99–110.

BISHOP I.R. & DELANY M.J. (1963b) Life histories of small mammals in the Channel Islands in 1960–61. *Proc. zool. Soc. Lond.* **141**, 515–26.

BOVEY R. (1949a) Les chromosomes des chiroptères et des insectivores. *Rev. suisse Zool.* **56**, 371–460.

BOVEY R. (1949b) La formule chromosomique de quelques insectivores indigènes. *Experientia* **5**, 72–3.

BRAMBELL F.W.R. (1935) Reproduction in the common shrew (*Sorex araneus* L.). *Phil. Trans.* B, **225**, 1–62.

BRAMBELL F.W.R. & HALL K. (1937) Reproduction of the lesser shrew (*Sorex minutus* L.). *Proc. zool. Soc. Lond.* 957–69.

BRINK F.H. VAN DEN (1967) *A field guide to the mammals of Britain and Europe.* London, Collins.

BROCKIE R.E. (1960) Road mortality of the hedgehog (*Erinaceus europaeus* L.) in New Zealand. *Proc. zool. Soc. Lond.* **134**, 505–8.

BROCKIE, R.E. (1974) The hedgehog mange mite, *Caparinia tripilis* in New Zealand. *N.Z. Vet. J.* **22**, 243–7.

BROCKIE R.E. (1976) Self anointing by wild hedgehogs in New Zealand. *Anim. Behav.* **24**, 68–71.

BUCHALCZYK T. & PUCEK Z. (1963) Food storage of the European water shrew, *Neomys fodiens* (Pennant, 1771). *Acta theriol.* **7**, 376–7.

BUNN D.S. (1966) Fighting and moult in shrews. *J. Zool., Lond.* **148**, 580–2.

BURTON M. (1957) Hedgehog self anointing. *Proc. zool. Soc. Lond.* **129**, 452–3.

BURTON M. (1969) *The hedgehog.* London, André Deutsch.

CALABY J.H. & POOLE W.E. (1971) Keeping kangaroos in captivity. *Int. zoo Yb.* **11**, 5–12.

CARLIER E.W. (1892–3) Contributions to the histology of the hedgehog (*Erinaceus europaeus*). *J. Anat. Physiol.* **27**, 334–46.

CORBET G.B. (1963) The frequency of albinism of the tail tip in British mammals. *Proc. zool. Soc. Lond.* **140**, 327–30.

CORBET G.B., CAMERON R.A.D. & GREENWOOD J.J.D. (1968) Small mammals and their ecto-parasites from the Scottish islands of Handa (Sutherland), Muck, Pabay, Scalpay and Soay (Inner Hebrides). *J. Linn. Soc. (Zool.)* **47**, 301–7.

COX F.E.G. (1970) Parasitic protozoa of British wild mammals. *Mammal Rev.* **1**, 1–28.

CRANBROOK EARL OF (1959) The feeding habits of the water shrew, *Neomys fodiens bicolor* Shaw, in captivity and the effect of its attack upon its prey. *Proc. zool. Soc. Lond.* **133**, 245–9.

CRANBROOK EARL OF & CROWCROFT P. (1958) The white-toothed shrews of the Channel Islands. *Ann. Mag. nat. Hist.* (13) **1**, 359–64.

CROIN MICHIELSEN N. (1966) Intraspecific and interspecific competition in the shrews *Sorex araneus* L. and *S. minutus* L. *Archs néerl. Zool.* **17**, 73–174.

CROIN MICHIELSEN N. (1967) Intraspecific and interspecific competition in the shrews *Sorex araneus* L. and *Sorex minutus* L. *Bull. Mammal Soc.* **28**, 6–7.

CROWCROFT W.P. (1954a) The daily cycle of activity in British shrews. *Proc. zool. Soc. Lond.* **123**, 715–29.

CROWCROFT W.P. (1954b) *An ecological study of British shrews.* D.Phil. thesis, University of Oxford.

CROWCROFT W.P. (1957) *The life of the shrew.* London, Max Reinhardt.

CROWCROFT P. & INGLES J.M. (1959) Seasonal changes in the brain-case of the common shrew (*Sorex araneus* L.). *Nature, Lond.* **183**, 907–8.

DAVIES J.L. (1957) A hedgehog road mortality index. *Proc. zool. Soc. Lond.* **128**, 606–8.

DEANESLY R. (1934) The reproductive processes of certain mammals, part 6. The reproductive cycle of the female hedgehog. *Phil. Trans.* B. **223**, 239–76.

DEANESLY R. (1966) Observations on reproduction in the mole (*Talpa europaea*). *Symp. zool. Soc. Lond.* **15**, 387–402.

DEHNEL A. (1950) [Studies on the genus *Neomys* Kaup.] *Ann. Univ. M. Curie-Skłodowska,* C, **4**, 17–102.

DELANY M.J. & HEALY M. (1966) Variation in the white-toothed shrews (*Crocidura* spp.) in the British Isles. *Proc. roy. Soc.* B **164**, 63–74.

EVANS A.C. (1948) The identity of earthworms stored by moles. *Proc. zool. Soc. Lond.* **118**, 356–9.

FONS R. (1972) La musaraigne musette, *C. russula* (Hermann 1780). *Sci. Nat. Paris* **112**, 23–8.

FORD C.E. & HAMERTON J.L. (1970) Chromosome polymorphism in the common shrew, *Sorex araneus. Symp. zool. Soc. Lond.* **26**, 223–36.

FRANKLAND H.M.T. (1959) The incidence and distribution in Britain of the trematodes of *Talpa europaea. Parasitology* **49**, 132–42.

FRASER F.C. & KING J.E. (1954) Faunal remains *in* Clark, J.G.D., *Excavations at Star Carr* ... Cambridge, University Press.

FREDGA K. & LEVAN A. (1969) The chromosomes of the European water shrew (*Neomys fodiens*). *Hereditas* **62**, 348–56.

FUNMILAYO O. (1971) *Population studies on the distribution of moles* (Talpa europaea *L.*) *relative to food supply and general habitat.* Ph.D. thesis, University of Edinburgh.

FUNMILAYO O. (1976) Age determination, age distribution and sex ratio in mole populations. *Acta theriol.* 21, 207–15.

GEBCZYŃSKA Z. & GEBCZYŃSKI M. (1965) Oxygen consumption in two species of water shrews. *Acta theriol.* **10**, 209–14.

GLUE D.E. (1974) Food of the Barn Owl in Britain and Ireland. *Bird Study* **21**, 200–10.

GODFREY G.K. (1955) A field study of the activity of the mole (*Talpa europaea* L.). *Ecology* **36**, 678–85.

GODFREY G.K. (1957) Observations on the movements of moles (*Talpa europaea* L.) after weaning. *Proc. zool. Soc. Lond.* **128**, 287–95.

GODFREY G.K. & CROWCROFT P. (1960) *The life of the mole.* London, Museum Press.

GRÜNWALD A. (1969) Untersuchungen zur Orientierung der Weisszahnspitzmäuse (Soricidae—Crocidurinae). *Z. vergl. Physiologie* **65**, 191–217.

GURNEY J.H. (1879) Notes on shrews observed in Norfolk. *Zoologist* 3, 123.

HAECK J. (1969) Colonization of the mole (*Talpa europaea* L.) in the Ijsselmeerpolders. *Neth. J. Zool.* **19**(2), 145–248.

HANZÁK J. (1966) Zur Jugendentwicklung der Gartenspitzmaus, *C. suaveolens* (Pallas, 1821). *Lynx* **6**, 67–74.

HAWKINS A.E. & JEWELL P.A. (1962) Food consumption and energy requirements of captive British shrews and the mole. *Proc. zool. Soc. Lond.* **138**, 137–55.

HAWKINS A.E., JEWELL P.A. & TOMLINSON G. (1960) The metabolism of some British shrews. *Proc. zool. Soc. Lond.* **135**, 99–103.

HERTER K. (1938) Die Biologie der europäischen Igel. *Kleintier und Pelztier* **14**, 1–222.

HERTER K. (1965) *Hedgehogs.* London, Phoenix House.

HEYDEMANN B. (1960) Zur Okologie von *Sorex araneus* L. und *Sorex minutus* L. *Z. Säugetierk.* **25**, 24–9.

IVANOVA E.I. (1967) New data on the nature of the rete mirabile and derivative apparatuses in some semi-aquatic mammals. *Dokl. (Proc.) Acad. Sci. USSR (biol.)* **173**, 1–3.

JALLOQ M.C. (1975) The invasion of molehills by weeds as a possible factor in the degeneration of reseeded pasture. *J. appl. Ecol.* **12**, 643–57.

KOZUCH O., GRULICH I. & NOSEK J. (1966) Serological survey and isolation of tick-borne encephalitis virus from the blood of the mole (*Talpa europaea*) in a natural focus. *Acta virol.* **10**, 557–60.

KRAL B. (1967) Karyological analysis of two European species of the genus *Erinaceus. Zool. Listy* 16, 239.

KRISTOFFERSSON R. & SUOMALAINEN P. (1964) Changes of body weight of hibernating and non-hibernating animals. *Ann. Ac. Sci. Fenn. (Ser. A)* no. 76, 1–11.

KRUUK H. (1964) Predators and anti-predator behaviour of the black-headed gull (*Larus ridibundus* L.). *Behaviour* suppl. 11.

LARKIN P. A. (1948) *Ecology of mole* (Talpa europaea *L.*) *populations.* D.Phil. thesis, University of Oxford.

LEHMANN E. VON (1969) Die Rückendrüse des europäischen Maulwurfs (*Talpa europaea*). *Z. Säugetierk.* **34**, 358–61.

LEWIS J.W. (1968) Studies on helminth parasites of voles and shrews from Wales. *J. Zool., Lond.* **154**, 313–31.

LINDEMANN W. (1951) Zur Psychologie des Igels. *Z. Tierpsychol.* **8**, 224–51.

LORENZ K.Z. (1952) *King Solomon's ring.* London, Methuen.

LORENZ K.Z. (1957) The European water shrew (*Neomys fodiens* Pennant, 1771). *In* Worden A.N. & Lane-Petter W. *The UFAW handbook on the care and management of laboratory animals* 2nd ed. London, University Fed. Animal Welfare.

McDIARMID A. & AUSTWICK P.K.C. (1954) Occurrence of *Haplosporangium parvum* in the lungs of the mole (*Talpa europaea*). *Nature, Lond.* **174**, 843–4.

McLAUGHLAN J.D. & HENDERSON W.M. (1947) The occurrence of foot and mouth disease in the hedgehog under natural conditions. *J. Hyg. Camb.* **45**, 474–9.

MATTHEWS L.H. (1935) The oestrous cycle and intersexuality in the female mole (*Talpa europaea* Linn.). *Proc. zool. Soc. Lond.* 347–83.

MEAD-BRIGGS A.R. & WOODS J.A. (1973) An index of activity to assess the reduction in mole numbers caused by control measures. *J. appl. Ecol.* **10**, 837–45.

MEESE G.B. & CHEESEMAN C.L. (1969) Radio-active tracking of the mole (*Talpa europaea*) over a 24-hour period. *J. Zool., Lond.* **158**, 197–224.

MELLANBY K. (1967) Food and activity in the mole *Talpa europaea*. *Nature, Lond.* **215**, 1128–30.

MELLANBY K. (1971) *The mole.* London, Collins.

MEYLAN A. (1964) Le polymorphisme chromosomique de *Sorex araneus* L. (Mammalia-Insectivora). *Rev. suisse Zool.* **71**, 903–83.

MEYLAN A. (1965) La formule chromosomique de *Sorex minutus* L. (Mammalia-Insectivora). *Experientia* **21**, 268.

MEYLAN A. (1966) Données nouvelles sur les chromosomes des insectivores européens (Mamm.). *Rev. suisse Zool.* **73**, 548–58.

MILNER C. & BALL D.F. (1970) Factors affecting the distribution of the mole (*Talpa europaea*) in Snowdonia (North Wales). *J. Zool., Lond.* **162**, 61–9.

MOLLISON B.C. (1960) Food regurgitation in Bennett's wallaby *Protemnodon rufogrisea* (Desmarest) and the scrub wallaby *Thylogale billardei* (Desmarest). *CSIRO Wildl. Res.* **5**, 87–8.

MORRIS B. (1961) Some observations on the breeding season of the hedgehog and the rearing and handling of the young. *Proc. zool. Soc. Lond.* **136**, 201–6.

MORRIS B. (1967) The European hedgehog. *In* Worden A.N. & Lane-Petter W. *The UFAW handbook on the care and management of laboratory animals.* 3rd ed. London, Livingstone.

MORRIS P. (1970) A method for determining absolute age in the hedgehog. *J. Zool., Lond.* **161**, 277–81.

MORRIS P. (1971) Epiphyseal fusion in the forefoot as a means of age determination in the hedgehog. *J. Zool. Lond.* **164**, 254–9.

MORRIS P. (1973) Winter nests of the hedgehog (*Erinaceus europaeus* L.). *Oecologia (Berl.)* **11**, 299–313.

MORRIS P. & ENGLISH M.P. (1969) *T. mentagrophytes* var. *erinacei* in British hedgehogs. *Sabouraudia* **7**, 122–7.

OGNEV S.I. (1928) [*Mammals of eastern Europe and northern Asia, vol. 1: Insectivora and Chiroptera.*] Moscow (English translation 1962: Jerusalem, Israel Program for Scientific Translations).

OUDEMANS A.C. (1913) Acarologisches aus Maulwürfnestern. *Arch. Naturgesch.* **79A** (8) 108–200, (9) 68–136, (10) 1–69.

PERNETTA J.C. (1973a) The ecology of *Crocidura suaveolens cassiteridum* (Hinton) in a coastal habitat. *Mammalia* 37, 241–56.

PERNETTA J.C. (1973b) *Field and laboratory experiments to determine the feeding ecology and behaviour of* Sorex araneus *L. and* Sorex minutus *L.* D.Phil. thesis, University of Oxford.

PRICE M. (1953) The reproductive cycle of the water shrew *Neomys fodiens bicolor*. *Proc. zool. Soc. Lond.* 123, 599–620.

PUCEK K. (1959) The effect of the venom of the European water shrew (*Neomys fodiens fodiens* Pennant) on certain experimental animals. *Acta theriol.* 3, 93–104.

PUCEK Z. (1960) Sexual maturation and variability of the reproductive system in young shrews (*Sorex* L.) in the first calendar year of life. *Acta theriol.* 3, 269–96.

QUILLIAM T.A. (ed.) (1966a) The mole: its adaptation to an underground environment. *J. Zool., Lond.* 149, 31–114.

QUILLIAM T.A. (1966b) The mole's sensory apparatus. *J. Zool., Lond.* 149, 76–88.

QUILLIAM T.A. (1966c) The problem of vision in the ecology of *Talpa europaea*. *Exper. eye Res.* 5, 63–78.

RANDOLPH, S.E. (1975) Seasonal dynamics of a host-parasite system: *Ixodes trianguliceps* (Acarina: Ixodidae) and its small mammal hosts. *J. Anim. Ecol.* 44, 425–49.

ROOD J.P. (1964) *Studies on the ecology of the small mammals of the Isles of Scilly*. Ph.D. thesis, University of Southampton.

ROOD J.P. (1965a) Observations on population structure, reproduction and molt of the Scilly shrew. *J. Mammal.* 46, 426–33.

ROOD J.P. (1965b) Observations on the home range and activity of the Scilly shrew. *Mammalia* 29, 507–16.

RUDGE A.J.B. (1966) Catching and keeping live moles. *J. Zool., Lond.* 149, 42–5.

RUDGE M.R. (1968) The food of the common shrew *Sorex araneus* L. (Insectivora: Soricidae) in Britain. *J. Anim. Ecol.* 37, 565–81.

SAINT GIRONS M.-C. (1959) Les characteristiques du rythme nycthéméral d'activité chez quelques petits mammifères. *Mammalia* 23, 245–76.

SCHAERFFENBERG B. (1940) Die Nahrung des Maulwurfs (*Talpa europaea* L.). *Z. angew. Ent.* 27, 1–70.

ŠEBEK Z. & ROSICKÝ B. (1967) The finding of *Pneumocystis carinii* in shrews (Insectivora: Soricidae). *Folia Parasit.* 14, 263–7.

SHILLITO J.F. (1960) The general ecology of the Common shrew (*Sorex araneus* L.). Ph.D. thesis, University of Exeter.

SHILLITO J.F. (1963) Field observations on the Water shrew (*Neomys fodiens*). *Proc. zool. Soc. Lond.* 140, 320–2.

SKOCZEŃ S. (1958) Tunnel digging by the mole (*Talpa europaea* Linné). *Acta theriol.* 2, 235–49.

SKOCZEŃ S. (1961a) On food storage of the mole (*Talpa europaea* Linnaeus, 1758). *Acta theriol.* 5, 23–43.

SKOCZEŃ S. (1961b) Colour mutations in the mole (*Talpa europaea* Linnaeus, 1758). *Acta theriol.* 5, 290–3.

SKOCZEŃ S. (1970) Food storage of some insectivorous mammals (Insectivora). *Przegl. zool.* 14, 243–8.

SMIT-VIS J. (1962) Some aspects of the hibernation in the European hedgehog *Erinaceus europaeus* L. *Archs. néerl. Zool.* 14, 513–97.

SOUTHERN H.N. (1954) Tawny owls and their prey. *Ibis* 96, 384–410.

SOUTHERN H.N. (ed.) (1964) *The handbook of British mammals*. Oxford, Blackwell Scientific Publications.

SPENCER-BOOTH Y. (1956) Shrews (*C. cassiteridum*) on the Scilly Isles. *Proc. zool. Soc. Lond.* **126**, 167–70.

SPENCER-BOOTH Y. (1963) A coastal population of shrews *C. s. cassiteridum*. *Proc. zool. Soc. Lond.* **140**, 322–6.

STEIN G.H.W. (1950) Zur Biologie des Maulwurfs, *Talpa europaea* L. *Bonn. zool. Beitr.* **1**, 97–116.

STEIN G.H.W. (1960) Schädelallometrien und Systematik bei altweltlichen Maulwürfen (Talpinae). *Mitt. zool. Mus. Berlin* **36**, 1–48.

STEIN G.H.W. (1961) Beziehung zwischen Bestandsdichte und Vermehrung bei der Waldspitzmaus, *Sorex araneus*, und weiteren Rotzahnspitzmäusen. *Z. Säugetierk.* **26**, 13–28.

STEIN G.H.W. (1963) Anomalien der Zahnzahl und ihre geographische Variabilität bei Insectivoren: I Maulwurf, *Talpa europaea* L. *Mitt. zool. Mus. Berlin* **39**, 223–40.

TARKOWSKI A.K. (1957) Studies on reproduction and prenatal mortality of the common shrew (*Sorex araneus* L.) Part II. Reproduction under natural conditions. *Ann. Univ. M. Curie-Sklodowska*, C, **10**, 177–244.

TUPIKOVA N.V. (1949) [Feeding and pattern of daily activity in shrews in the central zone of USSR]. *Zool. Zh.* **28**, 561–72 (in Russian).

TWIGG G.I., CUERDON C.M. & HUGHES D.M. (1968) Leptospirosis in small mammals. *Symp. zool. Soc. Lond.* **24**, 75–98.

TWIGG G.I. & HUGHES D.M. (1970) The 'Pancreas of Aselli' in shrews. *J. Zool., Lond.* **162**, 541–4.

VASARHELYI S. (1929) Beiträge zur Kenntnis der Lebensweise zweier Kleinsäuger. *Allat. Közl.* **26**, 84–91.

VOGEL P. (1969) Beobachtungen zum intraspezifischen Verhalten der Hausspitzmaus (*C. russula*). *Rev. suisse Zool.* **76**, 1079–86.

VOGEL P. (1972) Beitrag zur Fortpflanzungsbiologie der Gattungen *Sorex*, *Neomys* und *Crocidura* (Soricidae). *Verhandl. Naturf. Ges. Basel* **82**, 165–92.

VOGEL P. (1973) Vergleichende Untersuchungen zum Ontogenesmodus einheimischer Soriciden (*Crocidura russula*, *Sorex araneus* und *Neomys fodiens*). *Rev. suisse Zool.* **79**, 1201–1332.

WINDSOR D.E. & DAGG A.I. (1971) The gaits of the Macropodinae (Marsupialia). *J. Zool., Lond.* **163**, 165–75.

WODZICKI K. & FLUX J.E.C. (1967) Guide to introduced wallabies in New Zealand. *Tuatara* **15**, 47–59.

YALDEN D.W. (1966) The anatomy of mole locomotion. *J. Zool., Lond.* **149**, 55–64.

YALDEN D.W. (1976) The food of the Hedgehog in England. *Acta theriol* **21**, 401–24.

YALDEN D.W. & HOSEY G.R. (1971) Feral wallabies in the Peak District. *J. Zool., Lond.* **165**, 513–20.

ZUCKERMAN S. (1952) Breeding seasons of mammals in captivity. *Proc. zool. Soc. Lond.* **122**, 827–950.

BATS

ABEL G. (1967) Wiederfund von 2 Mopfledermäusen (*Barbastella barbastellus*) nach 18 Jarhen. *Myotis.* **5**, 19–20.

AELLEN V. (1962) La baguement des Chauves-Souris au Col de Bretolet (Valais). *Arch. Sci. (Geneva)* **14**, 365–92.

AUBERT A. (1963) Observations sur l'accouplement des Chiroptères. *Acta theriol.* **6**, 300–1.

BALCELLS R.E. (1956) Estudio Biologico y Biometrico de *Myotis nattereri* (Chir., Vesperti-lionidae). *Inst. Biol. Apl.* **23**, 37–81.

BAKER J.R. (1974) Protozoan parasites of the blood of British wild birds and mammals. *J. Zool. Lond.* **172**, 161–90.

BARBU P. & SIN G. (1968) Observatii asupra hibernarii speciei *Nyctalus noctula* (Schreber 1774) in Faleza Lacului Razelm–capul Dolosman-Dobrogea. *St. Si. cerc. Biol. Seria Zool.* **20**, 291–7.

BARRETT-HAMILTON G.E.H. (1910–11) *A History of British Mammals*. Vol. 1: *Bats*. London, Gurney & Jackson.

BAUER K. (1960) Die Säugetiere des Neusiedlersee-Gebietes (Oesterreich). *Bonn. zool. Beitr.* **11**, 141–344.

BELS L. (1952) Fifteen years of bat banding in the Netherlands. *Publtiës natuurh. Genoot. Limburg* **5**, 1–99.

BEZEM J.J., SLUITER J.W. & HEERDT P.F. VAN (1960) Population statistics of five species of the bat genus *Myotis* and one of the genus *Rhinolophus*, hibernating in the caves of S. Limburg. *Archs. néerl. Zool.* **13**, 511–39.

BEZEM J.J., SLUITER J.W. & HEERDT P.F. VAN (1964) Some characteristics of the hibernating locations of various species of bats in South Limberg. I and II. *Koninkl. Nederl. Akademie van Wetenschappen—Amsterdam* **67**(5), 235–350.

BLACKMORE M. (1956) An occurrence of the mouse-eared bat *Myotis myotis* (Borkhausen) in England. *Proc. zool. Soc. Lond.* **127**, 201–3.

BOVEY R. (1949) Les chromosomes des Chiroptères et des Insectivores. *Rev. suisse Zool.* **56**, 371–460.

BURESCH I.W. (1941) Die Fledermause ziehen wie die Zugvögel, *Schr. Bulg. Akad. Wiss.* **61**, 51–72.

CAPANNA E. & CIVITELLI M.V. (1964) Contributo alla conoscenza della cariologia dei Rinolofidi (Mammalia, Chiroptera). *Caryologia* **17**, 361–71.

CAPANNA E., CIVITELLI M.V. & CONTI L. (1967) I cromosomi somatici del pipistrello, Ferro di cavallo minore (Mammalia, Chiroptera). *Rend. Acc. Naz. Lincei* (s. 8) **42**, 125–8.

CAPANNA E., CONTI L. & DE RENZIS G. (1968) I chromosomi di *Barbastella barbastellus* (Mammalia, Chiroptera). *Caryologia* **21**, 137–45.

CAUBÈRE B., MENU H. & SAINT GIRONS M.–C. (1968) Notes sur les mammifères de France. VII. Dimensions de l'avant-bras de *Rhinolophus ferrumequinum*. *Mammalia* **32**, 97–103.

CHURCH H.F. (1957) The times of emergence of the pipistrelle. *Proc. zool. Soc. Lond.* **128**, 600–2.

CLARKE R.R. (1963) *Grime's graves, Norfolk*. London, HMSO.

CORBET G.B. (1964) The grey long-eared bat *Plecotus austriacus* in England and the Channel Islands. *Proc. zool. Soc. Lond.* **143**, 511–15.

CORBET G.B. (1970) Vagrant bats in Shetland and the North Sea. *J. Zool., Lond.* **161**, 281–2.

CORBET G.B. (1971) Provisional distribution maps of British mammals. *Mammal Rev.* **1**, 95–142.

CRANBROOK, EARL OF (1964a) Notes on the behaviour of hibernating Noctule (*Nyctalus noctula*). *Trans. Suff. Nat. Soc.* **12**, 446–7.

CRANBROOK, EARL OF (1964b) Notes on a foraging group of Serotine bats (*Eptesicus serotinus* Schreber). *Trans. Suff. Nat. Soc.* **13**, 15–19.

CRANBROOK, EARL OF, & BARRETT H.G. (1965) Observations on Noctule bats (*Nyctalus noctula*) captured while feeding. *Proc. zool. Soc. Lond.* **144**, 1–24.

DAAN S. & WICHERS H.J. (1968) Habitat selection of bats hibernating in a limestone cave. *Z. Säugetierk.* **33**, 262–87.

DEANESLY, R. & WARWICK, T. (1939) Observations on pregnancy in the common bat (*Pipistrellus pipistrellus*). *Proc. zool. Soc. Lond.* **109 A**, 57–60.

DE COURSEY G. & DE COURSEY P.G. (1964) Adaptive aspects of activity rhythms in bats *Biol. Bull.* **126**, 14–27.

DINALE G. (1964) Studi sui Chirotteri Italiani, II: Il raggiungimento della maturita sessuale in *Rhinolophus ferrumequinum* Schr. *Atti. Soc. Ital. Sci Nat. & Mus. Civ. Stor. Nat. Milano* **103**, 141–53.

DORGELO J. & PUNT A. (1969) Abundance and internal migration of hibernating bats in an artificial limestone cave (Sibbergroeve). *Lynx, Praha* **10**, 101–25.

DULIĆ B. (1963) Etude écologique des chauves-souris cavernicoles de la Croatie Occidentale (Yougoslavie). *Mammalia* **27**, 385–436.

DULIĆ B. (1966) Kromosomi somatickih stanica kao indikatori interspecificke srodnosti nekih rinolofida (Mammalia, Chiroptera). *Biol. Glasnik* **19**, 65–97.

DULIĆ B., SOLDALOVIC B. & RIMSA D. (1967) La formule chromosomique de la Noctule, *Nyctalus noctula* (Mammalia-Chiroptera). *Experientia* **23**, 945–8.

DUNITRESCO M. & ORGHIDAN T. (1963) Contribution à la connaissance de la biologie de *Pipistrellus pipistrellus* Schreber. *Annls Spéléol.* **18**, 511–17.

EGSBAEK W. & JENSEN B. (1963) Results of bat banding in Denmark. *Vidensk. Meddr. dansk Naturh. Foren.* **125**, 269–96.

EISENTRAUT M. (1936) Zur Fortpflanzungsbiologie der Fledermäuse. *Z. Morph. Okol. Tiere* **31**, 27–63.

EISENTRAUT M. (1937) Die deutschen Fledermäuse, eine biologische Studie. *Zbl. Kleintierk.* **13**, 1–184.

EISENTRAUT M. (1949) Beobachtung über Begattung bei Fledermäuse in Winterquartur. *Zool. Jahrb* (Syst. Oekol) **78**, 297–300.

ELIASSEN E. & EGSBAEK W. (1963) Vascular changes in the hibernating bat *Myotis daubentonii*. *Arb. Univ. Bergen—Mat. Naturv. Serie* **3**, 1–22.

ENGLANDER H. & LAUFENS G. (1968) Aktivitätsuntersuchungen bei Fransenfledermäusen (*Myotis nattereri*, Kuhl 1818). *Experientia* **24**, 618–19.

EVANS G.O. & TILL W.M. (1966) Studies on British Dermanyssidae (Acari: Mesostigmata). Pt II: Classification. *Bull. Br. Mus. nat. Hist.* (*Zool.*) **14**, 107–370.

FEDYK A. & FEDYK S. (1970) Karyotypes of some species of Vespertilionid bats from Poland. *Acta theriol.* **15**, 295–302.

FEDYK S. & FEDYK A. (1971) Karyological analysis of respresentatives of the genus *Plecotus* Geoffroy 1818 (Mammalia: Chiroptera). *Caryologia* **24**, 483–492.

FELDMANN R. (1967) Bestandsentwicklung und heutiges Areal der Kleinhufeisennase, *Rhinolophus hipposideros* (Bechstein, 1800), im mittleren Europa. *Säugetierk. Mitt.* **15**, 43–9.

FENTON M.B. (1970) Population studies of *Myotis lucifugus* (Chiroptera: Vespertilionidae) in Ontario. *Life Sci. Contr. R. Ont. Mus.* no. 77, 1–34.

GAISLER J. (1966a) Reproduction in the lesser horseshoe bat (*Rhinolophus hipposideros hipposideros* Bechstein 1800). *Bijdr. Dierk.* **36**, 45–64.

GAISLER J. (1966b) A tentative ecological classification of colonies of the European bats. *Lynx, Praha* n.s. **6**, 35–9.

GAISLER J. (1970) Remarks on the thermopreferendum of palearctic bats in their natural habitats. *Bijdr. Dierk.* **40**, 33–5.

GAISLER J. & HANÁK V. (1969a) Ergebnisse der zwanzigjährigen Beringung von Fledermäusen (Chiroptera) in der Tschechoslowakei: 1948–1967. *Acta Sc. Nat. Brno* **3**, (5), 1–33.

GAISLER J. & HANÁK V. (1969b) Summary of the results of bat banding in Czechoslovakia-1948–1967. *Lynx, Praha*, n.s. **10**, 25–34.

GILBERT O. (1948) On bats in West Suffolk. *Trans. Suffolk Nat. Soc.* **6**, 163–5.

GILBERT O. & STEBBINGS R.E. (1958) Winter roosts of bats in West Suffolk. *Proc. zool. Soc. Lond.* **131**, 321–33.

GRIFFIN D.R. (1958) *Listening in the dark*. New Haven, Yale University Press.

HANÁK V. (1969) Okologische Bemerkungen zur Verbreitung der Langohren (Gattung *Plecotus* Geoffroy, 1818) in der Tschechoslowakei. *Lynx, Praha* **10**, 35–9.

HANÁK V. (1970) Notes on the distribution and systematics of *Myotis mystacinus* Kuhl, 1819. *Bijdr. Dierk.* **40**, 40–4.

HANÁK V. (1971) *Myotis brandtii* (Eversmann, 1845) (Vespertilionidae Chiroptera) in der Tschechoslowakei. *Věst. čsl. Spol. zool.* **35**, 175–85.

HARMATA W. (1962) Sezonowa rytmika obyczajow i ekologia nietoperzy (Chiroptera) przebywajacych w niektorych zabytkowych budowlach wojewodztwa krakowskiego. *Zeszyty naukowe uniwersytetu jag.* **58**, 149–79.

HARMATA W. (1969a) Kolonia letnia nietoperza *Myotis bechsteini* (Kuhl) w Szymbarku kolo Gotlic w woj rzeszowskim. Uwagi o biologii ii wystepowaniu. *Przeglad Zool..* **13**, 233–8.

HARMATA W. (1969b) The thermopreferendum of some species of bats (Chiroptera). *Acta theriol.* **5**, 49–62.

HAYDEN J. & KIRKBY P. (1954) Bats in the Bishop's Stortford area. *Oryx* **2**, 325–8.

HEERDT P.F. VAN & SLUITER J.W. (1961) New data on longevity in bats. *Natuurh. Maandb.* **3–4**, 36.

HEERDT P.F. VAN & SLUITER J.W. (1965) Notes on the distribution and behaviour of the Noctule bat (*Nyctalus noctula*) in the Netherlands. *Mammalia* **29**, 463–77.

HOOPER J.H.D. (1969) Potential use of a portable ultrasonic receiver for the field identification of flying bats. *Ultrasonics* **7**, 177–81.

HOOPER J.H.D. & HOOPER W.M. (1965) Habits and movements of cave-dwelling bats in Devonshire. *Proc. zool. Soc. Lond.* **127**, 1–26.

HOOPER J.H.D. & HOOPER W.M. (1967) Longevity of Rhinolophid bats in Britain. *Nature, Lond.* **216**, 1135–6.

HURKA L. (1966) Beitrag zur Bionomie, Okologie und zur Biometrik der Zwergfledermaus (*Pipistrellus pipistrellus* Schreber, 1774) (Mammalia: Chiroptera) nach den Beobachtungen in Westböhmen. *Věst. čsl. Spol. zool.* **30**, 228–46.

HURKA L. (1971) Zur Verbreitung und Ökologie der Fledermäuse der Gattung *Plecotus* (Mammalia Chiroptera) in Westböhmen. *Fol. mus. rer. natur. Bohemiae. Occ. Zool.* **1**, 1–24.

HUTSON A.M. (1964) Parasites from mammals in Suffolk. *Trans. Suffolk Nat. Soc.* **12**, 451–2.

ISSEL W. (1958) Zur Ökologie unserer Waldfledermäuse. *Natur Landschaft* **1**, 1–4.

JEFFERIES D.J. (1972) Organochlorine insecticide residues in British bats and their significance. *J. Zool. Lond.* **166**, 245–63.

KEPKA O. (1960) Die Ergebnisse der Fledermausberingung in der Steiermark vom Jahr 1949 bis 1960. *Bonn. zool. Beitr.* **11**, 54–76.

KLEIMAN D.G. (1969) Maternal care, growth rate and development in the noctule (*Nyctalus noctula*), pipistrelle (*Pipistrellus pipistrellus*) and serotine (*Eptesicus serotinus*) bats. *J. Zool. Lond.* **157**, 187–211.

KLEIMAN D.G. & RACEY P.A. (1969) Observations on noctule bats *Nyctalus noctula* breeding in captivity. *Lynx, Praha* **10** (n.s.), 65–77.

KRZANOWSKI A. (1960) Investigations of flights of Polish bats, mainly *Myotis myotis* (Bork-hausen 1797). *Acta theriol.* **4**, 175–84.

KRZANOWSKI A. (1964) Three long flights by bats. *J. Mammal.* **45**, 152.

LAUFENS G. (1969) Untersuchungen zur Aktivitätsperiodic von *Myotis nattereri* Kuhl 1818. *Lynx, Praha* n.s. **10**, 45–51.

LOVETT W.V. (1961) A feeding population of pipistrelle bats (*P. pipistrellus* Lin.). *Trans. Suffolk Nat. Soc.* **12**, 39–43.

MASON C.F., STEBBINGS R.E. & WINN G.P. (1972) Noctules and starlings competing for roosting holes. *J. Zool. Lond.* **166**, 467.

MATTHEWS L.H. (1937) The female sexual cycle in the British horseshoe bats *Rhinolophus ferrumequinum insulanus* Barrett-Hamilton and *R. hipposideros minutus* Montague. *Trans. zool. Soc. Lond.* **23**, 229–66.

MAZÁK V. (1965) Changes in pelage of *Myotis myotis myotis* Borkhausen 1797. (Mammalia, Chiroptera). *Věst. čsl. Spol. zool.* **29**, 368–76.

MISLIN H. & VISCHER L. (1942) Zur Biologie der Chiroptera. II Die Temperaturregulation der überwinternden *Nyctalus noctula* Schreb. *Verh. Schweiz. Naturf. Ges. Bern.* **122**, 131–3.

MOFFAT C.B. (1900) The habits of the hairy-armed bat, *Vesperugo leisleri*. *Ir. Nat.* **2**, 235–40.

MOFFAT C.B. (1922) The habits of the long-eared bat. *Ir. Nat.* **31**, 105–11.

MOORE N.W. (1975) The diurnal flight of the Azorean bat (*Nyctalus azoreum*) and the avifauna of the Azores. *J. Zool. Lond.* **177**, 483–6.

NIEUWENHOVEN P.J. VAN (1956) Ecological observation in a hibernation-quarter of cave dwelling bats in South Limburg. *Publiës natuurh. Genoots Limburg* **9**, 1–55.

NORBERG U.M. (1970) Hovering flight of *Plecotus auritus* Linnaeus. *Bijdr. Dierk.* **40**, 62–6.

NYHOLM E.S. (1965) Zur Ökologie von *Myotis mystacinus* (Leisl.) und *Myotis daubentoni* (Leisl.) (Chiroptera). *Ann. Zool. fenn.* **2**, 77–123.

PALASTHY J. (1968) Casty Vyskyt Parcialneho Albinizmu U Uchane Ciernej (*Barbastella barbastellus* Schreber, 1774). *Biologia, Bratislava* **23**, 370–6.

PALASTHY J. & GAISLER J. (1965) K. Otazce tak zvanych 'Invazi' a zimnich Koloni netopyra hvizdaveho (*Pipistrellus pipistrellus* Schr. 1774). *Zool. Listy* **14**, 9–14.

PHILLIPS W.W.A. & BLACKMORE M. (1970) Mouse-eared bats *Myotis myotis* in Sussex. *J. Zool. Lond.* **162**, 520–1.

PIECHOKI R. (1966) Uber die Nachweise der Langohr-Fledermäuse *Plecotus auritus* L. und *Plecotus austriacus* Fischer im mitteldeutschen Raum. *Hercynia* **3**, 407–15.

PIEPER H. (1968) Neues Höchstalter für die Mausohrfledermaus (*Myotis myotis*). *Myotis* **6**, 29–30.

POULTON E.B. (1929) British insectivorous bats and their prey. *Proc. zool. Soc. Lond.* (1929) 277–303.

RACEY P.A. (1969) Diagnosis of pregnancy and experimental extension of gestation in the pipistrelle bat *Pipistrellus pipistrellus*. *J. Reprod. Fert.* **19**, 465–74.

RACEY P.A. (1970) The breeding, care and management of vespertilionid bats in the labora-tory. *Lab. Anim.* **4**, 171–83.

RACEY P.A. (1972) Aspects of reproduction in some heterothermic bats. Ph.D. thesis, Uni-versity of London.

RACEY P.A. (1973a) The viability of spermatozoa after prolonged storage by male and female bats. *Period. Biol.* **75**, 201–5.

RACEY P.A. (1973b) Environmental factors affecting the length of gestation in heterothermic bats. *J. Reprod. Fert. Suppl.* **19**, 175–89.

RACEY P.A. (1973c) The time of onset of hibernation in the pipistrelle (*Pipistrellus pipistrellus*). *J. Zool. Lond.* **171**, 465–7.

RACEY P.A. (1974a) Ageing and assessment of reproductive status in the pipistrelle bat (*Pipistrellus pipistrellus*). *J. Zool. Lond.* **173**, 263–71.

RACEY P.A. (1974b) The temperature of a pipistrelle hibernaculum. *J. Zool. Lond.* **173**, 260–2.

RACEY P.A. (1974c) The reproductive cycle in male noctule bats *Nyctalus noctula*. *J. Reprod. Fert.* **41**, 169–82.

RACEY P.A. (1975) The prolonged survival of spermatozoa in bats. *In* Duckell J.G. & Racey P.A. *The biology of the male gamete. Biol. J. Linn. Soc.* **7** Suppl. 1, 385–416.

RACEY P.A. & KLEIMAN D.G. (1970) Maintenance and breeding in captivity of some vespertilionid bats with special reference to the noctule *Nyctalus noctula*. *Int. Zoo Yb.* **10**, 65–70.

RACEY P.A. & STEBBINGS R.E. (1972) Bats in Britain—a status report. *Oryx* **11**, 319–27.

RACEY P.A. & TAM W.H. (1974) Reproduction in the male pipistrelle (*Pipistrellus pipistrellus*). *J. Zool. Lond.* **172**, 101–22.

RADFORD D. (1954) Observations on the fur mites (Acarina, Myobiidae). *Ann. Mus. Congo Belge, Zool.* (4) **1**, 238–48.

RANSOME R.D. (1968) The distribution of the greater horseshoe bat, *Rhinolophus ferrumequinum* during hibernation, in relation to environmental factors. *J. Zool. Lond.* **154**, 77–112.

RANSOME R.D. (1971) The effect of ambient temperature on the arousal frequency of the hibernating greater horseshoe bat, *Rhinolophus ferrumequinum*, in relation to site selection and the hibernation state. *J. Zool. Lond.* **164**, 353–71.

RANSOME R.D. (1973) Factors affecting the timing of births of the greater horseshoe bat (*Rhinolophus ferrumequinum*). *Period. Biol.* **75**, 169–75.

RITCHIE J. (1927) A long flight—the European particoloured bat (*Vespertilio murinus*) in Scotland. *Scot. Nat.* 1927: 101–3.

ROER H. (1968) Zur Frage der Wochenstuben—Quartierertreue weiblicher Mausohren (*Myotis myotis*). *Bonn. zool. Beitr.* **19**, 85–96.

ROER H. (1969) Zur Ernährungsbiologie von *Plecotus auritus* (L.) (Mam. Chiroptera). *Bonn. zool. Beitr.* **20**, 378–83.

ROER H. & EGSBAEK W. (1966) Zur Biologie einer skandinavischen Population der Wasserfledermaus (*Myotis daubentoni*) (Chiroptera) *Z. Säugetierk.* **31**, 440–53.

RUDNICK A. (1960) A revision of the mites of the family Spinturnicidae (Acarina). *Univ. Calif. Publ. Ent.* **17**, 157–284.

RUPRECHT A.L. (1971) Distribution of *Myotis myotis* (Borkhausen, 1797) and representatives of the genus *Plecotus* Geoffroy, 1818 in Poland. *Acta theriol.* **16**, 96–104.

RYBERG O. (1947) *Studies on bats and bat parasites.* Stockholm, Svensk Natur.

SAINT GIRONS M.–C. & CAUBÈRE B. (1966) Notes sur les mammifères de France. V. Sur la répartition de *Rhinolophus hipposideros hipposideros* (Bechstein, 1800) et *Rhinolophus hipposideros minimum* Heughlin 1861. *Mammalia* **30**, 308–26.

SALES G.D. & PYE J.D. (1974) *Ultrasonic communication by animals.* London, Chapman & Hall.

SKLENAR J. (1963) The reproduction of *Myotis myotis* Borkh. *Lynx, Praha* **2**, 29–37.

SLUITER J.W. (1954) Sexual maturity in bats of the genus *Myotis*. II: Females of *M. mystacinus* and supplementary data on female *M. myotis* and *M. emarginatus*. *Proc. K. ned. Akad. Wet.* C. **57**, 696–700.

SLUITER J.W. (1960) Reproductive rate of the bat *Rhinolophus hipposideros*. *Proc. K. ned. Akad. Wet.* C. **63**, 383–93.

SLUITER J.W. (1961) Sexual maturity in males of the bat *Myotis myotis*. *Proc. K. ned. Akad. Wet.* C. **64**, 243–9.

SLUITER J.W. & BOUMAN M. (1951) Sexual maturity in bats of the genus *Myotis*. I: Size and histology of the reproductive organs during hibernation in connection with age and wear of the teeth in female *Myotis myotis* and *Myotis emarginatus*. *Proc. K. ned. Akad. Wet.* C. **54**, 594–601.

SLUITER J.W. & HEERDT P.F. VAN (1966) Seasonal habits of the Noctule bat *Nyctalus noctula*. *Arch. néerl. Zool.* **16**, 423–39.

SMIT F.G.A.M. (1957) The recorded distribution and hosts of Siphonaptera in Britain. *Entomologist's Gaz.* **8**, 45–75.

STANSFIELD G. (1966) Parti-coloured bat *Vespertilio murinus* L. from a North Sea drilling rig. *J. Zool. Lond.* **150**, 491–2.

STEBBINGS R.E. (1960) Lesser horseshoe bat in West Suffolk. *Proc. zool. Soc. Lond.* **133**, 483.

STEBBINGS R.E. (1965) Observations during 16 years on winter roosts of bats in West Suffolk. *Proc. zool. Soc. Lond.* **144**, 137–43.

STEBBINGS R.E. (1966a) Bechstein's bat, *Myotis bechsteini* in Dorset 1960–65. *J. Zool. Lond.* **148**, 574–6.

STEBBINGS R.E. (1966b) Bats associated with a *Plecotus* colony. *J. Zool. Lond.* **150**, 492–3.

STEBBINGS R.E. (1966c) A population study of bats of the genus *Plecotus*. *J. Zool. Lond.* **150**, 53–75.

STEBBINGS R.E. (1967) Identification and distribution of bats of the genus *Plecotus* in England. *J. Zool. Lond.* **153**, 291–310.

STEBBINGS R.E. (1968a) Bechstein's bat (*Myotis bechsteini*) in Dorset 1965–67. *J. Zool. Lond.* **155**, 228–231.

STEBBINGS R.E. (1968b) Measurements, composition and behaviour of the bat *Pipistrellus pipistrellus*. *J. Zool. Lond.* **156**, 15–33.

STEBBINGS R.E. (1968c) Longevity of Vespertilionid bats in Britain. *J. Zool. Lond.* **156**, 530–1.

STEBBINGS R.E. (1970a) A comparative study of *Plecotus auritus* and *P. austriacus* (Chiroptera, Vespertilionidae) inhabiting one roost. *Bijdr. Dierk.* **40**, 91–4.

STEBBINGS R.E. (1970b) A bat new to Britain *Pipistrellus nathusii* with notes on its identification and distribution in Europe. *J. Zool. Lond.* **161**, 282–6.

STEBBINGS R.E. (1973) Size clines in the bat *Pipistrellus pipistrellus* related to climatic factors. *Period. Biol.* **75**, 189–94.

STEBBINGS R.E. (1974) Artificial roosts for bats. *J. Devon Trust Nat. Conserv.* **6**, 114–19.

STEBBINGS R.E. & PLACIDO C. (1975) Predation on a pipistrelle bat (*Pipistrellus pipistrellus*) by a mustelid. *Scot. Nat.* **19**, 179–80.

STRELKOV P. (1962) The peculiarities of reproduction in bats (Vespertilionidae) near the northern border of their distribution. *Int. Symp. Meth. mammal. Invest. Brno 1960*, 306–11.

STRELKOV P.P. (1969) Migratory and stationary bats (Chiroptera) of the European part of the Soviet Union. *Acta Zool. Cracoviensia* **14**, 393–440.

STRELKOV P.P. & VOLOBUEV V.T. (1969) Identicnost' Kariotipov v rode *Myotis*. *Mater. K. II-omu Vsesoj. Sov. po mlekopit.* (*Moskava, 23–27*) **12**, 14–15.

THEODOR O. (1967) *An illustrated catalogue of the Rothschild collection of Nycteribiidae (Diptera) in the British Museum (Natural History)*. London, British Museum (Nat. Hist.)

THOMPSON G.B. (1963a) The parasites of British birds and mammals XXXIX. The Blythborough tick—*Argas* (*Carios*) *vespertilionis* (Latreille, 1802) (Ixodoidea). *Entomologist's mon. Mag.* **98**, 241–50.

THOMPSON G.B. (1963b) The parasites of British birds and mammals. XLI: The long-legged bat tick *Ixodes vespertilionis* Koch, 1884 (Ixodoidea). *Entomologist's mon. Mag.* **100**, 18–20.

THOMPSON G.B. (1968) Further notes on *Argas* (*Argas*) *reflexans* (Fabr.), *Argas* (*Carios*) *vespertilionis* (Latreille) and *Ixodes vespertilionis* Koch (Ixodoidea). *Entomologist's mon. Mag.* **103**, 153–4.

TOPAL G. (1956) The movements of bats in Hungary. *Ann. Hist. Nat. Musei Nationalis Hung.* **1**, 477–89.

TOPAL G. (1966) Some observations on the nocturnal activity of bats in Hungary. *Vertebrata Hungarica* **8**, 139–65.

USINGER R.L. *et al.* (1966) Monograph of the Cimicidae. *Thomas Say Foundation* **7**, 1–585.

VAUGHAN T.A. (1972) *Mammalogy.* Philadelphia, Saunders.

VENABLES L.S.V. (1943) Observations at a pipistrelle bat roost. *J. Anim. Ecol.* **12**, 19–26.

WIMSATT W.A. (1970) *Biology of bats.* New York, Academic Press.

YALDEN D.W. & MORRIS P.A. (1975) *Biology of bats.* Newton Abbot, David & Charles.

LAGOMORPHS

ANDERSEN J. (1957) Studies in Danish hare–populations. 1: Population fluctuations. *Dan. Rev. Game Biol.* **3**, 85–131.

ANDRZEJEWSKI R. & PUCEK Z. (1965) Studies on the European hare. X: Results so far obtained from research in Poland and trends in continued studies. *Acta theriol.* **10**, 79–91.

BOBACK A. (1954) Zur Frage des Harnspritzens beim Feldhasen, *Lepus europaeus* Pallas, 1778. *Säugetierk. Mitt.* **2**, 78–9.

BRAMBELL F.W.R. (1942) Intra-uterine mortality of the wild rabbit, *Oryctolagus cuniculus* (L.). *Proc. roy. Soc. B.*, **130**, 462–79.

BRAMBELL F.W.R. (1944) The reproduction of the wild rabbit, *Oryctolagus cuniculus* (L.). *Proc. zool. Soc. Lond.* **114**, 1–45.

EABRY S. (1969) *A bibliography of European hare* Lepus europaeus. Delmar, N.Y.S. Conservation Dept.

FARROW E.P. (1925) *Plant life on East Anglian heaths.* Cambridge, University Press.

FENNER F. & CHAPPLE P.J. (1965) Evolutionary changes in myxoma virus in Britain. *J. Hyg. Camb.* **63**, 175–85.

FLUX J.E.C. (1965) Timing of the breeding season in the hare *Lepus europaeus* Pallas, and rabbit, *Oryctolagus cuniculus* (L.). *Mammalia* **29**, 557–62.

FLUX J.E.C. (1967) Reproduction and body weights of the hare *Lepus europaeus* Pallas, in New Zealand. *N.Z. Jl Sci.* **10**, 357–401.

FLUX J.E.C. (1970) Life history of the Mountain hare (*Lepus timidus scoticus*) in north-east Scotland. *J. Zool., Lond.* **161**, 75–123.

HEWSON R. (1954) The mountain hare in Scotland in 1951. *Scot. Nat.* **66**, 70–88.

HEWSON R. (1958) Moults and winter whitening in the mountain hare *Lepus timidus scoticus* Hilzheimer. *Proc. zool. Soc. Lond.* **131**, 99–108.

HEWSON R. (1962) Food and feeding habits of the mountain hare *Lepus timidus scoticus* Hilzheimer. *Proc. zool. Soc. Lond.* **139**, 415–26.

HEWSON R. (1963) Moults and pelages in the brown hare *Lepus europaeus occidentalis* De Winton. *Proc. zool. Soc. Lond.* **141**, 677–88.

HEWSON R. (1968) Weights and growth rates in the Mountain hare *Lepus timidus scoticus*. *J. Zool., Lond.* **154**, 249–62.

HEWSON R. (1970) Variation in reproduction and shooting bags of mountain hares in north-east Scotland. *J. appl. Ecol.* 7, 243–52.

HEWSON R. (1974) *Population changes and grazing preferences of mountain hares* Lepus timidus L. *in north-east Scotland.* M.Sc. thesis, University of Aberdeen.

HEWSON R. & TAYLOR M. (1968) Movements of European hares in an upland area of Scotland. *Acta theriol.* 13, 31–4.

HEWSON R. & TAYLOR M. (1975) Embryo counts and length of the breeding season in European hares *Lepus capensis* in north-east Scotland. *Acta theriol.* 20, 247–54.

IRVIN A.D. (1970) A note on the gastro-intestinal parasites of British hares (*Lepus europaeus* and *L. timidus*). *J. Zool., Lond.* 162, 544–6.

LIND E.A. (1963) Observations on the mutual relationships between the snowhare (*Lepus timidus*) and the field hare (*Lepus europaeus*). *Suomen Riista* 16, 128–35 (Finnish, English summary).

LLOYD H.G. (1963) Intra-uterine mortality in the wild rabbit *Oryctolagus cuniculus* (L.) in populations of low density. *J. Anim. Ecol.* 32, 549–63.

LLOYD H.G. (1968) Observations on breeding in the brown hare *Lepus europaeus* during the first pregnancy of the season. *J. Zool., Lond.* 156, 521–8.

LLOYD H.G. (1970) Variation and adaptation in reproductive performance. *Symp. zool. Soc. Lond.* 26, 165–87.

MEAD-BRIGGS A.R. (1964) The reproductive biology of the rabbit flea, *Spilopsyllus cuniculi* (Dale) and the dependence of this species upon the breeding of its host. *J. exp. Biol.* 41, 371–402.

MYERS K., HALE C.S., MYKYTOWYCZ R. & HUGHES R.C. (1971) The effects of varying density and space on sociality and health in animals. 148–87. In *Behaviour & Environment.* Plenum Press.

MYERS K. & POOLE W.E. (1959) A study of the biology of the wild rabbit, *Oryctolagus cuniculus* (L.) in confined populations. 1. The effects of density on home range and the formation of breeding groups. *CSIRO Wildl. Res.* 4, 14–26.

MYERS K. & POOLE W.E. (1961) A study of the biology of the wild rabbit, *Oryctolagus cuniculus* (L.) in confined populations. 2. The effects of season and population increase on behaviour. *CSIRO Wildl. Res.* 6, 1–41.

MYKYTOWYCZ R. (1958) Social behaviour of an experimental colony of wild rabbits, *Oryctolagus cuniculus* (L.). 1. Establishment of the colony. *CSIRO Wildl. Res.* 3, 7–25.

MYKYTOWYCZ R. (1959) Social behaviour of an experimental colony of wild rabbits, *Oryctolagus cuniculus* (L.). 2. First breeding season. *CSIRO Wildl. Res.* 4, 1–13.

MYKYTOWYCZ R. (1960) Social behaviour of an experimental colony of wild rabbits, *Oryctolagus cuniculus* (L.). 3. Second breeding season. *CSIRO Wildl. Res.* 5, 1–20.

MYKYTOWYCZ R. (1962) Territorial function of chin gland secretion in the rabbit, *Oryctolagus cuniculus* (L.). *Nature, Lond.* 193, 799.

MYKYTOWYCZ R. (1965) Further observations on the territorial function and histology of the submandibular cutaneous (chin) glands in the rabbit, *Oryctolagus cuniculus* (L.). *Anim. Behav.* 13, 400–12.

MYKYTOWYCZ R. (1966) Observation on odoriferous and other glands in the Australian wild rabbit, *Oryctolagus cuniculus* (L.) and the hare, *Lepus europaeus* P. 1. The anal gland. *CSIRO Wildl. Res.* 11, 11–29.

MYKYTOWYCZ R. (1967) Communication by smell in the wild rabbit. *Proc. ecol. Soc. Aust.* 2, 125–31.

MYKYTOWYCZ R. & GAMBALE S. (1969) The distribution of dung hills and the behaviour of free-living wild rabbits, *Oryctolagus cuniculus* (L.) on them. *Forma et functio* 1, 333–49.

PETRUSEWICZ K. (1970) Dynamics and production of the hare population in Poland. *Acta theriol.* **15**, 413–44.

PIELOWSKI Z. (1971a) The individual growth curve of the hare. *Acta theriol.* **5**, 79–88.

PIELOWSKI Z. (1971b) Length of life of the hare. *Acta theriol.* **6**, 89–94.

PIELOWSKI Z. (1972) Home range and degree of residence of the European hare. *Acta theriol.* **9**, 93–103.

RIECK W. (1956) Untersuchungen über die Vermehrung des Feldhasen. *Z. Jagdw.* **11**, 49–90.

ROTHSCHILD M. & MARSH H. (1956) Increase of hares (*Lepus europaeus* Pallas) at Ashton Wold, with a note on the reduction in numbers of the brown rat (*Rattus norvegicus* Berkenhout). *Proc. zool. Soc. Lond.* **131**, 320–3.

SHEAIL J. (1971) *Rabbits and their history.* Newton Abbot, David & Charles.

SOUTHERN H.N. (1940) The ecology and population dynamics of the wild rabbit, *Oryctolagus cuniculus* (L.). *Ann. appl. Biol.* **27**, 509–26.

SOUTHERN H.N. (1948) Sexual and aggressive behaviour in the wild rabbit. *Behaviour* **1**, 173–94.

TANSLEY A.G. (1939) *The British Isles and their vegetation.* Cambridge, University Press.

TAYLOR R.H. (1956) The use of pellet counts for estimating the density of populations of the wild rabbit, *Oryctolagus cuniculus* (L.). *N.Z. J. Sci. Tech.* **38**, 236–56.

TAYLOR R.H. (1959) Age determination in wild rabbits. *Nature, Lond.* **184**, 1158–9.

THOMPSON H.V. & WORDEN A. (1956) *The rabbit.* London, Collins.

WATSON A. (1963) The effect of climate on the colour changes of Mountain hares in Scotland. *Proc. zool. Soc. Lond.* **141**, 823–35.

WATSON A. & HEWSON R. (1973) Population densities of Mountain hares *Lepus timidus* on western Scottish and Irish moors and on Scottish hills. *J. Zool., Lond.* **170**, 151–9.

WATSON A., HEWSON R., JENKINS D. & PARR R. (1973) Population densities of mountain hares compared with red grouse on Scottish moors. *Oikos* **24**, 225–30.

WATSON J.S. (1957) Reproduction of the wild rabbit *Oryctolagus cuniculus* (L.) in Hawke's Bay, New Zealand. *N.Z. J. Sci. Tech.* **38**, 451–82.

YALDEN D.W. (1971) The mountain hare (*Lepus timidus*) in the Peak District. *Naturalist, Hull.* no. 918, 81–92.

RODENTS

ABE H. (1967) Notes on the ecology of *Sciurus vulgaris orientis* Thomas. *J. Mammal Soc. Japan* **3**, 118–24.

AIROLDI J.P. & MEYLAN A. (1974) Bibliographie du genre *Arvicola* Lacépède, travaux publiés en Europe (à l'exclusion de la Russie) de 1900 à 1972. *Plant Health Newsl.* (Publication of European and Mediterranean Plant Protection Organization, series B, no. 78, Paris.)

ALIEV F.F. (1966) Enemies and competitors of the nutria in USSR. *J. Mammal.* **47**, 353–5.

AL-KHATEEB A. & JOHNSON E. (1971) Seasonal changes of pelage in the vole (*Microtus agrestis*). *Gen. comp. Endocr.* **16**, 217–40.

ALLANSON M. (1933) The reproductive processes of certain mammals. Part V. Changes in the reproductive organs of the male grey squirrel (*Sciurus carolinensis*). *Phil. Trans.* B, **222**, 79–96.

ALLEN G.M. (1942) *Extinct and vanishing animals of the Western Hemisphere.* Spec. Publ. Amer. Comm. International Wild Life Protection, 11.

ANDERSON P.K. (1965) The role of breeding structure in evolutionary processes of *Mus musculus* populations. *Proc. Symp. Mutation Process, Prague*. Pp. 17–21. *Academia*.

ANON (1962) *The grey squirrel*. London, HMSO Forestry Commission Leaflet No. 31 (new edition in preparation).

ANON (1969) Of voles and men. *Br. med. Jn*. 1, no. 5643, 527–8.

ARDEN G.B. & SILVER P.H. (1962) Visual thresholds and spectral sensitivities of the grey squirrel (*Sciurus carolinensis leucotis*). *J. Physiol., Lond*. **163**, 540–57.

ARTIMO A. (1964) The baculum as a criterion for distinguishing sexually mature and immature bank voles *Clethrionomys glareolus* Schr. *Ann. Zool. fenn*. **1**, 1–6.

ARVY L. (1974) Contribution à la connaissance de l'appareil mammaire chez les rongeurs. *Mammalia* **38**, 108–38.

ASHBY K.R. (1972) Patterns of daily activity in mammals. *Mammal Rev*. **1**, 171–85.

BAAL H.J. (1949) The indigenous mammals, reptiles and amphibians of the Channel Islands. *Bull. Soc. Jersiaise* **15**, 101–10.

BAKER J.R. (1930) The breeding season in British wild mice. *Proc. zool. Soc. Lond*. 113–26.

BAKER J.R., CHITTY D. & PHIPPS E. (1963) Blood parasites of wild voles, *Microtus agrestis*, in England. *Parasitology* **53**, 297–301.

BAKER J.R. & RANSON R.M. (1932) Factors affecting the breeding of the field mouse (*Microtus agrestis*) Part 1—light. *Proc. R. Soc*. B. **110**, 313–22.

BAKER J.R. & RANSON R.M. (1933) Factors affecting the breeding of the field mouse (*Microtus agrestis*) Part 3—locality. *Proc. R. Soc*. B. **113**, 486–95.

BALFOUR A. (1922) Observations on wild rats in England, with an account of their ecto- and endoparasites. *Parasitology* **14**, 282–98.

BARKALOW F.S. (1967) A record gray squirrel litter. *J. Mammal*. **48**, 141.

BARKALOW F.S., HAMILTON R.B. & SOOTS R.F. (1970) The vital statistics of an unexploited gray squirrel population. *J. Wildl. Mgmt* **34**, 489–500.

BARNETT S.A. (1951) Damage to wheat by enclosed populations of *Rattus norvegicus*. *J. Hyg. Camb*. **49**, 22–5.

BARNETT S.A. (1958) An analysis of social behaviour in wild rats. *Proc. zool. Soc. Lond*. **130**, 107–52.

BARNETT S.A. (1963) *A study in behaviour*. London, Methuen.

BARRETT-HAMILTON G.E.H. & HINTON M.A.C. (1910–21) *A history of British mammals*. London, Gurney & Jackson.

BARRIER M.J. & BARKALOW F.S. (1967) A rapid technique for aging gray squirrels in winter pelage. *J. Wildl. Mgmt* **31**, 715–19.

BARRINGTON R.M. (1880) On the introduction of the squirrel into Ireland. *Sc. Proc. roy. Dublin Soc*. n.s., **2**, 615–31.

BARUDIERI B. (1953) Epidemiology of leptospirosis in Italian ricefields. *WHO Monograph Series* no. 19, 117–26.

BECKER K. (1952) Uber das Vorkommen schwarzer Wanderatten (*Rattus norvegicus*). *Zool. Gart. Lpz*. **19**, 223–33.

BENTLEY E.W. (1959) The distribution and status of *Rattus rattus* L. in the United Kingdom in 1951 and 1956. *J. Anim. Ecol*. **28**, 299–308.

BENTLEY E.W. (1964) A further loss of ground by *Rattus rattus* L. in the United Kingdom during 1956–61. *J. Anim. Ecol*. **33**, 371–3.

BERGSTEDT B. (1965) Distribution, reproduction, growth and dynamics of the rodent species *Clethrionomys glareolus* (Schreber), *Apodemus flavicollis* (Melchior) and *Apodemus sylvaticus* (Linné) in southern Sweden. *Oikos* **16**, 132–60.

BERRY R.J. (1963) Epigenetic polymorphism in wild populations of *Mus musculus*. *Genet. Res. Camb.* **4**, 193–220.

BERRY R.J. (1970b) The natural history of the house mouse. *Fld Stud.* **3**, 219–62. Lancaster, Pa. **18**, 468–83.

BERRY R.J. (1968) The ecology of an island population of the house mouse. *J. Anim. Ecol.* **37**, 445–70.

BERRY R.J. (1969) History of the evolution of *Apodemus sylvaticus* (Mammalia) at one edge of its range. *J. Zool. Lond.* **159**, 311–28.

BERRY R.J. (1970a) Covert and overt variation, as exemplified by British mouse populations. *Symp. zool. Soc. Lond.* **26**, 3–26.

BERRY R. J. (1970b) The natural history of the house mouse. *Fld Stud.* **3**, 219–62.

BERRY R.J. (1973) Chance and change in British Long-tailed field mice (*Apodemus sylvaticus*). *J. Zool., Lond.* **170**, 351–66.

BERRY R.J., EVANS I.M. & SENNITT B.F.C. (1967) The relationships and ecology of *Apodemus sylvaticus* from the Small Isles of the Inner Hebrides, Scotland. *J. Zool., Lond.* **152**, 333–46.

BERRY R.J. & JAKOBSON M.E. (1974) Vagility in an island population of the house mouse. *J. Zool., Lond.* **173**, 341–54.

BERRY R.J. & MURPHY H.M. (1970) The biochemical genetics of an island population of the house mouse. *Proc. R. Soc.* **B. 176**, 87–103.

BERRY R.J. & ROSE F.E.N. (1975) Islands and the evolution of *Microtus arvalis* (Microtinae). *J. Zool., Lond.* **177**, 395–407.

BERRY R.J. & SEARLE A.G. (1963) Epigenetic polymorphism of the rodent skeleton. *Proc. zool. Soc. Lond.* **140**, 577–615.

BERRY R.J. & TRICKER B.J.K. (1969) Competition and extinction: the mice of Foula, with notes on those of Fair Isle and St Kilda. *J. Zool., Lond.* **158**, 247–65.

BIRKAN M. (1968) Répartition écologique et dynamique des populations d'*Apodemus sylvaticus* et *Clethrionomys glareolus* en pinède à Rambouillet. *Terre Vie* **3**, 231–73.

BISHOP I.R. & DELANY M.J. (1963) Life histories of small mammals in the Channel Islands in 1960–61. *Proc. zool. Soc. Lond.* **141**, 515–26.

BLACKMORE D.K. & OWEN D.G. (1968) Ectoparasites: the significance in British wild rodents. *Symp. zool. Soc. Lond.* **24**, 197–220.

BOBEK B. (1969) Survival, turnover and production of small rodents in a beech forest. *Acta theriol.* **14**, 191–210.

BOCK E. (1972) Use of forest associations by bank vole population. *Acta theriol.* **17**, 203–19.

BOROWSKI S. (1963) *Apodemus flavicollis* in the tops of tall trees. *Acta theriol.* **6**, 314.

BOVET J. (1972) On the social behaviour in a stable group of long-tailed field mice (*Apodemus sylvaticus*). *Behaviour* **41**, 43–67.

BOYD J.M. (1959) Observations on the St Kilda field-mouse *Apodemus sylvaticus hirtensis* Barrett-Hamilton. *Proc. zool. Soc. Lond.* **133**, 47–65.

BRAMBELL F.W.R. & ROWLANDS I.W. (1936) Reproduction of the bank vole (*Evotomys glareolus* Schreber). I: The oestrous cycle of the female. *Phil. Trans.* B, **216**, 71–97.

BREED W.G. & CLARKE J.R. (1970) Effect of photoperiod on ovarian function in the vole *Microtus agrestis*. *J. Reprod. Fert.* **23**, 189–92.

BROOM J.C. (1958) Leptospiral infection rates of wild rats in Britain. *J. Hyg. Camb.* **56**, 371–6.

BROOM J.C. & COGHLAN J.D. (1958) *Leptospira ballum* in small rodents in Scotland. *Lancet* 1041–2.

BROWN J. CLEVEDON & TWIGG G.I. (1965) Some observations on grey squirrel dreys in an area of mixed woodland in Surrey. *Proc. zool. Soc. Lond.* **144**, 131–4.

BROWN J. CLEVEDON & TWIGG G.I. (1969) Studies on the pelvis in British Muridae and Cricetidae (Rodentia). *J. Zool., Lond.* **158**, 81–132.

BROWN J. CLEVEDON & TWIGG G.I. (1971) Mammalian prey of the Barn owl (*Tyto alba*) on Skomer Island, Pembrokeshire. *J. Zool., Lond.* **165**, 527–30.

BROWN L.E. (1956a) Field experiments on the activity of the small mammals (*Apodemus, Clethrionomys* and *Microtus*). *Proc. zool. Soc. Lond.* **126**, 549–64.

BROWN L.E. (1956b) Movements of some small British mammals. *J. Anim. Ecol.* **25**, 54–71.

BROWN L.E. (1966) Home range and movement in small mammals. *Symp. zool. Soc. Lond.* **18**, 111–42.

BROWN L.E. (1969) Field experiments on the movements of *Apodemus sylvaticus* L. using trapping and tracking techniques. *Oecologia, Berl.* **2**, 198–222.

BROWN R.Z. (1953) Social behaviour, reproduction and population changes in the house mouse (*Mus musculus* L.). *Ecol. Monogr.* **23**, 217–40.

BUJALSKA G. (1970) Reproduction stabilising elements in an island population of *Clethrionomys glareolüs* (Schreber 1780). *Acta theriol.* **15**, 381–412.

BUJALSKA G. & RYSZKOWSKI L. (1966) Estimation of the reproduction of the bank vole under field conditions. *Acta theriol.* **11**, 351–61.

CALDWELL L.D. (1964) An investigation of competition in natural populations of mice. *J. Mammal.* **45**, 12–30.

CALHOUN J.B. (1962) *The ecology and sociology of the Norway rat.* Maryland, US Dept. Health, Education and Welfare.

CAMERON T.M.W. (1949) Diseases carried by house mice. *Pest Control* **17** (9), 9–11.

CAPEL-EDWARDS M. (1971) The susceptibility of three British small mammals to foot-and-mouth disease. *J. comp. Path.* **81**, 433–6.

CARSON J.D. (1961) Epiphyseal cartilage as an age indicator in fox and gray squirrels. *J. Wildl. Mgmt.* **25**, 90–3.

CHARLES W.N. (1956) The effect of a vole plague in the Carron Valley, Stirlingshire. *Scot. For.* 201–4.

CHITTY D. (1938) A laboratory study of pellet formation in the short-eared owl (*Asio flammeus*). *Proc. zool. Soc. Lond.* A **108**, 267–87.

CHITTY D. (1952) Mortality among voles (*Microtus agrestis*) at Lake Vyrnwy, Montgomeryshire, in 1936–9. *Phil. Trans.* B, **236**, 505–52.

CHITTY D. (1954) The study of the brown rat and its control by poison. *In* Chitty & Southern (1954) (q.v.).

CHITTY D. (1957) The field vole (*Microtus agrestis*) and the Orkney vole (*Microtus orcadensis*, Millais, 1904). *In* Worden & Lane-Petter (1957) (q.v.).

CHITTY D. (1960) Population processes in the vole and their relevance to general theory. *Can. J. Zool.* **38**, 99–113.

CHITTY D. (1967) The natural selection of self-regulatory behaviour in animal populations. *Proc. ecol. Soc. Aust.* **2**, 51–78.

CHITTY D. (1970) Variation and population density. *Symp. zool. Soc. Lond.* **26**, 327–33.

CHITTY D. & CHITTY H. (1962) Population trends among the voles at Lake Vyrnwy 1932–60. *Symp. Theriologicum, Brno 1960*, 67–76.

CHITTY D. & PHIPPS E. (1966) Seasonal changes in survival in mixed populations of two species of vole. *J. Anim. Ecol.* **35**, 313–31.

CHITTY D. & SOUTHERN H.N. (eds) (1954) *Control of rats and mice.* 3 vols. Oxford, Clarendon Press.

CHITTY H. (1957) The oestrous cycle and gestation period in the lactating field vole *Microtus agrestis. J. Endocr.* **15**, 279–83.

CLARKE J.R. (1956) The aggressive behaviour of the vole. *Behaviour* **9**, 1–23.

CLARKE J.R. & CLULOW F.V. (1973) The effect of successive matings upon bank vole (*Clethrionomys glareolus*) and vole (*Microtus agrestis*) ovaries. *In* Peters, H. (ed.) *The development and maturation of the ovary and its functions.* Int. Congr. Ser. No. 267. Amsterdam, Excerpta Medica.

CLARKE J.R., CLULOW F.V. & GRIEG F. (1970) Ovulation in the bank vole. *J. Reprod. Fert.* **23**, 531.

CLARKE J.R. & FORSYTH I.A. (1964) Seasonal changes in the gonads and accessory reproductive organs of the vole (*Microtus agrestis*). *Gen. comp. Endocr.* **4**, 233–42.

CLARKE J.R. & KENNEDY J.P. (1967) Effect of light and temperature upon gonad activity in the vole (*Microtus agrestis*). *Gen. comp. Endocr.* **8**, 474–88.

CLEGG T.M. (1970) Introduced forms of the red squirrel in south Yorkshire and north Derbyshire. *Naturalist, Hull* **912**, 1–4.

COLLETT R. (1911–12) *Norges Pattedyr.* Kristiania, Aschehoug.

CORBET G.B. (1960) *The distribution, variation and ecology of voles in the Scottish Highlands.* Ph.D. thesis, University of St Andrews.

CORBET G.B. (1961) Origin of the British insular races of small mammals and of the 'Lusitanian' fauna. *Nature, Lond.* **191**, 1037–40.

CORBET G.B. (1963a) An isolated population of the bank vole *Clethrionomys glareolus* with aberrant dental pattern. *Proc. zool. Soc. Lond.* **140**, 316–19.

CORBET G.B. (1963b) The frequency of albinism of the tail tip in British mammals. *Proc. zool. Soc. Lond.* **140**, 327–30.

CORBET G.B. (1964) Regional variation in the bank vole *Clethrionomys glareolus* in the British Isles. *Proc. zool. Soc. Lond.* **143**, 191–219.

CORBET G.B. (1966) *The terrestrial mammals of western Europe.* London, Foulis.

CORBET G.B. (1971) Provisional distribution maps of British mammals. *Mammal Rev.* **1**, 95–142.

CORBET G.B. (1975) Examples of short- and long-term changes of dental pattern in Scottish voles. *Mammal Rev.* **5**, 17–21.

CORBET G.B., CAMERON R.A.D. & GREENWOOD J.J.D. (1968) Small mammals and their ectoparasites from the Scottish islands of Handa (Sutherland) Muck, Pabay, Scalpay and Soay (Inner Hebrides). *J. Linn. Soc. (Zool.)* **47**, 301–7.

CORBET G.B., CUMMINS J., HEDGES S.R. & KRZANOWSKI W. (1970) The taxonomic status of British water voles, genus *Arvicola. J. Zool., Lond.* **161**, 301–16.

CORKE D. (1970) The local distribution of the yellow-necked mouse (*Apodemus flavicollis*). *Mammal Rev.* **1**, 62–6.

CORKE D. (1974) *The comparative ecology of the two British species of the genus* Apodemus (*Rodentia, Muridae*). Ph.D. thesis, University of London.

CORKE D. & HARRIS S. (1974) The small mammals of Essex. *Essex Nat.* **33**, 32–59.

COTTON M.J. (1970) The comparative morphology of some species of flea larvae (Siphonaptera) associated with nests of small mammals. *Ent. Gaz.* **21**, 191–204.

COUTTS R.R. & ROWLANDS I.W. (1969) The reproductive cycle of the Skomer vole (*Clethrionomys glareolus skomerensis*). *J. Zool., Lond.* **158**, 1–25.

COX F.E.G. (1970) Parasitic protozoa of British wild mammals. *Mammal Rev.* **1**, 1–28.

CRAWLEY M.C. (1969) Movements and home ranges of *Clethrionomys glareolus* Schreber and *Apodemus sylvaticus* L. in north-east England. *Oikos* **20**, 310–19.

CRAWLEY M.C. (1970) Some population dynamics of the bank vole, *Clethrionomys glareolus* and the wood mouse, *Apodemus sylvaticus* in mixed woodland. *J. Zool., Lond.* **160**, 71–89.

CROSS R.M. (1970) Activity rythms of the harvest mouse, *Micromys minutus* Pallas. *Mammalia* **34**, 433–50.

CROWCROFT W.P. (1955) Territoriality in wild house mice, *Mus musculus* L. *J. Mammal.* **36**, 299–301.

CROWCROFT W.P. (1966) *Mice all over*. London, Foulis.

CROWCROFT W.P. & GODFREY G. (1962) Laboratory produced hybrids of the Guernsey vole (*Microtus arvalis sarnius* Miller). *Ann. Mag. nat. Hist.* (13) **5**, 408–19.

CROWCROFT W.P. & ROWE F.P. (1963) Social organisation and territorial behaviour in the wild house mouse (*Mus musculus* L.). *Proc. zool. Soc. Lond.* **140**, 517–31.

DAVIS D.E. (1953) The characteristics of rat populations. *Quart. Rev. Biol.* **28**, 373–401.

DAVIS D.E., EMLEN J.T. & STOKES A.W. (1948) Studies on home range in the brown rat. *J. Mammal.* **29**, 207–25.

DAVIS D.H.S. (1933) Rhythmic activity in the short-tailed vole, *Microtus*. *J. Anim. Ecol.* **2**, 232–8.

DAVIS D.H.S. (1950) Notes on the status of the American grey squirrel (*Sciurus carolinensis* Gmelin) in the south-western Cape (South Africa). *Proc. zool. Soc. Lond.* **120**, 265–8.

DAVIS R.A. (1963) Feral coypus in Britain. *Ann. appl. Biol.* **5**, 345–8.

DEANESLY R. & PARKES A.S. (1933) The reproductive processes of certain mammals. Part IV. The oestrous cycle of the grey squirrel (*Sciurus carolinensis*). *Phil. Trans.* B, 222, 47–78.

DEGN H.J. (1973) Systematic position, age criteria and reproduction of Danish red squirrels (*Sciurus vulgaris* L.). *Dan. Rev. game Biol.* 8(2), 1–24.

DELANY M.J. (1965) The application of factor analysis to the study of variation in the long-tailed field-mouse (*Apodemus sylvaticus* (L.)) in north-west Scotland. *Proc. Linn. Soc. Lond.* **176**, 103–11.

DELANY M.J. (1970) Variation and ecology of island populations of the long-tailed field-mouse (*Apodemus sylvaticus* (L.)). *Symp. zool. Soc. Lond.* **26**, 283–95.

DELANY M.J. & DAVIS P.E. (1961) Observations on the ecology and life history of the Fair Isle field mouse *Apodemus sylvaticus fridariensis* (Kinnear). *Proc. zool. Soc. Lond.* **136**, 439–52.

DELANY M.J. & HEALY M.J.R. (1964) Variation in the long-tailed field-mouse (*Apodemus sylvaticus* (L.)) in north-west Scotland. II: Simultaneous examination of all characters. *Proc. Roy. Soc.* B, **161**, 200–7.

DELOST P. (1966) Reproduction et cycles endocriniens de l'écureuil (*Sciurus vulgaris*). *Archiv. Scien. Physiol.* **20**, 425–57.

DEOL M.S. (1970) The determination and distribution of coat colour variation in the house mouse. *Symp. zool. Soc. Lond.* **26**, 239–50.

DRUMMOND D.C. (1960) The food of *Rattus norvegicus* Berk. in an area of sea wall, salt marsh and mud flat. *J. Anim. Ecol.* **29**, 341–7.

DUFOUR B. (1972) Adaptations du terrier d'*Apodemus sylvaticus* à la température et à la lumière. *Rev. suisse zool.* **79**, 966–9.

DUMAEVA T.N., DOBROKHOTOV B.P. & SHLYGINA K.N. (1967) Detection of listeriosis in wild rodents of the forest-tundra of the northern part of middle Siberia. *Zool. Zh.* **46**, 272–3.

DYKSTRA W. (1954) Rodent filth in food. *Pest Control* 22(7), 9–10, 12, 14.

EAST K. (1965) Notes on the opening of hazel nuts (*Corylus avellana*) by mice and voles. *J. Zool., Lond.* **147**, 223–4.

ECKE D.H. (1954) An invasion of Norway rats in South West Georgia. *J. Mammal.* **35**, 521–5.

EDWARDS F.B. (1962) Red squirrel disease. *Vet. Rec.* **74**, 739–41.

EIBL-EIBESFELDT I. (1951) Beobachtungen zur Fortplanzungsbiologie und Jugendentwicklung des Eichhörnchens (*Sciurus vulgaris* L.). *Z. Tierpsychol.* **8**, 370–400.

EISENTRAUT M. (1930) Beobachtungen über den Winterschlaf der Haselmaus (*Muscardinus avellanarius*). *Z. Säugetierk.* **4**, 213–39.

ELDRIDGE M.J. (1969) Observations on food eaten by wood mice (*Apodemus sylvaticus*) and bank voles (*Clethrionomys glareolus*) in a hedge. *J. Zool., Lond.* **158**, 208–9.

ELLERMAN J.R. & MORRISON-SCOTT T.C.S. (1951) *Checklist of Palaearctic and Indian mammals, 1758 to 1946.* London, Brit. Mus. (Nat. Hist.).

ELLIS A.E. (ed.) (1965) *The Broads.* London, Collins.

ELTON C. (1942) *Voles, mice and lemmings: problems in population dynamics.* Oxford, Clarendon Press.

ELTON C. (1953) The use of cats in farm rat control. *Brit. J. Anim. Behav.* **1**, 151–5.

ELTON C., FORD E.B., BAKER J.R. & GARDNER A.D. (1931) The health and parasites of a wild mouse population. *Proc. zool. Soc. Lond.* 657–721.

ENGLISH M.P. (1966) *Trichophyton persicolor* infection in the field vole and pipistrelle bat. *Sabouraudia* **4**, 219–22.

ENGLISH M.P. (1969) Ringworm in wild mammals: further investigations. *J. Zool., Lond.* **159**, 515–22.

ENGLISH M.P. (1971) Ringworm in groups of wild mammals. *J. Zool., Lond.* **165**, 535–44.

ENGLISH M.P. & SOUTHERN H.N. (1967) *Trichophyton persicolor* infection in a population of small wild mammals. *Sabouraudia* **5**, 302–9.

ERKINARO E. (1961) Seasonal change of the activity of *Microtus agrestis.* *Oikos* **12**, 157–63.

ERKINARO E. (1972) Fasväxling hos djur. *Fauna flora, Upps.* **5**, 215–19.

EVANS D.M. (1973) Seasonal variations in the body composition and nutrition of the vole *Microtus agrestis.* *J. Anim. Ecol.* **42**, 1–18.

FAIRLEY J.S. (1967) Wood mice in grassland at Dundrum, County Down, Northern Ireland. *J. Zool., Lond.* **153**, 553–5.

FAIRLEY J.S. (1970a) Form of the fieldmouse *Apodemus sylvaticus* (L.) in Ireland. *Ir. Nat. J.* **16**, 381.

FAIRLEY J.S. (1970b) Foetal number and resorption in wood mice from Ireland. *J. Zool., Lond.* **161**, 342–6.

FAIRLEY J.S. (1971a) The present distribution of the bank vole *Clethrionomys glareolus* Schreber in Ireland. *Proc. Roy. Ir. Acad.* **71B**, 183–9.

FAIRLEY J.S. (1971b) A critical reappraisal of the status in Ireland of the eastern house mouse, *Mus musculus orientalis* Cretzchmar. *Ir. Nat. J.* **17**, 2–5.

FAIRLEY J.S. (1972) The fieldmouse in Ireland. *Ir. Nat. J.* **17**, 152–9.

FAIRLEY J.S. & COMERTON M.E. (1972) An early-breeding population of fieldmice *Apodemus sylvaticus* (L.) in Limekiln Wood, Athenry, Co. Galway. *Proc. Roy. Ir. Acad.* **72B**, 149–63.

FERNS P.N. (1970) Unusual occurrence in the stomach of a field vole, *Microtus agrestis.* *J. Zool., Lond.* **162**, 540–1.

FISHER E.W. & PERRY A.E. (1970) Estimating age of gray squirrels by lens-weights. *J. Wildl. Mgmt* **34**, 825–8.

FITZWATER W.D. & FRANK W.J. (1944) Leaf nests of gray squirrels in Connecticut. *J. Mammal.* **25**, 160–70.

FLOWERDEW J.R. (1971a) The subcaudal glandular area of *Apodemus sylvaticus. J. Zool., Lond.* **165**, 525–7.

FLOWERDEW J.R. (1971b) *Population regulation of small rodents in relation to social behaviour and environmental resources.* D.Phil. thesis, University of Oxford.

FLOWERDEW J.R. (1972) The effect of supplementary food on a population of wood mice (*Apodemus sylvaticus*). *J. Anim. Ecol.* **41**, 553–66.

FLOWERDEW J.R. (1973) The effect of natural and artificial changes in food supply on breeding in woodland mice and voles. *J. Reprod. Fert.*, Suppl. **19**, 257–67.

FLOWERDEW J.R. (1974) Field and laboratory experiments on the social behaviour and population dynamics of the wood mouse, *Apodemus sylvaticus. J. Anim. Ecol.* **43**, 499–511.

FLYGER V.F. (1960) Movements and home range of the gray squirrel *Sciurus carolinensis* in two Maryland woodlots. *Ecology* **41**, 365–9.

FORMOSOV A.N. (1933) The crop of cedar nuts, invasions into Europe of the Siberian nutcracker (*Nucifraga caryocatactes macrorhynchus* Brehm) and fluctuations in numbers of the squirrel (*Sciurus vulgaris* L.). *J. Anim. Ecol.* **2**, 70–81.

FRANK F. (1956) Das Duftmarkieren der Grossen Wühlmaus, *Arvicola terrestris* (L.). *Z. Säugetierk.* **21**, 172–5.

FRANK F. (1957) Biologie der Zwergmaus. *Z. Säugetierk*, **22**, 1–44.

FRANK H. (1952) Über die Jugendentwicklung des Eichhörnchens. *Z. Tierpsychol.* **9**, 12–22.

FREEMAN R.B. (1941) The distribution of *Orchopeas wickhami* (Baker) (Siphonaptera), in relation to its host the American grey squirrel. *Entomol. mon. Mag.* **77**, 82–9.

FULLAGAR P.J. (1967) Moult in field mice and the variation in the chest markings of *Apodemus sylvaticus* (Linné, 1758) and *Apodemus flavicollis* (Melchior, 1854). *Säugetierk. Mitt.* **15**, 138–49.

FULLAGER P.J., JEWELL P.A., LOCKLEY R.M. & ROWLANDS I.W. (1963) The Skomer vole (*Clethrionomys glareolus skomerensis*) and long-tailed field mouse (*Apodemus sylvaticus*) on Skomer Island, Pembrokeshire in 1960. *Proc. zool. Soc. Lond.* **140**, 295–314.

GELMROTH K.G. (1970) Über den Einfluss verschiedener äusserer und innerer Faktoren auf die lokomotorische Aktivität der Waldmaus (*Apodemus sylvaticus* L.). *Z. wiss. Zool.* **180**, 368–88.

GEORGE R.S. & CORBET G.B. (1959) A collection of fleas from small mammals in the Scottish Highlands. *Ent. gaz.* **10**, 147–58.

GLUE D.E. (1970) Avian predator pellet analysis and the mammalogist. *Mammal Rev.* **1**, 53–62.

GODFREY G.K. (1953) The food of *Microtus agrestis hirtus* (Bellamy, 1839) in Wytham, Berkshire. *Säugetierk. Mitt.* **1**, 148–51.

GODFREY G.K. (1954) Tracing field voles (*Microtus agrestis*) with a Geiger-Müller counter. *Ecology* **35**, 5–10.

GODFREY G.K. (1955) Observations on the nature of the decline in numbers of two *Microtus* populations. *J. Mammal.* **36**, 209–14.

GODFREY J. (1958) The origin of sexual isolation between bank voles. *Proc. Roy. phys. Soc. Edinb.* **27**, 47–55.

GOSLING L.M. (1974) The coypu in East Anglia. *Trans. Norf. Nor. Nat. Soc.* **23**, 49–59.

GRATZ N.G. (1973) Urban rodent-borne disease and rodent distribution in Israel and neighbouring countries. *Israel J. med. Sci.* **9**, 969–79.

GREEN E.L. (1966) *Biology of the laboratory mouse*, 2nd edn. New York, McGraw-Hill.

GRODZIŃSKI W. (1959) The succession of small mammal communities on an overgrown clearing and landslip mountain in the Bestid Sredni (western Carpathians). *Ecol. Pol.* **7**, 83–143.

GRODZIŃSKI W. (1963) Seasonal changes in the circadian activity of small rodents. *Ecol. Pol. Ser. B* **9**, 3–17.

GROSZ S. (1905) Beiträge zur Anatomie der accessorischen Geschlechtsdrüsen der Insektivoren und Nager. *Arch. Mikr. Anat.* **66**, 567–608.

GRULICH I., NOSEK J. & SZABO L. (1967) The autecology of small rodents and insectivores of the Tribeč Mountain Range. *Bull. Wld Hlth Org.* **36**, suppl. 1, 25–30.

GUTHRIE D.R., OSBORNE J.C. & MOSBY H.S. (1967) Physiological changes associated with shock in confined gray squirrels. *J. Wildl. Mgmt* **31**, 102–8.

HACKER H.P. & PEARSON H.S. (1951) Distribution of the long-tailed field mouse, *Apodemus sylvaticus*, on South Haven Peninsula, Dorset, in 1937, with some observations on its wandering and homing powers. *J. Linn. Soc. (Zool.)* **42**, 1–17.

HALL E.R. & KELSON K.R. (1959) *The mammals of North America.* 2 vols. New York, Ronald Press.

HANSEN-MELANDER E. (1964a) The chromosomes of *Microtus agrestis*. *Hereditas* **52**, 241.

HANSEN-MELANDER E. (1964b) The relation of sex chromosomes to chromocenters in somatic cells of *Microtus agrestis* (L.). *Hereditas* **52**, 357–66.

HANSSON L. (1971a) Small rodent food, feeding and population dynamics. *Oikos* **22**, 183–98.

HANSSON L. (1971b) Habitat, food and population dynamics of the field vole *Microtus agrestis* (L.) in South Sweden. *Viltrevy* **8**, 267–378.

HARVIE-BROWN J.A. (1880–81) The squirrel in Great Britain. *Proc. Roy. phys. Soc. Edinb.* **5**, 343–8; **6**, 31–63, 115–82. (Also in book form: (1881) Edinburgh, Macfarlane & Erskine.)

HEDGES S.R. (1969) Epigenetic polymorphism in populations of *Apodemus sylvaticus* and *Apodemus flavicollis* (Rodentia, Muridae). *J. Zool., Lond.* **159**, 425–42.

HEWSON R. (1951) Some observations on the Orkney vole, *Microtus o. orcadensis* (Millais). *Northw. Nat.* **23**, 7–10.

HILLEMAN H.H., GAYNOR A.I. & STANLEY H.P. (1958) The genital systems of nutria (*Myocastor coypus*). *Anat. Research* **130**, 515–28.

HOFFMAN R.A. & KIRKPATRICK C.M. (1956) An analysis of techniques for determining male squirrel reproductive development. *Trans. N. Amer. Wildl. Conf.* **21**, 346–55.

HOFFMEYER I. (1973) Interaction and habitat selection in the mice *A. flavicollis* and *A. sylvaticus*. *Oikos* **24**, 108–16.

HOLIŠOVÁ V. (1969) Vertical movements of some small mammals in a forest. *Zool. Listy* **18**, 121–41.

HOLIŠOVÁ V. (1970) Trophic requirements of the water vole *Arvicola terrestris* Linn., on the edge of stagnant waters. *Zool. Listy* **19**, 221–33.

HOLLAND S.C. (1967) Mammal notes and records. *J. N. Gloucestershire Nat. Soc.* **18**, 225–6.

HOLMES R.G. (1962) Fascioliasis in coypus (*Myocastor coypus*). *Vet. Rec.* **74**, 1552.

HRABE V. (1971) Circumanal glands of central European Gliridae (Rodentia). *Zool. Listy* **20**, 247–58.

HSU T.C. & BENIRSCHKE K. (1970) *Sciurus vulgaris* (Hokkaido squirrel). *An atlas of mammalian chromosomes* **4**, folio 162. Berlin, Springer-Verlag.

HURRELL E. (1962) *Dormice.* London, Sunday Times Publications (Animals of Britain no. 10).

HYVÄRINEN H. & HEIKURA K. (1971) Effects of age and seasonal rhythm on the growth patterns of some small mammals in Finland and in Kirkenes, Norway. *J. Zool., Lond.* **165**, 545–56.

JEFFRIES D.J. & FRENCH M.C. (1972) Lead concentration in small mammals trapped on road-side verges and field sites. *Environ. Pollut.* 3, 147–56.

JEFFRIES D.J., STAINSBY B. & FRENCH M.C. (1973) The ecology of small mammals in arable fields drilled with winter wheat and the increase in their dieldrin and mercury residues. *J. Zool., Lond.* 171, 513–39.

JEWELL P.A. (1966a) Breeding season and recruitment in some British mammals confined on small islands. *Symp. zool. Soc. Lond.* 15, 89–116.

JEWELL P.A. (1966b) The concept of home range in mammals. *Symp. zool. Soc. Lond.* 18, 85–109.

JEWELL P.A. & FULLAGAR P.J. (1965) Fertility among races of the field mouse (*Apodemus sylvaticus* (L.)) and their failure to form hybrids with the yellow-necked mouse (*A. flavicollis* (Melchior)). *Evolution, Lancaster, Pa.* 19, 175–81.

JOHST V. (1969) Vergleichende Untersuchung des agonistischen Verhaltens einiger Arten von *Clethrionomys*. *Z. Tierpsychol.* 24, 558–79.

KACZMARSKI F. (1966) Bioenergetics of pregnancy and lactation in the bank vole. *Acta theriol.* 11, 409–17.

KAHMANN H. (1969) Die Alveolenmuster der Oberkieferzahnreihe der Waldmaus, Hausratte, und Hausmaus aus Populationen der grossen Tyrrhenischen Inseln. *Z. Säugetierk.* 34, 164–83.

KAIKUSALO A. (1972) Population turnover and wintering of the bank vole, *Clethrionomys glareolus* (Schreb.), in southern and central Finland. *Ann. Zool. fenn.* 9, 219–24.

KALABUKHOV, N.I. (1937). [Results of 20 years' research (1917–1937) on the ecology of rodent pests in the USSR] *Zool. Zh.* 16, 950–71.

KALELA O. (1962) On the fluctuations in the numbers of Arctic and boreal small mammals as problems of production biology. *Ann. Acad. Sci. fenn.* A4, 66, 1–38.

KARPUKHIN I.P. & KARPUKHINA N.M. (1971) Eye lens weight as a criterion of age of *Sciurus vulgaris*. *Zool. Zh.* 50, 274–7.

KÄSTLE W. (1953) Die Jugendentwicklung der Zwergmaus, *Micromys minutus soricinus* (Hermann, 1780). *Säugetierk. Mitt.* 1, 49–59.

KEELER B. (1961) Damage to young plantations by the bank vole at Bernwood forest, 1958–60. *J. For. Comm.* 30, 55–9.

KENNETH J.G. & RITCHIE G.R. (1953) *Gestation periods*, 3rd edn. Tech. Comm. Bur. Anim. Breeding, Edinburgh No. 5.

KHAMAGANOV S.A. (1972) Distribution of the common rat in the Far East. *Fauna i Ecologiya Gryzunov* 11, 149–56.

KIKKAWA J. (1964) Movement, activity and distribution of the small rodents *Clethrionomys glareolus* and *Apodemus sylvaticus* in woodland. *J. Anim. Ecol.* 33, 259–99.

KINDLER V. (1946) [Dormouse damage in the Sneznik Forests]. *Gozd. Vijesn.* 5, 104–5.

KING C.M. (1971) *Studies on the ecology of the weasel.* D. Phil. thesis, University of Oxford.

KIRIS I.D. (1937) [Method and technique of age determination of the squirrel and analysis of the age-group composition of squirrel populations]. *Byull. mosk. Obshch. Ispyt. Prir. Biol.* 46, 36–42 (Russian, French summary).

KIRKPATRICK C.M. & BARNETT E.M. (1957) Age criteria in male gray squirrels. *J. Wildl. Mgmt* 21, 341–7.

KIRKPATRICK C.M. & HOFFMANN R.A. (1960) Ages and reproductive cycles in a male gray squirrel population. *J. Wildl. Mgmt.* 24, 218–21.

KLETS E.I. (1936) [Susceptibility of *Mus minutus* Pall. to experimental pneumococcus infection, anthrax and Fridlandler's pneumobacillus.] *Izv, Gos. protivochumn. inst. Sibiri i DVK*, 4.

KNIGHT M. (1963) *Harvest mice*. London, Sunday Times Publications (Animals of Britain no. 19).

KOWALSKI K. (1970) Variation and speciation in fossil voles. *Symp. zool. Soc. Lond.* 26, 149–61.

KOWALSKI K. & SUTCLIFFE A.J. (1976) Pleistocene rodents of the British Isles. *Bull. Br. Mus. Nat. Hist.* (Geol.) 27, 31–147.

KRÁL B. (1970) Chromosome studies in two subgenera of the genus *Apodemus*. *Zool. Listy* 19, 119–34.

KREBS C.J. & MYERS J.H. (1974) Population cycles in small mammals. *Adv. ecol. Res.* 8, 267–399.

KUBIK J. (1952) [The harvest mouse—*Micromys minutus* Pall.—in the Białowieża National Park]. *Ann Univ. M. Curie-Sklodowska* 7, 449–82 (British Library Translation no. 7692).

KULICKE H. (1963) Kleinsäuger als Vertilger forstschädlicher Insekten. *Z. Säugetierk.* 28, 175–83.

LAMPIO T. (1972) Squirrel hunting based on the ecology of the species. *Riistat. Julk.* 8, 44–9.

LAURIE E.M.O. (1946a) The reproduction of the house mouse *Mus musculus* living in different environments. *Proc. Roy. Soc.* B, 133, 248–81.

LAURIE E.M.O. (1946b) The coypu (*Myocastor coypus*) in Great Britain. *J. Anim. Ecol.* 15, 22–34.

LEHMANN E. VON (1962a) Uber die Seitendrüsen der mitteleuropäischen Rötelmaus (*Clethrionomys glareolus* Schreber). *Z. Morph. Ökol. Tiere* 51, 335–44.

LEHMANN E. VON (1962b) Vorübergehende Veränderungen im Haar der Rötelmaus, *Clethrionomys glareolus*. *Bonn. zool. Beitr.* 12, 235–40.

LEMNELL P.A. (1970) Telemetry as a method for studying the home range—examples from a study on the red squirrel (*Sciurus vulgaris v.* L.). *Zool. Revy* 32, 51–6.

LEMNELL P.A. (1973) Age determination in red squirrels (*Sciurus vulgaris* (L.)). *Int. Congr. Game Biol.* 11, 573–80.

LESLIE P.H. & DAVIS D.H.S. (1939) An attempt to determine the absolute number of rats on a given area. *J. Anim. Ecol.* 8, 94–113.

LESLIE P.H. & RANSON R.M. (1940) The mortality, fertility and rate of natural increase of the vole *Microtus agrestis* as observed in the laboratory. *J. Anim. Ecol.* 9, 27–52.

LESLIE P.H., TENER J.S., VIZOSO M. & CHITTY H. (1955) The longevity and fertility of the Orkney vole, *Microtus orcadensis*, as observed in the laboratory. *Proc. zool. Soc. Lond.* 125, 115–25.

LESLIE P.H., VENABLES U.M. & VENABLES L.S.V. (1952) The fertility and population structure of the brown rat (*Rattus norvegicus*) in cornricks and some other habitats. *Proc. zool. Soc. Lond.* 122, 187–238.

LEVER R.J.A.W. (1959) The diet of the fox since myxomatosis. *J. Anim. Ecol.* 28, 359–75.

LEVER R.J., ARMOUR C.J. & THOMPSON H.V. (1957) Myxomatosis and the fox. *Agriculture* 64, 105–11.

LEWIS J.W. (1968) Studies on the helminth parasites of voles and shrews from Wales. *J. Zool. Lond.* 154, 313–31.

LEWIS J.W. & TWIGG G.I. (1972) A study of the internal parasites of small rodents from woodland areas in Surrey. *J. Zool., Lond.* 166, 61–77.

LINDEMANN W. (1953) Einiges über die Wildkatzes der Ostkarpathen. *Säugetierk. Mitt.* 1, 73–4.

LLOYD H.G. (1968) Observations on nut selection by a hand-reared grey squirrel (*Sciurus carolinensis*). *J. Zool., Lond.* **155**, 240–4.

LOCKIE J.D. (1955) The breeding habits and food of short-eared owls after a vole plague. *Bird Study* **2**, 53–69.

LOCKIE J.D. (1961) The food of the pine marten *Martes martes* in west Ross-shire, Scotland. *Proc. zool. Soc. Lond.* **136**, 187–95.

LOUARN H. LE & SCHMITT A. (1972) Relations observées entre la production des faines et la dynamique de population du mulot, *Apodemus sylvaticus* L., en forêt de Fontainebleau. *Ann. Sci. forest.* **30**, 205–14.

LOWE V.P.W. (1957) The wood mouse (common field mouse) (*Apodemus sylvaticus* L.). In Worden & Lane-Petter (1957) (q.v.).

LOWE V.P.W. (1971) Root development of molar teeth in the bank vole (*Clethrionomys glareolus*). *J. Anim. Ecol.* **40**, 49–61.

LOZAN M.N. (1961) [Age determination of *Dryomys nitedula* Pall. and of *Muscardinus avellanarius* L.]. *Zool. Zh.* **40**, 1740–3.

LUDWICK R.L., FONTENOT J.P. & MOSBY H.S. (1969) Energy metabolism of the eastern gray squirrel. *J. Wildl. Mgmt.* **33**, 569–75.

LÜHRING R. (1928) Das Haarkleid von *Sciurus vulgaris* L. und die Verteilung seiner Farbvarianten in Deutschland. *Z. Morph. Ökol. Tiere* **11**, 667–762.

MACKINTOSH J.H. & GRANT E.C. (1966) The effect of olfactory stimuli on the agonistic behaviour of laboratory mice. *Z. Tierpsychol.* **23**, 585–7.

MARELLI C.A. (1932) El nuevo y especie, *Pitrufquenia coypus* de Malófago de la Nutria Chilena. *La Chacra* **3**, 7–9.

MATHESON C. (1962) *Brown rats*. London, Sunday Times Publications. (Animals of Britain, no. 16).

MATTHEY R. (1956) Cytologie chromosomique comparée et systématique des Muridae. *Mammalia* **20**, 93–123.

MAZÁK V. (1963) Notes on the dentition in *Clethrionomys glareolus* Schreber, 1780 in the course of postnatal life. *Säugetierk. Mitt.* **11**, 1–11.

MAZURKIEWICZ M. (1972) Density and weight structure of populations of the bank vole in open and enclosed areas. *Acta theriol.* **17**, 455–65.

MIDDLETON A.D. (1930) The ecology of the American grey squirrel (*Sciurus carolinensis* Gmelin) in the British Isles. *Proc. zool. Soc. Lond.* 809–43.

MIDDLETON A.D. (1931) *The grey squirrel*. London, Sidgwick & Jackson.

MILLER G.S. (1912) *Catalogue of the mammals of western Europe*. London, Brit. Mus. (Nat. Hist.).

MILLER R.S. (1955) Activity rhythms in the wood mouse, *Apodemus sylvaticus* and the bank vole, *Clethrionomys glareolus*. *Proc. zool. Soc. Lond.* **125**, 505–19.

MILLER R.S. (1958) A study of a wood mouse population in Wytham Woods, Berkshire. *J. Mammal.* **39**, 477–93.

MINETTE H.P. (1964) Leptospirosis in rodents and mongooses on the island of Hawaii. *Amer. J. trop. Med. Hyg.* **13**, 826–32.

MOFFAT C.B. (1938) The mammals of Ireland. *Proc. Roy. Ir. Acad. B*, **44**, 61–128.

MOLYNEUX D.H. (1969) The morphology and life history of *Trypanosoma* (*Herpetosoma*) *microti* of the field vole *Microtus agrestis*. *Ann. trop. Med. Parasit.* **63**, 229–44.

MONTGOMERY W.I. (1976) On the relationship between yellow-necked mouse (*Apodemus flavicollis*) and woodmouse (*A. sylvaticus*) in a Cotswold valley. *J. Zool. Lond.* **179**, 229–33.

MORRIS P.A. (1968) Apparent hypothermia in the wood mouse (*Apodemus sylvaticus*). *J. Zool., Lond.* **155**, 235–6.

MORRISON-SCOTT Γ.C.S. (1938) A late Pleistocene vole from Guernsey. *Rep. Guernsey Soc. nat. Sci.* 13, 24–5.

MOSBY H.S. (1969) The influence of hunting on the population dynamics of a woodlot gray squirrel population. *J. Wildl. Mgmt* 33, 59–73.

NEWSOME A.E. (1969) A population of house mice permanently inhabiting a reed-bed in South Australia. *J. Anim. Ecol.* 38, 361–77.

NEWSON R. (1963) Differences in numbers, reproduction and survival between two neighbouring populations of bank voles (*Clethrionomys glareolus*). *Ecology* 44, 110–20.

NEWSON R.M. (1966) Reproduction in the feral coypu (*Myocastor coypus*). *Symp. zool. Soc. Lond.* 15, 323–34.

NEWSON R.M. & HOLMES R.G. (1968) Some ectoparasites of the coypu (*Myocastor coypus*) in eastern England. *J. Anim. Ecol.* 37, 471–81.

NIETHAMMER J. (1969) Zur Frage der Introgression bei den Waldmäusen *Apodemus sylvaticus* und *A. flavicollis* (Mammalia, Rodentia). *Z. zool. Syst. Evolutionsf.* 7, 77–127.

NIXON C.M. & McCLAIN M.W. (1969) Squirrel population decline following a late spring frost, *J. Wildl. Mgmt* 33, 353–7.

NIXON C.M., WORLEY D.M. & McCLAIN M.W. (1968) Food habits of squirrels in southeast Ohio. *J. Wildl. Mgmt* 32, 294–305.

NORRIS J.D. (1967) A campaign against feral coypus (*Myocastor coypus*) in Great Britain. *J. appl. Ecol.* 4, 191–9.

O'DONNELL T.G. (1971) *Ecology of the ectoparasites of three species of small rodents.* MS in Elton Library, University of Oxford.

OKON E.E. (1972) Factors affecting ultrasound production in infant rodents. *J. Zool., Lond.* 168, 139–48.

O'MAHONY E. (1935) Discovery of a second race of the house-mouse in Ireland. *Irish Nat. J.* 5, 218–19.

OSGOOD W.H. (1943) The mammals of Chile. *Zool. Ser. Field Mus. Nat. Hist.* 30, 1–268.

PACK J.C., MOSBY H.S. & SIEGEL P.B. (1967) Influence of social hierarchy on gray squirrel behaviour. *J. Wildl. Mgmt* 31, 720–8.

PANTELEYEEV P.A. (1968). [*Population ecology of the Water Vole.*]. Moscow.

PARKER J.C. & HOLLIMAN R.B. (1972) A method for determining ectoparasite densities on gray squirrels. *J. Wildl. Mgmt* 36, 1227–34.

PEARSON A.M. (1962) Activity patterns, energy metabolism and growth rate of the voles *Clethrionomys rufocanus* and *Clethrionomys glareolus* in Finland. *Ann. Soc. zool.-bot. fenn. Vanamo* 24, 1–58.

PEARSON O.P. (1966) The prey of carnivores during one cycle of mouse abundance. *J. Anim. Ecol.* 35, 217–35.

PELIKÁN J. (1966) [Comparison of the birth rates in four *Apodemus* species]. *Zool. Listy* 15, 129–30 (in Czech).

PELIKÁN J. (1967) Resorption rate in embryos of four *Apodemus* species. *Zool. Listy* 16, 325–42.

PERNETTA J.C. & HANDFORD P. (1970) Mammalian and avian remains from possible bronze age deposits on Nornour, Isles of Scilly. *J. Zool., Lond.* 162, 534–40.

PERRIN M.R. & GURNELL J. (1971) Rats on Lundy. *Ann. Rep. Lundy Field Soc.* 22, 35–40.

PERRY J.S. (1943) Reproduction in the water vole, *Arvicola amphibius* Linn. *Proc. zool. Soc. Lond.* A112, 118–30.

PETERS H. & CLARKE J.R. (1974) The development of the ovary from birth to maturity in the bank vole (*Clethrionomys glareolus*) and the vole (*Microtus agrestis*). *Anat. Rec.* 179, 241–52.

PETRIDES G.A. (1951) Notes on age determination in squirrels. *J. Mammal.* **32**, 111–12.

PIECHOCKI R. (1958) *Die Zwergmaus* Micromys minutus *Pallas*. (Die neue Brehm Bucherei no. 22.) Wittenberg, Lutherstadt.

POLLARD E. & RELTON J. (1970) Hedges. V: A study of small mammals in hedges and cultivated fields. *J. appl. Ecol.* **7**, 549–57.

RABUS A. (1881) Beiträge zur Kenntnis über den Winterschlaf der Siebenschläfer. *Zool. Gart. Frankfurt*, 321–5 (translation in *Zoologist*, 1882, **6**, 161–4).

RANDOLPH S.E. (1973) A tracking technique for comparing individual home ranges of small mammals. *J. Zool. Lond.* **170**, 509–20.

RANDOLPH S.E. (1975) Seasonal dynamics of a host-parasite system: *Ixodes trianguliceps* (Acarina: Ixodidae) and its small mammal hosts. *J. Anim. Ecol.* **44**, 425–49.

REICHSTEIN N. (1963) Beitrag zur systematischen Gliederung des Genus *Arvicola* Lacépède 1799. *Z. zool. Syst. Evolutionsforsch.* **1**, 155–204.

ROBEN P. (1969) Ein für europäische Kleinsäuger neues Haarwechselschema zur Gattung *Apodemus* im Rhein-Neckar-Gebiet. *Säugetierk. Mitt.* **13**, 31–42.

ROBINSON D.T. & COWAN I. Mc.T. (1954) An introduced population of the gray squirrel (*Sciurus carolinensis* Gmelin) in British Columbia. *Can. J. Zool.* **32**, 261–82.

ROBINSON R. (1970) Homologous mutants in mammalian coat colour variations. *Symp. zool. Soc. Lond.* **26**, 251–69.

ROOD J.P. (1965) Observations on the life cycle and variation of the longtailed field mouse *Apodemus sylvaticus* in the Isles of Scilly and Cornwall. *J. Zool., Lond.* **147**, 99–107.

ROWE F.P. (1961) Ectoparasites found on harvest mice. *Proc. zool. Soc. Lond.* **142**, 181–5.

ROWE F.P. & REDFERN R. (1969) Aggressive behaviour in related and unrelated wild housemice (*Mus musculus* L.). *Ann. appl. Biol.* **64**, 425–31.

ROWE F.P. & TAYLOR E.J. (1964) The numbers of harvest mice *Micromys minutus* in corn ricks. *Proc. zool. Soc. Lond.* **142**, 181–5.

ROWE F.P., TAYLOR E.J. & CHUDLEY A.H.J. (1963) The numbers and movements of house mice in the vicinity of four corn ricks. *J. Anim. Ecol.* **32**, 87–97.

ROWE J.J. (1973) *Grey squirrel control*. London, HMSO (Forestry Commission Leaflet 56).

ROWLANDS I.W. (1936) Reproduction of the bank vole (*Evotomys glareolus*, Schreber). II: Seasonal changes in the reproductive organs of the male. *Phil. Trans.* B, **226**, 99–120.

ROWLANDS I.W. (1938) Preliminary note on the reproductive cycle of the red squirrel (*Sciurus vulgaris*). *Proc. zool. Soc. Lond.* A, **108**, 441–3.

RUSSELL M.A. & SEMEONOFF R. (1967) A serum esterase variation in *Microtus agrestis*. *Genet. Res.* **10**, 27.

RYDER S.R. (1962) *Water voles*. London, Sunday Times (Animals of Britain, no. 4).

RYSZKOWSKI L. (1966) The space organization of nutria (*Myocastor coypus*) populations. *Symp. zool. Soc. Lond.* **18**, 259–65.

RYSZKOWSKI L. & TRUSKOWSKI J. (1970) Survival of unweaned and juvenile bank voles under field conditions. *Acta theriol.* **15**, 223–32.

SAINT GIRONS M.-C. (1957) Les mammifères des Pyrénées orientales. I. Observations sur quelques mammifères recueillis dans la région de Banyuls et plus particulièrement le mulot *Apodemus flavicollis*. *Vie et Milieu* **8**, 287–96.

SAINT GIRONS M.-C. (1966) Etude du genre *Apodemus* Kaup, 1829 en France. *Mammalia* **30**, 547–600.

SAINT GIRONS M.-C. (1967) Etude du genre *Apodemus* Kaup, 1829 en France (suite et fin). *Mammalia* **31**, 55–100.

SAINT GIRONS M.-C. (1972) Notes sur les mammifères de France. XII: Le reproduction du campagnol roussâtre *Clethrionomys glareolus* (Schreber, 1780) dans la nature et en captivité. *Mammalia* **36**, 93–107.

SALES G.D. (1972) Ultrasound and mating behaviour in rodents with some observations on other behavioural situations. *J. Zool., Lond.* **168**, 149–64.

SCHULZE W. (1970) Beiträge zum Vorkommen und zur Biologie der Haselmaus (*Muscardinus avellanarius* L.) und des Siebenschläfers (*Glis glis* L.) in Südharz. *Hercynia* **7**, 354–71.

SCHWARZ E. & SCHWARZ H.K. (1967) A monograph of the *Rattus rattus* group. *An. Esc. nac. Cienc. biol. Mex.* **14**, 79–178.

SELANDER R.K. (1970) Biochemical polymorphism in populations of the house mouse and old-field mouse. *Symp. zool. Soc. Lond.* **26**, 73–91.

SEMEONOFF R. & ROBERTSON W. (1968) A biochemical and ecological study of plasma esterase polymorphism in natural populations of the field vole, *Microtus agrestis* L. *Biochem. Gen.* **1**, 205–27.

SEWELL G.D. (1968) Ultrasound in rodents. *Nature, Lond.* **217**, 682–3.

SEWELL G.D. (1970) Ultrasonic communication in rodents. *Nature, Lond.* **227**, 410.

SHARP W.M. (1958) Aging gray squirrels by use of tail-pelage characteristics. *J. Wildl. Mgmt* **22**, 29–34.

SHILLITO E.E. (1963) Exploratory behaviour in the short-tailed vole *Microtus agrestis*. *Behaviour* **21**, 145–54.

SHORTEN M. (1951) Some aspects of the biology of the grey squirrel (*Sciurus carolinensis*) in Great Britain. *Proc. zool. Soc. Lond.* **121**, 427–59.

SHORTEN M. (1954a) The reaction of the brown rat towards changes in its environment. In Chitty & Southern (1954), 307–34 (q.v.).

SHORTEN M. (1954b) *Squirrels*. London, Collins.

SHORTEN M. (1957) Damage caused by squirrels in Forestry Commission areas 1954–6. *Forestry* **30**, 151–72.

SHORTEN M. (1962a) *Grey squirrels*. London, Sunday Times (Animals in Britain, no. 5).

SHORTEN M. (1962b) *Red squirrels*. London, Sunday Times (Animals in Britain, no. 6).

SHORTEN M. (1962c) *Squirrels*. London, HMSO (MAFF Bulletin no. 184).

SHORTEN M. & COURTIER F.A. (1955) A population study of the grey squirrel in May 1954. *Ann. appl. Biol.* **43**, 494–510.

SIDOROWICZ J. (1958) Geographical variation of the squirrel *Sciurus vulgaris* L. in Poland. *Acta theriol.* **2**, 141–57.

SIDOROWICZ J. (1959) Uber Morphologie und Biologie der Haselmaus (*Muscardinus avellanarius* L.) in Polen. *Acta theriol.* **3**, 75–91.

SIDOROWICZ J. (1961) Craniometrical measurements of Scandinavian squirrels and their distribution. *Acta. theriol.* **5**, 253–61.

SIERRA DE SORIANO B. (1960) Elementos constituvos de una habitación de *Myocastor coypus bonariensis* (Geoffroy). *Revta. Fac. Hum. Cienc. Univ. Repub. Urug.* **18**, 257–76.

SIERRA DE SORIANO B. (1961) Algunos modélos de las actividades en *Myocastor coypus bonariensis* Geoffroy ('nutria') en cautiverio. *Revta Fac. Hum. Cienc. Univ. Repub. Urug.* **19**, 261–9.

SLEPTSOV M.M. (1947) [The biology of *Micromys minutus ussuricus* Bar.-Ham.]. *Fauna i Ekologiya Gryzunov* **2**, 69–100 (British Library translation no. 7767).

SMIRNOV P.K. (1957) [Diurnal cycle of activity in *Micromys minutus* (Pallas).] *Proc. Acad. Sci. U.S.S.R.* **17**, 892–3.

SMIRNOV P.K. (1959) [The postembryonic development of the harvest mouse] *Nauch. Dokl. Vysshei Shk. Biol. Nauk* **3**, 40–2.

SMIT F.G.A.M. (1957) The recorded distribution and hosts of Siphonaptera in Britain. *Ent. Gaz.* **8**, 45–75.

SMITH N.B. & BARKALOW F.S. (1967) Precocious breeding in the gray squirrel. *J. Mammal.* **48**, 328–30.

SMITH W.W. (1958) Melanistic *Rattus norvegicus* in South-Western Georgia. *J. Mammal.* **39**, 304–6.

SMYTH M. (1965) Harvest mites on bank voles that have lost a leg. *J. Zool., Lond.* **147**, 221–2.

SMYTH M. (1966) Winter breeding in woodland mice, *Apodemus sylvaticus*, and voles, *Clethrionomys glareolus* and *Microtus agrestis*, near Oxford. *J. Anim. Ecol.* **35**, 471–85.

SOUTHERN H.N. (1954) Tawny owls and their prey. *Ibis* **96**, 384–410.

SOUTHERN H.N. (1970a) Ecology at the cross-roads. *J. Anim. Ecol.* **39**, 1–11.

SOUTHERN H.N. (1970b) The natural control of a population of Tawny owls, *Strix aluco*. *J. Zool., Lond.* **162**, 197–285.

SOUTHERN H.N. & CROWCROFT W.P. (1956) Terrestrial habits of the water vole (*Arvicola amphibius*). *Proc. zool. Soc. Lond.* **126**, 166–7.

SOUTHERN H.N. & LOWE V.P.W. (1968) The pattern of distribution of prey and predation in tawny owl territories. *J. Anim. Ecol.* **37**, 75–97.

STEIN G.H.W. (1956) Natürliche Auslese bei der Rötelmaus. *Z. Säugetierk.* **21**, 84–100.

STEVEN D.M. (1955) Untersuchungen über die britischen Formen von *Clethrionomys*. *Z. Säugetierk.* **20**, 70–4.

STODDART D.M. (1969) The frequency of unusual albinism in water vole populations. *J. Zool., Lond.* **158**, 222–4.

STODDART D.M. (1970) Individual range, dispersion and dispersal in a population of water voles (*Arvicola terrestris* (L.)). *J. Anim. Ecol.* **39**, 403–25.

STODDART D.M. (1971) Breeding and survival in a population of water voles. *J. Anim. Ecol.* **40**, 487–94.

STODDART D.M. (1972) The lateral scent organ of *Arvicola terrestris J. Zool. Lond.* **166**, 49–54.

TADROS W.A. (1968) The rediscovery of Findlay & Middleton's organism (the so-called *Toxoplasma microti*) in voles in the type locality in Wales. *Trans. Roy. Soc. trop. Med. Hyg.* **62**, 7.

TANTON M.T. (1965) Problems of live-trapping and population estimation for the wood mouse, *Apodemus sylvaticus* (L.). *J. Anim. Ecol.* **34**, 1–22.

TANTON M.T. (1969) The estimation and biology of populations of the bank vole (*Clethrionomys glareolus* (Schr.)) and wood mouse (*Apodemus sylvaticus* (L.). *J. Anim. Ecol.* **38**, 511–29.

TAPPER S.C. (1976) Population fluctuations of field voles (*Microtus*): a background to the problems involved in predicting vole plagues. *Mammal Rev.* **6**, 93–117.

TAYLOR J.C. (1966) Home range and agonistic behaviour in the grey squirrel. *Symp. zool. Soc. Lond.* **18**, 229–35.

TAYLOR J.C. (1968) The use of marking points by grey squirrels. *J. Zool., Lond.* **155**, 246–7.

TAYLOR K.D., SHORTEN M., LLOYD H.G. & COURTIER F.A. (1971) Movements of the grey squirrel as revealed by trapping. *J. appl. Ecol.* **8**, 123–46.

TELLE H.J. (1966) Beitrag zur Kenntnis der Verhaltensweise von Ratten verfleichend dargestellt bei *Rattus norvegicus* und *R. rattus*. *Z. angew. Zool.* **53**, 129–96.

THOMAS O. (1928) A special pro-odont race of water vole, occurring in Northumbria. *Ann. Mag. nat. Hist.* (10) **1**, 316–18.

THOMPSON H.V. (1953) The edible dormouse (*Glis glis* L.) in England, 1902–51. *Proc. zool. Soc. Lond.* **122**, 1017–24.

THOMPSON H.V. & PLATT F.B.W. (1964) The present status of *Glis* in England. *Bull. Mammal Soc. Br. Isles* **21**, 5–6.

TITTENSOR A.M. (1970) Red squirrel dreys. *J. Zool., Lond.* **162**, 528–33.

TITTENSOR A.M. (1975) *The red squirrel.* London, HMSO (Forest Record no. 101).

TROUT R.C. (1976) *An ecological study of wild populations of harvest mice.* Ph.D thesis, University of London.

TUPIKOVA N.V., SIDOROVA G.A. & KONOVALOVA E.A. (1968) A method of age determination in *Clethrionomys. Acta theriol.* **13**, 99–115.

TURNER D.T.L. (1965) A contribution to the ecology and taxonomy of the vole *Microtus arvalis* on the island of Westray, Orkney. *Proc. zool. Soc. Lond.* **144**, 143–50.

TWIGG G.I. (1966) Notes on the invertebrate fauna of some grey squirrel dreys. *Entomologist* **99**, 51–3.

TWIGG G.I. (1973) Rat-borne leptospirosis in wildlife and on the farm. *Mammal Rev.* **3**, 27–42.

TWIGG G.I. & CUERDEN C.M. (1966) Leptospirosis in British mammals: initial survey results. *J. Zool., Lond.* **150**, 494–8.

TWIGG G.I., CUERDEN C.M. & HUGHES D.M. (1968) Leptospirosis in British wild mammals. *Symp. zool. Soc. Lond.* **24**, 75–98.

UHLIG H.G. (1955) The determination of age of nestling and sub-adult gray squirrels in West Virginia. *J. Wildl. Mgmt* **19**, 479–83.

URSIN E. (1956) Geographical variation in *A. sylvaticus* and *A. flavicollis* (Rodentia, Muridae) in Europe, with special reference to Danish and Latvian populations. *Biol. Skr. Kong. Dansk Vidensk. Selsk* **8**, 1–46.

VARMA M.G.R. & PAGE R.J.C. (1966) The epidemiology of louping ill in Ayrshire, Scotland: ectoparasites of small mammals I. (Siphonaptera). *J. med. Ent.* **3**, 331–5.

VIETINGHOFF-RIESCH A.F. VON (1955) Siebenschläfermarkierung im Deister. *Z. Säugetierk.* **20**, 134–5.

VIETINGHOFF-RIESCH A.F. VON (1960) Der Siebenschläfer (*Glis glis* L.). *Monogr. Wildsäugetiere* **14**, i–vii, 1–196.

VIZOSO A.D. (1968) A red squirrel disease. *Symp. zool. Soc. Lond.* **24**, 29–38.

VIZOSO A.D., VIZOSO M.R. & HAY R. (1964) Isolation of a virus resembling encephalomyocarditis from a red squirrel. *Nature, Lond.* **201**, 849–50.

VOIPIO P. (1969) Some ecological aspects of polymorphism in the red squirrel *Sciurus vulgaris* L. in northern Europe. *Oikos* **20**, 101–9.

WACHTENDORF W. (1951) Beiträge zur Okologie und Biologie der Haselmaus (*Muscardinus avellanarius*) im Alpenvorland. *Zool. Jb. (Syst.)* **80**, 189–203.

WARKENTIN M.J. (1968) Observations on the behaviour and ecology of the nutria in Louisiana. *Tulane Stud. Zool.* **15**, 10–17.

WARWICK T. (1934) The distribution of the musk rat (*Fiber zibethicus*) in the British Isles. *J. Anim. Ecol.* **3**, 250–67.

WARWICK T. (1940) A contribution to the ecology of the musk rat (*Ondatra zibethica*) in the British Isles. *Proc. zool. Soc. Lond.* A, **110**, 165–201.

WATSON J.S. (1944) The melanic form of *Rattus norvegicus* in London. *Nature, Lond.* **154**, 334–5.

WATSON J.S. (1950) Some observations on the reproduction of *Rattus rattus* L. *Proc. zool. Soc. Lond.* **120**, 1–12.

WATSON J.S. (1951) *The rat problem in Cyprus.* London, HMSO (Colon. Res. Publ. no. 9).

WATTS C.H.S. (1968) The foods eaten by wood mice (*Apodemus sylvaticus*) and bank voles (*Clethrionomys glareolus*) in Wytham Woods, Berkshire. *J. Anim. Ecol.* 37, 25–41.

WATTS C.H.S. (1969) The regulation of wood mouse (*Apodemus sylvaticus*) numbers in Wytham Woods, Berkshire. *J. Anim. Ecol.* 38, 285–304.

WATTS C.H.S. (1970a) Long distance movement of bank voles and wood mice. *J. Zool., Lond.* 161, 247–56.

WATTS C.H.S. (1970b) Effect of supplementary food on breeding in woodland rodents. *J. Mammal.* 51, 169–71.

WELLS A.Q. (1937) Tuberculosis in wild voles. *Lancet* 232, 1221.

WELLS A.Q. (1946) The murine type of tubercle bacillus (the vole acid-fast bacillus). *Spec. Rep. Ser. med. Res. Coun.* no. 259.

WHITAKER J.O. (1966) Food of *Mus musculus*, *Peromyscus maniculatus bairdi* and *Peromyscus leucopus* in Vigo County, Indiana. *J. Mammal.* 47, 473–86.

WIJNGAARDEN A. VAN (1954) *Biologie en Bestrijding van de Woelrat*, Arvicola terrestris terrestris (*L.*) *in Nederland*. Eindhoven.

WILDHAGEN A. (1952) *Om vekslingene bestanden av Smånagere i Norge 1871–1949*. Drammen, Steenberg.

WORDEN A.N. & LANE-PETTER W. (eds.) (1957) *The UFAW handbook on the care and management of laboratory animals*. London, Univ. Fed. Animal Welfare.

WRANGEL H.F. VON (1939) Beiträge zur Biologie der Rötelmaus *Clethrionomys glareolus* Schr. *Z. Säugetierk.* 14, 52–93.

YOUNG H., STRECKER R.L. & EMLEN J.T. (1950) Localization of activity in two indoor populations of house mice *Mus musculus*. *J. Mammal.* 31, 403–10.

ZARROW M.X. & WILSON E.D. (1963) Hormonal control of the pubic symphysis of the Skomer bank vole (*Clethrionomys skomerensis*). *J. Endocrinol.* 23, 103–6.

ZEJDA J. (1961) Age structure in populations of the bank vole, *Clethrionomys glareolus* Schreber 1780. *Zool. Listy* 10, 249–64.

ZEJDA J. (1962) Winter breeding in the bank vole, *Clethrionomys glareolus* Schreb. *Zool. Listy* 11, 309–21.

ZEJDA J. (1965) Das Gewicht, das Alter und die Geschlechtsaktivität bei der Rötelmaus (*Clethrionomys glareolus* Schreb.). *Z. Säugetierk.* 30, 1–9.

ZEJDA J. (1971) Differential growth of three cohorts of the bank vole, *Clethrionomys glareolus* Schreb. 1780. *Zool. Listy* 20, 229–45.

ZEJDA J. & MAZÁK V. (1965) Cycle de changement du pelage chez le campagnol roussâtre, *Clethrionomys glareolus* Schreber, 1780 (Microtidae, Mammalia). *Mammalia* 29, 577–97.

ZEMANEK M. (1972) Food and feeding habits of rodents in a deciduous forest. *Acta theriol.* 17, 315–25.

ZIMMERMANN K. (1959) Über eine Kreuzung von Unterarten der Feldmaus *Microtus arvalis*. *Zool. Jb. Syst.* 87, 1–12.

CETACEANS

BEAMISH P. & MITCHELL E.M. (1971) Ultrasonic sounds recorded in the presence of a blue whale *Balaenoptera musculus*. *Deep-sea Res.* 18, 803–9.

CUMMINGS W.C., FISH J.F. & THOMPSON P.O. (1972) Sound production and other behaviour of southern right whales *Eubalaena glacialis*. *Trans. San Diego Soc. nat. Hist.* 17, 1–13.

EVANS P.G.H. (1975) An analysis of sightings of Cetacea in British waters. *Mammal Rev.* 6, 5–14.

EVANS W.E. (1967) Vocalisation among marine mammals. *In* Tavolga W. (ed.), *Marine bio-acoustics* 2. London, Pergamon Press.

FISHER D.M. & HARRISON R. (1973) Reproduction in the common porpoise. *J. Zool. Lond.* 161, 471–86.

FRASER F.C. (1934) *Report on Cetacea stranded on the British coasts from 1927 to 1932.* London, British Museum (Nat. Hist.).

FRASER F.C. (1937) Whales and dolphins. *In* Norman J. R. & Fraser F.C., *Giant fishes, whales and dolphins.* London, Putnam.

FRASER F.C. (1940) Three anomalous dolphins from Blacksod Bay, Ireland. *Proc. Roy. Ir. Acad.* 45, 413–41.

FRASER F.C. (1946) *Report on Cetacea stranded on the British coasts from 1933 to 1937.* London, British Museum (Nat. Hist.).

FRASER F.C. (1953) *Report on Cetacea stranded on the British coasts from 1938 to 1947.* London, British Museum (Nat. Hist.).

FRASER F.C. (1974) *Report on Cetacea stranded on the British coasts from 1948 to 1966.* London, British Museum (Nat. Hist.).

FRASER F.C. & NOBLE B.A. (1970) Variations of pigmentation pattern in Meyen's dolphin, *Stenella coeruleoalba* (Meyen). *Investigations on Cetacea* 2, 147–163.

FRASER F.C. & PURVES P.E. (1960) Hearing in cetaceans. Evolution of the accessory air sacs and the structure and function of the outer and middle ear in recent Cetaceans. *Bull. Br. Mus. nat. Hist. (Zool.)* 7, 1–140.

GAMBELL R. (1972) Why all the fuss about whales? *New Scientist*, 22 June.

GRAY J.E. (1864) *Eubalaena.* Proc. zool. Soc. Lond., 201.

HARMER S.F. (1914) *Report on Cetacea stranded on the British coasts.* British Museum (Nat. Hist.).

HARMER S.F. (1927) *Report on Cetacea stranded on the British coasts from 1913 to 1926.* London, British Museum (Nat. Hist.).

LAWS R.M. (1961) Southern fin whales. *Discovery Rep.* 21, 327–486.

LOCKYER C. (1972) The age at sexual maturity in the southern fin whale. *J. Cons. int. Expl. Mer* 34, 276–94.

MACKINTOSH N.A. & WHEELER J.F.G. (1929) Southern blue and fin whales. *Discovery Rep.* 1, 257–540.

MULLER J. (1954) Observations on the orbital region of the skull of Mysticeti. *Zool. Meded.* 32, 281–90.

OHSUMI S., MASAKI I. & KAWAMURA A. (1970) Stock of the antarctic minke whale. *Sc. Rep. Whales Res. Inst. Tokyo* 22, 75–123.

PAYNE R.S. (1970) *Songs of the humpback whale.* Del Mar, California, CRM Records (gramophone record with text).

PERKINS P.J. (1966) Communication sounds of finback whales. *Norsk Hvalvangsttid.* 55, 199–200.

PURVES P.E. & MOUNTFORD M.D. (1959) Ear plug laminations in relation to the age composition of a population of fin whales (*Balaenoptera physalus*) *Bull. Br. Mus. nat. Hist. (Zool.)* 5, 125–61.

SCHEVILL W.E., WATKINS W.A. & BACKUS R.H. (1964) The 20-cycle signals and *Balaenoptera* (fin whales). *In* Tavolga W. (ed.), *Marine bio-acoustics.* London, Pergamon Press, 147–52.

SERGEANT D.E. (1973) Biology of white whales (*Delphinapterus leucas*). *J. Fish. Res. Board Canada* 30, 1065–90.

SIMONS M.A. & WESTON R.D. (1958) Studies on the humpback whale in the Bellingshausen Sea. *Norsk Hvalvangsttid* 2, 53–81.

THOMPSON D.W. (1928) Whales landed at Scottish whaling stations. *Scient. Invest. Fishery Bd Scotl.* **3**, 1–40.

TOMILIN A.G. (1957) *Mammals of USSR and adjacent regions.* 9: *Cetacea.* Moscow (English translation 1967, Jerusalem, Israel Program for Scientific Translations).

WORTHINGTON L.V. & SCHEVILL W.E. (1957) Underwater sounds heard from sperm whales. *Nature, Lond.* **180**, 291.

CARNIVORES

AKANDE M. (1972) The food of feral mink (*Mustela vison*) in Scotland. *J. Zool., Lond.* **167**, 475–9.

ALBONE E.S. & PERRY G.C. (1976) Anal sac secretion of the red fox, *Vulpes vulpes. J. chem. Ecol.* **2**, 101–11.

ALDOUS S.E. & MANWEILER J. (1942) The winter food habits of the short-tailed weasel in northern Minnesota. *J. Mammal.* **23**, 250–5.

ANDERSEN J. (1955) The food of the Danish badger (*Meles meles danicus*) with special reference to the summer months. *Dan. Rev. Game Biol.* **3**, 1–75.

ANDERSON E. (1970) Quaternary evolution of the genus *Martes* (Carnivora, Mustelidae). *Acta Zool. fenn.* **130**, 1–132.

ANON (1949) Stoat essays long swim. *N.Z. Outdoor* **12**(3), 6.

ANON (1960) Vermin bag records. *Ann. Rep.* (*1959*) *Imp. Chem. Ind. Game Services.*

ANON (1969) The otter in Britain. *Oryx* **10**, 16–22.

ARTHUR D.R. (1963) *British ticks.* London, Butterworths.

ASDELL S.A. (1964) *Patterns of mammalian reproduction.* 2nd edn. Cornell University Press.

ASHTON E.H. (1955) Some characters of the skulls of the European polecat, the Asiatic polecat and the domestic ferret. *Proc. zool. Soc. Lond.* **125**, 807–9.

ASHTON E.H. & THOMSON A.P.D. (1955) Some characters of the skulls and skins of the European polecat, the Asiatic polecat and the domestic ferret. *Proc. zool. Soc. Lond.* **125**, 317–33.

ASPISOV D.I. (1959) [The population dynamics of the forest marten in the Volga–Kama area and some indexes for forecasting changes in its numbers]. *Trud. Vses. nauch. issled. Inst. Zhivotn. Syr'ya i Pushiniy* **18**, 29–45.

BATEMAN J.A. (1970) Supernumerary incisors in Mustelids. *Mammal Rev.* **1**, 81–6.

BÄUMLER W. (1973) Uber die Aktivitätsperiodik des Iltisses (*Mustela putorius*) und des Hermelins (*Mustela erminea*) sowie über dessen Farbwechsel. *Säugetierk. Mitt.* **21**, 31–6.

BEACOURNU J.C. & GRULICH I. (1968) A propos de la belette de Corse. *Mammalia* **32**, 341–71.

BREE P.J.H. VAN (1968) Deux exemples d'application des critères d'âge chez la Loutre *Lutra lutra* Linnaeus 1758. *Beaufortia* **15**, 27–32.

BRINK F.H. VAN DEN (1967) *A field guide to the mammals of Britain and Europe.* London, Collins.

BRODMANN K. (1952) *Mauswiesel frei im Hause.* Köln, Balduin Pick Verlag.

BROWN J.H. & LASIEWSKI R.C. (1972) Metabolism of weasels: the cost of being long and thin. *Ecology* **53**, 939–43.

BUCKTON K.E. & CUNNINGHAM C. (1971) Variation of the chromosome number of the red fox. *Chromosoma* **33**, 268–72.

BURKE N. (1963) *King Todd: the true story of a badger.* London, Putnam.

BURNHAM P.M. (1970) Kestrel attempting to prey on weasels. *Brit. Birds* **63**, 338.

BURROWS R. (1968) *Wild fox.* Newton Abbot, David & Charles.

CABRERA A. (1932) Los Mamiferos de Marruecos. *Trab. Mus. nac. Cient. nat. Ser. Zool.* **57**.

CAHN A.R. (1936) A weasel learns by experience. *J. Mammal.* **17**, 286.

CHURCHER C.S. (1960) Cranial variation in the North American red fox. *J. Mammal.* **41**, 349–60.

CLARK S.P. (1970) Field experience of feral mink in Yorkshire and Lancashire. *Mammal Rev.* **1**, 41–7.

CONDÉ B., NGUYEN-THI-THU-CUC, VAILLANT F. & SCHAUENBERG P. (1972) Le régime alimentaire du chat forestier (*F. silvestris* Schr.) en France. *Mammalia* **36**, 112–19.

CONDÉ B. & SCHAUENBERG P. (1969) Reproduction du chat forestier d'Europe (*Felis silvestris* Schreber) en captivité. *Revue suisse Zool.* **76**, 183–210.

CONDÉ B. & SCHAUENBERG P. (1971) Le poids du chat forestier d'Europe (*Felis silvestris* Schreber 1777). *Revue suisse Zool.* **78**, 295–315.

CORBET G.B. (1964) *The identification of British mammals*. London, British Museum (Nat. Hist.).

CORBET G.B. (1966) *The terrestrial mammals of Western Europe*. London, Foulis and Co.

CORBET G.B. (1971) Provisional distribution maps of British mammals. *Mammal Rev.* **1**, 95–142.

COUNCIL FOR NATURE (1973) *Predatory mammals in Britain*. Seel House Press.

COWAN I.M. & MACKAY R.H. (1950) Food habits of the marten (*Martes americana*) in the Rocky Mountain region of Canada. *Canad. Field Nat.* **64**, 100–4.

CRASTER J. (1970) Stoats and weasels: a new contrast. *Field* **236**(6144), 786–7.

CRIDDLE S. (1947) A nest of the least weasel. *Canad. Field Nat.* **61**, 69.

CUTHBERT J.H. (1973) The origin and distribution of feral mink in Scotland. *Mammal Rev.* **3**, 97–103.

DADD M.N. (1970) Overlap of variation in British and European mammal populations. *Symp. zool. Soc. Lond.* **26**, 117–25.

DANILOV P.I. & RUSAKOV O.S. (1969) [Special aspects of the ecology of the polecat (*Mustela putorius*) in the North-West regions of the USSR.] *Zool. Zh.* **48**, 1383–94 (translation British Library).

DAVIS W.B. (1942) Swimming ability of two small mammals. *J. Mammal.* **23**, 99.

DAY M.G. (1963) *An ecological study of the stoat* (Mustela erminea L.) *and the weasel* (Mustela nivalis L.) *with particular reference to their food and feeding habits*. Ph.D. thesis, Exeter University.

DAY M.G. (1968) Food habits of British stoats (*Mustela erminea*) and weasels (*Mustela nivalis*). *J. Zool., Lond.* **155**, 485–97.

DAY M.G. & LINN I. (1972) Notes on the food of feral mink *Mustela vison* in England and Wales. *J. Zool., Lond.* **167**, 463–73.

DEANE C.D. & O'GORMAN F. (1969) The spread of feral mink in Ireland. *Irish Nat. J.* **16**, 198–202.

DEANESLY R. (1935) The reproductive processes of certain mammals. Part 9—Growth and reproduction in the stoat (*Mustela erminea*). *Phil. Trans.*, Ser. B, **225**, 459–92.

DEANESLY R. (1943) Delayed implantation in the stoat. *Nature, Lond.* **151**, 365–6.

DEANESLY R. (1944) The reproductive cycle of the female weasel (*Mustela nivalis*). *Proc. zool. Soc. Lond.* **114**, 339–49.

DRABBLE P. (1957) *A weasel in my meatsafe*. London, Collins.

DULKEIT G. (1929) Biologie und Gewerbejagd des Zobels auf den Schantarskii-Inseln. *Bull. Pacific Fishery Res. Stn.* **3**(3), 1–119.

DUPLAIX-HALL N. (1971) La Bretagne, un des derniers refuges de la loutre *Lutra lutra* en France. *Penn Ar Bed* **8**(64), 8–16.

Duplaix-Hall N. (1972a) Notes on maintaining river otters in captivity. *Int. Zoo Yb.* 12, 178–81.

Duplaix-Hall N. (1972b) Otters of the world. *Animals* 14(10), 438–42.

Duplaix-Hall N. (1975) River otters in captivity: a review. *In* Martin R.D. (ed.) *Breeding endangered species in captivity.* London, Academic Press, 315–27.

East K. & Lockie J.D. (1964) Observations on a family of weasels (*Mustela nivalis*) bred in captivity. *Proc. zool. Soc. Lond.* 143, 359–63.

East K. & Lockie J.D. (1965) Further observations on weasels (*Mustela nivalis*) and stoats (*Mustela erminea*) born in captivity. *J. Zool., Lond.* 147, 234–8.

Eibl-Eibesfeldt I. (1955) Zur Biologie des Iltis (*Putorius putorius* L.). *Verh. dtsch. zool. Ges. Erlangen. 1955. Zool. Anz. Suppl.* 19, 304–14.

Eibl-Eibesfeldt I. (1956) Angeborenes und Erworbenes in der Technik des Beutetötens (Versuche am Iltis, *Putorius putorius* L.). *Z. Säugetierk.* 21, 135–7.

Enders R.K. (1952) Reproduction in the mink (*Mustela vison*). *Proc. Amer. Phil. Soc.* 96, 691–741.

Englund J. (1965) The diet of the fox (*Vulpes vulpes*) on the island of Gotland since myxomatosis. *Viltrevy* 3, 507–30.

Englund J. (1970) Some aspects of reproduction and mortality rate in Swedish foxes. *Viltrevy* 8, 1–82.

Erlinge S. (1967a) Home range of the otter *Lutra lutra* L. in Southern Sweden. *Oikos* 18, 186–209.

Erlinge S. (1967b) Food habits of the fish-otter *Lutra lutra* L. in South Swedish habitats. *Viltrevy* 4, 371–443.

Erlinge S. (1968a) Territoriality of the otter *Lutra lutra* L. *Oikos* 19, 81–98.

Erlinge S. (1968b) Food studies on captive otters *Lutra lutra* L. *Oikos* 19, 259–70.

Erlinge S. (1969) Food habits of the otter *Lutra lutra* L. and mink *Mustela vison* Schreber in a trout water in S. Sweden. *Oikos* 20, 1–7.

Erlinge S. (1972) Interspecific relations between otter *Lutra lutra* and mink *Mustela vison* in Sweden. *Oikos* 23, 327–35.

Erlinge S. (1974) Distribution, territoriality and numbers of the weasel *Mustela nivalis* in relation to prey abundance. *Oikos* 25, 308–14.

Erlinge S. (1975) Feeding habits of the weasel *Mustela nivalis* in relation to prey abundance. *Oikos* 26, 378–84.

Fairley J.S. (1969a) Destruction of foxes in Northern Ireland. *Ir. Nat. J.* 16, 187–9.

Fairley J.S. (1969b) A critical examination of the Northern Ireland fox bounty figures. *Ir. Nat. J.* 16, 213–15.

Fairley J.S. (1970) The food, reproduction, form, growth and development of the fox (*Vulpes vulpes* L.) in North-East Ireland. *Proc. Roy. Ir. Acad.* 69B, 103–37.

Fairley J.S. (1971) New data on the Irish stoat. *Ir. Nat. J.* 17(2), 49–57.

Fairley J.S. (1972) Food of otters (*Lutra lutra*) from Co. Galway, Ireland, and notes on other aspects of their biology. *J. Zool., Lond.* 166, 469–74.

Fairley J.S. & Wilson S.C. (1972) Autumn food of otters (*Lutra lutra*) on the Agivey River, Co. Londonderry, Northern Ireland. *J. Zool., Lond.* 166, 468–9.

Ferns P.N. (1974) Predation by weasels of eggs laid in nestboxes. *Bird Study* 21, 218–19.

Field R.J. (1970) Winter habits of the river otter (*Lutra canadensis*) in Michigan. *Mich. Acad.* 3, 49–58.

Fitzgerald B.M. (1977) Weasel predation on a cyclic population of the montane vole, *Microtus montanus* in California. *J. Anim. Ecol.* 46 (in press).

FLINTOFF R.J. (1935a) The weights and measurements of stoats and weasels. *Northwestern Nat.* **10**, 29–34.

FLINTOFF R.J. (1935b) Stoats and weasels, brown and white. *Northwestern Nat.* **10**, 214–29.

FOG M. (1969) Studies on the weasel (*Mustela nivalis*) and the stoat (*Mustela erminea*) in Denmark. *Dan. Rev. Game Biol.* **6**(2), 1–14.

FORREST H.E. (1907) *A handbook of the vertebrate fauna of North Wales.* London.

FORSYTH J.F. (1967) Stoated rabbits. *Shooting Times* 18.3.67, 327.

FOX M.W. (1971) *Behaviour of wolves, dogs and related canids.* London, Jonathan Cape.

GERELL R. (1970) Home ranges and movements of the mink *Mustela vison* Schreber in southern Sweden. *Oikos* **21**, 160–73.

GEWALT W. (1959) Optisches Differenzierungsvermögen einiger Musteliden. *Zool. Beitr. (Berl.)* **5**, 117–75.

GIBSON J.A. (1970a) The mammals of the Island of Bute. *Trans. Buteshire nat. Hist. Soc.* **18**, 5–20.

GIBSON J.A. (1970b) Additional mammal notes from the Island of Arran. *Trans. Buteshire nat. Hist. Soc.* **18**, 45–7.

GOETHE F. (1950) Vom Leben des Mauswiesels (*Mustela n. nivalis* L.). *Zool. Gart.* (*N.F.*) *Leipzig* **17**, 193–204.

GOETHE F. (1964) Das Verhalten der Musteliden. *Handbüch der Zöologie* (Band 8) **10**(19), 1–80.

GOSSOW H. (1970) Vergleichende Verhaltenstudien an Marderartigen. I. Über Lautäusserungen und zum Beuteverhalten. *Z. Tierpsychol.* **27**(4), 405–80.

GOSZCZYNSKI J. (1974) Studies on the food of foxes. *Acta theriol.* **19**, 1–18.

GULAMHUSEIN A.P. (1972) Reproductive studies in the stoat. Pre- and post-implantation changes in the ferret uterus. *J. Zool., Lond.* **166**, 574–7.

GUSTAVSON I. (1964). Karyotype of the fox. *Nature, Lond.* **201**, 950–1.

HABERMEHL K.H. & RÖTTCHER D. (1967) Die Möglichkeiten der Alterbestimmung beim Marder und Iltis. *Z. Jagdwiss.* **13**, 89–102.

HALL E.R. (1926) Abdominal scent gland in *Martes. J. Mammal.* **7**, 227–9.

HALL E.R. (1951) American weasels. *Univ. Kansas Publ. Mus. nat. Hist.* **4**, 1–466.

HALTENORTH T. (1953) *Die Wildkatzen der Altenwelt.* Leipzig.

HALTENORTH T. (1957) *Die Wildkatzes.* Wittenberg Lutherstadt, Ziemsen.

HAMILTON W.J. (1933) The weasels of New York. *Am. Mid. Nat.* **14**, 289–344.

HANCOX M.K. (1973) *Studies on the ecology of the European badger.* Unpubl. MSS in Elton Library, Oxford.

HANSSON I. (1967) Transmission of the parasitic nematode *Skrjabingylus nasicola* (Leuckart 1842) to species of *Mustela* (Mammalia). *Oikos* **18**, 247–52.

HANSSON I. (1970) Cranial helminth parasites in species of Mustelidae. II: Regional frequencies of damage in preserved crania from Denmark, Finland, Sweden, Greenland and the N.E. of Canada compared with the helminth invasion in fresh mustelid skulls from Sweden. *Ark. Zool.* **22**(15), 571–94.

HARRIS C.J. (1968) *Otters: a study of the recent Lutrinae.* London, Weidenfeld & Nicolson.

HARTING J.E. (1880) *British animals extinct within historic times.* London, Trübner.

HARTING J.E. (1894) The weasel. *Zoologist* **52**, 417–23, 445–54.

HARTMAN L. (1964) The behaviour and breeding of captive weasels (*Mustela nivalis* L.). *N.Z. Jl Sci.* **7**, 147–56.

HATTINGH I. (1956) Measurements of foxes from Scotland and England. *Proc. zool. Soc. Lond.* **127**, 191–9.

HAWLEY V.D. & NEWBY F.E. (1957) Marten home ranges and population fluctuations. *J. Mammal.* **38**, 174–84.

HEIDT G.A. (1970) The least weasel, *Mustela nivalis* L.: developmental biology in comparison with other North American *Mustela. Mich. State Univ., Publ. Mus. (Biol. Ser.):* **4**, 227–82.

HEPTNER V.G. (1964) Über die morphologischen und geographischen Beziehungen zwischen *M. putorius* und *M. eversmanni. Z. Säugetierk.* **29**, 321–30.

HEPTNER V.G. *et al.* (1967) [*Mammals of the Soviet Union*] vol. 2. Moscow. (pp. 636–86 on stoat and weasel, translation British Library: RTS 6458).

HERTER K. (1939) Psychologische Untersuchungen an einem Mauswiesel (*Mustela nivalis* L.). *Z. Tierpsychol.* **3**, 249–63.

HERTER K. (1959) *Iltisse und Frettchen.* Wittenberg Lutherstadt, Ziemsen.

HEWER H.R. (1974) The otter in Britain—a second report. *Oryx* **12**, 429–35.

HEWSON R. (1967) The wild cat in Banffshire. *Glasg. Nat.* **18**, 477–82.

HEWSON R. (1972) Changes in the number of stoats, rats and little owls in Yorkshire as shown by tunnel trapping. *J. Zool., Lond.* **168**, 427–9.

HEWSON R. & HEALING T.D. (1971) The stoat, *Mustela erminea*, and its prey. *J. Zool., Lond.* **164**, 239–44.

HEWSON R. & KOLB H.H. (1973) Changes in the number and distribution of foxes (*Vulpes vulpes*) killed in Scotland from 1948–1970. *J. Zool., Lond.* **171** 345–65.

HILL M. (1939) The reproductive cycle of the male weasel (*Mustela nivalis*). *Proc. zool. Soc. Lond.* B, **109**, 481–512.

HÖGLUND N.H. (1960) Studier över näringen vintertid hos mården *Martes m. martes* Linn. i Jamtlands län. *Viltrevy* **1**, 319–37.

HUFF J.N. & PRICE E.O. (1968) Vocalisations of the least weasel, *Mustela nivalis. J. Mammal.* **49**, 548–50.

HUMPHRIES M. (1962) In *Countryman*, Winter 1967, 751.

HURRELL H.G. (1968) *Wildlife: tame but free.* Newton Abbot, David & Charles.

JEFFERIES D.J. & PENDLEBURY J.B. (1968) Population fluctuations of stoats, weasels and hedgehogs in recent years. *J. Zool., Lond.* **156**, 513–17.

JENKINS D. (1962) The present status of the wild cat (*Felis silvestris*) in Scotland. *Scot. Nat.* **70**, 126–38.

JENSEN A. (1964) Odderen i Danmark. *Danske Vildtundersøgelser* **11**, 1–48.

JENSEN A. & JENSEN B. (1972) Ilderen (*Putorius putorius*) og Ilderjagten i Danmark 1969/70. *Danske Vildtundersøgelser* **18**, 1–32.

JONKEL C.J. & WECKWERTH R.P. (1963) Sexual maturity and implantation of blastocysts in the wild pine marten. *J. Wildl. Mgmt* **27**, 93–8.

KALELA O. (1940) Über die Einwanderung und Verbreitung des Iltis *P. putorius* L. in Finnland. *Ann. Ac. Sc. fennica* Ser. A, **54**, no. 6.

KALELA O. (1948) Changes in the distribution of the polecat in Finland. *Suomen Riista.* **2**, 93–6.

KALELA O. (1952) Changes in the geographic distribution of Finnish birds and mammals in relation to the recent changes in climate. *Fennia* **75**, 38–59.

KAVANAU J.L. (1969) Influences of light on activity of small mammals. *Ecology* **50**, 548–57.

KING C.M. (1971) *Studies on the ecology of the weasel* (Mustela nivalis L.). D.Phil. thesis, University of Oxford.

KING C.M. (1974) The nematode *Skrjabingylus nasicola* (Metastrongyloidea) in mustelids: a new record for New Zealand. *N.Z. Jl Zool.* **1**, 501–2.

KING C.M. (1975a) The sex ratio of trapped weasels (*Mustela nivalis*). *Mammal Rev.* **5**, 1–8.

KING C.M. (1975b) The home range of the weasel (*Mustela nivalis*) in an English woodland. *J. Anim. Ecol.* **44**, 639–68.

KING C.M. (1975c) (ed.) *The biology of mustelids: some Soviet research.* Boston Spa, British Library (translations of 18 Russian papers).

KING C.M. (1976) The fleas of a population of weasels in Wytham Woods, Oxford. *J. Zool. Lond.* **180**, 525–35.

KING C.M. (1977) The effects of the nematode parasite *Skrjabingylus nasicola* on British weasels. *J. Zool. Lond.* (in press).

KING R.J. (1958) The training of badgers in Pershore forest. *J. For. Com.* **2**, 45–50.

KIRK J.C. & WAGSTAFFE R. (1943) A contribution to the study of the Scottish wild cat (*Felis silvestris grampia* Miller). Part I: Size and weight. *Northw. Nat.* **18**, 271–5.

KOLB H.H. & HEWSON R. (1974) The body size of the red fox (*Vulpes vulpes*) in Scotland. *J. Zool., Lond.* **173**, 253–5.

KRATOCHVIL J. (1952) La nourriture et les races du *P. putorius. Acta. Univ. Agr. Silv, Brno.* **1**, 1–18.

KREBS J. (1971) Territory and breeding density in the Great Tit, *Parus major* L. *Ecology* **52**, 2–22.

KURTÉN B. (1965) On the evolution of the European wild cat. *Acta zool. fenn.* **111**, 3–29.

KURTÉN B. (1968) *Pleistocene mammals of Europe.* London, Weidenfeld & Nicolson.

LAMPIO T. (1951) On the sex ratio, sex differentiation and regional variation in the marten in Finland. *Pap. Game Res. Helsinki* no. 7.

LATHAM R.M. (1952) The fox as a factor in the control of weasel populations. *J. Wildl. Mgmt* **16**, 516–17.

LAWRENCE M.J. & BROWN R.W. (1973) *Mammals of Britain, their tracks, trails and signs.* London, Blandford.

LEUW A. DE (1957) Die Wildkatze. *Merkbl. Niederwildausschuss dtsch. Jagdschutzverb.* 16, Munich.

LEWIS J.W. (1967) Observations on the skull of Mustelidae infected with the nematode *Skrjabingylus nasicola. J. Zool., Lond.* **153**, 561–4.

LIERS E.E. (1951) Notes on the river otter (*Lutra canadensis*). *J. Mammal.* **32**, 1–9.

LIKHACHEV G.N. (1956) Some ecological traits of the badger of the Tula Abatis broadleaf forests. *In* Yurgensen, P.B. (ed.). *Studies of mammals in government preserves.* Moscow. (English translation 1961, Jerusalem, Israel Program for Scientific Translations.)

LINDEMAN W. (1955) Uber die Jugendentwicklung beim Luchs (*Lynx l. lynx* Kerr) und bei der Wildkatze (*Felis s. silvestris* Schreber). *Behaviour* **8**, 1–45.

LINN I. (1962) *Weasels.* London, Sunday Times Publications (Animals of Britain no. 14).

LINN I. & DAY M.G. (1966) Identification of individual weasels *Mustela nivalis* using the ventral pelage pattern. *J. Zool., Lond.* **148**, 583–5.

LLOYD H.G. (1968) The control of foxes. *Ann. appl. Biol.* **61**, 303–49.

LLOYD H.G. & ENGLUND J. (1973) The reproductive cycle of the red fox in Europe. *J. Reprod. Fert. Suppl.* **19**, 119–30.

LLOYD J.R. (1968) Factors affecting the emergence of the badger (*Meles meles*) in Britain. *J. Zool., Lond.* **155**, 223–7.

LOCKIE J.D. (1959) The estimation of the food of foxes. *J. Wildl. Mgmt.* **23**, 224–7.

LOCKIE J.D. (1961) The food of the pine marten *Martes martes* in west Ross-shire, Scotland. *Proc. zool. Soc. Lond.* **136**, 187–95.

LOCKIE J.D. (1964) Distribution and fluctuations of the pine marten *Martes martes* (L.) in Scotland. *J. Anim. Ecol.* **33**, 349–56.

LOCKIE J.D. (1966) Territory in small carnivores. *Symp. zool. Soc. Lond.* 18, 143–65.

McCABE R.A. (1949) Notes on live-trapping mink. *J. Mammal.* 30, 416–23.

MARDON D.K. & MOORS P.J. (1977) Records of fleas collected from weasels in Northeast Scotland. *Ent. Gaz.* (in press).

MARKLEY M.H. & BASSETT C.F. (1942) Habits of captive marten. *Amer. Midl. Nat.* 28, 604–16.

MARSHALL W.H. (1963) The ecology of mustelids in New Zealand. *DSIR (NZ) Information Series* 38, 1–32.

MATHESON C. (1963) The distribution of the red polecat in Wales. *Proc. zool. Soc. Lond.* 140, 115–20.

MATTHEY R. (1958) Les chromosomes des Mammifères eutheriens. Liste critique et essai sur l'évolution chromosomique. *Archiv. der Julius Klaus-Stiftung* 33, 253–97.

MATTHEWS L.H. (1941) Reproduction in the Scottish wild cat, *Felis silvestris grampia* Miller. *Proc. zool. Soc. Lond.* B. 111, 59–77.

MAZÁK V. (1963) Eruption of permanent dentition in the genera *Mustela* Linnaeus, 1758, and *Putorius* Cuvier, 1817, with a note on the genus *Martes* Pinel, 1792. *Vestn. ceskosl. zool. Spolec.* 27, 328–34.

MILLAIS J.G. (1905) *The mammals of Great Britain and Ireland,* vol. II, London, Longmans.

MOORS P.J. (1974) *The annual energy budget of a weasel* (Mustela nivalis L.) *population in farmland.* Ph.D. thesis, University of Aberdeen.

MOYSEY C.F. (1959) Badger activity automatically recorded. *Bull. Mamm. Soc.* 12, 19–23.

MÜLLER H. (1970) Beiträge zur Biologie des Hermelins, *Mustela erminea* Linné 1758. *Säugetierk. Mitt.* 18, 293–380.

MURIE A. (1935) Weasel goes hungry. *J. Mammal.* 16, 321–2.

MURR G. (1933) Aus den Fortpflanzungsbiologie des Frettchens (*Putorius furo*). *Z. Säugetierk.* 8, 26.

MURRAY R. (1970) Live trapping of badgers, their removal, release and rehabilitation in a new area. *Mammal Rev.* 1, 86–92.

MUSGROVE B.F. (1951) Weasel foraging patterns in the Robinson Lake area, Idaho. *Murrelet* 32, 8–11.

NASIMOVICH A.A. (1949) [The biology of the weasel in Kola Peninsula in connection with its competitive relations with the ermine]. *Zool. Zh.* 28, 177–82 (translation 257, Elton Library, Oxford).

NEAL E.G. (1948) *The badger,* London, Collins, 4th ed. 1975 (also Pelican Books, 1958).

NEAL E.G. (1962) *Otters.* London, Sunday Times (Animals of Britain no. 8).

NEAL E.G. (1972) National badger survey. *Mammal Rev.* 2, 55–64.

NEAL E.G. (1977) *Badgers.* Poole, Blandford.

NEAL E.G. & HARRISON R.J. (1958) Reproduction in the European badger (*Meles meles* L.). *Trans. zool. Soc. Lond.* 29, 67–131.

NORTHCOTT T.H. (1971) Winter predation of *Mustela erminea* in Northern Canada. *Arctic (Quebec)* 24, 141–3.

NOTINI G. (1948) Biologiska undersökinger över grävlingen (*Meles meles*). *Svenska Jägareförbundets Medd.* no. 13.

NOVIKOV G. A. (1956) [*Carnivorous mammals of the fauna of the U.S.S.R.*] Moscow & Leningrad (translation 1962 by Israel Program for Scientific Translations).

NYHOLM E.S. (1970) [On the ecology of the pine marten (*Martes martes*) in Eastern and Northern Finland]. *Suomen Riista* 22, 105–18.

OGNEV S.I. (1931) [*Mammals of Eastern Europe and Northern Asia. II: Carnivora (Fissipedia)*] (translation 1962, Jerusalem, Israel Program for Scientific Translations).

OGNEV S.I. (1935) [*Mammals of the U.S.S.R. and adjacent countries.* Vol. III: *Carnivora*].

Moscow & Leningrad (translation 1962, Jerusalem, Israel Program for Scientific Translations).

OSGOOD F.L. (1936) Earthworms as a supplementary food of weasels. *J. Mammal.* **17**, 64.

OWEN C. (1964) The status of *Putorius* in North Africa. *Bull. Mammal Soc.* **22**, 11–12.

PAGET R.J. & MIDDLETON A.C.V. (1974) *Badgers of Yorkshire and Humberside*. York, Ebor.

PAVLOV M.P. (1970) *Trans. 9th Int. Congr. Game Biologists, Moscow*, 129–35.

PEARSON O.P. & ENDERS R.K. (1944) Duration of pregnancy in certain mustelids. *J. exp. Zool.* **95**, 21–35.

PETSKOI P.G. & KOLPOVSKY V.M. (1970) [Neck glandular structure in animals of the family Mustelidae]. *Zool. Zh.* **49**(8), 1208–19.

POCOCK R.I. (1936) The polecats of the genera *Putorius* and *Vormela* in the British Museum. *Proc. zool. Soc. Lond.* 691–723.

POHL L. (1910) Wieselstudien. *Zool. Beobacht.* **51**, 234–41.

POLDERBOER E.B. (1942) Habits of the least weasel (*Mustela rixosa*) in Northeastern Iowa. *J. Mammal.* **23**, 145–7.

POOLE T.B. (1964) Observations on the facial pattern of the polecat. *Proc. zool. Soc. Lond.* **143**, 350–2.

POOLE T.B. (1967) Aspects of aggressive behaviour in polecats. *Z. Tierpsychol.* **24**, 351–69.

POPOV V.A. (1943) Numerosity of *M. erminea* Pall. as affected by *Skrjabingylus* invasion. *C.R. Acad. Sci. USSR* **39**, 160–2.

POWELL R.A. (1973) A model for raptor predation on weasels. *J. Mammal.* **54**, 259–63.

PRICE E.O. (1971) Effect of food deprivation on activity of the least weasel. *J. Mammal.* **52**, 636–40.

REINWALDT E. & ERKINARO E. (1959) Zur Taxonomie und Verbreitung des Baummarders, *Martes martes martes* (Linné, 1758). *Säugetierk. Mitt.* **7**, 97–100.

RITCHIE J. (1920) *The influence of man on animal life in Scotland*. Cambridge, University Press.

ROBINSON R. (1972) Hybridisation among the Mustelidae. *Carn. Genet. Newsl.* **2**, 91–2.

ROTHSCHILD M. (1944) Pelage change in the stoat, *Mustela erminea* L. *Nature, Lond.* **154**, 180–1.

ROWBOTTOM J. (1969) Watching otters in Scotland. *Animals* **12**, 159–61.

RUBINA M.A. (1960) [Some features of weasel (*Mustela nivalis* L.) ecology based on observations in the Moscow region]. *Byull. Mosk. Obshch. Ispyt. Prir., Ot. Biol.* **65**, 27–33 (translation, British Library: RTS 2292).

RUST C.C. (1962) Temperature as a modifying factor in the spring pelage change of short-tailed weasels. *J. Mammal.* **43**, 323–8.

RUST C.C. (1965) Hormonal control of pelage cycles in the short-tailed weasel (*Mustela erminea bangsi*). *Gen. Comp. Endocrinol.* **5**, 222–31.

RYDER R.A. (1955) Fish predation by the otter in Michigan. *J. Wildl. Mgmt* **19**, 497–8.

SARGEANT A.B. (1972) Red fox spatial characteristics in relation to waterfowl predation. *J. Wildl. Mgmt.* **36**, 225–36.

SCHAUENBERG P. (1969) L'identification du chat forestier d'Europe, *Felis s. silvestris* Schreber 1777, par une méthode ostéométrique. *Revue suisse Zool.* **76**, 433–41.

SCHMIDT F. (1943) Naturgeschichte des Baum- und des Steinmarders. *Monogr. Wildsäuget. Lpz.* **10**, 1–258.

SCHWALBE G. (1893) Ueber den Ferbenwechsel winterweissen Thiere. *Morph. Arbeiten Jena* **2**, 483–606.

SCOTT T.G. (1941) Methods and computation in faecal analysis with reference to the red fox. *Iowa State Coll. J. Sci.* **15**, 279–85.

SHERRELL D.A. (1953) Raids on nest boxes by weasels. *J. For. Comm.* **23**, 104–5.

SHORT H.L. (1961) Food habits of a captive least weasel. *J. Mammal.* **42**, 273–4.

SIEFKE A. (1960) Baummarder-Paarung. *Z. Säugetierk* **25**, 178.

SKOOG P. (1970) The food of the Swedish badger. *Viltrevy* **7**, 1–120.

SOEST R.W.M. VAN & BREE P.J.H. VAN (1969) On the moult in the stoat, *Mustela erminea* Linnaeus 1758, from the Netherlands. *Bijdr. Dierk.* **39**, 63–8.

SOEST R.W.M. VAN & BREE P.J.H. VAN (1970) Sex and age composition of a stoat population (*Mustela erminea* Linnaeus 1758) from a coastal dune region of the Netherlands. *Beaufortia* **17**, 51–77.

SOEST R.W.M. VAN, LAND J. VAN DER & BREE P.J.H. VAN (1972) *Skrjabingylus nasicola* (Nematoda) in skulls of *Mustela erminea* and *Mustela nivalis* (Mammalia) from the Netherlands. *Beaufortia* **20**, 85–97.

SOUTHERN H.N. & WATSON J.S. (1941) Summer food of the red fox in Great Britain. *J. Anim. Ecol.* **10**, 1–11.

STEELE-ELLIOTT J. (1936) *Bedfordshire 'Vermin' payments: concerning the destruction of 'vermin' by parish officials during the 16th–19th centuries.* Luton, Luton Museum.

STEPHENS M.N. (1957) *The natural history of the otter.* London, UFAW.

STEVENSON J.H.F. (1959) *Mink in Britain*, 3rd edn. Exeter, Pitts.

STIRLING E.A. & HARPER R.J. (1969) The distribution and habits of badgers on the southern outskirts of Durham city. *Bull. Mamm. Soc.* **32**, 5–6.

STROGANOV S.U. (1937) [A method of age determination and an analysis of the age composition of ermine populations (*Mustela erminea* L.)]. *Zool. Zh.* **16**, 113–29 (translation, DSIR Ecology Division, Wellington, NZ).

STUBBE M. (1968) Zur Populationsbiologie der *Martes*—Arten. *13th Working Fellowship for Game and Wildlife Research, Gatersleben, January 1968.* Berlin, German Acad. Agric. Sci. 195–203.

STUBBE M. (1969) Zur Biologie und zum Schutz des Fischotters *Lutra lutra* (L.). *Arch. Naturschutz Landschaftsforsch, Berlin* **9**, 315–24.

STUBBE M. (1970) Zur Evolution der analen Markierungsorgane bei Musteliden. *Biol. Zbl.* **89**, 213–23.

STUBBE M. (1972) Die analen Markierungsorgane der *Mustela*-Arten. *Zool. Garten NF. Leipzig* **42**, 176–88.

SUMINSKI P. (1962) Les caractères de la forme pure du chat sauvage *Felis silvestris* Schreber. *Archs. Sci., Genève* **15**, 277–96.

TAYLOR W.L. (1946) The wild cat (*Felis silvestris*) in Great Britain. *J. Anim. Ecol.* **15**, 130–3.

TEMBROCK G. (1957) Zur Ethologie des Rotfuchses (*Vulpes vulpes* L.) unter besondere Berucksichtigung der Fortpflanzung. *Zool. Gart. Lpzg.* **23**, 289–532.

TEMBROCK G. (1958a) Spielverhalten beim Rotfuchs. *Zool. Beitr. Berl.* **3**, 423–96.

TEMBROCK G. (1958b) Zur Aktivitätsperiodik bei *Vulpes* und *Alopex. Zool. Jb. (Allg. Zool.).* **68**, 297–324.

TEMBROCK G. (1963) Acoustic behaviour of mammals. In *Acoustic behaviour of animals* (ed. Busnel). Amsterdam, Elsevier.

TETLEY H. (1939) On the British polecats. *Proc. zool. Soc. Lond.* **B 109**, 37–9.

TETLEY H. (1945) Notes on British polecats and ferrets. *Proc. zool. Soc. Lond.* **115**, 212–17.

THOMPSON G.B. (1961) The ectoparasites of the badger (*Meles meles meles* L.). *Entomologists' mon. Mag.* **97**, 156–8.

THOMPSON H.V. (1971) British wild mink—a challenge to naturalists. *Agriculture* **78**, 421–5.

TUMANOV I.L. (1972) [Age changes in morphophysiological characters of some species of martens]. *Zool. Zh.* **51**, 694–703.

VAISFELD M.A. (1972) [Ecology of the stoat in the cold season in the European north]. *Zool. Zh.* **51**, 1705–14 (translation, DSIR Ecology Division, Wellington, NZ).

VENGE O. (1973) Reproduction in the mink. *Kgl. Vet.-og Landbohøjsk. Årsskr.* 95–146.

VESEY-FITZGERALD B. (1965) *Town fox, country fox.* London, Deutsch.

VIK R. (1955) Invasion of *Skrjabingylus* (Nematoda) in Norwegian Mustelidae. *Nytt. Magasin Zool.* **3**, 70–8.

VINCENT R.E. (1958) Observations of red fox behaviour. *Ecology* **39**, 755–7.

VOS A. DE (1952) Ecology and management of fisher and marten in Ontario. *Ontario Dept. Lands and Forests, Tech. Bull.*

WALKER D.R.G. (1972) Observations on a collection of weasels (*Mustela nivalis*) from estates in Southwest Hertfordshire. *J. Zool., Lond.* **166**, 474–80.

WALTON K.C. (1964) The distribution of the polecat (*Putorius putorius*) in England, Wales & Scotland, 1959–62. *Proc. zool. Soc. Lond.* **143**, 333–6.

WALTON K.C. (1968a) *Studies on the biology of the polecat* Putorius putorius (*L.*). M.Sc. thesis, University of Durham.

WALTON K.C. (1968b) The distribution of the polecat, *Putorius putorius* in Great Britain, 1963–67. *J. Zool., Lond.* **155**, 237–40.

WALTON K.C. (1968c) The baculum as an age indicator in the polecat *Putorius putorius. J. Zool., Lond.* **156**, 533–6.

WALTON K.C. & PAGE R.J.C. (1970) Some ectoparasites found on polecats in Britain. *Nature, Wales* **12**, 32–4.

WARD W. (1936) Hare versus stoat. *Northwestern Nat.* **11**, 265.

WAYRE P. (1972) Breeding the Eurasian otter at the Norfolk Wildlife Park. *Int. Zoo Yb.* **12**, 116–17.

WEIR V. & BANISTER K.E. (1972) The food of the otter in the Blakeney area. *Norfolk Bird Mammal Rep.* **22**, 377–82.

WIJNGAARDEN A. VAN & BRUIJNS M.F.M. (1961) De hermelijnen, *Mustela erminea* L., van Terschelling. *Lutra* **3**, 35–42.

WIJNGAARDEN A. VAN & PEPPEL J. VAN DE (1964) The badger (*Meles meles* L.) in the Netherlands. *Lutra* **6**, 1–60.

WILLIAMS M.B. (1976) The intestinal parasites of the red fox in southwest Wales. *Br. vet. J.* **132**, 309–12

WÜSTEHUBE C. (1960) Beiträge zur Kenntnis besonders des Spiel- und Beuteverhaltens einheimischer Musteliden. *Z. Tierpsychol.* **17**, 579–613.

YAZAN Y.P. (1970) [Pine marten, sable and kidas in the Northern Ural Foreland (winter observations)]. *Byull. Mosk. Obschchest. Ispty. Prir. Otd. Biol.* **75**(3), 16–28.

YURGENSON P.B. (1939) [Types of habitat and the forest marten: a contribution to the ecology of the marten]. *Voprosy. Ekologii i Biotenologii* (*Problems in Ecol. & Biocoenol.*) *Leningr.* **4**, 142. (Translation 84, Elton Library, Oxford.)

YURGENSON P.B. (1951) Ecological-geographical aspects of food of forest marten and geographical variation of ecomorphological adaptations of its masticatory apparatus. *Zool. Zh.* **30**, 172–85.

YURGENSON P.B. (1956) [Determining the age of pine martens] *Zool Zh.* **35**, 781–3. (Translation, British Library: RTS 1496.)

SEALS

ANDERSON S.S., BURTON R.W. & SUMMERS C.F. (1975). Behaviour of Grey seals (*Halichoerus grypus*) during a breeding season at North Rona. *J. Zool., Lond.* **177**, 179–95.

ARNLAUGSSON T. (1973) *Selir vid Island. Rannsóknastofun fiskidnadarins.* Oct. 1973. 25 pp. mimeo.

BACKHOUSE K.M. (1960) The grey seal (*Halichoerus grypus*) outside the breeding season: a preliminary report. *Mammalia* **24**, 307–12.

BACKHOUSE K.M. & HEWER H.R. (1957) A note on spring pupping in the grey seal (*Halichoerus grypus* Fab.). *Proc. zool. Soc. Lond.* **128**, 593–4.

BACKHOUSE K.M. & HEWER H.R. (1960) Unusual colouring in the grey seal, *Halichoerus grypus* (Fabricius). *Proc. zool. Soc. Lond.* **134**, 497–9.

BIGG M.A. (1969) The harbor seal in British Columbia. *Bull. Fish. Res. Bd Canada* **172**, 1–33.

BONNER W.N. (1971) An aged Grey seal (*Halichoerus grypus*). *J. Zool. Lond.* **164**, 261–2.

BONNER W.N. (1972) The grey seal and common seal in European waters. *Oceanogr. Mar. Biol. Ann. Rev.* **10**, 461–507.

BONNER W.N. (1976) The stocks of grey seals (*Halichoerus grypus*) and common seals (*Phoca vitulina*) in Great Britain. *Nat. Environment Research Council. Pub. Series C No. 16*, 16 pp.

BONNER W.N. & HICKLING G. (1971) The grey seals of the Farne Islands: report for the period October 1969–July 1971. *Trans. nat. Hist. Soc. Northumb.* **17**, 141–62.

BONNER W.N. & HICKLING G. (1974) The grey seals of the Farne Islands: 1971–1973. *Trans. nat. Hist. Soc. Northumbria* **42**(2), 65–84.

BONNER W.N., JOHNSTON L. & VAUGHAN R.W. (1973) The status of common seals in Shetland. *Biol. Conserv.* **5**, 185–90.

BONNER W.N. & WILTHAMES S.R. (1974) Dispersal of Common seals (*Phoca vitulina*), tagged in the Wash, East Anglia. *J. Zool., Lond.* **174**, 528–31.

BOYD J.M., LOCKIE J.D. & HEWER H.R. (1962) The breeding colony of grey seals on North Rona, 1959. *Proc. zool. Soc. Lond.* **138**, 257–77.

BURNS J.J. & FAY F.H. (1970) Comparative morphology of the skull of the Ribbon seal, *Histriophoca fasciata*, with remarks on systematics of Phocidae. *J. Zool., Lond.* **161**, 363–94.

COULSON J.C. (1959) The growth of grey seal calves on the Farne Islands, Northumberland. *Trans. nat. Hist. Soc. Northumb.* **13**, 86–100.

COULSON J.C. & HICKLING G. (1961) Variation in the secondary sex-ratio of the grey seal, *Halichoerus grypus* (Fab.), during the breeding season. *Nature, Lond.* **190**, 281.

DUNBAR M.J. (1949) The Pinnipedia of the Arctic and Subarctic. *Bull. Fish. Res. Bd Canada* **85**, 1–22.

FAY F.H., RAUSCH V.R. & FELTZ E.T. (1967) Cytogenetic comparison of some pinnipeds. *Can. J. Zool.* **45**, 773–8.

FOGDEN S.C.L. (1971) Mother–young behaviour at Grey seal breeding beaches. *J. Zool., Lond.* **164**, 61–92.

HARRISON R.J. (1960) Reproduction and reproductive organs in common seals (*Phoca vitulina*) in the Wash, East Anglia. *Mammalia* **24**, 372–85.

HARRISON R.J. (1963) A comparison of factors involved in delayed implantation in badgers and seals in Great Britain. *In* Enders, A.C. (ed.) *Delayed Implantation.* Pp. 99–114. Chicago & London, University of Chicago Press.

HAVINGA B. (1933) Der Seehund (*Phoca vitulina* L.) in der hollandischen Gewassen. *Tijdschr. ned. dierk. Vereen.* 3rd ser. 3, 79–111.

HEWER H.R. (1960) Behaviour of the grey seal (*Halichoerus grypus* Fab.) in the breeding season. *Mammalia* 24, 400–21.

HEWER H.R. (1964) The determination of age, sexual maturity, longevity and a life table in the Grey seal (*Halichoerus grypus*). *Proc. zool. Soc. Lond.* 142, 593–624.

HEWER H.R. (1974) *British seals.* London, Collins.

HEWER H.R. & BACKHOUSE K.M. (1959) Field identification of bulls and cows of the Grey seal, *Halichoerus grypus* Fab. *Proc. zool. Soc. Lond.* 132, 641–5.

HEWER H.R. & BACKHOUSE K.M. (1968) Embryology and foetal growth of the grey seal, *Halichoerus grypus. J. Zool., Lond.* 155, 507–33.

HICKLING G. (1962) *Grey seals and the Farne Islands.* London, Routledge & Kegan Paul.

HOOK O. (1960) Some observations on the dates of pupping, and the incidence of partial rust and orange colouration in grey seal cows, *Halichoerus grypus* (Fabricius), on Lunga, Treshnish Isles, Argyll. *Proc. zool. Soc. Lond.* 134, 495–7.

HOOK O. (1961) Notes on the status of seals in Iceland, June–July 1959. *Proc. zool. Soc. Lond.* 137, 628–30.

JAMIESON G.S. & FISHER H.D. (1972) The pinniped eye: a review. *In* Harrison R.J. (ed.) *Functional anatomy of marine mammals*, vol. 1, Pp. 245–61. London, Academic Press.

KING J.E. (1964) *Seals of the world.* London, British Museum (Nat. Hist.).

LOCKLEY R.M. (1966a) The distribution of grey and common seals on the coasts of Ireland. *Ir. Nat. J.* 15, 136–43.

LOCKLEY R.M. (1966b) *Grey seal, common seal.* London, Andre Deutsch.

MATTHEWS L.H. (1950) The natural history of the grey seal, including lactation. *Proc. zool. Soc. Lond.* 120, 763.

MATTHEWS L.H. (1952) *British mammals.* London, Collins.

MAWDESLEY-THOMAS L.E. & BONNER W.N. (1971) Uterine tumours in a grey seal (*Halichoerus grypus*). *J. Path.* 103, 205–8.

MOHL B. (1968) Auditory sensitivity of the common seal in air and water. *J. aud. Res.* 8, 27–38.

OYNES P. (1964) Sel på norskekysten fra Finnmark til Nore. *Fiskets Gang* no. 48, 694–707.

OYNES P. (1966) Sel i Sor-Norge. *Fiskets Gang* no. 45, 834–9.

PLATT, N.E., PRIME J.H. & WITTHAMES S.R. (1975) The age of grey seals at the Farne Islands. *Trans. nat. Hist. Soc. Northumbria* 42(4), 99–106.

RAE B.B. (1960) Seals and Scottish fisheries. *Mar. Res.* 1960 (2) 1–39.

RAE B.B. (1968) The food of seals in Scottish waters. *Mar. Res.* 1968(2), 1–23.

RAE B.B. (1969) Twin seals in Scotland. *J. Zool., Lond.* 158, 243–5.

RAE B.B. & SHEARER W.M. (1965) Seal damage to salmon fisheries. *Mar. Res. Scot.* 1965(2), 1–39.

SERGEANT D.E. (1951) The status of the Common seal (*Phoca vitulina* L.) on the East Anglian coast. *J. Mar. Biol. Assn UK* 29, 707–17.

SMITH E.A. (1966) A review of the world's grey seal population. *J. Zool., Lond.* 150, 463–89.

SUMMERS C.F., BONNER W.N. & HAAFTEN J. van (in press) Changes in the seal population of the North Sea. Proc. ICES Symp. Changes in the fish stocks of the North Sea and their causes. *Rap. P.-v. Réun. Cons. perm. vit. Explor. Mer.*

THIEL P.H. van (1962) Anisakiasis. *Parasitology* 52, 16–17.

VENABLES U.M. & VENABLES L.S.V. (1955) Observations on a breeding colony of the seal *Phoca vitulina* in Shetland. *Proc. zool. Soc. Lond.* 125, 521–32.

VENABLES U.M. & VENABLES L.S.V. (1957) Mating behaviour of the seal *Phoca vitulina* in Shetland. *Proc. zool. Soc. Lond.* **128**, 387–96.

VENABLES U.M. & VENABLES L.S.V. (1960) A seal survey of Northern Ireland, 1956–1957. *Proc. zool. Soc. Lond.* **133**, 490–4.

WALLS G.L. (1942) *The vertebrate eye and its adaptive radiation.* New York & London, Hafner.

WYNNE-EDWARDS V.C. (1954) Field identification of the common and grey seals. *Scot. Nat.* **66**, 192.

UNGULATES

AHLÉN I. (1965) Studies on the red deer, *Cervus elaphus* L., in Scandinavia. III: Ecological investigations. *Viltrevy* **3**, 178–376.

AITKEN R.J. (1974) Delayed implantation in roe deer (*Capreolus capreolus*). *J. Reprod. Fert.* **39**, 225–33.

AITKEN R.J. (1975a) Cementum layers and tooth wear as criteria for ageing roe deer (*Capreolus capreolus*). *J. Zool. Lond.* **175**, 15–28.

AITKEN R.J. (1975b) Ultrastructure of the blastocyst and endometrium of the roe deer (*Capreolus capreolus*) during delayed implantation. *J. Anat.* **119**, 369–84.

AITKEN R.J., BURTON J., HAWKINS J., KERR-WILSON R., SHORT R.V. & STEVEN D.H. (1973) Histological and ultrastructural changes in the blastocyst and reproductive tract of the roe deer, *Capreolus capreolus*, during delayed implantation. *J. Reprod. Fert.* **34**, 481–93.

AMRUD J. & NES N. (1966) The chromosomes of the roe (*Capreolus capreolus*). *Hereditas* **56**, 217–20.

ANDERSEN J. (1953) Analysis of a Danish roe-deer population (*Capreolus capreolus* (L.)) based upon the extermination of the total stock. *Danish Rev. Game Biol.* **2**, 127–55.

ANON (1931) The helminth parasites of deer. *J. Helminth.* **9**, 217–48.

ARMSTRONG N., CHAPLIN R.E., CHAPMAN D.I. & SMITH B. (1969) Observations on the reproduction of female wild and park fallow deer (*Dama dama*) in southern England. *J. Zool. Lond.* **158**, 27–37.

BAILLIE-GROHMAN W.A. (1896) *Sport in the Alps.* London, Adam & Charles Black.

BATCHELER C.L. (1960) A study of the relations between roe, red and fallow deer, with special reference to Drummond Hill Forest, Scotland. *J. Anim. Ecol.* **29**, 375–84.

BATTY A.F. & CHAPMAN D.I. (1970) Gastro-intestinal parasites of wild fallow deer (*Dama dama* L.). *J. Helminth.* **44**, 57–61.

BRAMLEY P.S. (1970a) Territoriality and reproductive behaviour of roe deer. *J. Reprod. Fert.*, Suppl. **11**, 43–70.

BRAMLEY P.S. (1970b) *Numbers and social behaviour of roe deer* (Capreolus capreolus) *in a Dorset wood.* Ph.D. thesis, University of Aberdeen.

BROMLEY G.F. (1956) Ecology of wild spotted deer in the Maritime Territory. In Yurgenson, P.B. (ed.), *Studies of mammals in government preserves.* Pp. 152–224 (translation, Jerusalem, Israel Program for Scientific Translations, 1961).

CADMAN W.A. (1966) *The fallow deer.* London, HMSO.

CAMERON A.G. (1923) *The wild red deer of Scotland.* Edinburgh, Blackwood.

CARTER H.B. (1965) Variation in the hair follicle population of the mammalian skin. In *Biology of the skin and hair growth.* Pp. 25–33. Sydney, Angus & Robertson.

CHAPMAN D.I. (1970) Observations on the sexual cycle of male deer in Britain. *Mammal Rev.* **1**, 49–52.

512

Bibliographies: ungulates

CHAPMAN D.I. (1972) Seasonal changes in the gonads and accessory glands of male mammals. *Mammal Rev.* **1**, 231–48.

CHAPMAN D.I. (1974) Reproductive physiology in relation to deer management. *Mammal Rev.* **4**, 61–74.

CHAPMAN D.I. (1975) Antlers—bones of contention. *Mammal Rev.* **5**, 121–72.

CHAPMAN D.I. & CHAPMAN N.G. (1969a) The incidence of congenital abnormalities in the mandibular dentition of fallow deer (*Dama dama* L.). *Res. vet. Sci.* **10**, 485–7.

CHAPMAN D.I. & CHAPMAN N. (1969b) Observations on the biology of fallow deer (*Dama dama*) in Epping Forest, Essex, England. *Biol. Consv.* **2**, 55–62.

CHAPMAN D.I. & CHAPMAN N.G. (1969c) Geographical variation in fallow deer (*Dama dama* L.). *Nature, Lond.* **221**, 59–60.

CHAPMAN D.I. & CHAPMAN N. (1970a) Development of the teeth and mandibles of fallow deer. *Acta theriol.* **15**, 111–31.

CHAPMAN D.I. & CHAPMAN N.G. (1970b) Preliminary observations on the reproductive cycle of male fallow deer (*Dama dama* L.). *J. Reprod. Fert.* **21**, 1–8.

CHAPMAN N. & CHAPMAN D. (1970c) *Fallow deer.* British Deer Society.

CHAPMAN D.I. & CHAPMAN N.G. (1971) Further observations on the incidence of twins in Roe deer, *Capreolus capreolus. J. Zool. Lond.* **165**, 505–9.

CHAPMAN D.I. & CHAPMAN N.G. (1973) Maxillary canine teeth in Fallow deer, *Dama dama. J. Zool. Lond.* **170**, 143–7.

CHAPMAN D.I. & CHAPMAN N.G. (1975) *Fallow deer: their history, distribution and biology.* Lavenham, Terence Dalton.

CHAPMAN D.I. & DANSIE O. (1969) Unilateral implantation in Muntjac deer. *J. Zool. Lond.* **159**, 534–6.

CHAPMAN D.I. & DANSIE O. (1970) Reproduction and foetal development in female muntjac deer (*Muntiacus reevesi* Ogilby). *Mammalia* **34**, 303–19.

CHAPMAN D.I. & HORWOOD M.T. (1968) Pregnancy in a Sika deer calf, *Cervus nippon. J. Zool. Lond.* **155**, 227–8.

CLARKE M. (1968) Fraying by muntjac. *Deer* **1**, 272–3.

CLARKE M. (1974) Deer distribution survey 1967–72. *Deer* **3**, 279–82.

CLAY T. (1966) Lice of the muntjac. *Deer* **1**, 17.

CUMMING H.G. (1966) *Behaviour and dispersion in roe deer* (Capreolus capreolus). Ph.D. thesis, University of Aberdeen.

DANIEL M.J. (1963) Early fertility of red deer hinds in New Zealand. *Nature, Lond.* **200**, 380.

DANSIE O. & WILLIAMS J. (1973) Paraurethral glands in Reeves' muntjac deer, *Muntiacus reevesi. J. Zool. Lond.* **171**, 469–71.

DARLING F.F. (1937) *A herd of red deer: a study in animal behaviour.* London, Oxford University Press.

DUNN A.M. (1969) The wild ruminant as reservoir host of helminth infection. *Symp. zool. Soc. Lond.* **24**, 221–48.

DZIECIOLOWSKI R. (1969a) *The quantity, quality and seasonal variation of food resources available to red deer in various environmental conditions of forest management.* Warsaw.

DZIECIOLOWSKI R. (1969b) Growth and development of red deer calves in captivity. *Acta theriol.* **14**, 141–51.

ELLERMAN J.R. & MORRISON-SCOTT T.C.S. (1951) *Checklist of Palaearctic and Indian mammals.* London, British Museum (Nat. Hist.).

ESPMARK Y. (1969) Mother–young relations and development of behaviour in roe deer (*Capreolus capreolus* L.). *Viltrevy* **6**(6), 461–540.

EVANS H. (1890) *Some account of Jura red deer*. Derby, Francis Carter.

EYGENRAAM J.A. (1963) Het sociale level van edelherten (*Cervus elaphus* L.). *Lutra* **5**, 1–8.

FLEROV K.K. (1952) *Fauna of USSR: Mammals*. Vol. 1, no. 2: *Deer and musk deer* (English translation, Jerusalem, Israel Program for Scientific Translations, 1960).

FRANKENBERGER Z. (1957) [Circumanal and circumgenital glands of our Cervidae.] *Cesk. morfol.* **5**, 255–65. (in Czech.).

GEIGER C. & KRÄMER A. (1974) Rank-order of roe deer at artificial winter feeding sites in a Swiss hunting district. *Z. Jagdwiss.* **20**, 53–6.

GILBERT B.K. & HAILMAN J.R. (1966) Uncertainty of leadership-rank in fallow deer. *Nature, Lond.* **209**, 1041–2.

GUINNESS F., LINCOLN G.A. & SHORT R.V. (1971) The reproductive cycle of the female red deer, *Cervus elaphus* L. *J. Reprod. Fert.* **27**, 427–38.

GUSTAVSSON I. & SUNDT C.O. (1968) Karyotypes in five species of deer (*Alces alces* L., *Capreolus capreolus* L., *Cervus elaphus* L., *Cervus nippon nippon* Temm. and *Dama dama* L.). *Hereditas* **60**, 233–48.

HAMILTON E. (1871) Remarks on the prolific nature of *Hydropotes inermis*. *Proc. zool. Soc. Lond.* 258.

HAMILTON W.J., HARRISON R.J. & YOUNG B.A. (1960) Aspects of placentation in certain cervidae. *J. Anat. Lond.* **94**, 1–32.

HARRINGTON R. (1973) Hybridisation among deer and its implications for conservation. *Irish Forestry* **30**, 64–78.

HARRIS R.A. & DUFF K.R. (1970) *Wild deer in Britain*. Newton Abbot, David & Charles.

HARRISON R.J. & HYETT A.R. (1954) The development and growth of the placentomes in the fallow deer (*Dama dama* L.). *J. Anat. Lond.* **88**, 338–55.

HEIDEMANN G. (1973) *Zur Biologie des Damwildes* (Cervus dama *L., 1758*). *Mammalia depicta* no. 9. Hamburg & Berlin, Parey.

HOFMANN R.R. & GEIGER G. (1974) Zur topographischen und functionellen Anatomie der Viscera abdominis des Rehes (*Capreolus capreolus* L.) *Zbl. Vet. Med.* C **3**, 63–84.

HOLMES F. (1974) *Following the roe*. Edinburgh, Bartholomew.

HORWOOD M.T. (1971) *Sika deer research—2nd progress report*. London, Nature Conservancy Council.

HORWOOD M.T. & MASTERS E.H. (1970) *Sika deer*. British Deer Society.

HOSEY G.R. (1974) *The food and feeding ecology of the roe deer* (Capreolus capreolus). Ph.D. thesis, University of Manchester.

HSU T.C. & BENIRSCHKE K. (1969) *An atlas of mammalian chromosomes*. folio 134. Berlin.

IMAIZUMI Y. (1970) Description of a new species of *Cervus* from the Tsushima Islands, Japan, with a revision of the subgenus *Sika* based on clinal analysis. *Bull. nat. Sci. Mus. Tokyo* **13**, 185–94.

JACKSON J.E. (1974) *The feeding ecology of the fallow deer* (Dama dama L.) *in the New Forest*. Ph.D. thesis, University of Southampton.

JENKINSON D.M. (1972) The skin structure of British deer. *Res. vet. Sci.* **13**, 70–3.

JENNINGS A.R. (1969) Tumours of free-living wild mammals and birds in Great Britain. *Symp. zool. Soc. Lond.* **24**, 275–87.

JENSEN P.V. (1968) Food selection of the Danish Red deer (*Cervus elaphus* L.) as determined by examination of the rumen content. *Danish Rev. Game Biol.* **5**, 1–44.

JEWELL P.A., MILNER C. & BOYD J.M. (1974) *Island survivors: the ecology of the Soay sheep of St Kilda*. London, Athlone Press.

KIDDIE D.G. (1962) *The Sika deer* (Cervus nippon) *in New Zealand*. Wellington.

KLEIN D.R. & STRANDGAARD H. (1972) Factors affecting growth and body size of roe deer. *J. Wildl. Mgmt* **36**, 64–79.

KURT F. (1968) The social behaviour of roe deer (*Capreolus capreolus* L.). *Mammalia depicta*, no. 3. Hamburg & Berlin, Parey.

LINCOLN G.A., YOUNGSON R.W. & SHORT R.V. (1970) The social and sexual behaviour of the red deer stag. *J. Reprod. Fert.* Suppl. 11, 71–103.

LÖNNBERG E. (1906) On the geographic races of the red deer in Scandinavia. *Ark. Zool.* 3(9), 1–19.

LOWE V.P.W. (1961) A discussion on the history, present status and future conservation of red deer (*Cervus elaphus* L.) in Scotland. *Terre Vie.* **108**, 9–40.

LOWE V.P.W. (1966) Observations on the dispersal of red deer on Rhum. *Symp. zool. Soc. Lond.* **18**, 211–28.

LOWE V.P.W. (1967) Teeth as indicators of age with special reference to Red deer (*Cervus elaphus*) of known age from Rhum. *J. Zool. Lond.* **152**, 137–53.

LOWE V.P.W. (1969) Population dynamics of the red deer (*Cervus elaphus* L.) on Rhum. *J. Anim. Ecol.* **38**, 425–57.

LOWE V.P.W. (1971) Some effects of a change in estate management on a deer population. *In* Duffey E. & Watt A.S. (eds) *The scientific management of animal and plant communities for conservation.* Pp. 437–56. Oxford, Blackwell Scientific Publications.

LOWE V.P.W. & GARDINER A.S. (1974) A re-examination of the subspecies of Red deer (*Cervus elaphus*) with particular reference to the stocks in Britain. *J. Zool. Lond.* **174**, 185–201.

LOWE V.P.W. & GARDINER A.S. (1975) Hybridization between Red deer (*Cervus elaphus*) and Sika deer (*Cervus nippon*) with particular reference to stocks in N.W. England. *J. Zool. Lond.* **177**, 553–66.

LYDEKKER R. (1898) *The deer of all lands.* London, Rowland Ward.

McDIARMID A. (1962) *Diseases of free-living wild animals.* Rome, FAO.

MATTHEWS L.H. (1952) *British mammals.* London, Collins.

MAUGHAN E. & WILLIAMS J.R.B. (1967) Haemoglobin types in deer. *Nature, Lond.* **215**, 404–5.

MIDDLETON A.D. (1937) Whipsnade ecological survey, 1936–1937. *Proc. zool. Soc. Lond.* A, **107**, 471–81.

MILLAIS J.G. (1897) *British deer and their horns.* London, Sotheran.

MITCHELL B. (1967) Growth layers in dental cement for determining the age of red deer (*Cervus elaphus* L.). *J. Anim. Ecol.* **36**, 279–93.

MITCHELL B. (1971) The weights of new-born to one-day-old Red deer calves in Scottish moorland habitats. *J. Zool. Lond.* **164**, 250–4.

NELSON G. (1966) A note on the internal parasites of the muntjac. *Deer*, 1, 16–17.

PRELL H. (1938) Die Tragzeiten der einheimischen Jagdtiere (II Nachtrag). *Tharandter Fortliches Jahrbuch* **89**, 696–701.

PRINS R.A. & GEELEN M.J.H. (1971) Rumen characteristics of red deer, fallow deer and roe deer. *J. Wildl. Mgmt* **35**, 673–80.

PRIOR R. (1968) *The roe deer of Cranborne Chase: an ecological survey.* London, Oxford University Press.

PUTTICK G. (1972) *Analysis of fallow deer population on Groote Schuur Estate.* Unpublished dissertation, University of Cape Town.

RAESFELD F. VON (1964) *Das Rotwild.* Hamburg & Berlin, Parey.

RIECK W. (1955) Die Setzzeit bei Reh-, Rot- und Damwild in Mitteleuropa. *Z. Jagdwiss,* 1, 69–75.

RIECK W. (1974) *Rehwildalter-Merkblatt.* Schaienwildausschuss des deutschen Jagdschutz-Verbandes.

RINEY T. (1951) Standard terminology for deer teeth. *J. Wildl. Mgmt* **15**, 99–101.

RINEY T. (1954) Antler growth and shedding in a captive group of fallow deer (*Dama dama*) in New Zealand. *Trans. Roy. Soc. NZ* **82**, 569–78.

RITCHIE J. (1920) *The influence of man on animal life in Scotland.* Cambridge, University Press.

ROBERTSON I.J.M. (1967) *The ecology and management of deer in temperate forests.* M.Sc. thesis, University of Edinburgh.

ROSS J. (ed.) (1925) *The book of the red deer.* London, Simpkin etc.

SCHUMACHER S. (1936) Das Stirnorgan des Rehbockes (*Capreolus capreolus capreolus* L.), ein bisher unbekanntes Duftorgan. *Zeit. Mikro-Anat. Forsch.* **39**, 215–30.

SHORT R.V. & HAY M.F. (1966) Delayed implantation in the roe deer *Capreolus capreolus. Symp. zool. Soc. Lond.* **15**, 173–94.

SHORT R.V. & MANN T. (1966) The sexual cycle of a seasonally breeding mammal, the roe-buck (*Capreolus capreolus*). *J. Reprod. Fert.* **12**, 337–51.

SPRINGTHORPE G. (1969) Long-haired Fallow deer at Mortimer Forest. *J. Zool. Lond.* **159**, 537.

STRANDGAARD H. (1972) The roe deer (*Capreolus capreolus*) population at Kalø and the factors regulating its size. *Danish Rev. Game Biol.* **7**(1), 1–205.

STUBBE C. (1966) Körperwachstum und Körpergrösse des europäischen Rehwildes (*Capreolus c. capreolus* L.). *Zool. Gart. Lpz.* **33**, 85–105.

TEGNER H. (1971) *The roe deer: their history, habits and pursuit.* London, Batchworth.

THOMPSON G.B. (1964) The parasites of British birds and mammals. XL: Ectoparasites of deer in Britain. *Entomologists' mon. Mag.* **99**, 186–9.

WATSON A. (1971) Climate and the antler-shedding and performance of red deer in north-east Scotland. *J. appl. Ecol.* **8**, 53–67.

WHITEHEAD G.K. (1953) *The ancient white cattle of Britain and their descendants.* London, Faber & Faber.

WHITEHEAD G.K. (1960) *The deer stalking grounds of Great Britain and Ireland.* London, Hollis & Carter.

WHITEHEAD G.K. (1964) *The deer of Great Britain and Ireland: an account of their history, status and distribution.* London, Routledge & Kegan-Paul.

WHITEHEAD G.K. (1972) *The wild goats of Great Britain and Ireland.* Newton Abbot, David & Charles.

WURSTER D.H. & BENIRSCHKE K. (1967) Chromosome studies in some deer, the springbock, and the pronghorn, with notes on placentation in deer. *Cytologia* **32**, 273–85.

YOUNGSON R.W. (1967) Behaviour studies on Rhum. In *Red deer research in Scotland, progress report* **1**, 30–3; Nature Conservancy.

Index